KU-616-878

NICK COHEN

You Can't Read This Book

Censorship in an Age of Freedom

FOURTH ESTATE • *London*

First published in Great Britain in 2012 by
Fourth Estate
An imprint of HarperCollins*Publishers*
77–85 Fulham Palace Road,
London W6 8JB
www.4thestate.co.uk

Copyright © Nick Cohen 2012

1

The right of Nick Cohen to be identified as the author
of this work has been asserted by him in accordance
with the Copyright, Design and Patents Act 1988

A catalogue record for this book is
available from the British Library

ISBN 978-0-00-730890-3

All rights reserved. No part of this publication may be
reproduced, transmitted, or stored in a retrieval system,
in any form or by any means, without permission
in writing from Fourth Estate.

Typeset in Minion by G&M Designs Limited,
Raunds, Northamptonshire

Printed and bound in Great Britain by Clays Ltd, St Ives plc

MIX
Paper from
responsible sources
FSC™ **C007454**

FSC™ is a non-profit international organisation established to promote
the responsible management of the world's forests. Products carrying the
FSC label are independently certified to assure consumers that they come
from forests that are managed to meet the social, economic and
ecological needs of present and future generations,
and other controlled sources.

Find out more about HarperCollins and the environment at
www.harpercollins.co.uk/green

For Christopher Hitchens

BURY LIBRARY SERVICE	
Bertrams	13/02/2012
323.443COH	£12.99
	CN

CONTENTS

There is an all-out confrontation between the ironic and the literal mind: between every kind of commissar and inquisitor and bureaucrat and those who know that, whatever the role of social and political forces, ideas and books have to be formulated and written by individuals.

CHRISTOPHER HITCHENS

INTRODUCTION

This book covers the power of the wealthy to silence critics, the conflict between religion and freedom of thought, and the determination of dictators to persecute dissenters. Let me begin with a problem older than them all: how can a woman discover if her man is cheating on her?

If she were married to a rich Englishman in the early twenty-first century, her husband could use the full force of the law to keep her in ignorance. After Parliament gave judges the power to develop a right to privacy in 2000, the judiciary rejected England's tradition of open justice with a breathtaking disdain for the past. The judges did not allow a free press to report what it knew, and punish editors only if they unjustifiably infringed the rights of others. Instead, they engaged in pre-publication censorship, the most suffocating form there is, and told newspapers in advance that they could never report forbidden facts. Under the terms of their injunctions, no one was able to say why a banker or celebrity had taken legal action. By the judiciary's logic, the ban on the reporting of the proceedings of the courts made sense. The secrets of the outwardly wholesome star who is sleeping with the wife of his best friend, or the outwardly respectable tycoon who hires prostitutes by the half-dozen to beat him in a London basement, would not be secret if the media could publish a description of his reasons for keeping his private life private.

Then the judges screwed the lid down tighter. They turned ordinary injunctions into 'super-injunctions', which not only barred reporters from revealing why claimants had gone to court, but barred them from revealing that claimants had gone to court at all. The censors censored the fact of censorship. The existence of their 'super-injunctions' was itself a secret.

The readiness of the judiciary to use the law of libel to stifle public debates in England and around the world had already provoked protests from the US Congress, the United Nations and journalists investigating oligarchs from New York to Kiev. True to their censorious form, the judges went on to shut down arguments about private life. They rejected the example set by American lawyers, who had created the concept of 'the right to be let alone' for ordinary citizens, but given public figures fewer protections. Instead, they invented rights to privacy that hardly anyone who went to work for a living thought justifiable.

The corporate-responsibility guidelines of modern corporations and state bureaucracies did not regard affairs at work as private matters. If a powerful man began a relationship with a subordinate, trade unions, supervisory boards and employment tribunals wanted to check that he had not pressured the woman into pleasuring him by hinting that her career would suffer if she did not. If there had been no sexual harassment, they wanted to know whether she had entered the affair in the expectation that pay rises and promotions would follow. The US Congress almost impeached Bill Clinton for having sex with an intern in the White House and lying about it under oath. In many companies, a philandering manager risked instant dismissal.

Everyone agreed that there was a public interest in the links between sex and the abuse of power and position – everyone, that is, except the judges. They gave Fred Goodwin, one of the most disastrous figures in the history of British finance, an injunction to suppress reporting of an extra-marital affair he enjoyed with a subordinate while he was leading his Royal Bank of Scotland to ruin – and half-bankrupting Britain as he did it. Even though Goodwin was in charge of a publicly traded company, the courts said the relationship was private. If the media wanted the gagging order lifted, they had to prove in advance that the affair was a specific abuse of power. The most hard-bitten hacks would have found clearing the hurdle the law had raised a formidable task. The judges had made it a contempt of court to identify the mysterious woman, so how could they ask questions about her?

Discovering what the judges censored in secret hearings was a difficult enterprise. The best information came from a tabloid journalist who risked contempt of court proceedings by piecing together snippets of information from newspapers' legal departments. Writing on the Web under the protection of a pseudonym, she said that a few of the super-injunctions she had been able to study were unobjectionable. Judges had intervened to protect children or private citizens who just wanted the press to leave them in peace. Most of the time, however, they came to the aid of people in the public eye: a first XI and full substitute bench of footballers, stars of stage and screen, singers and corporate executives. The majority of super-injunctions covered extra-marital affairs. They aimed to silence ex-mistresses, former wives or cuckolded husbands. In other instances, employers imposed them on former employees to keep accounts of professional incompetence or affairs in the workplace hidden. 'Some are absurd: one involves allegations that someone is losing his hair, while another is about a man who died after he got an injunction but it still can't be reported. Another is about failures by a doctor who was criticised by a judge in a social services case, but cannot be identified.'

When Ryan Giggs's lawyers tried to stop a beauty queen telling of her nights of passion with one of the most talented footballers in the English Premier League, they thought they had a straightforward case. She was preparing to sell her story, they said. The English legal system must silence her to protect Giggs's public image as a loyal husband and wholesome sporting role model. The judge told her to shut up, and warned the media that they must censor themselves or face the consequences. The sole option left to the frustrated tabloids was to run articles complaining that the courts had stopped them exposing an unnamed footballing 'love rat'.

No judge on earth can stop journalists gossiping, and many who worked in the media knew that the mysterious footballer was Ryan Giggs. Thirty years earlier, the gossip would not have spread far beyond the offices and pubs of Fleet Street. If editors had thought for a moment about sharing what they knew with their readers, the knowledge that the courts might have imprisoned them and hit their proprietors with substantial fines for breaking an injunction would have stopped them. This was the way it had always been.

Few in authority realised that their manageable world, where gatekeepers controlled the news and judges and politicians held gatekeepers to account, had gone. Word of Giggs's injunction reached Twitter. Account holders, some hiding behind pseudonyms, linked him to the beauty queen. His lawyers did what their predecessors would have done. Tweeters were publishing in defiance of a court order, so the lawyers' job was to identify and punish them. They announced that they would take legal action against Twitter, and compel it to reveal the identities of users who had placed themselves in contempt of court. Stuck in the last century, they did not understand how ridiculous their threats sounded.

Suing the Internet because they did not like what people were typing on Twitter? They might as well have sued the sky because they did not like the weather. The Internet is just there, like a force of nature. If one person, living in a court's jurisdiction, breaks an injunction, a judge can punish him. But how can a judge punish a thousand, ten thousand, a hundred thousand?

If the Web has a soul, then a loathing for censorship stirs it. Ever-larger numbers of bloggers and Facebook and Twitter users responded to legal intimidation by posting details of Giggs's affair. Most were English, but Manchester United is one of the best-supported clubs in the world. Many who were interested in Giggs or irked by the censorship he was trying to enforce lay beyond the jurisdiction of the English courts. Newspapers in Scotland and India saw the protest in cyberspace. They realised that English judges could not control them, and ran the story. Those who wanted to know about Giggs, and many who did not, knew about his adultery, but according to the law, no journalist or broadcaster in England could talk about it. Finally, a Liberal Democrat MP stood up in the House of Commons, the one space in England where free speech is protected and the lawyers cannot harm you. John Hemming said that seventy-five thousand people had reported on Twitter that Ryan Giggs was the adulterous footballer, and the courts could not punish them all. He would end the farce by naming him in the Commons, so that the mainstream media could escape the injunction and repeat what millions already knew.

No public interest was served by revealing details of Ryan Giggs's sex life – which does not mean the public was not interested in it. But optimists about the liberating potential of technology could find reasons to be euphoric even in the tacky tale of Giggs's betrayals. The Net had proved that it had no borders. National laws could not contain it. Attempts to press down on the free circulation of information in one country just pushed it into other countries. The ability of users to copy, link and draw others into their single-issue campaigns had stripped censors of their power.

On this cheerful reading, the Giggs affair was more than a story about the energetic sex lives of players in the English Premier League. It was a harbinger of revolution. Online citizens – puny as individuals but mighty as a collective – had come together to create an unstoppable flow of information. By connecting with each other and sharing their knowledge, they had prevented suppression. And their defiance of the law was so painless. Modern radicals did not need to slog through dull books and duller meetings. They did not need to enlist in a political party and campaign for politicians who might enact reform. Joining the revolution was the work of seconds. They had only to tweet 140 characters or, with a knowing wink, make a photo of Ryan Giggs their Facebook profile picture, and judicial power, whose writ had run for centuries, would collapse. The ease with which they had fought and won seemed to reveal the impossibility of censorship anywhere by anyone.

'An old way of doing things is dying; a new one is being born,' announced a US cyber activist just before Giggs sought his injunction. 'The Age of Transparency is here.'

So it appeared. WikiLeaks became the new age's journalistic phenomenon, as it dumped masses of confidential information onto the Web about the American war in Afghanistan and the American war in Iraq and the American prison at Guantánamo Bay and the American State Department. America, the most powerful country in the world, could not stop it. WikiLeaks was based in Sweden, beyond America's control, although everyone in America with access to the Net could read what it published.

The new technologies justified their revolutionary possibilities by playing a part in the Arab Spring of 2010–11, which had the potential to be the most optimistic moment the world had experienced since the fall of the Berlin Wall in 1989. In Syria and Libya, they allowed the victims of closed societies to talk to the rest of the world. In Egypt, Facebook became a means of organising revolutionary protest. The Arab dictators knew the arts of torture and repression well. They could break the bodies and the will of their traditional opponents. They could not cope with the mobilisations of the young the Net allowed, because they had never experienced anything like them before.

The promise of the Net inspired politicians as well as activists. In the late 1980s, after the fall of the Berlin Wall, optimistic leaders and intellectuals believed that history was over and any society that wanted to be wealthy had to embrace liberal capitalism. In the early 2010s, optimists switched from political to technological determinism. They predicted that genocides would become impossible when all it would take to stop an atrocity would be for witnesses to alert the conscience of humanity by uploading videos from their iPhones to YouTube. They warned dictators who censored that they were imperilling economic growth by stopping their businesses accessing the sources of knowledge they needed to compete in a global market. Any society that wanted to be wealthy had to embrace freedom of speech on the Net.

With tyrannies tumbling and computing power guaranteeing the triumph of liberal values, why write a book on censorship?

I am all for liberal optimism, and hope a new world is being born. Before euphoria carries us away, however, consider the following scenarios.

- A young novelist from a Muslim family writes a fictional account of his struggles with his religious identity. He describes religion as a fairy tale and mocks the prohibitions of the Koran he was taught as a child as bigoted and preposterous. His writing shows that he does not regard the life of Muhammad as exemplary. Quite the reverse, in fact. If word of his work seeped out in Pakistan, the courts would charge him with blasphemy, a 'crime' that carries the death sentence. In Iran or Saudi Arabia, the authorities would arrest him, and maybe kill him too. In India, they would confine themselves to charging him with 'outraging religious feelings'. In most Western states, prosecutors would not charge him with blasphemy, but he would receive the worst punishment the world can inflict on a writer other than depriving him of his life or liberty: no one would publish his work. He would find that although American and European countries do not have blasphemy laws that protect Islam, or in most cases Christianity, the threat of violent reprisals against Western publishers and authors is enough to enforce extra-legal censorship that no parliament or court has authorised.

- An African feminist comes to Europe and denounces its tolerance of the abuse of women in ethnic and religious minorities. Newspaper editors and television producers cannot get enough of her fresh and controversial voice. After religious fanatics murder one of her supporters and threaten to murder her, their mood changes. Intellectuals say she is an 'Enlightenment fundamentalist' who is as intolerant and extreme as the religious fanatics she opposes. Politicians and newspaper columnists complain about the cost to the taxpayer of her police protection and accuse her of bringing rancour to their previously harmonious multi-cultural society. No one bans her books, but her work inspires no imitators. She becomes a leader without followers, because women who agreed with her, and were prepared to support her arguments, look at the treatment she received, and put down their pens.
- Two bankers, one from New York and one from London, meet for lunch and discuss an issue that has troubled them both. Not one of the great newspapers that cover high finance saw the crash of 2008 coming. Nor did bloggers make it their business to find out about the risks their banks were running. The Net was as clueless as the 'dead tree' press. Insiders knew that the lust for bonuses and the pressure to accede to management demands for quick profits could have catastrophic consequences. But the information had never leaked. The two bankers discuss writing a joint article for the *Financial Times* or the *Wall Street Journal* exposing the continuing failure to address the structural problems in

Western banking. They think that their intervention could improve public debate, but dismiss the idea as too dangerous. They know that if they speak out, their banks will fire them and they will never work in banking again. No other bank will want people marked as troublemakers on its 'team'.

- A British newspaper reporter moves from the politics to the business desk. She resolves to start digging into the backgrounds of the Russian oligarchs who have set up home in London. She believes she can connect them to the kleptomaniac dictators the revolutionaries in the Middle East are challenging. She has criticised British politicians without fear of the consequences for years, but her editor turns pale when she talks about using the same tactics against plutocrats. The smallest factual mistake or unsupportable innuendo could lead to a libel action that could cost the paper a million pounds, 'and we don't have a million pounds'. She ploughs on, and produces an article that is so heavily cut and rewritten by the in-house lawyers no one can understand it. 'I want a thousand words on trends in fashion retailing by lunchtime,' the editor says when she starts work the next day.

- A member of the Central Committee of the Chinese Communist Party reads a speech by Hillary Clinton. 'When countries curtail Internet freedom, they place limits on their economic future. Their young people don't have full access to the conversations and debates happening in the world or exposure to the kind of free enquiry that spurs people to question old ways and invent new ones. Barring criticism of officials makes governments more susceptible to corruption, which creates economic distortions with long-term effects. Freedom of thought and the level playing field made possible by the rule of law are part of what fuels innovation economies.' The old communist is a man who has trained himself never to show his emotions in case they reveal weaknesses to his rivals in the party. But he thinks of China's booming economy and America's fiscal and trade deficits, and for the first time in years he throws back his head and roars with laughter.

What follows is an examination of how censorship in its clerical, economic and political forms works in practice. It is a history of the controversies of our times, and an argument that free speech is better than suppression in almost all circumstances. I hope that I will have convinced you by the end that the limits on free speech – for there are always limits – should be few, and that the law must refuse to implement them if there is a hint of a public interest in allowing debate to continue unimpeded.

My subject is censorship that hurts, not spin or the unstoppable desire of partisan newspapers, broadcasters and bloggers to preach to the converted and dismiss or ignore news their audiences do not wish to hear. I accept that press officers' manipulation of information is an attempt to limit and control. But manipulation becomes censorship only on those rare occasions when the law punishes those who expose the spin. I agree too that editorial suppression is a type of censorship, because it ensures that readers rarely find a good word about trade unions in a right-wing newspaper, or a sympathetic article about Israel in a left-wing journal. The effects are trivial, because those readers who do not wish to be spoon-fed opinions can find contrary views elsewhere, and a journalist who does not like the party line of one media organisation can choose to move to another. True censorship removes choice. It menaces and issues commands that few can ignore. Write a free-thinking novel, and religious terrorists will come to assassinate you. Tell the world about your employers' incompetence, and they will deprive you of your livelihood. Criticise a pharmaceutical corporation or an association of 'alternative health' quacks and they will seek to bankrupt you in the English courts. Speak out in a dictatorship, and the secret police will escort you to jail.

The invention of the Net, like all communications revolutions before it, is having and will have profound effects – which I do not seek to belittle. Its effect on the ability of the strong and the violent to impose their views is less marked than optimists imagine, because they fail to understand the difference between *total* control and *effective* control. Everyone who wants to suppress information would like to remove all trace of it. But when total power eludes them, they seek to impose limits. It may irk a Russian oligarch that readers can find accounts of his mafia past somewhere on the Web, or infuriate the Chinese, Iranian and Belarusian regimes that dissident sites escape their controls. But they are not threatened unless people can act on the information. Action requires something more than an anonymous post somewhere in cyberspace. It requires the right to campaign and argue in public. As we have seen in the Middle East, in dictatorships it can require the courage to risk your life in a revolution.

Censorship's main role is to restrict the scope for action. If Islamist violence ensures that every mainstream broadcaster in the West is frightened of exposing Islam's founding myths, or if the citizens of a dictatorship know that they will be arrested if they challenge their leaders' abuses of power, then censors are exercising effective control by punishing those who challenge them and bullying their contemporaries into silence. If these examples strike you as remote from everyday life, imagine that English lawyers find they can force Twitter to pass on the details of everyone who tweeted about a randy footballer's love life. Suppose then that the English legal system prosecuted the rumour-mongers for contempt of court. I guarantee you that the next time gossip began about a 'love rat' celebrity, it would not shoot across the Web with quite the speed of the news of Ryan Giggs's adultery.

'You can be a famous poisoner or a successful poisoner,' runs the old joke, 'but you can't be both.' The same applies to censors.

Ninety-nine per cent of successful censorship is hidden from view. Even when brave men and women speak out, the chilling effect of the punishments their opponents inflict on them silences others. Those who might have added weight to their arguments and built a campaign for change look at the political or religious violence, or at the threat of dismissal from work, or at the penalties overbearing judges impose, and walk away.

Technology can change the rules, but it cannot change the game. Freedom always has to be fought for, because it is rooted in cultures, laws and constitutions, not in microchips and search engines, and is protected by institutions that are obliged to defend it. The struggle for freedom of speech is at root a political struggle, not least because the powerful can use new technologies as effectively as the weak – often more effectively. Today's techno-utopianism is at best irritating and at worst a dangerous distraction, because it offers the comforting illusion that we can escape the need to fight against reactionary and unjust governments, regimes and movements with the click of a mouse.

Contrary to the shallow views of Net utopians, technology cannot ensure progress either. When it comes, progress in human affairs does not advance in a straight line. It bends and swerves; and sometimes it retreats. Today's debates assume that we are living in a better and more open world than our repressed ancestors. The most striking counter-argument against modern complacency is to begin by looking at that most contentious and dangerous of forces, and observe that we were freer to challenge religions that claimed dominion over men's minds and women's bodies thirty years ago than we are now.

In 1988, Salman Rushdie for one thought that a writer could criticise religious bigotry without running the risk that fanatics would murder him and everyone who worked with him, just for telling a story.

PART ONE

God

I cannot praise a fugitive and cloistered virtue, unexercised & unbreathed, that never sallies out and sees her adversary, but slinks out of the race, where that immortal garland is to be run for.

JOHN MILTON, 1644

ONE

'Kill the Blasphemer'

It would be absurd to think a book could cause riots. That would be a strange view of the world.

Of course it was blasphemous. A book that challenges theocracy is blasphemous by definition. Not just because it questions the divine provenance of a sacred text – Did God speak to Moses? Inspire the gospels? Send the archangel Gabriel to instruct Muhammad on how to live and what to worship? – but because it criticises the bigotries the sacred text instructs the faithful to hold. By this measure, any book worth reading is blasphemous to some degree, and *The Satanic Verses* was well worth reading.

To say that Salman Rushdie did not know his novel would cause 'offence' is not true in the narrow sense of the word. He and his publishers never imagined the viciousness of the reaction, but just before the book was published in 1988, he sent a draft to the Palestinian intellectual Edward Said. Rushdie wanted Said's opinion because he thought his new novel 'may upset some of the faithful'. Indeed it did, but in the late twentieth century, no honest writer abandoned his or her book because it might upset a powerful lobby. Lackeys working for a plutocrat's newspaper or propagandists serving a state or corporate bureaucracy guarded their tongues and self-censored, but not artists and intellectuals in free countries.

Rushdie was writing in one of the most optimistic times in history. The advances in political, sexual and intellectual freedoms were unparalleled. It seemed that decent men and women needed only to raise their angry voices for tyrants to totter and fall. First in the fascistic dictatorships of Spain, Portugal and Greece in the 1970s, then in the military dictatorships of South America in the 1980s, and from 1989 to 1991 in the Soviet Union, Eastern Europe and apartheid South Africa, hundreds of millions of people saw their oppressors admit defeat and embrace liberal democracy.

Those who fought on the side of liberty did not worry about offending the religious or challenging cultures. Forty years ago a campaigner against state-enforced racism knew that supporters of apartheid came from a white supremacist culture with deep roots in the 'communities' of Dutch and English Africans. Their clerics provided a religious justification for racism by instructing them that blacks were the heirs of Ham, whom God had condemned to be 'the servants of servants' because of a curse – vindictive even by the standards of the Abrahamic religions – that Noah placed on Ham's son Canaan. (Ham had had the temerity to gaze on a sleeping Noah when he was naked and drunk, and laugh at him. God therefore damned his line in perpetuity.) The opponents of oppression did not say that they must 'respect Afrikaans culture', however. They did not say that it was Afrikaanophobic to be judgemental about religion, or explain that it was imperialist to criticise the beliefs of 'the other'. If a religion was oppressive or a culture repugnant, one had a duty to offend it.

The liberal resurgence, which brought down so many tyrannies, was also an attack on the beliefs and values of the old democracies. The 1960s generation brought an end to the deference shown to democratic leaders and established institutions.

Many found its irreverence shocking, but no matter. The job of artists, intellectuals and journalists became to satirise and expose; to be the transgressive and edgy critics of authority. They did not confine themselves to politics. Cultural constraints, backed by religious authority, collapsed under the pressure of the second wave of feminism, the sexual revolution and the movements for racial and homosexual emancipation. The revolution in private life was greater than the revolution in politics. Old fences that had seemed fixed by God or custom for eternity fell as surely as the Berlin Wall.

Struggling to encapsulate in a paragraph how the cultural revolution of the second half of the twentieth century had torn up family structures and prejudices, the British Marxist historian Eric Hobsbawm settled on an account from a baffled film critic of the plot of Pedro Almodóvar's 1987 *Law of Desire*.

> In the film Carmen Maura plays a man who's had a transsexual operation and, due to an unhappy love affair with his/her father, has given up on men to have a lesbian, I guess, relationship with a woman, who is played by a famous Madrid transvestite.

It was easy to mock. But laughter ought to have been stifled by the knowledge that within living memory transsexuals, transvestites, gays and lesbians had not been subjects that writers and directors could cover sympathetically, or on occasion at all. Their release from traditional morality reflected the release of wider society from sexual prejudice.

That release offended religious and social conservatives who thought a woman's place was in the home, sexual licence a sin and homosexuality a crime against nature. Although the fashion for relativism was growing in Western universities in the 1980s, leftish academics did not say we had no right to offend the cultures of racists, misogynists and homophobes, and demand that we 'respect' their 'equally valid' contributions to a diverse society. Even they knew that reform is impossible without challenging established cultures. Challenge involves offence. Stop offending, and the world stands still.

Salman Rushdie was a man of his time, who would never have understood the notion that you should think twice before offending the powerful. *Midnight's Children*, the 1981 novel that made him famous, was an account of how the ideals of independent India, which Nehru announced as the chimes of midnight struck on 14–15 August 1947, degenerated into the tyranny of Indira Gandhi's state of emergency. Its successor, *Shame*, dissected the brutalities of military and religious tyranny in Pakistan. By the time he began *The Satanic Verses* Rushdie was the literary conscience of the subcontinent. He deplored the cruelties of post-colonialism, while never forgetting the cruelties of the colonists. It was not a surprise that after looking at post-partition India and Pakistan, he turned his attention to Islam. He had been born into a secular Muslim family in Bombay. He had studied the Koran at Cambridge University, as a literary text written by men rather than God's creation. The Islamic Revolution in Iran, which brought the Ayatollah Khomeini to power in 1979, had pushed religious conservatism to the centre of politics. Rushdie would no more treat religious authority uncritically than he would treat secular authority uncritically. If he had, he would have committed a real offence against the intellectual standards of his day.

A God of Bullies

Rushdie's title declared his intention. According to a contested religious tradition, the satanic verses were the lines the devil tricked Muhammad into believing were the words of God as he struggled to convert the pagan people of Mecca to Islam. Satan suggested that Muhammad tell the Meccans he would compromise his harsh new religion and allow Mecca's pagan goddesses

Al-Lat, Al-'Uzzá and Manāt to intercede with God on their behalf. The biographers of the Prophet claimed that the angel Gabriel chastised Muhammad for allowing Satan to deceive him. Mortified, the Prophet took back the satanic words and returned to uncompromising monotheism.

To modern and not so modern eyes, the episode raises pertinent questions about how believers can consider a sacred text to be the inerrant word of a god or gods when the devil or anyone else can insert their thoughts into it. The cases of the Koran, Old Testament and New Testament gave them excellent grounds for scepticism, because the texts were not prepared until decades after the supposed revelations. Rushdie endorsed scepticism by showing how well the Koran suited the prejudices of early medieval Arabia, and threw in the oppression of women for good measure.

Al-Lat, Al-'Uzzá and Manāt were goddesses, and Islam, like Judaism and Christianity, was determined to wipe out the goddess cults of the ancient world and replace them with the rule of a stern and unbending patriarch. It is worth mentioning Christianity and Judaism at this point, because although everyone who raises the subject of sexism and religion in the post-Rushdie world concentrates on Islam's attitude to women, liberalism's task of knocking misogyny out of the other mainstream religions is not over. As late as 2010, a modest proposal to allow women to become bishops with the same powers as their male counterparts pushed the Church of England close to schism. In any other area of public life, the suggestion that male employees could refuse to serve a woman boss would be greeted with derision. To a large faction within the supposedly modern and moderate Church of England, sexism remained God's will, and equality of opportunity an offence against the divine order. At about the same time as Anglicans were displaying their prejudices, gangs of Orthodox Jews were forming themselves into 'chastity squads'. They beat divorced women in Jerusalem for breaking religious law by walking out in the company of married men, and asked the courts to uphold men's 'right' to force Orthodox women to sit at the back of buses – an unconscious homage to the segregation of blacks and whites in the old American South.

Rushdie was touching therefore on a theme that was close to being universal. While there always have been and always will be men who wish to dominate women, the peculiar iniquity of religion is to turn misogyny into a part of the divine order: to make sexism a virtue and equality a sin.

The authors of a recent study of religious oppression dispensed with the circumlocutions of modern commentators, and put the case for an unembarrassed critique of religion plainly. They considered how Sharia adultery laws state that a raped woman must face the next-to-impossible task of providing four male witnesses to substantiate her allegation or be convicted of adultery; how when rapists leave Pakistani women pregnant courts take the bulge in their bellies as evidence against them; how in Nigeria, Sharia courts not only punish raped women for adultery but order an extra punishment of a whipping for making false accusations against 'innocent' men; how in the United States, the fundamentalist Church of Latter Day Saints gives teenagers to old men in arranged marriages and tells them they must submit to their wishes; and how the theocratic Saudi Arabian state stops women walking unaccompanied in the street, driving a car and speaking to men outside the family. Then – after drawing a deep breath – they asked, 'Does God hate women?'

Well, what can one say? Religious authorities and conservative clerics worship a wretchedly cruel unjust vindictive executioner of a God. They worship a God of ten-year-old boys, a God of playground bullies, a God of rapists, of gangs, of pimps. They worship – despite rhetoric about justice and compassion – a

God who sides with the strong against the weak, a God who cheers for privilege and punishes egalitarianism. They worship a God who is a male and who gangs up with other males against women. They worship a thug. They worship a God who thinks little girls should be married to grown men. They worship a God who looks on in approval when a grown man rapes a child because he is 'married' to her. They worship a God who thinks a woman should receive eighty lashes with a whip because her hair wasn't completely covered. They worship a God who is pleased when three brothers hack their sisters to death with axes because one of them married without their father's permission.

Although the authors looked at the abuse of children by the Catholic Church, and prejudice in Jewish, American Baptist and Mormon sects, most of their examples came from Islam and Hinduism. That is not a sign of prejudice on their part. Any writer tackling religious oppression has to accept that liberalism tempered the misogyny of mainstream Christianity and Judaism in the rich world after centuries of struggle, but left the poor world largely untouched. Christianity and Judaism are not 'better' than Islam and Hinduism. Free-thinkers have just made a better job of containing their prejudices and cruelties.

Rushdie's Muhammad does not always pretend that religious ordinances come from heaven. As he considers the Meccans' demand that their goddesses should be allowed to argue with his male god, he is no longer a prophet seeking to understand divine commands, but a politician weighing the options. The pagans of Mecca will accept his new religion in return for him allowing them to keep their old goddesses. That's the bargain. That's the offer on the table. God's will has nothing to do with it. Nor do the tricks of Satan. If Paris is worth a mass, is Mecca worth a goddess, or two, or three?

'I've been offered a deal,' he shouts, but his followers will have none of it. Like so many leaders, Rushdie's Muhammad is trapped by the fanaticism of disciples who deny him space for compromise. They had believed that every word he said came from God via Gabriel. If they changed their story to suit political pressures, they would become a laughing stock. Why should anyone trust them if they diluted their absolute faith and accepted that God's commands were open to interpretation and negotiation? Why should they trust themselves?

'How long have we been reciting the creed you brought us?' asks one. 'There is no god but God. What are we if we abandon it now? This weakens us, renders us absurd. We cease to be dangerous. Nobody will ever take us seriously again.' In any case, a second disciple tells Muhammad, 'Lat, Mamnat, Uzza – they're all females! For pity's sake! Are we to have goddesses now? Those old cranes, herons and hags?'

Muhammad realises that if he compromises, he will lose his followers and with them his power base. The Meccans will have no reason to deal with him. He falls into a crisis of self-doubt, a scene Rushdie carries off with great pathos, although neither his religious detractors nor many of his secular admirers could admit it.

As the book went on, Rushdie provided his enemies with more ammunition by continuing in the feminist vein. Can a man who has so many wives under his control be the leader of a new faith, he asks. Or as Aisha, Muhammad's youngest wife, says in the novel, 'Your God certainly jumps to it when you need him to fix things up for you.' When Rushdie's Muhammad confronts free-thinking women, 'bang, out comes the rule book, the angel starts pouring out rules about what women mustn't do, he starts forcing them back into the docile attitudes the Prophet prefers, docile or maternal, walking three steps behind or sitting at home being wise and waxing their chins'.

To illustrate how you cannot have blasphemy until there is a religion to blaspheme against, Rushdie had the men of Mecca go to a brothel where the courtesans were named after the Prophet's wives. He tested the belief that the Koran was the sacred word of God by having a sceptic rewrite the Prophet's divine revelations. As I said, to those with the mentalities of heretic-hunters and witch-burners, *The Satanic Verses* was a blasphemous book, and no one could deny it. The single point that his supporters should have needed to make in his defence was that Salman Rushdie was born in democratic India and moved to democratic Britain. He was a free man in a free country, and could write what he damn well wanted.

Events were to prove that his supporters needed additional arguments.

The first was to emphasise that the best novelists do not produce agitprop.

The Satanic Verses is not just 'about' religion and the rights of women. It is a circus of magical realism, with sub-plots, dream sequences, fantasies, pastiches, sudden interruptions by the author, a bewildering number of characters, and a confusion of references to myths and to the news stories of the day. If you insist on nailing down its political message – and trust me, you will whack your thumb with the hammer many times before you do – you will discover that the novel is 'about' migrants from India to the West who, like Rushdie, are contending with their changing identities and their dissolving religious and cultural certainties.

The protagonists – Gibreel Farishta, a Bollywood movie star who plays Hindu gods in religious epics, and whose fans worship him as a god, and Saladin Chamcha, an actor who has left India and makes a living doing voiceovers for London advertising agencies – confront the pressures on the psyche migration brings. Somewhat prophetically given what was to happen next, the Anglicised Saladin tells his Indian mistress, who is trying to find what remains of India inside him:

'Well this is what is inside … An Indian translated into English-medium. When I attempt Hindustani these days, people look polite. This is me.' Caught in the aspic of his adopted language he had begun to hear in India's Babel an ominous warning: don't come back again. When you have stepped through the looking glass you step back at your peril. The mirror may cut you to shreds.

If people wanted reasons to find offence – and as we will see, there are people who are offended if you *don't* give them reasons to find offence – then the British police and immigration services might have issued death threats, because Rushdie showed them as racists and sadists. When the controversy broke and he needed police protection, supporters of law and order complained about the lack of 'respect' for the British state Rushdie had displayed in his writings. The cops, however, took his satire on the chin and went on to guard him from assassins. If you wanted to be fussy, you could also notice passages which showed that Asian shopkeepers in London were not always comradely soldiers joined with their Afro-Caribbean brothers in the struggle against white prejudice, as the anti-racist orthodoxy of the 1980s said they must be. Rushdie's Asian Londoners are contemptuous of the black youths they assume must be criminals. Britain's black community once again lived with the offence.

But, and here is the second large point, to go through *The Satanic Verses* with the squinting eye of a censor searching for thought crimes, or even to seek to see it in the round, as I have tried to do, is to blind yourself to the real reason why the fatwa against Salman Rushdie became the Dreyfus Affair of our age. That reason is as brutal now as it was then.

Globalising Censorship (1)

Terror is why *The Satanic Verses* is still the novel that all modern arguments about the silencing of sceptical and liberal voices must deal with first. The terror unleashed by its opponents and the response of the inheritors of the liberal tradition to their enemies' demands for censorship and self-censorship. No terror, and *The Satanic Verses* would be one of several great works by a great novelist, rather than shorthand for a battle whose outcome defined what writers can and can't say.

Rushdie did not understand what he was fighting. 'The thing that is most disturbing is they are talking about a book which does not exist,' he said as the protests grew. 'The book which is worth killing people for and burning flags is not the book I wrote. The people who demonstrated in Pakistan and who were killed haven't actually read the book that I wrote because it isn't on sale there.' He had not grasped that reactionary mobs and those who seek to exploit them have a know-nothing pride in their ignorance. It was sufficient that clerical authorities said that the book was blasphemous, and could quote a passage or two to prove their case. The vast majority of religious fanatics who murdered or threatened to murder publishers, translators, booksellers and innocent bystanders did not want to read the book in the round, or to read it at all. Most would not have understood it if they had tried.

Their violence rolled around the world. The brutality of the reaction was beyond anything that Rushdie or his publishers anticipated or could have anticipated. Penguin released *The Satanic Verses* in 1988. Without pausing to consider its contents, President Rajiv Gandhi put it on India's proscribed list. The opposition MP who demanded that Gandhi ban the book had not read it either, but decided, 'I do not have to wade through a filthy drain to know what filth is.' Gandhi was frightened of communal riots and of losing the Muslim vote, and perhaps remembered how Rushdie had excoriated his mother, Indira, in *Midnight's Children*.

In India and Pakistan and later in Britain, Jamaat-e-Islami organised the protests. Its enmity was a compliment to Rushdie, for Jamaat's supporters were enemies any liberal should be proud to have. Jamaat's founder, Maulana Abu'l Ala Maududi, began agitating in British-occupied India in 1941, and had a good claim to be the first of the Islamists. He combined his version of a 'purified' Islam with European totalitarianism. From the communists he took the notion of the vanguard party, which would tell the masses what they wanted, regardless of whether the masses wanted it or not, and vague notions of a just future where all would be equal. From the Nazis, Jamaat, and its partners in the Arab Muslim Brotherhood, took the Jewish conspiracy theory. They explained that Muslims were weak because they were victims of the plots of sinister Jews, or 'Zionists', as they came to call them, who were everywhere seeking to undermine their faith and morals. Muslims would free themselves by building a caliphate, where the supreme ruler of a global empire would not be a Nazi führer or communist general secretary but a theocrat ruling with total power in accordance with Koran and Sharia.

After the British withdrew from India in 1947, leaving millions to die in the slaughters of partition, Jamaat supported the new Muslim state of Pakistan, which was split between its Bengali east wing and the Punjabi-dominated west. When the Bengalis of East Pakistan revolted against a system that made them second-class citizens, the Pakistani army's retaliation stunned a twentieth century that thought it had become inured to genocide. Jamaat aided the army's campaigns of mass murder and mass rape because it believed in the caliphate, and hence could not tolerate the secession of Bangladesh from Pakistan, because it broke Islamic unity. At the time this book went to press, Bangladeshi prosecutors were beginning war crime proceedings against Jamaat leaders they claimed were members of the paramilitary squads Pakistan recruited to help with killing.

Rushdie had already noticed that the Pakistani military dictatorship of the 1980s needed the Jamaatists to provide a religious cover for tyranny. 'This is how religions shore up dictators; by encircling them with words of power, words which the people are reluctant to see discredited, disenfranchised, mocked,' he said, as he gave Jamaat reasons to hate him as well.

The next countries to ban *The Satanic Verses* were Sudan, Bangladesh and apartheid South Africa. If you find the alliance of militant Islamists and white supremacists strange, then you have yet to learn that all the enemies of liberalism are the same. In its dying days, the regime tried to uphold the apartheid state by co-opting mixed-race and Asian South Africans into the system, the better to deny South Africa's black majority the vote. Most coloured and Asian South Africans refused to cooperate. But Islamists saw the chance to use apartheid's censorship laws against Rushdie. The left-wing *Weekly Mail* and the Congress of South African Writers had invited him to visit Johannesburg in 1988 to discuss the censorship of the opponents of white rule. Rushdie had to pull out because of death threats from Islamists. The white-skinned rulers learned they could now rely on brown-skinned religious extremists to intimidate a writer who was proposing to come to their country and denounce their regime.

Even before the Ayatollah Khomeini's fatwa, Rushdie had many enemies, but they were not dangerous enemies. The Indian government regularly banned books it thought might provoke communal violence. Jamaatists in Pakistan and white supremacists in South Africa had always threatened authors. An Anglo-Indian writer based in London had little to fear from them. Intellectuals who had made it to the West were beyond the reach of oppressive forces. They had a place of sanctuary.

The fatwa changed all that. It redrew the boundaries of the free world, shrinking its borders and erasing zones of disputation from the map of the liberal mind. It ensured that London, New York, Paris, Copenhagen and Amsterdam could no longer be places of safety for writers tackling religious themes.

Journalists throw around the word 'unprecedented' so carelessly and ceaselessly that we miss the new when it stares us in the face. Khomeini's incitement to murder was without precedent. Here was a head of state ordering the execution of the private citizens of foreign countries for writing and publishing a work of fiction. A grotesque regard for the forms of legality had accompanied previous outbreaks of state terrorism. Even Stalin forced his victims to confess at show trials so that when he murdered them, he did so with a kangaroo court's approval. No such concern with keeping up appearances inhibited Khomeini. On 14 February 1989, he said that the faithful must kill Rushdie and his publishers and 'execute them quickly, wherever they may find them, so that no one will dare insult Islam again. Whoever is killed in this path will be regarded as a martyr.' Just in case zealous assassins doubted that they would receive eternal life in paradise along with the services of seventy-two virgins, an Iranian foundation offered the earthly reward of $3 million.

There was not even a show trial. Khomeini did not listen to the religious scholars who said that as Rushdie was not a citizen of an Islamic state, he could not punish him for blasphemy or apostasy. And he took even less notice of the more substantial objections from secularists that no one had the right to order the murder of a writer for subjecting religion to imaginative scrutiny.

Far from making himself the object of repulsion, the Ayatollah's endorsement of state-sponsored murder won him many followers. After the death sentence, preachers whipped up mobs against Pakistani Christians in Islamabad. In Bombay, twelve died in battles with the police. A bomber murdered a security guard at the British Council offices in Karachi. In Dhaka, fifteen thousand people tried to break through police lines and ransack the British Council's library. In the United States, Islamists threatened bookstores and firebombers hit the offices of the *Riverdale Press*, a weekly paper in the Bronx, after it published an unexceptional editorial saying that the public had the right to read whatever novels it pleased.

In Britain, demonstrators in Bradford burned copies of *The Satanic Verses*. I doubt they had heard Heinrich Heine's line that 'Where they burn books, so too will they in the end burn human beings' – a condemnation from the German Enlightenment of the burning of the Koran by the Spanish Inquisition, ironically enough. Onlookers were entitled to wonder whether Heine was right, and Rushdie's British enemies would burn the human being in question if they could get hold of him. As in America and Europe, British bookshops withdrew the novel in the face of threats – two independent bookshops on the Charing Cross Road were bombed, as were Penguin bookshops and a department store. Police surrounded Penguin's head office with concrete barricades to stop suicide bombers crashing cars into the building. They X-rayed all packages for explosives and patrolled the perimeter with guard dogs. Meanwhile Special Branch officers moved their charge from safe house to safe house. Rushdie was at the beginning of a rolling programme of house arrest that was to deprive him of his liberty for years.

He had nowhere to run. If he had left Britain, no other country could have promised him safety. The global scale of the malice directed against him made him a refugee without the hope of asylum. Iranian or Pakistani writers who saw the violence in the West realised that if clerics issued fatwas against them in Tehran or Lahore, they could no longer expect to flee to a safe haven. If the controversy was raucous, if the media amplified the death threats, there would be nowhere on the planet to hide.

To justify their death threats and make the shocking seem reasonable, Rushdie's enemies aped the European fascists and communists of the twentieth century. Just as the Nazis said that the Germans were the victims of supernatural Jewish plots or the communists said that the proletariat was the target of the machinations of the treacherous bourgeoisie, so the Islamists told the faithful that they were being persecuted by a conspiracy of global reach and occult power. Ali Akbar Rafsanjani, the speaker of the Iranian parliament, declared that the West had been engaged in a cultural war from colonialism on to 'undermine the people's genuine Islamic morals'. Rushdie was at its forefront. He was the ideal undercover agent for Western intelligence, Rafsanjani announced – 'a person who seemingly comes from India and who apparently is separate from the Western world and who has a misleading name'. Rushdie was a white colonialist, hiding beneath a brown skin; a traitor hiding behind a Muslim name. The British secret service had paid him to betray the faithful, the Iranian theocracy explained as it added corruption to the list of charges against him. It gave him bribes, disguised as book advances, as it organised the assault on Islam by the cunning if curious means of a magical realist novel.

As with Nazism, the conspiracy theory needed Jews. The Iranian interior minister said that Zionists had 'direct involvement' in publishing the book. The Iranian president said that 'Zionist-controlled news agencies' had made Rushdie famous. In Syria, the Ba'athist dictatorship said that the novel was part of a plot to distract the world's attention from Israel's treatment of the Palestinians. In Pakistan, religious leaders talked of an 'American Jewish conspiracy'. Across the planet, the drums shuddered to the same beat: 'It's the Jews, it's the Jews, it's the Jews.'

The demonstrations against Rushdie were not confined to the poor world. The faithful marched in Bradford and London as well as Tehran and Lahore. They inspired a fear in the West that went almost unnoticed during the elation the 1989 revolutions in Eastern Europe produced.

Fear was a novel emotion for Western liberals, and I understand why they wanted to push it to the back of their minds. However much they talked about the bravery of the stands they were making, those in the West who campaigned against apartheid in southern Africa, and those, much fewer in number, who wanted to help the opponents of communism in Eastern Europe and the Soviet Union, had not had to put their lives on the line. They had not had to come to terms with the knowledge that the publication of a book or a cartoon, or the vigorous condemnation of an oppressive ideology, would place families, colleagues and themselves in danger. They had never felt the need to glance twice at dark doorways or listen for quickening footsteps coming up behind them in the street.

By the early 1990s, events seemed to have taught liberals that they could win without pain, in bloodless revolutions. After the fall of white South Africa and the break-up of the Soviet Union, fear appeared to be an unnecessary emotion. History's lesson was that dictatorships would collapse of their own accord without the usual wars and revolutionary terrors. Party hacks and secret policemen, who had never uttered a dissenting word in their lives, had of their own accord given up serving worthless ideologies and embraced the ideals of Western liberalism. 'The heroes of retreat', the German poet Hans Magnus Enzensberger, called them – Kadar, Suarez, Jaruzelski, Botha and above all Gorbachev: apparent 'yes men' who decided to say 'no' to the regimes they had promised to protect. Just like that, without anyone invading their countries or storming their palaces and holding guns to their heads. One day apartheid was there, the next Nelson Mandela was president of South Africa, and the world was granting him a status dangerously close to sainthood. For forty years the Iron Curtain had divided Europe, and then as if a magician had waved his wand, it vanished and tourists could gawp at what was left of the Berlin Wall, before going on to holiday in what had once been the forbidden territory of Eastern Europe.

Humanity had seen nothing on the scale of the bloodless revolutions of 1989 to 1991 before. Former enemies acknowledged their mistakes. They came to agree with our way of thinking without us having to risk our personal safety. The world lived through an age of miracles; but the trouble with witnessing miracles is that you come to expect more of them.

The tactless Rushdie spoilt the ecstatic mood. The reaction to his novel showed that history was not over. One enemy of liberalism was not coming round to our way of thinking, holding up its hands and admitting that we had been right all along. It asked questions of liberals that were close to home. Would they be able to defend their values, when their opponents were not Russian communists sending dissidents to Siberia, or right-wing dictators in faraway lands ordering the torture and murders of Latin American leftists, but fellow citizens who were threatening to kill novelists and bombing bookshops in the cities of the West? Would they defend free speech in murderous times? Or would they hold their tongues and accept that they must 'respect' views they knew to be false?

Demand a Respect You Don't Deserve

Do you believe in freedom of speech?

Are you sure?

Far be it from me to accuse you of living with illusions, but unless you are a tyrant or a lunatic – and the line between the two is thin – you will rarely speak your mind without a thought for the consequences. You would be friendless within a day if you put a belief in absolute freedom of speech into practice. If you propositioned complete strangers, or told them that they were fools, if you sat down at a meeting and announced that the woman next to you was ugly and the man next to her stank, you would run out of people willing to spend time in your company.

Humans are social primates, and socialising with the rest of our species requires a fair amount of routine self-censorship and outright lying, which we dignify with names such as 'tact', 'courtesy' and 'politeness'.

The appeal of censorship becomes evident when you consider whether you would be happy for others to say what they thought about you. Even if what they said was true – particularly if what they said was true – you would want to stop them saying that you were ugly, boring or smelly. You would expect them to lie to you, just as they would expect you to lie to them. Humans have a bias in favour of information that bolsters their prejudices and validates their choices. Above all, our species has a confirmation bias in favour of information that upholds our good opinion of ourselves. We want our status confirmed. We want others to lie to us so that we can lie to ourselves. We want to be respected.

As well as a provision for freedom of speech, most guarantees of basic liberties have a right to privacy sitting uneasily alongside them. It recognises that the full truth about an individual's life cannot be made public without crushing his or her autonomy. Under the pressure of exposure, his sense of who he was would change. He would become suspicious, fretful, harassed; he would be left exposed to gales of mockery and condemnation. In the interests of preventing a surveillance society, it is better that the state allows the citizen to live a lie. 'If you've nothing to hide, you have nothing to fear,' say authoritarians. But everyone has something to hide, and if there isn't a dirty secret, there is always something that your enemies can twist to make you look dirty.

Privacy was meant to offer the citizen protection against the over-mighty state. The emphasis on the right to a private life was an understandable and necessary reaction against the informers and spies the communist and fascist totalitarian regimes recruited to monitor daily life. But in the late twentieth century, at the same time as the *Satanic Verses* controversy began, judges began to adapt the law. Instead of stopping the secret service from tapping the phones or opening the mail of citizens, judges decided to stop the media revealing details of the private lives of wealthy celebrities and other public figures.

The privacy law they developed could not have been more different from traditional libel law. Libel is meant to protect the individual from the pain inflicted by malicious gossips who spread lies about him or her. Privacy protects against the pain that comes from hearing the truth broadcast. In libel, truth is an absolute defence. If writers and publishers can justify what they say, they may leave the court without punishment. In privacy cases, truth is not a defence but an irrelevance. The law intervenes not because the reports are false, but because they tell too much truth for the subject to cope with, and open him up to mockery, to pain … to disrespect. Privacy rights allowed the wealthy to suppress criticisms, even though the criticisms were true. They could demand respect, even though they were not respectable.

The persecution of Rushdie appeared to follow the old precedents. Contemporaries looking for a parallel to Khomeini's gangsterish order for assassins to 'hit' him recalled the Vatican's order to take out Elizabeth I in the 1570s. They talked about the re-emergence of the Inquisition, or quoted Voltaire's pointed question, 'What to say to a man who tells you he prefers to obey God than to obey men, and who is consequently sure of entering the gates of Heaven by slitting your throat?'

The comparison with the past fails, because there is an unbridgeable gulf between today's religion and the religious ideas which persisted for most of history. Until the Enlightenment, maybe until the publication of *On the Origin of Species*, believers could reassure themselves that the wisest thinkers of their time believed that a divine order structured the universe. As late as the 1690s, a belief in science and magic could co-exist even in the great mind of Isaac Newton, who divided his days between trying to understand the laws of motion and trying to work out when the Book of Revelation foretold the 'great tribulation and the end of the world'. (He thought that God would wind us up in 2060, readers expecting to make it through the mid-twenty-first century should note.)

Charges of blasphemy and heresy were once like accusations of libel. The wretched sinner had sought to spread falsehoods against the true religion, which the faithful exposed. The Protestant divines of Elizabethan England and the papacy that confronted them fought over what kind of supernatural power ordered the world. But they agreed on the fundamental question that a supernatural power must order the world. The Catholic believed that if the Protestant converted to Catholicism he would find the truth. The Protestant believed the opposite. Now you have to be a very isolated believer to imagine that your religion, or any religion, can provide a comprehensive explanation of the world. When they study beyond a certain level, all believers learn that the most reliable theories of the origins of life have no need for the God of the Torah, the New Testament or the Koran. The most brilliant modern scientists have little in common with Newton. They are atheists, or believers in a remote God who is nothing like the capricious, interventionist deity of the holy books. The best thought has moved beyond religion. It is for this reason that religion, which once inspired man's most sublime creations, can no longer produce art, literature or philosophy of any worth; why it is impossible to imagine a new religious high culture.

If you go to the chapel at King's College, Cambridge, you will see one response to the loss of religious authority. The inheritors of the priests and stonemasons who sent arches soaring heavenwards to show their confidence in a divinely ordained universe are now modest people. Their information for visitors makes no pretence that the gospels are accurate accounts of Christ's life and teaching. Cambridge Anglicans stress that unknown hands wrote them long after Christ's death. They offer worshippers a celebration of tradition, symbolic truths and parables, not literal truths. Everywhere liberal Christians, Jews and Muslims follow the same example. They worship in a narrow religious sphere, which is cautious and a touch vapid, and do not try to force the rest of society to accept their views. For them there is a secular world informed by science, and there is their world of faith.

Religious fanatics appear to be opposed to the liberal modernists. They would never accept that their holy books could be anything other than the word of God. The philosopher Ernest Gellner wrote just after the fatwa that Westerners ought to rethink the assumption that industrialisation undermined religious belief. The post-Khomeini world was showing that the forward march of secularism was not inevitable. Islam 'demonstrates that it is possible to run a modern, or at any rate a modernising economy, reasonably permeated by the appropriate technological, educational and organisational principles *and* combine it with a strong, pervasive, powerfully internalised Muslim conviction and identification'.

The differences between religious fundamentalists and religious modernists are not as great as either imagine. Both want to keep religion in a separate sphere; it is just that the religious sphere of the fundamentalist is wider and the means used to protect it from scrutiny more neurotic and brutal. Trying to maintain a 'strong, pervasive, powerfully internalised' religious conviction in a world that can manage without religious explanations creates perpetual tensions, however. The effort required to resolve them is harder than Gellner believed. At some level, even murderous fanatics know that their ideologies are redundant. They are not the vanguard for a new age of piety, but reactionaries, who hope that if they indoctrinate and intimidate they can block out modernity. Their desires mock their hopes. The rifles they fire, the nuclear weapons they crave come from a technology that has no connection to their sacred texts.

To prevent defeat, religious extremists stop the sceptical, evidence-based approach of science moving into the religious sphere and asking hard questions about the validity of their holy books. Rushdie crossed the boundary, and asked modern questions about the evidence behind the story of the founding of Islam. His persecution was just as modern. Rather than representing a continuation of the persecutions of medieval inquisitors, who thought they were protecting the truth from its enemies, his tormentors were closer to celebrities' lawyers, who claim that their client's feelings would be hurt and their image tarnished by the discussion of unwelcome facts. Rushdie's critics were more concerned about the effect of his writings on the psyche of believers than whether what he had said was true. The charge they threw at him was that he had 'offended' the faithful by 'insulting' their religion. It was as if he had invaded their privacy.

I accept that the individual needs protection from the surveillance of an over-mighty state. I accept too that the judges will have to tackle the explosion of character assassination on the Net directed at private citizens. I find the use of privacy law to restrict the media's reporting of public figures far harder to justify. The English judiciary does not put the public interest first, as its willingness to censor on behalf of bankers who had affairs at work shows. But if a new generation of judges could be trusted with the power to prohibit, then I would accept too that people in the public eye need not be exposed to the scrutiny they receive in the United States. All of these acts of censorship, however, are protections for *individuals*. No honest jurisdiction can defend using censorship to protect ideological systems from the harm or offence of criticism. You must treat ideologies which mandate wars, and govern the sexual behaviour of men and women and, in their extreme forms, every aspect of life for hundreds of millions of people, with the utmost candour. For they are ideas that seek to dominate.

Politics is as much a part of the identity of the committed leftist, green or conservative as religion is a part of the identity of the committed Christian, Jew, Muslim or Hindu. When the political partisan's beliefs are insulted or ridiculed, he feels the 'offence' as deeply as any believer who has heard his god or prophet questioned. We do not, however, prohibit or restrict arguments about politics out of 'respect' for political ideologies, because we are a free society. We call societies that prohibit political arguments 'dictatorships', and know without needing to be told that the prohibiting is done to protect the ruling elite. If political or religious believers are offended to the core of their being by criticism, free countries must reply, 'Tough. Learn to live with it. We know that we tell white lies about many things.

We accept that the truth can be suppressed on some occasions. But religion and politics are too important and too dangerous to risk handling with kid gloves.'

Respect for religion is the opposite of religious tolerance, because it allows the intolerant to impose their will on others. The Virginia Statute for Religious Tolerance, written by Thomas Jefferson in 1776, highlighted the distinction in flowing prose:

> Be it enacted by General Assembly that no man shall be compelled to frequent or support any religious worship, place, or ministry whatsoever, nor shall be enforced, restrained, molested, or burthened in his body or goods, nor shall otherwise suffer on account of his religious opinions or belief, but that all men shall be free to profess, and by argument to maintain, their opinions in matters of Religion, and that the same shall in no wise diminish, enlarge or affect their civil capacities.

Salman Rushdie was not free to abandon and criticise the religion of his childhood. The Islamists said that if he – and by extension all other Muslims – changed his religion or decided that he was an atheist, he would face assassination for the 'crime' of apostasy. They wanted to make Rushdie 'suffer on account of his religious opinions'; to restrain, molest and burthen his body for his blasphemy, and to do the same to anyone, Muslim or not, who echoed his ideas. In his most compelling line, Jefferson concluded that 'all men shall be free to profess, and by argument to maintain, their opinions in matters of Religion'.

'Argument' was his key word. Religious toleration did not limit argument, but removed the sanctions of the state and the established Church that had stood in argument's way. It did not rule out appeals to logic, reason, imagination and sympathy – but gave them the space to breathe without the threat of punishment. Argument involves the true respect that comes from treating others as adults who can cope with challenging ideas and expecting them to treat you with a similar courtesy. Looking back on his life in 2011, Rushdie echoed Jefferson: 'The question is who has power over the story. The response of anybody interested in liberty is that we all have a say and the ability to have an argument is exactly what liberty is, even though it may never be resolved. In any authoritarian society the possessor of power dictates, and if you try and step outside he will come after you.'

The 'respect' demanded by Rushdie's enemies infantilised both the giver and the receiver, and suited religious reactionaries well. They had every interest in keeping their subject populations in a state of infantile ignorance, and in spreading the fear that all who thought about arguing with them would know that they risked becoming the next target.

TWO

A Clash of Civilisations?

I see no way to secure liberalism by trying to put its core values beyond any but internal or consensual reasoning. The resulting slide into relativism leaves a disastrous parallel between 'liberalism for the liberals' and 'cannibalism for the cannibals'.

MARTIN HOLLIS

Islamism is a movement of the radical religious right. Its borrowings from fascism include the anti-Jewish conspiracy theory and the anti-Freemason conspiracy theory. It places men above women. It worships martyrdom and the concomitant cult of death. You do not have to stare too long or too hard at its adherents to realise that they are liberalism's enemies. Yet the most jarring aspect of Khomeini's denunciations was that he and his supporters implied that Western liberals should regard them as brothers in the struggles to defend the wretched of the earth. They used the anti-imperialist language the political left employed when it castigated the machinations of the White House and the CIA, and the anti-racist language it employed when castigating white oppression.

With a devious inversion, they turned the freedom to speak and to criticise into instruments of coercion the strong inflicted on the weak. If you wanted to be a genuine liberal, if you wanted to be on the side of the weak in their battle with the strong, you must be against Rushdie. Of all the lies that surrounded the fatwa, this was not only the most noxious but also the most farcical.

Rushdie was a typical leftist of the 1980s. He supported all the old causes. He was a candid friend of the Nicaraguan revolution, and wrote in defence of the Palestinians. At first, he welcomed the overthrow of the Shah of Iran and the arrival of the Islamic revolution, although he changed his mind long before its admirers tried to kill him. In Britain, he was the first great novelist English literature had produced to confront the disorientation felt by migrants. By necessity, his subject and his own experience made him a tough and on occasion vituperative enemy of racism. In the early 1980s, he broadcast a blood-chilling description of Britain as an island saturated with chauvinism. Unlike the Germans, who had come through painful self-examination to 'purify German thought and the German language of the pollution of Nazism', the British had never come to terms with the evils of Empire, he told the liberal viewers of Channel 4, who were doubtless suitably guilt-ridden. 'British thought, British society has never been cleansed of the filth of imperialism. It's still there, breeding lice and vermin, waiting for unscrupulous people to exploit it for their own ends. British racism, of course, is not our problem. It's yours. We simply suffer from the effects of your problem. And until you, the whites, see that the issue is not integration, or harmony, or multi-culturalism, but simply facing up to and eradicating the prejudices within almost all of you, the citizens of your new and last Empire will be obliged to struggle against you.'

If Rushdie was an agent of the imperialists, he was operating under deep cover.

Assessing the response of liberals to the assault on liberalism and the attempts to murder one of their own is blighted by the old problem that we remember the best writers' work, because it survives and moulds the future's thinking, but forget the lesser journalists and authors who dominate debate at the time. The best left-wing writers of the 1980s understood that the left's commitment to freedom of speech was far from certain. They knew that it had its own foul history of fellow travelling with tyranny. Their noses sniffed the air to catch the first whiff of treachery. In *Culture of Complaint,* his dissection of the politicisation of the arts and humanities in the 1980s, Robert Hughes lacerated the universities for their failure to defend Rushdie. Academics were forever berating dead white males for their failure to conform to exacting modern standards, he said, but stayed silent as murderers threatened the basic standards of intellectual life. On American campuses, they held that if a man so much as looked around with a lustful eye, or called a young female a 'girl' instead of a 'woman', he was guilty of gross sexual impropriety. 'Abroad it was more or less OK for a cabal of regressive theocratic bigots to insist on the chador, to cut off thieves' hands and put out the eyes of offenders on TV, and to murder novelists as state policy. Oppression is what we do in the West. What they do in the Middle East is "their culture".' Leftists could not make a stand, because to their minds defending Rushdie would at some level mean giving aid and comfort to racists and strengthening the hand of the one enemy they could admit to having: the imperialist warmongers in Washington, DC.

Rushdie's friend Christopher Hitchens saw the centres of British cities clogged with men who wanted to pass blasphemy laws and give the police the power to control what free citizens could read. 'That this ultra-reactionary mobocracy was composed mainly of people with brown skins ought to have made no difference. In Pakistan, long familiar with the hysteria of Jamaat Islami and other religio-dictatorial gangs, it would have made no difference at all. But somehow, when staged in the streets and squares of Britain it did make a difference. A pronounced awkwardness was introduced into the atmosphere.'

Too many of his former comrades were dodging the issue by imagining a false moral equivalence, he said. Rushdie and his oppressors were to their minds equally guilty. They could not see that 'all of the deaths and injuries – *all of them* – from the mob scenes in Pakistan to the activities of the Iranian assassination squads were directly caused by Rushdie's enemies. None of the deaths – *none of them* – were caused by him, or by his friends and defenders. Yet you will notice the displacement tactic used by … the multicultural left which blamed the mayhem on an abstract construct – "the Rushdie Affair". I dimly understood at the time that this kind of post-modern "left" somehow in league with political Islam was something new. That this *trahison* would take a partly "multicultural form" was also something that was ceasing to surprise me.'

The Western leftists Hughes and Hitchens had in their sights were making the elementary howler of confusing ethnicity – which no one can change – with religions or political ideologies – which are systems of ideas that men and women ought to be free to accept or reject. As that howler now howls like a gale through liberal discourse, we had better take the time to explain why its assumptions are false before moving on.

When Serb extremists killed Bosnian Muslims because of their religion, their lethal religious prejudice was indeed akin to lethal racial prejudice. When employers from the old Protestant ascendancy in Northern Ireland refused Catholics jobs because they were Catholics, a comparison with colour bars against black workers in the old American South applied. When people said that a conspiracy of American Jews controlled American foreign policy, or that Muslim immigrants were imposing a jihadi theology on Europe, they were propagating racist conspiracy theories. Moral equivalence held in all these cases.

When supporters of Rushdie opposed the murder of authors, however, their ideals could not have been further from the dark fantasies of racial hatred. Islamists could call them 'Islamophobes' if they wanted, for they were indeed opposing reactionary Islamic doctrines, but they were doing so because they were liberals who wanted to show solidarity with liberals from the Muslim world, not because they were filled with an irrational loathing. When Catholic reactionaries accuse opponents of papal doctrine on contraception and abortion of 'anti-Catholicism', and when believers in a greater Israel accuse opponents of Israeli expansion into the West Bank of anti-Semitism, they too are palming a card from the bottom of the deck. They are trying to pass off rational morality as an irrational hatred.

In 1989, such confusions lay in the future. Hitchens and Hughes may have realised that an ominous shift was taking place, but most commentators at the time did not. Liberal opinion seemed to me and many others to reel from the threats of the extremists, collect itself and fight back.

Liberalism's First (and Last) Stand

The staff and directors of Penguin, Rushdie's publishers, showed steadiness under fire. Led by Peter Mayer, the chief executive, they contemplated the consequences of withdrawing *The Satanic Verses*. Penguin would not suffer alone, they decided. Every other publisher putting out works that a demagogue could take offence at might become a target.

Mayer and his colleagues were living in fear. The sneering claim that they 'knew what they were doing' when they published *The Satanic Verses* was contradicted by their evident astonishment. As furious men plotted murder, they had to worry about keeping Rushdie from harm. They had to protect their buildings and shops in Britain, and their export offices all over the world. They had to agonise about their staff, most of whom did not realise that they were signing up to fight for freedom of speech when they signed on for mundane jobs. Despite what critics said against them, they had to and did worry about British Muslims, trying to integrate into a new culture. And when the heat was at its fiercest, they had to worry about protecting their own lives and the lives of their families.

They did not spend too much time thinking about Milton or Galileo, Mayer recalled, 'but I did think of books we and others had published that some Catholics probably did not like; other books that offended some Jews or evangelical Christians, or minorities who felt their beliefs, values or ethnicity had been treated negatively. And what of books that offend *majorities*, a subject I heard no one raise? Cease to publish those books, too, when someone raised a hand against them?'

Penguin stayed strong, as did the wider publishing industry. In an uplifting 'I am Spartacus' moment, Penguin's commercial rivals joined with it and formed a consortium to publish the paperback edition of *The Satanic Verses* so that Penguin did not have to face the terror alone. Workers in bookshops, who were neither well paid nor well protected, said that they must continue to stock it. Even bookshops Islamists bombed kept it under the counter when they reopened. The customer only had to ask.

'Although my board was profoundly uneasy, we came to agree that all that any one of us, or a company, could do was above all to preserve the principles that underlie our profession, and which have, since movable type, bought it respect,' said Mayer. 'We were *publishers*. I thought that meant something.'

So it did, and not just at Penguin.

The mediocrity of Rushdie's critics in the West strengthened the resolve of liberals. Most of his enemies came from the political right. American neo-cons, who a few years later would shout until they were hoarse about the threat of Islamism, were delighted that the dictatorial regimes and movements of the poor world were targeting a left-wing novelist. Whatever their politics, comfortable English intellectuals were equally incapable of seeing extremist blackmail for what it was. John le Carré, whose George Smiley seemed to understand that political freedom had to be defended, saw no similar case for a defence of religious freedom. There was 'no law in life or nature that says great religions may be insulted with impunity', he said, apparently unaware that the law of the land he lived in specifically protected its citizens from assassination. It was not that he supported the fatwa, of course. But his anger was directed at the writer, not the men who wanted the writer dead. 'When it came to the further exploitation of Rushdie's work in paperback form, I was more concerned about the girl at Penguin books who might get her hands blown off in the mailroom than I was about Rushdie's royalties. Anyone who had wished to read the book by then had ample access to it.'

In one of his rare public interventions during his underground life, an icy Rushdie wrote from his secret address to say that le Carré was taking 'the philistine, reductionist, militant Islamist line that *The Satanic Verses* was no more than an insult', and that anyone 'who displeases philistine, reductionist, militant Islamist folk loses his right to live in safety. He says that he is more interested in safeguarding publishing staff than in my royalties. But it is precisely these people, my novel's publishers in some thirty countries, together with the staff of bookshops, who have most passionately supported and defended my right to publish. It is ignoble of le Carré to use them as an argument for censorship when they have so courageously stood up for freedom.'

The Tory historian Hugh Trevor-Roper, who wasted his time and talent in snobbish feuds, revelled in Rushdie's suffering. 'I wonder how Salman Rushdie is faring these days,' he mused, 'under the benevolent protection of British law and British police, about whom he has been so rude. Not too comfortably, I hope ... I would not shed a tear if some British Muslims, deploring his manners, should waylay him in a dark street and seek to improve them. If that should cause him thereafter to control his pen, society would benefit and literature would not suffer.' Roald

Dahl said that Rushdie knew what he was doing, an assertion which was not true but allowed him to turn the blame from the potential murderers to their intended victim. 'This kind of sensationalism does indeed get an indifferent book on to the top of the bestseller list,' he continued, 'but to my mind it is a cheap way of doing it.'

The English establishment has a dictionary of insults for men and women who take on the futile task of making it feel guilty – 'chippy', 'bolshie', 'uppity', 'ungrateful' … It directed them all at Rushdie.

I do not think I am reading too much into Dahl's accusation of cheapness or Trevor-Roper's hope that Islamists would beat manners into an author in a dark alley when I say that members of the traditional intelligentsia could not support Rushdie because in his success they could sense their decline. The Indian and South American magical realists of the 1980s foretold a time when great literature would not come from the world they knew. Rushdie was the master of the English language, their language. He came to literary London and took their prizes at the Booker awards. Reviewers in their serious newspapers praised him for his ability to draw from different cultures and ideas. The immigrant from a Muslim family, the most famous Indian in England, seemed interested in everyone except them. He did not describe the agonies of the English upper-middle class or the life and loves of Oxbridge dons, but the slums of London and the politics of the subcontinent, while never forgetting to remind the well-bred among his readers of the shame of British imperialism and the persistence of white racism.

Those who have never believed in universal human rights described the persecution of Rushdie as the first manifestation in the West of a 'clash of civilisations'. We had 'our values' – human rights, freedom of speech – the Islamic world had theirs – fanatical blasphemy laws, the oppression of women – and never the twain would meet.

Rushdie's persecution and the reactions to it showed that from the beginning the clash-of-civilisations hypothesis was condescending and bovine. It flattered the West by ascribing to its leaders a virtue they did not possess. Hardly anyone in a position of authority was prepared to speak up for 'our' values. Religious leaders were as keen as upper-class intellectuals were on shutting up Rushdie. Immanuel Jakobovits, the then Chief Rabbi of Britain, said Penguin should not have published. Robert Runcie, the then Archbishop of Canterbury, proposed that the government extend England's blasphemy law to cover Islam. In these and similar statements from religious conservatives, you could see Christian and Jewish leaders sensing an opportunity. Maybe they could use the violence of Jamaat and the Khomeinists to create an ecumenical taboo that might protect all religions from criticism, even though those religions were incompatible, and their adherents had spent the best part of two millennia killing each other. If writers became frightened of taking on Islam, the reasoning ran, maybe they would keep away from Christianity and Judaism too.

The *Economist* looked at the trade unionism of the faithful and said, 'Rabbis, priests and mullahs are, it seems, uniting to restrain free speech, lest any member of their collective flock should have his feelings hurt … The Rushdie affair is showing not just that some Muslims do not understand the merits of free speech. It shows that many Western clerics do not either.'

Nor did many politicians in Margaret Thatcher's government and George Bush senior's administration understand either. 'The British government, the British people have no affection for this book,' said Britain's then Foreign Secretary, Geoffrey Howe. 'It compares Britain with Hitler's Germany.' Rushdie did not compare Britain with Nazi Germany, as it happens, and hundreds of thousands of British readers bought and enjoyed his novels. If these were forgettable mistakes from an ignorant man, Howe's next words proved fateful. 'We do not like that any more than people of the Muslim faith like the attacks on their faith.'

Western governments followed the same script. After anti-Rushdie riots in Islamabad, the US State Department said, 'The Embassy wishes to emphasise that the US government in no way associates itself with any activity that is in any sense offensive to Islam or any other religion.' Margaret Thatcher, adopting the royal 'we' as was her wont in her last days in power, said, 'We have known in our own religion people doing things which are deeply offensive to some of us. We feel it very much. And that is what is happening to Islam.' Thatcher's acolyte Norman Tebbit called Rushdie an 'outstanding villain', and asked, 'How many societies having been so treated by a foreigner accepted in their midst, could go so far to protect him from the consequences of his egotistical and self-opinionated attack on the religion into which he was born?'

From their different perspectives, Susan Sontag, one of Rushdie's most loyal defenders, Daniel Pipes, an American conservative, and, later, Kenan Malik, a British historian of the struggles for free speech, all noticed the dangers of London and Washington's stance. They were telling Muslim democrats, free-thinkers, feminists and liberals that human rights were Western rights, and not for brown-skinned people from a clashing 'civilisation'. You can call this cultural relativism, but 'racism' is a blunter and better word.

Consider the position of the West in 1989. It had looked upon Iran as a threat from the moment the ayatollahs took power in 1979. It had given air cover to Saddam Hussein's genocidal regime during the Iran–Iraq war because it thought that any enemy of Iran was better than none. Western politicians lectured their own Muslim citizens on the need to adapt to the Western way of life, but then assumed that all Muslims wanted to burn books and murder authors. Freedom of speech was a Western value, not a universal right. Muslims could not be expected to handle it.

The best in the Muslim world did not want Westerners to patronise them or protect them from dangerous books. They wanted the freedom to challenge theocracy and tradition. The bravest was the Egyptian novelist Naguib Mahfouz, winner of the Nobel Prize for Literature, who put his life on the line by condemning Khomeini as a terrorist. One hundred Arab intellectuals joined him when they came out in solidarity with Rushdie. One hundred and twenty-seven Iranians signed a declaration condemning the 'terrorist and liberty-cide methods' of the Islamic Republic.

The Rushdie affair was not a 'clash of civilisations' but a struggle for civilisation. On 27 May 1989, rival demonstrations in central London made the choice on offer clear to anyone willing to look. Thousands of anti-Rushdie protesters came to the capital. Malise Ruthven, author of one of the first accounts of the controversy, was shocked by the violence of their slogans. 'Rushdie is a devil'. 'Rushdie is a son of Satan'. 'Kill the bastard'. 'Jihad on Agnostics'. 'Devil Rushdie Wanted Dead or Alive'. One poster showed Rushdie, with devil's horns, hanging from a gallows. Another had his head on the body of a pig surrounded by the Star of David.

Shameless Labour MPs, who were prepared to court the ethnic vote by forgetting what liberal principles they had once possessed, addressed them. Ranged against them in Parliament Square were two counter-demonstrations. Skinheads from the neo-fascist National Front were hanging around on the fringes, looking for a fight. Meanwhile, in the lawn in the centre of the square, a small band of Asian women who ran hostels for battered wives and safe houses for the victims of misogyny staged a protest of their own.

'Here to doubt/Here to stay/Muslim leaders won't have their way,' they chanted. The police had to protect them from the

Asian religious demonstrators, who hated them for not being submissive, and from the British neo-fascist demonstrators, who hated them for not being white. The women never forgot the experience of seeing apparent enemies unite against them.

'Approximately fifty women were marooned between a march of young Asian men calling for a ban on *The Satanic Verses* and National Front supporters. Instead of tackling the National Front, the Asian men verbally and physically attacked Women Against Fundamentalism, which then had to rely on the police for protection whereas previously WAF members would have been marching alongside their Asian "brothers" against police and state racism!'

They were not all atheists, the women said. They just wanted to be modern British citizens, and to dispute the power of their fathers and brothers to force them into arranged marriages.

Gita Sahgal and her sisters at Women Against Fundamentalism did not have the smallest doubt that Rushdie's struggle was their struggle, and that Rushdie's enemies were their enemies. 'At the heart of the fundamentalist agenda is control of women's minds and bodies, such as the imposition of restrictions on the right to abortion, on free and equal education and on the right of women to organise autonomously,' said the group's statement on Rushdie. 'We reject the idea the fundamentalists can speak for us. We will continue to doubt and dissent and will carry on the fight for our right to determine our own destinies, not limited by religion, culture or nationality ... We are taking this opportunity to reaffirm our solidarity with Salman Rushdie.'

How hard was it to be on their side? Who in conscience would not choose to stand with them and against Jamaat-e-Islami, craven Indian politicians, apartheid South Africa, Islamist Iran, Wahhabist Saudi Arabia, the Tory intelligentsia, the Tory government, shabby Labour MPs playing Chicago politics, book-burners, life-deniers, witch-finders and murderers?

I can place public figures of my generation by where they stood on Rushdie. His friends believed in imaginative freedom and the right of the individual to argue with the world. Even if they did not agree with him, they knew that those who were trying to silence him would silence millions if they could. His enemies did then and have since put the collective before the individual. The conservatives among them talked about realpolitik and keeping the natives happy. The leftists talked of the rights of 'the other' and cultural imperialism. Both would throw out freedom of thought, freedom of speech and the rights of women, if sectarian power or realpolitik demanded it.

Hundreds of thousands of people thought that the choice between defending Rushdie or joining his critics was no choice at all. They ensured that the censors could not stop *The Satanic Verses*, although the censors inflicted a terrible price. An unknown assailant murdered Hitoshi Igarashi, *The Satanic Verses'* Japanese translator, by stabbing him in the face. Ettore Capriolo, the Italian translator, was knifed in his apartment in Milan, but lived. William Nygaard, Rushdie's Norwegian publisher, was shot three times and left for dead at his home in an Oslo suburb. Nygaard was not a man who frightened easily. He recovered, and published the Bangladeshi writer Taslima Nasrin, who had described the massacres of Hindus in the 1971 genocide, and received the obligatory death threats. In Turkey, the satirist Aziz Nesin started a translation. On 2 July 1993 he attended an Alevi cultural festival in the central Anatolian city of Sivas. Alevis are a tolerant and egalitarian Shia sect, and suffer the consequences. A mob gathered around the hotel where the Alevis were staying, calling for Sharia law and death to infidels. Nesin and many guests escaped. The killers murdered thirty-seven others.

The victims did not appear to have suffered in vain. Rushdie lived, and *The Satanic Verses* remained in print and sold around the world. Battered but unbeaten, liberalism triumphed.

Or appeared to triumph.

For here is something strange. Between the fatwa and the present, religious killers have murdered just one Western artist – the Dutch director Theo van Gogh, assassinated in 2004 for making a film with the Somali feminist Ayaan Hirsi Ali. Yet in the same period Western culture changed, and not for the better. The change can fit into a sentence. No young artist of Rushdie's range and gifts would dare write a modern version of *The Satanic Verses* today, and if he or she did, no editor would dare publish it.

RULES FOR CENSORS (2):

A Little Fear Goes a Long, Long Way

Free societies are not free because their citizens are fighting for their freedom. They are free because previous generations of citizens *have* fought for their freedom. When put under dictatorial pressure, they must start old fights anew. Once the struggle begins, you can never guarantee in advance that the citizens of the United States, Holland or Britain will be braver than the citizens of Iran, Zimbabwe or Burma. National and political differences are no protection against the universal emotion of fear. Not the immediate fear that causes the eyeballs to dilate and the fight-or-flight response to kick in, but the niggling fear at the back of the mind that warns of the pressing need to avoid a fight in the first place.

Hitoshi Igarashi was the only person associated with *The Satanic Verses* to pay for the Ayatollah's blood lust with his life. Compared to the millions killed in wars and genocides in the years that followed the fatwa, the pain the enemies of the novel inflicted was small. But it was sufficient. The threats against Rushdie produced a fear that suffused Western culture and paralysed its best instincts. From then on, authoritarians seeking to restrict civil liberties or members of the political right led the opposition to militant Islamism. Liberals, who had the best arguments against theocracy, and who might have offered immigrants to Europe – particularly women immigrants to Europe – a better future, went absent without leave.

The society around them imitated the craven politicians, bishops and rabbis rather than the workers in the bookshops and the editors at Penguin. It displayed little or no willingness to defend the potential victims of terror. In one of his rare interviews, Peter Mayer, Penguin's chief executive, praised the bravery of everyone in the book trade who had defended his right to publish, but then told a bleak story about how strangers treated his family. He had received many death threats. Someone went to the trouble to cut themselves and send him a letter scrawled in blood. An anonymous telephone caller told Mayer that 'not only would they kill me but that they would take my daughter and smash her head against a concrete wall'. Far from rallying to defend an innocent girl and her innocent father, the parents of her classmates demanded that the school expel her. What would happen, they asked, if the Iranian assassins went to the school and got the wrong girl?

And Meyer thought, 'You think my daughter is the *right* girl?'

The same cowardice greeted him when he applied for a co-op apartment in New York. 'There were objections that the Iranians could send a hit squad and target the wrong apartment. As if I had done something wrong.'

Mayer spoke truer than he knew. After Rushdie, the fear of a knife in the ribs or a bomb at the office meant that liberals who stuck by liberalism were in the wrong. They knew the consequences now. If someone killed them, they were guilty of provoking their own murder. In the eyes of most politicians and most of the journalists, broadcasters, academics and intellectuals whose livelihoods depended on the freedom to debate and criticise, the targets of religious violence had no one to blame but themselves. The intensity of the rage against Rushdie allowed them to turn John Stuart Mill on his head. Mill argued that censorship could be justified only if a writer or speaker caused a direct harm – by urging on a mob to commit a crime, was his example. Rushdie did not incite violence. His opponents did. The harm was all on their side. However, governments and cultural bureaucracies came to believe that when religious mobs showed that they were prepared to murder Rushdie, they provided the justification for the censorship they sought.

The attack on *The Satanic Verses* appalled liberals. The fight to defend it exhausted them. Knowing what they now knew, few wanted to put themselves through what Rushdie and Penguin had been through. Unlike the Western campaigns against apartheid, Franco, the Greek colonels and the Soviet Empire, a campaign for free speech would involve them running a slight risk of becoming the target of violence themselves. They soon found high-minded reasons to avoid it, and redefined their failure to take on militant religion as a virtuous act. Their preferred tactic was to extend arguments against racism to cover criticism of religion. Or rather, they extended them to cover arguments about minority religions in Western countries. It remained open season on Christianity for liberal writers and comedians, even though Islamist pogroms in Pakistan, Nigeria, Egypt and Iraq and communist oppression in China made Christianity the most persecuted of the major religions.

Writers taking on religious themes, journalists writing about Islamist extremism, or police officers, teachers and social workers investigating the abuse of women, knew that they now ran the risk of their opponents accusing them of a kind of racial prejudice. The charge of 'Islamophobia' would not always stick, but its targets understood that their employers would take it seriously and their contemporaries would regard them as tainted until they had cleared their names. The accusation was not always fatuous. As the millennium arrived, racists and nativist conservatives, who hated Muslims because they were immigrants or came from immigrant families, could develop the most unlikely interest in human rights. If liberalism gave them a new means of attack, they were prepared to feign an interest in it. The only principled response to their hypocrisy was to oppose racism and radical Islam in equal measure and for the same reasons. The best conservatives and liberals managed that, but most settled into the ruts described by a liberal Muslim think tank in 2011. 'Sections of the political left have not done enough to challenge Islamism, yet, encouragingly, they have challenged anti-Muslim extremism,' it said. 'Similarly, sections of the political right have been reluctant to challenge far-right extremism yet are willing to challenge Islamism.'

The fear the Ayatollah generated among liberals thus operated on several levels. Critics of religious obscurantism, most notably liberal Muslims and ex-Muslims, feared violent reprisals. Beyond the worries about direct threats lay the fear that religious groups, bureaucrats, left-wing politicians and newspapers would accuse critics of insensitivity or racism, and that racist groups or websites would confirm the accusation by repeating their critiques. The fear of the vilification and ostracism that would follow was often the most effective deterrent against speaking out. 'Society can and does execute its own mandates,' said John Stuart Mill. 'It practises a social tyranny more formidable than many kinds of political oppression, since, though not usually upheld by such extreme penalties, it leaves fewer means of escape, penetrating much more deeply into the details of life, and enslaving the soul itself.' He might have been writing of modern Europe.

The nature of intellectual life made retreat the likely option. Whatever radical postures they strike, writers and journalists in Western countries are not the equivalents of soldiers or police officers. Nor are they members of a revolutionary underground. They do not begin an artistic or journalistic career expecting to risk their lives. They do not work in well-protected police stations or military bases alongside colleagues who have access to firearms. They work in university campuses or offices, or, in the case of many authors, at home surrounded by their families. Rushdie's marriage broke down under the strain of the fatwa.

Police moved the couple fifty-six times in the first few months, and his wife walked out. The desperate Rushdie tried everything to persuade his pursuers to let him live in peace. He apologised to Iran and converted to Islam. Nothing worked. His enemies just laughed at him and pressed on with the terror campaign. Should other writers spend years in hiding with no hope of escape? Did they want to see their relationships disintegrate, as Rushdie had done?

They could rely on the police for protection, but only up to a point. Ordinary criminals, including ordinary murderers, want to escape from the scenes of their crimes. Visible security measures deter them. The likelihood of arrest and prosecution makes them think twice. Suicide bombers, brainwashed to believe they are on their way to paradise to ravish an assortment of virgins, do not care about arrest and prosecution once they have detonated their bombs. They reason that the police cannot prosecute a corpse.

If they had discovered a general resolve to take on militant religion, then writers and editors might have found safety in numbers. Instead, they were united by their fear. An inversion of the usual processes of publishing began. In normal circumstances, publishers look for controversy the way boozers look for brawls. Nothing delights them more than an author or newspaper columnist who arouses anger. When Margaret Thatcher's government tried and failed to suppress the memoirs of Peter Wright, a retired MI5 officer, his paranoid book became an international bestseller. The British authorities' trial of *Lady Chatterley's Lover* for obscenity in 1960 turned the lawyers and expert witnesses on D.H. Lawrence's side into liberal heroes, and the publishers into happy men and women. Forty years on, admiring newspaper features and television drama documentaries still recalled how E.M. Forster, Richard Hoggart and Raymond Williams had revealed to the jury the artistic merit behind Lawrence's use of the words 'fuck' and 'cunt'. The prosecutor, the hapless Mervyn Griffith-Jones, earned his dismal place in the history books when he revealed how out of touch the fuddy-duddy establishment of the 1960s had become by asking the jury if this was the kind of book 'you would wish your wife or servants to read'.

Before Rushdie, publishers praised themselves for their business acumen in buying a book that offended the authorities. After Rushdie, the smart business move was for a publishing house to turn down books that might offend religious zealots. Publishers knew that their business rivals would not pick up the discarded title; they would be equally frightened, and no more inclined to run risks. A cost-benefit analysis lay behind their calculations. Authors can be touchy creatures: vain, grasping and needy. But say what you must about us, no author has ever murdered an editor for *not* printing a book, or bombed the home of a television commissioning editor for *not* broadcasting a drama.

Censorship is at its most effective when its victims pretend it does not exist. If intellectuals had stated that they were too scared to cover subjects of public concern, then at least they would have possessed the courage to admit that they were afraid. Western societies would then have been honest with themselves, and perhaps that honesty would have given birth to a new resolution. But the psychological costs of a frank confession were too high to contemplate. Honesty would have exposed contemporary culture as a culture of pretence.

The grand pose of intellectuals and artists in liberal democracies in the years after the fatwa was that they were the moral equivalents of the victims of repressive regimes. Loud-mouthed newspaper columnists struck heroic postures and claimed to be dissenting voices bravely 'speaking truth to power'. Their editors never had to worry that 'power' would respond by raiding their offices. Publicly funded BBC comedians and state-subsidised playwrights claimed to be the edgy breakers of taboos as they denounced the wars of the Bush/Blair era. Although they never said it, they knew that Bush and Blair would not retaliate by cutting grants or putting artists on trial for sedition – nor did governments fighting wars on two fronts think of imposing military censorship on civilians. Few admitted that what made liberal democracies liberal was that 'power' would not throw you in prison, whether you spoke the truth to it or not, and that taboos had been broken for so long that the most 'edgy' thing an artist could do was conform to them. If the transgressive had come clean, they would have had to accept that they lampooned the bigotry of Christianity and the wickedness of Western governments because they knew that Christians were not so bigoted and Western leaders were not so wicked that they would retaliate by trying to kill them, while the Islamists they ignored just might. Their fear caused them to adopt out of nervousness an ideology that Islamists adopted out of conviction. A partisan of Hizb ut-Tahrir, the Muslim Brotherhood, Jamaat or al Qaeda would not tolerate criticism of Muhammad, but had no difficulty in attacking the greed of Western corporations and the double standards of Western governments. As for denunciations of Christianity and Judaism from Western commentators, Islamists welcomed them, because they echoed their own denunciations of Zionists and Crusaders.

Journalists hoped no one would notice that we were living with a similar double standard. Newspapers ran accounts of Western soldiers torturing or mistreating prisoners in Iraq or Afghanistan. They could well have put troops' lives in danger as the Internet and satellite television sent images of abuse round the world. If anyone raised the matter with us, we replied that freedom of the press and the need to expose torture trumped all other considerations. It would have been a conclusive argument, had we not refused to publish articles and cartoons that might have put *our* lives in danger. As it was when Grayson Perry, a British artist who produced what Catholics would consider to be blasphemous images of the Virgin Mary, said what everyone knew to be true, his candour was so rare *The Times* treated it as news. 'The reason I have not gone all out attacking Islamism in my art is because I feel the real fear that someone will slit my throat,' he told the audience at a debate on art and politics.

Few others could bring themselves to say the same in public, or admit the truth to themselves in private. In the chilling phrase of Kenan Malik, they 'internalised the fatwa', and lived with a fear that dare not speak its name. They ignored the Indians, Pakistanis, Arabs, Africans and Turks who just wanted to get on with building a new life in the West, they forgot about the refugees who had fled to Europe to escape militant Islam, and took militant Islam to be the authentic voice of European Muslims.

You only had to look around to understand why they accepted that there might be something in the clash-of-civilisations hypothesis after all. The 9/11 attacks on New York and Washington were planned in Hamburg. The 7/7 attacks on the London transport system were planned in Leeds and executed by men with broad Yorkshire accents. Most terrorist violence in Europe came from within. Meanwhile Britain exported terrorists to Pakistan, Israel, Iraq and Afghanistan, and Danish Muslims travelled the world to whip up trade boycotts against their own country.

Theirs were not typical cases. But those in charge of politics and culture were well aware that behind the terrorists were hundreds of thousands of people whose attitudes towards violence were at best ambivalent. In 2007 a survey of British Muslims found that, contrary to expectations, the sense of belonging to Britain was higher among the old, who were more likely to have been born abroad, than the young, who were more likely to have been born in Britain. A significant minority was turning to religious reaction. About one third of Muslims surveyed aged between sixteen and twenty-four wanted the introduction of Sharia law and supported the execution of apostates. Cheeringly, two thirds did not, but anxious cultural bureaucrats were more impressed by those who might do them harm than by those who would leave them alone, particularly when the forces of reaction appeared to have history on their side.

In his caustic *Reflections on the Revolution in Europe: Immigration, Islam and the West*, the American conservative writer Christopher Caldwell saw a continent that was declining in numbers and paralysed by political correctness. It had become too weak to face down the 'adversary culture' of militant Islam. He and others on the right held that post-Christian, post-imperial, post-Holocaust, post-modern, post-just-about-everything European countries lacked the patriotic pride and religious certainties of strong societies, and were wide open to attack from those who felt no comparable embarrassment about their beliefs. As I hope this book makes clear, I think that conservatives underestimate the power and appeal of liberalism. But the most striking feature of the twenty years after *The Satanic Verses* was that Western political and cultural grandees, who trumpeted their anti-Americanism, behaved as if American conservatives were right. They treated Muslims as a homogeneous bloc, and allowed the reactionaries to set the cultural agenda.

They might have looked to Salman Rushdie, to the feminists in Women Against Fundamentalism, to the Arab and Iranian dissidents and to liberals in immigrant communities struggling against the religious ultras. But a principled stand would have involved confronting their fears. However fantastic those fears were, they were not irrational. They could glance at the evening news and see Islamists slaughtering tens of thousands of civilians in Pakistan, Iraq, Nigeria and Afghanistan. They knew it could happen here, because in Rushdie's case it *had* happened here.

With religious censorship, as with censorship in all its forms, you should not just think about the rejected books, newspaper articles, TV scripts and plays, but remember the far larger class of works that authors begin then decide to abandon. The words that were never written, the arguments that were never made during two decades when argument was needed. In 2010, the BBC asked the Egyptian-American feminist Mona Eltahawy why ever-larger numbers of European women were allowing men to tell them that they must hide behind veils. 'I think it has become more prevalent because the space has been left completely uncontested to the Muslim right wing, which does not respect anyone's rights whatsoever except for this one right to cover a woman's face,' she replied. 'No one has pushed back against the Muslim right wing. Integration has largely failed across Europe, even in the UK.'

You can find many reasons why writers, journalists and politicians failed to push back against the Muslim right wing, or even to admit that a Muslim right wing existed. I accept that they were not always cowardly, and that an honourable wariness about the possibility of aiding the white right wing motivated many. But beneath the plausible arguments lay a base and basic fear.

It pushed the majority of Western liberals into adhering in whole or in part to the post-Rushdie rules of self-censorship:

1 They would defer to Islamists and engage in no criticism of the life and teachings of Muhammad.
2 They would treat the Koran as the inerrant word of God, as they would the sacred texts of any other religion which threatened violence, and not suggest that sacred texts are man-made.
3 They would carry on exercising their freedom to criticise, often justifiably, Western religions and governments, which were not threatening to kill them, while appeasing or ignoring those that might.
4 They would never admit to being hypocrites, or accept that their double standards favoured extremists.

5 They would minimise political differences within Muslim
   communities and refuse to risk their necks for Muslim or
   ex-Muslim liberals and feminists.
6 They would say that the dictatorial policies of religious regimes
   and movements were the fault of Western provocation.
7 They would argue that religious violence had nothing to do with
   religion.

If these rules were all there were, it would have been bad enough.
But rules imply limits, and there were no limits. After Grayson
Perry said he did not satirise Islam because he feared having his
throat slit, he added a shrewd observation. 'I'm interested in
religion and I've made a lot of pieces about it,' he said. 'With
other targets you've got a better idea of who they are, but
Islamism is very amorphous. You don't know what the threshold
is. Even what seems an innocuous image might trigger off a
really violent reaction, so I just play safe all the time.'

THREE

Manufacturing Offence

One nineteen p.m.
No one seems to be going in.
Instead a fat baldy's coming out.
Like he's looking for something in his pockets and
at one nineteen and fifty seconds
he goes back for those lousy gloves of his.

WISŁAWA SZYMBORSKA,
'THE TERRORIST, HE WATCHES'

No one doubted that Maqbool Fida Husain was India's greatest modern artist. Western conceptual art became so formulaic, so lost in mannerism and self-reference, that he may have been the world's greatest living artist, although writers risked ridicule when they made such ostentatious claims. I would defy any critic, however, to deny that Husain's work embodied the struggles and glories of India.

For half the year, he lived in London. If you had passed him in Mayfair before he died in June 2011 at the venerable age of ninety-five, you would have found him hard to ignore. He strode out from his studio to Shepherd's Market in bare feet or socks – he did not wear shoes, whatever the weather. Often he carried an oversized paintbrush, just to make sure that the curious could guess his trade. Yet most people in Britain who thought of themselves as cultured found it easy to ignore his work, because no one showed it to them. In part, the ignorance was the result of the parochialism of British culture. But that was not the only reason for Husain's obscurity.

London's Serpentine Gallery included a selection of his paintings in a wider exhibition of contemporary Indian art in 2008. Strange though it once would have been to say it, the gallery's staff deserved praise for their courage as well as their good taste. In 2006, the Asia House cultural centre in Marylebone tried to give the British public the first major solo exhibition of Husain's work. Threats from protesters closed it within days. Even though the Indian High Commissioner opened the show, they denounced Husain as an enemy of the Indian nation. Husain offended all Hindus, they said, with his pornographic and blasphemous art. The possibility of violence terrified the exhibition organisers, and they backed away from a confrontation with censorious extremism.

In India, Husain's position was worse. Hindu militants attacked his home and galleries showing his work. For twelve years, the Indian legal system aided and abetted them. Without understanding how his enemies were exploiting him, the old man became a cog in a machine that manufactured offence. Sectarian politicians exploited him to keep their supporters in a useful state of religious fury, a splenetic condition that delivers many votes to unscrupulous operators at election time.

Born into a Muslim family in Maharashtra in 1915, Husain began his career as a self-taught artist under the Raj. His family moved to Bombay when he was in his teens, and he went door to door offering to sketch portraits. 'What I discovered was that everyone, regardless of their looks, wanted to have their cheeks rosy. I could not do all these rosy cheeks, so I decided to paint Bollywood cinema hoardings instead.'

He painted posters for nearly twenty years, scaling scaffolding and sleeping on the pavement. 'I loved it, that street life. All art in India is viewed as celebration. That is what I've tried to put into my work.'

Husain's friends tell me that he travelled round India, and when he ran out of money he exhibited his drawings on railway station platforms and invited passing passengers to pay what they wanted for them.

When Nehru announced Indian independence in 1947, Husain joined the Bombay Progressive Artists' Group. It had the cosmopolitan project to make a new art for a new country by combining Indian traditions with the Western avant-garde. Husain stayed true to the progressive promises of the 1940s all his life. German expressionism and the modern movement influenced him, and Western critics called him 'the Indian Picasso', but he never lost his ability to straddle high culture and popular culture, which is as good a definition of greatness in art as I can find. In his paintings, gorgeous Bollywood stars appear alongside gods and goddesses of the Hindu tradition. 'For me, India means a celebration of life. You cannot find that same quality anywhere in the world,' he told an interviewer in 2008. 'I never wanted to be clever, esoteric, abstract. I wanted to make simple statements. I wanted my canvases to have a story. I wanted my art to talk to people.'

All India's religious traditions moved him. His family were from the Sulaimani Bohra branch of Shia Islam, which had absorbed many Hindu beliefs. His mother died when he was young, and his father sent him away from home when he was a teenager. 'I used to have terrible nightmares when I was about fourteen or fifteen. This stopped when I was nineteen. I had a guru called Mohammad Ishaq – I studied the holy texts with him for two years. I also read and discussed the Gita and Upanishads and Puranas. This made me completely calm.'

All of which is a long way of making a short point: Husain was from the roots of India. He painted for longer than the Indian republic has existed, and tried to tie its present to its past through his work. Until he was close to eighty, the suggestion that he had no right to include himself as a part of the Indian cultural tradition because he was from a Muslim family would have struck him and all who admired him as inexplicable. As would the notion that there was anything offensive about his nudes.

You only have to visit the Lakshmana temple at Khajuraho to see the erotic strain in Indian culture. The presence of naked gods and goddesses tells visitors that they are far from the taboos of the Abrahamic religions. Hinduism bears partial responsibility for the many crimes of the caste system, but its admirers defend it by saying that because it has no prophet or pope, it has room for those who believe in thousands of gods or none. 'You can cover up your goddess in the finest silk and jewellery,' wrote a sympathetic observer. 'Or you can watch her naked. You can look at the beauty of her face and admire the divinity of her halo, a sari wrapped around her, and her face made up like a Bollywood queen. Or you can see her with ample breasts heaving, her luscious lips parted seductively carved, her thighs wrapped in supreme sexual ecstasy around an athletic god or even goddess – carved for eternity on the walls of a Hindu temple … At least that's the theory, and it has been the practice in large parts of India for thousands of years.' The sculptors of the Tantric and Shaktic traditions openly celebrated eroticism. Others placed erotic carvings on the outer walls of temples – not to excite visitors, but as a reminder that they should leave their desires behind before they entered. More often, artists used nudity in religious painting and sculpture to symbolise purity. Their work carried no more sexual charge than the nudity of the sadhus who wade into the Ganges at Kumb Mela.

Husain's sketch of Saraswati, the goddess of learning, did not compare with temple carvings of goddesses wrapping their thighs around gods. You could not even call the drawing a fully realised nude. Saraswati sits cross-legged beside a lute, holding a lotus flower above her head. There is nothing erotic – let alone pornographic – about his stylised white-on-black sketch in which only the contours of the body are evident. Husain's goddess is pure to the point of being ethereal. He drew her in the mid-1970s. No one complained. In 1996, a Bombay art critic included the sketch in a book on Husain. A writer on a sectarian Hindu monthly picked up a copy, saw the line drawing of Saraswati, and decided to create a scandal out of nothing.

'M.F. Husain an Artist or a Butcher?' ran the headline above an article accusing the artist of insulting Hindus. The provocateur had picked the right time to start a culture war. By the 1990s, religious parties and sectarian militias had infested the supposedly secular Indian state. They wanted to – they *needed* to – inflame their supporters. If they could not find real offences, they were happy to manufacture them.

Shiv Sena, a thuggish bunch of rabble-rousers, dominated Husain's Bombay. They saw a copy of the article, and instructed the police to file charges. Three days later, Hindu activists stormed a gallery showing his work and trashed his paintings. Husain's enemies had thrown him into the self-pitying and vicious world of Hindu sectarianism, whose malignancies the West should treat as a warning.

Identity politics contains a trap. Of all the reasons to be wary of religious leaders asking the state to suspend freedom of speech to spare their tender feelings, not the smallest is that selective censorship leaves liberals with no argument against sectarians from the dominant denomination or ethnic group. The Indian version of identity politics has led to the majority – or demagogues claiming to represent the majority – *behaving as if it were a persecuted minority*. The various Hindu sectarian parties complained that the state gave special treatment to the descendants of India's former Muslim masters. Rajiv Gandhi's Congress government banned *The Satanic Verses* to please Muslim sentiment. It agreed to exempt Muslim men from paying the alimony to divorced wives the secular law demanded, while not allowing Hindu men to benefit from the cheap rate authorised by Sharia. Look, cried the Hindu sectarians, look at how the elite panders to the minority while penalising the majority.

The worst thing one could say about the Hindu nationalist charges was that they were true. By departing from equality before the law, Gandhi had left India with no argument against sectarianism, in whatever form it came. Hindu nationalists saw an opening, and poured through it. They told the mass of Indians that they remained the victims not just of their former Muslim conquerors, but of the former British conquerors too. The Raj's final imposition on India was to indoctrinate Nehru and his anglicised, British-educated contemporaries with alien democratic and secular ideas. Like militant Islamists and so many pseudo-leftist Western academics, Hindu nationalists damned human rights, including the right to free expression, as colonial impositions.

Bal Thackeray, Shiv Sena's leader, showed where the rejection of secularism led in one of his many declarations of admiration for that ultimate cultural relativist, Adolf Hitler. Thackeray announced that Hindus must 'shake off their stupor' and consider protecting their civilisation and culture. 'If telling it like it is makes one a Nazi, I say: Fine, better that than the spineless, deaf, dumb, numb and blind state exalted as Nehruvian secularism. I wouldn't even spit on it.' Thackeray and the many politicians like him said that Hindus were put upon and cozened. To end the injustice they must free themselves from their former Muslim and British oppressors and become a force the world must reckon with. Hence the destruction in December 1992 of the Ayodhya mosque, allegedly built by the conquering Mughals in the sixteenth century on the site of a Hindu temple, and the slaughter of thousands in the communal riots that followed. Hence the threats to the lives of historians who said that India had always been an amalgam of cultures, religions and ethnicities, and that some Hindu princes had been as keen on sacking Hindu temples as the Mughal invaders were. And hence the campaign to persecute Husain, who, as a supporter of Nehru's ideals and a Muslim to boot, was their perfect target.

As soon as Shiv Sena filed lawsuits against him, Husain had to cancel his planned attendance at a commemoration in the city of the achievements of the Progressive Artists' Group. If he had come, the police would have arrested him for 'disturbing communal harmony' – and there was a chance a religious mob might have killed him too. A group of young artists unfurled a banner at the party reading 'Husain, we miss you', but other guests were unimpressed when a Western collector insisted that they speak out on Husain's behalf. 'Why doesn't he understand?' said an artist's husband. 'This is like asking us to speak out in Berlin in 1936.'

As so often, the Hitler comparison was an exaggeration, although given Thackeray's pronouncements, you can see why the man reached for it. Fanatics threatened Husain and all associated with him with violence. They destroyed his paintings at every opportunity. When a TV network asked its viewers whether Husain should receive India's highest honour, religious yobs stormed the studios. In 1998, militants attacked Husain's Bombay home and wrecked it. Thackeray justified them and identified with them. 'If Husain can step into Hindustan, what is wrong if we enter his house?' he said as he redefined secular, multi-cultural India into mono-cultural 'Hindustan', and made Husain an enemy alien in his own city.

The logic of retaliatory sectarianism dictated that when Islamists offered a reward to anyone who would kill Danish cartoonists who had offended them, Hindu nationalist politicians offered a reward to 'patriots' who would chop off Husain's hands.

A dirty mind is a perpetual feast, and once they started look-ing for reasons to be offended, sectarians found them every-where. Husain painted a nude woman whose body curved around a map of India. His persecutors denounced it as porno-graphic, and claimed he was insulting Bharatmata (Mother India). In truth, Husain had painted a severe work because it was his contribution to a charitable campaign to raise money for the victims of the civil war in Kashmir, and the cause demanded restraint. As might have been expected, the fact that the aid was going to Muslim Kashmiris made his opponents angrier still.

When they had finished with what he had painted, Husain's enemies questioned him about the subjects he had never painted. Why did he not paint Muhammad? Why did he paint nudes of Indian goddesses, but not of the Prophet's favourite wife Aisha? On the Web, they contrasted his abstract nudes of gods and goddesses with his fully clothed portraits of his wife and daughter, and of the Prophet Muhammad's daughter Fatima. 'Husain depicts the deity or person he hates as naked. He shows Prophet's Mother, his own mother, daughter, all the Muslim personalities fully clothed, but at the same time Hindus and Hindu deities along with Hitler are shown naked. This proves his hatred for the Hindus.'

India's lawyers and politicians helped at every stage of the campaign of harassment. India and America are the world's greatest democracies. But whereas America's founding fathers wisely protected free speech with the First Amendment, India's founders took their lead from the British colonialists. They believed that censorship could promote national unity, as many European politicians and bureaucrats believe today. Article 19 of the constitution grants Indians free speech – but adds opt-outs to allow censors to intervene in every important area of debate – the 'sovereignty and integrity of India, the security of the State, friendly relations with foreign States, public order, decency or morality, or in relation to contempt of court, defamation or incitement'. Article 295 of the criminal code penalises 'deliberate and malicious acts, intended to outrage religious feelings or any class by insulting its religion or religious beliefs'. For good measure, Article 153 mandates the punishment of those who promote 'enmity between different groups on grounds of religion, race, place of birth, residence, language, etc., [by] doing acts prejudicial to maintenance of harmony'.

The courts and the police, who never seemed to be to hand when criminals attacked art galleries, besieged Husain for more than a decade. Censorship was not promoting harmony, let alone the interests of justice, but allowing sectarians to pick grievances out of thin air. It took until 2008 for the Delhi High Court to throw out all of the hundreds of criminal charges against Husain, and warn, 'In India, a new puritanism is being carried out … and a host of ignorant people are vandalising art and pushing us towards the pre-renaissance era.'

By then Husain had had his fill. In 2010, at the age of ninety-four, and after years of exile, he renounced his Indian citizenship. Speaking with sadness but not bitterness, he said, 'I have not intended to denigrate or hurt the beliefs of anyone through my art. I only give expression to the instincts from my soul. India is my motherland and I can never hate the country. But the political leadership, artists and intellectuals kept silent when Sangh Parivar [Hindu nationalist] forces attacked me. How can I live there in such a situation?'

India must carry the shame of being the first country to ban *The Satanic Verses*, the work of its greatest novelist, and of following up that miserable achievement by driving its greatest artist into exile.

Why pick on Husain for sketches no one found disturbing when he first released them? Read his accusers, and they cannot justify their charges of blasphemy or obscenity. How can they, when Husain's paintings are not remotely pornographic, but part of a deliberate attempt by the artist and his contemporaries to continue Indian traditions? Husain's real offences were to be born into a Muslim family almost a hundred years ago, and to defend the secular dream of Nehru. That was it. His enemies wanted to feed their supporters a diet of indignation, and needed to supply them with new targets for their rage. The identity of the target was irrelevant. If they had not gone after Husain, they would have gone after someone else.

In his study of the crisis in Indian secularism, Salil Tripathi emphasises how unIndian Indian nationalism has become. 'Whenever Hindu nationalists attack an art gallery, or tear down posters they consider obscene, or demand bans on books they don't want others to read, or vandalise a research institute, or destroy the home of an editor, or threaten an academic, or run a campaign against a historian they disagree with, or force film studios to change scripts, or extract apologies from artists, or hurl eggs at scholars, or destroy mosques, or rape Muslim women, or kill Muslim men and children, they take India into a deeper abyss [and] push Hinduism into a darker age. They look and act like the Nazis and the Taliban … [They] are untrue to the meaning of their faith and are disloyal to their nation's constitution. They shame a great nation and belittle how Rushdie saw India: "The dream we all agreed to dream".'

The self-satisfied might say how lucky we in Britain are that we do not suffer from India's censorship laws, and how proud we should be that we could offer Husain a sanctuary. Before we become too smug, we should go back to the forced closure of the Husain exhibition in London in 2006. The reaction to the attack on intellectual freedom in the heart of a city that boasted of being a great cultural capital was instructive. There was no reaction. The artists and intellectuals who are usually so keen to write round-robin letters to the press denouncing this policy or that injustice stayed silent. Journalists and politicians bit their tongues too, as they tacitly accepted the tyrannical proposition that if a writer or artist failed to show 'respect', then he or she must suffer the consequences. The denial by fanatics of the right of the public to see the work of a major artist did not warrant one paragraph in even the news-in-brief columns of any of the daily papers.

I must enter one further caveat. For all the bad faith behind their concocted accusations, the religious thugs had one good question: Why couldn't Husain paint Muhammad, or come to that, his favourite wife Aisha?

'God is love'

Sherry Jones gave every appearance of being a warm-hearted American. She covered Montana and Idaho for a business news service, until in 2002 she decided like so many reporters before her to try to break into fiction. She learned Arabic. She read academic studies of the history of early Islam. Then, like no other reporter before her, she sat down to write a novel about the life of Aisha bint Abu Bakr, whose father, according to popular accounts, betrothed her to Muhammad when she was six, and gave her away to be his wife when she was nine.

The wars of 9/11 moved Jones to seek reconciliation between peoples. 'We in the West know so little about Islam that we tend to demonise it,' she told an interviewer. Muhammad was 'fairly egalitarian in his attitudes to women', and got a 'bad rap' from feminists. The sooner Muslims, Christians, Jews, atheists and Buddhists realised that 'we are all human beings with needs, desires and fears … the closer we will be to achieving Paradise right here on Earth. Because Paradise means living continually in the presence of God, and, as the Bible says, God is love.'

Jones's novel, *The Jewel of Medina*, continues in this vein – at some length. The opening lines set the tone for the rest of the book: 'Join me on a journey to another time and place, to a harsh, exotic world of saffron and sword fights, of desert nomads living in camel-hair tents, of caravans laden with Persian carpets and frankincense, of flowing colourful robes and kohl-darkened eyes and perfumed arms filigreed with henna.'

As the above suggests, Ms Jones was writing a historical romance for the women's market. The New York office of Random House was impressed, and paid her an advance of $100,000 in a two-novel deal.

I defy any reader to guess how a religious, racial or other interest group could find grounds for offence in her work. As with the paintings of M.F. Husain, it is impossible for those who do not know what happened next to understand why even the most twisted censor would want to hurl Jones's book on the fire.

The Jewel of Medina is an anti-*Satanic Verses*. It replaces scepticism with reverence, and satire with solemnity. Jones's Aisha is a feisty girl, as all modern heroines must be. Muhammad is wise and good. Jones does not suggest for a moment that his teachings are inferior to Christianity or Judaism. For those who do not like to see their prophets or gods cast in a bad light, Jones puts the best possible gloss on an event that shocks modern sensibilities: an old man taking sexual possession of a young girl. Jones avoids the obstacle by pretending it isn't there. In the novel, they are married when Aisha is nine. Muhammad kisses the child and says goodbye. She reaches the age of fourteen. To her intense frustration, her marriage is still unconsummated. 'Each day flowered with hope – would Muhammad visit me today? – then dropped its petals like tears. The weeks dragged by like a funeral procession.' The waiting lasts for years, and the marriage is not consummated until after she reaches puberty.

This comforting view of Aisha's life is popular with apologists for religion, most notably Karen Armstrong, a former nun who now soothes modern readers by assuring them that there is little or nothing to worry about in Catholicism or any other creed she comes across. Her biographies of Muhammad and her history of Islam guided Jones as she worked on the plot of *The Jewel of*

Medina, and Jones seems to have been impressed by Armstrong's bold assertion that the emancipation of women was a cause dear to the Prophet's heart. To make it, Armstrong had to explain away the hadiths and verses in the Koran that support the beating and sexual exploitation of women, and the power the holy book gives husbands to divorce unwanted wives. On the question of men marrying little girls, Armstrong's Muhammad, like Sherry Jones's Muhammad, does the decent thing. He waits until Aisha reaches puberty before making love to her. As Armstrong explains:

> Finally about a month after she had arrived in Mecca, it was decided that it was time for the wedding of Muhammad with Aisha. She was still only nine years old, so there was no wedding feast and the ceremonial was kept to a minimum … Abu Bakr had bought some fine red-striped cloth from Bahrain and this had been made into a wedding dress for her. Then they took her to her little apartment beside the mosque. There Muhammad was waiting for her, and he laughed and smiled while they decked her with jewellery and ornaments and combed her long hair. Eventually a bowl of milk was brought in and Muhammad and Aisha both drank from it. The marriage made little difference to Aisha's life. Tabari says that she was so young that she stayed at her parents' home and the marriage was consummated there later when she had reached puberty. Aisha went on playing with her girlfriends and her dolls.

Tabari, the ninth-century Koranic scholar, is not in fact such a comforting source. In his collection of stories about the Prophet, he quotes Aisha as saying, 'the Messenger of God consummated his marriage with me in my house when I was nine years old'. In other traditions he cites, he puts her age at ten. The hadith collections of Bukhari, which Sunni Muslims consider to be the most authoritative, also say that Muhammad consummated the marriage when Aisha was nine. For most of the history of Islam, there was nothing controversial about her age at the time of the wedding. Because it confirmed her virginity, it reinforced Aisha's status among the Prophet's wives, and gave her wishes added force in the power struggles within Islam after Muhammad's death.

Perhaps Jones, Armstrong and all those like them who avert their eyes from inconvenient evidence do so because they worry about Western racists, who use Muhammad's marriage to Aisha to taunt ethnic minorities. But it is as important to worry about religious extremists who use the arguments for male supremacy, homophobia and the exploitation of women and children in holy books to justify oppression – and to notice that there is not a great deal of difference between the ideologies of the religious and the racial extremists.

In *Does God Hate Women?*, their scholarly study of the links between religion and misogyny, Ophelia Benson and Jeremy Stangroom criticise Armstrong by making the essential point that when sacred texts are taken to be divine instructions, you cannot allow nervousness to inhibit criticism.

In Iran after the 1979 revolution, the Islamists reduced the minimum age of marriage for girls to nine. In 2000, under pressure from women's rights activists, the Iranian parliament voted to raise it to fifteen. However, the Council of Guardians, an anti-democratic oversight body dominated by traditional clerics, vetoed the reform, saying that the new ruling was contrary to Islamic law. (They had the example of Ayatollah Khomeini on their side. He had availed himself of the law's blessings and married a ten-year-old girl.) The case of Yemen is equally instructive. In 1998, the Yemeni parliament revised a law that had set the minimum age of marriage at fifteen. The new ruling allowed girls to be married much earlier, so long as they did not move in with their husbands until they had reached sexual maturity. Conservative clerics take this to mean that the consummation of a marriage can take place at the age of nine. Human-rights activists have fought to reverse this ruling, but to date they have been unsuccessful, because Islamic clerics can point to Muhammad's marriage to Aisha to justify their views.

'Although it would be a massive oversimplification to claim that Islam is the cause of these patterns,' Benson and Stangroom conclude, 'it is nevertheless the case that Islamic beliefs are sometimes a factor in child marriage.' As the Iranian reformers found, religion makes the task of stopping girls becoming the possessions of older men – sometimes far older men – harder. The men can always say that religious authority is on their side. Unless religious authority is challenged, they will win.

There are three possible challenges. The first, and to my mind the simplest, is to give up on religion. To reject communism, you do not need to know why Marx's beliefs in the inevitability of proletarian revolution were wrong, you just need to look at the vast crimes the communists committed, and resolve to have nothing to do with the ideology behind them. Similarly, to reject religion you do not need to understand the scientific and philosophical arguments about the extreme unlikelihood of God's existence, or go through the archaeological and literary studies which tell us that the early years of Judaism, Christianity and Islam were strikingly different from the accounts presented to believers. Knowledge of the vast crimes committed in the name of religion is once again sufficient.

Religious reformers must try subtler strategies. They cannot abandon their faiths, therefore they take, say, the problematic lines in Leviticus, St Paul's epistles and the Koran that license the persecution of homosexuals and try to reinterpret them.

Leviticus says:

Thou shalt not lie with mankind, as with womankind: it is abomination.

The prohibition appears to leave no escape hatches, but liberal Jews and Christians must find a way out so they can continue to practise their religions without sacrificing their tolerant instincts. American Christian homosexuals made a dogged effort when they formed a group with the splendid title of the National Gay Pentecostal Alliance. (Sadly, they later changed its name.) They did their own translation of Leviticus, and came up with a new version of the prohibition:

> *And a man who will lie down with a male in beds of a woman, both of them have made an abomination; dying they will die. Their blood is on them.*

They updated the language into contemporary English to produce:

> *If two men engage in homosexual sex while on a woman's bed, both have committed an abomination. They are to be put to death; their blood will be on their own heads.*

It did not sound much of an improvement. But the gay Pentecostalists were undaunted. 'Rather than forbidding male homosexuality', they decided, Leviticus simply restricts where lovemaking may occur. According to their reading, if a bisexual man takes a gay lover into the bedroom he shares with his wife, he is committing an abomination in the eyes of the Lord. But if he sneaks him into the spare bedroom, then everything will be fine with God, although not, I imagine, with his wife.

An ingenious American rabbi by the name of Arthur Waskow decided that Leviticus could have meant:

> *Do not sleep with a man as it were with a woman.*

Once more, there seemed to be no substantial change to the rules of engagement. But the rabbi decided that Leviticus was saying that men must make love like men, not women. If two men have sex, neither should be the passive, womanly partner, he explained. They must come out of the closet and revel in their masculine sexuality when they get down to business. As the authors of Leviticus issued prohibitions against everything from bestiality to sacrificing donkeys, it is improbable that they wanted men to be out, loud and proud when they made love. But you can see why a liberal rabbi wanted to twist the Torah's words.

These arguments are casuistic, because if a conservative theologian could prove that Leviticus or St Paul had an unswerving opposition to homosexuality, liberal believers would not shrug and accept defeat, but would try to reconcile religion and liberalism by another tortuous method. However, the liberals' bad faith is not complete. They may be trying to get round inhumane prohibitions of homosexual love with arguments that are close to being ridiculous, but they never pretend that the inhumane verses do not exist. If they did, their conservative opponents would rout them. They would simply point to the relevant passages in the Torah or the New Testament and win the argument.

Muslim feminist reformers try a third and braver tactic when they confront Koranic justifications for sexism or the endorsement of child marriage. They tell believers 'to reject literal reads of the Koran and recognise that these verses were communicated during specific moments of war, and they aren't edicts for all time. We, as Muslims, must reject the notion that we read these words literally.' The reformers want to persuade the faithful that not every verse is true. Again, they do not wish away the difficulties of the enterprise by talking as if there is no conflict between modernity and tradition.

The task of pretending that a fundamental schism between liberalism and religious authoritarianism does not exist has fallen to the generation of post-Rushdie apologists. They do not say that believers should ignore the hadiths that describe Muhammad's consummation of a marriage to a nine-year-old girl. Nor do they reinterpret them, or argue that the hadiths do not constitute reliable evidence as their collectors did not find them and write them down until long after Muhammad's death. (Bukhari lived two hundred years after the Prophet died.) Instead, they write as if the uncomfortable passages are not there.

Sherry Jones strikes me as less culpable than others who self-censor to avoid offence. *The Jewel of Medina* is a novel. She is not offering readers a factual account, but telling a story. She ignores unpleasant evidence because she is a warm woman, with a heart throbbing to the passionate rhythms of sentimental fiction, and a soul brimming over with love for humankind.

Why would anyone want to hurt her for that?

The Rise of the Religious Informer

Random House was delighted with *The Jewel of Medina*. It set a publication date for August 2008, and told Sherry Jones it would send her on a nationwide tour.

Days later, it pulled the book. Random House explained that 'credible and unrelated sources' had given it 'cautionary advice not only that the publication of this book might be offensive to some in the Muslim community, but also that it could incite acts of violence by a small, radical segment'. For 'the safety of the author, employees of Random House, booksellers and anyone else who would be involved in the distribution and sale of the novel', it had to abandon its planned publication of *The Jewel of Medina*.

Jones was devastated. She could not understand how anyone in the Muslim community could have found her book offensive. *The Jewel of Medina* was her first novel. Random House had told her it would be a bestseller. Her chance to become a novelist, her hopes of a big break, had been snatched from her. There is no record of her reaction when she found that one of the 'credible sources' who had damned the book was not a Jamaat activist in the Indian subcontinent or an ayatollah in Tehran, but a Western academic.

One of the creepy consequences of living in an age of religious extremism is that readers start thinking like police spies. 'She can't expect to get away with that,' we mutter as we put down the book and wait for the inevitable protests. 'She must know she's asking for trouble.'

Usually, demands for censorship and retribution come from members of the confessional group that has been insulted, or can simulate an offended manner, but not always. In an atmosphere of cultural tension, the small-minded discover that they cannot allow debates to be won on their merits. They must take it upon themselves to play the informer and point the finger at offenders.

Of all people, academics ought to have a professional interest in unconstrained intellectual freedom. If an American president were to demand the dismissal of leftish professors on US campuses for criticising American foreign policy, his targets would cry 'McCarthyism'. Liberal opinion would rally behind them and defend their right to speak their minds. Yet academics who depend on freedom of thought are among the first to deny its benefits to others. The twisted legacy of the 1968 generation carries much of the blame. The original attempts of the baby-boomer 'New Left' to promote equality were honourable, and conservatives who sneered at political correctness revealed nothing more than their own brutishness. Those who spoke up for black, Hispanic, female and gay students were asking for fair treatment. They wanted universities to ensure that no man or woman was refused the education they deserved to receive.

Treating people as equals means treating them as adults who can handle robust argument, not as children who need to be told fairy stories and tucked up in bed. But as the culture wars raged, fairy stories were what the universities delivered. Topics and arguments were ruled off-limits; real and imagined heresies denounced with phlegm-spitting vehemence; and comforting histories promulgated on how black Egypt was responsible for the philosophies of ancient Athens, or how Amazonian tribes were noble savages living in a state of prelapsarian harmony until wicked whitey came along.

Islamism came into universities whose academics had the good liberal motive that they should not discriminate against students because of their race or religion, but whose intellectual defences had been weakened by the hysterical attitudes the culture wars fostered. By the end of the first decade of the twenty-first century, academia had acquired a further bias. In general, academics hated George W. Bush and Tony Blair's wars in Afghanistan and Iraq, and worried about illiberal restrictions on human rights that the post-9/11 anti-terrorism legislation imposed. Many academics went on to find justifications for terror. An interventionist foreign policy and an authoritarian criminal justice policy were 'recruiting sergeants' for terrorism, they said. When they met students and preachers who promoted hate-filled ideologies, they could not argue against them with the vigour with which they argued against the hatreds of the white far right, because they thought Islamist hatred was justified in part.

Fear caught their tongues, too: the fear of accusations of 'racism', 'neo-conservatism', 'Islamophobia' or 'orientalism'; the fear of having to admit that their vague commitments to anti-imperialist solidarity were feeding reactionary movements; and the fear of violence. At City University, London, an investigation by liberal Muslims found students who preached, 'When they say to us the Islamic state teaches to cut off the hand of the thief, yes it does! And it also teaches us to stone the adulterer ... When they tell us that the Islamic state tells us and teaches us to kill the apostate, yes it does! Because this is what Allah and his messenger have taught us, and this is the religion of Allah and it is Allah who legislates and only Allah has the right to legislate.' Lesbian, gay and Jewish students reported feeling intimidated, while journalists on the independent student newspaper received threats after they covered the story.

They were not alone in that. 'A couple of years ago, UCL allowed the Islamic Society to put on a show of Islamic art,' recalled Professor John Sutherland of University College, London, in 2010. 'A friend of mine, an eminent scientist, strolled in to take a look. Was he a believer, asked an obviously Muslim student. No, replied my friend, he didn't believe in any god, as it happened. "Then," the young man confidently informed him, "we shall have to execute you." He wasn't joking; he was predicting. He wasn't going to draw a scimitar that minute and lop off the godless one's head, but he implied that at some future point such things would happen.' Sutherland was dragging up his memories of this old confrontation because on Christmas Day 2009 a graduate of University College, Umar Farouk Abdulmutallab, tried to detonate plastic explosives hidden in his underwear and murder the 289 passengers and crew on a Northwest Airlines flight from Amsterdam to Detroit.

Abdulmutallab had come to Britain from a good home – his father had been chairman of the First Bank of Nigeria. He was radicalised in the Dostoyevskian world of London extremism where the white far left meets the Islamist far right. Lonely and sexually frustrated – 'The hair of a woman can easily arouse a man. The Prophet advised young men to fast if they can't get married but it has not been helping me,' he wrote on a Web forum for young Muslims – he drifted towards his university's Islamic society.

He found himself in a religious atmosphere saturated with conspiracy theory. Speakers at the UCL Islamic Society had advocated anti-Semitic hatred. Jews are 'all the same', said one.

'They've monopolised everything: the Holocaust, God, money, interest, usury, the world economy, the media, political institutions … they monopolised tyranny and oppression as well.'

A TV crew caught another on camera saying that homosexuals should be thrown off cliffs and that the testimony of a woman was worth half that of a man. A common theme was that although Westerners were murderous, tyrannical, corrupt and licentious, they were also perilously seductive. 'Today, the culture of Coke and the Big Mac, the culture of the Americans, the culture of the Europeans, these cultures are dominant and they are all-pervasive,' a third guest was on record as saying. 'We stand in awe of their culture and we are imitating them in everything. This culture, this evil influence, this imitation of the kuffar.'

After Abdulmutallab became president of the UCL Islamic Society in 2005, he organised martial-arts training and an 'anti-terror week', which featured a video of clips of violence, accompanied by a hypnotic soundtrack. The film-maker included footage of British left-wing politicians saying that the West believed that Palestinian blood was cheaper than Israeli blood, and of a former prisoner of war alleging that the Americans tortured him at Guantánamo Bay.

'When we sat down, they played a video that opened with shots of the twin towers after they'd been hit, then moved on to images of mujahedeen fighting, firing rockets in Afghanistan,' one member of the audience said. 'It was quite tense in the theatre, because I think lots of people were shocked by how extreme it was. It seemed to me like it was brainwashing, like they were trying to indoctrinate people.'

When the FBI arrested Abdulmutallab, journalists wanted to know why the university had not done more to fight extremism. The response of the university authorities was an education in itself. They denounced the 'quite disturbing level of Islamophobia' the case had aroused. Their inquiry decided that Abdulmutallab's radicalisation had happened after he left university, despite the evidence to the contrary. At a meeting at UCL to discuss the controversy, I watched academics and student leaders abuse the university's critics. They were the real racists and bigots, not the guests of the Islamic Society. They were the ones who needed 'de-radicalising', not the religious reactionaries.

It is less surprising than it ought to be that academics were on the side of repression when censors came for a harmless novel by a well-meaning writer.

Among those who received advance copies of *The Jewel of Medina* was Denise Spellberg, an associate professor of Islamic history at the University of Texas in Austin. Jones had read Spellberg's *Politics, Gender, and the Islamic Past: The Legacy of 'A'isha Bint Abi Bakr* while researching her novel, and the publishers might have hoped that Spellberg would supply a puff quote.

If they did, they were disappointed. Spellberg phoned Shahed Amanullah, a lecturer at her university, and the editor of altmuslim.com, a popular site for American Muslims. 'She was upset,' Amanullah told the *Wall Street Journal*. She asked him to 'warn Muslims' that a novel that 'made fun of Muslims and their history' was on its way. Spellberg confirmed to the paper that she hated the book. It was a 'very ugly, stupid piece of work', she said and quoted a scene which takes place on the night when Muhammad consummates his marriage with Aisha. Spellberg said that Jones was guilty of a 'deliberate misinterpretation of history', and of producing soft porn. She did not seem to grasp that novelists are not historians, and in any case, if *The Jewel of Medina* was misinterpreting history, it was misinterpreting it in Muhammad's favour.

Amanullah dashed off an email to his graduate students: 'Just got a frantic call from a professor who got an advance copy of the forthcoming novel, *Jewel of Medina* – she said she found it incredibly offensive.'

The next day, a blogger posted Amanullah's email on a website for Shia Muslims, Hussaini Youth, under the headline 'Upcoming Book, *Jewel of Medina*: A New Attempt to Slander the Prophet of Islam'. His readers rallied to the new cause. 'In the garb of Freedom of Speech enemies of Islam are attacking Islam,' said one poster. 'You have the freedom of throwing the stones in the sky. But you can be prosecuted if it injures or kills someone.'

The publishers soon heard the commotion. A manager at Random House told her colleagues, 'There is a very real possibility of major danger for the building and staff and widespread violence. Denise says it is a declaration of war … explosive stuff … a national security issue … thinks the book should be withdrawn ASAP.'

In a letter she later wrote to the *Wall Street Journal*, Spellberg said that she was not alone in wanting to see the book stopped. 'I never had this power [to cancel publication], nor did I single-handedly stop the book's publication. Random House made its final decision based on the advice of other scholars, conveniently not named in the article, and based ultimately on its determination of corporate interests. I felt it my duty to warn the press of the novel's potential to provoke anger among some Muslims.'

The good, old cause of freedom of speech was upheld not by editors in New York, still less by academics in American universities determined to defend their country's Bill of Rights, but by American Muslims. Asra Q. Nomani wrote the *Wall Street Journal*'s story about the incident, and concluded her piece with a personal note: 'This saga upsets me as a Muslim – and as a writer who believes that fiction can bring Islamic history to life in a uniquely captivating and humanizing way. For all those who believe the life of the Prophet Muhammad can't include stories of lust, anger and doubt, we need only read the Quran (18:110) where, it's said, God instructed Muhammad to tell others: "I am only a mortal like you."'

Shahed Amanullah, Denise Spellberg's colleague, met Sherry Jones and liked her. 'Unlike so many other times in our recent history where we are struggling against people who are really out to vilify us, I sensed from the beginning that you were doing this out of appreciation or respect,' he told her, and then found the words that ought to have been in the mouths of American professors and publishers. 'The best response to free speech ought to be more speech in return. Anyone should have the right to publish whatever he or she wants about Islam or Muslims – even if their views are offensive – without fear of censorship or retribution. In an ideal world, both parties would open their minds enough to understand the other point of view.'

Even the protests on the Shia website were not as menacing as they appeared. Its readers' action plan consisted of a letter-writing campaign.

Rival publishers realised that Random House had not just failed to defend free speech, but worse – much, much worse – had failed to think about the bottom line. Beaufort Books decided the fears of a violent attack were twaddle, and snapped up *The Jewel of Medina*. Sherry Jones had her bestseller, and foreign houses bought the overseas rights. Jones and everyone associated with her book seemed safe.

In her eerie poem 'The Terrorist, He Watches', the Polish poet Wisława Szymborska describes a terrorist looking at a bar in the minutes before his bomb will explode. Some people escape danger just in time, although they do not know it. Others walk into the bar and to their deaths. It is the terrorist's detachment that gives the poem its power. Everyone in and around the bar is in his killing zone. Whether they live or die is down to luck. The terrorist sees a bald man leave, then turn back to collect his gloves. He will die. Another man gets on a scooter and rides off. He will live. The terrorist does not mind who his targets are, as long as he has targets.

The publishers who bought *The Jewel of Medina* did not realise that they were now in the zone. It did not matter that Jones had avoided the issue of sex with children in an admiring account of Muhammad's life, and that American Muslims had praised her work. However briefly, her name had been associated with an 'insult to Islam'. Whether someone would respond by targeting her or her publishers was now down to chance.

Ali Beheshti was an admirer of Omar Bakri Muhammad, a Syrian-born militant living in London, and founder of the British extremist group al-Muhajiroun. 'We don't make a distinction between civilians and non-civilians, innocents and non-innocents,' Bakri said as he explained the group's ideology, 'only between Muslims and unbelievers.' Beheshti was not a sleeper, hiding from the police until the moment came to strike. He made no effort to play the undercover agent. He embraced radical Islam and thrust himself in front of the police. He gained international notoriety in 2006 when he took his twenty-month-old daughter on a demonstration outside the Danish embassy against cartoons of the Prophet Muhammad which had appeared in the Danish newspaper *Jyllands-Posten*. He made her wear a hat carrying the slogan 'I ♥ Al Qaeda'. Around her, furious men chanted 'Bomb, bomb the UK' and 'Europe, you will pay with your blood.'

Beheshti had the motive. The opportunity was there for the taking. The owner of the Gibson Square publishing house, which bought the British rights to *The Jewel of Medina*, ran his business from his home, and his promotional literature carried its address. Beheshti found the means on the night of 27 September 2008, when he and two accomplices put a barrel of diesel into the boot of a Honda Accord. The police had bugged the car, and heard Beheshti ask his co-conspirator, 'You wanna be the emir [leader], yeah?'

'That would be you.'

'You know what we gotta do, anyway, innit?' Beheshti added.

They poured the diesel through the letterbox in the publisher's front door and set it on fire. They failed to kill anyone, and the police picked them up. Iraqis or Pakistanis looking at the terrorist slaughters that were taking place in their countries would have thought the failed firebombing a lame effort. But in the Western democracies the attack on Gibson Square reinforced the message that capricious violence might strike anyone, anywhere. All it needed was for someone to denounce an author, and for that denunciation to spread on the Net. In the 1980s, mullahs in Tehran and clerical reactionaries in Pakistan ignited violence. By the 2000s, anyone could deliberately or inadvertently set off a panic – a blogger, a reviewer, an academic or indeed a reporter.

The muscling in of my trade of journalism into the business of manufacturing offence was an ominous development, because journalists are skilled at making news out of nothing. We come across a fact we suspect will outrage a pressure group/political party/guardian of the nation's morals. We call the pressure group/political party/guardian of the nation's morals and ask, 'Are you outraged?' 'Yes we are,' the pressure group/political party/guardian of the nation's morals replies, allowing us to generate the headline 'Pressure Group/Political Party/Guardian of the Nation's Morals Outraged by …'

In 2009, Ophelia Benson and Jeremy Stangroom published *Does God Hate Women?*, which criticised the soothing story about Aisha's life that Karen Armstrong, Sherry Jones and others promoted, and presented evidence that contradicted it. The *Sunday Times* greeted the book's arrival with the headline 'Fears of Muslim Anger Over Religious Book'. The report explained that it 'could cause a backlash among Muslims because it criticises the Prophet Muhammad for taking a nine-year-old girl as his third wife'.

The word to concentrate on in that sentence is '*could*'.

Religious militants were not in fact preparing a 'backlash', because they did not know of the book's existence. The journalist who wrote the piece phoned Anjem Choudary, a self-styled Sharia judge from al-Muhajiroun, the group Ali Beheshti was associated with when he had targeted Sherry Jones's British publishers. The obliging 'judge' told the *Sunday Times* that as well as targeting Sherry Jones's book, Islamists could also target the critics of Sherry Jones's version of history. 'Talk of Aisha as a child when she married is not true,' he said. 'At nine, she reached her menses and in those days a girl was considered to be mature when that happened. No one will swallow talk about child brides. It would lead to a huge backlash, as we saw with *The Jewel of Medina*.'

The journalist phoned the publisher of *Does God Hate Women?*, and told him he was being 'brave'. The poor man had not appreciated that he was being brave, and called on the services of an 'ecumenical adviser', a religious censor modern Europe thought it had seen the last of. The ecumenical adviser said that although he did not like the book, the authors had substantiated their claims, and that in his opinion the publisher should allow the public to read their work.

Because of an inoffensive sketch he drew in the 1970s, Hindu fanatics drive an Indian artist from his country in the 1990s. Because an academic from Texas denounces an American romantic novelist, terrorists firebomb a publisher's home in north London. Because two intellectuals write a study of feminism and religion, and a journalist invites extremists to find offence, an editor calls in a religious adviser to rule if he can publish a book in a country that was once proud to number John Milton, John Stuart Mill and George Orwell among its greatest writers.

Go Postal!

Imagine a dictatorship. Let us call it Authoritania. It could be a gulf sheikhdom, an African nationalist kleptocracy, a relic of pan-Arabism, a post-Soviet republic or a communist 'people's democracy'.

Our imaginary dictator has learned from the twentieth century that cooperating with crony capitalists is more profitable than spouting slogans about proletarian revolution. He pushes most of his subject country's earnings through a sovereign wealth fund, and forms alliances with oligarchs in the private sector. Public and private enterprises – the distinction between the two is fine – provide jobs that bring maximum reward for minimal effort to the dictator's supporters, relatives and mistresses. In return, he harries free trade unions and allows both state and private companies to operate without restraint. Corruption and exploitation follow. The state's medical service publishes no official records of industrial injuries, or of the high rates of depression, for fear of what they may reveal about the state's luckless subjects. Doctors play down the Aids epidemic, because they know that honest reporting would show how many desperate women have become prostitutes. The secret police arrest opposition leaders and deny them access to the state-controlled television channels. The state's prosecutors harass the few opposition newspapers and radio stations. Although Authoritania's constitution declares its commitment to freedom of speech and of the press, its 'Law of Social Responsibility' allows the courts to impose hefty fines on journalists and editors found guilty of 'offending' or 'denigrating' the authorities. The official 'Press Law' goes further, and imposes prison terms on writers who criticise the president or incite actions that 'undermine state security'. The police arrest journalists who cover 'illegal' strikes – legal strikes are impossible – or protests by the owners of small businesses, who face continuous demands for bribes from bureaucrats. With considerable initiative, prosecutors charge reporters with organising the demonstrations they had gone to observe.

Authoritania seems sewn up. But it remains a dictatorial, not a totalitarian state. Opposition parties can stand in elections, although the bureaucracy ensures that they can never win. Writers and journalists face intimidating restrictions, but because the government casts the restrictions as laws, dissidents can work round them and subvert the apparently rigorous censorship. The bureaucracy is not a monolith, but contains competing interests and rival factions. Many in authority are happy to see mild criticism of the leader, and give journalists the leeway to target their enemies in the state apparatus.

Like Andrzej Wajda in post-Stalinist Poland, or the writers and directors of the Iranian new wave, the country's film-makers produce haunting tales of fear and disillusionment, which are far better than the offerings of Hollywood. Their films are not explicitly political, but the audience finds the political message just below the surface. Theatres produce surrealist and absurdist dramas to avoid the laws banning direct criticism of the regime. Their favourite play, however, is a traditional story. They keep staging an apparently innocuous folk tale about an official who stands up to a tyrannical king. Everyone knows why it interests them so.

The small opposition press uses similar tactics. It does not tackle the fraud of the kleptomaniac state head-on, for a direct assault would be too dangerous. It focuses on small cases of corruption instead, and uses them to hint at the sickness of the wider society.

To the president's fury, his power and pomp mean nothing to visiting foreign journalists and human-rights groups. In their eyes, it is the marginal artists, writers and trade unionists who speak for his country, rather than his ministers in their air-conditioned offices and bulletproof cars.

He summons the chief of the secret police.

'How can I silence these shits?'

'Go postal!'

'What?'

'It's a phrase from neo-con America, Excellency. A man with a gun, often a postal worker for reasons no one understands, walks into an office or school where he thinks he was once humiliated and kills people at random.'

'You mean I should kill the leaders of the opposition?'

'I will happily do so, Excellency, if you command it. But that's not the idea. You need to pick on slights and humiliations that are so small they seem not to be humiliations at all, and punish them with unreasonable ferocity. Random violence creates the necessary conditions for order. A leader of the opposition expects us to arrest him from time to time, but a writer making a veiled criticism of your rule, or a man who grumbles about you in a shop queue, does not. By randomly attacking a few people who speak sedition, we tell many people that the only safe option is to avoid all talk about politics. The aim is to create a state where everyone knows it is best to say nothing, and the bastards shut up.'

A story from Mao's China illustrates the hopelessness engendered by a truly random terror. Mao imitated Stalin by purging the Communist Party of anyone who might defy or threaten him. He prepared the ground by turning society upside down, so that it would be in no position to resist. Mao changed the balance of power between the old and the young by telling schoolchildren that they could torture and murder their teachers for filling their minds with 'bourgeois ideology'. However bestially they behaved, the police would not intervene. The students killed their first recorded victim on 5 August 1966, when pupils at a Peking girls' school seized their headmistress. The girls kicked and trampled the fifty-year-old mother of four, and poured boiling water over her. They ordered her to carry heavy bricks back and forth, and thrashed her with leather belts with brass buckles until she collapsed and died. If the teacher had seen her life flash by her in her dying moments, she would have realised that nothing she might have done could have spared her. She had obeyed the communists, spouted their dogmas, taught Mao's own daughters … but Mao still killed her. There had never been a smart move to make, no moment when she might have chosen a safer course, and escaped her execution.

Most modern dictators are not like communist totalitarians. They do not kill loyalists as well as enemies. When they slip towards terror, they use disproportionate violence against minor critics instead. Just as the relatives of the victims of a mass murderer who goes berserk in a school because he felt its teachers humiliated him can find reasons for the deaths, so the victims of dictatorial violence can understand the reasons for their suffering. It is just that the 'offence' is out of all proportion to the retribution visited on the offenders.

Robert Mugabe was not the equivalent of Saddam Hussein or the organisers of the genocide in Darfur. After taking power in 1980, he presided over one act of mass terror, when he sent the 5th Brigade of the Zimbabwean Army to Matabeleland and the Zimbabwean Midlands to murder three thousand of his opponents. After that atrocity, he practised cruelty at a lower level. He wrecked the economy by seizing white-owned farms and handing them over to cronies, and failed to tackle the Aids epidemic.

But although parliament was neutered, the judiciary subverted and the country reduced to beggary, Mugabe allowed some opposition – at the time of writing there are opposition politicians in his government. Wilf Mbanga, the editor of the *Zimbabwean*, told me that outsiders would be surprised at how much journalists and artists can get away with – when the security services relax.

In 1999, Oliver 'Tuku' Mtukudzi's song 'Wasakara' was the hit of the year. The chorus ran:

> Admit, hey, admit
> Admit you have gotten old
> Admit you are worn out.

As Mtukudzi sang, helpful members of the concert crew beamed a spotlight onto a portrait of the wizened Mugabe. When the police questioned him, Mtukudzi told them that his lyrics came from observing his family and acquaintances, and criticism of the geriatric despot could not have been further from his mind.

Such small acts of resistance are typical of stable times in dictatorships. In Burma, an official in the national bank protested against the arrest by the military junta of Aung San Suu Kyi, whose National League for Democracy had been the legitimate winner of a free general election in 1990, by enhancing rather than debasing the national currency. His superiors had asked him to design a new one-kyat note. It had to include a picture of Aung San Suu Kyi's father General Aung San, who in 1945 had led Burma to independence. The designer used light strokes to soften the jawline as he gently transformed the face of the father into that of the daughter. Around the portrait he drew four circles of eight petals to mark the date of Burma's democratic uprising on 8 August 1988 – 8/8/88. For months the portrait of 'the lady', as Aung San Suu Kyi was known, was admired by the citizenry, until the generals realised their mistake, withdrew the 'democracy note' from circulation, and made possessing it a criminal offence.

Like the Burmese generals, Mugabe did not tolerate veiled criticism for long. He retained power because he mixed periods of relative quiet with outbreaks of capricious repression. The courts sent an unemployed man to prison for asking two boys with Mugabe's face emblazoned on their T-shirts, 'Why would you want to wear a wrinkly old man on your clothes?' The police arrested a human-rights campaigner who exposed the brutal conditions in an army-controlled diamond mine. 'That kind of behaviour, if proved, is treacherous and abominable, particularly in these times of national economic strife,' the judge said as he denied him bail. Such inflated rhetoric is characteristic of dictatorships on the rampage. To justify censorship their lackeys magnify the offence, as the judge did when he turned a criticism of the working conditions of miners into an act of economic treason.

Neither the campaigner for workers' rights nor the man talking to the boys in the Mugabe T-shirts was a direct threat to the regime. But as Wilf Mbanga said, 'Every now and again he wants to send a message to all and sundry. He wants to keep journalists and activists on their toes, so we don't know what we can get away with from one day to the next.'

The prudent Mr Mbanga edits the *Zimbabwean* from a seaside town in southern England.

A Cartoon Crisis

Modern religious violence, even in its most barbaric forms, is not comparable to the absolute terror of communist totalitarianism. In Afghanistan, Pakistan and Iraq, men can stay alive if they do not cross the Taliban or al Qaeda (women, obviously, face additional dangers). Like the Nazis, Islamists do not slaughter their own supporters. In the democracies, the fear spread by religious violence is closer to the fear of excessive punishments for inconsequential slights that modern dictatorships generate.

To put the same thought another way, we are living through a Mugabification of religious argument.

Even conscious acts of anti-clericalism, an essential part of any campaign to cut down over-mighty religions, bring a response as disproportionate as the assault on Sherry Jones's unconscious 'insult'.

The Danish cartoon crisis of 2005 – and it tells you everything about the overwrought state of democratic opinion that policy-makers and pundits could talk about a 'cartoon crisis' with a straight face – was almost as phoney as any manufactured act of outrage. The religious censorship it engendered met the criteria of dictators engaged in random retaliation:

- A modest critique produced an excessive reaction.
- Legitimate criticism of terrorist murder and the oppression of women was turned into something it was not, in this instance a prejudiced hatred of all Muslims.
- The threat of violent punishment hung in the air.
- Critics learned that the safe course was to say nothing, because they did not know where fanatics would draw their lines.

Intellectuals discuss freedom of speech in the abstract. But it always arises as a political issue in response to changes in society. The Danish press did not commission cartoons of Muhammad for a laugh, but because they could see new forces at work in their country. A group of Muslim fundamentalists had attacked a lecturer at Copenhagen University because he had quoted from the Koran to non-Muslims. Sunni traditionalists had threatened Sufi Muslims for staging a concert, because they claimed that music was unIslamic. The most disturbing story came in press reports about how a writer called Kåre Bluitgen could not find an artist prepared to illustrate a guide to

Muhammad and the Koran for schoolchildren. The artists he approached muttered about the murder of Theo van Gogh, and the assaults on the lecturer at Copenhagen University. They maintained that Islam proscribed representations of Muhammad, although that was not true, as the portraits of Muhammad from the golden age of medieval Islam demonstrate. More probably, the wavering Danish illustrators reasoned that certain sects in modern Islam denounce images of Muhammad as idolatry, and that those sects were, as it happens, the sects most likely to kill them.

Flemming Rose, the editor of *Jyllands-Posten*, a Danish daily with a circulation of about 150,000, invited cartoonists to treat Islam as they treated other religions, and show that demands for censorship were incompatible with contemporary democracy and freedom of speech. 'One must be ready to put up with insults, mockery and ridicule,' Rose said in an article accompanying the cartoons. Reject that idea and 'we are on our way to a slippery slope where no one can tell how the self-censorship will end'. Despite his defiant words, his blasphemy fell short of being a full-frontal satirical assault on religious conviction. The twelve cartoons that were to provoke such fury were a tame collection.

Among them was an image of Muhammad with a bomb in his turban. The drawing suggested that extremists had used Islam as an excuse for terrorism, a view that was hard to argue with. It caused the most offence, because it could also be interpreted as suggesting that all Muslims supported terrorism, an argument which was not true, although the protesters against the newspaper undermined their case when they resorted to violence. The tender-minded found three other drawings offensive. An ambiguous portrait of Muhammad may or may not have been insulting. The artist drew him with a glowing object above his head. Readers could interpret it as a halo, a pair of devil's horns or Viking's horns, or the Islamic crescent. You had to work hard to find the 'devil' insult, although, as always, that did not stop those determined to be offended from putting in the effort. Next was a cartoon which showed a Muhammad in heaven, greeting suicide bombers with the words, 'Stop, stop, we've run out of virgins!' Of all the cartoons, it came closest to making a joke that was actually funny. Complainants also decried a picture of an aggressive Muhammad, in which the artist had blocked out his eyes with a black line to prevent his identification. The line paralleled the eyeholes in the hijabs of two women with frightened expressions behind him, the rest of whose bodies were draped in black robes.

Several cartoonists mocked Flemming Rose, Kåre Bluitgen and themselves rather than Muhammad. In one drawing, a cartoonist sweats with fear as he draws a straight portrait of Muhammad. A self-fulfilling prophecy, since the artists duly received death threats. In another, a figure (presumably Muhammad) attempts to calm down two furious armed followers with the words, 'Relax, it's just a drawing by a cartoonist from the south-west of Denmark.' One artist showed Bluitgen wearing a turban and holding up a stickman portrait of Muhammad. An orange bearing the slogan 'PR Stunt' is perched on the turban's top. The orange baffled foreigners, but local readers got the point that Bluitgen was seeking to up his profile and make money out of the controversy, because in Danish the phrase 'to have an orange drop into your turban' means to receive undeserved good fortune. Another artist had an every-man character saying that he is unable to pick out Muhammad from an identity parade of religious figures. Among them is Kåre Bluitgen, who is holding up a sign which says 'Kåre's public relations, call and get an offer'.

Nor did the cartoonists miss the argument that in Saudi Arabia, Pakistan and Iran, Islam was the religion of clerics with real power to ruin the lives of others, but in Denmark it was the religion of immigrants on the margin of society. In one drawing, by Lars Refn, a schoolboy captioned as 'Mohammed' from 'Valby

School class 7A' – which identified him as coming from a poor immigrant area of Copenhagen – taunts the editors at *Jyllands-Posten*. The boy has written a slogan in Farsi on a blackboard, which reads '*Jyllands-Posten* journalists are a bunch of reactionary provocateurs'. Little good did Refn's decision to attack the newspaper and defend immigrants do him: he was the first of the cartoonists to receive death threats. Apparently there are people who will kill you for drawing pictures of boys called 'Mohammed'. The remaining cartoons were unremarkable. One was an abstract drawing of a group of women whose heads are formed from traditional Arabic symbols of a star and a crescent, along with a poem criticising the Prophet for 'keeping women under yoke'. Then there was a picture of Muhammad with a star and crescent forming one eye and the outline of his face. And finally, a reverent picture of the Prophet leading a donkey through the desert, entirely suitable for use in a children's book.

If writers and artists were required under pain of death to be careful about how they mocked the papacy's ban on contraception, they would not be able to make an effective critique of how religious dogma facilitates the spread of the Aids epidemic. Satire generalises. It speaks with a clear voice or no voice at all. Satirists cannot argue with caveats, particularly when the caveat the religious insist on is that satirists remove religion from criticisms of religious violence and religious oppression.

I will not pretend that the publication of the cartoons was met with equanimity. Jamaat-e-Islami, inevitably, urged the Pakistani government to issue a reward for anyone who killed the cartoonists, and many Danish Muslims were offended. About 3,500 people attended a protest in Copenhagen, and the police moved two cartoonists to safe houses. Imams and ambassadors from Muslim countries demanded meetings with the Danish prime minister, Anders Fogh Rasmussen. He replied that a meeting was pointless, because 'free speech goes far and the Danish government has no influence over what the press writes'.

Quite properly for a democratic leader, he said that what the press printed was not the business of his government, or of foreign dictatorships for that matter. The police found no grounds for prosecution because, as the prime minister had said, Denmark was a free country.

For all the initial demonstrations, the fact remained that Rose published the cartoons on 30 September 2005, but the violence did not begin in earnest until January 2006. In the interval, newspapers in many countries, including the Egyptian weekly *El Fagr*, printed the cartoons, without raising significant protests.

Much of the credit for turning a mild satire into a crisis must go to three reactionary imams, to whom Denmark had offered asylum. French television gave viewers a glimpse of their ideology when it caught one of them, Ahmed Akkari, on camera implicitly threatening a liberal Muslim leader, Naser Khader, a member of the Danish parliament. According to the footage, Akkari said: 'If Khader becomes minister of integration, shouldn't someone dispatch two guys to blow up him and his ministry?' He later said he was 'jesting'. For a man who wanted to ban cartoons, he had a broad sense of humour. The imams had a political as well as a religious interest in whipping up a crisis that might place them at the head of Danish Islam. A survey in March 2006 found that Khader was Danish Muslims' most popular spokesman, followed by a left-wing Pakistani doctor who shared Khader's beliefs in secularism and sexual equality. Akkari and his friends trailed well behind their liberal rivals.

In December 2005 – two months after the paper published the cartoons – the three imams went to an Arab League meeting in Hosni Mubarak's Egypt. The league issued a statement condemning freedom of speech being used as a pretext to defame religion. A separate delegation briefed Bashar Assad's Ba'athist dictatorship in Syria. The imams carried with them a forty-three-page dossier which contained all twelve of the *Jyllands-Posten* cartoons. Helpfully, someone had added three other images, supposedly of Muhammad – one of a man wearing a plastic pig mask, one of a praying man being sodomised by a dog, and one of a devilish Muhammad – all of which were considerably more offensive than anything the paper had published. The imams claimed that they had been included for context, to 'give an insight into how hateful the atmosphere in Denmark is towards Muslims'. But where did these pictures originate? In two cases, no one knows if they were anything more than the sort of scrawl which is regularly found on toilet walls. Bloggers quickly identified the 'pig' picture as an Associated Press photograph taken in August 2005 at an agricultural fair in Trie-sur-Baïse, in the French Pyrenees, which had nothing to do with Muhammad. Instead of showing the Prophet, it showed Jacques Barrot, a French farmer, who was competing in the village's annual 'pig-squealing competition', complete with plastic snout and pig's ears. Along with other locals, he was dressing up and demonstrating his pig-imitating skills as part of an annual promotion of the region's excellent pork dishes. Barrot didn't even win.

After the briefing by the imams came a direct call at the beginning of February 2006 from Yusuf al-Qaradawi, the spiritual leader of the Muslim Brotherhood, for 'an international day of anger for God and his prophet'. Danes and anyone associated with them became a target.

As the crisis grew, *Jyllands-Posten* received more than a hundred credible threats. Syria, Kuwait, Saudi Arabia and Libya withdrew their ambassadors from Denmark. In Gaza, gunmen stormed the EU offices demanding that Europe apologise. In Libya, the police shot fifteen people dead who were protesting against reports that an Italian minister had worn a T-shirt with the cartoons on it. In all 139 people were to die, as police fired into crowds in Nigeria and Afghanistan as well as Libya. The owners of *France Soir* fired the paper's editor for running the cartoons as a gesture of solidarity with his Danish colleagues, and then rehired him. In Damascus, demonstrators attacked the

Danish embassy and the Norwegian embassy. Iranian militants attacked the Danish embassy in Tehran and firebombed it. Demonstrators in Lahore attacked branches of the American-owned Pizza Hut, Kentucky Fried Chicken and Holiday Inn chains, while Muslim customers boycotted Lego, Bang & Olufsen and Arla Foods, which at least had the merit of being Danish-owned. Osama bin Laden blamed Jews and Crusaders for the cartoons, and said no apology could stop the rage.

As late as January 2010, a Somali armed with an axe and a knife broke into the home of Kurt Westergaard, who had drawn the picture of Muhammad with a bomb in his turban. Westergaard dived into a panic room and pressed the alarm, as the Somali tried to batter the door down. The police shot the intruder in the leg, but a spokesman for the Somali al-Shabaab terror group implied that there would be plenty more where he came from: 'We appreciate the incident in which a Muslim Somali boy attacked the devil who abused our prophet Muhammad and we call upon all Muslims around the world to target the people like him.'

As striking as the violence was the reaction of liberals. Across the world, demonstrators were attacking the embassies and nationals of a small social democratic country in northern Europe and boycotting its goods because of twelve cartoons. Its prime minister had held true to the values of anti-fascism and anti-communism and refused to abandon freedom of speech within the law, despite the pressure on him to go along with repression. The assault on Denmark was political, and not only because radical imams were seeking to supplant their liberal rivals and make themselves the 'authentic' voice of Danish Islam. The countries that demanded that Denmark apologise had political agendas of their own. George W. Bush's plan to extend democracy to the Middle East appalled the Egyptian dictatorship. By manufacturing a scandal about Danish cartoons, Mubarak hoped he could show the naïve Americans that 'Western' freedoms were not for Egyptians, and it was better to leave them under the control of the elite, a fiction he succeeded in maintaining until his subject people contradicted him in Tahrir Square in 2011. The Iranian and Syrian dictatorships used the crisis to bolster their regimes by whipping up hatred against the Western enemy, the better to distract attention from their grim rule.

From the behaviour of the majority of Western liberals, you would never have guessed that dictatorial regimes and ideologies were attacking fundamental principles for self-interested reasons. In 1989, a large section of liberal opinion rallied to Salman Rushdie, regardless of whether it thought *The Satanic Verses* was a good book or not. By 2006, many liberals had abandoned the basic tenet of a free society that the intention of a speaker or writer is irrelevant to his or her right to enjoy freedom of speech and publication. If Flemming Rose had commissioned cartoons mocking America and the Bush administration had protested, liberals would have clasped him to their pounding chests, because his intention would have been *good*. But because he had allowed cartoonists to criticise Islam, albeit mildly, his intention was *bad*, and therefore the enemies of liberalism could take their revenge on him, his cartoonists and his country.

Bill Clinton and European rabbis said the drawings reminded them of the anti-Semitic cartoons of fascist Europe – an odd comparison, because the leaders of Syria, Iran and the Muslim Brotherhood were anti-Semites. Jack Straw, the then British Home Secretary, praised the British press for not running the cartoons, while the Council of Europe criticised the Danish government for invoking the apparently irrelevant concept of 'freedom of the press' when it refused to take action against the 'insulting' cartoons.

The reaction of the Yale University Press encapsulated Western deference. Without waiting to receive a threat, it censored pre-emptively, and refused to carry pictures of the cartoons in a supposedly serious academic book about the controversy. The book's author treated arguments about free-dom of speech and women's rights as if they were ancient notions that need not detain the modern reader, and could not have been 'fairer' to their opponents. Nevertheless, Yale said it would have had 'blood on its hands' if it had shown readers the cartoons its author was analysing. Murders would not be the responsibility of the murderers, but of the publishers, because 'republication of the cartoons by the Yale University Press ran a serious risk of instigating violence'.

Until the twentieth century, Western writers were frightened of criticising Christianity. Britain took until 2008 to abolish its blasphemy law, although it had fallen into disuse long before then. America's constitutional protection of free speech and press freedom meant that blasphemy had never been an offence in the United States, but social pressures and the potential of Christian groups to stage protests and boycotts made it a de facto crime. That power to censor has gone. Trey Parker and Matt Stone, the creators of *South Park*, acknowledged its passing at the time of the cartoon crisis: 'It really is open season on Jesus. We can do whatever we want to Jesus, and we have. We've had him say bad words. We've had him shoot a gun. We've had him kill people. We can do whatever we want.'

Islam was another matter. *South Park*'s network Comedy Central would not allow the show to run a simple image of Muhammad during the affair, but at least it was honest about its reasons. Other US networks that banned images of Muhammad said they were censoring because they were liberals who wanted to display their respect and tolerance. 'No you're not,' Stone said. 'You're afraid of getting blown up. That's what you're afraid of. Comedy Central copped to that, you know: "We're afraid of getting blown up."'

In autumn 2011, the French satirical magazine *Charlie Hebdo* responded to the depressing success of an Islamist party in Tunisia's first election after the Arab Spring. As its target was a religious group, it satirised religious beliefs – what was it meant to do? The cover featured a cartoon of Muhammad with a bubble coming from his mouth saying, 'One hundred lashes if you don't die laughing.' An arsonist bombed *Charlie Hebdo*'s office. French politicians defended freedom of speech, but the guardians of liberal orthodoxy could not match their fortitude. *Time* deprecated the 'notoriously impertinent paper' and others who 'openly beg for the very violent responses from extremists their authors claim to proudly defy'. By then the notion that religious criminals did not have moral responsibility for their crimes was everywhere. Muslims were an undifferentiated block, naturally prone to violence, rather than a vast denominational group with reactionary and liberal strands.

As the old Christian punishments withered, Islamists pushed the West into accepting a new blasphemy law. It was not a law debated by congresses or parliaments. No legitimate authority spelt out its limits in a statute book. No judge protected defendants' rights to a fair trial. No jury said that it must find the accused guilty beyond reasonable doubt before conviction. The accused could break the law without knowing it, and be condemned without appeal. It was sufficient that someone, somewhere, deemed that the defendant had failed to show proper respect, and had the means to threaten retribution.

When I spoke to Flemming Rose he made a direct link between the modern acceptance that an 'insult' to a religion justified punishment, and the ideologies of the twentieth-century dictatorships. Rose had worked as a foreign correspondent in the old Soviet Union, and had learned to despise 'the trick of labelling any critique as an anti-Soviet insult to the state. You can catch anyone that way: Andrei Sakharov, Vladimir Bukovsky, Alexander Solzhenitsyn, Natan Sharansky, Boris Pasternak ... the regime accused them all of anti-Soviet propaganda, and many in the West went along with that.'

His comparison was not as far-fetched as it seemed.

FOUR

The Racism of the Anti-Racists

It is time to extend our solidarity to all the rebels of the Islamic world, non-believers, atheist libertines, dissenters, sentinels of liberty, as we supported Eastern European dissidents in former times. Europe should encourage these diverse voices and give them financial, moral and political support. Today there is no cause more sacred, more serious, or more pressing for the harmony of future generations. Yet our continent kneels before God's madmen, muzzling and libelling free-thinkers with suicidal heedlessness.

PASCAL BRUCKNER, 2007

Affectation had no place in Ayaan Hirsi Ali's writing. She did not play the coy dissident and smuggle coded messages past the censors, or imitate the magical realists by wrapping a critique inside a spinning narrative. She wrote plainly, in a precise voice of restrained outrage, and behaved as if she were a free woman with no reason to fear those who would silence her permanently – although she had reasons aplenty.

You needed to spend just five minutes in her company, or read a few pages of her work, to realise that indignation about the oppression of women drove her forward. The baby-boomer cliché that 'The personal is political' ignored the reality that in most of the world, and for most of history, the personal could not be political for women, because the power of religious and cultural authority prevented a political response to personal oppression. For a moment when Hirsi Ali was young, that power seemed to be breaking. Her father was a Somali socialist involved in revolutionary politics. But revolution in Somalia, like revolutions everywhere, turned to dictatorship. The local strongman threw her father in jail. The family fled into exile, and found a haven in Kenya, where Hirsi Ali learned that, revolution or no revolution, her sex determined her fate. When she and her sisters went to pray in a mosque, her father explained to the confused girl that she must stand behind him and the rest of the men. At school, she saw her friends dreaming of marrying a husband they loved, but then being forced to marry old men by their parents. Her grandmother arranged for what euphemists call 'female circumcision' – that is, for an amateur surgeon to cut away a girl's clitoris and her outer and inner labia, and scrape the vaginal walls. Hirsi Ali learned the hard way that she 'was a Somali woman and therefore my sexuality belonged to the owner of my family: my father or my uncles. It was obvious that I absolutely had to be a virgin on marriage, because to do otherwise would damage the honour of my family and whole clan – uncles, brothers, male cousins – forever and irretrievably. The place between my legs was sewn up to prevent it. It would be broken only by my husband.'

The retreat of poor-world radicals from the dying creed of socialism and into religious and tribal fanaticisms was well underway in Kenya by the time Hirsi Ali was a teenager. In Europe and America as well as Africa and the Middle East, the Muslim Brotherhood was the vehicle for religious reaction. Although conceived in Egypt as a totalitarian movement, which would impose a theocratic caliphate on the whole of humanity, the Brothers were not always agents of dictatorial revolution. In the West, they sought to 'engage' with liberal establishments to ensure that their sectarian version of Islam received state funds, and that they were allowed to define who was and was not an authentic Muslim among immigrant populations. Elsewhere, they could be plotting to seize control of Arab states or lying low. The Brotherhood followed the tactics of twentieth-century Marxists-Leninists. It could adopt an entryist strategy of infiltrating existing power structures or try insurrection depending on circumstances.

The Brotherhood's willingness to play along with Western governments should not disguise its extremism. It was the world's largest anti-Semitic organisation. Yusuf al-Qaradawi, the Egyptian scholar the Brotherhood most admired, declared that throughout history, God had imposed upon the Jews avengers who would punish them for their corruption. 'The last punishment was carried out by Hitler. By means of all the things he did to them – even though they exaggerated this issue – he managed to put them in their place. This was divine punishment for them. Allah willing, the next time will be at the hand of the believers.' His combination of partial Holocaust denial – 'even though they exaggerated it' – with genocidal fantasy – divine punishment awaits the Jews – marked him as a religious counterpart of Europe's neo-Nazis, whose fantasies allowed them to pretend that Auschwitz wasn't a death camp while dreaming of the death of the Jews.

The young Hirsi Ali was briefly attracted to the Brotherhood, but it was no place for an independent-minded woman. Qaradawi permitted husbands to beat disobedient wives, and allowed genital mutilation – 'Whoever finds it serving the interest of his daughters should do it, and I personally support this under the current circumstances in the modern world' – while the Brotherhood recommended a lifetime of submission. She got enough of that at home, and drifted away.

More useful to her was an altogether less holy tradition. At her Kenyan school, she read the novels of Charlotte Brontë, Jane Austen and Daphne du Maurier. Outside class, she and her friends swapped trashy paperback romances. Not a particularly radical education, you might think. But romance contains an idea more subversive than half the political philosophies devised by men. Hirsi Ali's heroines fell in love and defied their families to marry the husbands of their choice. In East Africa, and in much of the world, this was then, and remains now, a thrillingly revolutionary idea.

Her father arranged for her to marry a distant cousin from Canada she had never met. En route to Canada, she turned romance into rebellion. The plane touched down in Germany. She made a dash from the airport, and crossed the Dutch border. Realising that in refugee law the personal was not political, and that no country would grant her asylum so that she could escape an arranged marriage, she claimed to be a victim of political persecution in Somalia. Once she had secured asylum, her intelligence and determination ensured that she could build a new life. She helped fellow refugees find work, went to university, became a Dutch and therefore a European citizen, and began to publish her thoughts on her new homeland.

I can think of no better antidote to Western ennui than the writings of poor-world liberals. Hirsi Ali came to Europe, and was liberated and inspired. The notion that the world could be explained without reference to the 'fairy tales' of monotheism enchanted her. Secularism, stability, peace, prosperity and rights for women were wonders. 'The very shape of Holland seemed like a challenge to Allah,' she said at one point. 'Reclaiming land from the sea, controlling flooding with canals – it was like defying God.' At university in Holland, she embraced the liberal tradition of free speech and religious tolerance, and studied, Locke, Mill, Russell, Popper and Baruch Spinoza, whom Amsterdam Jews excommunicated for his free-thinking in the 1650s, and whose works Catholic and Protestant divines banned for their blasphemy. Given her sufferings and her intellectual self-confidence, it was always likely that she would abandon her religion.

She found a ready supply of Western moralists willing to denounce her as a 'new atheist'. Their label was self-evidently foolish – the 'new atheists' of the twenty-first century were not so different from the old atheists of the twentieth (they still did not believe in God, to mention the most prominent continuity). The newness of the 'new atheists' lay solely in their determination after 9/11 to state their beliefs without embarrassment. The dangers of religious extremism were clear, even to those who had not wanted to see. The new atheists thought that the best argument against Islamist terror, or Christian fundamentalism, or Hindu or Jewish nationalism, was to say bluntly that there is no God, and we should grow up. Fear of religious violence also drove the backlash against atheism from those who felt that appeasement of psychopathic believers was the safest policy; that if we were nice to them, perhaps they would calm down. Prim mainstream commentators decried the insensitivity and downright rudeness with which the new atheists treated the religious. The complaints boiled down to a simple and piteous cry: 'Why can't you stop upsetting them?'

You cannot, if like Ayaan Hirsi Ali you are confronting clerical oppression. In 1792, Mary Wollstonecraft's *Vindication of the Rights of Woman* stood alongside the pamphlets of the French revolutionaries as a founding feminist text. Wollstonecraft was alert to the danger that religion could suffocate her belief that 'It is vain to expect virtue from women till they are in some degree independent of men.' Although a radical dissenter from the English non-conformist tradition rather than an atheist, she took on the myths Judaism and Christianity had thrust on humanity: that God made Eve from Adam's rib to be his helpmate, and that Eve damned women by taking the apple from the tree of knowledge.

Suppose, Wollstonecraft wondered in the liberated intellectual climate after the French Revolution, that the conservative clerics of the 1790s were right, and God had formed women from Adam's rib to please men. The conclusion that 'she ought to sacrifice every other consideration to render herself agreeable to him: and let this brutal desire of self-preservation be the grand spring of all her actions' would be just, and women must submit to being stretched on the 'iron bed of fate'. But Wollstonecraft thought that dependence made an 'ignoble base' for human society – unworthy of a supreme being. So she begged leave to doubt whether God had created woman to please man. 'Though the cry of irreligion, or even atheism, be raised against me, I will simply declare, that were an angel from heaven to tell me that Moses's beautiful, poetical cosmogony, and the account of the fall of man, were literally true, I could not believe what my reason told me was derogatory to the character of the Supreme Being.'

In the later 1790s, as the reaction against the French Revolution swept Britain, anti-Jacobin writers denounced women's emancipation as the doctrine of 'hyenas in petticoats'. They seized on the miseries of Wollstonecraft's private life, and held them up as a terrible example to other women of the dangers of rebelling against God and nature. After her death in childbirth, her husband, the silly radical philosopher William Godwin, supplied her critics with the ammunition they needed. He stripped 'his dead wife naked' in the words of Robert Southey, by publishing frank accounts of her love affairs, illegitimate child and suicide attempt. Conservatives could not have been more grateful. Challenge traditional society and you will end up like her, they said – deprived of feminine charm, cursed with bastard children, betrayed, dejected and suicidal. But Wollstonecraft won a posthumous victory. Not even Tories and bishops can bring themselves to read the anti-Jacobin attacks on her now, while her work survives to enthuse succeeding generations. The triumph of her ideas did not happen by some benign process of osmosis. The opponents of the subjugation of women had to fight for their ideas, and endure abuse and hatred.

Ayaan Hirsi Ali reacted to life in Holland with a feminist revulsion Wollstonecraft would have recognised. Freedom was everywhere except in the lives of refugee women, who were still tied to the 'iron beds' fate had prescribed for them. As an interpreter, she visited Somali wives whose husbands beat them. Alongside the bruises and broken bones, she found Vitamin D deficiency. Dutch social workers thought it was the result of a poor diet caused by poverty. Hirsi Ali had to explain that the women were sick because their husbands would not let them leave their homes and walk in sunlit streets. The women did not complain, because they believed that in 'accepting systematic merciless abuse, they were serving Allah and earning a place in heaven'.

Hirsi Ali protested against the white society which tolerated such abuses as much as she did against the abuse itself. She came to believe that guilt crippled Europe: guilt about imperialism, guilt about Nazism, guilt about the Holocaust; guilt about the past but never about the present. Like many others, Hirsi Ali noticed that in the name of anti-racism European liberals were following a racist policy. When mass immigration began, they resolved to emphasise what divided rather than what united people, and to show their compassion by respecting the culture of 'the other'. Compassion sounds a fine virtue, which ordinarily leads the compassionate to help those less fortunate than themselves. In Europe, it produced indolence and indifference: a squishy liberal version of apartheid in which the authorities downplayed the genital mutilation of girls on kitchen tables and the murder of women who refused to accept arranged marriages because the women on the receiving end of the abuse were not white.

The appeal of respectable reasons for doing nothing should not be underestimated. Nor should the readiness of Ayaan Hirsi Ali to confront the double standard.

The first thing that strikes you when you meet her is her extraordinary calm. She is chatty and funny, but when the conversation turns to politics, stillness envelops her, as if her life had brought her to one unshakeable conclusion: the oppression of women by whatever authority must be fought. Blasphemous though her simple idea may be to some, she reasoned that Holland was a land where sex and drugs were openly on sale, and where comedians could fire at Christianity at will. Surely there would be no repercussions if she asserted the obvious? She campaigned against male violence, and renounced Islam on national television. By 2000, she was active in politics, an achievement worth mentioning for a black immigrant who arrived in Holland unable to speak Dutch in 1992. She marched under the banner of the Labour Party, before the left's hypocrisies pushed her into joining the centre-right liberals. I would be being unfair if I suggested that the whole of the Dutch left was too frightened to support her. Hirsi Ali's memoirs record the camaraderie of individual social democratic politicians. She joined the centre-right because as a collective the European left remained stuck in the identity politics of the 1968 generation. They were interested in group rights – the rights of blocs of immigrants not to be penalised for their colour or creed – rather than rights of individuals not to be persecuted by their own 'community'.

If the historians of the future have one ounce of morality, they will damn the European left for its inability to oppose racism and support individual liberty simultaneously. Hirsi Ali was not prepared to wait for posterity's judgement, and forced the Dutch police to recognise the extent of 'honour' killings of women in her country. After she renounced her religion and criticised the abuse of women, she learned that the descendants of the clerics who had banned Spinoza's books remained at large in Amsterdam. The police sent bodyguards to protect her. Her fellow MPs wondered if they needed to 'protect her from herself', a true example of white condescension towards 'the other' which she rejected with disdain.

She linked up with Theo van Gogh, a distant relative of the painter. Friends and critics alike described him as a provocateur: a typical loud-mouthed showman, who was always trying to get himself noticed by épatering the bourgeoisie. *Submission*, the ten-minute film he directed in 2004 from Hirsi Ali's script, belied much that critics said about him, and much of what he said about himself. It is a formal, sombre work, in which the camera flits over the faces and bodies of young women. The first woman describes how she fell in love, and was whipped in accordance with the Koranic injunction that 'The woman and the man guilty of adultery or fornication, flog each of them with a hundred stripes; let no compassion move you in their case, in a matter prescribed by God, if ye believe in God and the Last Day; and let a party of the believers witness their punishment.' A second describes how her family compels her to marry a man who repels her. She pretends to be 'unclean', but when she can pretend no longer he forces himself on her. She submits because the Koran tells men, 'When they have purified themselves, ye may approach them in any manner, time or place ordained for you by God.' A third is raped by her uncle. 'When I told my mother, she said she would take it up with my father. My father ordered her – and me – not to question his brother's honour.' Now she is pregnant, and knows her father will kill her for losing her virginity. She wants to kill herself, but cannot. The film ends with her saying, 'I know that in the hereafter the one who commits suicide shall never count on Your mercy. Allah, giver and taker of life. You admonish all who believe to turn towards You in order to attain bliss. I have done nothing my whole life but turn to You. And now that I pray for salvation, under my veil, You remain silent as the grave I long for. I wonder how much longer I am able to submit!'

If van Gogh had produced a film on the religious oppression of puritan women in seventeenth-century Holland, or Orthodox Jewish women in nineteenth-century Poland, the jury at Cannes might have applauded. But he and Hirsi Ali wanted to challenge contemporary injustice, not to excavate the past.

He laughed when the first death threats arrived. 'No one kills the village idiot,' he told Hirsi Ali.

On the morning of 2 November 2004, Mohammed Bouyeri, a second-generation Moroccan immigrant who had joined the local jihadist sect the Hofstad Network, approached van Gogh on an Amsterdam street with a handgun. Van Gogh's last words were, 'Can't we talk about this?'

There was to be no conversation.

Bouyeri shot van Gogh eight times in the chest, slit his throat and stuck a letter to Hirsi Ali onto his warm corpse with a butcher's knife.

In the millions of words that have been written about Hirsi Ali, few commentators discuss what Bouyeri, or the ideologue who drafted the letter for him, said. The contents were too embarrassing, for they placed Europeans under an anti-fascist obligation to stir themselves. Hirsi Ali was going to be next, Bouyeri said. Because she had argued for women's rights, she, like Salman Rushdie before her, had become the tool of 'Jewish masters': 'It is a fact, that Dutch politics is dominated by many Jews who are a product of the Talmud schools; that includes your political party-members.' Hirsi Ali was not Jewish – how could she be? – so the Hofstad group decided that because she had renounced religion she was 'an infidel fundamentalist' manipulated by the Elders of Zion. She did not 'believe that a Supreme Being controls the entire universe'. She did not 'believe that your heart, with which you cast away truth, has to ask permission from the Supreme Being for every beat'.

You can find the same reasoning among all varieties of religious rightists. The American evangelical Jerry Falwell said the 9/11 attacks on New York and Washington were God's punishment on 'the pagans, and the abortionists, and the feminists, and the gays and the lesbians who are actively trying to make that an alternative lifestyle, the ACLU, People for the American Way, all of them who have tried to secularize America'. Like Bouyeri, Falwell saw a vengeful God enforcing his punishments on decadent secularists.

In Amsterdam, the city of Spinoza and Anne Frank, anti-Semites had murdered a director for making a feminist film, and forced a black liberal into hiding. Hirsi Ali had good reasons to criticise European liberals, but she might have expected that they would have stood with her as she faced down murderous enemies. She was to learn a hard lesson. The response to van Gogh's murder could not have been more different from the response to the attempts to assassinate Salman Rushdie. Instead of defending the victims of armed reaction, liberal opinion turned on them.

The New Anti-Jacobins

Liberal immigrants to Europe are caught on a fork. Native conservatives in their new country are against them because they are immigrants. Religious conservatives in their 'community' are against them because they are liberals. They ought to be able to turn to white liberals for support, but liberalism in Europe has turned septic. In the name of tolerance it is happy to abandon its friends and excuse its enemies.

The Dutch media went to work on Ayaan Hirsi Ali after van Gogh's murder. A television crew travelled to East Africa and revealed that she had not fled from the war in Somalia, as she had said on her asylum application, but from a comfortable home in Kenya. The story was true, but it was not a revelation:

she had told the leaders of her party long before that she was fleeing an arranged marriage. The journalists then alleged that she was not fleeing an arranged marriage. Of course I was, Hirsi Ali replied. My father had said that I must marry a distant cousin – and 'My father is not a man who takes no for an answer.'

Once, attacks on bogus asylum seekers and illegal immigrants were confined to the right-wing press. But those who attacked Ayaan Hirsi Ali used the language of the left. One Dutch commentator explained that the Dutch public did not support her because the 'neo-conservative wave that swept Holland in recent years is running out of steam and turning in on itself'. Let me remind you that Hirsi Ali and van Gogh had made a film that criticised rape, wife-beating and the flogging of 'immoral women'. The response of elements in the Dutch left was to assert that opposition to the oppression of women made a feminist a neo-conservative. Ordinary Dutch society behaved no better. Just as the neighbours of Penguin's Peter Mayer did not want him or his children near them, so Hirsi Ali's neighbours wanted to remove her from the safe flat where the Dutch police had hidden her. Appeal court judges accepted a suit from families living in the apartment block. In a ruling beyond satire, the court said that the decision of the Dutch police to put her in a place of safety was a breach of her new neighbours' human rights. Because Hirsi Ali defended the rights of immigrants, she was a threat to the human rights of the natives. Her presence endangered their security, the court said, and lowered the value of their properties – an unforgivable offence in the eyes of the European bourgeoisie. Of the fourteen apartment-owners in the complex, only three were prepared to offer her their solidarity.

Rita Verdonk, a leading figure in Hirsi Ali's Liberal Party, moved against her next. Verdonk was a populist, who gave the Dutch electorate a tough line on immigration. True to form, she said that because Hirsi Ali had lied in her asylum application, the state must strip her of her Dutch citizenship. Her attack on

Hirsi Ali split her party, and Verdonk had to back down. But it remained an eye-opening event. After the courts ejected an atheist feminist from her place of safety, Dutch politicians threatened to make her a stateless woman again. If they had succeeded, the Dutch authorities would have been under no obligation to protect her. They could call off her police escort and leave Hirsi Ali in a free-fire zone. Such was the price elements in the Dutch establishment wished Hirsi Ali to pay for upholding the ideals they professed to hold themselves.

Nor were the majority of the wider liberal intelligentsia prepared to offer support to a woman hitmen wanted to assassinate because she had protested against patriarchy. Their assaults on Hirsi Ali were ominous in the extreme, for they revealed the retreat from universal values.

Even before her neighbours demanded that the courts eject Hirsi Ali from her secure apartment, anyone could see that large numbers of European liberals did not want to defend their principles, if defending them put their lives and property at risk. The Dutch journalist's accusation that standing up for human rights made you a 'neo-con' was widely held by his contemporaries. They could not maintain a belief in universal human rights and criticise George W. Bush at the same time. The accusation became a self-fulfilling prophecy in Hirsi Ali's case. Rejected by Dutch leftists and the Dutch Liberal Party, she eventually found a home at the neo-conservative American Enterprise Institute in Washington, DC. She became what her enemies said she was because when her natural allies abandoned her, their opponents were the only people who would take her in.

Identity politics played their part too. The proposition that 'Europeans believe defending Muslim women from mutilation and abuse constitutes a racist attack on Muslims' is an oxymoron that is so morally and logically contemptible it demolishes itself. Few of Ayaan Hirsi Ali's enemies could admit to holding such a detestable notion, although many behaved as if they did.

Liberal intellectuals did not force their readers to be honest with themselves. Instead the Anglo-Dutch journalist Ian Buruma and the Oxford academic Timothy Garton Ash stepped forward to provide a 'liberal' critique of Hirsi Ali. The unthinking consensus in which they operated was best revealed by their failure to explain why they felt it necessary to add to her troubles. Nothing in their writing betrayed the smallest awareness that others would find it strange that men who called themselves liberals should turn on a woman clerical censors were persecuting because of her commitment to the equality of the sexes. When the fashion in Manhattan, London and Paris is to slide away from universal principles, those leading the slither can never admit that modern liberalism contains contradictions and dark motives that require an explanation. Self-awareness and self-criticism would puncture the assumption of moral superiority, which is liberal culture's greatest strength.

In Buruma's book *Murder in Amsterdam* and in a series of articles for the *New York Review of Books* and the *New York Times*, Buruma and Garton Ash acknowledged Hirsi Ali's bravery with a passing nod, and then men who had no fear in their own lives passed judgement on a marked woman who could not step outside without bodyguards.

Her call for the emancipation of women marked her as an extremist, they decided. Van Gogh's assassin had denounced her as an 'infidel fundamentalist'; Garton Ash and Buruma adapted the insult, and denounced her as an 'Enlightenment fundamentalist'. As if those who believed in the subjugation of women, the Jewish-conspiracy theory of history and the murder of homosexuals, adulterers and apostates were the moral equivalents of those who did not. As if there was nothing to choose between the two. As if the principled liberal response to the conflict between them was to dedicate time and energy to condemning Enlightenment 'fundamentalism' while ignoring the Enlightenment's enemies.

Buruma decided that Hirsi Ali was not a victim but a victim-iser, an elitist with contempt for ordinary women. The way she waved her hand at a guest arguing with her during a debate at a refuge for battered women unsettled him. It was a 'gentle gesture of disdain', he decided, an 'almost aristocratic dismissal of a noisome inferior'. Her attitude towards the Dutch was no better. The ingrate immigrant regarded the inhabitants of her new homeland as being in a pit of 'moral decadence'. She said she supported Enlightenment values, but Buruma maintained she had no right to compare herself to Voltaire. He was a brave man who fought the mighty Catholic Church of the eighteenth century. She was, he implied, a bully who was picking on weak Muslims, 'a minority that was already feeling vulnerable'. By renouncing Islam, he concluded, she had made herself a woman of no importance. She had cut herself off from European Muslims. Her voice had no legitimacy among the women she sought to address, so she was an irrelevance as well as an elitist and a bully. It apparently never occurred to him that Mary Wollstonecraft and her successors in the nineteenth century had to take on established Christianity. Although devout women at the time would not have liked their repudiation of Genesis, their lives and the lives of their daughters could not have been improved until divinely sanctioned oppression had been challenged.

Garton Ash and Buruma dwelt on Hirsi Ali's brief interest in the Muslim Brotherhood when she was young. She had walked away, as we saw, but they decided that the change in her politics was more superficial than real. She was a Muslim fundamental-ist then, and an 'Enlightenment fundamentalist' now. Politic Europeans should have nothing to do with her. Garton Ash concluded by turning Hirsi Ali's good looks against her. 'It is no disrespect to Ms Ali,' he said with the condescension Oxford dons habitually mistake for wit, 'to suggest that if she had been short, squat and squinting, her story and views might not have been so closely attended to.'

The West still had intellectuals prepared to defend the honour of liberalism, and Garton Ash and Buruma's attacks on Hirsi Ali, and the willingness of the liberal *New York Times* and *New York Review of Books* to run them, provoked rousing counterblasts in North America and Europe. The New York intellectual Paul Berman filled half of an issue of the *New Republic* with a dissection of how the affair exposed the 'reactionary turn' twenty-first-century liberal thought had taken. In a ringing conclusion, he declared:

> A sustained attack in the intellectual world on a persecuted liberal dissident from Africa, a campaign in the press that has managed to push the question of women's rights systematically to the side, a campaign that has veered more than once into personal cruelty, a soft vendetta but a visible one, presided over by the normally cautious and sincerely liberal editors of one distinguished and admired journal after another, applauded and faithfully imitated by a variety of other writers and journalists, such that, in some circles, the sustained attack has come to be accepted as a conventional wisdom – no, this could not have happened in the past.

In Paris, Pascal Bruckner, heir to the best traditions of the French Enlightenment, said that as well as living in fear, Ayaan Hirsi Ali has had 'to endure the ridicule of the high-minded'. In the eyes of the 'genteel professors' she had 'committed an unpardonable offence: she has taken democratic principles seriously'. For that they called her a 'fundamentalist', and could not see that 'the difference between her and Muhammad Bouyeri is that she never advocated murder to further her ideas'.

For all the brilliance of the polemics in the pamphlet war over Hirsi Ali, no fair observer could doubt that Buruma and Garton Ash represented the dominant tendency in liberal opinion in the West. In Britain, the Archbishop of Canterbury and the Lord

Chief Justice supported the use of Sharia law in divorces and other family disputes – the Lord Chief Justice in a Jamaat-e-Islami-influenced mosque, appropriately. The women priests of the Church of England, so keen to have their equal right to be bishops asserted, and women lawyers at the Bar, who complained so vociferously about the law's glass ceiling, did not accuse the archbishop and the judge of sexism. They left the fight to a group of ex-Muslim women, who pointed out that Sharia law already existed informally in Britain, and 'women are often pressured by their families into going to these courts and adhering to unfair decisions. If they refuse to go they faced threats and intimidation, or at best being ostracised.' Too many liberals ignored the protest, and showed they were prepared to endorse one law for women with white skins and another for women with brown skins.

With equal insincerity, the nominally left-of-centre and perennially two-faced Labour Party instructed the Foreign Office to appease Islamist sentiment at home and abroad. It embraced the Muslim Brotherhood and Jamaat-e-Islami, and declared that they were 'reformist groups' with a 'moderate' and 'progressive' ideology. Britain's 'progressives', nitpickingly politically correct in all other matters, stayed silent as they did it.

Ayaan Hirsi Ali was not the only dissident they left behind.

The Scaremongers and the Scared

In 2009, I was standing with a group of young men and women whose courage made me want to hug them. They called themselves British Muslims for Secular Democracy, and they had come together to defend freedom of speech and demand the separation of Church and state. We were demonstrating in central London against Islam4UK, a front organisation for radical Islamists, whose fellow travellers were more than willing to turn violent, as the publishers of *The Jewel of Medina* had learned. 'Laugh at those who Insult Islam', read one of my companions' placards. 'Liberal democracy will rule the world', read another. 'Secularism is coming to Britain,' their organisers said. 'We are all free to worship or not to worship according to our own conscience.'

Well, I thought, I've waited a long time to see this. Behind us on the steps of Eros at Piccadilly Circus was a separate protest organised by beery football fans, draped in Union flags. Its members explained that they were from a new organisation called the English Defence League. They had had enough of Islamists wrecking the solemn ceremonies to mark the return of the bodies of British troops from Iraq and Afghanistan. They would fight back, they told me, but not as racists. I had been waiting a while for that, too. Liberal-left politicians could not deplore prejudice and then welcome Islamists into Whitehall without expecting a backlash. The Archbishop of Canterbury and the Lord Chief Justice could not call for Sharia law, and think that no one would notice. There was bound to be a reaction, and it was good to see that it appeared to be of an earthy and democratic kind. Or as the wife of an EDL member said to me, 'I'm not walking three paces behind any fucking man.'

My illusions lasted less than an hour. I walked into a nearby bar with a young woman who was as British as anyone else in London that day. 'You're not welcome here,' EDL members spat at a Muslim so integrated that she would walk into a pub with a casual acquaintance. 'Fuck off back to Pakistan.' I learned then that the English Defence League was not against Islamists, but against all Muslims. As I expected, the League soon became home to those far-rightists who hated Muslims more than they hated Jews.

A few weeks later, I addressed a meeting of students, and praised the secular Muslims for defending liberal values. A leftist in the audience was having none of it. He denounced British Muslims for Secular Democracy as the English Defence League's allies and collaborators, citing as evidence the 'joint demonstration' at Piccadilly Circus. I told him there had been no joint demonstration, and I had seen with my own eyes the white racists abuse the secular Muslims. I was there, he was not; but it did not matter what I said. He and his comrades had already spread the required smear round the Net. To their minds, liberal Muslims were Uncle Toms. Authentic Muslims could only be bearded men with a Koran in one hand and a Kalashnikov in the other.

By that time, it was hard to know whether left or right was more culpable of inciting violence. With a neat symmetry, campaigners against white neo-fascism wrote to the right-wing *Daily Star* in 2010 to complain that the paper exaggerated 'the importance of tiny Muslim extremist groups', and risked creating 'a dangerous backlash among non-Muslims which in turn will feed groups such as the EDL and the British National Party'. Within weeks, liberal Muslims at the Quilliam Foundation complained to the leftish executives of Channel 4 that they took speakers from Islamist groups and supporters of the Iranian theocratic regime to 'represent mainstream Muslim opinion', and reinforced 'negative stereotypes of Islam to non-Muslims' by doing so. Right-wing newspapers pretended extremists were immigrants' authentic representatives because they wanted to whip up the fear of the other. The liberal media gave platforms to reactionary and paranoid men because they wanted to revel in the exoticism of the other. The motives were different, but the effect was the same.

In Holland, the Islamophobic Party for Freedom overtook the Christian Democrats to become the largest conservative force in the country. The French National Front enjoyed a resurgence of support, while the Sarkozy government banned women from wearing the burqa – a direct assault on freedom of choice and freedom of religion. American conservatives believed that Muslim immigration was turning Europe into 'Eurabia', as the example mentioned earlier from Christopher Caldwell's writing shows. Immigrants, the theory ran, had huge families and an uncompromising religion. Godless, pacifist Europeans, their will sapped by secularism and relativism, their numbers diminished by their hedonistic determination to have sex without having babies, lacked the moral certainty to fight militant Islam and the birth rate to outbreed it. They were losing the battle of ideas and the battle in the maternity wards. Muslims would make up 30, 40 or 50 per cent of the population of Europe by 2050, according to which alarmist forecast you read. It would become an anti-American, anti-Semitic, anti-Western continent, too frightened of its new inhabitants to stand up for democratic values.

These figures were nonsense. Even when they were not outright inventions, they included the assumption that current immigrant birth rates would remain high, when statistics suggested they were falling. The premise behind conservatives' fears was equally dubious. European Muslims did not form a cohesive bloc capable of collective action in favour of the causes of Islamist militants. The best reason for rejecting the paranoia of the right, however, was that it did not look at the victims of violence.

Extremists of all persuasions committed atrocities. Islamists murdered 191 civilians in Madrid in March 2004 and fifty-two in London in July 2005. The neo-fascist Anders Breivik murdered seventy-seven in Norway in July 2011. Both the religious far right and the white far right were convinced that they were fighting diabolic conspiracies. The London bomber Mohammad Sidique Khan justified random murder by invoking a Western plot to destroy Islam. 'Your democratically elected governments continuously perpetuate atrocities against my people all over the world,' he said in a videotape released after he killed himself and murdered six others on the London Underground's Circle Line. 'And your support of them makes you directly responsible, just as I am directly responsible for protecting and avenging my Muslim brothers and sisters.' Breivik cut and pasted a manifesto from anti-Muslim blogs, and justified his massacre by saying that leftish multi-cultural elites were plotting to destroy Europe's old nations and create 'Eurabia' by flooding the continent with immigrants. His charge was not that European establishments were naïve or cowardly in their treatment of religious extremism – which they were on many occasions – but that a quasi-Marxist hatred of traditional Christian culture pushed them into collaboration with an alien enemy.

Although the two sides seemed to be diametrically opposed, when they went for specific targets, rather than bombing random collections of civilians, they showed that what united them was more important than what divided them. Breivik's victims were not militant Islamists: most of them were young members of the Norwegian Labour Party. To his mind they were 'traitors' to their race and culture. Similarly, those Islamists marked for suffering were not far-rightists who dreamed of an all-white Europe, or conservatives who bewailed the decline of the Christian West. The leaders of most European far-right parties could operate without fearing a bullet in the head. It never occurred to Tea Party Republicans, who wittered about a demographic explosion producing a jihadist Europe, that jihadis might retaliate by gunning them down. With the exception of Geert Wilders of the Dutch Party of Freedom, who was the target of threats and one assassination attempt, the scaremongers knew no fear.

Unlike panic-stricken conservatives, Islamists did not regard European Muslims as a bloc which was theirs to command. They understood that there was no unified Islam, that most immigrants were just trying to make a living, and many were experimenting with new ideas and freedoms. The first aim of religious violence is to stop experiment by the faithful and to enforce taboos. Naturally, the first targets of Islamists in Europe were liberal Muslims and ex-Muslims, who like Salman Rushdie were 'traitors' to their religion. Potential victims ought to have been able to count on the steady support of a European mainstream that opposed Islamism and neo-fascism in equal measure, and recognised that both drew on a common totalitarian impulse. But as the example of Ayaan Hirsi Ali showed, principled anti-fascism was hard to find.

Liberal societies treated the Islamist wave with a disastrous mixture of authoritarianism and appeasement. On the one hand, they passed anti-terrorist laws that conflicted with basic liberties, banned burqas and imposed new immigration controls, which were controls on Muslim immigration when you stripped away all the humbug around them. On the other, they complemented their anti-terror strategy with a policy of 'engaging' with Islamists of the Muslim Brotherhood variety, who were extreme but not violent. They hoped that by co-opting religious zealots, they could reduce the pool of potential terrorists. If we concede ground and don't challenge them too rigorously, they thought, perhaps they won't turn malevolent. The consequence of their double standards was that they had to attack Hirsi Ali and those like her who were not afraid to point out their hypocrisy or ignore the suffering of immigrant women 'engagement with Islamists' brought.

Naser Khader, the Danish Muslim politician whose defence of free speech during the cartoon crisis provoked one radical imam to discuss the possibility of him being blown up – as a 'jest', you will remember – viewed the manoeuvres of mainstream opinion with abhorrence. 'They take a minority in a minority to represent everyone,' he told me. 'When the minority in the minority demands the right to oppress the majority within the minority, they give it to them.' Khader has had to live with threats from extremists of all kinds. The intimidation from white racists bothered him less than the threats from Islamists from the religious far right. The police ought to know the identities of activists in local white extremist movements, he reasoned, and be able to monitor them. But radical Islam had a global network – a Comintern of the faithful – that stretched far beyond the jurisdiction of the Danish state. Just before I spoke to Khader, he had suggested in a television debate that schools should spare Muslim children the Ramadan fast because teachers had told him that hungry pupils were tired and listless during lessons. Someone in Denmark heard him, and passed details of his offence to the Middle East. A threatening message ordering him to mend his ways or suffer the consequences arrived from Jordan. Maybe nothing would come of it, maybe it would, but the Danish police could not investigate a threat from extremists living almost two thousand miles away.

Maryam Namazie, who fled with her family to Britain to avoid the persecutions of the Iranian theocracy, responded to the Archbishop of Canterbury and the Lord Chief Justice by organising campaigns against Sharia. 'To safeguard the rights and freedoms of all those living in Britain, there must be one secular law for all and no religious courts,' she said. As with Hirsi Ali and Khader, religious extremists threatened her as soon as she spoke out. She received a message warning, 'You are going to be decapitated.' If the American government or the British state had menaced her, she would have been a heroine. The press and the broadcasters would have defended and succoured her, and given encouragement to all who wanted to defy authority. As it was, she remained a virtually unknown figure.

On occasion, liberal society stirred itself. The self-taught Moroccan-Dutch artist Rachid Ben Ali responded to the murder of Theo van Gogh by producing pictures of 'hate imams' spewing bombs and excrement. As if to prove his point, death threats followed. Ali, like so many others, confessed to being frightened, but said that he remained determined to use his art to show that people of Muslim origins can be 'absolutely free in their thinking'. His gallery stood by him, and paid for his security guards.

Such moments of solidarity were rare. Ali's fellow artist Sooreh Hera was not so fortunate after she tried to confront religious hypocrisy. 'They condemn homosexuality, but in countries like Iran or Saudi Arabia it is common for married men to maintain relations with other men,' she said as she explained her project. 'Works of art can be provocative. It is not an artist's job just to paint flowers. Art should shine a light on social issues.' She photographed gay Iranian exiles wearing masks of Muhammad and Ali, the Prophet's son-in-law, sitting half-naked in modern bedrooms. The director of her Dutch gallery loved her protests against the execution of gays by the Iranian regime – Such a transgressive critique of hegemonic power structures! So edgy! So fizzing with contemporary relevance! – until he realised that 'Certain people in our society may perceive them as offensive,' and removed them from the show. Hera went into hiding, after receiving charming emails along the lines of 'We're going to burn you naked or put a bullet in your mouth.' Like Khader, she was well aware of the international reach of her enemies, and feared that agents of the Iranian state might target her. The Dutch government and the left-wing press refused to support her. 'Freedom of expression has become an illusion in Europe,' she said. 'We think we have freedom of expression, but in fact we live under a sort of hidden censorship.'

Because it was fighting a religious culture war and targeting newspapers, artists and novelists who offended it, radical Islam posed the greatest threat to freedom of speech of the anti-liberal movements. There is no guarantee that others will not imitate its tactics. In the summer of 2011, a British literary festival cancelled an event featuring an Islamist speaker after the English Defence League threatened to disrupt the meeting. Maybe I should not make too much of an isolated event, but the white extreme right could not have failed to have noticed that the habit of agreeing to the demands of menacing men had become ingrained in cultural bureaucrats. Religious radicals could dictate who spoke and wrote, so why shouldn't they do the same?

If the fears of feminists, artists, politicians and writers seem remote from ordinary life, consider the case of Deepika Thathaal, who like many girls did not dream of growing up to be a painter or a novelist, but a pop star. She started as a child singer in her native Norway. By seventeen, she was doing what teenage girls do, rebelling against authority, dressing in skimpy outfits and listening to the music of her day. Her second album, released in 1996, was a sensation in Norway. She mixed the influences of Asian music, Massive Attack and Portishead, and looked stunning as she did it. She thought she was on a smooth path to success, until the intimidation began.

Her parents had to change their phone number because of the hate calls. Five men burst into her school calling her 'a slut, a whore, a prostitute'. The confused teenager could not see why they were upset. 'I had the first brown face to appear on the front of the showbiz magazines. They ought to have been pleased.' She was attacked on the street and on stage during a concert in Oslo. She moved to London, where she decided to relaunch her career as Deeyah, 'the Muslim Madonna'. With a naïvety that could make you weep, she thought Britain would be a safer and better country than Norway because she had visited it as a child, and been impressed to see Asian women in Western clothes. Performers like her would be freer here, she reasoned, because immigrants had had longer to integrate.

'I first realised that something was wrong when my new manager told me that there was no competition. No other Muslim woman was doing what I was doing. He thought it was great, but I wondered, "Why am I the only one?"'

She soon found out. In 2006, she released a single, 'What Will it Be'. 'We don't take it lightly when you threatenin' women/How you have so much hate and faith in religion?' she sang on the video as she danced in a bikini top. To pile offence on offence, she supported women's refuges and campaigns against 'honour killings'.

British religious reactionaries forced her to hire bodyguards. Middle-aged men spat at her in the street and phoned her to say they would cut her to pieces not just because of her clothes, she told me, but because the sight of a woman making any kind of music was anathema to them. Callers demanded that Asian music channels ban her videos, and the channels' abject managers agreed. A spokesman for the Islamist organisations the Labour government, the Archbishop of Canterbury and the Lord Chief Justice were appeasing condemned her by saying women should not draw unnecessary attention to themselves.

'It was just the same in Britain as it was in Norway,' Deeyah said. She moved to an American city where no one knew her to find peace of mind and the time to pull herself together.

Deeyah talks as if liberal Europe had betrayed her, a common feeling among dissidents. Naser Khader, whose defence of gay rights and freedom of speech would once have marked him as a leftist, has given up on the liberal left and has joined the Danish conservative party. Gita Sahgal, who organised the pro-Rushdie demonstrations in Parliament Square in 1989, went on to work for Amnesty International. She and the organisation seemed natural allies. Sahgal was a feminist. Amnesty International was the world's pre-eminent liberal campaign group. She resigned in 2009 because she could no longer tolerate Amnesty allying with Islamists. Liberal-leftists in Europe and North America assume that good people will always recognise the inherent goodness of the liberal left and join it. I would not count on that happening with the coming generation of dissenters from Muslim backgrounds. The most radical voices – to use 'radical' in its true sense for once – have good reason to turn away. The first principle of liberalism, a principle that predates the Enlightenment, was freedom of conscience. No man should have the power to force others to accept his religion. Europe had hundreds of politicians, activists, intellectuals, writers, artists and exiles who found that freedom denied to them as they tried to criticise religious beliefs. Beyond Salman Rushdie and Ayaan Hirsi Ali were many others whose cases rarely made the papers. They had come to Europe because they wanted freedom of speech and freedom of conscience. When they tried to exercise those rights, they were threatened, attacked or forced to go into hiding. Mainstream society, which could cry so piteously for the persecuted in far-off lands, did not even know their names, let alone find the courage to defend their liberties.

Say that it is Bigoted to Oppose Bigotry

Attempting to define 'chutzpah', and finding that 'gall, brazen nerve, effrontery, incredible guts, presumption plus arrogance' did not quite capture the awe the word carried with it, the Yiddish linguist Leo Rosten tried again. Chutzpah, he said, is 'that quality enshrined in a man who, having killed his mother and father, throws himself on the mercy of the court because he is an orphan'.

The skill of the practised chutzpahean lies in his ability to manipulate his listeners' guilt. He knows that no one wishes to be accused of picking on the vulnerable, and so will make you forget that the self-made orphan is a murderer, and the self-anointed victim an oppressor.

From Salman Rushdie on, Islamists have supplemented the threat of violence with appeals to the sometimes irritating but often well-justified arguments for fair treatment made by the politically correct. They have claimed that they are the victims of racism or religious phobia, and said that democratic countries must punish or ostracise those who affront their prejudices or question their faith. It is a breath-catching demand, because blasphemy is a victimless crime. What has the blasphemer injured? Is it religious ideas? If so, must we protect ideas from criticism as we protect children from abusers? Are we to regard concepts as persons who can suffer physical harm and financial loss? Perhaps the tender feelings of believers are the victims. If so, is their faith so weak that mockery and doubt can threaten it? Or maybe the defendant stands accused of insulting whatever god or gods the faithful follow. If that is the case, are the delicate deities in question so thin-skinned that their 'self-esteem' can only recover if their followers perform human sacrifices and present them with the corpses of their critics?

In practice, the injured party on whose behalf the state brings its action or the terrorist kills his victim is the tribe or imagined community. Blasphemy is the means by which it enforces group identity by condemning internal critics as heretics and apostates, and silencing sceptical outsiders. The religious transfer legal rights from individuals, where they belong, to abstractions such as faith or God. The 'insults' and 'offences' they penalise are vague and subjective. Given the impossibility of defining what they mean with anything like the clarity we expect in law, let alone of demonstrating real physical or financial harm, the 'crime' of blasphemy gives censors, judges and poisonous nuisances enormous leeway. Reviewing the blasphemy laws not just of the Islamic world but also of Poland and Greece, the human-rights group Freedom House said in 2010 that blasphemy allowed extremists to cement a mobbish alliance between Church and state. 'No matter what the political environment, blasphemy laws lend the power of the state to particular religious authorities and effectively reinforce extreme views, since the most conservative or hard-line elements in a religious community are generally the quickest to take offence and the first to claim the mantle of orthodoxy. Virtually any act has the potential to draw an accusation and prosecution' – a sentiment that M.F. Husain and Sherry Jones would have agreed with.

Religious freedom – including freedom from religion – requires freedom of speech. Restrict freedom of speech, and Christians can persecute Muslims and Jews for denying that Jesus was the son of God. Muslims can persecute Jews and Christians for denying that Muhammad was God's messenger.

Jews can persecute Christians and Muslims for saying that Christian and Muslim doctrines superseded theirs. And every religion can persecute free-thinkers.

To cite the most striking example, the United Nations Human Rights Council demanded in 2009 that member states forbid the 'defamation of religion'. The council is a sick joke, which has included Russia, China, Saudi Arabia and many another dictatorship among its members. Its proclamations are a regular source of shame, but its attack on freedom of speech was its nadir. The UN did not say that states should forbid persecution on religious grounds – if it had, China and Saudi Arabia would have been in the dock – but that they should forbid criticism of religion. It gave no definition of the meaning of defamation, but Pakistan, the promoter of the motion, said it was against the 'negative stereotyping of religions [and] the frequent and wrong association of Islam with human-rights violations and terrorism'. Irony is always lost on the authoritarian mind, and the representative of Pakistan could not allow himself to remember that Islamists were reducing his country to a failed state by using religion to justify human-rights violations and terrorism.

Clearly floundering as he tried to find a moral justification for censorship, he went on to say that the motion must be passed, because laws against the defamation of religion were needed to protect religious minorities from 'discrimination and acts of violence'. The insincerity behind the worthy sentiment was plain to see. As Pakistan talked of the need to end discrimination, its judiciary and Islamist terrorists persecuted Christians, and Shia, Ahmadi and other 'heretical' versions of Islam.

The most notorious case was that of Asia Bibi, a Christian mother of five. The police arrested her after she argued with Muslim women who refused to drink water she had carried, saying that she was impure. A mob surrounded the police station in her village in the Sheikhupura district of the Punjab. Its leaders told the authorities that she had insulted Muhammad.

For this blasphemy, the court sentenced her to death. Not much respect shown for her minority rights, then. Nor for the rights of Salmaan Taseer, the governor of the Punjab, who denounced the death sentence as the work of a 'black law'. He and his wife visited Asia Bibi in prison, and promised that she would receive a presidential pardon. Taseer's fellow politicians, from the president downwards, could not emulate his bravery. Fearing a religious backlash, they abandoned him. (One went so far as to say that not only would he not soften or repeal the blasphemy law, he would personally kill anyone who blasphemed.) Their cowardice left religious talk-show hosts free to run a hate campaign against Taseer. A police constable, charged by the state to protect him, then pumped twenty-six bullets into his body, while other members of his bodyguard stood by and let him do it.

Once you concede ground to religious extremists, their demands grow more impertinent. The supporters of Taseer's killer did not claim that the governor had blasphemed by asserting that the Koran was the work of men, not God, or that he had insulted the Prophet Muhammad. He was murdered for criticising the workings of a lethal blasphemy law, and urging judicial restraint. He had not blasphemed against God, only blasphemed against blasphemy law, but for that small 'offence' he had to die.

Pakistan's use of the language of victimhood to sweeten repression was not a one-off. In 1990, the foreign ministers of the Organisation of the Islamic Conference launched the Cairo Declaration on Human Rights in Islam. It established Sharia as 'the only source of reference' for the protection of human rights in Islamic countries, thus giving it supremacy over the principles of the United Nations Declaration of Human Rights. Both documents claim to protect freedom, but the former is a sickly and deceitful alternative to the latter. On 10 December 1948 the United Nations responded to the gas chambers and saturation bombings of the Second World War and the crimes of Stalin and

Hitler by stating that 'disregard and contempt for human rights have resulted in barbarous acts which have outraged the conscience of mankind'. Article 1 of the Declaration consists of the straightforward statement that 'All human beings are born free and equal in dignity and rights. They are endowed with reason and conscience and should act towards one another in a spirit of brotherhood.' Article 1 of the Cairo Declaration of 1990 is a more shifty piece of prose: 'All human beings form one family whose members are united by submission to God and descent from Adam,' it asserts, as it at once distances itself from universal brotherhood by limiting membership of the human family to those who believe in God and submit to Him. If the Cairo Declaration had upheld human rights, the appeal to religion would have mattered less. Instead, the drafters offered human rights with one hand and then snatched them away with the other. Article 2 says: 'Life is a God-given gift and … it is prohibited to take away life except for a Sharia prescribed reason.' The Declaration says that safety from bodily harm is a guaranteed right, and 'it is prohibited to breach it without a Sharia prescribed reason'. Murder and torture are prohibited, except when Sharia says they are not. The Declaration asserts the right to free speech, and then removes it from those who 'violate sanctities and the dignity of Prophets, undermine moral and ethical values or disintegrate, corrupt or harm society or weaken its faith'. Its authors produced a human-rights declaration that from the point of view of free speech offers no protection against terrorists killing cartoonists, or courts passing death sentences for blasphemy, or ayatollahs ordering the murder of novelists for apostasy.

The Islamic states' hypocrisy shows that in our time opposing religious censorship means concentrating on authoritarian Islam. You can find many examples of appalling Jewish and Christian attitudes towards women and gays. Orthodox Judaism is a misogynistic creed, and Christian Africa is one of the most dangerous places in the world for homosexuals. In the past, Judaism and Christianity threatened freedom of speech as a matter of course. But their censorious power in the rich world has largely been contained by secularism – which is not to say that extremist Jews and Christians do not want to see it rise again. Israel has a blasphemy law. America does not, but it has a legal campaign group called the Alliance Defense Fund that employs Christian lawyers to force schools and libraries to censor when it can. As I have argued, the West underestimates the threat Hindu nationalism poses to Indian writers, academics and artists. When all the exceptions have been made, however, Islamic states and paramilitaries are in a league of their own when it comes to religious censorship.

Given the ethnic spread of the faith, their targets will usually have brown skins; yet a large section of white Western liberal opinion does not recognise that it is truly racist to refrain from condemning the clerics who seek to oppress them. Half-educated academics and gutless politicians maintain that, on the contrary, it is racist to argue that human rights are universal. They instruct us that formerly colonised peoples should have different human rights, even if these turn out on close examination not to be human rights at all. The chutzpah of the authoritarian regimes and movements which maintain that it is bigoted to criticise religious bigotry is dazzling. More dazzling still is the eagerness of fercockt Western putzes to go along with them.

HOW TO FIGHT BACK:

John Milton and the Absurdity of Identity Politics

The English unleashed the contemporary idea of freedom of speech in the 1640s. Ever since, the English establishment has being trying to rein it in. John Milton's *Areopagitica* – his title paid homage to the free-speaking assembly of ancient Athens – was the first critique of religious censorship to push ideas about freedom of conscience into the modern age. His words ring down the centuries, providing arguments and inspiration to all who must take on secular and religious tyranny.

Milton supposed that the Parliamentarians he supported in the war against Charles I were fighting to end the power of the state to tell men what they must believe and how they must worship. When the king ruled without Parliament from 1629 to 1640, his determination to impose religious orthodoxy, in the form of a Catholicised Anglicanism, on England helped convince Milton – and his fellow rebels – of the necessity of revolution against a monarch who appeared to be aiming for absolute power. Charles's Court of Star Chamber had lopped off the ears and sliced the cheeks of Protestant dissidents, and branded their faces with 'SL' – seditious libeller – for contradicting the king's theology, and questioning the authority of the king's bishops. (Such was Star Chamber's reputation for extracting confessions through torture that even now in England you hear people denounce kangaroo courts and arbitrary verdicts as 'Star Chamber justice'.) A 1637 Star Chamber decree made it a crime to print 'any seditious, scismaticall, or offensive Bookes or Pamphlets'. A publisher must obtain state approval, in the form of a licence, before he could sell a book. Charles, like his predecessors, insisted on pre-publication censorship – the most effective censorship there is – and mutilated those who refused to submit to the screening process.

When the costs of war with the Presbyterian Scots forced Charles I to recall Parliament in 1640 and England began its slide towards revolution, one of the first acts of the new House of Commons was to abolish the state licensing of book publishers, along with the Court of Star Chamber. For the first time in their history, the English enjoyed the freedom to publish and read what they wanted.

Milton revelled in the new liberty. He dived into the controversies about religion and politics, and briefly was more famous for his polemics than his poetry. As with so many revolutionaries since, he soon found it hard to tell the difference between the new boss and the old. The Presbyterian faction in the Westminster Parliament, strengthened by its alliance with the Scots, wanted to replace the uniformity Charles I had imposed through his bishops with a uniformity of its own. It reintroduced licensing in 1643. All printers had to register with the state and submit to pre-publication censorship. Parliament's officer had the power to seize and destroy books and arrest offensive writers and publishers.

Milton watched the vanquishing of his hopes for religious liberty with increasing alarm. His bitter quip, 'New presbyter is but old priest writ large,' anticipated Orwell's concluding scene in *Animal Farm*, in which the creatures looked 'from pig to man, and from man to pig, and from pig to man again; but already it was impossible to say which was which'.

Milton had personal as well as intellectual reasons for opposing the return of censorship. Orthodox Protestants had demanded that a pamphlet on divorce he had written in 1643 should be burned for contradicting Christ's teachings in the gospels and St Paul's in his epistles. For recommending that men and women should be free to separate if their characters were incompatible, the poet became 'Milton the divorcer', a dangerous thinker who threatened the family and promoted lasciviousness.

Milton wrote *Areopagitica* in 1644, when the outcome of the war between Parliament and the king was still uncertain. It takes apart the reasoning of those who would censor authors' works with the fury of a great writer directing all his intelligence against the mean-minded. As a mark of his intent, Milton refused to send his pamphlet to the licensers, but published it freely and at some risk to his safety. He argued as if his life depended on it, because what was at stake for Milton was the principle that was to inspire *Paradise Lost*. God had endowed man 'with the gift of reason to be his own chooser'. Censors denied the God-given right to find religious truth in the world. They wanted to impose a 'yoke of outward conformity' and push England back into a 'gross conforming stupidity'. It told Milton much about the contempt with which religious leaders held their flocks that they appeared to believe that 'the whiffe of every new pamphlet should stagger them out of their catechism'. What were they frightened of? If a writer was leading the faithful astray, why could they not challenge his arguments? Christ preached in public 'wherewith to justify himself [and] writing is more public than preaching; and more easy to refutation'.

The most stirring lines in the *Areopagitica*, which still have the power to bring a tear to English eyes, show Milton arguing for England to become a free-thinking country. 'Lords and Commons of England,' he said to Parliament, 'consider what nation it is whereof ye are, and whereof ye are the governors: a nation not slow and dull, but of a quick, ingenious, and piercing spirit, acute to invent, subtle and sinewy to discourse, not beneath the reach of any point the highest that human capacity can soar to.' The English should not allow clerics and politicians to infantilise them. Only by engaging in the battle of ideas, including the battle with false, foolish and blasphemous ideas, could they discover religious truth. When Milton said that he could not praise a 'fugitive and cloistered virtue, unexercised and unbreathed, that never sallies out and sees her adversary', he meant that religious truth could not be imposed from above by a king, priest, minister, rabbi, guru, ayatollah, 'community leader', judge or bureaucrat. The individual had to find it for himself in the heat of argument. The sentence all readers remember – 'Give me the liberty to know, to utter, and to argue freely according to conscience, above all liberties' – is an assertion that authority is no guarantee of truth, if authority is not tested.

Milton's advantage over modern writers and academics is that he had experienced censorship. He knew the humiliation of having to take work to a censor, and had a justifiable contempt for the type of man who would choose bowdlerising as a career. He wondered who would want to tell others what they could and could not write, and found that his question answered itself. No writer with any talent or respect for liberty would consider accepting the job. Censoring was 'tedious and unpleasing journey-work'. Only the 'ignorant, imperious, and remiss, or basely pecuniary' would wish to take money for blacking out the thoughts of others.

'*Milton! Thou shouldst be living at this hour,*' cried William Wordsworth in his sonnet to liberty of 1802.

> England hath need of thee: she is a fen
> Of stagnant waters: altar, sword, and pen ...

Then as now, the temptation to see Milton as a modern man, whose words are weapons we can use to defend our freedoms, is overwhelming.

But the author of *Paradise Lost*, one of the greatest poems Christianity inspired, was not a forerunner of the Enlightenment, but a writer formed by the wars of religion. He could not bring himself to offer toleration to persecuted Catholics, and wrote a hack propaganda work for Oliver Cromwell before the general sailed off to massacre the Irish. Papists were so wicked to Milton's mind that they must be silenced. His pamphlet on divorce, that infuriated the clerics of seventeenth-century London, did not anticipate Mary Wollstonecraft and the first feminists. As his biographer Anna Beer says, Milton had no interest in the horrendous abuse of women by men that the seventeenth century tolerated. In *Paradise Lost*, he created one of the most loathsome images in English literature when he imagined 'Sin', a female figure who guards Hell's gates. Her own son has raped her, and she gives birth to fiendish dogs,

> hourly born, with sorrow infinite
> To me; for, when they list, into the womb
> That bred them they return, and howl, and gnaw
> My bowels, their repast; then, bursting forth
> Afresh, with conscious terrors vex me round,
> That rest or intermission none I find.

I think it is fair to say that John Milton was not wholly at ease with women's sexuality. I am certain that he could no more contemplate the emancipation of women than could his contemporaries. Milton did not support divorce because he wanted to free battered wives from private hells, but because he thought marriage was a restriction on the dominant male's right to live as he wished. He wanted to 'make it easier for men to divorce their wives' so that men could be 'masters of themselves again'. Later, in the 1650s, he reneged on the principles of *Areopagitica*, and censored on behalf of Parliament. His work survives despite, not because of, the man.

To put that thought more kindly, Milton was a creature of his time, as we all are. His relevance lies not just in his arguments for freedom. The reaction against him illustrated how supporters of the status quo justify suppression. Monarchs believed that their subjects must share their religion. Charles I had no difficulty in justifying the censorship of Milton's contemporaries, because he thought – rightly, as events were to show – that his power depended on his ability to suppress religious dissent. Seventeenth-century Presbyterians thought that they possessed the revealed truth, and had every right to use force to stop the 'lies' of blasphemers leading the faithful to perdition. Once again, their reasons for suppression strike us as dictatorial, but struck them as self-evident.

Today's supporters of religious censorship claim that they are different. They say they are not advocating censorship because they believe we must bow down before Church and state, but because we must respect different cultures and say nothing that might offend them.

If those who said, from the Ayatollah Khomeini's fatwa onwards, that we must censor and self-censor in the name of 'respect' could be transported to the London of the 1640s, how would they make their case?

I said that Milton was a creature of his time, and they might reply that Milton was offending the culture of his time and inviting punishment. But how would they define culture? Milton's views on divorce and freedom of speech undoubtedly conflicted with the views of the majority of his compatriots. But not even Milton's opponents would have said he was an enemy of English culture. He was one of the most English Englishmen who ever lived, whose patriotism is obvious to all who read him. In any case, what could a charge of offending

English culture have meant in the 1640s? Cultures are not unified or sealed in aspic; they change because men and women, propelled by circumstances and their own intelligence, fight to change them. Then as now, the English had many attitudes in common, but there was no such thing as a unified English culture, as the English of the 1640s proved by fighting a civil war to determine how the politics and culture of their country should change.

Our time travellers would fare no better if they substituted religious cultures for national cultures. It would take some nerve to accuse Milton of being a 'Christianophobe', and not only because of *Paradise Lost*. With Catholics fighting Protestants across Europe, a unified Christianity did not exist in the seventeenth century, any more than a unified Christianity, Hinduism, Judaism or Islam exists now. Could you say then that Milton was a heretical Protestant? His opponents claimed that he was, but the charge lacked force when Protestantism was itself divided into warring factions. The Presbyterians wanted to impose their views. A smaller group of independent Protestants, who believed in freedom of conscience, opposed them. Milton supported the independents, but the ranks of his comrades contained further divisions.

The faster you strip cultures down, the more you find contrariness and disputation, rather than a solid core, until eventually you reach the individual, a mammal shaped by evolution, material needs, cognitive biases and historical circumstances no doubt, but still a creature with a better right to state his opinions than kings and clerics have to silence them.

The faster you strip down the respectful arguments for religious censorship, the more you see the nation, tribe or community splintering, until you are left with one group of individuals with coercive power behind them demanding the right to censor another group of individuals because they disagree with them.

The one escape left from *reductio ad absurdum* for those who say we must censor to protect the majority within a religious group or any other community from the psychic harm that comes from hearing a strongly held view challenged, is for the 'liberal' proponents of censorship to admit that they support censorship on utilitarian grounds. They must believe that the harm to the tender feelings and brittle minds of believers caused by the publication of an argument, satire or exposé outweighs the benefit to the individual author of exercising his or her rights and of readers exercising theirs. They must take the possibility of violent reprisals as an honourable reason to ban a book rather than the best of reasons for defending it. To this way of thinking, even if the ayatollahs issuing death threats have not read the novel, and if the exposé of the subjugation of women is correct in all factual respects, liberals must join the religious in demanding suppression. They must hold that if the majority of a nation or community agrees on one issue – that divorce is immoral, in Milton's case; that mockery of the Prophet is blasphemous, in Rushdie's – it has the right to demand silence. (Even if the 'community' or nation is in other respects proving its lack of 'social cohesion' by fighting civil wars, as Protestants were in the 1640s.) They must mount the barricades against new thoughts that might torment and enrage the faithful, and say that no one can be the first to clamber over them, as Milton was the first Englishman to begin the argument for freedom of speech, or Mary Wollstonecraft was the first woman to argue for women's rights, or Salman Rushdie was the first novelist to subject the myths of the creation of Islam to ironic enquiry, or Ayaan Hirsi Ali was the first politician from the poor world to warn Europeans of the dangers of tolerating religious abuse.

In short, they must favour mob rule, the policy of demagogues, which liberals once earned what distinction they possessed by opposing.

PART TWO

Money

If any opinion is compelled to silence, that opinion may, for aught we can certainly know, be true. To deny this is to assume our own infallibility.

JOHN STUART MILL, 1869

FIVE

The Cult of the Supreme Manager

Stardom isn't a profession; it's an accident.

LAUREN BACALL

In 2003, I was trying to find a way of dramatising the widening gap between the broad mass of society and the emerging plutocracy. I hit on the idea of comparing the money the British public raised on Red Nose Day with the wealth of the super-rich. Foreign readers may need me to explain that after much consciousness-raising in the preceding weeks, the BBC devotes a day in March to exhorting the populace to donate to charities dedicated to the relief of poverty at home and abroad. As in every other year, the mandatory 'fun' in 2003 took the form of comedians filling the screens and cajoling viewers to help the cause. Tens of thousands of adults pestered their friends to sponsor their stunts – dressing up as a chicken, sitting in a bath filled with cold baked beans, going to work on a unicycle or some other rib-tickling wheeze. Twelve thousand telecom workers gave up their spare time to man phone lines, while a million or so school-children wore red clown noses and extorted money from their parents. The relentless cheeriness ground down all but the most miserly. The organisers estimated that about five million people gave money, if only so the chickens and children would leave them in peace. The appeal raised £35,174,798 in total.

That sum, I cried in a voice that hit the soprano C of right-eous indignation, *those hard-won proceeds* of Britain's largest exercise in communal altruism, counted for nothing when set against the rewards of the mighty. Red Nose Day's takings were dwarfed by the £157.7 million pocketed in 2002 by one man: Sir Philip Green, a retail tycoon the British Labour Party knighted even though he vested ownership of chain stores in the name of his wife, a resident of Monaco, so the family could avoid the taxes Labour imposed on the common people it once claimed to represent. The income of one tycoon made the charitable efforts of a large slice of the British public seem pathetic.

How risible my comparison seems now. The incomes of plutocrats have flown far beyond the levels of the early years of the century.

Statistics and anecdote dramatise how much wealth and potential power is now in the hands of a global elite. Between 2002 and 2007, 65 per cent of all income growth in the United States went to the top 1 per cent of the population. The financial crisis interrupted their enrichment, but after American and British governments, by which I mean American and British taxpayers, bailed out the financial system, the super-rich bounced back. The top twenty-five hedge-fund managers received on average more than $1 billion each in 2009, and over-took the records set in the bubble year 2007. They were the beneficiaries of a longer trend that began with the break-up of the post-war social democratic consensus in the 1970s. The pre-tax income of the richest 1 per cent of American earners increased from about 8 per cent of the total in 1974 to more than 18 per cent in 2007. The richest 0.01 per cent (the fifteen thousand richest families in the US) saw their share of pre-tax income rise from 1 per cent in 1974 to 6 per cent in 2007.

In 1997, the year Labour came to power promising to govern for 'the many, not the few', the collective wealth of the richest thousand people in Britain stood at £98.99 billion. By the time the tribunes of the masses were preparing to leave office in 2009, it stood at £335.5 billion. In the former Soviet Union, sharp operators moved in to plunder the assets of the defunct communist state by buying them cheaply or for nothing at all. In 1989, there were no Russian billionaires. By 2003, the country had more dollar billionaires in proportion to gross domestic product than any other major economy – thirty-six in all, fourteen more than in Japan, a markedly less corrupt, miserable and unhealthy society. Russia's wealthiest man was then Mikhail Khodorkovsky, with $15.2 billion. Vladimir Putin had Khodorkovsky jailed for crossing the autocracy, but those oligarchs who stayed out of opposition politics and found ways to – how shall we say? – make the burdens of office easier for the ruling clique to endure, saw their wealth grow and their numbers swell. Despite the crash of 2008, Forbes counted sixty-two Russian billionaires in 2009. In China, the number of billionaires ballooned to 128 in 2009, from seventy-nine in 2008. Only the United States, with four hundred, had more. It is the same in India, Brazil and Mexico … everywhere in the world you look, the ranks of the super-rich are growing.

In 2005 Ajay Kapur, global strategist at Citigroup, and his colleagues described societies where a minority controls the majority of the wealth, and where economic growth becomes dependent on the fortunes of that same wealthy minority. The strategists said that it made sense to forget about national divisions and divide the world between the men and women at the top and the rest.

There is no such animal as 'the US consumer' or 'the UK consumer', or indeed the 'Russian consumer'. There are rich consumers, few in number, but disproportionate in the gigantic slice of income and consumption they take. There are the rest, the 'non-rich', the multitudinous many, but only accounting for surprisingly small bites of the national pie.

Beneath the obscenely wealthy are the filthy rich. J.P. Morgan, the austere American financier, is reputed to have said that his executives should not earn more than twenty times the wages of workers at the bottom of his firms. How quaint his puritan limits seem a hundred years on. In 2009, the chief executive of the pharmaceutical company Reckitt Benckiser received £37 million – 1,374 times the pay of the average (not the lowest-paid) worker beneath him. The salaries of just two of the chief executives of the companies in the FTSE-100 passed Morgan's test. In the United States, the ratio of CEO pay to average worker pay rose from 42:1 in 1960 to as high as 531:1 in 2000 during the dotcom bubble, and fell back to 263 times more than the average worker in 2009.

Wealth always has its intellectuals, eager to find high-minded justifications for acquisitiveness. They have filled many books and many pages in the business press with their efforts to explain why fears of a plutocracy are groundless. I will not deny that they have a case. The collapse of Marxism was one of the most beneficial revolutions in history. In China alone, the end of Mao's terror and the replacement of his command economy with a limited market economy lifted hundreds of millions out of poverty. Globalisation, its defenders argued, inevitably created billionaires, because the global market and new technologies have allowed superstar brands, and with them superstar entrepreneurs, to emerge. Companies needed the best talent to handle disruptive technologies, because the difference between an average and a great manager was the difference between success and bankruptcy. If an Apple laptop delights, if Facebook puts its users in touch with the world, why should the citizen care about the incomes of the companies' founders? Lives for an increasing proportion of humanity are more comfortable, longer and healthier than they have ever been. In the rich world, the majority of what we used to call the working class is no longer engaged in hard manual labour, and mechanisation has removed the need for a peasantry to toil in the fields. Class hatred of the rich is therefore muted when set against the passions of the socialist era. Even the modern resentment of the bankers is a conservative emotion, comparable to the resentment of trade unionists who demanded state subsidies in the 1970s. Taxpayers loathe bankers not for being capitalists but for being failed capitalists, who picked the public's pockets. If they had been successes, the public would not despise them. Why worry?

The crash of 2008 showed a reason for not viewing the established order with complacency that is beyond the scope of this book. Financiers make up the bulk of the super-rich – a study of wealth in America in 2004 found that for every one company executive earning over \$100 million there were nine Wall Street tycoons. When their speculative gambles pay off, they privatise the profits; when they fail, they nationalise the losses. America and Britain have a parasitic version of financial capitalism that exploits the taxpayer to cover the failings of wealthy and dangerous citizens. Andrew Haldane of the Bank of England estimated that between 2007 and 2009 the average annual subsidy for the top five UK banks was £50 billion – roughly equal to UK banks' annual profits prior to the crisis. With the understatement the British mandarin deploys when he thinks the world has taken leave of its senses, he added, 'These are not small sums.'

For the purposes of this book, there is a further harm. I can think of few more important subjects for democratic citizens than the influence of the rich over politics, the damage business can do to the atmosphere and the environment, and the risks high finance brings to economic stability. Yet extreme wealth is creating societies in which it is harder to hold economic power to account. Writers in the Anglosphere concentrate on the failings and corruptions of our own elites – who, to give them their due, provide us with an abundance of material – and fail to see the wider corruption. In the rich world, the crash of 2008 hit democratic countries and public limited companies hardest.

However useless they proved to be, they remained institutions whose structures allowed accountability, albeit imperfect. Citizens who questioned their behaviour did not run a personal risk. The new concentrations of wealth are not in democratic Europe or North America. Oligarchies with no traditions of freedom of speech or democratic government now hold much of the world's wealth, and those who try to hold them to account run considerable risks. In China, Russia and the Middle East, sovereign wealth funds or oligarchs who have paid off the local elites own the biggest banks and oil companies. Government-run energy companies in Saudi Arabia, Iran, Venezuela, Russia, China, India and Brazil control 80 per cent of the world's oil and gas supplies. India and Brazil are the only real democracies on that list, and the populations of both have to live with astonishing levels of inequality and corruption. It is not hysterical leftism to see a link between the two. In democratic India and America, and maybe soon in Britain and Europe too, corrupting the political system is the natural strategy for oligarchs to follow. It is a statement of the obvious to say that as inequality increases, 'the rich are likely to both have greater motivation and opportunities to engage in bribery and fraud to preserve and advance their own interests while the poor are more vulnerable to extortion'. But after making it, the American economists Jong-sung You and Sanjeev Khagram went on to demonstrate that while countries with authoritarian regimes are likely to have greater levels of corruption, the effect of greater inequality on levels of corruption will be higher in democracies. In free societies, the wealthy cannot employ direct repression by hiring private armies. They have to act covertly. One only has to look at how Wall Street's contributions to American presidential campaigns have prevented effective bank reform to see You and Khagram's theory operating in practice.

Contrary to all who believed that liberalism's triumph in 1989 was permanent, oligarchic countries did not suffer from the Great Recession of 2008. China boomed, and overtook Japan to become the world's second largest economy. It began to boast that it had nothing to learn from the Western model, and that the West should learn from China, which in the worst of ways we may do. For believers in liberal economics and for social democrats, who wanted to regulate market economies to produce the funds for welfare, 2008 was an ominous year. Vince Cable, now Britain's Business Secretary, saw an alignment of state and private interests across the world that 'promises all the worst features of capitalist economies – unfettered greed, corruption and inequalities of wealth and power – without the benefits of competitive markets'. The crimes and excesses of the age that has passed notwithstanding, we may look back fondly on the liberal supremacy of 1989–2008, and see the merits of its naïve belief that the world was destined to witness a victory of the free market and free societies.

I am not pretending that there is a clear division. The oligarchic world and the Western world are not separate entities, as NATO and the Warsaw Pact were in the Cold War. They are interlaced. At the level of the plutocracy there is no 'us' and 'them', and most certainly no 'other'. Of the fifty-three billionaires resident in London and the south-east of England for all or part of the year in 2010, twenty-four were foreign-born. Banks in New York handle the money made by 'high net-worth individuals', from whichever corner of the globe they come. German social democrat politicians promote the interests of the Russian gas giant Gazprom while they are in office, and take jobs from it when they retire. Libel lawyers in London protect the reputation of Saudi petro-billionaires and post-Soviet oligarchs.

Beyond the intermingling of their finances and interests, the Western rich and the oligarchic rich share an ideological affinity that is worth worrying about too: they are unshakeable in their belief that they are entitled to their wealth, and have every moral right to resist attempts to reduce it. It never occurs to them that they are lucky; that if they are Western speculators, they are lucky to have lived during a time when the negligent governments of America and Britain failed to regulate finance and allowed them to take incredible risks at no personal cost; that if they are post-communist oligarchs, they were lucky to be in place when the Soviet Union collapsed, and to have the connections and muscle to take control of the old empire's raw materials. To outsiders their luck seems self-evident. Yet nowhere in the recorded utterances of the plutocracy does one find a glimmer of an understanding that time and chance played a part in their good fortune.

Chrystia Freeland, a business journalist who works for Reuters, provided an archive of attitudes when she published interviews with the super-rich. As one might expect, the 'new men' of Putin's Russia were the most brazenly self-aggrandising. While he was still the richest man in Russia, Mikhail Khodorkovsky told her, 'If a man is not an oligarch, something is not right with him. Everyone had the same starting conditions, everyone could have done it.' American financiers were more careful in their choice of words, but their self-justifications were no different. They could accept no blame for the financial crisis, even though the public had bailed out the banks and lent hundreds of billions of dollars nearly free of charge to the financial system. The real culprits were the plebs who had bought homes they could not afford, or small-time investors who had over-extended their property portfolios. After hearing much more in this vein, Freeland ended on a portentous note: 'The lesson of history is that, in the long run, super-elites have two ways to survive: by suppressing dissent or by sharing their wealth.'

There are several forms of suppression available. The use of expensive lawyers to punish critics in libel courts, most notably in Britain, but in France, Brazil and Singapore as well, is an under-explored form of censorship that allows the wealthiest people on the planet to intimidate their opponents. The control by the wealthy of parts of the media is a kind of censorship, if not in the age of the Internet a censorship that is as effective as it once was. The most obvious restriction on freedom of speech, and the one which can cause the most damage to the common good, is so ubiquitous and accepted we do not even call it censorship, or think of tearing off the gag that silences us.

The Censor in a Suit

Every time you go into your workplace, you leave a democracy and enter a dictatorship. Nowhere else is freedom of speech for the citizens of free societies so curtailed. They can abuse their political leaders in print or on radio, television and the Web as outrageously as they wish, and the secret service will never come for them. They can say that their country's leader is a lunatic, their police force is composed of sadists and their judiciary is corrupt. Nothing happens, even on those occasions when their allegations are gibberish. The leniency of free societies is only proper. Freedom of speech includes the freedom to spout clap-trap, as regular surfers of the Web know. If employees criticise their employers in public, however, they will face a punishment as hard as a prison sentence, maybe harder: the loss of their career, their pension, and perhaps their means of making a livelihood.

Britain has a formal legal protection for whistleblowers, but as so often with laws about free speech, the theory is one thing and the practice another. Workers are allowed to make 'qualifying disclosures' and warn of criminal offences, failure by their firms to comply with legal obligations, miscarriages of justice, threats to an individual's health and safety, and threats to the environment. The list sounds impressive, but the law says that an employee must first take his or her concerns to their employer. Only then can they raise the alarm and claim compensation if the boss fires them.

'It's like telling a mouse to go see the cat,' one of London's best employment lawyers told me. If the employer thinks for a moment that the employee may go to the press or a Member of Parliament, he will suspend him or her and deny them access to the computer system. In theory again, the law is aware of the problem, and allows an exception to the rule. If employees reasonably believe that they will suffer a 'detriment', or the employer will destroy evidence, they can go public without notifying their bosses. In practice, any worker who took the law at its word because he 'reasonably believed' his employer would destroy evidence or silence him would find himself in a catch-22. When his compensation case came to court, he would have to say, 'I went to the press without consulting my employers because I thought my employers would fire me.' To which the employer would respond, 'No we wouldn't, and because you didn't come to us first, you have no evidence that will stand up in this court that we would have.'

As soon as a whistleblower brings unwelcome news to his or her superiors, the human-resources department of any major public or private bureaucracy knows what it must do next. It will instruct its lawyers to secure a gagging injunction from the courts. All employment contracts include confidentiality clauses stating that the employee cannot release information about the organisation and its clients under any circumstances. Many now contain an additional catch-all clause stating that the employee must take no action that could bring the organisation into disrepute. Britain is a country where a council can sack a dinner lady for bringing her 'school into disrepute' by telling parents that their daughter was being bullied in the playground. Workers here do not speak their minds if they suspect their employers may find out. Even medics, who have a professional duty to protect the interest of patients, are exposed. The Nursing and Midwifery Council struck off a nurse who revealed the neglect of elderly patients by taking a camera crew into her hospital. The

British Medical Journal said that when a doctor raised concerns about unsafe heart surgery in his hospital, 'his career stalled' and he moved to Australia to find work. Medical whistleblowers, whose concerns touch on vital questions of who lives and who dies, 'find themselves the subject of retaliatory complaints and disciplinary action'. In one case of alleged research fraud, whistleblowers were advised to 'keep quiet or their careers would suffer'. When they did not, the regulatory authorities investigated them first, rather than the abuses they had uncovered.

In theory again, the courts will not issue a gagging order if the defendant can prove that he was seeking to release information that the public ought to know about. In practice, judges rarely refuse to gag, because the odds are stacked against the employee. Imagine a woman who has gone to her boss, maybe nervously, maybe filled with trust in her superiors' good faith. Instead of listening to her concerns, the employer tells security to escort her from the building. Her swipe card no longer works. She has no access to the computer system. Her belongings are in bin bags in reception, and she cannot afford expensive legal representation. Her case is lost before it has begun.

Lawyers know of just a handful of instances where employees have received compensation because they followed the correct procedure: first raising their concerns with their managers, and going public only when the company failed to address them. By one of those serendipities that can make the most atheist of authors believe that a supernatural power orders the universe, among the few was Gita Sahgal, who organised the Asian feminists who protested in defence of Salman Rushdie in Parliament Square in 1989. After her employer, the human-rights group Amnesty International, required her to leave for complaining to the press about its alliances with Islamists, her lawyers secured compensation for her.

Few have chosen to follow her path, because the driving desire in the minds of the overwhelming majority of employees is not the intricacies of the legislation or the possibility of compensation, but keeping their jobs and avoiding the need to go to law that speaking their minds would bring. Every whistle-blower I have known has ended up on the dole. Their colleagues know without needing anyone to spell it out for them that self-censorship is necessary if they are to enjoy future wealth and security. Speaking out in the public interest guarantees financial loss and unemployment. The primary concern of employees, public and private, is to avoid a confrontation. They work in hierarchies organised like armies. The managing director or CEO is the general, and a princely salary bolsters his or her status and pride. Beneath him or her are the staff officers, whose first duty is to show mindless obedience; and beneath them are the grunts, who are expected to take orders without question and not to answer back. The radical British economist Chris Dillow describes the strangeness of today's hierarchical organisations well. As the collapse of communism approached in 1989, conservative and soft-left commentators 'told us, rightly, that no one had enough knowledge and rationality to manage an economy. But they also told us that managers had enough knowhow to manage a firm.' While they condemned the hierarchical centrally planned economy, they praised the hierarchical centrally planned corporation or state bureaucracy.

If we take one lesson from the economic crisis, it should be that excessive wealth rendered the managers of banks unfit to run complex organisations. They had the most persuasive of economic incentives not to investigate the dangers of collapse thoroughly, because prudent banking would have cut the size of their extraordinary bonuses.

We should not be surprised that the managerial system that was so successful in the nineteenth and twentieth centuries experienced such a breakdown. Modern economies do not depend on producing goods on assembly lines, but on creative thinking, and you cannot command and control creativity, or order it to appear on time like a replacement machine tool. In the most advanced areas of the economy, most notably computing and biotechnology, small, light firms overtake established corporations because they know that information is scattered across organisations, not confined in the offices of executives. They tap it by encouraging cooperation, not subservience. As the costs of storing and retrieving information have collapsed, sharing expertise ought to be easy. But the cooperative approach based on openness and trust undermines the status of managers, whose wealth depends on the ability to create the impression that they have knowledge that their subordinates cannot be trusted to share.

All of the above are strong arguments against the managerialism that blights free countries. But the strongest stares us in the face. If managers looked to the inspiration for the technologies they deploy, they would find it comes from a scientific method that has no connection to the cramped, fearful ideologies of the managerial economy. The scientific method insists that researchers must go where the evidence leads, whatever the consequences. Status, salary and position should offer no protection from criticism, because no idea or person is sacred. Richard Feynman said that the differences between true sciences and the pseudo-sciences – a category that includes the management-speak of the business schools – was that the former try to be honest, while the latter do not.

Richard Dawkins illustrated the scientific ideal of egalitarian openness with the affecting story of a young zoologist challenging an old professor in Dawkins' zoology department. The professor believed that the Golgi apparatus (a microscopic feature on the interior of cells) was an illusion. 'Every Monday afternoon it was the custom for the whole department to listen to a research talk by a visiting lecturer. One Monday, the visitor was an American cell biologist who presented completely compelling evidence that the Golgi apparatus was real. At the end of the lecture, the old man strode to the front of the hall, shook the American by the hand and said – with passion – "My dear fellow, I wish to thank you. I have been wrong these fifteen years." We clapped our hands red. No fundamentalist would ever say that. In practice, not all scientists would. But all scientists pay lip-service to the ideal, [and] the memory of the incident still brings a lump to my throat.'

The scientific method is opposed to secrecy, and has no respect for status. It says that all relevant information must be open to scrutiny. The ideal it preaches – not always successfully, I grant you – is that men and women must put their pride to one side and admit mistakes. It is the opposite of the hierarchical cultures of business and the state, where status determines access to information, and criticism is met with punishment.

Nearly all of us work in hierarchies. Nearly all of us bite our tongues when we should speak freely. Yet few of the classic or modern texts on freedom of speech discuss freedom of speech at work, even though, as the crash of 2008 showed, self-censorship in the workplace can be as great a threat to national security as foreign enemies are.

On the Psychology of Financial Incompetence

'The bullying is all I remember about him,' said a former executive as he recalled how dictatorial folly had brought down the Royal Bank of Scotland, and helped to almost bring down the British economy with it. 'He was just another angry guy.'

I could add that he was also a deluded, petty and ruthless man who terrified his subordinates, but the dismissive tone of 'just another angry guy' is better than a sackful of adjectives. When tyrants fall, and the chief executive of the Royal Bank of Scotland was a tyrant of the workplace, people shake themselves as if snapping out of a dream, and wonder why they ever feared the reduced and ridiculous figure before them.

'Fred the Shred', or to give him his full title, Sir Frederick Anderson Goodwin, was born in 1958. His father was an electrician in Paisley, a suburb of Glasgow, who sent him to the local grammar school. Young Fred went on to Glasgow University, the first Goodwin from the family to receive higher education. He graduated, and began to work his way up the corporate ladder. He was not a fool. In 1991, as a young accountant, he helped wind up the Bank of Credit and Commerce International, which had financed Saddam Hussein, the Medellín drug cartel and many another gangster and terrorist. He impressed his superiors by recovering money they thought had disappeared into crime families' safe-deposit boxes for good.

Goodwin earned his nickname by shredding jobs after he moved from accounting to become a manager at the Clydesdale Bank. His determination to cut costs may not have impressed his junior colleagues, but it won him many admiring glances from institutional shareholders and directors. RBS made him its deputy CEO in 1998, and he took overall control shortly after it purchased the National Westminster Bank in 2000.

The takeover was a triumph for RBS, and you can understand why success inflated Goodwin's pride. Despite the glories of Scottish culture, there is a strong sense of inferiority among the Scottish elite. However well careerists do in Edinburgh, they cannot escape the feeling that the prizes worth having in politics, business, the arts and the media are won on the big stage down south; that if they do not make it in London, their achievements will feel trifling. The battle for NatWest overturned English superiority. Edinburgh beat London. The men from the New Town outsmarted the men from Chelsea. NatWest managers had precedent and money on their side, and few gave the Scots a chance. RBS was one third of the size of its English rival. The deal RBS was offering was seven times the size of the previous biggest hostile takeover in the UK, and no hostile takeover of a major European bank had been successful before. City analysts assumed it would fail, but their scepticism could not stop RBS, whose dynamism and aggression saw it through.

Goodwin's triumph was twofold. He believed that 'naysayers' ran the NatWest, cautious and to his mind lazy bankers, who turned down good lending opportunities and missed the seductive prospect of speculating in the derivatives market. Once in charge, he tore into the bank's costs, slashing staff and merging departments, and ordered its remaining bankers to go out and find business. Profits ballooned, and Goodwin could say to himself that not only had he fought the City in a takeover battle and won, he had also gone on to show that the supposed superstars of London finance had missed an opportunity for profit that had been staring them in the face.

In 2002, *Forbes* named him its businessman of the year – not bad for a boy from Paisley who had been working for an Edinburgh bank in a backwater of global capitalism. As his fame grew, all the psychological flaws of the egotistic authoritarian personality feasted on his mind. He had no time for collaborative decision-making, or respect for collective wisdom. He was the meritocratic master, the proven winner, who instinctively knew what was right. 'I always work on the five-second rule,' he told *Forbes*. 'How a job offer makes you feel in the first five seconds when you hear the idea, before you spend ages agonising, is what you should do.' He required his subordinates to obey without question. At 9.30 a.m. he held his 'prayer meetings', at which he would caustically review the performance of his lieutenants, and assert his power with exercises in public humiliation. 'Executives would hate going to meetings with him,' a senior manager told me. 'They would sit at the table, eyes down, chin on chest, thinking, "I hope he doesn't pick on me this time."' Goodwin was adept at using his control of targets to frighten those below him. 'People would work for months on plans for the next year, trying to get costs down and profits up. Then he would tear up what they had done in front of their faces and say that the plans were too timid. Costs must always go down; profits must always go up, even if the targets were impossible. So back we would go, and try again.' The culture of the quick buck and the fast deal demoralised the corporation. Anyone who raised doubts about the tiny amounts of capital backing lending, or the failure to invest in computer systems that could cope with the bank's trades, heard managers tell them in threatening voices that they were 'Business Prevention Officers'. Carry on getting in the way, and the hierarchy would mark them as fifth columnists whose naysaying was destroying the bank's viability and the chance for bonuses for everyone working in it.

Let one vignette stand for the whole man. RBS was about to move staff into an office on Bishopsgate in the City. Goodwin inspected it just before it opened, and noticed that the carpet colour was not quite right. The minor breach with corporate branding did not matter: Bishopsgate was a home for administrative workers, not a place for customers. The exception was Goodwin's suite, which filled the eleventh and twelfth floors, and had an express lift so he and his guests could reach his private hospitality lounge without encountering the riff-raff. Linking the eleventh and twelfth floors was a sweeping staircase, which Goodwin descended to greet important guests as if he were a star in his own movie (the 'Fred Astaires', his underlings called it). Goodwin had previously insisted that every RBS branch in the world must have matching fixtures and fittings, that every RBS executive must wear a white shirt with a tie sporting the RBS logo, and that every plate of biscuits for RBS executives must include digestives, but not pink wafers. One of his guests might notice that the carpet was slightly wrong, so Goodwin ordered it to be ripped up and replaced, at a cost of £100 per square yard. His employees were reminded that he was their capricious lord, whose lives were his to control.

As an amateur psychologist could have predicted, Goodwin believed he could find fortune in the future by sticking to the strategies that had turned him from a provincial banker into a global player. The result was a bank collapse that made the failure of Bank of Credit and Commerce International seem like a blip.

Goodwin's insistence on making deals had transformed the culture of his corporation. RBS was once a bank whose conservatism was a source of pride to Scots. Before Goodwin, it specialised in 'value' banking. It would try to spot the best asset-financing opportunities – by setting up the Tesco Bank, say, or developing Canary Wharf – and profit when the deals came good. The trouble with value banking in a bonus-hungry City was that even if a bank invested early in a good venture, it would take years for the profits to come through. Equally depressingly, it would have to set capital aside as a regulatory cost in case the deal turned sour. Dealing in derivatives and using securities as collateral was much more satisfying. Bankers at RBS and everywhere else could claim their deals created no regulatory costs, and their banks did not have to hold capital against default because AAA securities were free of credit risk. Hence they could increase paper profits – and boost the bonus pot. The deals depended on everyone forgetting that the securities in question were ultimately dependent on saps in American trailer parks who had fallen for introductory teaser rates on sub-prime mortgages they would never be able to repay to buy condos whose keys they would have to return. RBS said it had 'stress tested' its securities, but like the geniuses in so many other banks, its geniuses never worked out that the securities might be worth 50p, 5p or 0p in the £1, and that they did not have the regulatory capital set aside to absorb the bad debts. 'Don't get high on your supply,' say drug dealers. As elsewhere, bankers at RBS ignored the wise advice of their colleagues in the opium-derivative markets. They did not offload the risk by selling on securities to the greater fool, but treated them as their own capital and held on to them.

Goodwin continued with his takeover binge. The battle for NatWest had made him famous, and he carried on expanding into Asia and the US at a frenetic rate. At the top of the market, just when liquidity was vanishing, he won a takeover battle against Barclays and paid £48 billion for the Dutch bank ABN AMRO, which he thought would give him a 'global platform'. The crash revealed what RBS should have known: bad debts weighed ABN down. Far from being a global platform, it was a sprawling mess of a bank with fifty-seven IT structures in eighty countries that would take years for a properly run business to integrate or even understand.

Goodwin's career ended in a scene so perfect it might have been taken from fiction. On 7 October 2008, three weeks after the collapse of Lehman Brothers had frozen the global financial markets, he stood in front of a roomful of investors in the ballroom of the Landmark Hotel near London's Marylebone station. In a thirty-minute presentation, he described the company's broad portfolio of businesses, strong balance sheet and opportunities for growth in Asia. Despite the turmoil in the markets, RBS remained as solid and reliable as it had always been. As he talked, word reached the hotel that the market had fallen again. A fund manager put up his hand. 'In the time that you have been speaking, your share price has fallen 35 per cent. What is going on?'

Goodwin went pale, and mumbled an answer. He cancelled his remaining meetings and rushed back to RBS's offices. A few days later the state nationalised the bank, and pumped in £37 billion from the British taxpayer. Goodwin retired with a pension pot of £16.5 million, also from the British taxpayer.

Keep Mum, it's not so Dumb

Insiders knew. The greatest crash in the financial markets since 1929 did not come without warning. In the wake of the catastrophic loss of the jobs and homes of millions of workers, whose employers had never paid them a bonus in their lives, the previously somnolent media belatedly paid tribute to those who had tried to raise the alarm. In 2005, Raghuram Rajan of the International Monetary Fund addressed a meeting of central bankers. In the audience were Alan Greenspan of the US Federal Reserve, and Larry Summers, who along with Greenspan had done Wall Street's dirty work for it by preventing a few honourable officials in the Clinton administration from regulating the new derivatives market. Rajan's speech was prescient. He warned that derivatives and credit default swaps were providing lucrative financial incentives to bankers to take risks in the mistaken belief that the deals would never unwind.

Also mentioned in dispatches was Nouriel Roubini of New York University, who warned in 2006 that changes in economic fundamentals – real income, migration, interest rates and demographics – could not account for the surge in US property prices. America was in the grip of a speculative bubble pumped up by hot money and extraordinarily risky lending that would end with a 'nasty fall', he said. Again, his prescience was faultless.

But singling out the few – shamefully few – financiers, business journalists and economists who emerged from the early 2000s with their reputations intact is to miss a wider point. Thousands of people in banking knew the deals they were closing were dangerous, and suspected that money and egomania had turned their masters' heads. They may not have been able to predict a global liquidity crisis, but they knew that in their firms a lust for self-enrichment had replaced the principles of prudent banking. Goldman Sachs persuaded its gullible customers to invest in sub-prime securities that the company's investment bankers privately dismissed as 'crap' and 'shitty deals'. They knew. In Iceland, where a tiny population sat on a heap of volcanic rock, three banks ran up loan books of $110 billion – 850 per cent of Iceland's GDP. The official inquiry into the

Icelandic financial collapse, which left every Icelandic man, woman and child nominally liable for $330,000, said that insiders were withdrawing their funds days before the bubble banks went bust. I think it is fair to say that they knew too. At RBS, everyone except Fred Goodwin knew that they were paying over the odds for ABN AMRO. As early as 2005, City analysts diagnosed that their chief was suffering from 'megalomania'. His staff did not need outsiders to tell them that. They knew from experience that he was also a sociopath, who was capable of leading their bank to ruin.

Goodwin's sociopathic tendencies seem exceptional, but if Barclays rather than NatWest had won the battle for ABN AMRO, Barclays would have collapsed, and journalists would now be writing about the character flaws of its executives. One cannot reduce the failures of management to the failures of a few bad apples that somehow ended up at the top of the sack. Instead, you have to look at the structural weaknesses of managerialism that encourage delusion. A fundamental flaw of modern capitalism is that businesses promote bombastic people. As Cameron Anderson and Sébastien Brion of the University of California, Berkeley, showed experimentally, 'In conditions where there is any ambiguity in competence and performance (which is common in organisations), overconfident individuals will be perceived as more competent by others, and attain higher levels of status, compared to individuals with more accurate self-perceptions of competence.' They think even better of themselves when they are promoted – 'If my employers say I'm a top dog, I must be' – and their elevation gives them the hiring power to surround themselves with sycophants, or 'my team', as they describe them.

The question therefore ought not to be who knew, but why so few spoke out. The answer reveals why financial institutions pose greater potential dangers to society than any other private business. The strongest link between the inequalities of wealth at the top and the destruction of the living standards of those underneath lies in the incentives the hierarchical system gives its participants to self-censor.

All bubble markets carry perverse incentives. During the dotcom bubble of the 1990s, analysts and fund managers on Wall Street and in the City who warned that worthless companies had issued bubble stocks were not thanked by their employers for their honesty, or congratulated when the crash in the dotcom market vindicated their scepticism. By staying out of the bubble, they missed the chance to profit as the bull market roared ahead. The investors who made money suspended their disbelief, feigned ecstasy about the market's prospects, and sold on before the crash. It was not enough to be right. One had to be right at the right time. The bonus culture of the first decade of the twenty-first century institutionalised financial false consciousness. Everyone in the City I interviewed emphasised that you should not just look at the money made by the alleged stars of the dealing rooms and the CEOs. All employees in a position of power or knowledge within the organisation were caught up by the determination to run risks and to jack up their bonuses. 'An ordinary risk manager or accountant at a bank can make £100,000 basic and £100,000 bonus,' said one. 'There is no way he can get that kind of money anywhere else. He is going to be as keen as the CEO on authorising risky trades.'

Suppose, though, that junior employees or indeed senior bankers realise that their managers are making catastrophic mistakes. They still have no reason to speak out. In the good years they will have pocketed salaries and bonuses. The state will not confiscate their homes and empty their accounts if their bank collapses, but will allow them to hold on to their assets and their winnings. If they have not caused trouble, they should be able to find another job in another bank. If the state coerces the taxpayer into bailing out the failed institution, they can carry on in their old job as if nothing had happened – but now drawing their salaries and bonuses at public expense. Within three years of the taxpayer bailing out RBS, two hundred of its staff were receiving million-pound bonuses. The recession, unemployment, higher taxes, reduced public services fell hard on everyone except the originators of the banking crash.

Silence in a banker's private interest brings no penalty. Speaking out in the public interest, however, would mean that he would never work in banking again. Even if he could use whistleblowing legislation – and as we have seen, that is no easy matter – the compensation he would receive would usually be one year's wages – pin money in comparison to the wealth the bank or the taxpayer would give him if he bit his tongue. Perhaps the banker could go to the regulatory authorities privately. Even assuming that they were not slumbering, his employers would find ways to force him out if they found out what he had done. And executives in rival hierarchies would ensure that he would *never work in banking again*. Therein lies the ultimate sanction. Whistleblowing in banking, and many another trade, does not mean you lose just your job, but *all other possible jobs* in your field. No rival manager would want you on his 'team', because you might expose him as you exposed his predecessor. In banking, business and the public sector, challenge one hierarchy and you challenge them all. Speaking out within the firm is equally dangerous. 'A risk manager once told me that to raise an issue that undermined the bank's multi-billion-dollar profits would have been to "sign his own death warrant",' said a Wall Street derivatives trader after the crash. 'This inability to challenge trading desks generating billions in phantom profits was endemic.'

If a whistleblower had gone to journalists privately, there is no guarantee that they would have listened to him, because the same forces that were boosting high finance were destroying good financial reporting. In the 1840s, *The Times* thundered against the railway mania which ruined so many Victorian investors. In the 1990s, the *Economist* heaped scorn on the boosters of dotcom stocks, and won many admirers for its forthright journalism. In the 2000s, not one of the media organisations that covered business – not the *Wall Street Journal*, Bloomberg News, the *New York Times*, the *Economist*, *Forbes*, the *Financial Times* or, I should add, the mainstream British press and the BBC – saw a crash coming, or campaigned for a change in regulatory policy. Individual journalists served their readers well, but to pretend that the writing of Allan Sloan of *Fortune* or Gillian Tett of the *Financial Times* represented the media is like pretending that the work of Rajan and Roubini represented the collective wisdom of economists and financial analysts.

A post-mortem examination by the *Columbia Review of Journalism* noticed an alarming deterioration in the ability of reporters to investigate the wealthy and hold them to account. In the early 2000s, the American press printed much it could be proud of. Journalists found stories worthy of Upton Sinclair or Émile Zola as they exposed how Lehman, Citigroup and other Wall Street banks were throwing money at poor Americans to generate securities from sub-prime debt. The most haunting was the tale of an illiterate quarry worker who was already $1,250 in debt because he had borrowed money to buy food. Citigroup's sub-prime subsidiary bought the debt and convinced him to refinance ten times in four years until he owed $45,000, more than half of it in fees. Repayment took more than 70 per cent of his income.

Such was the rock on which Alan Greenspan and George W. Bush built their economic miracle. Here were the 'economic fundamentals' that underlay Gordon Brown's boast that there would be 'no return to boom and bust'.

As the market went manic, it left the press behind. Wholesale fraud and forgery were rampant. Wall Street's demand for mortgages became so frenzied that managers expected female wholesale buyers to trade sex with retail brokers for securities. Bank underwriters, who approved mortgage loans, demanded bribes from wholesalers before they would pretend that the deals were prudent. Yet the American press ignored the wave of white-collar crime, and offered its readers pap pieces in which reporters praised the dynamism of CEOs and gasped like porn actresses at the size of their bonuses. Every bubble market captures journalists as it captures regulators and investors. The longer a speculative mania goes on, the more normal it seems. Journalists who ignore the euphoria that grips their colleagues and warn that the collapse will be all the worse when it comes risk hearing their editors tell them that they are bores who are not worth publishing. 'Where's the crash you promised me? Where's my story? All I can see are happy people out there working hard and making money.'

The *Columbia Review of Journalism* found other reasons for the media's inability to anticipate the crash of 2008. The decision of the Bush administration to call off the regulators, copied by Gordon Brown in Britain, was the most prominent among them. Regulators had provided reporters with leads. Once they dried up, the stories dried up as well. To anyone who worked on a newspaper in the early 2000s, however, one reason the *Review* gave for the failure of journalism rang as true as a funeral bell: 'The financial press is … a battered and buffeted institution that in the last decade saw its fortunes and status plummet as the institutions it covered ruled the earth and bent the government.'

The instant electronic communications that allowed speculators to deal globally were destroying newspapers' business models by taking readers and advertisers away to the free sites of the Internet. A whistleblower who risked the sack and went to an old media institution with a possible story could not be sure that it would have the resources to follow the lead. The British media faced the further fear of libel actions. Fred Goodwin threatened to sue the *Sunday Times* for saying that he had wanted his own private road built from Edinburgh airport to RBS's Scottish headquarters, and had tried to jump the waiting list for membership of an elite golf club. The legal action never came to anything – the golf club backed the newspaper, and confirmed that Goodwin's 'people' had passed on words to the effect of 'Do you know who I am?' But as the decade progressed, newspapers that could see money haemorrhaging from their balance sheets could not afford to accept the costs of taking on the plutocracy's lawyers.

Nor were the British and US governments interested in learning the truth from insiders. The nominally left-wing Tony Blair, Gordon Brown and Bill Clinton, as well as the confidently right-wing George W. Bush, were certain that the best regulation of finance was less regulation.

One of the few honourable men monitoring the crazed market that followed was Paul Moore, the risk manager of the Halifax, a bank whose history tracked the decline of British self-reliance. It had once been a mutual building society formed by respectable working- and lower-middle-class families in Victorian Yorkshire to pool their savings and allow them to buy homes. Margaret Thatcher – who, contrary to myth, was the enemy of the best Victorian values – allowed the building societies' managers to enrich themselves by converting the mutuals into banks. The Halifax merged with the Bank of Scotland (which was not the same institution as the Royal Bank of Scotland, but was just as spivvishly managed), and the new company spewed out mortgages.

As its risk manager, Moore was under a legal duty to ensure it behaved prudently. He found a hyperactive sales culture. Managers rewarded sales teams if they sold mortgages, and mocked and demeaned them if they failed to persuade punters to take the bait. Moore thought that there 'must have been a very high risk if you lend money to people who have no jobs, no provable income and no assets. If you lend that money to buy an asset, which is worth the same or even less than the amount of the loan, and secure that loan on the value of that asset purchased, and then assume that asset will always rise in value, you must be pretty close to delusional. You simply don't need to be an economic rocket scientist or mathematical financial-risk-management specialist to know this.' When he tried to make the case for responsible lending, one manager told him he could never hit his sales targets if he behaved ethically. Another leaned across a desk and said, 'I warn you, don't make a fucking enemy out of me.'

Moore was a Catholic gentleman, who was educated at Ampleforth and trained as a barrister. He saw no conflict between business and morality. He went to the board and warned that its demand for sales growth at any price was putting the company at risk. The board received him warmly. A month later, the chief executive, James Crosby, called him to his office.

'I'm doing a reorganisation, and your job is being made redundant,' Moore remembered him saying.

'My job cannot be made redundant,' replied Moore. 'It is a regulatory requirement to have my job.'

'You lost the confidence of key executives and non-executives.'

'Who?' asked Moore.

'I don't have to explain myself to you,' said Crosby.

The subsequent fates of the two men encapsulate the perverse incentives the Western financial system offers. Moore left Crosby's office bewildered. 'It was a terrible shock. I felt absolutely devastated. I went outside on the street and just cried. A million thoughts going through my head. How am I going to tell my wife? How am I going to tell my kids? What are people going to think of me?'

HBOS paid him off. Not one headhunter phoned him to sound him out for a job, even though he was one of the most experienced risk managers in Britain. He had broken the *omertà* of a hierarchical culture, and rendered himself unemployable.

In his spare time, and he had plenty of spare time, Moore conducted a survey of 563 risk managers about the causes of the financial crisis. 'Most risk professionals saw the technical factors which might cause a crisis well in advance,' it concluded. 'These included easy availability of global capital, excessive leverage and accounting standards which permitted over-valuation of assets. The risks were reported, but senior executives chose to prioritise sales. That they did so is put down to individual or collective greed, fuelled by remuneration practices that encouraged excessive risk-taking. That they were allowed to do so is explained by inadequate oversight by non-executives and regulators, and organisational cultures which inhibited effective challenge to risk-taking.'

James Crosby went to Buckingham Palace to meet no less a personage than Her Majesty the Queen. Gordon Brown had instructed her to knight Crosby for his services to the financial industry, as he had asked her to knight Fred Goodwin and Alan Greenspan before him. Crosby's decision to sack Moore and carry on lending as before had been endorsed by his senior colleagues, auditors and the financial regulators. Trapped in the group-think of a bubble market, no one in a position of responsibility could guess how a strategy of borrowing on the wholesale markets to fund an exponential growth in a bank's loan book could possibly go wrong. Fresh honours followed. Brown appointed Sir James, the manager who had sacked his risk manager for warning of risks, to the financial regulatory authority that was supposed to guard against risk. There Sir James remained until HBOS went bust in the crash, and Moore forced him to resign by going to Parliament to reveal all.

*   *   *

With millions in excessive debt and millions jobless, one might have expected a surge of protest against managerialism and hierarchy. By the autumn of 2011, the banks had received almost £1 trillion in subsidies in the form of cheap Bank of England loans and deposit and debt guarantees, given by the state on condition that they improved lending to British businesses. The banks took the money, but did not lend, because there were no easy profits or easy bonuses in business loans. The most unjustly rewarded executives in the world had wrecked Western economies and shown no willingness to change their ways. Yet it never occurred to the supposedly liberal-left governments of Barack Obama and Gordon Brown to provide incentives to allow employees to speak up and speak truthfully, or to impose penalties on those who stayed silent. Governments did not promise to provide full compensation to bankers who revealed their corporations' risky policies. They did not say that all bureaucracies, public as well as private, should allow elected workers' representatives on their boards, who might provide a fair hearing to those who suspected their managers were going haywire. They did not say that bailed-out banks should remain under accountable state control because the government could not do a worse job than the private sector. Nor was there irresistible public pressure on them to reform.

It was as if the citizens of the West did not want to know.

RULES FOR CENSORS (5):

People Don't Want to Know

In most cultures for most of history, speech has not been free. Criticise the state, and the state punished you. Break with the religion or defy the taboos of the tribe, and the tribe punished you. The powerful cannot afford to lose face, because as soon as they do, the authority of the state and the tribe begins to drain away.

The democrats of ancient Athens John Milton admired were among the few to escape from hierarchical control. Citizens exercised *parrhesia*, which translates as 'all speech', or sometimes 'true speech'. They had the right to say anything to anyone: to speak truth to power. Aristophanes mocked the city's generals and demagogic politicians. They responded with lawsuits alleging that he was slandering the *polis*. Their threats did not silence Aristophanes, but provoked him into producing more satires. It sounds stirring, until you remember that women and slaves did not enjoy the freedom allowed to male citizens, and liberty in Athens as elsewhere broke down in moments of crisis. Frightened after their defeat in the Peloponnesian War, Athenian citizens sentenced Socrates to death for corrupting the minds of the young and – inevitably, given the persistent link between religion and censorship – for refusing to honour the city's gods. For Xenophon and Plato, Socrates' nobility lay in his refusal to flee from prison when the opportunity presented itself. He preferred accepting his punishment to showing a fear of death, and died a free man.

By drinking the hemlock, Socrates was truer to the Athenian ideal than were his persecutors. 'To be happy means to be free and to be free means to be brave,' Pericles said in his oration for the Athenian war dead, as he emphasised that ancient ideas of free speech have a notion of courage behind them. Citizens of modern democracies, who are at liberty to talk about politics in whatever manner they please, may find the insistence on bravery puzzling, but if they think about how careful they are to 'respect' employers and religious militants they will understand the link.

Michel Foucault believed that speech was truly free only when the weak took a risk and used it against the strong: 'In *parrhesia*, the speaker uses his freedom and chooses frankness instead of persuasion, truth instead of falsehood or silence, the risk of death instead of life and security, criticism instead of flattery, and moral duty instead of self-interest and moral apathy.'

On Foucault's reading, the worker who criticises his boss uses *parrhesia*. The boss who shouts down his worker does not. The woman who challenges religious notions of her subordination is a *parrhesiastes*. The priest and her relatives who threaten her with ostracism or worse are not. In the ancient Chinese story, the mandarin who knows he must tell the emperor that his policies are foolish orders carpenters to build him a coffin and takes it with him to court. Pericles would have approved.

So far, so commonplace. For who does not admire the brave dissident, and who does not flatter themselves into believing that they would be equally brave in the same circumstances? It is one thing to admire, however, another to emulate. Anyone who has worked in a hierarchical organisation must have noticed that bravery is rarely on display when a superior enters the room.

The best proponents of freedom of speech do not just demand courage. They say we must not only tell truth to power, we must also tell truth to ourselves. John Stuart Mill was more concerned about the self-censorship imposed by the received opinion of Victorian Britain than by the small British state of the nineteenth century. When he says in *On Liberty* that 'If all mankind minus one, were of one opinion, and only one person were of the contrary opinion, mankind would be no more justified in silencing that one person, than he, if he had the power, would be justified in silencing mankind,' he sounds like an intellectual reducing his argument to absurdity. But Mill, who had to fight the religious conformity of his day as well as the self-satisfied culture of Britain at its imperial zenith, meant what he said. The majority had no right to use social pressure to silence arguments, because without argument it could never be sure if its opinions were true: 'Complete liberty of contradicting and disproving our opinion, is the very condition which justifies us in assuming its truth for purposes of action; and on no other terms can a being with human faculties have any rational assurance of being right.' If an argument is false, then exposure produces greater trust in truth. If it is true, or partially true, then there is no case for repressing it. Censorship was the enemy of human progress.

Mill's Victorian belief in progress strikes those who know the history of the twentieth century as naïve – although I note that parts of humanity have progressed in their treatment of women, homosexuals and the races Mill, to his shame, dismissed as 'inferior'. Victorian liberals had the advantage over us in one respect, however. Because they believed that humanity was moving forward, they had few relativist qualms about saying that liberal society was better than what had gone before, and could be better still. For Mill, the decisive argument against censorship was that 'ages are no more infallible than individuals'. Just as we now regard ideas that were the common sense of the past as false and ridiculous, so many opinions we now take for granted will strike the future as cruel and absurd. I believe that posterity will look back on our treatment of animals, and the insouciance with which we have presided over the sixth mass extinction of species in the earth's history, and shudder. Even if I am wrong, I can be certain that, for ill as well as good, the ideas that some small and derided groups of men and women are discussing now will one day be in the mainstream.

Nor was Mill's demand for openness utopian. Modern societies fit Mill's ideal in several respects. The scientific method demands that its practitioners must be prepared to accept that they are wrong. A Nobel laureate cannot rely on his status to protect him from ridicule. If the evidence does not support his theories, he must either lose face and admit his error, or exclude himself from the debate. At their best, science and the humanities follow Mill's dictum that 'The beliefs which we have most warrant for, have no safeguard to rest on, but a standing invitation to the whole world to prove them unfounded.' Democratic societies also expect their politicians to have thick skins. Elected leaders can rarely call out the police to punish those who subject them to criticism, even if their opponents are malicious, ill-informed and self-serving – as they often are. Nor, in most circumstances, can the citizens of democracies call on the law to punish those who produce arguments they regard as immoral, threatening, false or scandalous. *Parrhesia* brings many benefits. Democracy, science, intellectual excellence and the ability of citizens to live as autonomous adults depend on the right to criticise and accept criticism.

Let no one pretend that it is easy. Along with the bravery the Athenians recommended, which most people do not possess, Mill insists on an open mind, which most people do not possess either. We must not only be ready to make the powerful lose face, we must be prepared to lose face ourselves. We must not only run the risk that our country/tribe/confessional group will punish us for questioning its taboos. We must be ready to confront our own taboos, our idea of ourselves, and give people who may well be unhinged and spiteful a hearing. Few are prepared to do it. In Richard Landes' nice phrase, most societies regard self-criticism at an 'individual and collective level, as akin to chewing on broken glass', and 'have elaborate ways of enforcing silence'.

Beyond Mill lies Marx. Anyone who has engaged in political controversy will have experienced a moment of elation when they produce an argument that is so clear, so logical, so morally certain, so factually accurate and so elegantly presented that they cannot imagine how anyone could read it and fail to be convinced. It is best to get these delusions out of your system early in a writing career, because readers rarely accept arguments that challenge their interests. Even if they acknowledge at some level that there may be truth in what you say, they will blank out the unwelcome knowledge. By blanking out, I do not mean that they fall for one of the standard cognitive biases that push people into delusion and denial, simply that they decide that it is not advantageous to act on what you have said, even though they suspect that you may be right. Political information is not neutral. It always helps someone and hinders someone else. If you show that a conservative politician is corrupt or incompetent, conservatives worry that your work will help bring to power left-wing politicians who will raise their taxes. If you show that a left-wing politician is a charlatan, left-wing readers worry about the boost you are giving to conservatives who will reduce the welfare state on which they depend. During the Arab Spring, outsiders thought that once the subject peoples had risen up, the dictators would vanish like mist before the wind. As it turned out, the dictators had supporters, not just among servants of the regime who feared the loss of their jobs, but among those who preferred tyranny to chaos. China, the world's most populous country, and Russia, the world's largest country, are autocracies whose rulers convince a proportion of the population that it is better to blank out knowledge of their arbitrary abuses of power and concentrate instead on the deluge that could follow if their arbitrary power collapsed.

As we have seen, Westerners who know perfectly well that the God of the Torah, the Bible and the Koran is a fable nevertheless refuse to condemn the bigotry of the faithful for fear of provoking a violent reaction or laying themselves open to accusations of religious prejudice. Instead of denouncing oppression, they concentrate their energy on denouncing 'new atheists' and 'enlightenment fundamentalists' for voicing what they know to be true. Meanwhile, in any business or state bureaucracy, it is far from certain that a whistleblower will win the admiration of his or her colleagues. Even if their supposedly secret information is not false or is beside the point, even if they are not leaking commercially confidential information that an organisation has every right to keep private, their actions will damage their firm or institution. The scandal will delight its private or bureaucratic rivals, and in extreme cases threaten the whistleblowers' colleagues' income or jobs.

Employers, like kings, dictators, politicians, bishops, rabbis, imams, priests, civil servants, judges and censors, can urge their fellow citizens to shut up and forget for fear of the consequences.

Given the political, cultural, psychological and economic forces ranged against freedom of speech and freedom of the press, the wonder of free societies is not that they are rare, but that they exist at all. In these circumstances, one might have hoped a country that boasted of being a bastion of liberty would have protected its precious inheritance.

SIX

A Town Called Sue

TOM CRUISE: *You made me look stupid! I'm gonna sue you too!*
STAN: *Well fine! Go ahead and sue me!*
TOM CRUISE: *I will! I'll sue you … in England!*

SOUTH PARK,
'TRAPPED IN THE CLOSET' (2005)

The threat of sexual violence hangs over *Chinatown*, the last film Roman Polanski was to make in Hollywood. Jack Nicholson plays Jake Gittes, a private detective who thinks he has seen it all. In the best *noir* tradition, a beautiful and mysterious woman comes to his office. Evelyn Mulwray says she wants to hire him to follow her husband, an official with the local water company. She suspects he is having an affair, and Gittes thinks he has a simple case. He realises that he does not when the real Evelyn Mulwray appears and tells him that the first woman was an impostor engaged by her husband's enemies – rich men, led by the monstrous Noah Cross, who are creating a desert in the mountain valleys east of LA by diverting the water supply. They intend to buy out the parched farmers cheaply, then turn on the sluices and enjoy possession of valuable real estate. They sent a fake Evelyn to the detective's office because they need to find and silence Mulwray, who knows too much about their plot.

Greed is not the only sin on display. Noah Cross is Evelyn Mulwray's father. She tells Gittes he raped her when she was fifteen, and left her pregnant. He now wants to find his daughter/granddaughter, and rape her too. In the dismal finale, despairing even by the standards of the post-Vietnam 'new Hollywood' of 1974, Gittes fails to expose the criminals or to save Evelyn's daughter. Cross seizes the child with the assistance of police officers, who shoot Evelyn Mulwray dead, and tell the powerless Gittes to forget what he has seen.

The film ends with a string of quotes that anticipate Polanski's later career, and the careers of men richer and nastier than Polanski. 'I don't blame myself,' Cross tells Gittes, as he admits to incest. 'You see, Mr Gittes, most people never have to face the fact that at the right time and the right place, they're capable of *anything*.'

Gittes plays with that thought. 'He's rich!' he says, as he begins to make sense of the corruption he is witnessing. 'Do you understand? He thinks he can get away with *anything*.'

Sex and money were pertinent themes in Polanski's life. Dandyish and talented, he enjoyed the Swinging Sixties. His marriage in 1968 to the beautiful actress Sharon Tate – star of his daft but appealing caper movie *The Fearless Vampire Killers* – was one of the great parties of the fashionable London of the day. If one had to fix a moment when the swinging stopped and the sixties turned rancid, the night of 9 August 1969, when Charles Manson's 'family' went berserk in Polanski's Hollywood home, could be it. Manson was a petty criminal who moved into Haight-Ashbury, San Francisco's bohemian quarter. He found that babbling about the joys of drugs and free love attracted a large following of counter-cultural drifters and that perennial type of middle-class girl whose revolt against parental authority consists of a search for more domineering masters than her parents had ever been. As well as worshipping big daddy and agreeing to subject themselves to his sexual demands, 'family' members ticked the boxes on the checklist of late-sixties radical chic. 'The Karma is turning, it's blackie's turn to be on top,' Manson told his followers. 'The cities are going to be mass hysteria, and the piggies won't know what to do, and the system will fall and the black man will take over.' Black power would be short-lived, however, because Manson, the true ruler of the world, would emerge from the chaos and 'scratch blackie's fuzzy head and kick him in the butt, and tell him to go pick cotton. It would be our world then. There would be no one else, except us and our black servants.'

As a prelude to Armageddon, Manson's followers went to Polanski's isolated mansion, cut the telephone lines and slaughtered everyone inside for no reason at all. The heavily pregnant Sharon Tate's last words were, 'Please, I don't want to die. I want to live. I want to have my baby. I want to have my baby.' Her killers showed her no mercy, and inscribed 'PIG' in her blood on the front door.

For conservatives, the Manson murders were an overdue comeuppance for everything they loathed about their permissive age. The police regarded Polanski as a suspect. The press treated him abysmally. Reporters asked him whether his wife was having an affair, and one suggested that he might have arranged her murder to ingratiate himself with occult friends. One newspaper ran the headline 'Live Freaky, Die Freaky'. The dead were not the victims of a psychopathic cult leader and his followers, but of their and Polanski's promiscuity.

After all that distress and humiliation, Polanski appeared to have known too much suffering. As a child he had survived the Kraków ghetto. He had grown up in the drab dictatorship of communist Poland. He had come to America and seen a jeering press blame him for the murder of his wife and unborn child. He was entitled to a little slack.

The forty-three-year-old Polanski began to pull on the rope when he had an affair with the fifteen-year-old Nastassja Kinski in 1976, and hosted 'children's parties' for his new love. Explaining himself later to Martin Amis, he said, 'Fucking, you see, and the young girls. Judges want to fuck young girls. Juries want to fuck young girls – *everyone* wants to fuck young girls!' He tugged harder when he decided to photograph 'sexy, pert' thirteen- and fourteen-year-olds for a 'gentlemen's magazine'. And he gave himself enough rope to hang himself when he raped a child in 1977.

Polanski met Samantha Gailey's mother in an LA nightclub, and offered to get her daughter into *Vogue*. When he had secured possession of the thirteen-year-old, he took her to Jack Nicholson's mansion. He gave her a glass of champagne and told her to take her top off. In her subsequent testimony to a California grand jury, she did not come across as a 'sexy, pert' Lolita but a frightened child, miles out of her depth.

Polanski gave her Quaaludes, a relaxant, and told her to go into a nearby bedroom and lie down, she told a grand jury.

'I was going, "No, I think I better go home," because I was afraid. So I just went and I sat down on the couch.'

'What were you afraid of?' asked the prosecutor.

'Him. He sat down beside me and asked me if I was OK.'

'What did you say, if anything?'

'No.'

'What did he say?'

'He goes, "Well, you'll be better." And I go, "No, I won't. I have to go home."'

'What happened then?'

'He reached over and he kissed me. And I was telling him, "No," you know, "Keep away."'

Polanski began to engage in oral sex. 'I was ready to cry. I was kind of – I was going, "No. Come on. Stop it." But I was afraid … he goes, "Are you on the pill?" And I went, "No." And he goes, "When did you last have your period?" And I said, "I don't know. A week or two. I'm not sure."'

'And what did he say?'

'He goes, "Come on. You have to remember." And I told him I didn't.'

Polanski had heard all he needed to know. The girl could not remember when she last had a period, and had told him she was not on the pill. So, she alleged, he decided to sodomise her.

If you happen to know any thirteen-year-old girls, the final scene is the most convincing. Instead of running away and raising the alarm, Samantha obediently returned to Polanski's car after the assault, and sat and cried while she waited for him to drive her home.

Polanski arrived and said, 'Don't tell your mother about this and don't tell your boyfriend either,' she told the jury. 'He said something like, "This is our secret."

'And I went, "Yeah."'

When Samantha's mother saw the pictures Polanski had taken of her semi-naked daughter, she called the police. A grand jury charged him with giving a drug to a minor, committing a lewd act upon a person less than fourteen, rape of a minor, rape by use of a drug, oral copulation and sodomy. As so often in rape cases, the victim did not want to testify. To spare her a cross-examination, and the coverage of the salivating media, the prosecution allowed Polanski to make a plea bargain. He would admit statutory rape of a minor in return for the state dropping the other five charges. The judge sent Polanski to prison for a psychiatric evaluation before sentencing. Once free, Polanski and his lawyers convinced themselves that the judge was preparing to give him a long sentence to appease a press that was running pictures of him chatting in bars with attractive women.

Christopher Sandford, Polanski's biographer, could find no evidence that the judge intended to renege on a deal to keep Polanski's sentence short, but Polanski did not trust the court, and other biographers have said that he had reason to be suspicious. Instead of returning to face his punishment, he fled to

France, where he had citizenship. The French would not extradite him. If, however, he entered a country with a stiffer extradition treaty with the United States, the local police could arrest and deport him to face the wrath of American judges, who are not at their most lenient when they sentence fugitives from justice.

Hollywood forgave him, and the French loved him. In his first days in France, 'when he strolled outside on the Champs-Élysées, a large crowd invariably gathered to applaud him. The men signified their approval by clapping. The women by jostling among themselves to touch his hem, and frequently much more.' *Le Matin* said Polanski was a victim of America's 'excessively prudish petite bourgeoisie'. Others compared him to Alexander Solzhenitsyn and Nelson Mandela.

Treated as a star and a victim, Polanski never showed regret for his crime. In 1988, Samantha Gailey sued him. He paid out a large sum, and in return she said that she wanted the case dropped so she could get on with her life. But the law does not allow the private resolution of criminal prosecutions. Polanski remained an exile from Hollywood. Whenever his name came up, he could count on someone saying that his considerable artistic merits notwithstanding, he remained a self-confessed rapist on the run from justice. There seemed to be no way he could escape his past and silence those who wanted to drag up the old unpleasantness in Jack Nicholson's mansion, until 2002, when *Vanity Fair* ran a long feature on Elaine's, the favourite restaurant of New York's artistic old guard. Among the stories regulars told about its good old days was an anecdote from Lewis Lapham, a left-wing essayist. What with its artistic clientèle, Lapham had learned to leave prudishness behind when he went through Elaine's doors. Still, a scene from 1969 stuck in his mind. Polanski had entered Elaine's shortly after the murder of Sharon Tate, Lapham remembered. He made a beeline for a 'Swedish beauty' sitting next to Lapham.

'Polanski pulled up a chair and inserted himself between us, immediately focusing his attention on the beauty, inundating her with his Polish charm. Fascinated by his performance, I watched as he slid his hand inside her thigh and began a long, honeyed spiel which ended with the promise, "And I will make another Sharon Tate out of you."'

Polanski had had enough of the attacks. He announced from France that he would sue *Vanity Fair* for libel.

But how could he? An important objection that I think only writers will grasp was that the magazine had not set out to attack Polanski. *Vanity Fair* buried the anecdote near the end of a long, star-struck piece about a fashionable New York restaurant. Polanski now wanted the legal system to focus on a few sentences – to magnify them as if they were bugs under a microscope – and ignore the likelihood that most readers would have skim-read them, if they had read them at all. Every fact in a work of non-fiction ought to be correct, but proving the veracity of an anecdote from a generation back is formidably hard. All a writer can say is that he or she checked with people who were there at the time. *Vanity Fair* should have checked with Polanski. But he would have denied it, as everyone denies unflattering stories.

A stronger objection was that the story may have been wrong, and Lapham's memory of the incident may have been false. He was certain that it was not, and another witness remembered the model asking Polanski to leave. *Vanity Fair* later admitted getting the date of the incident wrong – the alleged encounter with the blonde took place after Sharon Tate's funeral, not before it, as the magazine had said. More than thirty years after the event, the Swedish beauty said that all she could remember was that 'Roman Polanski came over to the table when I was eating and it was as if he tried to say something but he didn't … He just stared at me for ages.'

In normal circumstances, falsely saying that a man proposi-tioned a woman just after the murder of his wife would be a cruel slur, even if a journalist made it in a throwaway paragraph. The claimant would have the right to demand compensation for damage to his reputation and a correction. But Polanski later admitted that he had started having casual sex with women within a month of his wife's murder, so he could not claim that it was libellous to suggest that he would have made a pass at the time. In the end, it was not the alleged pass but the alleged chat-up line that was the sole defamatory issue at stake.

It may be a terrible thing to say of a bereaved husband that he used his dead wife's name to entice another woman into bed, but why was it such a terrible thing to say about Polanski? Libel law protects men and women of good reputation. How could a man who had pleaded guilty to the statutory rape of a minor, after a thirteen-year-old girl had accused him of getting her alone, giving her drinks and drugs and, after checking the date of her period, anally raping her, maintain that he had a reputation on matters sexual that was worthy of the law's protection? Any sensible judge would say that he could not possibly give Polanski damages. Even if the offending lines were false, Polanski had no good reputation to lose.

There was a further logistical difficulty. *Vanity Fair* published in New York. But if Polanski had gone to America to sue, the police would have arrested him as a fugitive from justice and sent him to face a vengeful judge in California.

His plan would have been hopeless, were there not one jurisdiction he could turn to. A legal system that strained its sinews and besmirched its country's good name to help rich men who thought they could get away with *anything*.

Writing in Stilted English

Nothing destroys clichés about the gentle temperament of the British so thoroughly as reading what the British read. In political journalism, the British pick their side and line up their targets. Right-wingers inflame prejudices against gypsies, immigrants and all public-sector workers except the police and the armed forces. Left-wingers inflame prejudices against social conservatives, Jews, and all members of the upper and upper-middle classes except the public-sector great and good. Both suspect the white poor. The right regard them as scroungers, who steal the money of the middle classes, either by breaking into their homes or by taking their taxes in benefit cheques. The left regard them as sexist and racist homophobes.

The chavs or the toffs, the niggers or the yids – the thuggish British journalist never forgets that hate sells better than sex.

Away from politics, the popular press keeps millions happy with gossip, soft-core pornography, health scares and sport. Its journalists work with the sneer of the sadist on their lips. The *Daily Mail*, whose online paper is one of the most visited news sites in the world, specialises in running cruel examinations of women in the public eye. They can never do anything right. They are too fat or too thin, too old or too young, too pretty or too plain, too fertile or too barren, too promiscuous or too frigid. To find stories on celebrities or anyone else in the news, national papers hacked the phones of their targets. The main player in the criminal enterprise was Rupert Murdoch's News International, whose quasi-monopoly control of the privately owned media ensured that elected British leaders debased themselves and their country by bending the knee to the tycoon. Initially, the police backed away from mounting a full investigation into the hacking scandal that might have brought the perpetrators to justice. Some officers were frightened that Murdoch's papers would turn on them, and the suborned politicians would not defend the rule of law. Others were taking bribes from reporters in return for information. Yet more were dining with newspaper executives and looking forward to casual work with the Murdoch press after their retirement. The media company and the police got away with blaming the scandal on a 'rogue' royal correspondent of the *News of the World* and a private detective he hired. The police were forced to reopen the case by questions from Labour MPs, and dogged reporting of a story everyone else thought was dead by the *Guardian* – which I should say in the interests of transparency is the sister paper of my employers at the *Observer*. The truth began to trickle out that men in Murdoch's pay (and the employees of other newspapers) had hacked thousands of phones. No trick was too contemptible for them to pull. They hacked into the phones of the families of dead soldiers, the parents of murdered schoolgirls and of the victims of the 7/7 Islamist atrocity. When the *Guardian* revealed that they had hacked the phone of Milly Dowler, a teenage girl who had been abducted and murdered, and deleted voicemail messages that might have helped the police to identify her killer, the public outcry was such that Murdoch was forced to close the *News of the World* to save his wider business interests – which include the publishers of this book, I should add in the interests of further transparency.

The sincerity of the public's outrage was open to doubt. The *News of the World* had been Britain's most popular newspaper because it gave its audience what it wanted. When typical British readers tossed it aside to snuggle up with a good book, they did not bury their noses in works of moral improvement. Often they reached for one of the many detective novels that competed to give the nastiest accounts imaginable of the abuse of women. After reading fantasies of men imprisoning, binding, gagging, stringing up, raping, slicing, burning, blinding, beating, eating, starving, suffocating, stabbing, boiling and burying women alive, one critic on a London literary magazine gave up. She refused to review any more crime novels, because 'each psychopath is more sadistic than the last and his victims' sufferings are described in detail that becomes ever more explicit'. Popular non-fiction was little different. In the first decade of the 2000s, 'misery memoirs' were the surprise bestsellers of the book trade.

The purportedly true stories of abuse 'survivors' spared the reader nothing in their accounts of bestial violence against children.

Compare today's prurience with the gentility of the past. In the shock they caused and the voyeuristic interest they provoked, the British equivalent of the Manson murders of 1969 was the 'Moors murders' of 1963–65. On 7 May 1966, the morning after the jury convicted Myra Hindley and Ian Brady of murdering five children and burying their bodies in the hills outside Manchester, readers had to stare hard at the front page of *The Times* to find the news. The lead story was a less than gripping piece about the then Home Secretary visiting the US to discover what lessons, if any, he could learn about law enforcement. The second lead was an account of HM Government's difficulties with the white settler revolt in Rhodesia. Squeezed between them, and filling about half of one column of a seven-column broadsheet, was a curt summation of the case. *The Times* gave no details of the sadism involved. So disdainful was its editor of sensational journalism that he gave equal prominence to a speculative story on whether a ban by the Irish government on the movement of horses might hit the English racing season.

The popular press was more forthcoming, as you might expect. In the frantic search for a scoop, editors hired helicopters to follow the police investigation, and bought the stories of witnesses. But the reporting was restrained, almost refined, and written in better prose than journalists on most serious papers can manage today. The police had found a suitcase Hindley and Brady had hidden in a left-luggage locker, with pornographic pictures of Lesley Ann Downey, one of their victims, and a tape of the child pleading for her life. No one who heard it in court ever forgot the experience. The *News of the World* of the 1960s did not dwell on the horror. It confined itself to saying, 'There were sixteen minutes of tape with a child – her mother has said it was Lesley Ann's voice – screaming and whimpering and crying, "Please God, help me ... please, please." And there was a woman's voice – Myra Hindley's say police who have heard her at interviews – saying "Shut up or I will forget myself and hit you one." Throughout these sixteen minutes there was not another sound in the court, not a cough, not a whisper.'

Beyond that description, there was no attempt to intrude on the girl's last moments. It never occurred to the paper to run the contents of the tape in full.

Reading the old clippings, I felt an ache for the lost age of popular literacy, when the *News of the World* could fit almost as many words onto a page as *The Times*, and expect its working-class audience to appreciate fine writing. Everyone at some point must feel an equal regret for the loss of British reticence and the coarsening of public life. The foul-mouthed celebrities on the television, the Peeping Toms of the tabloid press, the mob-raising screamers of talk radio and Twitter, and the emotionally incontinent blabbermouths who reveal their 'secrets' when they have nothing worth hiding, are representatives of the collapse of the values of the old Britain, which *The Times* and the *News of the World* once held to in their different ways.

The compensation for the decline in civility is the decline of deference. Investigative journalism did not exist in the 1960s. The colleagues of my first editor regarded him as a brave pioneer because he had revealed how detectives had beaten a confession out of a suspect. Local newspapers had never given the police such a hard time before. The rich of the day could operate without scrutiny. Business journalism consisted of bland reports on companies' results, rather than investigations into whether those results were genuine, while celebrities could present entirely false pictures of themselves to their fans.

Britons' automatic deference to monarchy, Parliament, Church and peerage has gone, and good riddance to it. We are meant to have become a more raucous and bawdy society, but a more honest society as well. So we are, in all respects except the one that matters most.

At their best, journalists expose the crimes of the powerful, and there were plenty of powerful people worthy of examination in the Britain of the early 2000s. London was awash with money, as it competed with Manhattan to be the hub of global finance. The despots challenged in the Arab Spring channelled their stolen wealth through the City. Oligarchs from around the world flocked to Britain because it offered them the rule of law, protection from assassins, luxury stores, art galleries, Georgian town houses, country estates and public schools that could train their sons in the gentlemanly style. If journalists tried to do what they should do and investigate them, Britain also gave them a further privilege: the power to enforce a censorship that the naïve supposed had vanished with the repressions of the old establishment. Among the many attractions London offered the oligarchs was a legal profession that served them as attentively as the shop girls in the Harrods food hall.

With an aristocratic prejudice against freedom of speech, the judges imposed costs and sanctions on investigative journalism which would have been hard to endure in the best of times, but were unbearable after the Internet had undermined the media's business models. Instead of aiming its guns at the worst of British writing, the law of libel aimed at the bravest.

The system the judges upheld had its roots in feudalism. Edward I, one of England's most barbarous kings, introduced the crime of *scandalum magnatum* while he colonised Wales, hammered the Scots and expelled the Jews. 'Henceforth none be so hardy to tell or publish any false News or Tales, whereby discord, or occasion of discord or slander may grow between the King and his People, or the Great Men of the Realm,' Edward declared in the Statute of Westminster of 1275. Although the statute fell into disuse, and was overtaken by the libel law Star

Chamber used in the 1630s, an element of the feudal concern to defend the mighty remains in English libel law and the laws of many former British colonies.

Contrary to natural justice and the Common Law, the burden of proof is on the defendant. Once a claimant has shown that the words in question are likely to provoke hatred, ridicule or contempt, the alleged libeller has to prove that what he or she has written is true, or a fair comment based on true information. English libel law, and the laws of Scotland, Ireland and all the former British colonies that take it as its guide, works on the assumption that a gentleman's word is his bond, and that anyone who impugns his honour must prove his case.

A second archaic quirk makes wealthy litigants appreciate English law all the more. The judiciary treat a gentleman's reputation as if it were his personal property, the defilement of which is a wrong in itself. Libel and trespass on land are the only torts the law says are actionable *per se*. A claimant does not have to prove that a writer has caused him to suffer financial loss or personal injury, any more than a landlord has to prove that a trespasser has damaged his land. The claimant can still sue even if no one has formed a bad opinion of him or read and remembered the offending words.

'The only purpose for which power can be rightfully exercised over any member of a civilized community, against his will, is to prevent harm to others,' said John Stuart Mill. The English law does not believe him. A litigant does not need to prove that he has been harmed. It is sufficient that the author has published the offending words in question, and that they *may* make a person or persons unknown think less of him.

The judges invoke a quasi-feudal precedent to justify compensating claimants. The Duke of Brunswick's Rule of 1849 states that every republication of an offending statement is actionable. It says much about how the dead hand of the past weighs on my country that I need to explain that twenty-first-century law takes its lead from the case of a corpulent and despised German princeling, whom the good people of Brunswick had had the sense to throw out in the revolutions of 1830. In 1849, while living in exile in Paris, the duke sent his servant to the offices of the *Weekly Dispatch* in London to get an old copy of the paper, which contained an unflattering article about him. The six-year time limit on bringing a libel action had long passed. The offending issue was gathering dust in an archive. But the helpful judiciary obliged His Grace by deciding that because his manservant had been able to purchase a back copy of a seventeen-year-old newspaper, the publishers had repeated the original libel, even though the duke himself had instigated the repetition of that libel by sending his manservant to buy the back copy in the first place. No precedent could be more dangerous in the age of the Internet, when readers can access blog posts, Twitter feeds, Facebook pages and online newspaper articles afresh with every new day. Because of a case from the 1840s, any one of the millions of people who have published on the Web could be sued for something they wrote years before.

To many onlookers, the law's biases seem reasonable. If writers produce a character assassination, what is wrong with the law requiring them to justify their words? As for putting a price on the value of a good reputation, who can measure the damage caused by smears and innuendos?

English lawyers are fond of quoting Iago's lines to Othello:

> Who steals my purse steals trash; 'tis something, nothing;
> 'Twas mine, 'tis his, and has been slave to thousands;
> But he that filches from me my good name
> Robs me of that which not enriches him,
> And makes me poor indeed.

They forget that Iago is a liar, and never admit that the English law does not confine itself to defending the reputation of men and women of good standing, but will come to the aid of any criminal who is not behind bars.

In the 1980s, the most fevered writ-generator was Robert Maxwell, a conceited and crooked media mogul. After fleeing to Britain from his native Czechoslovakia, he established business relationships with the communist dictators of the old Eastern Europe. In Britain, the Department of Trade and Industry said after one of his many dubious takeovers, 'he is not in our opinion a person who can be relied on to exercise proper stewardship of a publicly quoted company'. This condemnation, and his warm relations with tyrannies, did not prevent Maxwell from bombarding newspapers and book publishers with writs threatening to take anyone who impugned his reputation to the courts. 'His purpose was to make it impossible for any editor of a newspaper or book to consider writing about him critically without considering the enormous cost both financially and in time wasted that would entail,' said his unauthorised biographer Tom Bower. 'He would come down on them with the force of a bulldozer.' The scores of writs had their effect. When presented with leads, editors wondered whether they wanted the trouble and expense following them would entail. Those who took him on learned that sources from inside the Maxwell organisation, who had spoken to their reporters off the record, were too frightened of losing their jobs to appear in court, and that Maxwell was not above bribing witnesses outside his employ to change their testimony.

The law takes no account of the difficulty of getting on-the-record affidavits from sources in dictatorial corporations, and offers another benefit to litigants that Maxwell took full advantage of. The ordinary citizen might suppose that if a newspaper or a book publisher ran an unflattering portrait of a wealthy man, the wealthy man would sue the newspaper or book publisher. It was likely to have the resources to pay for damage to his fine reputation, after all. But nothing in English law stops the wealthy man suing the author personally, so his or her home and savings would be on the line unless they retract and grovel, or the shops that distribute books and newspapers. Maxwell calculated that the owners of bookshops or newsagents would not stock a controversial work if standing up for the freedom of publication might cost them money, and they had other titles to place on their shelves. His tactic of suing bookshops was not as violent a means of reprisal as the Islamists' tactic of hitting them with bombs, but the intent was the same.

Which is not to say that Maxwell eased up on his direct attacks on publishers. He targeted *Private Eye*, the most courageous British news magazine, and won colossal damages from the courts. The *Eye* had the distinction of receiving his last writ, in 1991, after it reported suspicions that Maxwell was 'gambling' with his employees' pensions. Sources in his corporation told its journalists that Maxwell was reducing their benefits and sacking those who spoke out. His lawyers maintained that it was outrageous to suggest that Maxwell was a criminal, who was raiding the employee pension fund to shore up the share price of his ailing businesses. Maxwell had 'suffered a very serious injury to his feelings and reputation', they said, as they demanded an apology with the usual damages.

A few weeks later, Maxwell either fell or jumped from his yacht. His businesses went bankrupt, and his employees found that he was indeed a criminal who had stolen £727 million from their pension fund.

The writs Maxwell issued against Tom Bower, *Private Eye*, the *Sunday Times*, the *Independent* and others were directed at stories covering his business activities. All those stories turned out to be true, or on the right lines. If they had a fault, it was that they were nowhere near as scathing as they should have been. The judges and law officers showed no regrets. They never paused to ask why the English law had punished investigations into a man who had never had a good name, and always deserved a worse one.

In 1998, the English judiciary hit its nadir when it allowed David Irving, one of Europe's leading neo-Nazis, to sue the American historian Deborah Lipstadt for saying that he manipulated evidence to 'prove' that the Holocaust had never happened. Penguin defended its author, as it had defended Salman Rushdie, and had to spend several million pounds, money it never recovered. After a full trial, the learned judge – one Mr Justice Gray – announced that in his considered opinion, and after weighing all the relevant evidence, he had concluded that the Nazis were indeed a bad lot who had gassed millions of Jews at Auschwitz and elsewhere, and that Irving and others who said they had not were likely to be liars.

Where would the English be without their lawyers to guide them?

The law's readiness to censor writers and order their publishers to pulp books and pay costs and fines weakens conservative claims that England and the rest of Europe are afflicted with an over-mighty 'liberal judiciary'. The judges are not true liberals, but the successors to the aristocratic Whigs of pre-democratic Britain. William Hazlitt defined a Whig as neither liberal nor conservative, but 'a coward to both sides of the question, who dare not be a knave nor an honest man, but is a sort of whiffling, shuffling, cunning, silly, contemptible, unmeaning negation of the two'. Modern judges prove Hazlitt's point for him. After presiding over the false convictions of the Birmingham Six, the Guildford Four and other innocent men and women in the terrorist trials of the 1970s, they were obliged to learn to uphold the rights of defendants to fair trials in the criminal courts. However, when citizens are not prisoners of the state, but are exercising their right to be full participants in the deliberations of society, they shut them up. British and European 'liberalism' is uncomfortable with freedom of speech. Liberal judges do not have the instinctive democratic belief that citizens in open societies should be free to argue without restraint. Instead, they think they have a duty to intervene in open arguments, invariably on the wrong side. They subvert the right to freedom of speech protected by the First Amendment of the American Constitution, sanctified by custom in Britain and enshrined in the European Convention on Human Rights, as they try to create a journalism that never runs the risk of provoking the anger of the wealthy.

A prissy nervousness afflicts writers when they tackle people who can afford to sue: plutocrats, banks and corporations; or those who have a reputation for using no-win, no-fee lawyers to sue even if they are not personally wealthy themselves: front organisations for Jamaat-e-Islami and the Muslim Brotherhood, alternative-health cranks and other vexatious litigants. The people writers ought to have gone into journalism to scrutinise are the very people the law requires them to treat with exaggerated caution. Instead of writing about them with the required vigour, we switch to stilted English and pepper our pieces with 'we are not suggesting thats' – when we want to suggest just that – 'allegedlys', 'could be saids', 'mays', 'seems', 'some may thinks' and 'appears', inside ugly sentences that are hacked back by lawyers; when, that is, they are published at all. In newspaper offices, lawyers are powerful figures who start to worry as soon as reporters mention a litigious man. Often they spike pieces, saying that no amount of cuts and caveats can avert the risk that a plutocrat will begin lengthy and expensive litigation before a hostile judiciary.

The service the courts provided the Dutch base metals and oil trading company Trafigura best illustrates the readiness of the legal profession to censor on behalf of the wealthy. Trafigura had hired a ship to deliver toxic waste to Amsterdam in July 2007. Waste-disposal companies tested the load, noted its foul stench, and refused to touch it unless Trafigura gave them a generous fee. Trafigura would not pay, and went round the world to find a country willing to take it. The Estonians and Nigerians turned the ship away. Finally, it docked in the poverty-stricken Ivory Coast, where dealers took the waste at a bargain rate, and did not treat it but dumped it. Many people became sick, and several died.

Trafigura said the waste could not have caused the suffering. When the BBC contradicted its account, Trafigura sued for libel. The BBC backed down, and withdrew any allegation that the toxic waste dumped in Africa had caused deaths. That would have been the end of the controversy in Britain, had not Trafigura had a draft internal report – the 'Minton Report' – whose authors said that on the 'limited information' they had received the harmful chemicals 'likely to be present' in the waste included sodium hydroxide, cobalt phthalocyanine sulphonate, coker naphtha, thiols, sodium alkanethiolate, sodium hydrosulphide, sodium sulphide, dialkyl disulphides and hydrogen sulphide.

The report was not the final word on the dumping. Other experts had reached different conclusions, as experts are wont to do. When the case for compensating the alleged victims came to court, lawyers for the sick Ivorians could not prove that the waste had harmed them, but Trafigura could not prove that it had not, and paid compensation without admitting liability. The contest between the two sides ended in a tie. Nevertheless, news organisations facing the prospect of legal action, and the families of the dead living with ongoing grief, would have liked to have read what the report's author had to say.

To stop the press publishing the findings, Trafigura hit the media with that ingenious legal invention, the super-injunction: a court order so secret it is a contempt of court to reveal that it even exists. Paul Farrelly, a Labour MP, ignored the judge's ruling and tabled a question in Parliament, which stated that Trafigura's solicitors had secured an injunction from the High

Court to prevent publication of the report on the 'alleged dumping of toxic waste in the Ivory Coast'. Trafigura's solicitors told journalists that reporting what the MP had told Parliament, and mentioning the 'existence of the injunction would, absent a variation to the order', place them in contempt of court.

It is worth pausing to contemplate how many principles the English legal system was prepared to overturn. The civil wars of the seventeenth century, in which John Milton and his contemporaries lined up, concluded with the settlement enshrined in the 1689 Bill of Rights. It asserted that Members of Parliament had absolute freedom of speech, and no monarch or court could interfere with their proceedings. The radicals of the eighteenth century fought and won a hard battle to allow the press to report Parliament, so that MPs' constituents could know what their supposedly accountable representatives were saying on their behalf.

To no avail. Only a public outcry forced a U-turn, and pushed Trafigura's lawyers into saying that the injunction had not 'been obtained for the purpose of restricting publication of a report of proceedings in Parliament'. Just all other reporting of the Minton Report's contents.

The belief that 'If you are telling the truth, you have nothing to fear' does not apply in England. The courts say that you are guilty until you prove yourself innocent. They take no account of the difficulty in persuading confidential sources to place their careers at risk by taking the witness stand. They tell the claimant that he does not need to prove that he has suffered damage or harm. They do not consider whether the claimant has a good reputation the law is obliged to defend. They are presided over by judges drawn from the pseudo-liberal upper-middle class who have no instinctive respect for freedom of speech or gut understanding of its importance. The judges are willing to look on as claimants go for individual writers, who cannot afford to fight back, or retailers, who have no commercial interest in fighting back. The single concession they make to the democratic age is the so-called 'Reynolds Defence', that allows editors to defend statements they cannot prove are true, if they can nevertheless prove that they acted responsibly and in the public interest when they printed them. I will not detain you with the details of how an editor can show he has acted in the public interest. The Reynolds Defence carries so many conditions it is as if the lawyers designed it to fail. The senior judiciary complain that the judges in the libel courts disregard what protections it offers, and few writers or defence lawyers think it worth their while invoking its terms.

Scandalous though these barriers to justice are, they would not be so intimidating if the English legal system had not given a further and overwhelming advantage to the moneyed classes. Civilised countries must find ways for citizens to take action against poisonous writers who cause real harm. They must insist on prominent corrections, and if editors refuse to carry them, the law must punish them. But if justice is to be done, it must be speedy, or the powerful will be able to close down stories for years. And it must be cheap, otherwise most members of the public will not be able to protect their reputations, and most publishers will be unable to afford the risk of defending their work, and will fall into silence.

In Britain, money buys silence. The cost of libel actions in England and Wales is 140 times higher than the European average. If you lose a case, lawyers operating on a no-win, no-fee contract force you to pay damages, your costs, your assailant's costs, a 'success fee' for the victorious lawyers – which doubles their real costs – and a payment to cover insurance bills. In 2010, Lord Justice Jackson added these together, and estimated that the costs of civil litigation in England could amount to ten times the damages the court awarded.

A chill descended on English writing as publishers realised that punitive costs could cripple them. Libel law became the strangest branch of English jurisprudence. It was a law that lawyers hardly ever tested in court. Libel judges had to find other work for much of the year. The overwhelming majority of libel actions never ended in a hearing to determine if a work was true or its opinions fair, but remained hidden from public view. Publishers quietly settled, coughed up and withdrew offending material rather than run the risk of facing extortionate bills. Beyond these cases of censorship lay the unknowable number of writers and publishers who self-censored. As when you contemplate religious censorship, you must always think of the books that were never written, and the investigations that were never begun, because of the overweening power of money.

Lawyers began to wonder about the point of defamation law. The London media solicitor David Allen Green said, 'Almost all the statements which can actually damage a person's reputation – employers' references, credit searches, complaints to police and regulatory authorities – are covered by "qualified privilege".' The person making the statement was free to defame – regardless of the damage caused – 'as long as he or she is not being malicious'. Police officers could have records that falsely suggested that you were a child abuser, but you could not sue them. A credit agency could erroneously claim that you were a serial debt defaulter, and you could not sue them either, when a bank denied you an essential loan, unless the agency had acted with a negligent disregard for the truth. If a newspaper, academic journal, book publisher, blogger or TV station made any kind of accusation, you could sue them, and in all likelihood the case would never come to court because of the horrific costs of fighting and losing an action.

The denial of access to the courts was a final malign consequence of the English system. Censorship only made sense if judges weighed the evidence in a fair hearing. But cases rarely went to court. Therein lay the beauty of the English system for the rich litigant. He need not risk a trial in open court, where the defence could air the argument against him on the record. He could secure an apology through fear of financial loss, while sparing himself unwelcome publicity. Instead of being a means of establishing facts, the law became a device deployed by lawyers, who tellingly began to call themselves 'reputation managers'. A dubious businessman trying to make his way in English society would make a show of contributing to charities. He might buy some fine art, or donate to the opera, so he could pose as something more refined than a money-grubbing philistine. He would contribute to a political party in the hope, nearly always realised, of buying himself a peerage. And if anyone tried to query his philanthropic reputation, he could divert a small part of his fortune to a 'reputation manager' who would manage the offender with writs, and deter others from following the story.

In 2006, reporters on the Danish newspaper *Ekstra Bladet* decided to investigate the stunning rise of the Icelandic bank Kaupthing, which was buying assets across Denmark. How, they asked, had a bank from a volcanic island, without the resources to support a huge and voracious financial sector, become so powerful? The newsdesk decided they should concentrate on the links between the bank, Russian oligarchs and tax havens. Kaupthing was furious. It was accustomed to receiving praise from the financial press for the entrepreneurial dynamism of its managers. It threatened to sue *Ekstra Bladet* in Copenhagen, and at the same time filed a complaint with the Danish Press Council, which handled cases of breaches of press ethics.

The paper defended its journalism, and the Danish Press Council rejected the bank's complaint. Kaupthing withdrew its Danish lawsuit, and the argument seemed to be over until *Ekstra Bladet*'s bewildered editors heard that the bank was now suing them in London. The costs were beyond anything they had experienced before. In Denmark, lawyers consider a libel action that costs £25,000 expensive. In London, lawyers for Kaupthing and *Ekstra Bladet* ran up costs of close to £1 million *before* the case came to court. *Ekstra Bladet* could not run the risk of doubling, maybe trebling, the bill if it lost. It agreed to pay substantial damages to Kaupthing, cover its legal expenses and carry a formal apology on its website.

A few months later, Kaupthing, along with the other entre-preneurial, go-ahead Icelandic banks, collapsed. Iceland's GDP fell by 65 per cent, one third of the population said they were considering emigration, and the British and Dutch governments demanded compensation equivalent to the output of the entire Icelandic economy for the lost deposits of their citizens in Kaupthing and other banks.

Two points are worth flagging. The Danish journalists did not predict the collapse, but instead showed they had the nose for trouble that all good reporters possess. They could sense that there was something wrong with banks from a country with a population no larger than that of Coventry or Peoria, Illinois, buying overpriced foreign assets and acquiring the debts to match without having a government capable of acting as a lender of last resort in an emergency. Kaupthing went for the paper in England – not just because it wanted to kill the original story, but because it also wanted to deter others from spreading the idea that Iceland was not a safe place for investors. The English legal profession obliged. It placed the bank off-limits. Newspapers lawyers thought once, twice … a hundred times before authorising critical stories. As events were to turn out, the English legal profession had also stopped the British investors who were to lose deposits worth $30 billion in Iceland from learning that there was a whiff of danger around the country's banks, although no lawyer showed any remorse about that.

A second point staggered foreigners. Even though Kaupthing was an Icelandic bank challenging a Danish newspaper, it was able to go to London and find a legal system willing and able to provide the coercive pressure it required. Most people would assume that what Danes wrote about Icelanders was none of England's business. England's lawyers thought differently. Their meddling did not shock all foreigners, however. Roman Polanski for one realised that England could give him what no other country would offer: a chance to sponge his reputation clean.

Globalising Censorship (2)

On 21 July 2008, the United Nations declared that the practical application of English libel law 'has served to discourage critical media reporting on matters of serious public interest, adversely affecting the ability of scholars and journalists to publish their work'. England's authoritarianism was not a local concern, but created the global danger that one country's 'unduly restrictive libel law will affect freedom of expression worldwide on matters of valid public interest'.

Libel law was making England look like a pariah state. The Internet ensured that all online publications everywhere on the planet could be read in England. Thanks to the Duke of Brunswick and his obedient servant, a single view of a Web page in the UK constituted a publication of the libel in England, however old the offending words were. True, wealthy men could sue only if they had a reputation in England that critical reporting could damage. But as many oligarchs had a London home, or had business dealings in the City, they could overcome that obstacle with ease. The courts retained the option of saying that a rich man should sue in the country where the offending article was published, but the judges wanted to catch passing trade, and on most occasions welcomed plutocrats to the courts of old London town.

The first casualty was the British reading public, which could not buy works published in free America in their bookshops. The threat of legal action either banned or ensured the mutilation of Kitty Kelley's muckraking biography of the royal family, virtually every American discussion of the funding of Islamist terrorism, and *The Best Democracy Money Can Buy*, Greg Palast's account of the dark side of corporate life.

An admirably vulgar episode of *South Park* highlighted the absurdity of banning material in one part of the democratic world that was freely available elsewhere. In an episode entitled 'Trapped in the Closet', Scientologists decide that the child character Stan is the reincarnation of L. Ron Hubbard, the herder of credulous souls who founded a sci-fi cult in the 1950s. Celebrity Scientologists John Travolta and Tom Cruise join the crowd on Stan's lawn in South Park that has gathered to worship him. When Stan tells Cruise he does not think he's as good an actor as Leonardo DiCaprio, but is 'OK, I guess', the despairing Cruise buries his face in his hands. 'I'm nothing,' he says. 'I'm a failure in the eyes of the Prophet!' He runs into Stan's wardrobe and locks himself in, allowing assorted characters to shout, 'Tom Cruise, come out of the closet!' with all the false but funny innuendo that implied, for the rest of the show.

In the final scene, Stan refuses to become the Scientologists' new guru, and renounces L. Ron Hubbard and all his works. Hearing this blasphemy, Cruise comes out of the closet and cries, 'I'll sue you … *in England!*' To make the joke complete, the Scientology episode was the one episode of *South Park* British television managers dared not show, in case they were sued … *in England.*

English broadcasters' fear of the law spared the producers of *South Park* an experience common to human-rights campaigners and investigative journalists around the world: the bewilderment that came with receiving a letter threatening to initiate proceedings in the High Court in London. Far from being a beacon of liberty, a place where people from authoritarian regimes or working for authoritarian corporations could hear arguments about their masters aired, England was liberty's enemy. Saudis who could not investigate a petro-billionaire in

Riyadh for fear of punishment found that London punished exposés when they were printed elsewhere. Ukrainian and Russian journalists, who took no small risk when they confronted their native oligarchs, discovered that the English legal system was as willing as their native jurisdictions to punish them for insubordination.

I still recall the shame I felt when the legal director of Human Rights Watch in New York told me she spent more time worrying about legal action from England than from any other democratic country when she signed off reports on torture, political persecution and tyranny. In the late 1990s, her colleagues had collected eyewitness testimony and Rwandan government documents, and named those who played a role in the Rwandan genocide. In 2005, one of the men named in the report threatened a defamation suit in the UK, although only a few readers had accessed the report online from Britain. Her colleagues had to go back to Rwanda, reconfirm facts and relocate sources, and amend the report to avoid a full-blown legal case, even though the new Rwandan government was investigating the complainant and he had gone into hiding.

It was a familiar pattern. English judges allowed Boris Berezovsky to sue the American *Forbes* magazine for accusing him of being involved in the gangsterism that marked the arrival of Russian capitalism. The magazine sold around 780,000 copies in the United States, while readers accessed about six thousand copies in print or via the Net in the UK. Among the reasons the judges gave for allowing Berezovsky to avail himself of the services of the English rather than the Russian or American law was that his daughter was studying at Cambridge. *Forbes* retracted. The Ukrainian oligarch Rinat Akhmetov successfully pursued *Kyiv Post*, which had just a hundred British subscribers, and a Ukrainian website which did not even publish in English. The son of the ruler of the Republic of the Congo tried to sue Global Witness for a breach of privacy after it published details of how he was spending a fortune on luxury hotels and goods, while the country's inhabitants suffered from miserable poverty.

These were mere part-time litigants when set against the foreigner who exploited the reach of the English libel law more than any other: Sheikh Khalid bin Mahfouz, a Saudi banker, whom I think I can write about now because he is dead – and the dead cannot sue, not even in England.

'Behind every great fortune there is a great crime,' Balzac is meant to have said. And as with so many other oligarchs, bin Mahfouz's fortune had a whiff of the gutter about it. He was in charge of the National Commerce Bank of Saudi Arabia, and worked with the Bank of Credit and Commerce International. In 1992, after BCCI's spectacular collapse, the New York District Attorney indicted him as a front man for a 'Rent a Sheikh' fraud. Bin Mahfouz was a principal shareholder and director in the BCCI Group, whose presence on the board reassured trusting investors, the DA said. Without their knowledge, he withdrew his investment, an action that resulted 'in a gross misstatement of the true financial picture of the bank'. Luckless investors, who did not realise that bin Mahfouz had got out before the balloon went up, suffered 'larger losses when BCCI's worldwide Ponzi scheme finally collapsed'. Bin Mahfouz denied all allegations, but he agreed to pay a fine of $225 million, and accept a ban on any further activities in the American banking system. England did not hold it against him. When investigative journalists began to talk about his alleged links to al Qaeda, London lawyers pounded them with writs with a ferocity not seen since Robert Maxwell's day.

In one respect, however, bin Mahfouz differed from the old brute. He defended his 'reputation' in the English courts while not being a British citizen. Nor, somewhat surprisingly, was he a Saudi citizen. In 1990, the billionaire acquired Irish passports for himself and ten members of his family over a convivial lunch at the Shelbourne Hotel in Dublin with the Irish Taoiseach

Charles Haughey. Bin Mahfouz promised to invest in the country. Haughey promised him citizenship. A subsequent inquiry found that Haughey breached statutory procedures in the interest of pleasing bin Mahfouz.

Time and again, bin Mahfouz used the law or the threat of legal action to ban books which tied him to Islamist violence. It was not that he denied the charge in its entirety. He admitted that he had given money, but said it was only when Islamists were fighting the Soviets. Writers seeking to test his assertions, and see if there were grounds for the relatives of the dead of 9/11 naming him in their lawsuits, or the US Treasury Department treating him with suspicion, were clobbered. The serial litigant did not allow any disobliging reference to him, however hedged with lawyerly caveats, to go unpunished. Terrified publishers pulped rather than run the risk of a trial.

To be fair to the ghost of the billionaire, he could raise legitimate doubts about some of the claims against him. In a normal country, an argument would have taken place, freely and in the open, about the merits of the case. But in this respect, Britain was closer to Saudi Arabia than a free country, and bin Mahfouz was a man only *Private Eye* dared write about.

The legal actions went on without a hitch – he launched thirty-three suits – until bin Mahfouz lawyers issued a writ against *Funding Evil: How Terrorism is Financed and How to Stop It* by the American author Rachel Ehrenfeld. In truth, Ehrenfeld's was not the best book on the subject – that distinction belonged to *Charity and Terrorism in the Islamic World*, by J. Millard Burr, a former USAID relief coordinator in Sudan, and Robert O. Collins, a history professor, which the Cambridge University Press pulled to avoid a libel trial. Ehrenfeld's case stood out because of where her book was published rather than what she said. She published in New York, not London. No British publisher bought the rights for fear of the law, and that fear denied the British public yet another book others could read.

Bin Mahfouz still sued, because twenty-three copies reached Britain via Amazon.

Despite this paltry sale, the courts allowed his action to proceed, and ordered that Ehrenfeld should withdraw her book and pay him $225,000 even though bin Mahfouz was not English, Ehrenfeld was not English, and her book had not been published, publicised or reviewed in England. The imperialism of the English judiciary, its belief that it could punish books whose connection to England was virtually non-existent, finally made the world wake up to the danger London posed to freedom of speech. American writers, from leftists to neo-cons, realised that the availability of books on the Net was overriding their constitutional rights. English law 'constitutes a clear threat to the ability of the US press to vigorously investigate and publish news and information about the most crucial issues before the US public', said a coalition of American publishers. England was organising 'book burnings', added a Republican senator, not entirely hyperbolically, because chastened publishers withdrew defamatory books from the shelves and pulped them. Rory Lancman, a stout member of the New York State Assembly, stood on the steps of the New York Public Library and began a campaign to make English verdicts unenforceable in America with a magnificent speech: 'When American journalists and authors can be hauled into kangaroo courts on phoney-baloney libel charges in overseas jurisdictions who don't share our belief in freedom of speech or a free press,' he said, 'all of us are threatened.'

Polanski Redux!

Naturally, England had no difficulty in satisfying Roman Polanski. *Vanity Fair* was an American magazine, but it sold in Britain, and that was enough to justify his action in London. There was the slight problem that if Polanski appeared at the Royal Courts of Justice to give evidence, the police would arrest him and deport him to America to face an overdue appointment with an angry judge. The judiciary spared him that indignity by saying that he did not need to give his evidence in person, but could deliver it via a video link from the safety of France. Just because he was a fugitive did not mean he was an 'outlaw' whose 'property and other rights could be breached with impunity', said the House of Lords, then the highest court in the land. Not one judge on its benches had the wit to realise that Polanski was not seeking to protect his property from theft or his body from torture, but asserting that he could still say he had a sexual reputation worth defending after his rape conviction, and demand damages from those who doubted it.

Polanski looked magnificent on the video link. The camera focused close on his face as he told the jury that the offending paragraph about the Scandinavian model was 'an abominable lie' which implied he possessed a 'callous indifference' to his wife's murder. He admitted under cross-examination, however, that a month after Sharon Tate's death he had been sleeping with other women. Mia Farrow added more stardust to the proceedings, by arriving in court to give evidence on Polanski's behalf. She said she had been with him on the night he went to Elaine's, and he could not possibly have made a pass at a strange woman because he was in no mood for seduction.

Even if the jury ultimately decided that the story as told in *Vanity Fair* was untrue, the magazine would have had a chance to reduce the damages, perhaps to vanishing point, if it had been allowed to show in court the full testimony of the girl Polanski had raped. 'The jury in London was permitted to hear only the outline of the formal conviction and not the background,' the editor recalled. 'The details could not be published in the UK during Polanski's suit against *Vanity Fair*; after the verdict, the reporting restrictions were lifted.'

The judge went on to tell the jury that 'We are not a court of morals. We are not here to judge Mr Polanski's personal lifestyle'

– even though others might have thought that the 'lifestyle' of a convicted sex offender had some bearing on the case. The jury found for Polanski, and the court awarded him damages of £50,000 and costs estimated at £1.5 million.

If Polanski was seeking to stop discussion of his crime, the 2005 libel action was a failure. Not all the lawyers in England could make the case go away. In 2010 he strayed into Switzerland, where the gendarmerie arrested and threatened to deport him. Nor did readers suffer: they could easily find the details the judge told the jury not to consider on the Web. His action seemed futile.

Yet you risk misunderstanding the nature of censorship if you assume it is always concerned with the obliteration of information. For a few years, Polanski could say that a court had considered the evidence about his sex life, and upheld his reputation and punished his detractors. And not just any court, but an *English* court, whose judgements in other areas of law were – correctly – respected.

Location matters as much in censorship as it does in property development. London gave the powerful something as useful as the suppression of secrets: it gave dignity and authority to their claims of innocence. Even if unwelcome information about them remained in circulation, rich claimants could tell all fair-minded people that an impartial legal process had vindicated their reputations and damned their critics as knaves, fools or liars. They could warn anyone who thought about repeating the allegations against them that the English courts would hit them with stupendous damages, and costs as well.

From Robert Maxwell onwards, they had the satisfaction of making their enemies learn that they could not criticise them without feeling the consequences. They taught their opponents a lesson in 'respect'; showed them that there were still punishments for offending the mighty. The cases they brought could consume their critics' lives, and threaten on occasion to bankrupt them, but they did not consume the lives of the oligarchs. They could hand the job of imposing retribution to their lawyers and reputation managers, and cover the costs of litigation from their loose change.

Censorship is not always about hiding secrets. Sometimes it is just an assertion of raw power.

Money Makes You a Member of a Master Race

On 1 February 1960, four black students – Joe McNeil, Frank McCain, Dave Richmond and Ezell Blair – went to the lunch counter at Woolworth's in Greensboro, North Carolina, and ordered hot dogs and coffee, a courageous request to make at that time and in that place. Despite the US Supreme Court announcing that segregation was unconstitutional, white supremacists still ruled the American South. Most whites could vote, and most blacks could not – poll taxes, literacy tests and intimidation kept them off the electoral rolls. White Southern politicians did not just fail to represent black interests; they were the beneficiaries of a political system whose first purpose was to keep blacks disenfranchised. If they wanted to be re-elected, they knew they had to defend segregation or pay the political price. Political disenfranchisement had a further consequence. Because blacks were not on electoral rolls, they could not serve on juries, let alone aspire to be judges. They were at the mercy of racists in the legal system who could.

Segregation did not just mandate separate services for blacks and whites. Blacks' inferior political and legal status ensured that the services provided to them were in every respect shabbier and meaner. It is extraordinary that within a generation of the struggle against segregation, liberals and leftists could forget the importance of treating citizens without regard for their colour or creed, and embrace identity politics. In the Deep South, 'respecting difference' and 'celebrating diversity' meant that whites went to white schools and universities, and blacks went to underfunded black schools and universities. Whites drank at whites-only water fountains, and blacks at blacks-only fountains. Blacks had to sit at the back of buses, and could not use the 'white' seats at the front; and in Woolworth's and other dime stores they could shop, but they could not sit down at the whites-only counter and order a hot dog and a cup of coffee.

McCain ordered a hot dog and a cup of coffee. The waitress consulted the manager.

'Sorry, I can't serve you. We don't serve coloureds here.'

'But you do have hot dogs and coffee,' said McNeil, pointing at whites eating and drinking further down the counter.

'I can't serve you.'

The boys didn't argue, but they didn't move. They just sat at the counter until the store closed.

The next day twenty-seven black Greensboro students went to Woolworth's. The waitress wouldn't serve them either. So they just sat there too.

The sit-in movement spread across the American South. Blacks occupied whites-only beaches, parks and libraries as well as cafés and dime stores. In Nashville, Tennessee, eighty students put on their smartest clothes, picked up their textbooks and Bibles and divided into relay teams. The first fourteen sat down at a lunch counter.

'Right away the toughs started throwing things over us and putting out cigarette butts on our backs,' recalled Candice Carawan. 'I've got to say that didn't surprise me. What did surprise me is that when the police came they just watched. Finally, they turned to the students at the lunch counter: "OK nigras, get up from the lunch counter or we're going to arrest you." When nobody moved, they just peeled those people with their neat dresses and their Bibles right off their seats and carried them out to the paddy wagons. Before they were out of the store, another fourteen of us took their places at the counter. They got peeled off, and another fourteen sat down. By the end, eighty of us got arrested. Boy it was something!'

At no point did they resist. Christian pacifism and American idealism inspired the black Civil Rights movement of 1955 to 1968. When Carawan's white 'toughs' smeared food over blacks sitting at lunch counters, the blacks did not stand up and hit them. When white employers sacked black workers for trying to register to vote, the workers did not turn violent. When the police stood aside and gave the Ku Klux Klan fifteen minutes' free time to inflict ferocious injuries on 'freedom riders' trying to travel on the segregated buses of the Deep South, the protesters did not fight back. When the police inflicted injuries of their own on protesters in jail cells, the protesters did not retaliate. Even after white supremacists dynamited the Sixteenth Street Baptist Church in Birmingham, Alabama, and murdered four little girls, blacks did not bomb white churches in return.

At the start of the Civil Rights movement, Martin Luther King said that it would adhere to the tactics of non-violent civil disobedience. 'Don't let anyone compare our actions to the Ku Klux Klan. There will be no crosses burned. There will be no white persons pulled out of their homes and taken out on some distant road and murdered. If we protest courageously and with dignity, future generations of historians will pause and say, "There lived a great people, a black people, who injected new meaning and dignity into the veins of civilization."'

Civil disobedience against unjust laws or an occupying power is a hard tactic, that demands intelligence and courage. Only rarely does it work in full democracies. When there are iniquitous laws that have no popular mandate, and require popular cooperation, a mass refusal to obey can destroy them. Hundreds of thousands refused to pay Margaret Thatcher's poll tax, a naked piece of class legislation which said that a dustman must meet the same tax bill as a duke. As large parts of British society withdrew their consent for the tax, it collapsed, as did her premiership shortly afterwards. In most instances, however, the proponents of civil disobedience have to justify breaking the law rather than campaigning to change it. This is the catch that usually snags leftists in Western democracies when they feel the urge to turn militant. They rarely have a respectable answer to the question, 'If you say you have the right to break the law, why can't people you find repellent – racists, fascists – break the law too?'

Debates about the morality of law-breaking in a democracy did not concern the Civil Rights movement. The American South in 1960 was anything but a democracy. To the question, 'Why do you not use the ballot box to seek change?', blacks had the irrefutable answer that white supremacists stopped them voting.

The courage in civil disobedience comes from the dignified nature of the resistance. Protesters never sink to the level of their opponents. As well as refusing to meet violence with violence, true believers in civil disobedience respect the law as they break it. They do not try to escape arrest like common criminals, but use their trials to dramatise their cause and alert public opinion. It follows that peaceful civil disobedience can work in oppressive societies that nevertheless allow protesters to protest. The example Martin Luther King drew on was Gandhi's campaign of the 1930s and 1940s against British imperial rule in India. Like Gandhi, King directed his protests against a system that was repressive, but not so repressive as to make disobedience futile. If King had called on the masses to defy the law and take to the streets, and the masses had known the police would have gunned them down, the masses would have stayed at home.

Writing about Gandhi's belief that the victims of Nazism should arouse the conscience of the world by passively protesting, a sympathetic George Orwell said that Gandhi did not understand the impossibility of protest in totalitarian states. 'It is difficult to see how Gandhi's methods could be applied in a country where opponents of the regime disappear in the middle of the night and are never heard of again. Without a free press and the right of assembly, it is impossible not only to appeal to outside opinion, but to bring a mass movement into being, or even to make your intentions known to your adversary.'

A civil disobedience movement needs a civil society to agitate, and a free or at least half-free press to report its case. It uses the power of publicity against the power of the police baton, and cannot succeed if censorship stops domestic and international opinion from learning of its struggles.

In March 1960, the Committee to Defend Martin Luther King tried to use publicity to stir the conscience of America. It united Northern liberals, black Southern ministers and celebrities such as Harry Belafonte, Marlon Brando, Nat King Cole and Sidney Poitier, who risked losing income by challenging the prejudices of a large section of their audiences. They declared their solidarity with the sit-in movement in a two-page advertisement in the *New York Times*. Under the stirring headline 'Heed Their Rising Voices', they pledged their support to the American teenagers whose 'courage and amazing restraint have inspired millions and given a new dignity to the cause of freedom'.

The committee picked out details of the black struggle to heighten their readers' indignation. In Montgomery, Alabama, they said that after students sang the patriotic anthem 'My Country, 'Tis of Thee' on the State Capitol steps, 'their leaders were expelled from school, and truckloads of police armed with shotguns and tear-gas ringed the Alabama State College Campus. When the entire student body protested to state authorities by refusing to register, their dining hall was padlocked in an attempt to starve them into submission.' The committee went on to describe how the authorities harassed King. 'Again and again the Southern violators [of the US Constitution] have answered Dr. King's peaceful protests with intimidation and violence. They have bombed his home almost killing his wife and child. They have assaulted his person. They have arrested him seven times – for speeding, loitering, and similar offences. And now they have charged him with perjury – a felony under which they could imprison him for ten years. Obviously, their real purpose is to remove him physically as the leader to whom the students – and millions of others – look for guidance and support, and thereby to intimidate all leaders who may rise in the South.'

Not everything the liberals, ministers and celebrities endorsed in the advertisement was correct, for it is rare for every word in a piece of political writing to be true. Writers do their best, but even if we manage to fact-check everything, an argument is not a rendition of pure information. Unlike speak-your-weight machines, writers select facts, emphasise and arrange them. Critics and censors can always find reasons for offence if they put their minds to it, because there is always something – an unchecked fact, an unsupported innuendo – to object to.

The defenders of Martin Luther King knew two great truths, which no one could deny: racial oppression was everywhere in the United States; and the authorities were determined to use force to maintain the status quo. The detail did not bother them, and when they said that the police had arrested Martin Luther King seven times, they made a mistake. In fact the police had hauled him in four times. King said officers had assaulted him on one occasion. The officers denied it. Students had staged a demonstration on the State Capitol steps in Montgomery, as the advert stated, but they sang 'The Star-Spangled Banner', not 'My Country, 'Tis of Thee'. The State Board of Education had expelled nine students, but not for leading the demonstration at the Capitol, but for demanding service at a whites-only lunch counter in the Montgomery County Courthouse on another day. The defence committee also overestimated the extent of police complicity in subduing the protests. Although the state authorities deployed the police near the campus in large numbers, they did not at any time 'ring' the campus. Nor was there any attempt to 'starve' the students into submission.

These were undoubtedly blemishes. No writer who does not try to get his or her facts right can demand the trust of the reader. However, it was not the mistakes that infuriated Alabama's officials but the truths the campaigners were telling about the official harassment of the leaders of the Civil Rights movement, and the punishment of students asking for racial equality. That the proclamation of support for King appeared in a do-gooding Yankee newspaper written for the Confederacy's traditional enemies in the North did nothing to improve their temper. They wanted to stop publicity for the Civil Rights movement, because they understood that press coverage was putting pressure on a reluctant Kennedy administration to end the abuse of power.

But how could they stop it? America in 1960 did not have official censors to vet reports and send writers and editors to prison. Instead it had Thomas Jefferson and James Madison's First Amendment to the US Constitution, which guaranteed freedom of speech and freedom of religious conscience:

> Congress shall make no law respecting an establishment of religion, or prohibiting the free exercise thereof; or abridging the freedom of speech, or of the press; or the right of the people peaceably to assemble, and to petition the government for a redress of grievances.

But America had also inherited the English libel law, and the ideas of English judges became the tools of Southern politicians and bureaucrats as they sought to work their way around constitutional guarantees of freedom of the press.

On the face of it, no official appeared able to sue the *New York Times*, because it had not mentioned any official by name. But libel law covered whatever innuendos or suggestions the court could find, as well as the words on the page. The defenders of Martin Luther King had denounced the police's treatment of students and of King. Lawyers for L.B. Sullivan, Montgomery's police commissioner, decided that the *New York Times* was accusing him of answering 'Dr. King's peaceful protests with intimidation and violence'.

Libel law got round a further difficulty. Hardly anyone in Alabama read Yankee newspapers. In 1960, only 394 of the 650,000 copies the *New York Times* sold daily went to news-stands and subscribers in Alabama. But because libel, almost alone among civil torts, did not require the alleged victim to prove that he or she had suffered damage or financial loss, the fact that a mere few hundred people in Alabama had read the offending advert did not matter. If the *New York Times* had sold one copy in Alabama, that would have been sufficient.

Sullivan demanded a retraction. The *New York Times* refused, as the advertisement had not mentioned him. Sullivan sued. To give his action a local touch he included in his libel writ four black Alabama ministers who had put their names to the advert, and he took his case to an Alabama court. A white judge and jury heard the case and, naturally, found for Sullivan. They awarded him $500,000. Bailiffs seized the ministers' cars, while the court told the *New York Times* to find the equivalent of well over $3 million in today's money.

No newspaper could then or can now take many fines of that size. But the Southern courts had created the principle that criti-cism of a public body was a direct criticism of the person in charge of it, who could then sue for libel. The writs kept on coming. Alabama city commissioners sued the *New York Times* again, this time for $3 million, after its reporter Harrison Salisbury filed a piece that spared the reader nothing. Alabama's authorities, he wrote, had segregated everything from parks to taxis, and created an American Johannesburg. They even banned a book showing black rabbits and white rabbits playing together. 'Every channel of communication, every medium of mutual interest, every reasoned approach, every inch of middle ground has been fragmented by the emotional dynamite of racism, enforced by the whip, the razor, the gun, the bomb, the torch, the club, the knife, the mob, the police and many branches of the state's apparatus.'

The white legal system did not only target newspapers. Anthony Lewis, in his history of the struggle for civil rights and press freedom in America, tells the story of what happened to the publishers of a pamphlet issued by a citizens' committee which recounted how the police stopped a black man, forced him out of his car and shot him in the back. The FBI identified and charged a local policeman, but an all-white jury in a segregated court acquitted him. Alabama lawyers told the police they could sue the citizens' committee for criminal libel for suggesting that it had a racist killer in its ranks.

All sides realised what was at stake. The newspapers of the old Confederacy welcomed the prospect of libel law denying publicity to the Civil Rights movement. Sullivan's victory over the *New York Times*, said the *Alabama Journal*, 'could have the effect of causing reckless publishers of the North ... to make a re-survey of their habit of permitting anything detrimental to the South and its people to appear in their columns'. The South was 'libelled every day'. Now Southern lawyers were fighting back, and calling editors from hundreds of miles away to make them answerable to Alabama's courts. Or as the *Montgomery Advertiser* headlined the verdict: 'State Finds Formidable Legal Club to Swing at Out of State Press'.

The Civil Rights movement knew that the intimidation, the bombing of black churches, the attacks on black children going to white schools, had to be publicised if they were to be stopped. But as lawyers for Alabama's black ministers said after the Sullivan verdict, 'If the libel action is not struck down not only will the struggles of Southern negroes toward civil rights be impeded but Alabama will have been given permission to place a curtain of silence over its wrongful activities.'

The American Supreme Court intervened, and its decision in the 1964 case *New York Times Co. v. Sullivan* is one of those rare moments in history when freedom of speech made an unequivocal advance. Herbert Wechsler, the *New York Times*' lawyer, who had earned the right to be respected by prosecuting Nazi war criminals at Nuremberg, made a bold argument. He did not confine himself to saying that Alabama had no right to impose punishments on newspapers that sold only a few hundred copies in the state. Nor did he look at the racist nature of the Alabama legal system. Rather he examined the history of American liberty from the Revolution on, and argued that politicians and their officials should not be allowed to punish citizens in the libel courts for freely expressing their opinions, even if some of their facts were wrong and some of their views offensive.

No court had ruled that libel law was an attack on free speech before. Judges and legislators had exempted defamation, slander and calumny from protections for freedom of speech and freedom of the press. They reasoned that lies stuck, and the malicious could sully good reputations. Citizens needed protection from poison pens, and it was not a restriction on freedom to give it to them. But the *New York Times* argued that the law was not being used by citizens seeking to protect themselves from scurrilous journalists. Instead, it had become the chosen instrument for state officials and police chiefs seeking to punish citizens protesting about their abuses of power.

On its own, this argument was not enough. The English tradition of libel authorised the punishment of the 'seditious' who libelled the state and its officers. In 1704, Lord Chief Justice Holt ruled that 'It is very necessary for all governments that the people should have a good opinion of it. And nothing can be worse to any government than to endeavour to procure animosities, as to the management of it; this has always been looked on as a crime, and no government can be safe without it be punished.'

Ruling classes have always wanted to silence critics, and the rulers of America were no exception. Within a decade of Congress accepting the First Amendment, John Adams persuaded it to pass a Sedition Act, which punished the press for publishing 'false, scandalous, and malicious writing' against the government or its officials. The president wanted to muzzle press criticism of America's conflict with revolutionary France, whose seditious agents he saw everywhere. Among the dissidents the state arrested were Benjamin Franklin's grandson, who edited an anti-government newspaper, and a blunt citizen who saw townspeople in Massachusetts welcoming President Adams with a cannon salute and remarked to the man standing next to him that he would not mind if they fired the cannonball through the president's 'ass'.

The panic passed, and Congress repealed the authoritarian law. But the Supreme Court was packed with Adams's supporters, and it never declared the punishment of 'seditious' newspapers unconstitutional. It was still open for public officials to do what Sullivan had done, and haul his critics before the courts.

Wechsler and the *New York Times* showed that Adams' two immediate successors as president, Thomas Jefferson and James Madison, as well as many others, regarded Adams' political censorship of 'seditious' newspapers that criticised the state as a clear breach of the First Amendment and an attack on democracy. 'The censorial power is in the people over the Government,' said Madison, 'and not in the Government over the people.' Moreover, Wechsler could quote a string of rulings by American judges from succeeding decades who had defended freedom of speech and of the press against the state. (My favourite being from a judge in the 1940s, who dismissed contempt of court accusations against a union leader by saying, '[I]t is a prized

American privilege to speak one's mind, although not always with perfect good taste, on all public institutions.')

The Supreme Court agreed. Debate on public issues should be 'uninhibited, robust and wide-open', it ruled. If the government and its officials were on the receiving end of 'vehement, caustic and sometimes unpleasantly sharp attacks', that was the price they paid for exercising power in a democracy. They had to learn to live with it.

The judges did not force the American government to reveal all, and leave it powerless to punish those who leaked its secrets. Instead they established new rules for the conduct of public debate. They were careful not to allow absolute liberty. Private citizens can sue as easily in America as anywhere else, if writers attack them without good grounds. Poison pens are still punished, and individual reputations are still protected. If, however, a private citizen is engaged in a public debate, it is not enough for him or her to prove that what a writer says is false and defamatory. They must prove that the writer behaved 'negligently'. The judiciary protects public debates, the Supreme Court said in 1974, because 'under the First Amendment, there is no such thing as a false idea. However pernicious an opinion may seem, we depend for its correction not on the conscience of judges but on the competition of other ideas.'

Finally, the judges showed no regard for the feelings of politicians and other public figures. They must prove that a writer was motivated by 'actual malice' before they could succeed in court. The public figure must show that the writer knew that what he or she wrote was a lie, or wrote with a reckless disregard for the truth. Unlike in Britain, the burden of proof was with the accuser, not the accused.

The US today is not a free-speech utopia. Various states have had to pass laws against SLAPP actions – 'strategic lawsuits against public participation'. The corporations which brought cases of libel, breach of confidence, invasion of privacy or conspiracy did not expect to win, but to slap down protesters with expensive litigation that could drag on for years. But the black students who sat in their best suits and dresses at whites-only lunch counters could still claim a victory. They had opened up American society, and forced the judiciary to recognise a paradox. Free societies living under the rule of law can only be free if the law's reach is limited. As with religion, the political arguments of a democracy are too important to allow the courts to police them.

If the disputes of 1960s America feel like ancient history, think about the similarities between yesterday's white supremacists and today's super-rich.

- The racist expected deference because he was in a superior position. To his mind, the colour of his skin should guarantee that others 'respect' him or face punishment. Flatterers surround today's wealthy, whether they are subordinate employees, supplicants looking for favours or politicians looking for campaign donations. They spend large parts of their professional lives hearing deferential voices, and regard criticism when it comes as an assault on their dignity.
- A white politician or bureaucrat in the 1960s upheld a segregationist political order and knew that the political order would protect him if he played the game. A critic could not take a case against him to any regulatory institution – the Alabama courts, the state police or the state legislature. If you attacked one part of the system, you attacked it all. A modern employer knows that rival firms will refuse to employ a whistleblower if he fires him. Even if the information the whistleblower releases is in the public interest or to the benefit of shareholders, an attack on one employer is an attack on every employer.
- In the courts of the old South, a white skin conferred an overwhelming advantage. In the British courts, money confers an

overwhelming advantage. In neither instance do the courts accept that the powerful and wealthy have the means to refute or rebut criticism without the need for legal sanctions.

The most striking continuity, however, lies in the failure to look at the wider interests of society. For it takes an almighty effort to make an established order recognise that free debate, even hurtful, raucous, inaccurate and disrespectful debate, causes less harm than the bludgeon suppression.

John Stuart Mill and the Struggle to Speak Your Mind

John Stuart Mill is an easy philosopher to love, but a hard one to follow. On first reading, his harm principle, that the 'only purpose for which power can be rightfully exercised over any member of a civilized community, against his will, is to prevent harm to others', seems mild when set against the vast systems of the Continental philosophers. While his nineteenth-century contemporary Karl Marx dreamed that the workers would free themselves from wage slavery, and unleashed the slavery of revolutionary tyranny as a consequence, Mill dreamed of allowing people to do as they pleased as long as they did not harm others. What could be more polite – more English – than his injunction to mind your own business? Do not be deceived by the apparent modesty. Mill's ideas are at the root of more revolutions in human behaviour than Marx and all his followers managed.

Mill's father, the utilitarian philosopher James Mill, brought up his son to be a genius. Young John could speak Greek by the time he was three. By the age of eight, he was reading Plato's dialogues, and by thirteen he was helping his father compose a treatise on political economy. His autobiography describes the mental breakdown his hothouse childhood induced, and hints with Victorian reticence at how he fell for Harriet Taylor, a married woman, who was the love of his life and his salvation.

Under her influence, he became the first British Member of Parliament to make a case for the emancipation of women. If men should have the freedom to express themselves and experiment with their lives as long as they did not harm others, Mill argued, why should not women enjoy the same rights? He dismissed the objection that women's natures meant that they were not fit to exercise freedom. Under the condition of oppression, women could not reveal their true nature; and until equality came, 'no one can possibly assess the natural differences between women and men, distorted as they have been'. Nor would he allow the customs of the past to dictate the future, if custom did more harm than good. The religious fanaticism of our time devotes much of its energy to keeping women down. Its bombs and thunderous declarations are an attempt to silence Mill's argument that nature and tradition cannot justify the suffering caused by male oppression.

The fight for homosexual equality is also a Millian struggle. His harm principle held that what consenting adults did in private was no business of the state. Even if the rest of society disapproved of pre-marital, promiscuous or gay sex, even if it thought that homosexual love harmed homosexuals, it had no right to intervene. Notice how broadly Mill set his harm principle. It is not enough to say that people who hate the idea of homosexuality suffer mental distress at the knowledge that it is legal. They must suffer actual harm, and as they do not, they cannot prohibit it. His most glaring failure was one that the colonial subjects of Queen Victoria would have noticed at once. Mill gave freedom to people in the 'maturity of their faculties', and did not include blacks and Asians as full adults. Just as Milton could not extend liberty to Catholics, so Mill could not extend it to the subject peoples of the British Empire.

If today's governments took Mill seriously, they would end the 'war on drugs'. They would remove restrictions on all pornography apart from child pornography, whose producers by definition harm children, who cannot give informed consent. They would have to allow incest between consenting adults – although I think we could rely on instinctive human revulsion to prevent it – and they would have no argument against public nudity. As I mentioned, Mill is not an easy philosopher to follow, but look at the misery and corruption caused by the war on drugs before you are tempted to dismiss him.

Mill did not believe in absolute freedom of speech – no one can, because it denies man's nature as a social animal – instead he argued for the limits on censorship to be set as broadly as possible. He and Harriet Taylor went over the arguments in *On Liberty* repeatedly before publication, and chose their example of where the boundary should be set with care. If agitators claim that corn dealers starve the poor, they said, the law has no right to punish them. Only if they say the same to an angry mob gathered outside a corn dealer's home, or hand placards to the mob denouncing the corn dealers' wickedness, can the state intervene. Mill does not say that the law should punish the incitement of hatred against corn dealers. Even if their critics made their neighbours despise them as rapacious capitalists, even if the criticism was unfair and caused them financial harm, corn dealers could not go to court. The law should restrict itself to punishing speech that directly provokes crime – incitement to murder, incitement to violence or incitement to arson. It should not punish incitement to hatred, because it is not a crime to hate people, any more than it is to envy them or to lust after them.

The enemies of Mill's liberalism were once on the right, and in many parts of the world they still are. Conservatives said Mill could not brush aside the views of the societies, tribes and communities just because individuals seeking to break with taboos were not harming others. When Britain discussed legalising homosexual acts between consenting adults in the 1950s, on the Millian grounds that what gays did in the privacy of their bedrooms was no one's business but their own, the conservative jurist Patrick Devlin said that the law was still entitled to punish them. 'Invisible bonds of common thought' held society together, he argued, and individual homosexuals must accept legal penalties because no one could live apart from society. Opponents of social conservatives make a mistake when they think they can ignore these objections or overcome them without effort. The conservative may well suspect that his God is a fabrication and his holy book is a fable, but he will none the less fear for the future if the traditions and taboos his society holds are cast aside. The best liberal response is to reassure conservatives that change will not be as bad as they think – in all likelihood their daughters will not run off with the first man they meet, and their sons will not start trying on their wives' dresses. If they look as if they might, social conservatives remain free to try to persuade them that they are wrong. All that is forbidden to them is the argument that if a majority in a society finds the law's tolerance of gay lovemaking or women's emancipation revolting, the majority is entitled to demand retribution. If the knowledge that others are engaging in taboo behaviours inflicts a psychic wound and provokes the deepest feelings of revulsion, that's tough. Conservatives just have to learn to live with it.

Today's liberals lack the self-confidence to say the same about intellectual freedom, and have become as keen on censorship as conservatives once were. They want to silence those who pose no direct harm comparable to Mill's rabble-rouser urging on the mob outside the corn dealer's home. Like homophobic conservatives, who worry that if societies' taboos go, the promotion of homosexuality will turn young people gay, they worry that if the law allows unpalatable views to escape unpunished, hatred will turn to violence. Hence, they support laws against incitement to racial and religious hatred in Britain and across Europe, against Holocaust denial in Germany and Austria, and against Holocaust denial *and* denial of the Armenian genocide in France. Hence, they enforce speech codes that mandate the punishment of transgressors in the workplace and the universities. Few liberals have the confidence to say that free speech, like sexual freedom, would not create a terrible society, because they do not trust their fellow citizens. They do not realise that most people in modern democracies do not harbour secret fascist fantasies, and that the best way to respond to those who do is to meet their bad arguments with better arguments.

In trying to find the best argument against censorship, John Stuart Mill wanted to be true to his father's utilitarianism – that happiness is the only good and pain the only evil – and to his own respect for intellectual freedom. He could not do both. His formulation that we should allow the widest possible freedom to argue because it is 'Better to be Socrates dissatisfied than a fool satisfied' may affirm the desirability of knowing thyself and knowing as much as you can about the world, but it is not a utilitarian calculation. Fools may well be happier in their ignorance than wise people are in their knowledge; certainly, there is no way of proving that they are not. Removing censorship and challenging taboos allows people to live as autonomous adults. Such liberations may be desirable – in my view, they are essential – but they are not always happy or free from pain.

Mill is more convincing when he moves from happiness to harm. We lack the certainty of the Victorians that the world can be made better, but we know that it can be made worse. Breaking with Mill's insistence on the widest possible freedom for individuals is one of the surest ways of doing it.

We are relearning a lesson we ought never to have forgotten: you cannot be a little bit free. You cannot have one law for civilised people who read the *New York Times* and know the difference between a Bordeaux and a Burgundy, and another for beer-swilling bigots who watch Fox News. Saul Bellow explained why when he said, 'Everybody knows there is no fineness or accuracy of suppression; if you hold down one thing, you hold down the adjoining.'

Equality before the law means what it says. As Bellow understood, those who demand the suppression of others must expect to be suppressed themselves. Naïve liberals were once comfortable with punishing expressions of racism, homophobia and misogyny. Whereas Mill would only allow the police to arrest a demagogue whipping up a mob outside a mosque or a gay bar, they wanted to regulate writing and speech which did not directly cause crime. To use the phrase of the philosopher Joel Feinberg, they replaced Mill's harm principle with an 'offence principle', which held that societies are allowed to punish speech that people find exceptionally offensive.

Leave aside if you can the sensible objection that the offence principle justifies courts censoring political debates – for do not many politically committed people find the views of their opponents 'exceptionally offensive'? – and instead look at the boomerang that has whirled back through the air and smacked the children of the 1960s in the face.

They knew that racists, homophobes and misogynists were bad people with terrible ideas, and too few worried about the ground they were conceding when they accepted excessive restrictions on free speech. They ought to know better now. Because they decided that they must do more than fight bad ideas with better ideas, and allowed 'offence' to a faith or racial group, rather than actual harm, to be grounds for censorship, they could not defend liberal principles against Islamists who were also racists, homophobes and misogynists. The same failure to look at wider consequences bedevils the other examples of censorship discussed in these pages. There are many excellent reasons for maintaining corporate secrecy, but the excessive faith in managerial command and control has led to criticism being silenced, and left us with half-ruined societies that still do not dare think about new ways to bring transparency to the workplace. The feudal assumptions behind libel laws are not all bad. Judges have punished newspapers which deserved chastisement, and deterred editors from publishing nasty and worthless work. If democracies in Europe and beyond were to import the principles of the US First Amendment, the amount of rubbishy and 'exceptionally offensive' work in circulation would grow. Preventing its publication by maintaining current laws seems as worthy as banning hate speech or preventing the publication of commercial secrets, until you remember Bellow's warning that truth and falsehood, the moral and the immoral, do not come in separate packages but are mixed together. You cannot hold down one without holding down the other.

The Inaccuracy of Suppression

Of all the notions least worthy of legal protection, the idea that a chiropractic therapist can cure a patient's sickness by pounding his joints with low-amplitude, high-velocity thrusts must be close to the top of the list. The therapy is as rough as it sounds – to imagine a chiropractor at work on a joint, hold your hand flat as if you are a waiter carrying a tray of drinks, bend it backwards below the horizontal as far as you can, then hit it with your free hand. The theory behind the treatment is equally disquieting.

Daniel David Palmer already had an interest in spiritual and magnetic healing when he moved from Canada to Iowa in the 1860s. Once established in the US, he invented his own form of the laying on of hands. In September 1895, he met a deaf janitor by the name of Harvey Lillard. Palmer noticed that Lillard had a vertebra racked from its normal position in his spine. Lillard roused Palmer's amateur curiosity when he told him that he had lost his hearing seventeen years before, when he had bent over and heard something pop in his back. 'I reasoned that if that vertebra was replaced, the man's hearing should be restored. With this object in view, a half hour's talk persuaded Mr Lillard to allow me to replace it. I racked it into position by using the spinous process as a lever and soon the man could hear as before.'

Palmer had performed the founding miracle of the chiropractic faith, a wonder his disciples venerate to this day. With typical bombast, he said that if all he had achieved was the healing of the janitor, 'This of itself, should have been hailed with delight.' But new wonders kept on coming. As Palmer manipulated joints and shoved backs, he convinced himself that he had found a cure for deafness, heart disease and just about everything else. Displaced vertebrae caused 95 per cent of all diseases, he announced. Viruses and bacteria were irrelevant. The key to the cure of all sicknesses lay in the back. To be specific, he concluded that 'innate intelligence' – a substance unknown to science – flowed up and down the spine. A chiropractor who manipulated its joints could therefore heal the body and for good measure 'correct abnormalities of the intellect as well'.

'I am the originator, the Fountain Head,' he bragged. 'It was I who combined the science and art and developed the principles thereof. I have answered the time-worn question – what is life?' He compared himself to Muhammad, Jesus and Martin Luther, and built the Palmer School of Chiropractic in Davenport, Iowa, in 1897 to spread his new religion.

Midwestern doctors were outraged, and had the courts send him to jail for failing to pay a fine for practising medicine without a licence. Far from convincing his followers that he was a fraud, the sentence persuaded them that he was a martyr persecuted by the bullies of conventional medicine. His son Bartlett moved into the family business, and made so much money from trusting patients that he was able to buy the first car Davenport, Iowa, had seen. Alas, in 1913 he used it to run down his father on the day of the Palmer School of Chiropractic's homecoming parade. Daniel died in hospital a few weeks later.

His death may not have been an accident. Father and son had fought for control of the movement, and Bartlett had many reasons to loathe Daniel. His father's violent therapy had its antecedents in the violent treatment of his children. He had pummelled them when they were young, and thrown them onto the street when they were eighteen, telling them to make their own way in the world. 'All three of us got beatings with straps, for which father was often arrested and spent nights in jail,' recalled Bartlett.

Once he was filling his father's shoes, Bartlett Palmer proved himself an astute huckster. He sold expensive, if medically worthless, equipment to muscular initiates to the back-racking trade, established his own radio station to promote it, and pushed the chiropractic empire into Europe.

Doctors scoffed at the chiropractors' belief that they could channel the mysterious force of innate intelligence. Along with satirists and journalists, they laid into the therapy without restraint. The alternative practitioners joined the argument by fighting among themselves. All mystical movements are prone to schism, and believers in the chiropractic gospel were no exception. Therapists who made a fleeting contact with reality began to doubt the movement's claims to provide a cure for all sicknesses. They still believed that chiropractic therapy could treat musculoskeletal problems, but they doubted it was a panacea, and rejected the concept of innate intelligence. They called themselves 'mixers', because they accepted elements of conventional medicine. The 'straights', on the other hand, remained committed to the belief that chiropractic therapy could treat almost any condition. The arguments between the two sects added to the commotion. At no point did a court feel that it was its business to silence anyone taking part in the debate.

Scientists examining the therapy faced a special difficulty, which those who laughed at Palmer did not readily appreciate. Just because he was a violent mystic, with a mind clouded by ignorant mumbo-jumbo and egotistical self-delusion, that did not mean his treatments were necessarily worthless. His therapy could provide the right results for the wrong reasons; be effective in practice although ludicrous in theory. The scientific method insisted that it was not sufficient to say that an alternative therapist walked like a quack and talked like a quack – critics had to demonstrate that his treatments were quackery.

The task of doing so fell to a free-ranging researcher called Edzard Ernst. He was a professor at Vienna University's medical school, whose prolific research record might have allowed him to take a job in the grandest of universities anywhere in the world. Instead, he decided in 1993 to become the world's first professor of complementary medicine, at Exeter University, a fine institution, but something of a backwater in the opinion of his fellow academics.

Ernst's decision was not so eccentric. Although alternative or complementary medicine was a neglected scientific subject, establishing what merit, if any, it possessed was of pressing public importance. Ernst estimated that the global spend on alternative health care stood at £40 billion in 2008. The pseudo-science of homeopathy generates the largest profits, because the cost of the raw material for homeopathic 'remedies' is so low. Homeopaths believe, on the basis of no evidence at all, that the smaller the proportion of an allegedly beneficial substance in a 'remedy', the more effective that remedy becomes. Their theory ensures that the most valuable animal on the planet is not a rare Chinese panda or endangered Siberian tiger, but a common French duck. Every year, functionaries working for a French homeopathic firm kill one. They extract its heart and liver, then dilute them with water to a ratio of $1:100^{200}$ – that is, 1 part duck to 1 plus two thousand zeroes of water. Not a molecule of the offal survives the drenching; water is all that remains. The company drips it into sugar pills, and in keeping with homeopathic orthodoxy, claims that a 'memory' of the dead duck lingers in the medicine. Its remembrance of the unfortunate *canard* gives the sugar pills curative powers. From one bird, they produce warehouses-full of 'medicines' that they sell for millions of dollars.

Ernst resisted the temptation to dismiss the popularity of alternative medicine as the product of the silly obsessions of the rich world's 'worried well'. There are thousands of homeopaths in Britain, but hundreds of thousands in India, he noted. In the poor world as well as the rich, not just homeopaths and chiropractic therapists but the sellers of aromatherapy, hypnotherapy, magnet therapy, massage therapy, flower and crystal remedies, acupuncture, feng shui and colonic irrigation claim that there is no need for modern drugs. They offer 'natural', 'herbal', 'holistic' and 'traditional' remedies to desperate people with little money to waste on useless treatments as well as to the wealthy.

Ernst understood that practitioners of alternative medicine pose two dangers to rich and poor alike. First, their treatments may not cause actual harm, but because patients believe in the remedy and trust the therapist, they fail to visit clinicians who might actually help them. Second, the treatments may cause actual harm, while still deterring patients from visiting competent clinicians.

In the case of chiropractic therapy, Ernst and his colleagues conducted systematic reviews and meta-analyses of the available clinical trials. They showed that spinal manipulation could do nothing to relieve headaches, period pains, colic, asthma, allergies and all the other conditions therapists claimed to be able to treat. This was not a startling finding. If there were anything in the 'straight' version of chiropractic claims, trouble with the back would bring on a host of apparently unrelated medical problems. No one has been able to show that it has. For neck pain, the evidence was more mixed. Two reviews concluded that spinal manipulation was futile. A third found its effects were more beneficial, although Ernst pointed out that the lead reviewer in this case was a chiropractic therapist. There was more of a scientific consensus that spinal manipulation was as effective in treating back pain as conventional physiotherapy and anti-inflammatory drugs. But there's the rub – no variety of back rubbing, conventional or alternative, does much to relieve back pain: they are all equally ineffective.

A credulous patient who believes that chiropractic treatment can cure or alleviate illnesses that have nothing to do with musculoskeletal conditions may well avoid seeking trustworthy advice, and suffer the consequences. Believers in the efficacy of nearly all other alternative treatments run the same risk – a traveller who believes that homeopathic treatments can protect her from malaria, for example, risks her life if she refuses to take conventional medicines as well. As for the further risk that the patient could suffer positive harm at the hands of the alternative therapists, chiropractic therapy stands out as one of the few alternative treatments that are dangerous in themselves. In 2001, a systematic review of five studies revealed that roughly half of all chiropractic patients experienced temporary adverse effects, such as pain, numbness, stiffness, dizziness and headaches. Patients put themselves in jeopardy when they allowed therapists to execute high-velocity, low-amplitude thrust on their necks – one of the most vulnerable parts of the body, as hangmen know.

Manipulating the neck risks attacking the arteries that carry the blood to the brain. Because there is usually a delay between damage to the arteries and the blockage of blood to the brain, the link between chiropractic treatment and strokes went unnoticed for many years. Typical of the suffering Ernst revealed was the case of a twenty-year-old Canadian waitress who visited a chiropractor twenty-one times between 1997 and 1998 to relieve pain in her lower back. On her penultimate visit, she complained of stiffness in her neck. That evening she began dropping plates at the restaurant, so she returned to the chiropractor. As the chiropractor manipulated her neck, she began to cry, her eyes started to roll, she foamed at the mouth and her body began to convulse. She slipped into a coma and died three days later. At the inquest, the coroner declared that she died of a 'ruptured vertebral artery, which occurred in association with a chiropractic manipulation of the neck'. Hers was not an isolated case. A 2001 study by the Association of British Neurologists found thirty-five cases of neurological complications, including nine strokes, occurring within twenty-four hours of neck manipulation.

Conventional medicine can have fatal consequences. But medical regulators assess drugs before allowing them on the market, and doctors monitor their effects and seek the informed consent of patients. Neither of the first two checks exists in chiropractic treatment, and a 2005 study of British chiropractors found that 77 per cent did not seek informed consent.

Ernst did not start with a prejudice against alternative medicine – he had trained in herbalism, homoeopathy, massage therapy and spinal manipulation – but the good scientific principle of basing beliefs on evidence shook him out of his complacency. The Exeter University researchers found that 95 per cent of alternative medical treatments had no reliable evidence to support claims for their effectiveness, and suggested that we dropped terms like 'alternative', 'complementary' and 'conventional' medicine, and instead tried 'medicines that work' and 'medicines that do not work'.

Leaving all medical questions to one side, Ernst's research was a great story. The British alone spend £1.6 billion a year on alternative treatments that do not work except as placebos, and there was a pool of potential readers who wanted to know why. Ernst teamed up with Simon Singh, one of the best modern science writers, to bring his work to a wider audience. Singh trained as a scientist at Cambridge University. He completed his PhD at the CERN laboratory, where he learned about the demands of the scientific method. Before his colleagues would allow him to put a scientific paper into the public domain, they tore into his ideas, challenging his premises, doubting his methods and questioning his ability. It never occurred to Singh that he could sue a critic of his work, even if the criticism was damaging to his reputation or wholly misguided. If the criticisms were wrong, he could expose their falsity. If they were right, they would stop him making a mistake. It tells us something about our times that I need to labour this point, but freedom to speak includes the freedom to be wrong. In science, as in any other intellectual pursuit, free debate without fear of the consequences is the only way of allowing facts to be established and arguments to be tested. As Carl Sagan beautifully explained, 'At the heart of science is an essential balance between two seemingly contradictory attitudes – an openness to new ideas, no matter how bizarre or counterintuitive, and the most ruthlessly sceptical scrutiny of all ideas, old and new. This is how deep truths are winnowed from deep nonsense.'

Singh had written acclaimed books on the history of codebreaking and the efforts of generations of mathematicians to find a proof for Fermat's last theorem. He explained scientific ideas to a lay audience without glossing over difficulties the reader needed to understand – one of the hardest forms of prose writing there is, in my opinion.

In 2008, Singh and Ernst released *Trick or Treatment*, a history of how the various alternative therapies came about, why they once seemed plausible, and why patients and governments should now reject most of them. A few months after the book was published, the British Chiropractic Association held National Chiropractic Awareness Week. Singh noted that it offered its members' services to the anxious parents of sick children, and wrote an article for the *Guardian*, 'Beware the Spinal Trap'. He began by saying that readers would be surprised to learn that the therapy was the creation of a man who thought that displaced vertebrae caused virtually all diseases. A proportion of modern chiropractors still believed in Palmer's 'quite wacky' ideas, as the British Chiropractic Association was proving by claiming that its members could treat children with colic, sleeping and feeding problems, frequent ear infections, asthma and prolonged crying. There was 'not a jot of evidence' that these treatments worked, said Singh. 'This organisation is the respectable face of the chiropractic profession and yet it happily promotes bogus treatments.' He went on to explain that he could label the treatment as 'bogus' because Ernst had examined seventy trials exploring the benefits of chiropractic therapy in conditions unrelated to the back, and found no evidence to suggest that chiropractors could treat them.

By the standards of polemic, it was an even-tempered piece; far angrier articles have been written with less cause. Singh was warning that parents would be wasting their money if they took children to chiropractors, and could risk harming them too. He backed up his comments with reliable evidence, and concluded that 'If spinal manipulation were a drug with such serious adverse effects and so little demonstrable benefit, then it would almost certainly have been taken off the market.' This unexceptionable thought was no more than a statement of the obvious.

On the offence principle, one could see why chiropractors would find Singh's argument extremely offensive, even if it were true or mainly true. According to the harm principle, there was no reason to punish him even if his argument was not supported by strong evidence but was false. On the contrary, John Stuart Mill believed that if all reasonable people thought an opinion was false, they still had no right to suppress it. They must allow the debate to run its course. The courts of his native country turned Mill's idea on its head. Instead of praising Singh for contributing to a debate on children's health that all reasonable people should welcome, the judges allowed the British Chiropractic Association to sue him for libel.

The March of the Nerds

On a wet evening in 2009, I addressed a meeting in a London pub close to the law courts. I gave a speech along the lines I have presented in this book. I warned that the Internet was opening up the possibility of extra-territorial censorship, and that authoritarian jurisdictions could ban books, impose fines and use international agreements to enforce their verdicts. British judges were the worst offenders in the democratic world, I continued. They allowed sex offenders to sue. They allowed criminals to collect damages, and did not reform the law when their criminality was exposed. They presided over a system that was so biased and so expensive it compelled honest men and women to deny what they knew to be true. Suing scientists engaged in essential arguments about public health was the logical continuation of a policy of suppression.

Simon Singh's case was not unique. The American health conglomerate NMT sued the British doctor Peter Wilmshurst in London for criticising its treatments in an online American scientific journal. Another pharmaceutical company was to go after a Danish radiologist after he alleged at a scientific conference in Britain that there was evidence of a link between one of its treatments and a rare and crippling muscular condition. The editors of medical journals were admitting that they refused to print or censored scientific papers they feared might bring them to the attention of the courts. A vitamin salesman sued Ben Goldacre, Britain's pre-eminent demystifier of pseudo-science, after Goldacre condemned him in the *Guardian* for peddling his pills to sufferers from Aids in southern Africa, and telling them that retro-viral drugs were poisons. The libel action failed, but for more than a year all British newspapers, and all foreign newspapers the vitamin salesman might sue in London, risked a writ if they talked about his sales techniques.

My glum account of English oppression was a warm-up act for Singh, who was preparing to take the microphone and announce whether he was prepared to fight the libel writ.

The chiropractors had not sued the *Guardian*, but had gone for Singh personally, hoping that the threat of financial ruin would force him to grovel. The *Guardian* withdrew his article from their website, thus lessening any 'offence' caused, and offered the chiropractors the right of reply, so they could tell their side of the story and convince readers by argument rather than by threats that Singh was in the wrong.

The chiropractors carried on suing Singh, and demanded that he pay them damages and apologise. Singh did not see why he should, considering he was reporting reputable evidence that chiropractic therapy was the invention of a faith healer, whose claims that his mystical method could cure sicknesses that had nothing to do with backache were nonsense. At a preliminary hearing to determine the 'meaning' of Singh's article, the judiciary soon showed why English law was feared and despised across the free world. Determined to draw him into the law's clutches, the judge put the worst possible construction on Singh's words.

He ruled that because Singh had said 'there is not a jot of evidence' that chiropractic therapists could cure colic, sleeping and feeding problems, frequent ear infections, asthma and prolonged crying, the courts would at enormous expense see if they could find one piece of evidence, however small, to support the chiropractors. Maybe if a child stood up in court and breathlessly announced that a chiropractor had cured her, that would be a jot. Maybe if the judge could find a smidgeon of doubt in one of the studies, Singh would have to pay for a phrase that may have been ever so slightly inaccurate.

If Singh could prove that no such doubt existed, he would still not be free of the law. The judge ruled that when Singh said of the British Chiropractic Association, 'This organisation is the respectable face of the chiropractic profession and yet it happily promotes bogus treatments,' he was accusing it of dishonesty. It seemed clear to those of us who did not have the benefit of a legal training that he was doing no such thing. In his article, Singh said that chiropractic therapists had 'wacky ideas', and accused the hard-line among them of being 'fundamentalists'. In normal English usage, to describe someone as a fundamentalist who holds wacky ideas is to accuse him of folly, not of mendacity.

Not according to the judge. In his role as a definer of hidden meanings, he ruled that when Singh wrote 'happily promotes', he did not mean that chiropractors 'carelessly' promoted bogus therapies without a thought for the available evidence, or 'stupidly' promoted them because they did not understand the findings of clinical trials. No. Singh was accusing therapists of deliberately and fraudulently promoting quack remedies they knew to be worthless. 'That is in my judgement the plainest allegation of dishonesty and indeed it accuses them of thoroughly disreputable conduct,' the judge told Singh.

Proving whether a believer in magical medicine, the 'faked' moon landings, the 'truth' about Obama's birth certificate or any other mystical or paranoid theory is a fool or a liar is a next to impossible task. The most disturbing thing about fantasists is that they are often sincere. Yet on the ruling of the English courts, a writer who described a neo-Nazi or an Islamist as 'happily promoting bogus conspiracy theories' about the global reach of the Elders of Zion, for which there is 'not a jot of evidence', could be sued for libel in London. And unless the writer could prove that the object of the critique was a liar instead of a fool, the writer would lose.

After hearing the judge's ruling, Singh's friends, his lawyers and everyone else who had his best interests at heart advised him to get out of the madhouse of the law while he still could. He had already risked £100,000 of his own money. If he fought the case, it would obsess his every waking moment for a year, possibly longer, and he could lose ten times that amount if the verdict went against him. Even if he won, he would still lose, because another peculiarity of the English law is that the victor cannot recoup his full costs. It was as if the judiciary had put Singh in a devil's version of *Who Wants to be a Millionaire?*

Singh's wife, the BBC journalist Anita Anand, understood the principle at stake, and backed her husband. Whatever happened, she said, the case would not divide them. But the question remained for Singh, how far could he go before deciding that the risk to his family's finances was too great? To cap it all, the judge had come up with a reading of Singh's words that made a defence impossible.

No one would have blamed him for backing down. There would have been no dishonour in withdrawing from the fray. Thousands of publishers and writers in England and beyond have looked at the cost and biases of the English law and thought surrender the only option. Singh said that if he were a twenty-five-year-old with no money he would have apologised. But his bestselling books had given him financial independence. He resolved to refuse to put his name to a lie by authorising an apology. He knew what his enemies would do with it. Ernst and Singh had spent years investigating alternative medicine. No potential patient would spend more than a few days doing the same. If he apologised, chiropractic therapists would wave his retraction at potential patients, and say that Singh had admitted that their philosophy was not gibberish, and their claims to treat children were not bogus. As shamefully, an apology would also make Singh complicit in silencing other journalists, scientists and editors, who would think hard before challenging alternative therapists after seeing how the law had forced him to retract.

From Stalin in his show trials to oligarchs suing investigative journalists, censors want recantations as well as exemplary punishments. I have seen billionaires, including convicted criminals, extract admissions of guilt from British newspapers too poor or too frightened to fight, and use them to convince journalists and politicians around the world that legitimate criticisms of their actions were groundless. Singh did not wish to join such sorry company.

He told the audience in the pub that night that he cared about health and the health of children, and thought that his article was fair and reasonable. He had spoken to his lawyers, and they had promised to try to find a way to appeal the judge's ruling. 'I should be able to write about scientific issues without the fear of being intimidated,' he said. 'It's about more than just me. Bloggers, journalists and scientists … we should all have the right to write about important issues without fear of being intimidated. It's not just about science. It's about all journalists being able to write fairly and reasonably.'

The audience who had gathered to hear him were science bloggers, members of the 'skeptic' movement the Internet had empowered to argue for evidence-based politics and against official toleration of superstition. They did not need newspaper editors or broadcasters to give their views a hearing. They knew that they could reach any interested reader with access to a computer anywhere in the world, and revelled in the new opportunities the Web had opened up.

The normal response of the British to a speaker's description of an abuse of power is to say 'Tut-tut,' often quite sternly. But instead of shrugging their shoulders and muttering, 'It's a bad business but what can we do?', Singh's audience of Net-literate skeptics turned into a heaving mass of whooping, hollering geeks. They roared their defiance as a red mist descended over their spectacles, and vowed they would not rest until they had brought the rotten system of English censorship crashing to the ground.

Shocked and awed, I said to Ben Goldacre, 'The nerds are on the march. I wouldn't like to be standing in their way.'

An uncharacteristically spiritual look passed over the great debunker's face. 'Yes,' he said. 'Strike us down, we shall become more powerful than you could possibly imagine.'

I realised this was what Obi-Wan Kenobi said to Darth Vader in *Star Wars*, and mockingly commented that the skeptic movement's highest cultural reference point was a 1970s sci-fi movie.

I should have been more courteous.

Goldacre was right about this, as so much else. The 'Streisand effect' – first seen in 2003, when the actress tried to remove pictures of her Malibu home from a publicly available collection, and ensured that they were copied around the world – kicked in with a vengeance. Dozens of websites reprinted Singh's original article. What had been a small piece on the comment pages of a British newspaper became a global phenomenon read by anyone with an interest in science and free debate. Although newspapers and broadcasters were careful about what they said for fear the chiropractors would sue them too, bloggers were uninhibited. They seemed beyond the control of the censors. Individually, each writer or tweeter appeared too small to go after. Collectively, there were too many of them. Because skeptics were informed readers of science blogs, Singh's solicitor Robert Dougans, a brilliant young lawyer on his first big case, and Adrienne Page, his QC, found they could call on the knowledge of hundreds of scientists just by logging on to the Net and crowd-sourcing their appeal.

The chiropractors produced pleadings for the court that said there was reliable evidence that they could cure sick children. Bloggers put them up, and their readers picked them apart. The chiropractors claimed that a study suggested that they could cure babies with colic. One online commentator noticed, 'There was no control group at all. It simply follows 316 babies and found that most of them eventually got better. Well, they do, don't they?' The chiropractors said a second study found that their treatments worked. The bloggers said that this study consisted of 'two case reports and they refer to use of a mechanical device, not the usual chiropractic manipulation'. Computer-literate scientists, who understood the investigative power of the Net, tracked down six hundred chiropractic therapists in Britain who claimed they could treat childhood illnesses, and reported them for breaching advertising standards requirements. The regulators at the General Chiropractic Council were so overwhelmed with complaints that they had to take on more staff. At one point in 2010, one in four chiropractors was under investigation.

A justifiable paranoia descended on British chiropractic therapists. Their trade associations warned them to take down their websites and to refuse to talk to strangers, who might be undercover skeptics. If they had leaflets 'that state you treat whiplash, colic or other childhood problems in your clinic or at any other site where they might be displayed with your contact details on them. DO NOT USE them until further notice.'

The Singh case brought home to English law the interactive possibility of the Net. It was not just that the courts could no longer stop an article being read, or that their threat of censorship turned readers into active citizens who could help Singh and his lawyers in building a defence. Libel law had created a virtual community that was ready to turn into the most successful British free-speech movement since the campaign fifty years previously against the obscenity laws the state used to prosecute Penguin Books for publishing *Lady Chatterley's Lover*.

On the one hand, the legal establishment faced a traditional reform campaign which William Wilberforce would have recognised. Sense about Science, Index on Censorship and English PEN mobilised elite scientific, media and political figures. Running alongside the traditional reformers was the exuberant and anarchic reform campaign on the Web, which Wilberforce could never have imagined.

The judiciary backed down. Faced with growing alarm from politicians and courtrooms packed with protesters, and maybe the dim realisation that they were sitting on the benches of a democracy, the judges of the Court of Appeal reversed all previous rulings. The legal reasoning they used was technical – when Singh said there was 'not a jot' of evidence to support the therapists' claims, the judges decided he was making a 'fair comment' based on facts truly stated rather than stating a plain fact. It seemed to outsiders to be a distinction without a difference, but the ruling meant that the chiropractors now faced fearsome difficulties in pressing forward with their case. They dropped their action, and Singh, and all the campaign groups and Net activists who stood by him, savoured a rare triumph.

Those of us who thought that English judges did not know the difference between John Milton and Milton Keynes listened with wonder as the Lord Chief Justice remembered which country he came from, and aligned himself with its best traditions. 'To compel an author to prove in court what he has asserted by way of argument is to invite the court to become an Orwellian ministry of truth,' he said, and then quoted the passage from the *Areopagitica* where Milton recalled meeting the persecuted Galileo in Florence in 1638. 'I have sat among their learned men', Milton said of the Italians who entertained him, and 'for that honour I had, and been counted happy to be born in such a place of philosophic freedom, as they supposed England was, while themselves did nothing but bemoan the servile condition into which learning among them was brought; … that nothing had been there written now these many years but flattery and fustian. There it was that I found and visited the famous Galileo, grown old a prisoner of the Inquisition, for thinking in astronomy otherwise than the Franciscan and Dominican licensers thought.'

The judge did not quite say that English libel law was as great a threat to scientific thought as the Inquisition's order to Galileo to recant his belief that the earth went round the sun. But he saw a valid comparison, and said 'that is a pass to which we ought not to come again'.

Modern culture despises politicians. In newsrooms or on satire shows, no lawyer stops journalists and comedians from mocking them, because politicians generally don't sue. Most have thick skins, and those who do not know they will look ridiculous in the eyes of their voters if they go to court. In my experience, politicians are more open than the supposedly liberal judiciary. They are certainly more protective of the reputation of their country. The United Nations had condemned Britain. After the Saudi plutocrat Khalid bin Mahfouz used English law to attack books that American houses had not even published in England, President Obama signed a law that stated that the US courts should not enforce the orders of English judges against American authors. Now scientists were telling the judges that lawyers for cranks and pharmaceutical corporations were threatening free debate about public health.

Politicians honoured Simon Singh's bloody-minded refusal to bow before pressure by agreeing to reform. In the run-up to the general election of 2010, all three main political parties made a manifesto commitment to reforming the libel laws, after fifty thousand voters signed a petition defending free speech and free enquiry. The victorious Conservative/Liberal coalition government honoured its promises and proposed making it far harder for libel tourists to use the London courts to punish their critics. Ministers also wanted a strengthening of the defences available to writers, and in a nod to John Stuart Mill, they added that claimants must prove they had suffered substantial harm before they could sue. There were many gaps in the draft Bill. The presumption of guilt still lay on the accused, and more seriously, the cost of libel actions looked as if it would remain formidably high.

At the time this book went to the printers, it was not certain that Parliament would pass the measure into law. Even if it does, the most striking feature of the reform campaign was its timidity. English radicals are remarkably conservative, and the reformers did not ask Parliament to adopt the American system and allow citizens to say and write what they pleased about public figures, as long as they did so without a negligent disregard for the truth. The police and credit reference agencies can pass on false information and the citizen cannot sue them for libel unless they act with malice, yet the law continues to demand that the public debates of a democracy must be constrained.

If reformers had been braver, they might have argued that giving primacy to freedom of speech would not allow the worst aspects of American culture to implant themselves in Britain. The First Amendment did not permit radio shock jocks and Fox News to flourish in the US. On the contrary, the courts had ruled that America's 'fairness doctrine' – which required broadcasters to cover matters of public importance and to give airtime to contrasting views – was compatible with constitutional protections for freedom of speech. The judges held that because only a limited number of stations could fit onto the broadcast spectrum, the state had a right to prevent their owners from delivering unbalanced or propagandistic journalism. 'There is nothing in the First Amendment which prevents the Government from requiring a licensee to share his frequency with others,' the Supreme Court said in 1969. 'It is the right of the viewers and listeners, not the right of the broadcasters, which is paramount.'

Free-speech legislation did not undermine the fairness doctrine, rather in the 1980s the American political right, led by officials in the Reagan administration, began the task of dismantling the regulatory controls which required broadcasters to air balanced journalism. Today's European broadcasters who yearn to deliver similarly hectoring and prejudiced journalism say that cable television and the Internet have destroyed the reasons for legally enforced impartiality. Technological advance has removed the spectrum scarcity which limited the number of channels, so how can countries like Britain justify restricting what they broadcast? But even though cable and the Web have created a space for every type of political view, one can still argue that television and radio broadcasters should be treated as special cases.

In everyday life we accept differing standards in differing circumstances. We have a right to swear when we are at home or with friends. If an employer were to dismiss us for swearing at customers or clients, we would not say that he or she was infringing our rights to freedom of speech. There is no public-interest defence for swearing at customers, and we could still swear in other circumstances. Similarly, society is entitled to say that there should be a corner in the marketplace of ideas where journalists and their managers and owners must respect notions of fairness and balance, particularly when radio and television stations continue to be controlled by the state or by wealthy individuals and corporations.

A more dangerous American development has been the ability of lobbyists to use free-speech legislation to overturn restrictions that had existed since the early twentieth century on corporations and trade unions funding attack ads during elections. A US Supreme Court decision passed by a margin of 5–4 in 2010 effectively gave every organisation the right to sponsor propaganda. At first glance the ruling appeared logical: why should corporations not enjoy the same rights as individuals, newspapers and bloggers to say what they wanted in an election debate? Its logic fell apart under closer examination, and the perverse verdict is ripe for overturning. Corporations and trade unions are not individuals but collectives, which is why the law should never allow them to sue for libel. They cannot vote or run for office, and corporations may be controlled by foreigners who cannot vote or run for office either. It is unlikely that every shareholder, customer or employee of a company, or every member of a trade union, will agree with the political stance the controllers of the collective take in an election campaign. When a company board or a trade-union committee takes a political stance, it forces dissenters to pay a de facto tax to subsidise views with which they profoundly disagree.

The US Supreme Court ignored the distorting effects of big money on debate. Or as Justice John Stevens said when he dissented from the view of the majority of his fellow judges, 'At bottom, the Court's opinion is a rejection of the common sense of the American people, who have recognized a need to prevent corporations from undermining self-government since the founding, and who have fought against the distinctive corrupting potential of corporate electioneering since the days of Theodore Roosevelt. It is a strange time to repudiate that common sense. While American democracy is imperfect, few outside the majority of this Court would have thought its flaws included a dearth of corporate money in politics.'

Arguments about the distorting effects of special interests on democracy are as old as representative government. The novelty of the present lies in the new argument that we no longer need to worry about the power of religion, money or the state. The Singh case and many battles like it appeared to prove that the Web had made the old debates about restrictions on freedom of speech redundant. Singh's supporters, like the supporters of so many other modern causes, had used the new technologies to circumvent legal restrictions. Optimists could say that their success showed that we were moving into a new world, whose liberalism would make past generations blink with astonishment. All of a sudden, debates about blasphemy, libel, electoral laws, campaign finance and constitutional protections appeared leftovers from the analogue age. The wonder of the Web had dispatched the concerns of the past to the dustbin of history. Now we could write what we wanted, and no one could stop us.

PART THREE

State

In our age there is no such thing as 'keeping out of politics'. All issues are political issues.

GEORGE ORWELL, 1946

SEVEN

The Internet and the Revolution

Tyranny's new nightmare: Twitter

LOS ANGELES TIMES, 24 JUNE 2009

If I had been writing a book on censorship before the invention of the Internet, I would have concentrated on two subjects that have hardly featured in these pages: the power of the state in its dictatorial and democratic forms to suppress criticism; and the power of private and public media conglomerates to control debate. They dominated thinking about freedom of speech in the twentieth century, but by the twenty-first appeared less important than at any time since the highpoint of Victorian liberalism.

To understand how the culture has changed, look at what George Orwell wrote about censorship after he attended a meeting in 1944 to commemorate the tercentenary of the publication of Milton's *Aeropagitica*. At that time, the dominant mood in intellectual London was one of sympathy for Stalin's Soviet Union. Although Milton had argued for freedom of thought, Orwell found that communists and their fellow travellers at the celebration adopted the Marxist position that bourgeois freedoms were illusions, and intellectual honesty was a form of anti-social selfishness: 'Out of this concourse of several hundred people, perhaps half of whom were directly connected with the writing trade, there was not a single one who could point out that freedom of the press, if it means anything at all, means the freedom to criticise and oppose.'

Democratic Britain imposed its own censorship during the war and before it: through direct state controls on what writers and reporters might say, and more circuitously through the informal pressure publishers put on writers to say nothing that might undermine the nation's struggle against its enemies. The pressure was subtle but unremitting, and Orwell sighed that no one had been able to escape the 'continuous war atmosphere of the past ten years'.

He was as depressed by the economic constraints on writers as the ideological pressures. 'In our age, the idea of intellectual liberty is under attack from two directions. On the one side are its theoretical enemies, the apologists of totalitarianism, and on the other its immediate, practical enemies, monopoly and bureaucracy.' The unwillingness of the public to buy books meant that if writers wished to see their work published, they had to seek work in newspaper offices or film studios, which were in the hands of a few rich men, or at the stations of the publicly owned BBC radio monopoly. The alternative was to sell themselves as propagandists and draw wages from the Ministry of Information or the British Council, 'which help the writer to keep alive but also waste his time and dictate his opinions'. 'Everything in our age conspires to turn the writer and every other kind of artist as well, into a minor official, working on themes handed down from above and never telling what seems to him the whole of the truth.'

The tight-fisted public is as unwilling to buy books as ever, but much else about Orwell's description feels dated. Although Western troops have been fighting since 9/11, Orwell's 'war atmosphere' has not intimidated writers as varied as investigative reporters trying to find the truth about the second Iraq war, and malign fantasists peddling conspiracy theories. Far from fearing or respecting war leaders, journalists have treated them with the utmost contempt. As they did, they illustrated an unacknowledged truth about contemporary writing: reporters, editors and artists in Britain, America and most of Europe are not afraid of politicians. They are frightened of Islamists, and do not run cartoons that might offend them. They are frightened of oligarchs and CEOs, and worry about libel and the ability of the wealthy to bend the ear of their proprietors. But they are not frightened about leaking the secrets or criticising the actions of elected governments. One can map the shift of power from the state by tracing journalists' fears as the twentieth century progressed. In 1936, all British newspaper proprietors reached a 'gentlemen's agreement' not to mention Edward VIII's affair with Wallis Simpson for fear of offending the monarchy. In 2006, all British newspaper editors made an unspoken agreement not to run the Danish cartoons for fear of offending Islamists. In the 1930s, the public woke up to discover that their king was about to abdicate because he was determined to marry a divorcee, without their media forewarning them. In our time, the public woke up to discover that their banking system was about to collapse, without their media forewarning them.

In Western countries, the power of the state to intimidate its civil servants was little greater than the power of businesses to enforce silence on their employees. America and Israel were the exceptions, as so often, and clung on to the traditions of the old nation state that were fading in Europe. The Israeli courts imprisoned a soldier who leaked military secrets which suggested the army followed an illegal shoot-to-kill policy. Meanwhile, when the American soldier Bradley Manning passed thousands of cables from the US State Department to WikiLeaks, a vindictive Pentagon held him in solitary confinement. But even the American authorities made no attempt to stop US newspapers publishing the WikiLeaks secrets. The cases of two British civil servants who released batches of secrets provided a better guide to the weakness of the twenty-first-century democratic state. In 2003 Katherine Gun revealed how the British intelligence services were bugging the United Nations at the behest of the Americans in the run-up to the second Iraq war, and in 2006 Derek Pasquill showed how his employers at the Foreign Office were allowing the Muslim Brotherhood to influence British policy. In both instances, the government threatened to teach its servants not to embarrass their masters in wartime by prosecuting them for breaking the Official Secrets Act. In both instances, it dropped the threat of trial and imprisonment for fear that jurors would show how unimpressed the public was by the 'continuous war atmosphere' by acquitting them.

Warriors in the War on Terror attempted to attack freedom of speech, although nearly all the arrests were in Russia, China and the Arab dictatorships, who used the war as another excuse for clampdowns they would have authorised anyway. The British Labour Party tried to enforce a new offence that would punish anyone who 'glorifies, exalts or celebrates the commission, preparation or instigation (whether in the past, in the future or generally) of acts of terrorism'. Prosecutors might have used it legitimately against people who were directly inciting murder, or illegitimately against citizens who expressed sympathy with terrorists. As it was, they did little worth recording. Politicians in the 1997–2010 Labour government became notorious for issuing bloodcurdling threats to please press and public, and then doing nothing. Their attempt to restrict freedom of speech in wartime was no exception to the rule. The handful of cases where the state attempted to censor alleged Islamist sympathisers showed only how far Britain was from martial law.

Managers at Nottingham University reported a student to the police for downloading an al Qaeda training manual. It turned out that the material was freely available in the US, and that the suspect was researching rather than practising terrorism. He was released without charge, and successfully sued the police for false arrest. The courts jailed five men from Bradford who had down-loaded pro-jihadi sermons featuring all the usual hatreds. The Court of Appeal freed them on the Millian grounds that in England the state should prosecute you for what you did, not for what you read. The strangest case was that of a young Muslim woman who worked at Heathrow Airport, a likely terrorist target. She collected books on how to poison, shoot and bomb, and wrote poems in praise of murder. In 'How to Behead', she said:

> No doubt that the punk will twitch and scream
> But ignore the donkey's ass
> And continue to slice back and forth
> You'll feel the knife hit the wind and food pipe
> But don't stop
> Continue with all your might.

She was in love with death, but there was no evidence that she was involved in terrorism, and the court gave her a suspended prison sentence. Her mild punishment, which was subsequently overturned by the Court of Appeal, stood out because sentences for any kind of anti-government speech were so rare. Western democracies managed to fight without imposing restrictions on freedom of speech. Instead of Orwell's 'war atmosphere', there was an anti-war atmosphere. If the government had wanted to charge those who said that Islamist violence had nothing to do with Islamist ideology and was solely a response to Western provocation, it would have had to arrest a quarter of the public and three-quarters of the intelligentsia.

Meanwhile, Orwell's world of media monoliths that writers must appease if they wished to be published vanished. The BBC's monopoly was broken in the 1950s. By the 2000s, there were hundreds of TV channels and radio stations. If a writer, producer, journalist or actor crossed the BBC, it no longer meant an end to a broadcasting career. Newspapers remained under the control of corporations and plutocrats, but the

Internet so undermined what power they had that by the 2010s media commentators were wondering if the 'dead tree' or 'legacy' press could survive.

The Net achieved more than that. For all his fame as a futurologist, Orwell never predicted a final change. Enthusiasts hailed the Internet as the most important advance in communications technology since the invention of movable type in the 1450s. They may have been right, although it is too early to say. When they went on to announce, however, that the new age of transparency would free humanity from the constraints imposed by political power, they endorsed a faith as utopian as the communism that Orwell opposed.

Welcome to Utopia

In 1996, as the jubilation about the possibilities of the new technology was building, John Perry Barlow, a former lyricist for the Grateful Dead, stood as defiantly as Martin Luther and issued a thunderous manifesto. His audience was not a revolutionary crowd outside a dictator's palace, but the politicians and CEOs meeting at the global elite's annual beanfeast at Davos in the Swiss Alps. The object of his protest was as bewildering as its location: a proposal from the Clinton administration to deregulate the telecommunications industry.

The president was as prepared to annul America's old controls on cross-media ownership, as he was willing to shred the old restrictions on bank ownership. But Barlow had no complaints about corporations funding the politicians who passed the laws that increased corporate control of the airwaves. What stirred his passion and ignited his radical rage was a rider to the main Bill. Christian conservatives had insisted that there should be provisions to control the circulation of indecent material on the Internet. Their protests were ludicrous posturings to please the Christian core vote. As they must have known, their planned censorship conflicted with the First Amendment. The Supreme Court duly stuck down the measure as unconstitutional. But Congress's suggestion that democratic legislatures might regulate the Internet, even though in this instance they could not, provoked Barlow to issue a ferocious denunciation of the futility of state regulation, which must have pleased the bankers and executives enjoying the Alpine air.

'Governments of the Industrial World,' his Declaration of Independence of Cyberspace began, 'you weary giants of flesh and steel, I come from Cyberspace, the new home of Mind. On behalf of the future, I ask you of the past to leave us alone. You are not welcome among us. You have no sovereignty where we gather … We are creating a world that all may enter without privilege or prejudice accorded by race, economic power, military force, or station of birth. We are creating a world where anyone, anywhere may express his or her beliefs, no matter how singular, without fear of being coerced into silence or conformity. I declare the global social space we are building to be naturally independent of the tyrannies you seek to impose on us. You have no moral right to rule us nor do you possess any methods of enforcement we have true reason to fear.'

Barlow cut a ridiculous figure: 'a Deadhead in Davos' who dressed an argument for unregulated markets in the clothes of red revolution. 'Barlow may have sounded like an alienated counter-culturist as he railed against the Telecoms Act,' wrote the left-wing American critic Thomas Frank, 'but he essentially agreed with the suit-and-tie media execs on the big issue – that markets enjoyed some mystic, organic connection to the people, while governments were fundamentally illegitimate.'

Everyone with knowledge of recent history now realises that Clinton's deregulation of the banks led to a disaster, and new controls are essential. But most people who think about censorship agree with Barlow that attempting to censor what appears on the Net is not only pernicious but pointless.

What seemed in the mid-1990s to be the burblings of the plutocracy's pet hippy is the conventional wisdom of our day. The Internet had rendered traditional diplomacy obsolete, declared a wide-eyed Parag Khanna of the New America Foundation, a think tank for futurologists. There is no point worrying about old-style foreign policy, because non-governmental organisations and ad hoc networks linked by social media will soon replace it. Networking will achieve 'universal liberation' – no less – 'through exponentially expanding and voluntary interconnections'. The liberators will not be philosophers, the radicalised masses or political leaders, but celebrities, who 'possess one of the core ingredients of diplomatic success: prestige'. He held out the example of Madonna to convince doubters: 'Her resilience and tirelessness [are] the reasons why she remains at the top of her game. Regular diplomats should learn from her staying power.' Gordon Brown said that the new technologies ensured that 'foreign policy can no longer be the province of just a few elites'. The world was becoming a global village, where 'you cannot have Rwanda again because information would come out far more quickly about what is actually going on and public opinion would grow to the point where action would need to be taken'. It never occurred to Brown that a genocide comparable to Rwanda had taken place in Darfur in western Sudan in 2003, and the wired world had done nothing to stop it. Hillary Clinton and many others believed that dictatorships would soon go the way of genocidal militias. If a despotic regime censored the Net, its businesses would not have access to global sources of news, and their trade would suffer, she argued. They must allow the free flow of information or pay the economic price, because 'from an economic standpoint, there is no distinction between censoring political speech and commercial speech'.

The Internet inspires such ecstatic visions because it feels as if it has rolled all previous communications technologies into one. The experience of using it crosses all the old boundaries.

The reader becomes a writer by commenting on other people's work. The writer becomes a reader by looking at other people's comments. One minute the audience is passive, as if it were reading an old-fashioned book or watching a twentieth-century film, music video or television programme; the next it is active: intervening, copying, linking and recommending. Readers who are writers and writers who are readers can speak to each other personally, as if they were using a telephone. But they can extend their range of contacts beyond the possibilities of ordinary social life on social-network sites. Through trawling personal blogs, Facebook or Twitter they can listen in to private conversations between friends as if they were spies tapping a phone. Yet if they stumble across an obscure piece of writing, or a video that interests them, they can make the private public by linking to it. If enough people copy their link, they will have created a viral phenomenon, as if they were an A&R man discovering a new talent. Because they can copy and upload information painlessly, they can build sites in a day with more words than a Victorian novelist could produce in a lifetime. Because they can allow crowd sourcing and Wiki editing, they can gather more opinions than the compilers of the *Oxford English Dictionary* or the *Encyclopaedia Britannia* had at their disposal.

No wonder the new technologies went to people's heads, and they began to believe that the citizen was 'no longer a passive consumer of political information and occasional voter, but an active player monitoring what governments and politicians were doing and demanding a seat at the table'.

Beyond these attractions lay a wonderful gift: working on the Net was no more expensive than the price of a laptop or a session in an Internet café. The communist-influenced intelligentsia Orwell despised may have denied some of the greatest mass murders in history, lied so often it no longer understood the difference between truth and falsehood, and disgraced socialist politics irredeemably, but it had one good argument: freedom of the press was a hollow ideal when freedom came at such a high price. Only wealthy men and corporations with access to capital, or governments with access to taxes, could afford to run a newspaper, television or radio station. Only they could hire professional journalists, with the skills required to deliver news in the limited time and space available, and the star performers who could attract a mass audience. Like the joke about capitalist freedom guaranteeing everyone an equal right to book a room at the Ritz, freedom of the press meant freedom for Orwell's private tycoons and state-funded broadcasters.

Now the costs of publication were effectively nothing, the space available was effectively limitless, and the potential audience was an ever-increasing proportion of the world's population. Journalists felt as obsolete as blacksmiths – the products of an outdated technology which required a now-redundant professional caste. Blogging, online videos and podcasts meant that everybody could be a journalist, broadcaster or artist. If they produced material the public wanted to read or see, they did not, in theory, need a promotional budget to attract attention – search engines and links would direct readers to them. If they wanted to share their interest in a hobby or an obscure political cause they did not need to buy special-interest magazines, because the same processes allowed them to connect to others. No one needed an editor or a proprietor's permission to publish. No gatekeepers kept out innovators or writers. Even if conglomerates such as Apple are beginning to restrict what the public can read on the Net, they do not for the time being have anything like the influence of the old press barons.

Supporters and opponents alike overestimated proprietors' power to sway the electorate even in the media moguls' heyday, but what influence proprietors had became negligible when the new technologies subverted their business plans and smashed their control of the news agenda. The economic facts of publishing life were on the side of the many, not the few. In every advanced country, millions of people could scrutinise elected and unelected power with an intensity the old media could not manage, and publish their findings.

Consider how the terms of trade for investigative journalism had changed. In the twentieth century, journalists who tried to persuade state or corporate officials to give them classified documents faced many obstacles that still exist. Then as now, they had to convince them to risk their careers. They had to prove to them that they were worthy of their trust, and would protect their anonymity in all circumstances. But computer processing power has rendered a fearsome logistical difficulty irrelevant. Until the 1990s, journalist and informant faced the physical problem of copying. Suppose, in the late twentieth century, a source in the British House of Commons had wanted to leak approximately 1.2 million receipts to the *Daily Telegraph* that revealed how MPs were claiming expenses for everything from the cost of cleaning their moats to duckhouses for their ponds. Or think of a disillusioned soldier in the American military who wanted to leak 251,287 documents recounting the conversations between the US State Department and its embassies. Even in the unlikely event of the information all being in one building that the source had access to, he would still have to go through dozens of filing cabinets without arousing suspicion. He would have to photocopy on site or 'borrow' every piece of paper, and again hope that his colleagues did not begin to suspect what he intended to do with the information. Even if he fooled them, either he would need a truck to move the documents out of the building in one go, or he would have to divide them into manageable batches and walk past police officers or military guards hundreds of times. In both cases, the likelihood of them stopping and checking his load would be so high as to be a deterrent in itself.

Suppose he overcame his fear, duped everyone in his building and transported his documents to a newspaper office. Its editors would be able to publish just a small part of what he had given them in an old-fashioned print newspaper – assuming, that is, the authorities allowed the editor to publish, and did not threaten the paper with court action or worse.

Before the Net, just one information dump made it from behind the security fence to the press: the Pentagon Papers, a secret study prepared by the US Defense Department which Daniel Ellsberg leaked in 1971 to show how the Johnson administration of the 1960s had lied about the course of its disastrous Vietnam War. The papers made up forty-seven volumes. Their two million words filled four thousand pages of original documents and three thousand pages of analysis. The US government was so conscious of the damage the secret history of the war could do, it had printed just fifteen copies. Fortunately for Ellsberg, he could target a copy that was not in the Pentagon or another heavily guarded military base, but was kept at the offices of the RAND Corporation, a think tank where he worked. Ellsberg had access to the papers, and with the help of a friend spent three months in the autumn of 1971 carrying documents in his briefcase to a safe flat, and returning them before anyone noticed their absence. The task of copying them was so lengthy he co-opted his children to help. If he had leaked secret information of comparable sensitivity in any other major power in the 1970s, he would never have seen it published. The Russians and the Chinese would have shot him and the journalists who helped him. The French and the British would have arrested them. As it was, the editors of the *New York Times* and other American papers who ran his stories had to fight in court to assert the rights of the free press that the First Amendment to the US Constitution guaranteed. Now, if you have security clearance or can hack a system, you can simply copy documents to a memory stick and slip it in your pocket.

The traditional enemies of freedom of thought could attempt to manage information when it came via a few publishers and broadcasters with assets to seize, and editors and publishers they could fine and imprison. If the *Daily News* published an attack on its government in the twentieth century, the authorities knew before they knew anything else that it had originated in the offices of the *Daily News*, and that they could hold the paper to account. Mass-circulation titles had to deliver millions of copies overnight. They had to publish in the countries they covered, and submit to the jurisdiction of national authorities.

Today, if the law stops you publishing in your own country, you can publish abroad and still reach your target audience. WikiLeaks based itself in Sweden because of that country's exceptionally strong legal protections for journalists, and was well aware that the constraints of geography no longer limited its ability to distribute news. It installed military-grade encryption on its laptops to prevent secret services breaking into its systems, and instructed its workers to speak to each other on protected Skype networks. To say that journalists in the twentieth century did not enjoy such advantages is to understate the case. The CIA and the KGB did not enjoy them either. When John Perry Barlow announced in the 1990s that governments did not 'possess any methods of enforcement we have true reason to fear', he appeared to have seen beyond the constraints governments placed on the writers of the time to a free future.

Nor did twentieth-century reporters enjoy the advantages of unrestricted space. Thirty years ago, a news programme would rarely devote more than a couple of minutes to a subject, while a broadsheet newspaper rarely had the space to reproduce more than three or four pages from a stash of leaked documents. The editors would decide what was significant, and would make the wrong decisions on occasion. On the Net, you can run all the footage or reproduce all the documents in searchable format online, and leave it to thousands of readers, in some cases hundreds of thousands of readers, to examine every detail and look for significant facts and damning connections the best of editors or reporters might have missed.

The importance of viewing evidence can never be underestimated. Politicians worry more about video footage that makes them look ridiculous or a document that incriminates than the most scathing polemics, because they understand that direct evidence is more damning than any critical review. The Web allows more evidence to be presented to the court of public opinion than ever before.

Before I get to work, I should add that just because the Net inspires techno-utopian fantasies it does not mean the fantasies are always mistaken. To talk of a 'Twitter revolution' in Iran is to be wrong on both counts: Twitter had just twenty thousand subscribers in Iran in 2009, and the disgusting brutality of the clerical regime ensured there was no revolution. But when those same neophiliacs talked of the Arab Spring being made up of 'Facebook revolutions', they were not wholly deluded. Ahmed Maher, who launched the April 6 Youth Facebook group in Egypt, which linked bloggers and activists, did not create a mass movement on the Net. There were not enough users of Facebook in Egypt to form a mass movement. If you wanted to belittle April 6's achievements, you might say that the millions attracted to groups supporting fashionable causes in the West made the support the movement attracted seem paltry. But as an astute writer for *Wired* magazine said before the revolution, you cannot use the number of people from a democracy who click on an 'I like' button to damn the efforts of dissidents in dictatorships. 'In places like Egypt, these virtual gatherings are a big deal. Although freedom of speech and freedom of religion may be democracy's headliners, it's the less sexy-sounding freedom of assembly that, when prohibited, can effectively asphyxiate political organization. Uniting seventy thousand people is no easy feat in a country where collective action is so risky. Social networking has changed that. In turn, it is changing the dynamics of political dissent.'

The youth movement in Egypt was a new opposition force the regime did not understand. It had not been able to infiltrate its ranks or buy off its members, as it had always done with its traditional opponents. It understood the danger of individual bloggers, and arrested them, then tortured and sodomised them in prison. But it could not cope with a new form of political association which could mobilise demonstrators. In Syria, the heartbreaking bravery of the activists who risked their lives as they filmed the atrocities of the Ba'athist death squads would have counted for nothing if the Web had not allowed them to publish their videos. There, as in Iran and Egypt, the Web broke the dictatorship's illusion of omnipotence. Once dissenters sat in jails tormented by the knowledge that not only could their captors murder them, but the secret police could erase most of the records of their movements' struggles. The Web provides a space where no censor can wipe them from the record of history.

When the first popular hero of the revolution against the Egyptian dictatorship was Wael Ghonim, a Google executive, persecuted by the police for running a Facebook campaign of an opposition candidate, those who doubt the power of the Web have some explaining to do.

Clay Shirky, a typically can-do American optimist and the most engaging of the cyber-utopians, picked on the example of Belarus as he explored the apparently limitless possibilities for human freedom the Net had opened. This small country, squeezed between Russia and Poland, had experienced the worst the twentieth century could offer: Tsarism with its persecution of non-Russian minorities, most notably the Jews; the First World War and the terrible battles on the Eastern Front; the Russian Revolution; the civil war that followed it; Lenin's terror; Stalin's terror; Hitler's invasion and its massacres; the Holocaust; the terrible battles of the Soviet reconquest; and the return of Stalin's terror once the war was over. After Stalin's death, there was only a modest respite: the life-denying rulers of late-vintage Soviet communism governed the unlucky land.

The fall of the Berlin Wall liberated Eastern Europe, but not

Belarus. It broke away from Russia, but the local strongman Alexander Grigoryevich Lukashenko maintained a Brezhnevian state. He ruled 'the last dictatorship in Europe' by censoring the press, killing opposition leaders and rigging elections. The United States and the European Union protested, but what could they do? If the men with the guns do not want democratic change, it takes other men with guns to make them change their minds. The West was not going to invade. Russia, the regional superpower, tolerated the dictator, and there was no domestic military force capable of organising a revolution.

The Web appeared to lift the dead weight of history from the shoulders of the oppressed. 'The use of flash mobs as a tool of political protest has reached its zenith in Belarus,' Shirky said as he explained how citizens could organise against oppression in the most unpromising circumstances. The ability of Belarusian dissidents to arrange fast, spontaneous protests via online chatrooms and the community pages of LiveJournal inspired him. In 2006, after Lukashenko 'won' his third term with another rigged election, an anonymous activist working under the name of 'by_mob' proposed a demonstration. Instead of urging opponents of the regime to chant slogans, he suggested that they show up in central Minsk and eat ice cream. The police arrested them, as they arrested anyone engaged in unauthorised public gatherings. Activists retaliated by posting pictures on the Web of the cops leading away citizens for the anti-state crime of eating ice cream in a public place. Other flash mobs followed, and demonstrators caught the overreactions of the authorities on camera and posted them to an international audience. Before the gift of new technology, the state-controlled media would not publicise protests, nor would it report on them accurately afterwards – if at all. The local public and international observers need never know they had happened.

The new technology blew away the old advantages the state's media monopoly gave it. Anonymous bloggers could arrange demonstrations without revealing their identities. Anyone on the Net could read about them and come along, or read accounts of the protest afterwards and see pictures and videos taken with mobile phones. Meanwhile, Shirky thought, the knowledge that electronic eyes were monitoring them limited the brutality of the secret police. Understandably impressed, he said that the Belarusian protesters were showing us that the Web was delivering freedoms that men and women once needed liberal constitutions and democratic governments to guarantee. 'To speak online is to publish, and to publish online is to connect with others. With the arrival of globally accessible publishing, freedom of speech is now the freedom of the press and freedom of the press is freedom of assembly. Naturally the changes occasioned by new sources of freedom are most significant in a less free environment.'

He could not have been more wrong. The Net, like all previous revolutions in communications technology, will change the world. But, like all previous revolutions in communications technology, it will give advantages to those who already enjoy power and wealth. As well as empowering the citizens of democracies and dissidents in dictatorships, it empowers elected governments, dictatorial regimes, police forces, spies, employers, blackmailers, frauds, fanatics and terrorists. Meanwhile the ideology of the Net activists who command attention and admiration in the West can be a sly and parochial creed which actively works against the interests of Belarusian dissidents and all others living with oppression. Worst of all, those who claimed that the 'Age of Transparency' had dawned did not think about how censorship works. If they had, they would have grasped that those 'weary giants of flesh and steel' are tougher than they look. For there is one prediction about the next decade that one can make with certainty: after watching protests from the Belarus flash mobs to the Arab Spring, no dictatorship will make the mistake of ignoring social networking again.

RULES FOR CENSORS (7):

Look to the Past/Think of the Future

Cyber-utopians do not study history. If they did, they would not be utopians. The one story from the past they love to recall is the tale from the Middle Ages of Johannes Trithemius, Abbot of Sponheim near Bad Kreuznach in the Rhineland, and his unintentionally revealing polemic against Gutenberg's new printing presses.

The abbot venerated the traditions of the medieval scribes. With skill and persistence, they preserved the culture and the religious doctrines of medieval Europe by copying manuscripts which would otherwise have rotted away. Their labour was arduous, and their manuscripts were expensive; only the wealthiest individuals and institutions could afford a library. Gutenberg's movable type destroyed the scribes' monopoly and rendered their skills obsolete. For the first time, printers could make a copy of a book in less time than it took to read it. Like the Internet, the new presses of the 1450s were a revolution in communications technology, massively increasing the ability to view the written word.

The loss of his old culture appalled the abbot. Rude mechanicals with elementary skills were supplanting holy men who had studied for years to master the art of producing illuminated manuscripts. The abbot's polemic against the new technology, *De Laude Scriptorum* ('In Praise of Scribes'), dwelt on the producer interest of the scribes. The wider interests of readers and authors did not concern him. He did not write about how movable type allowed an explosion in the number of books and the number of writers who could reach an audience. He did not praise the printing press for allowing readers to purchase books at a fraction of the cost of illuminated manuscripts, or for encouraging the spread of literacy. Instead the abbot praised the art of copying for allowing monks to spend their time enlightening their minds and lifting their hearts as they painfully transcribed the scriptures in monastic solitude.

To the delight of all who tell the story, the abbot did not send his manuscript to the monks so that they might labour in their cells scratching out copies by candlelight. He wanted as many people as possible to read his denunciation of the new technology. So naturally, when he completed his manuscript in 1492, he sent it to the printers, who set it in movable type so he could produce his book denouncing the press and praising scribes quickly and cheaply, and ensure that everyone who wanted to read it could obtain a copy.

A merry little tale the abbot's hypocrisy has made. Enthusiasts for the Web use it to mock the 'reactionary cant' of today's gatekeepers as they try to resist the new expressions of democratic will and personal fulfilment Web 2.0 brings. As a putdown for practitioners of my grubby trade of journalism, I accept that it is hard to better. But I notice that the excursion into history stops almost as soon as it begins. No one goes on to say what happened to Europe after Gutenberg's presses began to roll.

Let me attempt to fill in the gaps. Try to imagine a fifteenth-century Clay Shirky or Julian Assange. Suppose he is a young monk at Sponheim, and is so enthused by the promise of the new presses that he blows a raspberry at the abbot and renounces holy orders to join the 'Gutenberg revolution' that is promising to bring 'a new age of transparency' to late-medieval Europe. If he predicted that printing would vastly increase the number of people who could write books, the subjects they could cover and the size of their potential audience, he would have been stating the obvious. If he imitated today's Net boosters, and predicted that generals would be less likely to massacre civilians because the new technology would spread word of their crimes, later events would disappoint him. The slaughters of the post-Gutenberg wars of religion between Catholics and Protestants in the sixteenth and seventeenth centuries were catastrophic crimes against humanity that foreshadowed the barbarism of the total wars of the twentieth century. They tore the heart out of Europe, killing perhaps a quarter of all Germans and laying waste to areas of Central Europe to such a degree that many towns never recovered. Although printing helped the Protestant cause by allowing Bibles to be distributed in native tongues, countries that saw Protestantism triumph at the wars' end did not experience a blossoming of free speech or a flowering of civilised values. In Oliver Cromwell's England and John Calvin's Geneva, Protestants were as censorious as the Catholic monarchies in France and Spain, and equally determined to persecute heretics, witches and dissenters.

And if our neophiliac monk had been so foolish as to think that print would encourage political liberty, he would have been history's fool. The most striking feature of Europe from the fifteenth to the eighteenth centuries was the rise of royal absolutism in France, Castile, Prussia and Russia, and the emasculation or abolition of the medieval estates and parliaments. France had a revolution in 1789, but the Jacobin terror and the Napoleonic Empire followed. You cannot say that France achieved anything resembling a stable, liberal democracy that protected free speech until 1871. Most of Western Europe did not achieve that goal until 1945. Eastern Europe was not free until 1989. Russia is still waiting. Our freedoms are an exception, not a norm.

Absolute monarchs could live with the printing press. They could censor opponents of the established order by licensing printers or sending critics to jail for their uncomfortably enlightened views, and – here is where everyone gets the radical possibilities of new technologies hopelessly wrong – they could *use* the presses to produce propaganda on behalf of the monarchical order and its religion. The works of political and religious dissenters could still be smuggled into the country, but as long as their circulation was small, monarchs were secure.

Nazism, communism and George Orwell's depiction of Airstrip One in *Nineteen Eighty-Four* have such a hold on our minds that we forget that most dictatorships do not want *total* control, but *effective* control. Their modus operandi is closer to France under Louis XIV or Russia under Nicholas I than to the Soviet Union or Nazi Germany. As in the Europe of the absolute monarchs, most modern dictatorships effectively license publishers, broadcasters and Internet service providers. They tell them they can make money as long as they protect the interests of the regime. Material from dissidents circulates, but its authors and publishers must live with continual harassment.

Vladimir Putin's Russia is typical of dictatorships old and new. It does not try to censor everything. The regime understands that the total control of communism failed because it suppressed too much. On a personal level, the men at the top in the Kremlin do not want to go back to a time when the bribes they received were worth little because the luxuries of capitalism were on the other side of an iron curtain. Their underlings, meanwhile, have no nostalgia for the 1930s and '40s, when Stalin murdered loyal apparatchiks who were working in jobs that look disturbingly like theirs. The elite wants a safe and profitable autocracy, and will tolerate dissent as long as its effects are limited.

Opposition journalists in Russia can find work, and the Net provides an important space for critical thought. But the Kremlin controls the main sources of information, and never lets its critics forget that freedom of thought comes at a price. As in England and the old American South, libel is used to intimidate the enemies of the powerful – Art Troitsky, the country's bravest music critic, faced defamation suits that could cost him millions of roubles and his liberty for mocking police officers who cover up the crimes of the oligarchs and artists who suck up to the governing clique. As in Western Europe, apparently liberal laws the authorities say are aimed against the hate crimes of extremists suffocate wider debates. Edward Lucas, a historian of the return of Russian autocracy, described their potential to harass thus:

> The radio station Ekho Moskvy has maintained its feisty journalistic tone. Its editor, Aleksei Venediktov, says that he will fire any staff he sees practising self-censorship. It broadcasts interviews with hated figures such as the American-educated president of Estonia, and opposition leaders. It is a refuge for independent-minded journalists who would scarcely gain airtime elsewhere. But in just two months of 2007, Ekho Moskvy received fifteen letters from prosecutors invoking the extremism law. Why was the station carrying interviews with such provocative figures? Even an editor as gutsy as Mr Venediktov, a hippy-like workaholic with a burning faith in press freedom, may not withstand such pressure for long.

As in democratic countries, a corporation that wants government favours makes sure its newspapers and its websites do not offend the mighty. The difference between Russia and a free society is that there is no prospect of the government changing, and the Kremlin's ability to punish businesses that cross it includes the seizing of its assets and the jailing of its journalists. Businesses with close links to the Kremlin buy critical TV stations. The new owners sideline the old editors, and the coverage becomes a lot less critical. *New Times*, one of the few independent weeklies left in Russia, hired an editor the Kremlin disapproved of. The regime made its feelings clear to the proprietor. She refused to find an acceptable replacement, but advertisers rewarded her stand on principle by taking their custom elsewhere. Once the authorities had made their unhappiness plain, giving *New Times* money 'would be commercial suicide in a business climate where official disfavour means harassment by every state agency, followed usually by bankruptcy'.

In these conditions, the best one can say about the existence of opposition websites and newspapers is that they are an advance on the blanket repression of the communist era. To exaggerate their importance is to ignore the fact that supporters of the Kremlin so dominate the old and the new media that no opposition candidate can reach a mass audience. Worse, it is to misunderstand the nature of censorship.

Putin and his mafia friends do not worry overmuch that their opponents can publish somewhere in cyberspace or in a few highbrow journals, as long as they cannot break away from the fringe and reach the mainstream. State harassment, up to and including the murder of journalists, ensures that dissidents know the consequences of 'going too far'. Similarly, Bashar Assad's Syria, Hosni Mubarak's Egypt and the Islamists they supported did not care that anyone with access to the Net could find the Danish cartoons of 2005 with the click of a mouse. It was enough that newspapers and book publishers refused to run them, and that other artists and writers who might have satirised religion thought again before doing so. The persecutors of Ayaan Hirsi Ali wanted to silence her dissenting voice permanently. When they failed, they too were prepared to settle for warning Muslim and ex-Muslim women of the high price they might pay if they spoke out against misogyny. Go back to Roman Polanski and the Russian, Ukrainian and Saudi oligarchs England's wretched legal profession welcomed to the High Court in London. They would, if they could, have wiped every unflattering word about them from the Web. A few tried, but for the rest the readiness of the English judiciary to punish their critics and announce that they were men of good reputation was compensation enough.

Writers in the West have already found that the Web does not set them free. Like the Gutenberg press, the Web has hugely expanded the number who can publish – and shown that while it is not true that everyone has a book inside them, they most certainly have a blog. But to reach an audience you must find a way of making yourself heard above the cacophony of millions of competing voices, and understand the importance of putting your name to your work.

An anonymous blogger can print a leaked document or run a denunciation of an abuse of power. But if the abuse is to be tackled, then the blogger or the people who have read his or her work must go out and campaign for change in public. Those who throw off the coward's cloak of anonymity find the law of the land applies as much to them as to anyone else. If they live in a dictatorship, they run into the secret police. If they live in a democracy, they face legal constraints, and find that all the old arguments about what the law should allow or punish acquire a pressing importance.

A refrain heard in the Ryan Giggs and Simon Singh affairs was that individually, each writer or tweeter is too small to go after. Collectively, there are too many of them. That has not been true in all cases. In Britain, libel lawyers use Google alerts to flag every mention of their clients. As soon as Google draws their attention to unfavourable coverage by bloggers, they threaten critics with writs. The costs of English libel law are beyond the means of many newspapers, let alone individual bloggers, and in all but two of the many examples I know of, the blogger has retracted rather than run the risk of litigation.

The Net gives writers in democracies new tools, but it does not spare them the burden of campaigning, lobbying and enlisting support that their predecessors in the analogue age had to carry. As they try to organise reform movements, they may find that the decline of the old media is not wholly benign. The Net's advantages are palpable. Online communities can devote more space to airing grievances than television stations and newspapers ever could. The achievements of Web-based campaigns against corruption in India and child abuse in the Catholic Church speak for themselves. Mass-circulation newspapers and national television stations in free countries, however, can put a country's political class under overwhelming pressure. That power is fading. Replacing gatekeepers' quasi-monopolies with the myriad of sites on the Net also means replacing one knock-out punch with hundreds of jabs. The powerful of the future may find it easier to ignore the pinpricks of little websites than the bludgeon of the mass media.

Meanwhile, politically active Westerners can find that the Web seduces them away from the public they need to influence. It gives them unrestricted freedom, and then denies them the audience that makes freedom effective. The Web has made it easier for them to write than ever before – and easier still to be ignored. Potentially, anyone writing on the Web can reach a global audience. In practice, hardly anyone ever does.

The Web keeps the politically committed on sites which confirm their prejudices, and never forces them to tackle a wider society that has little interest in or knowledge of their political ideas. As for wider society, when there were only a few television channels, the mass audience had little choice but to watch national news programmes. Now they can surf the multi-media world, and avoid all contact with current-affairs journalism. The Web and satellite television risk confining interest in the vital concerns of the day to a minority of politically engaged hobbyists.

Evgeny Morozov, the most bracing critic of modern optimism, emphasises the anaesthetising effects of perpetual amusement. People use new means of communication not to engage in political activism, but to find entertainment. The Net is no exception, and has increased the opportunities for the masses to find pleasing diversions to a level that no one had previously imagined possible. In Russia, China, Vietnam and the other formerly puritan communist countries, the decision by the new market-orientated regimes to allow Western-style media to provide high-quality escapism, sport, dating and gossip sites was a smart move that made their control of the masses more effective. In Belarus, Morozov discovered Internet service providers that were offering free downloads of pirated movies and music. The dictatorship 'could easily put an end to such practices, [but] prefers to look the other way and may even be encouraging them'. Unlike so many who write about the Net, Morozov was brought up in a dictatorship – Belarus, as it happens – and the knowledge that freedom is hard to win explains his impatience with wishful thinking.

I hope I am not making the insulting error of pretending that democracies are as oppressive as dictatorships – such comparisons are the self-pitying and self-dramatising whines of spoilt Western children. I am merely saying that the Web cannot free individuals from the need to challenge the constraints of politics, law and popular indifference, whatever system governs their country. Writers in democracies have fewer constraints, and for that we should be more grateful than we are. But if we want to achieve political change, the new possibilities of reaching and talking to people are offset by the difficulties in breaking out of the ghetto and preaching to the unconverted.

Meanwhile, the Net-induced death of dictatorial systems is far from certain, or even likely. They can adapt, as absolutist regimes have always adapted. They may indeed find the task of controlling easier, because of one benefit the Net brings that none of the old communications systems offered.

With the exception of North Korea, modern dictatorships are not as oppressive as the Stalinist state Orwell dissected in the

1940s. On one point, though, he almost predicted the future. Every reader of *Nineteen Eighty-Four* remembers the 'telescreens' the party installed in homes, that had the potential to watch every movement and record every sound.

Early in the novel, Winston Smith half-heartedly attempts the mandatory morning exercises. He assumes that no one is watching him, and allows his mind to wander, when:

> 'Smith!' screamed the shrewish voice from the telescreen. '6079 Smith W.! Yes, YOU! Bend lower, please! You can do better than that. You're not trying. Lower, please! THAT'S better, comrade. Now stand at ease, the whole squad, and watch me.'

Orwell's image of a dictatorship that could turn televisions into spies in the home never became a reality.

Computers, on the other hand ...

EIGHT

The Internet and the Counter-Revolution

Polish border guards were put on alert when they received orders to detain a runaway herd of several hundred cows, which swam across the Bug River from Belarus to Poland. Belarusian authorities now plan to build a fence to prevent livestock from crossing the EU's longest eastern border into Poland.

RADIO POLONIA, OCTOBER 2006

In the summer of 2010, actors from the Belarus Free Theatre landed in London looking like time travellers from another century. They were dressed in shabby clothes. They smoked cigarettes, and wondered why people tutted so. Their hosts were old-timers too, with records of solidarity with those struggling against dictatorship that stretched back into the Cold War. Index on Censorship, an organisation Stephen Spender founded in 1972 to help dissidents in the old Soviet bloc, greeted them. Tom Stoppard, who had written some of his finest plays about communist oppression, praised their bravery. It was as if nothing had changed since Stoppard was defending Václav Havel in the 1970s.

The stories the company told had an equally traditional feel. Natalia Koliada, its founder, described how the secret police had threatened her and her husband, and forced the company to perform in private houses or in the woods before audiences she had to vet to ensure they did not contain informers. Koliada had an ironic intelligence and an open heart. Even as she talked about her family's suffering, she could not stay glum for long. The absurdity of the dictatorship matched its cruelty, and she was soon bursting into astonished laughter. The company rejoiced in the story of how a herd of Belarusian cows had made a mass break for freedom and swum the River Bug to escape to Poland. Polish border guards had captured and deported the beasts back across the frontier, and the Belarusian authorities had promised to build a fence to keep them in. The human parallels the story offered of an unconcerned world cooperating with a dictatorship were too good for the theatre's writers to miss.

Koliada said that I should never forget that even in Russia the regime renamed the KGB the 'FSB' because of the unfortunate memories the old initials aroused. 'Not so in Belarus. Our dictator still calls our secret police the KGB. The nature of their job has not changed, why change the name? At least he's honest.'

That was the only honesty on offer. The censors and the censored had to play elaborate games, in which neither could admit their true motives. The actors had to pretend they wished to stage a work for artistic reasons, and not because they wanted to criticise the regime. The censors had to pretend that there were no reasons why any rational Belarusian would wish to criticise the regime, and yet find reasons for banning the work anyway.

One of the first plays the company tried to perform was *4.48 Psychosis* by Sarah Kane, a wrenching dramatisation of depression the British playwright completed just before she committed suicide in 1999, at the age of twenty-eight. (4.48 a.m. was the time her night terrors awoke her.)

The censor was in a quandary. He knew why the Free Theatre was drawn to Kane, and why the audience would appreciate the work. Along with prostitution and industrial injuries, mental illness stands at an extremely high level in Belarus. But as a functionary of Lukashenko's dictatorship, the censor could not accuse the company of trying to highlight a social evil the regime presided over, because that would mean admitting that mental illness *was* at an extremely high level in Belarus. He thought hard before passing judgement.

'You can't show it, because there is no depression in Belarus.'

'We're not saying there is,' the actors replied sweetly. 'Sarah Kane was British, so if any government is being criticised it is the British government.'

The logic of their argument stumped the censor for a moment. Then he rallied.

'Ah, but people who see the play may *think* that there is depression in Belarus – even though there isn't – so I'm still banning it.'

Andrei Sannikov, whose good manners and carefully chosen words signalled that he had once worked as a diplomat, accompanied the actors to London. He was preparing to stand as an opposition candidate in the December 2010 elections, and was trying to mobilise indifferent European publics to the Belarusian opposition's cause. He and his friends acknowledged that the Internet helped the opposition at home and abroad. It hosted their websites, and allowed them to mobilise domestic and international support. On occasion hundreds of thousands of people read articles on the Charter 97 dissident site. The Free Theatre told audiences of upcoming performances through blogs. The flash mobs which so impressed Westerners also inconvenienced the police. I will not pretend that the Net made no difference. For the Belarusian as for the Arab opposition, it gave them a new and welcome advantage. When the crunch came, however, it was as if it had never been invented. Belarusians learned the hard way that it takes a little more than flash mobs to shift a tyranny.

Before the election campaign began, Sannikov's press secretary committed suicide by hanging himself. Or that is what the police said. Sannikov did not believe a word of it. There was no suicide note, and his friend had not been depressed in the days before his death, but was looking forward to the coming struggle. Opponents of the regime had a habit of 'disappearing', and Sannikov had good reasons for fearing the worst.

The regime rigged the December 2010 election, and demonstrators came out onto the streets. A ferocious police response met them. Contrary to the predictions of Net utopians, phones that could upload to YouTube in no way inhibited the police, or caused them to worry about what outsiders might think, any more than they restrained the behaviour of the forces of the clerical regime in Iran or the Ba'athist regime in Syria when they turned on the revolutionaries. The police set on every demonstrator they could find. They arrested the entire staff of Charter 97, along with a thousand others. They marched Natalia Koliada to a prison van – 'a kind of mobile jail' – where they made her lie face-down. 'It was dark inside, and I couldn't see a thing. The guard said, "My only dream is to kill you; if you so much as move you'll feel my baton all over your body, you animal." Then he threatened to rape me.' In every corridor of the jail they took her to 'men were standing facing the walls with their hands behind their backs. It was like a scene out of films about fascism.' Perhaps the regime did not realise that it had captured a prize target – either that or a KGB clerk bungled the paperwork. When they arraigned Koliada in court the next day, they charged her under someone else's name with a minor offence. She escaped with a fine, and got out of the country.

They made no mistakes with Andrei Sannikov. The police picked him out at the post-election demonstration. They beat him with truncheons, and held the crowd back so it could not come to his aid. The KGB took his wife too, and once they were in jail they worked out a bestial way to destroy their sanity. The couple had left their three-year-old son with his grandparents. The police threatened to snatch the child and put him into state care, a tactic they had tried previously with Koliada's twelve-year-old daughter.

When they sentenced Sannikov to five years' hard labour for 'organising mass disturbances', spectators in the courtroom cried out, 'Andrei, you are our president!' Battered but dignified, Sannikov declared his support for democracy, the rule of law and enforceable international standards of behaviour from the dock: 'We all want one thing – to live in our own country, participate in fair elections and not to fear for our lives or the lives of our loved ones. That's exactly why we are being tried today, facing fabricated evidence from those who ignored the law. I want to warn all those who neglected the law today – you are bound to appear in court and incur deserved punishment. What's worse – you will inevitably have to look into the eyes of your children.'

They will have to look into the eyes of their children. Whether they will receive the punishments they so well deserve is an open question, whose answer depends on political calculations. Will the growing economic crisis push the populace into revolt? Will Russia abandon its support for the dictator? Whatever scenario one imagines, it is hard to imagine the Net making a decisive difference. As in democracies, the new technologies do not just allow citizens of dictatorships to expand their knowledge. They also help the authorities control the population. With people as with cattle, electric fences can always contain them.

Welcome to Dystopia

An age of revolution provokes counter-revolution, as elites fight to hold on to power. Their success in crushing democratic movements ought to destroy the whimsical notion that technology determines political freedom. The Iranian and Belarusian regimes suppressed the opposition with the utmost brutality – and survived the revolt. The Syrian and Bahraini governments taught demonstrators that if they took to the streets they would kill them. In Libya, the revolutionaries required the support of the full force of NATO air power before they could overthrow the dictatorship. If in Egypt the Muslim Brotherhood and the army unite to form a common reactionary front, the Egyptians will find that revolution has replaced a bad regime with a worse one – as the Russians found after 1917 and the Iranians after 1979.

Liberals have been able to use the Internet in the struggles of our time. Like the printing presses, it has opened novel possibilities. But the Net does not make democratic change inevitable, because liberalism's enemies can use it as well. As with all other advances in communications technology, the Net adds to the influence of those who already possess it.

Dissidents in China, like dissidents in dictatorial regimes everywhere, welcome the Web. It allows environmental campaigns and protests against official incompetence that would once have been impossible – although it is worth noting that liberal bloggers avoid full-frontal attacks on the Communist Party.

The most popular sites in China offer entertainment, not politics, however, and the authorities see no reason to stop the masses losing themselves in escapism and fantasy. Overwhelmingly, those sites that cater for the niche current affairs market are not written by liberal bloggers, but by nationalists and authoritarian party-liners. They criticise the government not for denying human rights, but for not asserting China's interests with sufficient ruthlessness. The most sinister sites target dissidents. When a professor complained that the cult of Mao in China venerated a tyrant, who killed more people in the twentieth century than any other dictator, the hard-line Utopia website responded by collecting ten thousand signatures demanding that the police prosecute him for subversion. Utopia called him a 'capitalist running dog', 'cow ghost' and 'snake spirit' – insults that outsiders found quaint but that Chinese readers recognised as anathemas the party used to describe Mao's enemies when he began the massacres of the Cultural Revolution. Pro-regime websites, like pro-regime novelists, artists and journalists, face none of the harassment the state metes out to its political and religious opponents.

Liberals regarded China as an oddity after the fall of the Berlin Wall. History was over, and if the Chinese Communist Party wanted to continue to see its country grow, it would have to accept the democratic reforms that Westerners assumed the expanding middle class was bound to demand. When China grew into the world's second largest economic power, without the middle class demanding or the Communist Party granting democratic reforms, the deterministic argument changed. The Internet would now undermine communist rule, and the rule of all other repressive regimes. If dictatorial states tried to restrict and censor it, they would see their economies shrink as open societies reaped the economic benefit of free speech in cyberspace. The crash of 2008 ought to have thrown a bucket of cold water over the excited futurologists. Open societies suffered far more than closed regimes. A member of the Central Committee of the Chinese Communist Party was entitled to wonder why Americans were telling him he must allow free speech when China was booming and the First Amendment had not stopped debt-laden America going through a deep recession.

On a technical level, controlling the Net caused the party few headaches. From the beginning, the Chinese state had been able to dominate the medium, shape its growth, control its structure and limit its users' access to the rest of the world. With the cooperation of every large Western Web company except Google, China blocks the addresses of dissident sites or hijacks users' sessions when they search for suspicious words – 'Tibet' and

'Tiananmen' to name two. The state requires online censors – 'Big Mamas' – to remove politically sensitive postings in chat forums. (The cosy name for the not-so-cosy job comes from the title Chinese families accord to the wife of the eldest uncle, who has the responsibility of guiding and taking care of everyone else.)

Net censorship in China and elsewhere is a private–public partnership. After human-rights groups accused the American communications corporation Cisco of helping China construct firewalls and keyword-searching facilities, a bland spokeswoman was entirely unconcerned. 'Our customers determine the specific uses for the capabilities of these products,' she said. The company was doing what all good businesses must do, and keeping the customer satisfied. When Google pulled out of China after it found that hackers had broken into dissidents' accounts, presumably with state approval, no other Western technology company followed it. They were content to abide by the 'pledge of self-discipline' for the Chinese Internet industry, and to 'refrain from producing, posting or disseminating pernicious information that may jeopardize state security and disrupt social stability' in return for the chance of making money. China licenses Internet service and content providers in the same manner that authoritarian seventeenth-century governments licensed printers. The effects are the same. An official for Sohu. com, a Chinese search engine and content provider, admitted in the early days of the Net that his company was 'very much self-censoring', and would not link to news that might anger the Party.

Attacks on the complicity of Western corporations with censorship came regularly from human-rights groups, and only Google took notice. How long Westerners will have even a minimal capacity to influence decision-making in China and other authoritarian states is open to doubt. Western dominance of the Net cannot last. The speed with which the Chinese economy is growing will ensure that new censorship technologies are developed in an environment where human-rights groups are banned rather than politely ignored.

Authoritarian regimes and organisations do not just censor the Net – they mine it for information. On a scale greater than any other communications technology, the Net offers states the power to spy and to entrap. A traditional secret service that wanted to watch a target could tap his phone and open his mail. The technology was cheap, but listening to every call and reading every letter required agencies to employ teams of eavesdroppers, at considerable expense. If they wanted to hear private conversations, they needed to break into homes and bug them, and send trained agents to shadow the dissident to discover the identities of his contacts.

Now they can simply watch how suspects use the Web. If they can hack into their accounts, they can access all their contacts by monitoring their emails, Facebook friends and Twitter followers. 'Informants and covert surveillance are no longer required when we have vast databases, telecommunications companies, and Internet service providers who accumulate information on our political interests, hobbies, loves, hates, and fetishes,' concluded one security specialist as he looked at the new possibilities opening up for intelligence-gathering. Information is not scattered around in dusty filing cabinets, but collected in easily accessible and searchable files. You might object that true underground dissidents would act like al Qaeda terrorists, and send encrypted emails. The main targets of oppressive regimes are not always psychopaths or potential revolutionary leaders, however. Ordinary citizens concern them as much. Letting them fear that they are under surveillance has as much of a chilling effect on their engagement in political debate as punishments for dissident writers. The knowledge that the state is watching you, or might be watching you, is a powerful deterrent against activism.

The misnamed 'Twitter revolution' in Iran displayed the oppressive power of the new technologies. The authorities posted pictures of protesters on the Net, and asked supporters of the regime to identify them and hunt them down. They used text messages and email to warn Iranians of the dire consequences of 'being influenced by the destabilising propaganda which the media affiliated with foreign countries have been disseminating. In case of any illegal action and contact with foreign media, you will be charged as a criminal consistent with the Islamic Punishment Act.' At Tehran airport, passport control questioned Iranians who were leaving the country – maybe to go into political exile – about Facebook, and went onto their pages to note down the names of their friends.

In Belarus the state's agents have developed their own intimidatory techniques. They write threats beneath politically incorrect posts to spread fear, and act as agents provocateurs on the Web. 'It's very dangerous to be a blogger who writes against the regime,' says Natalia Koliada. 'The Belarusian regime has a special department of people who work at the KGB and Belarusian Republican Union of Youth to monitor the Net.'

Western companies that have supplied China with technology that can track dissidents justify themselves by saying that they sell the same technology to Western governments and organisations. Their implication that the power of the new surveillance technologies knows no borders is correct. In the free and unfree worlds alike, snoopers can accumulate information with a thoroughness that would have made their predecessors salivate.

A Janus-Faced Technology

Let a small incident, which seems trivial when set against the clashes in Belarus, China, the Arab world and Iran, illustrate the Janus-faced nature of the new technologies.

Paul Chambers worked in a car-parts factory in the north of England, and tweeted in his idle moments. His friends and the friends of a young woman from Northern Ireland overlapped. The two did not know each other, and lived far apart. They probably would never have met had not the social network brought them together. Their friends organised a Twitter party in a London pub to which everyone in the ad hoc network was invited. Boy met girl, and boy and girl liked each other very much. Chambers arranged to fly from Robin Hood airport in the East Midlands to see her in Belfast.

Technological advances allow sexual advances. The invention of the bicycle expanded the gene pool of many a remote region, as it allowed young men to cycle beyond their villages to find mates. In the 1950s, teenage couples appreciated the value of cars that took them away from their parents' homes more than any other demographic. At times today, the sole point of the Web seems to be to allow the dissemination of pornography or, in the case of social network sites, the arrangement of assignations. Chambers was embarking on a romance that Twitter had nurtured and enabled. Just as previously isolated dissidents in Belarus, Iran, Russia, the Middle East and China found that the Web allowed them to make previously impossible connections with political sympathisers, so Chambers found that the Web allowed him to form a connection with a woman he would otherwise never have met.

The joy the Web spread appears plain. But consider the sequel. Before he flew to Belfast, Chambers saw a news report that snow had grounded all flights. 'Robin Hood airport is closed,' he tweeted. 'You've got a week and a bit to get your shit together, otherwise I'm blowing the airport sky high!!'

I should not need to explain that he was joking; engaging in the mock-bombast people use in private conversation all the time. When a woman says to her friends, 'I'll strangle my boyfriend if he hasn't done the washing up,' or one man tells another, 'I'll kill my boss if he makes me work late and miss the match,' they are not announcing a murder. The forces of law and order can rest easy. They do not mean it.

Staff at Robin Hood airport once had to patrol its precincts looking out for unattended baggage, and liaise with the police about credible terrorist threats. The Net gave them new sources of information, and they began to search Twitter for mentions of the airport's name. When a manager came across Chambers' tweet, he passed it to security officers. They saw no reason to panic. They realised that Chambers had not posted a 'credible' threat. But the procedures stated that every 'threat' must be referred up the line, and the airport staff had to obey orders.

A plain-clothes detective arrived at Chambers' workplace and arrested him under anti-terrorist legislation. A posse of four more anti-terrorist officers was waiting in reception.

'Do you have any weapons in your car?' they asked.

'I said I had some golf clubs in the boot,' Chambers said. 'But they didn't think it was funny. I kept wondering, "When are they going to slap my wrists and let me go?" Instead, they hauled me into a police car while my colleagues watched.'

The sight of detectives arresting Chambers scandalised his employers. They sacked him. The police realised that he wasn't a terrorist, just a guy who wanted to see his girl. State prosecutors could not let the matter rest, however, and decided to charge him with sending menacing messages over a public telecommunications network, even though no one took the message seriously, and business had carried on at the airport as usual. The magistrate did not allow common sense to make one of its rare appearances in an English courtroom, and ordered Chambers to pay £1,000 in costs and fines.

Shaken but still determined to give the new relationship a try, Chambers eventually reached Northern Ireland. He and his new friend got on so well that he found work in Belfast and they settled down as a couple. But the case did not go away. The ham-fisted behaviour of the authorities caused outrage on the Web. Friends and strangers came together to urge him to appeal. The week before the case went back to court, he told his new employers in Northern Ireland that there could be renewed press interest in the bomb threat that never was when the hearing began. All they heard were the words 'bomb' and 'threat'. They fired him too.

Paul Chambers' story has become a *cause célèbre* in Britain, because it would once have been unimaginable for a man to lose two jobs for making one lame joke. Security guards at airports could not have listened in to the conversations of random members of the public who had given no reason to arouse suspicion, and would never have wanted to do so. Their employers would never have told them to hang around bars on the off-chance that they might hear someone say, 'If it doesn't get its shit together, I am going to blow the airport sky high,' in a moment of mock rage. Security guards might have spent a lifetime eavesdropping and never heard the offending words uttered.

Suddenly, technology had made the impossible possible, and the possible has a nasty habit of becoming mandatory.

The blessings and curses the Net bestowed on Paul Chambers serve as a wider metaphor. The future may be one of greater information-sharing and informed collective action as people exploit new resources, or one of suspicion as people understand the growing likelihood of surveillance. What happens will depend on where you live, what rights you have, and how persistently you and your fellow citizens engage in political struggles to defend or expand those rights.

All new forms of technology change societies, but how they change them depends on the limits the politics of those societies set.

The Primacy of Politics

Democratic governments are the natural targets for Net activists. It is easier to find and publish information in free societies that offer legal protections for press freedom. Rights to trial by jury ensure that even those writers who have broken the law can be spared punishment if they have taken on the state in the public interest. Sensible jurors do not like their rulers getting ideas above their station, and will acquit the technically guilty rather than do the state's bidding.

At the most basic level of protecting a writer's personal safety, democratic countries offer a further advantage. If you steal hundreds of thousands of documents from the Russian state and put them online, the FSB will try to kill you. Steal American secrets, and the CIA will not.

This mismatch between the coercive powers of democracies and dictators produces many morbid symptoms. The most prominent is the tendency of democratic elites to succumb to dictator-envy. Rather than despising their opponents, they despise the free traditions of their own countries. How, they wonder, can their decadent, flabby, argumentative societies defeat an enemy who fights to win and lets nothing stand in his way? They think that they can beat their enemy by imitating him, and do not realise that when they become their opponents they defeat themselves. A craving by the US government to have the same ability Islamist militias and Saddam Hussein possessed to torture suspects and hold them outside the Geneva Convention is the shortest and best explanation for the moral and political disasters of extraordinary rendition and Guantánamo Bay.

On the left side of the argument, Western radicals fall for an equally inane error. Because it is easier to expose abuses of power in democracies, and because Western radicals are most concerned about abuses of power in their own countries, they assume that democratic abuses are the major or only abuses of power worth protesting about. Their parochial reasoning leads to the most characteristic of left-wing betrayals. Radicals either dismiss crimes committed by anti-Western forces as the inventions of Western propagandists or excuse them as the inevitable, if regrettably blood-spattered, consequences of Western provocation. The narcissism behind their reasoning is too glaring to waste time on. (In their minds, Western societies, their corporations and foreign policies remain responsible for the ills of the world half a century on from the end of colonialism. This myopic vision has the flattering consequence of making them – the brave Western opposition – humanity's dearest friends, because they, and only they, can take on hegemonic power in its Western citadels.)

The duplicity the illusion sanctions ought to be a true cause for liberal guilt. Because they believe the real enemy is at home, Western radicals ignore the victims of dictatorial states and movements, and provide excuses for their oppressors. They see dissidents in countries like Belarus as tainted, because their sufferings cannot be blamed on the West. At their worst, Western leftists will follow through the logic of their position and collaborate with the oppressors.

Given the persistence of the old pathology, no one should have been surprised that the supposedly radical movement for Net 'transparency' turned on the victims of oppression.

Transparency purports to be a depoliticised ideal. Its supporters say they want information on what governments are doing and on who is trying to influence them. When they obtain it, they wish to use the Net's processing power and crowd-sourcing techniques to root out corruption. On a more elevated level, they hope that transparency will create a more democratic system that enables citizens to participate in the decision-making of previously secretive bureaucracies, as governments put data on the Net and allow the public to analyse it. They do not say what decisions citizens should reach once they have the data. They do not discuss wider political questions – how should a good society share its wealth, deal with the rest of the world, protect its environment, care for its sick and educate its children? More pertinently, they reveal their privileged background by taking the democratic state for granted. They assume that the public they address is already living in a society where freedom of information and open government are at least possible, and spend too little time thinking about all those living in countries without democratic rights.

Transparency campaigners accept that their aims are narrow. They make a virtue of their limited and depoliticised ambitions by saying that all they are doing is 'allowing people to make their own minds up'. They carry no responsibilities for what happens next. Outsiders can judge others by how they use the information they provide, but they cannot judge them. They are the enablers of debates. Where those debates go once transparency has been achieved, and what conclusions the participants reach, is no concern of theirs.

I do not mean 'depoliticised' as an insult, and there is much that is admirable about demands for transparency. Democracy and freedom of information go together, because if the electorate does not know what has been done in its name, it cannot pass a fair verdict on its rulers. Democracy's advantage over other systems is that it allows countries to replace rulers without violence. But electorates cannot 'throw the scoundrels out' if censorship prevents them from learning that the scoundrels are scoundrels in the first place. The limiting of state corruption, meanwhile, is also an ambition that is beyond conventional politics, because it is a universal human aspiration that everyone who has experienced the insolence of office shares.

The emptiness of the transparency movement does not lie in its limited aims, but in the phoniness of its claim that it has escaped politics. WikiLeaks, the supposed source of sunlight for the twenty-first century, which ignorant celebrities and unprincipled activists instructed 'everyone who believes in the power of transparency' to 'stand up for', had a political programme that allowed it to intervene on the side of the world's darkest forces. To quote him for the last time, the transparency movement amply proved the truth of Orwell's remark that 'So much of left-wing thought is a kind of playing with fire by people who don't even know that fire is hot.'

WikiLeaks could not leave the Belarusian dissidents alone. They did not fit into the narrow mentality of modern radicalism. The American and European governments offered the Belarusian opposition nominal support, as they offered support to the opponents of the Taliban, the Iranian mullahs and other anti-Western dictatorships. To a certain type of Western radical, Belarusian dissidents were therefore suspect and tainted. They had collaborated with the great satan. They were not real dissidents at all. So, in Belarus WikiLeaks' conduit was a believer in the fascist conspiracy theory who wished to help former communists fight the democratic opposition. Julian Assange's chosen emissary was Israel Shamir, a renegade Russian Jew who converted to Greek Orthodoxy and embraced every variety of contemporary anti-Semitism. A French court convicted him in his absence of stirring up racial hatred. His published writing showed him to be a Holocaust denier who believed that a secret conspiracy of Jews controlled the world.

The dalliances of the 'radical' WikiLeaks with a proponent of neo-Nazi thought are not as surprising as they once would have been. If you believe that Western democracies are the sole or prime source of oppression, then you are wide open to the seduction of fascistic ideologies, because they come from a radical anti-democratic tradition that echoes your own. If you think that Israel or the West is the sole or prime source of conflict in the Middle East, your defences against anti-Semitism are down, and ready to be overrun.

Assange made Shamir WikiLeaks' associate in Russia. Shamir gave the KGB in Belarus information it could use when he printed WikiLeaks documents that told the dictatorship there had been conversations between the opposition and the US. Shamir went to Belarus, praised the rigged elections and compared Natalia Koliada and her friends to football hooligans. Whether he handed over a batch of US cables without blacking out the names of Belarusian political activists who had spoken to American officials was an open question. The Russian Interfax news agency said Shamir 'confirmed the existence of the Belarus dossier'. The Belarusian state media added that he had allowed the KGB to 'show the background of what happened, to name the organizers, instigators and rioters, including foreign ones, without compromise, as well as to disclose the financing scheme of the destructive organizations'. Given Shamir's record, it was prudent to fear the worst.

WikiLeaks said in public that Shamir had never worked for it, and that Assange and his colleagues did not endorse his writings. Privately, Assange told Shamir that he could avoid controversy and continue to assist WikiLeaks by working under an assumed name. When the BBC revealed Assange's double-dealing, his lawyers accused it of using stolen documents to expose their client – a priceless accusation for the apostle of openness to level after he had received 250,000 stolen US cables.

WikiLeaks then sunk lower. For all my liberalism, I cannot think of one honourable reason why governments should not be allowed to keep information secret that might be used by the Taliban to compile a death list. Yet a death list was what the founder of WikiLeaks appeared ready to give men who would crush freedom of speech and every other human right. The US State Department cables Bradley Manning leaked to Julian Assange contained the names of Afghans who had helped allied forces fight the Taliban. One of the histories of WikiLeaks describes how journalists took Assange to a London restaurant in 2010. The Taliban had massacred religious minorities, murdered teachers for the 'crime' of teaching girls to read and write, and confined women to darkened rooms where passing men could not see them. Aware of its record, the reporters wondered whether Assange would endanger Afghans who had helped the Americans if he put their names online. 'Well, they're informants,' he replied. 'So, if they get killed, they've got it coming to them. They deserve it.'

No man is under oath when the wine is flowing at a restaurant table. Assange denied at a public meeting that the conversation had taken place. His actions justified his assertions. Like a journalist who realises he has a moral obligation to protect confidential sources, he carefully suppressed documents that named Afghans the Taliban would want to kill. His decent behaviour did not last. In late 2011 WikiLeaks put all the US State Department cables on the Net, unedited, unredacted, with the names of better and braver people than Assange could ever be in Afghanistan, China, Ethiopia and Belarus for their dictatorial enemies to find and charge with collaboration with the US.

As I said at the beginning of this book, all the enemies of liberalism are essentially the same. Opposing them requires not just a naïve faith in technology, but a political commitment to expand the rights that we possess to meet changing circumstances, and a determination to extend them to the billions of people from Afghanistan to Zimbabwe who do not enjoy our good fortune.

HOW TO FIGHT BACK:

Advice for Free-Speaking Citizens

1 The political is not personal

The private life of civilised society is built on white lies. Everyone except sociopaths self-censors when talking to friends and strangers. Our relations with others would break down if we did not restrain free speech and treat them with respect. No one, however, should demand respect for public ideas that have the power to oppress others as long as criticism is not a direct incitement to crime. Religious and political ideas are too important to protect with polite deceits, because their adherents can seek to control all aspects of public and private life.

2 The personal is not political

However hard journalists find it to argue for the suppression of the truth, demands for a right to privacy are justifiable. They will grow as the Net replaces the anonymity of the twentieth-century city, which was so well suited to anonymous liaisons, with a global village. As in all villages, tell-tales, Peeping Toms and poison pens will proliferate. The Net makes ineradicable proofs of past indiscretions available to every cyber-bully and Net-spy with a search engine. As it opens up previously unavailable information to employers, police forces, corporations, democratic governments and dictatorial states, many will realise that the new technologies are a secret policeman's dream, and ask for the law's protection.

It is symptomatic of the banality of what ought to be a complicated debate that the only argument we hear about privacy is the argument between celebrities' lawyers and tabloid editors – a struggle which recalls the joke about the Iran–Iraq war that 'It's a pity they can't both lose.' As we must deal with celebrities before we can move on, the best solution would be for the courts to offer public figures protection, but to override their privacy rights and allow publication if there is a public interest, even a small public interest, in their exposure. To do that we need judges who instinctively value free debate and are alert to the dangers of the powerful and wealthy manipulating the law. If such judges are impossible to find – and they may be, as we have seen – we should restrict privacy rights for all public figures, as the Americans do.

3 Respect is the enemy of tolerance

The loud calls from the religious for censorship in the name of 'respect' reveal the fatuity of modern faith. The religious do not say that they are defending the truth from libellous attack, because in their hearts they know that the truth of the holy books cannot be defended. Instead, like celebrities' lawyers trying to hide secrets, they threaten the gains made in the struggle for religious toleration by saying that those who ask searching questions of religion must be punished for invading the privacy of the pious.

Religious toleration freed men and women from the blasphemy laws and religious tests for office that Church and state enforced. It allowed argument, apostasy, free-thinking, satire, science and fearless criticism – freedom of religion and freedom from religion. The demand to 'respect' religion is an attempt to push back the gains of the Enlightenment by forbidding the essential arguments that religious toleration allowed.

4 If you are frightened, at least have the guts to say so

Once one did not write the word 'liberal' and add 'hypocrite'. Since the Rushdie Affair, the reflex has become automatic. The worst aspect of the fear the ayatollahs spread was that Western intellectuals were afraid of admitting that they were afraid. If they had been honest, they would have forced society to confront the fact of censorship. As it was, their silence made the enemies of liberalism stronger.

5 Once you have paid him the Danegeld, you never get rid of the Dane

The slide from religious fanatics calling for the murder of Salman Rushdie because he had written a blasphemous novel, to murdering Salmaan Taseer merely for opposing the death penalty for blasphemy, shows how appeasement feeds the beast it seeks to tame. All dictatorial systems, secular and religious, have a capacity to go postal: to move from attacks on their enemies which can be rationally explained to random, almost meaningless assaults on the smallest transgressions. It is best to stop them before they get started.

6 If you have the chance to enact one law …

… make it the First Amendment. For all the crimes and corruptions of American democracy, the stipulation that 'Congress shall make no law respecting an establishment of religion, or prohibiting the free exercise thereof; or abridging the freedom of speech, or of the press; or the right of the people peaceably to assemble, and to petition the Government for a redress of grievances' is the best guarantor of freedom yet written.

7 Democracy does not end at the office door

Demands for elected worker-directors and stronger protections for whistleblowers are always justifiable, because they restrict the power of the plutocracy. The banking crisis revealed that they could also protect national security. Sensible countries should treat banks as if they were hostile foreign powers, and enable, protect and honour those who reveal the threats they pose to wider society.

8 The wealthy have means enough to defend themselves, they do not need the law to add to them

Free speech has advanced by a process of declaring subjects too important for states to censor. The American revolutionaries of 1776 said the law had no right to interfere in religious debates. The victories of liberalism and the struggle against the European dictatorships led to the acceptance by democracies that no one should regulate political ideas. The battles of the Civil Rights movement in the American South established that public figures in the United States could not seek the law's protection unless they were victims of 'malicious' attack – that is, of assaults from critics who showed a reckless disregard for the truth. Europe should import that protection, and ensure it covers business as well as politics. Given the power of plutocratic wealth and the dangers the financial system poses to modern democracies, the law should not allow CEOs, corporations and financiers the right to use their considerable wealth to limit free discussion of their affairs.

9 Free-speaking societies are rare …

… so protect them, and seek to extend the liberties they offer. Do not imitate the Dutch state and the liberal intellectuals who turned on Ayaan Hirsi Ali for speaking her mind, or the readiness of WikiLeaks to aid the Belarusian dictatorship. If rights are good enough for you, then they are good enough for everyone else.

10 Beware of anyone who begins a sentence with, 'There's no such thing as absolute free speech, so ...'

... for they will end it by saying something scandalous. There are legitimate limits on free speech. Governments and companies are entitled to keep secrets, as are individuals. There is a need for a libel law, although on American not English lines, and laws against direct incitement to crimes, rather than vague charges against the incitements of various hatreds. But John Stuart Mill's principle that censorship should be applied only in extreme circumstances remains the best guide to follow. The example of the British legal profession's assault on scientists shows that when society gives censors wide and vague powers they never confine themselves to deserving targets. They are not snipers but machine-gunners. Allow them to fire at will, and they will hit anything that moves.

11 Location, location, location

It is not what you say, but where you say it. Most who try to censor want total control, but will settle for the effective control brought by isolating and punishing critics. The freedom the Net brings is illusory if it confines writers to working under pseudonyms in obscure corners of the Web. Writers who wish to be heard must break from the fringe into the mainstream by arguing for their ideas in the open. If they live in a dictatorship or a democracy with oppressive laws, they will find that on their own the new technologies offer few ways around the old restrictions on free debate.

12 The Net cannot set you free

Only politics can do that.

ACKNOWLEDGEMENTS

I owe debts to many people. First and foremost to Christopher Hitchens, who gave me permission to dedicate this book to him. I do so with affection and gratitude. Ophelia Benson of Butterflies and Wheels, who combines broad sympathies with a narrow insistence on accuracy, read the proofs and helped at every stage along the way. Padraig Reidy and Michael Harris of Index on Censorship treated my repeated enquiries with patience and good humour.

This book has on occasion had hard words to say about the English legal profession. I must add in mitigation that Robert Dougans of Bryan Cave, David Buckle of Cubism Law, David Allen Green of Preiskel & Co. and Joanne Cash of One Brick Court found the time to break away from their busy practices to provide me with legal advice. If you are ever in trouble with the law, I commend them to you. I am equally appreciative of the informed advice of Anna Beer on John Milton, Kiara Chulupta on Internet censorship, Chris Dillow on managerialism and its discontents, Edzard Ernst on the scientific study of pseudo-science, Ghaffar Hussain on the difference between Islam and Islamism, Natalia Koliada on the long struggle for Belarusian freedom, Naomi McAuliffe on corporate lawyers, Christopher Mitchell on M.F. Husain, Douglas Murray on the silencing of dissident Muslim and ex-Muslim voices, Gita Sahgal on the Rushdie protests, Jean Seaton on media history, Simon Singh on fighting the law and winning, Jeremy Stangroom on identity politics, and Salil Tripathi on Hindu nationalism. Many of my colleagues offered me the benefit of their experience, including Tim Adams, Peter Beaumont, Henry Porter and Mark Townsend of the *Observer*; David Leigh and Luke Harding of the *Guardian*; Hilary Lowinger, Ian Hislop and Francis Wheen of *Private Eye*; Heidi Plougsgaard Jensen of *Jyllands-Posten*; Edward Lucas of the *Economist*; Ben Brogan of the *Daily Telegraph*; and the 'Fleet Street Fox' and others who must remain anonymous because of court orders covering their work.

The lines from Wisława Szymborska's 'The Terrorist, He Watches' were translated by Robert Maguire and Magnus Jan Krynsky, and can be found in *Sounds, Feelings, Thoughts*, a 1981 collection of her poetry. I am grateful to Princeton University Press for its permission to reproduce them here.

The hospitality of Christine and Colin Clark and Mary Elford allowed me to collect my thoughts, and Anne-Marie cleared me a space to write.

Robin Harvie of Fourth Estate and Natasha Fairweather of A.P. Watt waited for a manuscript and did not flinch as deadlines whooshed by. If there were a God, he would reward them in the hereafter for their forbearance. There is no God, so my thanks must suffice.

No journalist can write without editors who will back him, and I thank John Mulholland of the *Observer* and Daniel Johnson of *Standpoint* for allowing me to develop my ideas in their pages.

As ever, all errors of taste and judgement remain the sole responsibility of the author.

NICK COHEN
November 2011

NOTES

ix **'There is an all-out confrontation'** *For the Sake of Argument,* Christopher Hitchens on Salman Rushdie, Verso, 1993, pp.301–2

INTRODUCTION

xiii **'Some are absurd'** 'Do Not Read This', The Fleet Street Fox, 23 May 2011; http://www.fleetstreetfox.com/2011/05/do-not-read-this.html

xvi **'An old way of doing'** *WikiLeaks and the Age of Transparency,* Micah L. Sifry, Yale University Press, 2011, p.42

xix **'When countries curtail'** Hillary Rodham Clinton, speech at George Washington University, Washington, DC, 15 February 2011

CHAPTER 1: 'KILL THE BLASPHEMERS'

3 **'It would be absurd'** *Times of India,* 13 October 1988, quoted in *A Satanic Affair,* Malise Ruthven, The Hogarth Press, 1991

3 **'may upset some of the faithful'** *Hitch-22,* Christopher Hitchens, Atlantic Books, 2010, p.267

5 **'In the film Carmen Maura'** *Age of Extremes,* Eric Hobsbawm, Michael Joseph, 1994, p.320

8 **'Well, what can one say?'** *Does God Hate Women?,* Ophelia Benson and Jeremy Stangroom, Continuum Press, 2009, pp.29–30

13 **'The thing that is most disturbing'** *Guardian,* 13 February 1989, quoted in *The Rushdie Affair,* Daniel Pipes, Birch Lane Press, 1990, p.113

13 **'I do not have to wade'** Ruthven, p.86

18 **'undermine the people's'** Pipes, p.124

18 **'direct involvement'** Ibid., p. 131

RULES FOR CENSORS (1)

25 **'demonstrates that it is possible'** *Postmodernism, Reason and Religion*, Ernest Gellner, Routledge, 1992, p.22

28 **'The question is who has power over the story'** 'Salman Rushdie is Not Afraid', Gidi Weitz, *Haaretz*, 14 October 2002

CHAPTER 2: A CLASH OF CIVILISATIONS?

30 **'British thought, British society'** *Imaginary Homelands: Essays and Criticism 1981–1991*, Salman Rushdie, Granta, 1992

31 **'Abroad it was more or less OK'** *Culture of Complaint*, Robert Hughes, Oxford University Press, 1993, p.115

34 **'Although my board'** Peter Mayer, *Index on Censorship*, Vol. 37, No. 4, p.125

35 **'no law in life'** Exchange of letters in the *Guardian*, available at http://www.rjgeib.com/thoughts/burning/le-carre-vs-rushdie.html

36 **'This kind of sensationalism'** 'How One Book Ignited a Culture War', Andrew Anthony, *Observer*, 11 January 2009

37 **'Rabbis, priests and mullahs'** Pipes, p.165

37 **'The British government, the British people'** Press Association, 2 March 1989

38 **'The Embassy wishes to emphasise that the US government'** *Philadelphia Inquirer*, 14 February 1989, quoted Pipes, p.155

39 **'Rushdie is a devil!'** Ruthven, p.2

40 **'Approximately fifty women'** 'An All-Too Familiar Affair', Rahila Gupta, *Guardian*, 21 February 2009

40 **'At the heart of the fundamentalist'** *Women Against Fundamentalism Journal*, No. 1, 1990, p.12

RULES FOR CENSORS (2)

44 **'Not only will they kill me'** *From Fatwa to Jihad*, Kenan Malik, Atlantic Books, 2010, pp.12–13

46 **'Sections of the political'** 'Before and After the Norway Massacre – Symbiosis Between Anti-Muslim Extremists and Islamist Extremists', Quilliam Foundation, 28 July 2011

49 **'Artists too frightened to tackle radical Islam'** *The Times*, 19 November 2007

50 **'About one third of Muslims'** Populus poll for *Living Apart Together*, Policy Exchange, 2007

52 **'I think it has become more prevalent'** Mona Eltahawy, BBC
Newsnight, 20 July 2010

CHAPTER 3: MANUFACTURING OFFENCE

54 **'The Terrorist, He Watches'**, Wisława Szymborska, trans. Robert
Maguire and Magnus Jan Krynsky, in *Sounds, Feelings, Thoughts*,
Princeton University Press, 1981

55 **'What I discovered'** Tim Adams, unpublished interview. I am grateful
to the author for making his work available to me

56 **'For me, India means a celebration of life'** Interview with Shoma
Chaudhury, *Tehelka*, Vol. 5, Issue 4, 2 February 2008

56 **'I used to have terrible nightmares'** Ibid.

57 **'You can cover up your goddess'** *Offence: The Hindu Case*, Salil
Tripathi, Seagull Books, 2009, pp.17–19

60 **'If Husain can step into'** 'Assault on Art', *Frontline*, May 1998

62 **'In India, a new puritanism'** 'Only 3 Cases are Pending Against
Husain', *The Hindu*, 26 February 2010

62 **'I have not intended to denigrate'** *The Hindu*, 3 March 2010

63 **'Whenever Hindu nationalists attack an art gallery'** Tripathi,
pp.105–6

64 **'We in the West know so little about'** *The Jewel of Medina*, Sherry
Jones, Beaufort Books, 2008, p.358

64 **'Join me on a journey'** Ibid., p.vii

66 **'Finally about a month after she had arrived in Mecca'** *Muhammad:
A Biography of the Prophet*, Karen Armstrong, Phoenix, London, 1992,
p.157

67 **'In Iran after the 1979 Islamic revolution'** *Does God Hate Women?*,
Benson and Stangroom, p.59

68 **'Although it would be a massive oversimplification'** Ibid., p.58

68 **'Thou shalt not'** Leviticus 18:22, King James Bible

69 **'And a man who will lie down with a male'** *What Does Leviticus 18:22
Really Say?*, National Gay Pentecostal Alliance

69 **'Do not sleep with a man'** *Homosexuality and Torah Thought*, Rabbi
Arthur Waskow

70 **'to reject literal reads'** 'Get Over the Quran Burning', Asra Q.
Nomani, *The Beast*, 9 September 2010

74 **'A couple of years ago'** 'Our Universities Face a Radical Upheaval',
John Sutherland, *The Times*, 2 January 2010

74 **'All the same'** Centre for Social Cohesion press briefing, 5 January 2010

75 **'When we sat down'** 'Lonely Trek to Radicalism for Terror Suspect', *New York Times*, 16 January 2010

75 **'Quite disturbing level of'** 'Freedom of Thought is All we Foment', Malcolm Grant, *Times Higher Education Supplement*, 31 December 2009

76 **'She was upset'** Ibid.

77 **'There is a very real possibility'** Ibid.

77 **'I never had this power'** 'I Didn't Kill *The Jewel of Medina*', Denise Spellberg, *Wall Street Journal*, 9 August 2008

78 **'Unlike so many other times'** 'Me and Mrs Jones', altmuslim.com, 4 September 2008

78 **'The best response to free speech'** Ibid.

79 **'We don't make a distinction between'** 'Radical Cleric Warned of Big Operation', *The Times*, 10 July 2005

80 **'Fears of Muslim Anger Over Religious Book'** Christine Toomey, *Sunday Times*, 31 May 2009

RULES FOR CENSORS (3)

83 **'Law of Social Responsibility'** In Venezuela, 'While freedoms of speech and the press are constitutionally guaranteed, the 2004 Law of Social Responsibility in Radio and Television contains vaguely worded restrictions that can be used to severely limit these freedoms. Criminal statutes assign hefty fines and long prison terms for "offending" or "denigrating" the authorities. Legal defenses in insult cases are complicated by the unpredictability of courts' rationale, often resulting in a more cautious approach on the part of the press.' Freedom House, World Report on Freedom of the Press, 2009

83 **'The official "Press Law"'** 'Bahrain's Press Law contains 17 categories of offenses and prescribes up to five years' imprisonment for publishing material that criticizes Islam or the king, inciting actions that undermine state security, or advocating a change in government.' Ibid.

83 **'organising the demonstrations'** In Belarus, 'the government subjected the independent media to systematic political intimidation, while the state media consistently glorified Lukashenko and vilified the opposition. Local reporters working for foreign services with

programming aimed at Belarus – like Radio Free Europe/Radio Liberty, Deutsche Welle, and the Warsaw-based Radio Polonia – and those working for local Polish-language publications faced arbitrary arrest and aggressive harassment from the security services. A number of reporters were detained in retaliation for unauthorized demonstrations. In January, a freelance photographer for the independent weekly *Nasha Niva*, Arseny Pakhomov, was detained and beaten by the police for covering a rally against new restrictions on small businesses. He was then sentenced to two weeks in prison on charges of organizing and participating in an unsanctioned rally.' Ibid.

83 **'a tyrannical king'** Mao began the terror of the Cultural Revolution when officials ignored his orders to theatres to stop showing the opera *Hai Rui Dismissed from Office*, a traditional story of a mandarin who stood up to the king on behalf of the peasants. Chinese audiences whose families had died in the Great Leap Forward did not need to have the opera's contemporary significance explained to them. See *Mao: The Unknown Story*, Jung Chang and Jon Halliday, Jonathan Cape, 2005, p.525

85 **'The students killed their first'** Ibid., p.537

86 **'In Burma, an official'** *Small Acts of Resistance*, Steve Crawshaw and John Jacks, Union Square, 2010, pp.44–5

87 **'Why would you want to wear'** 'Zimbabwean Man Jailed for Ten Months Hard Labour After Calling President Mugabe "Old and Wrinkly"', *Daily Mail*, 7 September 2010

87 **'The police arrested a human-rights'** '"Blood Diamond" Activist Kept in Zimbabwe Jail', BBC News, bbc.co.uk, 22 June 2010

89 **'One must be ready to put up with'** Flemming Rose, *Jyllands-Posten*, 30 September 2005

91 **'free speech goes far'** *The Cartoons that Shook the World*, Jytte Klausen, Yale University Press, 2009, p.186

92 **'If Khader becomes minister of integration'** 'Politisk Bestyrtelse over Imam-udtalelser', DR (Danmarks Radio), *Nyheder/Politik*, 23 March 2006

94 **'We appreciate the incident'** 'Somali Charged Over Attack on Danish Cartoonist', BBC News, 2 January 2010

96 **'republication of the cartoons'** 'Yale Surrenders', Christopher Hitchens, *Slate*, 17 August 2009

96 **'It really is open'** 'Secrets of *South Park*', Jake Tapper and Dan Morris, ABC News, 22 September 2006

97 **'notoriously impertinent paper'** 'Firebombed French Paper is no Free Speech Martyr', Bruce Crumley, time.com, 2 November 2011

CHAPTER 4: THE RACISM OF THE ANTI-RACISTS

99 **'I was a Somali woman'** *Infidel*, Ayaan Hirsi Ali, Free Press, 2007, p.72

100 **'The last punishment'** Al Jazeera TV, 28 January 2009

100 **'Whoever finds it serving'** Gay and Lesbian Humanist Association response to the Mayor of London's dossier concerning Sheikh Yusuf Al-Qaradawi, February 2005

103 **'She ought to sacrifice'** *A Vindication of the Rights of Woman*, Mary Wollstonecraft, London, 1791, Chapter V

104 **'accepting systematic merciless abuse'** Hirsi Ali, p.244

109 **'My father is not'** 'Yes, Hirsi Ali Lied. Wouldn't You?', Isabella Thomas, *Observer*, 21 May 2006

109 **'neo-conservative wave'** 'Secrets and Lies that Doomed a Radical Liberal', Jason Burke, *Observer*, 21 May 2006

112 **'gentle gesture of disdain … so closely attended to'** For a full discussion of the attacks on Hirsi Ali see *The Flight of the Intellectuals*, Paul Berman, Melville House, 2010, pp.242–63

113 **'A sustained attack'** Ibid., p.264

114 **'women are often pressured'** *Sharia Law in Britain: A Threat to One Law for All and Equal Rights*, One Law for All, June 2010

114 **'reformist groups'** 'Panic in Whitehall', Martin Bright, *New Statesman*, 5 December 2005

116 **'the paper exaggerated'** *Tone Down the Shrill*, Hope Not Hate, November 2010

116 **'represent mainstream Muslim'** Letter to Chief Executive of Channel 4, Quilliam Foundation, November 2010

117 **'Your democratically elected governments'** London bomber: Text in full, BBC News, 1 September 2005

120 **'Absolutely free in their'** '¿Pueden convivir en paz el islam y Occidente?', John Carlin, *El País*, 20 February 2005

121 **'They condemn homosexuality'** 'Woman Artist Gets Death Threats Over Gay Muslim Photos', *Sunday Times*, 6 January 2008

HOW TO FIGHT BACK

135 **'to make it easier for men'** *Milton: Poet, Pamphleteer and Patriot*, Anna Beer, Bloomsbury, 2008, p.147

CHAPTER 5: THE CULT OF THE SUPREME MANAGER

142 **'Between 2002 and 2007, 65 per cent of all income growth'** Emmanuel Saez of Berkeley and Thomas Piketty of the Paris School of Economics, quoted in 'The Rise of the New Global Elite', Chrystia Freeland, *Atlantic*, January 2011

142 **'The pre-tax income of the richest 1 per cent'** 'Winner-Take-All Politics: Public Policy, Political Organization, and the Precipitous Rise of Top Incomes in the United States', Jacob S. Hacker and Paul Pierson, *Politics and Society*, June 2010

142 **'stood at £98.99 billion'** *Sunday Times* Rich List 2010

143 **'Russia had more dollar billionaires'** 'The 100 Richest Russians', *Forbes*, 23 July 2004

144 **'received £37 million – 1,374 times the pay'** 'Pay Gap Widens Between Executives and their Staff', *Guardian*, 16 September 2009

144 **'the ratio of CEO pay to average'** *St Petersburg Times*, political fact. com, 20–21 December 2010

145 **'a study of wealth in America in 2004'** 'The Inequality that Matters', Tyler Cowen, *The American Interest*, January 2011

145 **'These are not small sums'** 'The $100 Billion Question', Andrew G. Haldane, Bank of England, March 2010

146 **'the rich are likely'** 'Inequality and Corruption', Jong-sung You and Sanjeev Khagram, *Hauser Center for Nonprofit Organizations Working Paper No. 22, KSG Working Paper No. RWP04-001*

147 **'promises all the worst features'** *The Storm*, Vince Cable, Atlantic Books, 2009, p.122

147 **'Of the fifty-three billionaires resident'** *Sunday Times* Rich List 2010

148 **'If a man is not an oligarch'** Freeland

150 **'her school into disrepute'** '"You Deserved to be Sacked": Dinner Lady Dismissed for Exposing Bullying in School Gets Just £302.73 Compensation', *Daily Mail*, 4 February 2011

151 **'his career stalled'** 'Changing the Face of Whistleblowing', *British Medical Journal*, May 2009

152 **'told us, rightly, that'** *The End of Politics*, Chris Dillow, Harriman House, 2007, p.277

153 **'Every Monday afternoon'** *The God Delusion*, Richard Dawkins, Bantam, 2006, pp.283–4, cited in ibid., p.272

156 **'How a job offer'** 'Brisk and Brusque', *Forbes*, 6 March 2003

159 **'In the time that you'** 'Goodwin's Undoing', *Financial Times*, 4 February 2009

163 **'A risk manager'** 'Inside Job: How Bankers Caused the Financial Crisis', Peter Bradshaw, *Guardian*, 17 February 2011

166 **'Do you know who I am?'** 'New Witness Emerges in Libel Claim by Royal Bank's Chief', *Independent*, 27 March 2004

167 **'I warn you, don't make'** *The Choice*, BBC Radio 4, 3 November 2009

167 **'I'm doing a reorganisation'** Ibid.

168 **'Most risk professionals'** 'The RiskMinds 2009 Risk Managers' Survey: The Causes and Implications of the 2008 Banking Crisis', Cranfield University School of Management

RULES FOR CENSORS (5)

174 **'individual and collective level'** 'Freedom of Speech and the Thrash of Globalizing Cultures: Lessons from Ancient Athens for the 21st Century', Richard Landes, available at www.theaugeanstables.com

CHAPTER 6: A TOWN CALLED SUE

178 **'The Karma is'** *Polanski*, Christopher Sandford, Arrow Books, 2009

179 **'Fucking, you see'** Interview with Roman Polanski by Martin Amis, republished in the *Observer*, 6 December 2009

179 **'I was going, "No, I think I better go home"'** Transcript of evidence available at http://www.thesmokinggun.com/archive/polanskicover1.html

181 **'when he strolled outside'** Sandford, pp.321–2

182 **'Roman Polanski came over to the table'** 'Polanski Model Says he Didn't Make Advances', *Sunday Times*, 24 July 2005

185 **'each psychopath is more'** 'Crimes Against Fiction', Jessica Mann, *Standpoint*, September 2009

192 **'suffered a very serious injury'** Writ of Summons 1991 – M-6464, High Court (Queen's Bench Division)

196 **'existence of the injunction'** Inquiry into Press Standards, Privacy and Libel by Culture, Media and Sport Committee. Written evidence submitted by Guardian News and Media Ltd, 23 February 2010

197 **'The cost of libel actions in England and Wales is 140 times'**
'Comparative Study in Defamation Proceedings Across Europe,
Programme in Comparative Media Law and Policy', Centre for Socio-
Legal Studies, University of Oxford, December 2008

201 **'unduly restrictive libel law'** Quoted in *Free Speech is Not for Sale*,
Libel Reform Campaign, 2011, available at http://www.libelreform.
org/the-report

206 **'constitutes a clear threat'** 'Libel Without Borders', Rachel Donadio,
New York Times, 7 October 2007

206 **'When American journalists'** Office of Rory Lancman, 14 January
2008

207 **'The jury in London'** 'How I Spent my Summer Vacation in
London', Graydon Carter, *Vanity Fair*, September 2005

207 **'We are not a court of morals'** 'Polanski Called "Sexual Predator"',
BBC News, 21 July 2005

RULES FOR CENSORS (6)

211 **'Sorry, I can't'** *Everybody Says Freedom*, Pete Seeger and Bob Reiser,
W.W. Norton, 1989, pp.7–8

212 **'Don't let anyone compare'** Ibid., p.17

214 **'It is difficult to see how Gandhi's methods'** 'Reflections on Gandhi',
George Orwell, *Partisan Review*, 1949

218 **'If the libel action'** *Make No Law: The Sullivan Case and the First
Amendment*, Anthony Lewis, Random House, New York, 1991, p.110

220 **'[I]t is a prized'** Mr Justice Black, *Bridges v. California*, 1941

HOW TO FIGHT BACK

230 **'reasoned that if'** *The Chiropractor's Adjuster*, Daniel David Palmer,
Portland Printing House Company, 1910, p.17

231 **'I am the originator'** Ibid., p.19

236 **'ruptured vertebral artery'** *Trick or Treatment*, Simon Singh and
Edzard Ernst, Bantam, 2008, pp.175–6

236 **'a 2005 study of British chiropractors'** Ibid., p.178

237 **'At the heart of science'** *The Demon-Haunted World: Science as a
Candle in the Dark*, Carl Sagan, Ballantine Books, New York, 1996,
pp.304–6

238 **'not a jot of evidence'** 'Beware the Spinal Trap', Simon Singh,
Guardian, 19 April 2008

241 **'That is in my judgement'** MR JUSTICE EADY [2009] EWHC 1101 (QB), High Court, London

244 **'There was no control group'** http://www.dcscience.Net/?p=1775

245 **'that state you treat'** 'Furious Backlash from Simon Singh Libel Case Puts Chiropractors on Ropes', *Guardian*, 1 March 2010

248 **'There is nothing'** Decision of the Supreme Court in *Red Lion Broadcasting Co., Inc. v. Federal Communications Commission, June 1969*

250 **'At bottom, the Court's'** Opinion of Stevens, J., *Supreme Court of the United States, Citizens United, Appellant v. Federal Election Commission*

CHAPTER 7: THE INTERNET AND THE REVOLUTION

253 **'Out of this concourse of several hundred'** 'The Prevention of Literature', George Orwell, *Polemic*, 1946

257 **'No doubt that the punk'** Islam Online, 1 January 2008

259 **'Deadhead in Davos'** *One Market Under God*, Thomas Frank, Secker and Warburg, 2001, p.ix

260 **'universal liberation'** Parag Khanna quoted in 'The New Thinking', Leon Wieseltier, *New Republic*, 27 January 2011

260 **'foreign policy can no longer be the province'** 'Internet has Changed Foreign Policy Forever', Katherine Viner, *Guardian*, 19 June 2009

260 **'from an economic standpoint'** 'Remarks on Internet Freedom', Hillary Clinton, speech delivered at the Newseum, Washington, DC, 21 January 2010

261 **'no longer a passive'** *WikiLeaks and the Age of Transparency*, Micah L. Sifry, Yale University Press, 2011, p.48

266 **'In places like Egypt'** 'Cairo Activists Use Facebook to Rattle Regime', David Wolman, *Wired*, October 2008

268 **'The use of flash mobs'** Shirky, p.169

269 **'To speak online'** Ibid., p.171

RULES FOR CENSORS (7)

271 **'reactionary cant'** Shirky, p.69

274 **'Art Troitsky'** 'The Dangers of Satire', Emily Butselaar, *Index on Censorship*, 17 May 2011

274 **'The radio station Ekho Moskvy'** *The New Cold War*, Edward Lucas, Bloomsbury, 2009, p.78

275 **'would be commercial'** Ibid., p.80

278 **'could easily put an'** Evgeny Morozov, *The Net Delusion*, Penguin, 2011, p.73

CHAPTER 8: THE INTERNET AND THE
COUNTER-REVOLUTION

284 **'We all want one thing'** Charter 97, Speech to the judges at the Partyzansky court, 13 May 2011 http://charter97.org/en/news/2011/5/13/38527/

286 **'capitalist running dog'** 'China: Mao and the Next Generation', Kathrin Hille and Jamil Anderlini, *Financial Times*, 4 June 2011

287 **'is very much self-censoring'** *Asian Wall Street Journal*, 29 August 2000

288 **'Informants and covert'** 'Privacy as a Political Right', Gus Hosein, Privacy International, February 2010

289 **'being influenced by'** Morozov, p.11

291 **'Do you have any weapons in your car?'** 'Twitter and a Terrifying Tale of Modern Morality', Nick Cohen, *Observer*, 19 September 2010

296 **'everyone who believes'** Sifry, p.188

297 **'confirmed the existence'** 'Holocaust Denier in Charge of Handling Moscow Cables', David Leigh and Luke Harding, *Guardian*, 31 January 2011

297 **'Show the background'** Belarus *Telegraf*, 19 December 2010

298 **'Well, they're informants'** *WikiLeaks*, David Leigh and Luke Harding, Guardian Books, 2011, p.113

INDEX

12. Sedel, L. (1977) Traitement palliatif d'une série de 103 paralysies par élongation du plexus brachial. Evolution spontanée et résultats. *Rev. Chir. Orthop. (Paris)*, **63**, 651–663.

13. Ransford, A. O. and Hughes, S. P. F. (1977) Complete brachial plexus lesions. *J. Bone Joint Surg.*, **59B**, 417–420.

14. Allieu, Y. Triki, F. and de Godebout, J. (1987) Complete brachial plexus paralysis. The value of preservation of the limb and restoration of active elbow flexion (in French). *Rev. Chir. Orthop. (Paris)*, **73**, 665–673.

15. Allieu, Y. Privat, J. M. and Bonel, F. (1984) Paralysis in root avulsion of the brachial plexus. Neurotization by the spinal accessory nerve. *Clin. Plast. Surg.*, **11**, 133–135.

16. Alnot, J. Y., Jolly, A. and Frot, B. (1981) Traitement direct des lésions nerveuses dans les paralysies traumatiques du plexus brachial chez l'adulte. *Int. Orthop. (SICOT)*, **5**, 151–168.

17. Millesi, H. (1987) Brachial plexus injuries: management and results. In: *Microreconstruction of Nerve Injuries* (ed. J. K. Terzis, W. B. Saunders, Philadelphia, pp, 347–360.

18. Narakas, A. (1987) Plexus brachialis und na-heliegende periphere Nervenverkletzungen bei Wirbelfrakturen und anderen Traumen der Halswirbersale. *Orthopäde*, **16**, 81–86.

19. Narakas, A. (1984) Thoughts on neurotization or nerve transfers in irreparable nerve lesions. *Clin. Plast. Surg.*, **11**, 153–159.

20. Sedel, L. (1987) The management of supraclavicular lesions clinical examination, surgical procedures, results. In *Microreconstruction of Nerve Injuries* (ed. J. K. Terzis), W. B. Saunders, Philadelphia, pp. 385–392.

List of abbreviations

AX:	axillary nerve
DS:	dorso-scapular nerve for rhomboids and levator scapulae
GR:	graft
inf pect:	anterior thoracic rami for the sternal portion of pectoralis major
Long. thor.:	thoracicus longus nerve
M:	median
ME:	musculo-cutaneous nerve
MC prox.:	proximal stump of transected musculo-cutaneous nerve
MC distal:	distal stump of the same nerve on which the nerve transfer with intercostal nerves is performed
Med cut:	medial cutaneous nerve of forearm
R:	radial nerve
SS:	suprascapular nerve
sup pect:	rami to the clavicular portion of the pectoralis major
T3 MOT:	motor ramus of third intercostal nerve
XX:	spinal accessory nerve

Part 2 Associated Injuries and Complications

P. M. Yeoman

Vascular lesions associated with injuries of the brachial plexus have already been discussed by Narakas in his experience with 57 cases of injury either to the subclavian or axillary arteries. In my own experience vascular injuries were more commonly associated with infraclavicular lesions of the brachial plexus where the prognosis for the plexus lesion is considered to be more favourable [1] and possibly due to less severe violence. As it happened, the outcome was a disaster in some of my patients who were referred to me for assessment and further care. They had already developed a Volkmann's ischaemic contracture of

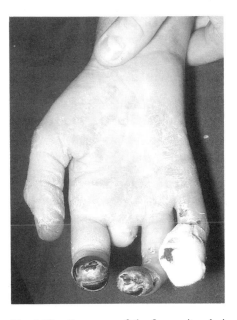

Fig. 16.7 Gangrene of the fingers in a lesion of the brachial artery and an infraclavicular traction injury of the brachial plexus. Appropriate treatment would have prevented the loss of the fingers in a patient whose nerve lesion recovered.

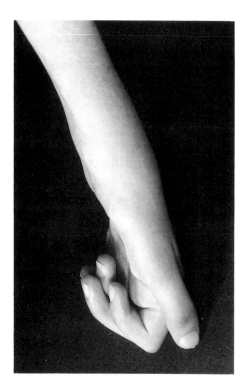

Fig. 16.8 Volkmann's ischaemic contracture of the flexor and intrinsic muscles in a patient whose plexus injury recovered.

the flexor muscles of the forearm and the intrinsic muscles of the hand (Fig. 16.8).

Volkmann's ischaemic contracture

It is an agreed fact that ischaemia of muscle is painful, and we teach that, passively to stretch a potentially ischaemic muscle will increase the pain. Hence the important test of stretching the flexor muscles of the forearm or the extensor and/ or flexor muscles of the foot and toes when a 'compartment syndrome' is suspected. If a traction lesion of the plexus is superimposed then painful stimuli will be abolished and the ischaemic pattern will persist unrecognized. Twenty-two patients who were referred to me for further care out of a total of 532 were examples of Volkmann's ischaemic contracture superimposed on their brachial plexus traction injuries. I estimate that half of them (11 patients) could have made an excellent recovery if the vascular lesion had been recognized and dealt with. As a result of the author's previous experience at the Institute

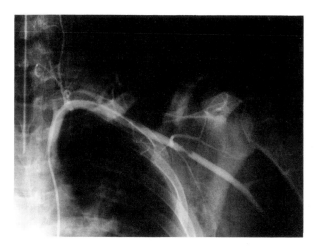

Fig. 16.9 Arteriogram (femoral) revealing a block of the brachial artery in continuity due to avulsion of the intima; associated haemothorax, open fracture of clavicle and complete rupture of infraclavicular brachial plexus. Recovery excellent after arterial and nerve grafts, nerve repairs and internal fixation of clavicle.

of Orthopaedics in London when engaged in assessing patients at a later stage of their plexus injuries [2], it was clear that a surgeon should be advised to exclude a vascular lesion within 4 hours' from the time of injury. Delay could be disastrous for the limb.

Arteriography (Fig. 16.9) must be available and indeed used if there is the slightest suggestion of an associated vascular lesion. This may inevitably involve early exploration of the lesion, even if it means calling up a team of experienced surgeons at any time of day or night. Exploration

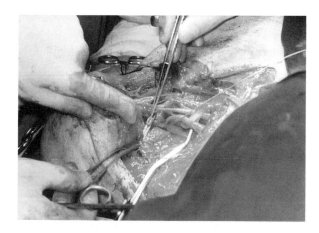

Fig. 16.10 Resection of brachial artery at damaged segment before graft.

is surprisingly easy at the acute stage compared with the lengthy and potentially meddlesome dissections through a minefield of fibrous tissue a few months later. Arteries and veins are restored by direct suture or graft (Fig. 16.10); then the nerves can be traced and the extent of their damage assessed before repair or graft. Fibrin glue is a quick and a well tried alternative [3] to meticulous but lengthy microscopic fascicular suture. The author has first hand experience of 17 such problems in the acute stage and ten went on to worthwhile recovery in that they achieved not only a useful and fairly strong hand grip (power 4: MRC grading) but protective skin sensibility. Sadly the other ten patients failed to recover any satisfactory function because there was either a long drawn out traction injury extending proximally from the site of vascular repair or associated avulsion of nerve roots.

Nerve pedicle graft

The survival of nerve graft has concerned us for years and there is a critical diameter but not necessarily length of free graft that will survive [4]. A vascular bed is an obvious requirement but not always easy to achieve amidst a thick sheet of fibrous tissue. The nerve pedicle graft [5] was designed to by-pass impenetrable and potentially hostile avascular territory for free nerve tissue. The blood supply was carried intact with the projected nerve and because the first stage involved ligature of one end of the loop it was possible to achieve a pre-degenerate length of nerve and thereby satisfy the metabolic requirements as a result of Wallerian degeneration. The final diameter of the graft tube would not be further reduced by fibrous tissue. This led to further research on the relative merits of pre-degenerate nerve grafts; some were impressed [6], others were not [7]. An example of the successful use of a two stage nerve graft is illustrated in a patient aged 24 who was sitting in the front passenger seat of a car when the car skidded off the road and careered through a fence and into a field. A fencing post pierced the front of the car and transfixed him to the seat (Fig. 16.11). The post entered his axilla and chest. In addition to the major wound he sustained a severe haemothorax, lung damage, a fractured shaft of humerus and a complete brachial plexus injury.

Fig. 16.11 Fencing post transfixed this patient, penetrating the chest, axilla and causing considerable vascular and nerve damage, as well as a fractured humerus.

After the wounds had healed and 3 months after the accident he was referred to me with an un-united fracture of the humerus and a flail arm lacking in shin sensibility. An arteriogram (Fig. 16.12); revealed that the axillary artery was not filling but there was a fairly adequate collateral circulation, and indeed the radial pulse was palpable. The outlook was not favourable; but a myelogram failed to reveal any traumatic meningocoeles or distortion of the cervical nerve

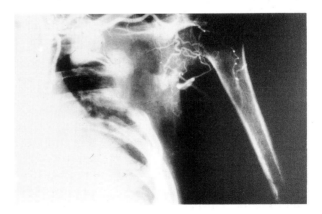

Fig. 16.12 Radiograph and arteriogram revealed an inadequate filling of the brachial artery but a reasonable secondary collateral flow to the distal part of the limb.

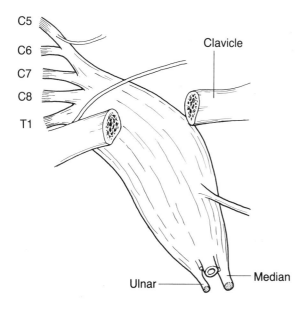

Fig. 16.13 Extensive scar tissue around the clavicle area with intact nerve roots and distal peripheral nerves.

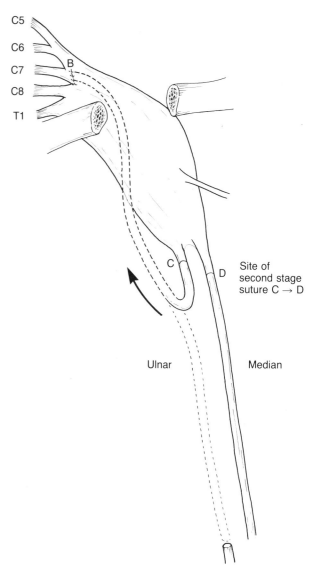

Fig. 16.14 First stage pedicle nerve graft; ulnar nerve mobilized and distal end doubled back to be sutured to C7 nerve root.

roots. A lengthy exploration was made of the supraclavicular part of the brachial plexus and the nerve roots and main nerve trunks were found to be intact (Fig. 16.13). I decided that any dissection around the clavicle and beyond in the axilla might damage the vital collateral vessels and thereby compromise the viability of the upper limb. A second exploration was made below the axilla and the ulnar nerve was mobilized down to the wrist together with its vessels. It was divided just proximal to the wrist and looped up through a tunnel made by a blunt nosed instrument in the scarred axillary area to emerge in the root of the neck where I sutured it to the proximal divided end of the root of C7 (Fig. 16.14). The fracture of the shaft of the humerus was secured with a plate and cancellous bone graft packed round. The second stage was achieved 3 months later and involved a relatively easy dissection to identify the loop of ulnar nerve, divide it and suture it to the distal end of the divided median nerve (Fig. 16.15). At 1 year there was a definite contraction in the flexors of the wrist and at 18 months it was possible to restore reasonable function in the hand by an arthrodesis and tendon transplants to the fingers. At 2 years there was not only recovery in skin sensibility in the median but strangely in the ulnar distribution as well. He must have been one of those fortunate

enough to have cross connections between the ulnar and median nerves in the wrist and hand.

This rather lengthy account must not detract from the later successful free vascularized ulnar nerve grafts including microscopic restoration of the vessels [8]. It serves to focus attention on the sacrifice of the ulnar nerve and its remarkable use in grafting the brachial plexus. The term 'sacrifice' may be misleading but it is written in the context relating to the negligible chances of recovery in the ulnar distribution in the hand after a degenerative lesion of the ulnar nerve in the

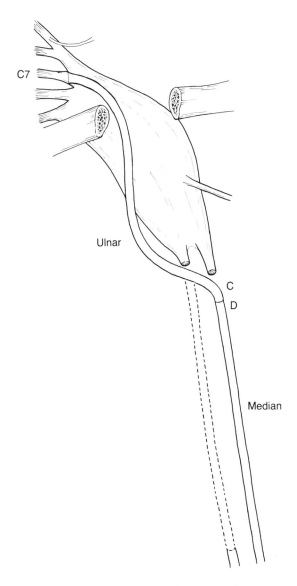

C7

Ulnar

C

D

Median

Fig. 16.15 Second stage pedicle nerve graft; ulnar nerve sutured to divided median nerve below level of scar tissue (mid-humerus).

Nerve root avulsion

The nearer the nerve injury is to the spinal cord the worse the prognosis.

It is necessary to determine nerve root avulsion because there is no way at present to successfully re-implant it. Isolated nerve root avulsion is barely possible without some other damage to the plexus in the type of traction injuries which are currently familiar. A myelograph [9] may well reveal a single traumatic meningocoele (Fig. 16.16) but it does not necessarily indicate that all the nerve root is avulsed; a CT or MRI scan would give a more accurate definition. Recovery in that nerve root might be very misleading and would throw doubt on the validity of the abnormal radiographic finding. A pre- or post-fixed plexus would explain the anomaly and there are many deviations from the accepted anatomical patterns [10]. Multiple meningocoeles (Fig.

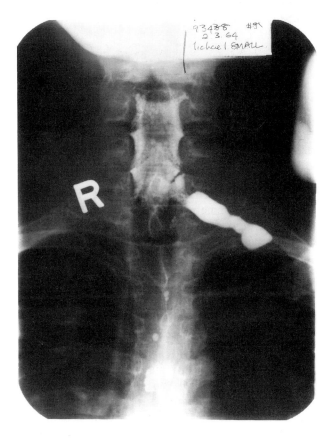

Fig. 16.16 A single traumatic meningocoele.

axilla. The quality of recovery in the intrinsic muscles is very poor indeed because of the long distance between the axilla and hand and the time taken for any recovering nerve fibrils to reach an intrinsic muscle; which in the long interval degeneration has taken place not only in the motor end-plate but in the muscle fibres.

We can afford to lose the ulnar nerve in those circumstances because it has an important part to play in restoration of function in the proximal part of the totally paralysed upper limb.

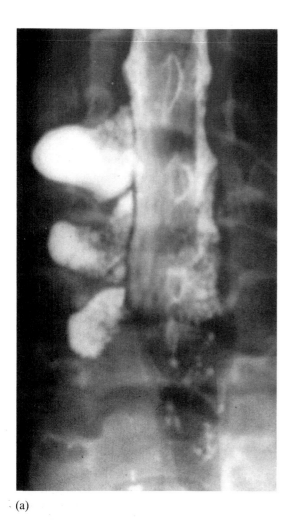

(a)

Fig. 16.17   Multiple meningocoeles at C7–C8–T1.

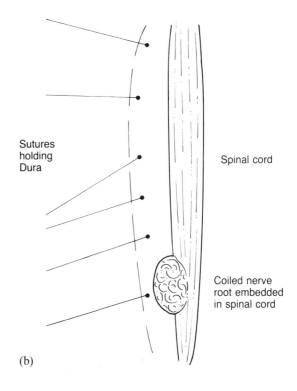

Sutures holding Dura

Spinal cord

Coiled nerve root embedded in spinal cord

(b)

16.17) are much more serious and when combined with the clinical picture of a painful flail arm, lacking sensibility, produced by an accident of high velocity and with an associated Horner's syndrome (Fig. 16.18) the outlook is very gloomy.

Haemorrhage into the subarachnoid space has been mentioned by Narakas and the author has confirmed this on three occasions when a lumbar puncture was performed on three patients who had been struck on the shoulder by a heavy object on a building site; there was no associated head injury. It is not surprising that bleeding occurs when a nerve root is torn because it is enveloped by small nutrient vessels both within and on the surface of the meningeal sleeve; it is, however, surprising to find relatively few reports of spinal cord damage. Exploration of the spinal

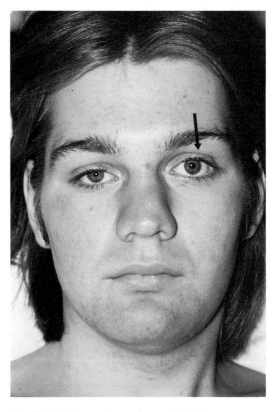

Fig. 16.18   Horner's syndrome left side.

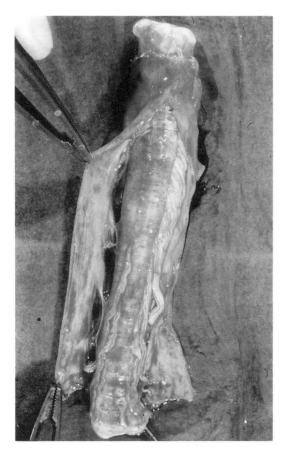

Fig. 16.19 Nerve roots totally avulsed from the spinal cord (autopsy specimen).

cord frequently reveals that the nerve rootlets have been avulsed, leaving a clean surface on the side of the spinal cord (Fig. 16.19). It is likely that pain is one of the unfortunate consequences of local spinal cord trauma.

Long term complications of nerve root avulsion

The author has seen two patients with long tract signs leading to spasticity and later more widespread signs of multiple sclerosis arising 15 and 18 years after a complete traction injury of the brachial plexus. The immediate diagnosis was not evident and it was hoped that the abnormal late onset spasticity was due to fibrous adhesions withdrawing the spinal cord into the mouth of a traumatic meningocoele [11], but sadly other

signs were found which discounted the mechanical cause. Another patient sustained a severe traction injury to the plexus at the age of 10 when tobogganing and 20 years later he was referred owing to difficulty in walking over a period of 2 years. There was no doubt that he had a spastic gait with all the signs of an upper motor neurone lesion. A myelograph revealed a filling defect compressing the lower cervical spinal cord. At operation the author found a coiled up piece of nerve root which was adherent to the cord (Fig. 16.20). The compression was relieved by removal of the coiled stump of nerve root and there was worthwhile but not full improvement in his gait over the next 3 years.

In conclusion, there has undoubtedly been an advance in both the diagnosis and management of brachial plexus injuries during the last decade. It is likely that further advances will be made, particularly with nerve grafts [12], fibrin glue for nerve repair and more detailed knowledge of the pharmacological activity at nerve endings. The more severe injuries could be reduced immediately by banning motor cycles.

References

1. Leffert, R. D. (1985) *Brachial Plexus Injuries*, Churchill Livingstone, New York, pp. 3–57.
2. Yeoman, P. M. and Seddon, H. J. (1961) Brachial plexus injuries: treatment of the flail arm. *J. Bone Joint Surg.*, **43B**, 493.
3. Seddon, H. J. and Medawar, P. B. (1942) Fibrin suture of human nerves. *Lancet*, **2**, 87.
4. Seddon, H. J. (1972) *Surgical Disorders of the Peripheral Nerves.* Churchill Livingstone, London, pp. 16–286.
5. Strange, F. G., St. C. (1950) Case report on pedicled nerve graft. *Br. J. Surg.*, **37**, 331.
6. Ballance, C. and Duel, A. B. (1932) Operative treatment of facial palsy by the introduction of nerve grafts into the fallopian canal and by other intratemporal methods. *Archs Otolaryngol.*, **15**, 1.
7. Bunnell, S. and Boyes, J. H. (1939) Nerve grafts. *Am. J. Surg.*, **44**, 64.
8. Bonney, G., Birch, R., Jamieson, A. J. and Eames, R. A. (1984) Experience with vascularized nerve grafts. *Clin. Plast. Surg.*, **2,1**, 137.
9. Yeoman, P. M. (1968) Cervical myelography in traction injuries of the brachial plexus. *J. Bone Joint Surg.*, **50B**, 253.
10. Kaplan, E. B. and Spinner, M. (1980) Normal and anomalous innervation patterns in the upper ex-

tremity. In *Management of Peripheral Nerve Problems* (ed. G. E. Omer and M. Spinner), Saunders, Philadelphia, pp. 77–89.

11. Penfield, W. (1972) Late spinal paralysis after avulsion of the brachial plexus. *J. Bone Joint Surg.*, **31B**, 40.

12. Glasby, M. A., Gilmour, J. A., Gschmeissner, S. E. *et al.* (1990) The repair of large peripheral nerves using skeletal muscle autografts: a comparison with cable grafts in the sheep femoral nerve. *Br. J. Plast. Surg.*, **43**, 169.

Part 3 Rehabilitation

C. B. Wynn Parry

Lesions of the brachial plexus are ideally explored immediately after injury or within the first 2 or 3 weeks. The operation is much less difficult than at a later stage. However this is often not possible, either because of the co-existence of head injuries or chest injuries or the lack of availability of a specialist unit. Thus many patients with brachial plexus lesions are seen months after injury. Elevation and the wearing of an appropriate sling will prevent formation and organization of oedema, and trophic lesions can be avoided by careful education of the patient to avoid damage to the insensitive hand. Should these basic principles have been neglected, patients may present for consideration of surgery some months after injury with a very stiff shoulder and an oedematous brawny arm and very stiff hand. The shoulder is particularly likely to stiffen as are the metacarpophalangeal joints and the thumb web. It is essential to have a good range of external rotation to allow adequate exposure of the plexus at operation and it may therefore be necessary to insist on a preoperative spell of intensive rehabilitation to prepare the patient for surgery. This is best done as an in-patient with an intensive programme of physiotherapy and occupational therapy, but at the very least, several hours a day as an outpatient should be required with progressive passive stretching of stiff joints, hydrotherapy and intensive re-education of spared muscles. If any oedema has organized then a spell of elevation may be necessary. It is surprising how rapidly even chronic oedema can subside if continuous elevation in bed is insisted upon. At this stage it is necessary to establish whether the patient has a pre- or post-ganglionic lesion. If the lesion is pre-ganglionic then there is no hope of repairing the plexus although some form of reconstruction such as neurotization may be considered. If the lesion is postganglionic it may be either in continuity or there may be ruptures of one or more roots.

Electromyography can be most valuable to assess the situation. Routine electromyography in our unit comprises sampling of at least two muscles supplied by each root to determine if there are any surviving motor units indicating that the lesion is not total.

Secondly, sensory conduction studies stimulating the index, middle and little fingers and recording over the median and ulnar nerves at the wrist; stimulating the radial nerve in the mid-forearm, and recording over the first dorsal interosseous space; stimulating the ulnar nerve at the wrist and recording over the ulnar nerve above the elbow. In the presence of total anaesthesia the presence of an action potential will indicate a pre-ganglionic lesion. The absence of sensory action potentials in an anaesthetic digit unfortunately does not mean that the lesion is certainly post-ganglionic, for it is possible to have pre- and post-ganglionic elements and the post-ganglionic element will show on electrical investigation. Sensory evoked potentials can be very helpful. Median and ulnar nerves are stimulated at the wrist and recordings made over the brachial plexus, over the cervical spine at the level of C2 and over the contralateral parietal cortex. The detection of a potential over the plexus at the root of the neck in the presence of anaesthesia in the distribution stimulated, will indicate a pre-ganglionic lesion and the degree of attenuation between that and C2 will indicate the relative degree of post- and pre-ganglionic involvement. We have shown that the most valuable results are obtained by a combination of the two techniques [1].

Myelography has been disappointing in the past for it is possible to have a meningocele and yet an intact root, and conversely it is possible to have a normal myelogram but an intra-dural root avulsion. However the combination of a CT scan and myelography appears to be giving very promising results.

The more information that can be gathered

before operation, the more certainly the diagnosis of the exact type and level of the lesion can be made.

Whether there has been rupture of nerve roots which are repaired at operation or whether spontaneous recovery is going to occur after a degenerative lesion in continuity, it is going to be months or years before the patient regains function; and in the case of a total avulsion lesion proved at surgery, it is clear that recovery will never occur.

For suitable patients with a permanent paralysis of the plexus and for the months or years before recovery occurs in those with reparable or recoverable lesions, functional splinting has been adopted in our unit. For the patient with a total paralysis, the full flail arm splint is provided. This is, in effect, an artificial arm over the patient's own limb. It consists of a shoulder support, elbow locking device, forearm support and a platform on the wrist piece into which a variety of tools may be fitted. The tools can be operated by a harness from movement of the contralateral shoulder, just as in a standard artificial arm, so that the patient has his good hand free to operate tools. The splint is ready-made and modular and comes in three sizes. The orthotist makes adjustments to suit the individual patient and the occupational therapist supervises a detailed training programme in which the patient learns to use the splint for a variety of activities of daily living, hobbies, recreations and appropriate work. The occupational therapist and the workshop technician will make every effort to simulate the patient's normal work and try out the splint in this realistic situation. Ten days is allowed for intensive training by which time the majority of patients will be fully conversant with its use (Fig. 16.20). The value of these splints is that they allow the patient to retain the arm in his body image during the stage of paralysis. It relieves the strain on the shoulder and it allows a variety of functional uses. It is in effect a mobile vice and is most valuable for steadying tools while the other hand directs the operation. A wide range of trades and professions have been made possible using this splint including draughtsmanship, spray painting, spot welding, engineering, car maintenance, gardening and a whole variety of recreations and hobbies. We have three patients who are able to go deep sea fishing with totally paralysed arms using the flail arm splint and we

(a)

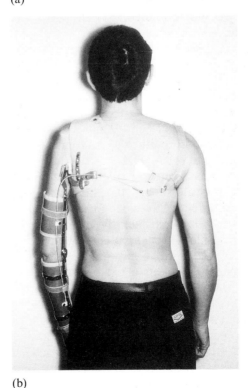

(b)

Fig. 16.20   Front (a) and rear (b) views of the flail arm splint. On rear view note shoulder support, shoulder joint and elbow ratchet.

have patients who can play golf, cricket and carry out all activities around the house, including painting and decorating [2].

Clearly patients must be motivated towards use of the splint and somebody who rejects it as clumsy and has no wish to try it should not be coerced into so doing. With experience the occupational therapist and the workshop technician can assess within a day or two whether a patient is likely to be a splint user. At a recent 2-year follow-up, 70% of patients were using the splint for hobbies, recreation or work. Patients may use the splint for a few months and then discard it, either when recovery occurs or when they become used to working. If it can be demonstrated to an employer that the patient has useful function with his paralysed arm, he may be much more ready to accept him for employment.

There are a variety of modifications of this splint for less severe paralysis. For example a patient with a C5/6 palsy who has no elbow flexion, a simple elbow lock splint is provided which weighs virtually nothing and allows the patient to position his arm in one of five positions. We have many patients who have been able to return to full work immediately on provision of this splint. For a patient with a C5/6/7 palsy with added paralysis of wrist and finger extension, a dropped wrist and finger appliance can be added. In a patient who has either recovered or has spared proximal muscle function and there is paralysis below the elbow, the forearm trough alone is all that is required and the shoulder piece can be discarded. A number of patients in the Armed Forces with total paralysis following brachial plexus lesions have been fitted with this splint and as a result of proving that they have excellent function they have been retained for full service careers. It is particularly important to help these patients get back to employment. In many cases they may well not be able to return to their former employment, e.g. labourers, brick layers, and the like. Many, however, by simple adjustments at work may be able to return to work and it is here that the services of a Resettlement Officer are invaluable. In our unit we have a full-time Resettlement Officer who is experienced in industry and in the niceties of trade union law. His role is to make immediate contact with the employer and indicate to him the extent of the injury and the likely time the patient will be off

work. Throughout the course of rehabilitation, he will contact the employer and keep him informed of progress. The vast majority of employers are perfectly happy to keep the job open for a patient and to modify it accordingly if only they are kept informed. So often the employer hears nothing for many months or years and naturally gives up hope and employs someone else in his place. In many instances the Resettlement Officer will visit the place of work and discuss with the personnel officer and the foreman what modifications could be made to allow the patient to return to work. It is very helpful if a trial period of work for a day or two can be arranged at an early stage of the rehabilitation so that the patient does not lose hope.

Seventy-four patients with total paralysis of the arm were referred to our Resettlement Officer and 81% were able to be returned to work.

Some 30 years ago, the standard treatment for a person with a total avulsion lesion of the brachial plexus was early amputation, arthrodesis of the shoulder and fitting of a prosthesis. It was shown that few patients actually use their artificial limb. The situation is even more radical now because well over half our patients have total avulsion lesions which involve avulsion of all five roots of the spinal cord. In such a situation there is total loss of proximal control and even with amputation and arthrodesis, such patients will never be able to operate a prosthesis because they have paralysis of the thoracoscapular muscles. Twelve of our patients had been advised elsewhere to have immediate amputation and 11 of them regained significant shoulder and elbow function some years later. Very few patients wish to have amputation. Young men do not want to be seen on the beach and in the swimming pool with a stump but most people are unobservant enough not to notice a withered arm. Only one out of our series of over a thousand patients with total paralysis of the arm developed trophic lesions severe enough to require amputation. The main indication for amputation is in an athletic person in whom the limb gets in the way when running or in a rugger scrum. Amputation of course has no effect whatsoever on the severe pain that so many of these patients suffer. It is deeply distressing for the patient to wake up after an amputation to find that his pain has not improved.

Reconstructive surgery

There are various procedures to restore elbow flexion, such as the Steindler operation, pectoralis major transfer, triceps to biceps transfer and the latissimus dorsi transfer. For a patient with a C7 paralysis, the standard radial nerve tendon transfers are appropriate to restore wrist and finger extension. However, re-education after tendon transfers for the brachial plexus lesions present greater problems than after peripheral nerve injuries. Joints are often stiff and there may well be contractures, there is often cross innervation causing co-contraction which makes re-education difficult and muscles may not be as strong for transfer as in the standard peripheral nerve lesion. In brachial plexus lesions objectives are more limited and it is common practice to transfer a muscle that is less strong than one would like, e.g. a 3 plus muscle. Although only limited power may develop it may make all the difference to the patient's function [3].

Pain

One of the most devastating effects of these tragic lesions is the severe pain that so many patients with avulsion lesions of the plexus suffer. Wynn Parry [4] showed that some 90% of patients with avulsion lesions of the plexus suffer severe pain at some stage. The pain is characteristically crushing or burning and felt in the anaesthetic and paralysed hand. The pain may feel as if the hand is being tightened in a vice or is having boiling water poured all over it. This pain is usually constant and unremitting, In addition, there may be severe shooting pains of the paroxysmal type lasting a few seconds and being particularly violent, causing the patient to cry out or turn away and double up in pain. These paroxysms are often quite unpredictable and may occur many times an hour throughout the day. It is these paroxysmal attacks of pain that are the most devastating and to which the patient finds most difficulty in adjusting. When the spinal cord is deafferented by avulsion of nerve roots, the nerve cells in the dorsal horn that have lost their input begin to discharge with high frequency impulses, increasing in frequency and intensity as

times goes on. This is the cause of the severe pain. Anderson *et al.* [5] showed in an experimental model in the cat that within 8 days of de-afferentation of the spinal cord, nerve cells start firing spontaneously and more cells discharge with an increasing frequency so that by a month there was massive discharge throughout the whole of the dorsal horn. This pain may come immediately after the accident but we have patients in whom the onset has been delayed by 3 or 4 months. This pain is notoriously resistant to standard analgesics and indeed does not respond to the narcotics such as morphine or heroin. The single most helpful way of coping with this pain is by mental distraction. This allows the patient to bring in his own central inhibitory pathways, for it is known that there is an inhibitory pathway for pain running from the hypothalamus through the para-ventricular grey through the raphe nucleus in the medulla down to laminae 1 and 5 in the dorsal horn where all the nociceptive traffic is arriving. Involvement in absorbing work or hobbies can often either completely or materially reduce this pain. Often the patients find that when they relax in the evening, the pain comes back with a vengeance and many patients have taken a second job in order to try and cope with the pain [4].

By far the most valuable modality in our hands has been transcutaneous electrical stimulation. Electrodes are applied just proximal to the site of lesion. In a total lesion, for example, the electrodes will be placed on the neck and on the front of the chest over the C3/4 dermatomes and over the inner side of the upper arm over the T2 dermatome. The aim is to stimulate the afferent input above and below the lesion in order to produce maximum release of endorphins at that site to try and damp down the transmission of the spontaneous firing. We insist that all our patients are admitted to our intensive rehabilitation unit where our physiotherapists, who are particularly skilled in this technique, will try various positions of the electrodes and various settings of the parameters, stimulating for many hours a day for 2 weeks before the treatment is abandoned as unhelpful. Far too often we have found that patients have been given stimulators at pain clinics without proper instruction in their use and advised to try it for half an hour at a time. This is quite useless. The stimulation has a cumulative effect as is well shown by Melzak [6]. The patients must be encouraged to use the stimulator for many hours a day, if necessary all day and sometimes all night for long periods before giving up [7].

Sixty percent of the patients we have treated with severe pain from avulsion lesions have had substantial or complete relief. Most patients can give up the treatment within 6 months but some have continued to use it for up to a year and keep the stimulator by them if there is an exacerbation of pain with an intercurrent infection or a particularly stressful period in their lives.

We cannot emphasize enough the importance of the correct use of this invaluable technique. Fortunately the vast majority of patients either lose their pain within an average time of 3 years or come to terms with it to the extent that it no longer impinges on their life. Many patients respond to transcutaneous stimulation but a few – some 1% of all our patients with severe pain – find themselves in a desperate state with unremitting pain which gradually increases with time and totally destroys their life. Such patients are quite unable to work and the whole family suffers. It is for these patients that the dorsal root entry zone lesion is suitable. Nashold [8] described an operation to destroy the nerve cells in laminae 1 and 5 and although it is a destructive lesion it is aimed at the seat of the problem rather than tracts carrying nociceptive information. It is well recognized by neurosurgeons that destruction of tracts such as cordotomies, rhizotomies and mesencephalic tractotomies is no longer indicated in 'benign' pain. Sooner or later pain will certainly recur and usually at a considerably greater intensity than before. Thomas at the National Hospital for Nervous Diseases in London has carried out operations on 27 of our patients with severe unremitting intractable plexus pain. These are patients in whom the whole family has been affected by the pain and in which it is quite clear that desperate measures are required. Patients must of course be subjected to the full rehabilitation programme already described with a trial of return to work, functional splinting, transcutaneous stimulation and anti-paroxysmal drugs such as Tegretol and Tripatfen. In both Nashold's [9] and Thomas's [10,11] series, between 60 and 70% of patients can be expected to achieve substantial and complete relief of pain. There are, however, serious drawbacks to the operation for there is a significant incidence of complications. In Thomas's series, 10% of patients had significant neurological defects such as weakness of the ipsilateral leg, unpleasant dysaesthesiae of the trunk, weakness of the neck muscles and affection of balance. One of our patients was rendered impotent and two were impotent for 6 months. It is therefore vital to make sure the patient understands the serious risk that he may be running, the least of which may be a lack of relief of pain and at the worst a neurological disability in addition. Provided the patient is psychologically robust and has been carefully assessed by the clinical psychologist, and provided the rehabilitation team is satisfied that every possible measure has been tried exhaustively and that the patient is in a really desperate state, then he is referred for this procedure.

Conclusions

Surgery is only one episode, albeit an all important one, in an ongoing saga in patients with brachial plexus lesions. The best results cannot be expected without the backup of a comprehensive and intensive rehabilitation regime. The rehabilitation team will provide the best conditions for surgery by restoring as full a range of passive movement to joints as possible and reducing oedema and regaining maximum function in spared muscles. They will provide skilled re-education after surgery, whether reparative or reconstructive. They will make determined attempts to help the pain and explain to the patient the nature of the pain and how he can best cope with it. They will provide appropriate functional splinting and help the patient return to work.

References

1. Jones, S. J., Wynn Parry, C. B. and Landi, A. (1980) Diagnosis of brachial plexus traction lesions by sensory nerve action potentials and somatosensory evoked potentials. *Injury*, **12**, 376–382.
2. Wynn Parry, C. B. (1980) Management of traction lesion of the brachial plexus and peripheral

nerve injuries in the upper limb. The Ruscoe Clark Memorial Lecture for 1979. *Injury*, **11**, 265–285.

3. Frampton, V. M. (1986) Problems involved in the management of reconstructive surgery in brachial plexus lesions contrasted with peripheral nerve injuries. *J. Hand Surg.*, **11**, 3–9.

4. Wynn Parry, C. B. (1980) Pain in avulsion lesions of the brachial plexus. *Pain*, **9**, 41–53.

5. Anderson, L. S., Black, R. G., Abraham, J. *et al.* (1971) Neuronal hyperactivity in experimental trigeminal deafferentation. *J. Neurosurg.*, **35**, 444.

6. Melzack, R. (1975) Prolonged relief of pain by brief intense transcutaneous stimulation. *Pain*, **1**, 357–374.

7. Frampton, V. (1982) Pain control with the aid of the transcutaneous stimulator. *Physiotherapy*, **68**, 77–71.

8. Nashold, B. S., Urban, B. and Zorab, D. S. (1976) Phantom pain relief by focal destruction of the substantia gelatinosa of Rolando. In: *Advances in Pain and Research Therapy* (eds J. J. Bonica and D. Albe Fessard) Vol. 1. Raven Press, New York, pp. 959–963.

9. Nashold, B. S. and Ostdahl, R. H. (1979) Dorsal root entry zone lesions for pain relief. *J. Neurosurg.*, **57**, 9–69.

10. Thomas, D. G. T. and Sheehy, J. R. R. (1983) Dorsal root entry zone lesions (Nashold's procedure for pain relief following brachial plexus avulsion. *J. Neurol. Neurosurg. Psychiat.*, **46**, 924–928.

11. Thomas, D. G. T. and Jones, S. J. (1984) Dorsal root entry zone lesions (Nashold's procedure) in brachial plexus avulsion. *Neurosurgery*, **15**, 966–967.

17

Rotator cuff injury

M. F. Swiontkowski

The rotator cuff is the term given to the confluence of the supraspinatus, infraspinatus, teres minor, and subscapularis. Its structure and function are essential to the stability and motion of the glenohumeral joint. The unconstrained articulation of the large radius convexity of the humeral head and the very shallow concavity of the glenoid surface must be enhanced by this confluence of tendons. Degeneration of this essential structure leads to pain, weakness, and sometimes stiffness of the glenohumeral joint. When degeneration progresses to a complete tear, superior instability of the glenohumeral joint can result. This phenomenon, with its resultant weakness of abduction and external rotation as well as pain, can lead to permanent, irreversible worsening of shoulder function.

Smith [1] credited by Codman [2] as the first investigator to report tears in the region of the insertion of the supraspinatus tendon. Smith was also the first to note the association of ruptures of the long head of the biceps with these tears. Additionally, he observed that 'the undersurface of the acromion process was found hardened by the friction of the head of the humerus and covered by a peculiar enamel-like secretion'. This was, of course, a description of an associated osteophyte of the undersurface of the acromion process. In the majority of the younger-aged cadavers Smith examined, he suspected acute trauma was the cause of the tendon avulsions. In two older cadavers he reported bilateral findings with communication of larger tears with the subacromial bursae, and noted synovial hyper-

trophy. One hundred years later Smith's findings were confirmed by Codman [2], Skinner [3], and Cotton [4], who reported a high incidence of these findings in older patients and frequent bilaterality. Codman was the first to recommend prompt recognition and repair to avoid 'much pain and disability as well as great economic loss' [2]. Functional improvement following repair was later confirmed by McLaughlin [5].

Presentation

Patients with tears of the rotator cuff are frequently older than 40 years of age and present with pain and weakness. Most patients have a prolonged history of intermittent aching in the shoulder associated with forward elevation and internal rotation of the arm. Older patients will often have no history of trauma, while those in the 40–55 year age group, particularly males, generally report a fall or forced abduction–external rotation of the arm [6].

Unless an element of adhesive capsulitis is associated with a longstanding rotator cuff tear, the patient will have a full passive range of glenohumeral motion. Initiation of abduction is typically severely limited, as is active internal rotation and forward elevation. These findings contrast with the partial tear stage or earlier 'impingement lesions', in that weakness and loss of active motion are present. The pain reported in both conditions is frequently aggravated by use of the arm in internal rotation and forward elevation. Patients report a dull, moderate to severe ache in the shoulder region. A frequent complaint is the inability to sleep on the affected side. The pain frequently radiates to the deltoid insertion and occasionally to the lateral elbow region. Deltoid motor function and axillary nerve sensation should be normal.

Diagnostic methods

Because of variability in history, degree of weakness of external rotation, initiation of abduction, and degree of pain, it is often impossible to make a definitive diagnosis of a rotator cuff tear. For this reason, ancillary diagnostic methods are of critical importance. Arthrography remains the cornerstone of diagnostic technique; however, the importance of plain radiography is frequently underestimated. In patients with large cuff tears, the classic radiographic findings are a decreased space between the superior humerus and undersurface of the acromion (less than 7 mm), cyst formation at the insertion of the supraspinatus, sclerosis of the undersurface of the acromion, irregularity of the greater tuberosity, and deepening of the groove between the articular surface and cuff attachment. A high quality AP of the scapula (allowing the clear visualization of the glenohumeral articular surface) and an axillary view must be obtained in every patient where the diagnosis of a rotator cuff tear is considered.

Standard arthrography has correlated with surgical findings in 90–100% of cases in multiple series of rotator cuff tears [7,8]. Pneumoarthrotomography is thought by several authors to improve the accuracy of diagnosis, but this is generally restricted to partial tears of the inferior surface of the cuff. The size of the tear is difficult to estimate from the arthrogram, and the differentiation of a small to medium size tear from a massive tear is best made on the basis of clinical examination and plain radiographs.

Recently, the use of ultrasonography has been shown to be an excellent alternative to the use of arthrography. A newer design probe head is required, as well as an interested and experienced ultrasonographer. Using these criteria, Mack *et al.* have demonstrated a 91% sensitivity and a 100% specificity compared to surgical findings [9]. This diagnostic tool is especially useful in patients with contrast allergies. Shoulder arthroscopy, although useful in treating labral tears and lesions of the biceps tendon, is of little help in the management of rotator cuff tear [10].

Rotator cuff anatomy and physiology

The confluence of the tendons of the subscapularis anteriorly with the teres minor, infraspinatus, and supraspinatus tendons posteriorly to superiorly is illustrated in Fig. 17.1. As shown by Smith [1] and Codman [2], the supraspinatus is involved with the vast majority of rotator cuff tears. This is due to its function in initiating abduction as well as to its position in relation to the inferior acromion and coracoacromial ligament.

Rotator cuff vascular anatomy may play a critical role in the degeneration of the rotator cuff [11]. Using injection studies, Laing investigated the arterial supply of the humerus in detail [12]. He noted the perforation of vessels of the anterior humeral circumflex into the humeral head and rotator cuff in the region of attachment of the supraspinatus tendon. Lindblom and Palmer were the first to demonstrate hypovascular areas in the region of the rotator cuff [13]. They noted a low perfusion area near the insertion of the supraspinatus tendon into the tuberosity, and a second region within the long head of the biceps near its origin at the superior glenoid. Based on clinical experience, Codman [2] had pointed to a 'critical portion' of the supraspinatus tendon which was renamed the 'critical zone' by Neer [14]. This region was shown in the injection studies of Rothman and Parke to have relatively low perfusion [15]. Rathburn and MacNab's study confirmed this finding and hypothesized that the resting position of the arm in adduction and vertical rotation causes the humeral head to place pressure on this region, which further decreases perfusion and predisposes this region to degeneration [16]. In the author's experience, preliminary studies utilizing laser Doppler flowmetry have shown this region to be hypervascular in terms of real-time measurement of capillary level blood flow [17]. It may be that repeated trauma to the tendon due to impingement on the undersurface of the acromion (see below) produces hyperaemia, which weakens the substance of the tendon and predisposes this region to rupture. This may correspond to Neer's phase I (haemorrhage and oedema) at the periphery of a cuff disruption [18].

The spectrum of rotator cuff disease

Neer has carefully and clearly delineated the spectrum of rotator cuff disease, based on experience in the anatomy laboratory and in surgery [18]. Stage I is oedema and haemorrhage within the 'critical zone' due to repeated trauma of the humeral head riding superiorly and crushing the tendon against the anterior surface of the acromion. Statistically, this is more common in the under 30 age group and is associated with overhead sports (i.e. tennis), but can occur in any patient with a new onset of activity above the horizontal plane. A common scenario is the 50-year-old weekend house painter or tree trimmer. With this history and mechanism of injury, conservative treatment is successful in all but the rarest cases. Treatment includes the use of an anti-inflammatory drug and resistive internal and external rotator strengthening exercises. Isometric exercises using surgical tubing for mechanical resistance have proven very effective, but must be performed at least three times a day for several weeks and then continued on an intermittent basis for several months. This treatment should be employed when there is no element of adhesive capsulitis restricting the active and passive range of shoulder motion. When adhesive capsulitis is present, assisted ROM exercises and/or manipulation should be included in the treatment plan. In the athlete, shoulder subluxation may play a role in the development of these symptoms. Shoulder instability and apprehension with the arm in abduction and external rotation must be examined for and treated appropriately. In all three stages of the disease, Radiographs must be carefully studied for osteophytes and narrowing of the acromioclavicular (AC) joint, reflecting AC arthritis which can mimic the symptoms of rotator cuff disease. A careful examination will often reveal direct tenderness over the AC joint, and the symptoms in this case can be relieved by a 2–3 ml injection of lidocaine into this joint. The cross body adduction test, which produces pain both in subacromial impingement stage I and AC arthritis, can thereby be eliminated.

The second stage of rotator cuff disease is that of fibrosis and tendinitis. With prolonged, repeated impingement of the rotator cuff on the undersurface of the acromion and coracoacromial (CA) ligament, the single cell layer, thin, overlying subacromial bursae becomes hypertrophied, and fibrotic. Because of the chronicity of the condition, this population of patients is generally 10–15 years older than the first stage patient. The history is that of refractory shoulder pain exacerbated by forward flexion and internal rotation. Frequently, patients presenting with this history of symptoms of intermittent severity for several years will have had multiple subacromial injections of steroids. This provides excellent temporary relief of the condition due to the patent anti-inflammatory properties of these compounds. Unfortunately, these compounds also result in weakening of the tensile strength of tendons and predispose to rupture of the rotator cuff – the next stage in the natural history of the disease. The use of these compounds on a chronic basis of this disease process must therefore be condemned.

As with the patient presenting in stage I, an element of adhesive capsulitis may be present in the stage II patient. This patient would present with limitations of active *and* passive ROM, evident primarily in loss of forward elevation and internal rotation. As the age of presentation moves into the 40–50 year age group, calcific tendinitis must enter the differential diagnosis. On the initial screening X-rays, calcific deposits in the insertion of the supraspinatus will be evident. The history is most often quite different from that of impingement syndrome with the rapid onset of severe shoulder pain unprovoked by activity. Calcific tendinitis is effectively managed by heat and anti-inflammatory drugs or with aspiration of the calcific deposit followed by administration of a single dose of long-acting steroid into the area of calcific degeneration.

In the second stage of impingement, correct conservative treatment as outlined for stage I should be employed for at least 12 months. In refractory cases, surgical management is recommended. This consists of resection of the thickened bursae, removal of the CA ligament, inspection of the tendon for a tear, and an anterior acromioplasty of the type advocated by Neer [14,18]. Removal of the lateral acromion is to be condemned, as it does not address the problem of the zone of impingement and weakens the deltoid origin [18]. The anterior–inferior one-third of the acromion should be inspected for overhang or osteophytes and if either of these is present, this segment of the acromion should be removed with a thin beveled osteotome or high-speed burr. The approach to the region should be an oblique incision one finger breadth lateral to the acomion in Langer's lines to optimize cosmesis. The interval between the anterior and middle one-third of the deltoid should be split $1\frac{1}{2}$–$2\frac{1}{2}$ cm distal from the tip of the acromion within the tendinous portion. Minimal deltoid (1 cm or less) from the lateral portion of the acromion as well as the anterior portion should be taken down. Care must be taken to leave enough deltoid fascia on the superior acromion to allow repair and, when this is not possible, repair should be performed with non-absorbable sutures through drill holes.

The final phase of the disease spectrum is that of acromial bone spurs and tendon ruptures. As this represents the endpoint on a continuum of chronic disease, patients in this phase are generally 45 or more years old. Almost invariably, the symptoms are of many years' duration. As noted earlier, patients presenting with tendon ruptures have frequently had multiple steroid injections, which play a role in pathogenesis. Because of the older age range of these patients, the differential diagnosis of chronic shoulder pain must include cervical radiculopathy, superior sulcus (Pancoast) tumors, and coronary artery disease. The biceps tendon is involved in the zone of impingement, and irritation of the biceps tendon is often present with tenderness in the bicipital groove. Neer has stated that the biceps tendon ruptures infrequently in this stage, and that the ratio of rupture of the supraspinatus to rupture of the long head of the biceps is seven to one [18]. Anatomical variability within the bicipital groove (shallowness, sharp lateral margin) may predispose some patients to early rupture of the long head of the biceps.

With further impingement on a fibrotic cuff, two phenomena develop. The anterior–inferior edge of the acromion becomes hypertrophic, and osteophytes and bone cysts develop in response to the pressure phenomenon. The second development is thinning and atrophy of the rotator cuff. The cuff tendon in the zone of impingement has become hypervascular from irritation [17] and eventually becomes weakened in terms of tensile strength. At this point, minor trauma leads to a rupture of the tendon. Routine radiographs may reveal the acromial changes and in cases of moderate to large size tears the distance between the humeral head and the acromion may be narrowed. Other than these radiographic signs present in large tears, there are no plain radiographic findings diagnostic for a cuff tear. The utility of arthrography and ultrasound has been referred to previously.

It is unlikely that partial or full thickness rotator cuff ruptures will heal if they remain untreated. This is due to the pathophysiology which produced the tensile weakness and the continued stress on the tendon in the region of the tear. In the setting of chronic shoulder pain where the indications for anterior acromioplasty are present (positive impingement test with symptoms refractory to conservative care for 12 months) in association with a proven cuff rupture, the acromioplasty should be performed as outlined by Neer and the rotator cuff concomitantly repaired directly using non-absorbable inverted sutures or brought into a groove in the greater tuberosity and sutured into bone through drill holes. Every effort must be made to mobilize the edges of the retracted cuff in the case of large (greater than 4 cm) tears and repair the tendon to bone. Where this is not possible, interposed synthetic materials or freeze dried dura or fascia lata have not proven effective and a simple debridement of the tendon combined with resection of the CA ligament, bursal resection, and inferior acromioplasty should be performed. Advancement of the supraspinatus posteriorly as described by Debeyre may be an effective alternative [19]. Great care must be taken to evaluate the acromioclavicular joint preoperatively as noted above. A resection of the lateral 1.5 cm of the calvicle should be performed when the AC joint is arthritic and pain is relieved by preoperative local anaesthetic injection or when an inferior osteophyte is impinging on the rotator cuff.

If a full thickness rotator cuff tear remains untreated, the disease may progress further. This progression takes the form of further superior migration of the humeral head until it eventually articulates with the acromion and loss of glenohumeral joint space results, with cyst formation and erosion of the atrophic humeral head and glenoid. The later articular changes occur because of the pathomechanical joint forces which introduce extreme shear forces across the glenohumeral joint and result in cartilage degradation and subchondral bone atrophy. Neer has termed this process 'cuff tear arthropathy' [20]. The recommended treatment is total shoulder arthroplasty with repair of the cuff whenever (although this occurs rarely) possible. Following this procedure, a special rehabilitation program must be designed to offset the loss of the constraining function of the rotator cuff and, in fact, special glenoid components may be necessary to prevent excess shear force across the glenoid surface with subsequent increased risk of loosening. It is not suggested that all rotator cuff tears result in this severe joint destruction, but this must be taken into consideration when recommending treatment of a full thickness rotator cuff rupture.

In the continuum of rotator cuff impingement disease, the impingement sign is helpful in differentiating symptoms referable to the rotator cuff from those due to calcium deposit tendinitis, AC arthritis, instability, and other non-glenohumeral aetiologies. As the test for the sign is described by Neer [18], the examiner stands to the rear of the seated patient and stabilizes the scapula with one hand and raises the arm with the other into forward elevation. Prevention of scapular rotation forces impingement of haemorrhagic, fibrotic, or torn supraspinatus region onto the anterior–inferior edge of the acromion, which reproduces the patient's complaint. This manoeuvre will also produce pain with glenohumeral arthritis, mild adhesive capsulitis, subluxation, and calcium deposition disease. The final confirmation of the diagnosis of impingement related rotator cuff disease can be made with the 'impingement test', also described by Neer [18]. The subacromial space is injected with 10 ml of 1.0% xylocaine and the above-described manoeuvre repeated. This is best accomplished with the patient seated, the shoulder sterilely prepared, using a long $1\frac{1}{2}$ inch 25 gauge needle, and with an assistant pulling the arm distally. This injection will not relieve symptoms due to the other problems listed above.

Results of operative repair

When ruptures of the rotator cuff are repaired primarily after debriding the frayed edges or suturing them into bone troughs in the greater tuberosity, excellent results in terms of pain relief can be expected in 84–95% of patients [7,8].

Patients with smaller tears tend to have better results, although the size of the tear is not the critical indicator. Duration of symptoms is inversely proportional to the percentage of excellent results, which mandates an early investigation into the possibility of rotator cuff rupture. Duration of symptoms is directly related to the size of the tear and to the distance between the humeral head and acromion, both of which directly influence the results. Loss of passive ROM and strength of abduction and external rotation preoperatively negatively affect the results of surgical treatment and suggest that an element of adhesive capsulitis negatively influences final motion and function in terms of pain [4]. Loss of strength, however, is not directly related to the size of the cuff defect. Despite the fact that many of the cuff repairs are not 'water tight' when reexamined arthrographically postoperatively, pain relief and improvement in function are achieved in approximately 98% of patients [8]. Because the majority of patients with irreparable cuff tears improve after debridement and acromioplasty, the author believes that the key to relieving pain and improving function is the acromioplasty. The implication is that removing the compressive forces on a thickened, hyperaemic tendon, torn or not, produces pain relief.

The future

The educational efforts of Neer, Hawkins, Rockwood *et al.* will continue to have the effect of improving both the knowledge base and the experience of the general orthopaedist, which will most likely result in earlier diagnosis and treatment of the impingement syndrome. The best approach to the treatment of massive rotator cuff tears and cuff-tear arthropathy is to prevent them from developing. New information on the response of the rotator cuff to injury and repair will be forthcoming, due in part to the development of new techniques for studying soft tissue blood flow and repair [17]. Improved techniques for arthroscopy may play an important role in the clinical study of the rotator cuff, as well as investigations into less traumatic techniques for its repair [10]. Improved substitutional materials may one day make the repair of massive cuff tears with interpositional material a reality, which should yield improved functional results. Much investigative work is being conducted into the clinical problems of rotator cuff function degeneration and repair.

References

1. Smith, J. G. (1834) Pathological appearances of seven cases of injury of the shoulder joints with remarks. *London Med. Gaz.*, **14**, 280.
2. Codman, E. A. (1937) Rupture of the supraspinatus – 1834 to 1934. *J. Bone Joint Surg.*, **19**, 643–652.
3. Skinner, H. A. (1937) Anatomical considerations relative to rupture of the supraspinatus tendon. *J. Bone Joint Surg.*, **19**, 137.
4. Cotton, R. E. and Rideout, D. F. (1964) Tears of the humeral rotator cuff – a radiological and pathological necropsy survey. *J. Bone Joint Surg.*, **46B**, 314–328.
5. McLaughlin, H. L. (1944) Lesions of the musculotendinous cuff of the shoulder – the exposure and treatment of tears with retraction. *J. Bone Joint Surg.*, **26**, 31–51.
6. Post, M., Silver, R. and Singh, M. (1983) Rotator cuff tear, diagnosis and treatment. *Clin. Orthop.*, **173**, 78–91.
7. Ellman, H., Hanker, G. and Bayer, M. (1986) Repair of the rotator cuff – end result study of factors influencing reconstruction. *J. Bone Joint Surg.*, **68A**, 1136–1144.
8. Hawkins, R. J., Misamore, G. W. and Hobeika, P. A. (1985) Surgery for full thickness rotator cuff tears. *J. Bone Joint Surg.*, **67A**, 1349–1355.
9. Mack, L. A., Matsen, F. A. III, Kilcoyne, R. F., Davies, P. K. and Sickler, M. E. (1985) US evaluation of the rotator cuff. *Radiology*, **157**, 205–209.
10. Ogilvie-Harris, D. J. and Wiley, A. M. (1986) Arthroscopic surgery of the shoulder – a general appraisal. *J. Bone Joint Surg.*, **68B**, 201–207.
11. Moseley, H. F. and Goldie, I. (1963) The arterial pattern of the rotator cuff of the shoulder. *J. Bone Joint Surg.*, **45B**, 780–789.
12. Laing, P. G. (1956) The arterial supply of the adult humerus. *J. Bone Joint Surg.*, **38A**, 1105–1116.
13. Lindblom, K. and Palmer, I. (1939) Ruptures of the tendon aponeurosis of the shoulder joint – the so-called supraspinatus rupture. *Acta Chir. Scand.*, **82**, 133–142.
14. Neer, C. S. (1972) Anterior acromioplasty for the chronic impingement syndrome in the shoulder – a preliminary report. *J. Bone Joint Surg.*, **54A**, 41–50.
15. Rothman, R. H. and Parke, W. W. (1965) The vascular anatomy of the rotator cuff. *Clin. Orthop.*, **41**, 176–186.
16. Rathburn, J. B. and MacNab, I. (1970) The microvascular pattern of the rotator cuff. *J. Bone Joint Surg.*, **52B**, 540–553.
17. Swiontkowski, M. F. Unpublished data.
18. Neer, C. S. (1983) Impingement lesions. *Clin. Orthop.*, **173**, 70–77.
19. Debeyre, J., Patte, D. and Elmelik, E. Repair of ruptures of the rotator cuff of the shoulder – with a note on advancement of the supraspinatus muscle. *J. Bone Joint Surg.*, **47B**, 36–42.
20. Neer, C. S., Craig, E. V. and Fukuda, H. (1983) Cuff tear arthroplasty. *J. Bone Joint Surg.*, **65A**, 1232–1244.

Osteoarthritis of the hip

C. H. Wynn Jones

Incidence

Population surveys show the incidence of osteo-arthritis of the hip increases with age. In females almost all have pain with marked radiological changes but in males only just over half those with moderate radiographic changes admitted to pain.

The overall incidence in female and male adults of all ages was 1%.

Aetiology and pathogenesis

Primary, idiopathic

This group is diminishing as identifiable causes or related factors are discovered.

Secondary, congenital

Skeletal dysplasia generalized.
Congenital hip dysplasia [1].
Strong inherited tendency yet no actual identified lesion.

Secondary, acquired

Acute injury and late effects.
Overload or repetitive minor injury.

Infection.
Suppuration/T.B.
Nutrition, rickets, metabolic and endocrine disorders, gout, acromegaly, slipped upper femoral epiphysis.
Inflammatory.
Immune deficiency disorder, rheumatoid arthritis.
Lysozome or storage diseases.
Following avascular necrosis:
Perthes' disease;
Idiopathic;
Associated with alcohol;
Other storage diseases, Gaucher's etc.;
Steroids.

Histological, biochemical and mechanical changes in cartilage and bone in osteoarthritis

Histology

The earlier changes can be seen as a natural process of aging and may not be associated with osteoarthritis either clinically or radiologically.

The earliest findings are zones of granularity especially of the anterior head.

Cartilage fibrillation may vary from minor to full thickness crevices down to bone. There may be cartilage loss, subchondral sclerosis and trabecular thickening.

Synovial inflammation is evident with increased vascularity, mononuclear cell infiltrate, fibrin deposits and villous hypertrophy.

Crystals are frequently associated with a high degree of inflammation in the synovium and may be of monosodium urate, as seen in gout or calcium pyrophosphate in chondrocalcinosis.

Biochemical changes

Proteoglycan molecules become smaller, synthesized at an increased rate and they appear to aggregate less well. There is overall less proteoglycan and there is an increased chondroitin component compared to the keratin sulphate component within the cartilage. The water content in arthritic cartilage is increased and the collagen bundle arrangement is altered; the meshwork structure becomes deficient.

Mechanical changes

Failure of lubrication cannot be implicated at present. There are glycoproteins in the synovium fluid that have particular lubricating qualities. Pseudonym 'Lubricin'.

Cartilage mechanical strength

The creep test under load of cartilage shows that the cartilage is softer and there is an increased rate of creep with an overall reduction in the compressive stiffness. The cartilage is thinned down overall. Freeman found that the cartilage at the zenith of the femoral head was much thicker and had different compression qualities from the cartilage at the antero inferior aspect of the head.

Vascular changes in osteoarthritis

These may be secondary to the initial development of osteoarthritis. There is certainly increased flow in the subchondral area in the cancellous bone beneath arthritic joints as demonstrated by isotope investigations There is also an increased venous intraosseus pressure.

Classification

Radiographic morphology of hip osteoarthrosis

There is no generally agreed radiological classification of osteoarthritis of the hip. Wroblewski and Charnley [2] describe such a classification but do not relate it to the outcome in total hip replacement. Such a classification becomes more important if osteotomies of various types are considered because it is now generally agreed that certain types of osteotomy may be better for specific radiological varieties of osteoarthritis.

Bombelli, in his classic monograph on osteoarthritis [3] of the hip treated by osteotomy, describes such a classification. The author commends the following (differs little from Charnley's).

Superolateral (Fig. 18.1)

Type a

Spherical head polar osteoarthritis, i.e. superior narrowing of the joint space with sclerosis or cyst formation. The medial cartilage joint space may be normal and there are minimal osteophytes.

Type b

Ellipsoid head. The acetabulum is more oblique and the head in the corresponding plane is flattened. There are major medial osteophytes on the femoral head with a capital drop. The head is beginning to glide antero-cranially out of the acetabulum.

Type c

Subluxated. There is extreme obliquity of the articular acetabular surface with uncovering of the femoral head. Shenton's line is severely interrupted and there are often marked floor osteophytes.

Type d

Lateralized.

  (i) Early stage.
  (ii) Middle stage.
  (iii) Later stage.

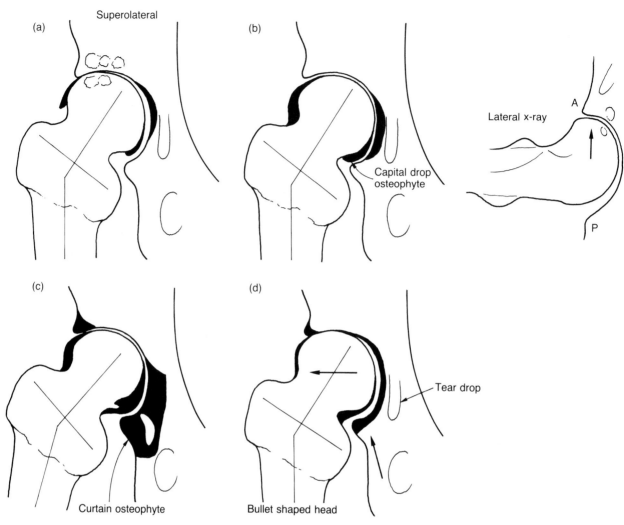

Fig. 18.1 (a) Loss of joint space superiorly and anteriorly polar OA. Neck slightly valgus (normal CCD < 126° 3). Weight bearing surface horizontal. (b) As (a) but head gliding more anterosuperior – WBS oblique. Valgus neck (CCD > 126°). (c) Congenital abnormal acetabulum with severe obliquity. Valgus anteverted femoral neck (new acetabulum formed). (d) Floor curtain osteophytes, extruding head, i.e., floor very deep. Often normal neck shaft angle.

The femoral head tends to migrate laterally. The head is usually fairly round, the weight bearing surface is horizontal and according to the grade the capital drop, i.e. the medial head osteophyte and the curtain osteophyte, i.e. the inferior floor osteophyte, become well developed. There may be a small roof osteophyte. (dii may be confused with type a.)

The superolateral group a,b,c belong to those arthritides that result from hip dysplasia and Perthes' disease. (The lateral radiograph demonstrates anterior osteoarthritis between femoral head and acetabulum and there may be a great deal of anteversion of the femoral neck in the congenital varieties.) There may be a strong preceding history of injury or heavy sport in superolateral type d.

Concentric (Fig. 18.2)

The head is spherical and well centred even on a lateral radiograph and there is even cartilage wear on acetabulum and femoral head. Osteophytes are scarce. The bone may be eburnated and sclerotic. There may not be widespread cyst formation because of even stress on the femoral head and acetabulum.

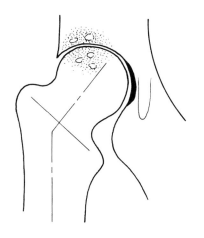

Fig. 18.2 Concentric round head, even wear acetabular cartilage and femoral head.

Medial (Fig. 18.3)

Type a (equatorial)

The femoral head points to the deeper aspect of the acetabulum. There is loss of joint space medially. Good superolateral cartilage joint space can be seen to be preserved. There may be a lateral acetabular osteophyte and a modest varus disposition on the femoral neck.

Type b (coxa profunda)

In such a case there is often a very varus disposition of the femoral neck, perhaps CCD angle 110. Superolateral cartilage joint space may be well preserved. In the main there is inferomedial

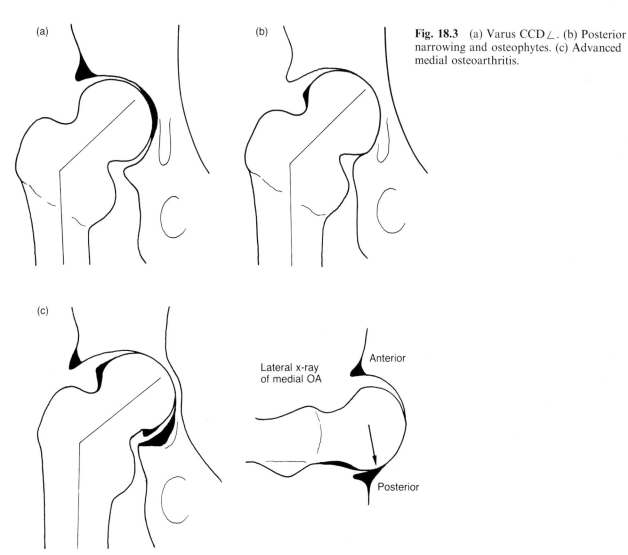

Fig. 18.3 (a) Varus CCD∠. (b) Posterior narrowing and osteophytes. (c) Advanced medial osteoarthritis.

narrowing of the joint space. The head is well sunk into the acetabulum, the medial wall of which may be very thin.

Type c (protrusio acetabuli)

The floor of the acetabulum is often interrupted and the head deeply penetrates into the acetabulum with medial osteoarthritis. The femoral head often loses its normal shape. On the lateral radiograph there is often good anterior joint space but posteriorly it may be lost and the head may be directed posteriorly, i.e. retroverted.

Other features that can be radiologically interpreted are the biological reaction of the bone to the arthritic process. The reaction may be atrophic, normotrophic or hypertrophic. In the former there is often collapse of the femoral head with very little attempt at osteophyte formation. It could be considered a metabolic problem and in such cases there are often marked inflammatory synovial changes, oedema and a high degree of vascularity. The latter hypertrophic osteoarthrosis is where the hip has a completely distorted shape and there is marked over growth of osteophytes. There are often protruding roof osteophytes and the capital drop is often high and with a large medial osteophyte in the acetabular floor; a so-called curtain osteophyte. It could be interpreted that in such cases the bone is still very reactive. Frequently there is a good cortical thickness in the femoral shaft. Such cases often respond well to osteotomy because the bone is reactive. A concomitant of this radiological feature is often marked stiffness which may be a contraindication to osteotomy.

Such a classification is helpful in choosing which sort of osteotomy to undertake. In terms of success rate after conventional cemented arthroplasty there are the obvious problems that may be predicted. For example, a gross protrusio with loss of the medial floor may mean that special measures will have to be undertaken to lateralize the cup into its anatomical position perhaps with bone grafting or the use of a non-cement cup with perimeter bearing. Similarly, a superolateral type b or in particular c with a marked degree of subluxation, an arthritic high false acetabulum is formed which has a very deficient roof. Special techniques are required to obtain the correct relationship of the prosthesis and true acetabulum; bone grafting or a small acetabular component may be required.

In osteotomy the implications for classification are much more profound as the success in any particular sort of osteotomy depends upon the type of arthritis.

Although not widely practised now, resurfacing arthroplasty is generally unwise for patients with radiological features more of metabolic inactivity than mechanically reactive osteoarthritis. The incidence of femoral neck failure is high in such patients. The bone density can be quantified with CT scans and should not be under 200 CT units.

Biomechanics of the hip

1. Normal.
2. The hip after osteotomy.
3. Biomechanical aspects of T.H.R. and design.

Normal hip joint

To assess the forces across the hip joint one has to simplify the hip down to a simple system of levers. A static analysis in one plane only is the simplest.

Uniplanar static analysis

The magnitude and direction of the forces acting on the joint are represented in Figs 18.4 and 18.5.

Figure 18.6 represents the analysis of the hip joint force with the subject standing on one leg,

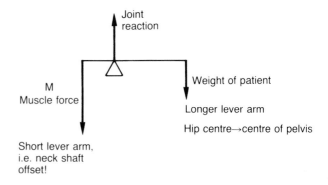

Fig. 18.4 Torque equilibrium in one-legged stance.

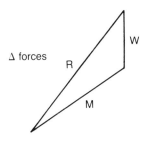

Fig. 18.5 Where length is proportionate to amount. direction is direction of force.

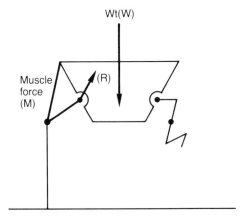

Fig. 18.6 One leg weight-bearing stance: W = weight of patient; M = muscle force of abductors; R = joint reaction force.

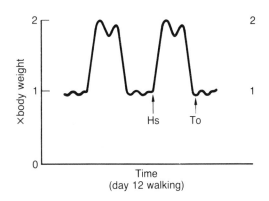

Fig. 18.7 Load trace from instrumented femoral component during walking.

when the subject is in equilibrium and Newton's first law is fulfilled. Newton's third law states that in equilibrium for each force there is an equal and opposite force. A simple balance principle, as in the diagram above, shows this.

Due to its small lever arm about the hip joint the abductor force must be large to achieve equilibrium. The sum of the abductor force and the body weight must equal the force on the hip joint to achieve force equilibrium. The force across the hip joint is large, for example four times the body weight.

The femoral neck must therefore withstand a large bending moment.

Dynamic stress analysis

The more sophisticated analyses consider the body in locomotion. Skin markers and light emitting diodes are placed over bony prominences in relation to the axial points of the joints of the lower limb. The patient is filmed in two planes at right angles during walking. Simultaneously, ground to foot forces readings in various directions are measured by a force-plate recessed in the floor, and thus the components of total joint force can be obtained by computer analysis. The phasic actions of muscles can be recorded by EMG synchronous recordings and relayed by trailing leads or telemetry. From these studies Paul suggested a figure of four times the body weight as a peak during walking. Walking up an incline or going upstairs increases this to about five times body weight [4].

It is estimated that certain sporting activities may increase the hip joint load to 15 times body weight, but these figures are difficult to analyse.

In vivo prosthetic joint force recordings have been undertaken English [5] implanted prostheses from which direct readings of force transmitted during ambulation were recorded. The load cycle achieved with walking by English is shown in Fig. 18.7.

Figure 18.8a shows that the resultant force across the hip joint varies according to the gait phase. When seen after total hip replacement the angle varies less. The inclination of R as viewed laterally is shown in Fig. 18.8b. This implies a twisting force which is applied to the proximal femur (Fig. 18.8c).

These findings in general suggest that load variability induced by walking and physical activity has a greater effect upon the magnitude and direction of R; thus the stress across the hip joint has a bearing on implant design and/or surgical technique.

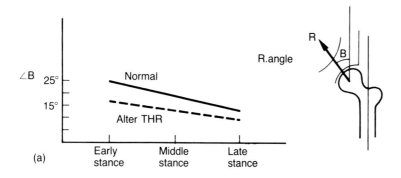

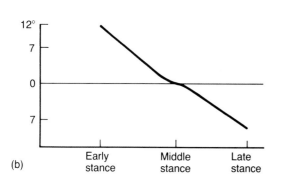

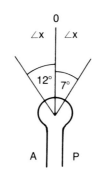

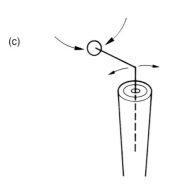

Fig. 18.8 Load angle and direction during walking. (a) ∠ of R in coronal plane. (b) Load ∠ change during walking: sagittal plane. (c) Torsional moment on femoral component induced by alternating ∠R with respect to coronal plane.

Biomechanics of the hip joint and osteotomy

Osteotomy and the soft tissue release can affect the forces across the hip joint in three ways:

(1) Alteration of the neck shaft angle alters the lever arm. The effect of this can be considered in the coronal and sagittal planes. A more varus disposition of the neck shaft angle reduces the joint force and medializes R, because it effectively increases the load taken by the abductor muscles. Valgus osteotomy on the other hand increases R and makes it more steeply inclined (Fig. 18.9a). As viewed in the horizontal plane the extension component to an osteotomy must tend to put R posterior to the vertical line of the hip joint (Fig. 18.9b).

(2) Osteotomy can influence the load distribution within the joint, an osteotomy (Fig. 18.9c) can improve congruency increasing the load bearing area. A valgus osteotomy brings osteophytes that were previously not load bearing into load contact with the acetabulum and must reduce joint stress (Fig. 18.9d). Muscle or tendon release (Voss procedure) can also reduce hip joint force.

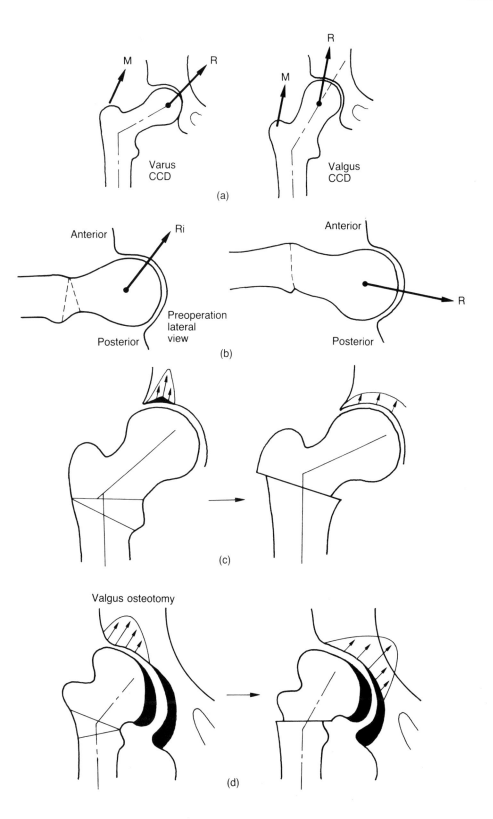

Fig. 18.9 (a–d) Alterations of Resultant force R with osteotomy. Improving congruency 'evens up' bad distribution.

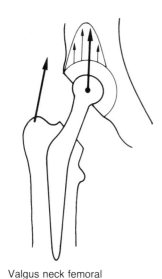

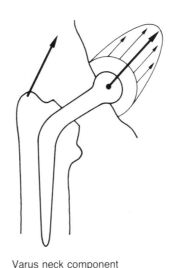

Fig. 18.10   (a) Valgus neck femoral component. (b) Varus neck component.

Valgus neck femoral
component

Varus neck component

Biomechanical alterations after hip joint replacement

Femoral component

Wroblewski's analysis of fractured femoral stems demonstrates that the initiation point for a fatigue failure is the anterolateral corner of the prosthesis. This supports the biomechanical analysis demonstrating a torsional force on the proximal femur. An increased offset prosthesis would increase the anterolateral load on the prosthesis. Anteversion of the prosthetic component tends to reduce the torsional moment. Similarly, a very valgus disposition of the neck shaft angle would decrease the torsional moment. A valgus neck shaft angle can minimize the lateral skin stress in the prosthesis but a side effect of the use of such a prosthesis would be to localize force R more superolaterally within the acetabular component with the potential for uneven load distribution at the cement bone interface (Fig. 18.10).

Implant design

An intramedullary femoral prosthesis alters the load distribution within the femur. Abnormal bending, shear and hoop stresses are induced. The design of the prosthesis and fixation must be such as to minimize each of these.

Axial

Calcar contact theoretically facilitates proximal load transmission but clinical studies when cemented arthroplasty is used suggest that calcar contact is quickly lost and there is remodelling of the calcar with rounding and loss of the axial loading. However, theoretical and experimental analysis supports the use of a collar. With an uncemented component, however, with a collar, definite axial loading can be determined as evidenced by sclerosis.

Radial and hoop stress

A wedge type of prosthesis, either cemented or uncemented, can induce these. The induction of hoop stresses in the more proximal femur may be beneficial. With cemented arthroplasty loss of bone density proximally suggests that weight is taken more distally through the prosthesis and this may enhance implant fatigue. Hoop stresses may be uniformly induced in the femur if the prosthesis is evenly tapered. Certainly any proximal muscle attachment forces will compliment the implant-induced hoop stresses.

Choices of treatment in hip osteoarthritis including historical perspectives

Conservative management

The obvious straight forward lines of management should not be forgotten, weight reduction is paramount but not always easily achieved. A whole range of non-steroidals are available but none obvious best in osteoarthritis.

Physiotherapy is usually tried but the results are disappointing. There are two specific areas where physiotherapy in the author's opinion is definitely beneficial:

(a) The occasional patient has minimal radiological changes and yet a marked degree of stiffness. If associated with a great deal of pain, an intra-articular injection of steroid and Marcain combined with intensive physiotherapy can produce a long lasting improvement.

(b) There are patients who without gross radiological changes appear to have developed quite a severe fixed flexion deformity. This can be aided greatly by preoperative advice from a physiotherapist and hydrotherapy. Hydrotherapy is an important line of treatment in the slightly stiff younger male patient where the symptoms are not quite bad enough for total hip replacement and the surgeon may be undecided about the benefits of osteotomy. Hydrotherapy can be used as a waiting manoeuvre before total hip replacement and the increased range of movement produced may be very beneficial, though pain may not be much reduced.

Operative treatment

The choice in general terms is between osteotomy or total hip replacement and the latter may be cemented or non-cemented. The choice is fairly straight forward in a patient over about 60 years. Cemented arthroplasty of a conventional design gives very satisfactory results in more than 90% of patients.

In active, very young patients the results of conventional cemented total hip replacement are worse than osteotomy. If there are the ideal indications for osteotomy, i.e. a moderate fixed flexion deformity and one of the more classic indications for osteotomy (see later under subsection osteotomy), then this treatment should be preferred. Osteotomy does not preclude a satisfactory total hip replacement, because modern osteotomy does not involve much displacement of femoral shaft.

Between the ages of 45 and 60 many surgeons would use conventional and time tested cemented total hip replacement and it is the author's view that it is much better to use a well cemented total hip replacement performed by a surgeon familiar with a good technique than the occasional non-cemented total hip replacement.

A non-cemented prosthesis can be used if there is excellent quality of bone stock and the geometry of the bone can be matched by an appropriate well fitted non-cemented prosthesis. There are patients, however, particularly those who have had osteotomy previously, where the accurate reaming required for non-cement prosthesis would be extremely difficult. In this small group of patients with advanced changes with abnormal bone geometry resurfacing may still have a place. The bone density of the femoral head and neck must be above 200 units as measured by CT scan.

Arthrodesis in the younger patient should be considered. A young male patient of short stature probably does best with this operation. The other hip and ipsilateral knee must be entirely normal. The technique of arthrodesis is not described as it is outside the scope of this chapter, but a method should be adopted probably using internal fixation and bone grafting, that does not derange the geometry of the proximal femur and acetabulum. The arthrodesis can then be converted to a total hip replacement if required years later.

Historical perspectives

The reader is referred to the original papers to obtain detail of osteotomies used historically and for the techniques and results of the early workers in total hip replacement. McMurray popularized the high offset osteotomy which was not internally fixed; later Wainwright described internal fixation methods leading up to Pauwell's work published in 1976. This latter is the forerunner of the modern osteotomy technique.

In hip arthroplasty the very earliest varieties were those of Rehn: 'Interposition arthroplasty'

1930 [6], although Girdlestone's operation is in a sense an excision arthroplasty. Wiles in London in 1938 was probably the first to use replacement of both the acetabular and femoral surfaces. Thompson (1954) and Moore (1952) popularized the hemiarthroplasty (femoral) for arthritis.

Indications, techniques and follow-up of osteotomy of the hip

General indications for osteotomy

Generally patients less than 50 years of age.
No obesity.
A good range of movement; preferably 90° of flexion.
A clerical rather than a manual worker.
Good congruence in a functional radiograph.
The radiographs should show signs of mechanical overload with secondary arthritis rather than atrophic or inflammatory arthritis.
Patients must be motivated to comply with the rehabiliation process with partial weight bearing and intensive exercises.
Morphological radiographic classification is vital to determine which osteotomy is likely to give the best result.
The key to the choice of osteotomy is the size, shape and direction of the weight bearing surface; 'sourcil' of Pauwells and Bombelli.

Options

Femoral osteotomy:

Varus, plus or minus extension and derotation component.
Valgus, plus an extension or flexion component.
Trochanteric lateralization procedure (Maquet).

Pelvic osteotomy:

Chiari operation.

Pelvic rotation operation including cover:

Salter
Triple (Berne or Steele).
Wagner osteotomy.

Often included particularly with the valgus

femoral osteotomy is the Voss procedure with a widespread soft tissue release further decreasing the stress on the hip. A femoral osteotomy is best utilized when there is adequate cover of the femoral head. If the head is uncovered in early disease in the younger patient a rotational osteotomy of the acetabulum would be preferred but the acetabulum must be congruous with the femoral head. In an older person with more major secondary arthritic changes and loss of cover an operation such as a Chiari may be more suitable. The neck shaft angle, i.e. CCD angle, is a guide to which osteotomy might be used. Coxa valga tending to give an extrusive arthritis might suggest that the varus femoral osteotomy is preferred to render the neck shaft angle more normal, and vice versa for a congenital coxa vara tending to produce a protrusive arthritis when a valgus osteotomy is often indicated.

Choice of osteotomy according to classification of osteoarthritis
(See previous subsection)

Superolateral

(a) Varus osteotomy.
(b) Early stage pelvic rotational osteotomy later valgus osteotomy alone or with pelvic osteotomy.
(c) Early stage pelvic osteotomy or shelf later valgus osteotomy.
(d) (i) Varus extension osteotomy
    (ii) Valgus extension osteotomy.
    (iii) Total hip replacement.

In dealing with (b) (c) and (d)ii, potential adduction of at least 15° range of movement should be available. Patients with a flattened head do well with a valgus osteotomy.

Medial osteoarthritis

(a) and (b) valgus extension osteotomy
(c) total hip replacement.

Principles of osteotomy

Anteroposterior radiographs centred on the hip and lateral radiographs are required. A weight bearing 60° oblique (Berne View) shows the loss of cover of the anterior head. The two methods available to plan the angular correction by osteotomy are:

(a) Tracings are made of the femur and acetabulum from the neutral position as in the original radiograph. Where a valgus osteotomy is considered an ideal may be perfect congruence with placement of the femur in adduction. It is advisable to plan extra superolateral clearance. The capital drop should approximate to the curtain osteophyte.

(b) The patient can be examined under image intensifier with films taken in adduction and abduction. Similarly, the extension component can be assessed by examining the abduction and adduction with the hip in flexion. If there appears to be increased joint space and superolateral opening out of the joint space the actual position of the leg in relationship to the image intensifier table determines the correct position for osteotomy. An ordinary lateral radiograph may give some idea of the anteversion of the neck. The extension component overcomes this. If there is clinically a fixed flexion deformity, enough extension must be put into the osteotomy to align the leg normally. With the joint capsule open the hip can be flexed until the anterior uncovered head is covered. Modern imaging with 3D CT reconstruction allows accurate planning. Some centres are using computer assisted techniques derived from the CT information to plan 3 dimensional corrections possible with a pelvic rotational operation.

Other points to assess in planning:

1. *Leg lengthening*. Leg length is increased with valgus osteotomy and vice versa with varus – with a valgus of 30° and extension component of 10° in a patient with a CCD of 130° there will be approximately 5 mm lengthening.

2. *Trochanteric osteotomy*. This can be added (a) to a valgus osteotomy. A bone graft can be wedged underneath to effectively lateralize the greater trochanter to maintain abductor power. (b) In a varus osteotomy of more than 20° the greater trochanter can be brought back to a more anatomical level to produce correct tension on the abductors and reduce the tendency to a postoperative limp.

3. Correction of a rotational element, i.e. severe external rotation deformity.

4. Reduction of the stress on the hip by muscle release (a). The abductors are in small part released in such a valgus osteotomy by lateralizing the greater trochanter and allowing the trochanter to ride up slightly but maintaining some soft tissue connection to stabilize the bone graft. (b) Adductor and psoas release is performed in a valgus osteotomy as the valgus would otherwise increase tension (Voss procedure).

5. Maintenance of load line in relationship to the knee. If a valgus osteotomy is undertaken the shaft should be lateralized to keep the load line satisfactory and to prevent a tendency to valgus deformity of the knee. *Vice versa* with a varus osteotomy.

6. Any major obstructing osteophyte should be identified, such as a so-called elephant trunk osteophyte on the head or a hypertrophic acetabular floor osteophyte.

7. If the valgus has been planned by plain radiographs the valgus component achieved may be under estimated, i.e. if a planned valgus of 20° is required and this is to be associated with an extension component of 15° or so, the surgeon will actually need to perform a 25° valgus angulation at operation in order to achieve the planned valgus as on the preoperative radiographs. The reverse is true in varus osteotomy. For more details the reader is referred to Bombelli's classic text [3].

Technique of valgus osteotomy

The patient should be supine on the operating table. An incision along the line of the shaft of the femur going from the tip of the greater trochanter to the anterior superior iliac spine is used. The femur is reached by deepening along the line of the skin incision through the fascia. Vastus lateralis is lifted forward. The capsule is exposed and opened and it is suggested that an AO angle blade plate of 130° is utilized. Figure 18.11 illustrates the calculation for the insertion angle for the seating chisel.

The line of the seating chisel is easy to find after direct inspection of the femoral neck. Operative radiographs are not required in general but an inexperienced surgeon might find them useful. Attention must be paid to the plane of insertion of the seating chisel, the coronal plane for the valgus component, the sagittal plane for the

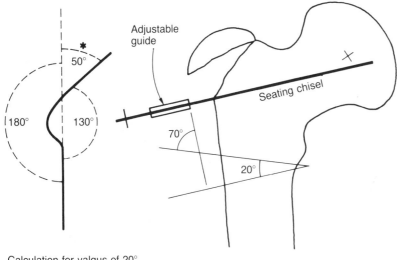

Fig. 18.11 Planning calculations for a 20° valgus osteotomy using a 130° blade plate.

Calculation for valgus of 20°

* 50° + 20° = 70°

Desired correction ∠of seating chisel to shaft of femur

extension component and the horizontal plane for the rotational component.

It is recommended that a long cancellous or cortical screw be inserted into the proximal osteotomy fragment to prevent the blade pulling out of the head and neck when compression is undertaken.

N.B. When the bone is sectioned the ilio-psoas muscle can be transected. The adductor release should be through a separate incision and due allowance must be made for this when draping.

Postoperative rehabilitation

(a) No passive movements; hydrotherapy.
(b) Six months elbow crutches if possible with partial weight bearing and graduated increments of weight bearing over this period.

Varus osteotomy

In general this osteotomy is beneficial in a rather earlier stage of osteoarthritis with minimal osteophytes, a valgoid femoral neck and a round femoral head. A particular indication may be in coxa vara subluxans when the weight bearing surface is horizontal and osteoarthritis is at its most early stage. It is in this sort of case that progressive arthritis can be predicted with certainty and a prophylactic operation may be justified. A varus osteotomy is not indicated when the head is flattened or osteophytes are too bulky.

The approach is much as in a valgus osteotomy. There is no need for adductor release or a psoas release. If more than 20° of varus is planned it is necessary to osteotomize the greater trochanter and more distally fix it. If 25° of varus is planned from a radiograph and there is an extension component also planned, it is necessary to under form the osteotomy at the actual operation. If in the coronal plane a 25° angle of varus from radiograph template is planned it would be necessary to put in only 20° of varus at the operation. A 90° AO blade plate is suggested with an offset and this automatically tends to maintain the knee alignment. To minimize shortening bone should not be resected; the calcar area of the proximal femur can be impacted into the shaft of the femur and securely held with a blade plate.

Assessment of angle of insertion of seating chisel

Using a 90° blade plate, if a varus of 20° is planned it is obvious that a 70° angle of the seating chisel is required in relationship to the long axis of the shaft of the femur.

Postoperative management as in valgus.

Follow-up after proximal femoral osteotomy

Bombelli [3] reports in a 6–8 year follow-up of valgus extension osteotomy that the results of pain relief are very good, i.e. 308 patients out of 471 had no pain. With medial osteoarthritis grade a and b Maquet [7] reports on the results of a valgus extension osteotomy that in an 8-year follow-up of 150 cases 83% were painfree. Bombelli on the follow-up of varus osteotomy over a similar period of time reports that 198 patients out of 212 had no pain. A fifth of patients had a slight limp after varus osteotomy. Morscher [8] reports from a multicentric continental trial that 80% had a good relief of pain and an improvement in 60% walking ability.

Cemented total hip arthroplasty. General principles and techniques including approaches to the hip joint

General principles

The general success rate after primary hip cemented arthroplasty is more than 90%. Some 350 000 are performed each year worldwide and it competes with heart and renal transplant surgery in reducing disability. The results of primary surgery are so much better than revisional surgery and there is no doubt the principle of 'get it right first time' applies.

A cemented total hip replacement will always have a finite life span. It is only with improvements in materials and techniques that survivorship will continue to improve. Major design changes are unlikely. The success rate in terms of prosthetic survival are higher in low demand users, i.e. the older patient and in patients with multiple joint problems. The clinical test bed for any hip replacement implant is a younger more active patient.

Whilst cemented total hip replacement may not be denied to patients who are in higher risk groups there are factors that have been identified that can be modified to improve implant survival.

High body weight has been related to early failure in many studies. High activity levels after surgery have been correlated with increased failure rates. Importantly positively restricting activity levels after surgery in younger patients can enhance implant survival. In this study the failures frequently did not use walking aids in the early postoperative period. More controlled trials are needed in such patients.

Careful planning and choice of implant is critical to the early success of insertion and a trouble free perioperative period. Clinical assessment demonstrates any severe degree of fixed flexion, external rotation or adduction deformity. Mild deformities need no special attention, but, for example, failure to correct a severe external rotation deformity by radical release of the posterior capsule and piriformis may spoil the result and the author considers that if this is not done at the time of operation, no amount of physiotherapy postoperatively will correct such a rotational deformity.

A fixed flexion deformity in a unilateral hip will correct spontaneously after pain relieving surgery. If the deformity is present in a younger patient with bilateral disease both hips should be replaced followed by hydrotherapy.

Preoperative counselling of the patient should be undertaken well before surgery. The choice of type of operation and implant suggested must be spelled out and the potential complications of note.

A full and frank discussion of these including overlengthening – nerve palsy and infection may save later medico-legal difficulties – the notes must include the details of the counselling.

Bilateral hip replacement

In patients with bilateral hip arthritis an extremely careful evaluation of the overall medical status of the patient is required. The author's experience is that patients under 60 who are slim and have no other medical problems can safely undertake this procedure particularly if anti-embolic measures are undertaken. In patients over 70 it is only the exception that bilateral simultaneous hip arthroplasty can be safely undertaken.

There is no authoritative agreement on the optimum interval between two hip operations.

The author's experience is that in the older patient where the primary indication is relief of pain a planned second admission is acceptable; between 6 months and a year after the first. For a younger patient the best results after bilateral operations are obtained within a smaller time interval.

Leg length inequality needs to be assessed. Often this is apparent due to an adduction contracture and is relieved in the painful stiff hip by arthroplasty. Occasionally, a severe contracture merits an adductor release which is performed percutaneously at the end of the hip operation. True leg length inequality of 1–1.5 cm can be corrected during ordinary arthroplasty and capsulotomy, but for greater length of inequality special measures need to be undertaken.

Planning for this needs to be undertaken prior to operation. Again a balance should be struck. In an elderly patient often the quickest operation consistent with a good straightforward technique may not equalize the leg length but is acceptable; the patient needs to be warned before the operation. A younger patient will seek perfection and the leg length can be achieved by a longer operation involving greater blood loss because of the wide capsular and muscular release; instability in the early stages is a likely hazard.

Accurate measurement of leg length discrepancy is required before operation and any fixed deformity is taken into account. At operation fixed reference points are determined either by:

(a) The most accurate; parallel pins are driven into the pelvis and femur prior to dislocation.
(b) The radiological tear drop, often obscured by floor osteophyte or ossification of the transverse ligament is identified and a point on the femur best made by burning a deep diathermy mark.

The desired length can be achieved by measurement after transecting in this order (a) capsule, (b) psoas, (c) piriformis and lastly (d) gluteus maximus tendinous insertion at the linea aspera.

Surgical Approach

Osborne [9] has described the history of surgical access for hip replacement. There are occasion-ally specific indications for particular approaches to the hip and these need to be assessed preoperatively. The author's view is that a severe fixed flexion deformity is better approached by an anterolateral or trochanteric osteotomy approach following a radical anterior release. A very severe fixed external rotation deformity is more easily corrected by a posterior approach. If the patient has a spastic element which is due to coincidental disease an anterior approach is preferable as the spasm tends to produce a flexion contracture and instability is likely with a posterior approach.

In all these approaches it is vital that soft tissue tension be determined from trial insertion and reduction of the femoral component. Gross pistoning of the femoral prosthetic head out of the acetabulum must not occur. In the posterior or anterior approaches trial reduction is critical, as no easy adjustment of the soft tissue tension can be undertaken once the prosthesis is inserted with cement.

In the trochanteric osteotomy approach the trochanter can be attached a little more distally to tighten up the soft tissues but the leg may be short. With the modified McFarland approach there is only a minimal capacity to tighten up soft tissues. In this approach the hip is usually perfectly stable in full internal rotation but if put in rather slackly in external rotation it may dislocate. It is vital that the hip is inserted with neutrality of both components with a 22 mm head prosthesis. If, for example, slight anteversion of the femoral component is combined with slight anteversion of the acetabular component then dislocation at trial reduction can be very apparent. The only safeguard against this is very accurate repair of the anterior fibres of medius. It is better to rely in the greater part on the stability from the prosthetic component position than the repair of anterior fibres of gluteus medius.

It is vital that the nursing staff understand the principles of the approaches used for the hip joint. In any one unit varying approaches may be used and various protocols of postoperative management may be instituted. This frequently leaves the nursing staff confused unless the principles of possible instability with the different approaches are explained. With any of the approaches described, if there is adequate soft tissue tension and correct component positioning, no special safeguards in postoperative rehabilitation are required.

Bone cement surgical technique

Improvement in mechanical properties of polymerized methacrylate

Inclusions of blood, air, radio-opaque agents and antibiotics should be minimized. Ling, Lee *et al.* [10], describe an elegant study of these factors. To avoid admixture of too much air the cement should be mixed rather than beaten like egg white. The dough should be used early so reducing laminations. Any technique that minimizes the amount of blood in the acetabulum or the femur and preventing lamination of blood in the cement should be utilized. The mechanical properties of the cement are enhanced if after delivery the cement is highly contained and preferably polymerized under pressure. There is clearly an overlap between the factors improving mechanical properties of cement and improving cement penetration into bony irregularities.

The recently advocated method of limiting air admixture into the cement is for the cement to be mixed in a vacuum and the cement to be centrifuged. It does alter the cement handling characteristics and laboratory rehearsal is advised. This may produce more cement shrinkage and is not widely adopted.

Under this context the overall mechanical behaviour of the cement mantle can be considered. There is no doubt that an even cement mantle is required. There may be sites that for particular mechanical reasons concerned with cement properties the cement should be thicker, e.g. in the superomedial femoral area. The techniques to achieve the above principles are described later.

Improved fixation of cement to the bone

First generation techniques did not involve brushing or lavage. The so-called second generation techniques have produced the greatest advances.

Halawa [11], working in Ling's unit describes the benefits of washing the trabecular bone with a pulsatile lavage system. The debris is thereby removed and there is enchanced cement penetra-tion into the trabecular bone. Subcortical strong trabecular bone should be pressurized for fixation. The penetration of cement into trabecular bone can be enhanced by pressurizing the cement. On the femoral side this can be undertaken by inserting the cement from distal to proximal using either a gun or a vent tube and digitally inserting the cement. The cement can be pressurized if a less viscous cement is used and a dam is applied to the proximal femur or the mouth of the acetabulum; it is easier where the cement is fully contained.

If in doubt the inexperienced surgeon should not use very non-viscous cement because it is difficult to handle and a deficient technique may provide a worse result than a sensibly used ordinary dough. It must be remembered that Charnley in his earlier work did not use these sophisticated methods and he inserted the cement dough with digital thrusts into the medullary cavity of the femur. When any pressurization technique is used the surgeon must be careful not to let the cement polymerize too far which would make insertion of the prosthesis almost impossible. With such containment techniques the surgeon has less tactile feedback and must rely on a knowledge of the time and temperature setting qualities of the cement rather than his finger tips.

If the femur is narrow and distally plugged the femoral component should be inserted early into the cement because too firm a dough stage may prevent correct component placement. The component should *not* be inserted with hammer blows because of the hydraulic damper effect of bone and cement; a firm and prolonged thrust is more effective.

Pressurizing the cement reduces the thickness of the blood film at the interface and adequate pressurizing prevents capillary flow. Blood at the interface can be reduced by:

(a) Lavage;
(b) Irrigation with hydrogen peroxide acts as a haemostatic;
(c) Packing with gauze or other similar absorptive agents from distal to proximal.

On the acetabular side a flanged cup helps to enhance cement interdigitation with bone. Shelley shows that the flange on the Charnley cup enables some 20 mm mercury pressure to be maintained within the cement mantle prior to setting. This is because of the containment of the cement by the flange. When an ordinary cup is used cement extrudes around the edge of the cup and although modest pressure may be effective for a minute or two, it is not maintained during the time the cement takes to set; any reduction of pressure allows capillary flow of blood produce a film at the interface.

A similar effect is developed within the femur when a tapered femoral component is thrust into the cement. Maximal pressure is developed distally but is not uniform throughout the cavity.

Cemented acetabular component choice and insertion

With a 22 mm headed femoral component there is adequate thickness of the acetabular component in the average case to prevent excess stress developing in the cement. If a 32 mm headed component is used or smaller outer diameter sizes a metal backed component is recommended. The size should be predetermined by examination of radiographs and assessment with templates. An acetabular component should not have deep grooves for cement purchase. An adequate exposure of the acetabulum by removing the capsule and osteophytes is mandatory.

Adequate depth should be achieved in the acetabulum so that the largest component can be inserted maintaining adequate cover anteriorly, superiorly and posteriorly and yet allowing an adequate cement mantle of at least 3 mm. It should be flanged to maintain pressurization of the cement during polymerization, and to avoid bottoming out and an uneven cement mantle. The placement of the acetabular component is somewhat determined by the pathological anatomy of the arthritic hip. The 22 mm ID acetabular components are placed in neutral in the coronal plane, i.e. no anti- or retroversion and 45° to the horizontal, large ID sizes 28 mm should be slightly 10–15° anteverted. The O.G. cup of Charnley with its anterior flange allows a neutral placement (of the cup) where there is a deficient anterior acetabular wall yet it contains the cement and allows coverage of the ischial keyhole. This elegant implant can be shaped with scissors to accurately occlude the mouth of the acetabulum.

There is clinical evidence that three large keyholes produce less evidence of loosening than multiple small holes. Such large key holes should be perhaps 12–15 mm in diameter and depth. Ideally, to minimize cement stress concentration the edges of the hole should be bevelled and there should be some undercutting within the key holes.

There is much debate about whether the subchondral bone plate should be removed. Total removal of the subchondral bone plate with opening out of all trabecular bone can allow cement to intrude within the substance of the trabecular bone almost up to the inner pelvic table. Charnley [12] traditionally advocated leaving as much subchondral bone as possible consistent with adequate placement of the acetabular component. Multiple drill holes into good quality subchondral bone are utilized with a flanged acetabular cup to pressurize the cement. Long term advantages of any specific technique have not been reported.

Protrusio acetabuli

Physiological placement of the acetabular component is important to prevent the tendency for protrusion of the component into the pelvis. A flanged cup is used and bone grafting of the acetabular floor. Ordinary cement pressurization in such a case can be used. This author prefers a non cement porous coated acetabular component with a tight perimeter bearing placed to provide a physiological centre of rotation. Bone graft can be placed beneath before impaction.

Cemented femoral component design and technique

There is general agreement now that the femoral component stem should be straight and of even taper with no sharp edges. The size is predetermined with templates. An adequate range of implants is required. There is evidence that the femoral component of the implant should fill between some 70–80% of the canal but still allow for a 2–3 mm even cement mantle. There is no doubt that a slim femoral component with a lot of cement around it leads to premature failure.

Oversize rasps used with a plastic head as a trial are very useful for the trainee surgeon to assess soft tissue tension and stability.

The author believes that there should be no cement beyond the tip of the prosthesis, and even the tip of the prosthesis protruding for a millimetre or two beyond the tip of the cement mantle is advantageous. Whether the prosthesis should be polished to allow subsidence within an intact viscoelastic cement mantle or roughened or pre-coated to bond to the cement mantle is as yet unresolved.

Postoperative care and rehabilitation

The patient and nursing staff are advised about the postoperative care particularly if there is any risk of instability.

If there is a tenuous trochanteric reattachment or if the tissues are very slack, bed rest for 2 weeks after the operation is a justifiable post-operative plan to allow the soft tissues to firm up and prevent instability.

Intensive physiotherapy postoperatively is not required for most patients but advice about walking aids and how to tackle the simple aspects of daily life should be described to the patient by a physiotherapist.

There is no doubt that it is wise to advise the patient to limit impact activities and not to run or play any contact sports for the rest of their lives. Soft heeled shoes reduce shock waves during brisk walking.

What is not proven, however, is whether in younger patients total restriction of weight bearing with crutch walking for 3 months after cemented arthroplast is beneficial.

Complications of total hip replacement, incidence, aetiology, avoidance, identification and management

Since the more widespread use of total hip replacement for arthritis of the hip in the 1970s, published incidences of loosening have been reduced by refinement in surgical technique; and similarly local operative complications have been reduced by improved surgeon training. Peri-operative fatality due to general systemic prob-

lems may be of the order of 1%. This figure will probably remain as the operation is increasingly being offered to more elderly patients with systemic disease.

The main medical complication that threatens our patients is thromboembolism with a reported fatality rate of 1–2%. Only recently, a large series has been published without any fatalities using prophylactic anticoagulation and a very low 0.8% (probably acceptable) bleeding complication rate.

Systemic operative complications of total hip replacement surgery

General medical assessment of patients preoperatively is essential to identify those patients at higher risk. There is an 8% incidence of coronary infarction in patients with pre-existing ischaemic heart disease even if there has been no recent infarct. Operation should not be undertaken if the patient has had a myocardial infarct in the last 6 months as the re-infarction rate in such patients is unacceptably high.

In patients with diabetes, coronary disease or a past history of thromboembolic disease it is necessary to institute measures to limit post-operative complications. Cervical spine instability in the rheumatoid patient or those with ankylosing spondylitis should be identified because of their anaesthetic risks.

There is no doubt that hypotensive anaesthesia cuts down blood loss during and in the early postoperative period by some two-thirds. Post-operative blood loss is generally equal to the operative loss. For surgical technical reasons hypotension is desirable to minimize blood film development at the cement bone interface.

Local complications

Vascular

Femoral artery damage is rare in primary hip replacement. More care is required with the anterior approach. Sharp Homan retractors should never be thrust into the tissues anteriorly to demonstrate the anterior acetabular margin. They should be insinuated gently between bone and soft tissues. Complications are rare with the posterior approach. Intrapelvic vessels occasionally have been damaged by sharp cutting instruments in the acetabulum. There should always be guards on keyhole cutting tools. It is the author's view that blunt drills are probably more dangerous than sharp. Providing power drills have a guard, i.e. end stop, they are satisfactory. 'Cheese grater' acetabular reamers are safe. The highest risk of intra pelvic damage arises in revision surgery where there has been cement intrusion into the pelvis. The fashioning of a Charnley central guide hole drilled right through into the pelvis is therefore inadvisable even if a cement retaining mesh is used.

Although thromboembolic complications are described later in this section, femoral vein occlusion can be demonstrated by venography when the hip is fully adducted and externally rotated, i.e. at dislocation with the anterior approach. The thromboembolic rate is much less with a posterior approach perhaps because of a different method of dislocation.

Neurological

More than 1% incidence of femoral or sciatic nerve damage in total hip replacement has been reported. The femoral nerve in the anterior approach is damaged less often than the sciatic nerve. In the posterior approach large retractors should not be forced around the posterior lip of the acetabulum and the sciatic nerve should be carefully identified and safeguarded before incising the posterior capsule with scissors. There is a risk of entrapping the sciatic nerve with any trochanteric attachment method that involves wire encirclement of the femoral shaft. Wroblewski suggests that a simple way of identifying this is to touch the encircling wire with a diathermy. If a sciatic nerve palsy is discovered postoperatively and the cause was not clearly identified intraoperatively, early exploration is advised. Early evacuation of haematoma may result in return of nerve function. An isolated apparently lateral popliteal nerve palsy may be localized by nerve conduction studies but it does appear that this section of the sciatic nerve is more vulnerable to local damage than the tibial nerve component of the sciatic nerve. Particular

care is required if significant limb lengthening is planned. The knee should be kept flexed during surgery to restrict intraoperative tension. Evoked cortical neurological potentials monitoring is recommended when significant limb lengthening is attempted during THR for dysplasia or CDH, to identify dangerous sciatic nerve tension.

Fracture

This is a real risk for inexperienced surgeons. It is more common in patients with osteoporosis caused either by age or rheumatoid arthritis. There are three stages of the operation when the femoral shaft is especially vulnerable.

(a) *Dislocation*; it is advised that only one surgeon manipulates the leg, and it is generally safer to lever on the head but adequate soft tissue release around the hip is also necessary. In an anterior approach any forceful demonstration of the proximal femur by an enthusiastic assistant before reaming may well result in a fracture of the lesser trochanter. Generous exposures produced by the modified McFarland's, posterior or trans-trochanteric approach reduces this complication.

(b) *Shaft penetration* by a 'T' handled or femoral reamer is similarly minimized by an adequate exposure. Femoral shaped reamers should never be hammered into the femur blindly without first identifying the general line of the shaft of the femur by the hand introduction of a taper pin reamer. A false passage can be created by this sharp instrument which should never be hammered into the shaft.

(c) *Rasp or trial impaction*; it almost goes without saying that careful choice of implants based upon preoperative measurement with templates reduces the risk when attempting to drive an over-size prosthesis into a femoral shaft. A trial prosthesis should always be used prior to final prosthetic insertion.

The current trend towards non-cement arthroplasty undoubtedly will lead to a much higher incidence of fractured femur. A blind assumption that all these fractures will heal because of the absence of cement is probably justified but no studies have been published on whether such patients go onto to have a pain free prosthesis.

Postoperative complications

Dislocation

Dislocation develops after 3% of total hip replacements. Charnley reports a 2% incidence of subluxation [12]. The incidence has little relationship to head size except with the posterior approach. Thus the 22 mm head size does not have a higher risk of dislocation. The component position in relationship to the approach is the most important factor. As might be expected, the posterior approach carries a higher likelihood of posterior dislocation and this increases when there is also a combination of retroversion of the components, slack soft tissues and a small head diameter. Care with patient positioning on the operation table, the use of a trial prosthesis to determine stability and soft tissue tension are vital. Reported incidences of early and late dislocation, are at variance. The author's experience is that early dislocation, if the prosthetic component looks satisfactory radiologically, can be treated successfully by reduction and immobilization to allow the soft tissues to heal. Late or recurrent dislocation if associated with a technical error of prosthetic insertion may need revision.

Revision arthroplasty itself has a much higher incidence of postoperative dislocation. The techniques that may be required to treat early dislocation are bed rest and traction for 3 weeks. The author has used successfully a pelvic abduction hinge orthosis. If operative revision is required, high speed cutting instruments to remove the prosthetic acetabular component from within its cement mantle are useful. The surgeon should not risk fracturing the acetabulum. It is easier to revise an acetabular component than a femoral. Soft tissue tension can often be taken up by more laterally placing an acetabular component, cementing with new cement into the old cement mantle. Special 22mm head anti-dislocation acetabular components are available. Similarly, soft tissue tension can be adjusted by correct reattachment of the trochanter if this is at fault.

Infection

The classic work of Charnley with ultra-clean air is reinforced by the recent Medical Research

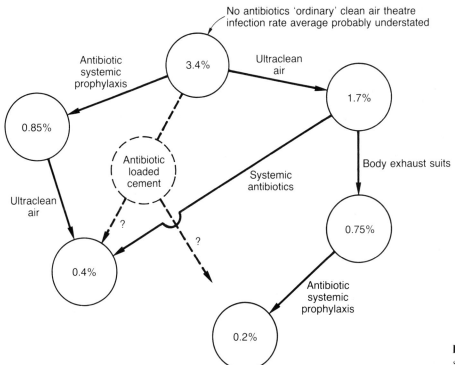

Fig. 18.12 MRC trial results in summary.

Council trial identified techniques that can minimize infection after hip arthroplasty [13] (Fig. 18.12).

Other principles of surgery should be followed. Any patient with active infection should have this treated. Body hair should be shaved with clippers rather than a razor as near to the time of surgery as possible. Whole body bathing with an antiseptic such as chlorhexidine gluconate can reduce dermal bacterial colonization. Skin preparation with either Povidone iodine or chlorhexidine in spirit for an adequate time, i.e. 1–2 minutes, exclusion of the skin edges, the use of double gloves and impervious gown sleeves or body exhaust suits are all factors that traditionally reduce infection.

High risk groups

These are rheumatoid arthritis 1.2% as compared with osteoarthritis 0.3%, diabetics 5.6%, psoriasis 5.5%, second operations 5% and males who have to be catheterized 6.6%

Bucholz has popularized the use of antibiotic loaded cement. Figures have been produced that are as low as those in the MRC trial when extra safety factors have been added. The general view is that in revision surgery or in patients with higher risks, antibiotic loaded cement is advised. The theoretical risk of late development of resistant organisms has not been reported. In any systemic study of infection after hip arthroplasty the following factors should be identified:

(a) Bacterial counts in settlement plates in the operating theatre and operative field.
(b) Bacterial counts in wound washings.
(c) Eventual infection rate bacteriologically identified.

A conventional operating theatre may have 500 colony forming particles per square metre. The ultra-clean air system with clothing impervious to bacteria or a total body exhaust system may limit the count to less than 1 per m³. If fewer than 10 colony forming particles per m³ is not achieved the theatre should really not be used for total joint replacement surgery. The addition of systemic antibiotics to the bone cement does not make up for deficient surgical environment. Down flow ultra clean air is advised with either side walls or high air velocity of at least 0.4 metres per second.

Thromboembolism

Fatal pulmonary embolism develops in between 0.5% (recent studies) and 3.0% (past studies) of patients without prophylaxis [14]. Calf vein thrombi occur in 50% of patients after total hip replacement. The peak incidences being on the 4th postoperative day with a second peak on the 14th day. There is a 6% pulmonary embolism rate. The relationship of calf vein thrombi to large vein potentially embolic thrombi is documented. Thus in any study where there is prophylaxis, isotopic assessment of calf vein thrombi probably can assess those methods of prophylaxis that could reduce this danger. Physical or pharmacological prophylactic methods are widely used.

Pharmacological prophylaxis has the hazard of excess bleeding. The surgeon must balance the risks and the benefits. A recent study [15] has demonstrated the effectiveness of dihydrogotamine and low molecular weight heparin in combination in reducing the incidence of calf vein thrombi from 50% in the placebo group to 25% in the prophylactically treated group. There are inadequate numbers to relate this statistically to a fatal pulmonary embolism rate. Recently the study described by Amstutz [16] with low dose warfarin has resulted in a nil rate of fatal pulmonary embolism, 3% of pulmonary embolism and a 0.8% of bleeding complications none of which was fatal in 2500 hip replacements. The incidence of bleeding complications is much higher in non-cement total hip replacements. The method used is to give 10 mg of warfarin the night of surgery (this is reduced if the patient's body weight is below 50 kg). The prothrombin time or the normalized international ratio is thereafter daily monitored. There is a preoperative control, and based on the prothrombin at postoperative day two the dose of warfarin is adjusted to a prothrombin time of 1.5 times control at a maximum. This level can be reached by postoperative day 4. To minimize the later risk of pulmonary embolism after discharge, the patient should be maintained on established low dose for at least 5 weeks.

Heterotopic ossification

The incidence is perhaps between 2% and 5%. Some cases are related to infection. The only known association is heterotopic ossification on a previous hip replacement. Statistically heterotopic ossification is much more common in a non-cement hip arthroplasty and ankylosing spondylitis. It may be associated with the extensive reaming. Although Indocid treatment has been used postoperatively, irradiation is the only method that has been proven to reduce the incidence of ossification. One thousand rads given in 5 divided doses in the first two weeks is the lowest dose that can give adequate control. The specific indication for this is a second side THR in a patient who on the opposite side had disabling ossification.

Loosening

The incidence is between 10% and 30% in long term follow-up depending on many variables. Two factors can be implicated in aseptic loosening:

(a) Inadequate strength of fixation.

(b) *biological factors*, including the abnormal host response to the implant primarily, which is rare, or the more common 'normal' biological response to wear debris from ground up cement or implant.

Implant fracture

Wroblewski described a high incidence of Charnley femoral implant fracture in heavy patients or those where there was inadequate proximal cement support for the prosthesis. It was almost exclusively in prosthesis of earlier design (flat backed Charnley). The incidence of stem failure is now virtually nil with the advent of high fatigue strength alloys. Acetabular component fracture is rare, the highest incidence being in thin walled high density polythene components and especially if there are deep cement retaining grooves. Higher incidences have been described in acetabular cups of the Muller design.

Assessment of results after total hip replacement

In the United Kingdom the most generally accepted method of assessment of results by clinical means is that of Charnley which was modified from d'Aubigne and Postel, although in the USA the method of Harris is preferred. The methods rely on a numerical scoring (see Fig. 18.13).

There are some studies which include in the assessment the activities of daily living. From such a comparative study it is evident that although the great majority of patients achieve almost total pain relief, the scatter of results in terms of hip movement, walking mobility and daily living postoperatively are more widely scattered, most patients moving up two grades. This study allows quantification of the benefit of total hip replacement in other than clinical terms.

Score	Range of hip movement	Pain	Mobility
1	0–30°	Severe spontaneous pain	Bedridden, or walks few yards with two sticks or crutches
2	31–60°	Prevents walking or severe on walking	Duration and distance very limited with or without sticks
3	61–100°	Tolerable with limited activity	Limited with one stick, difficult without sticks. Can stand for long periods
4	101–160°	Present only after activity; disappears quickly with rest	Long distance possible, but limited without aids
5	161–210°	Slight or intermittent, decreasing with activity	No aids required, but has a limp
6	210–260°	None	Normal

Fig. 18.13 Charnley hip score.

The results of total hip arthroplasty can be assessed by:

(a) Clinical follow-up based on a Charnley score indicating the percentage of patients that over a given period, say 10 years, have had a high score.
(b) Radiological follow-up with defined criteria for loosening.
(c) Absolute failure incidence as indicated by the revision rate.
(d) Statistical survival analysis.

For any study using any of the above methods the groups of patients, techniques and implants must be broadly comparable.

Cemented total hip replacement follow-up

The 15 year plus results have been described from the first era of cemented arthroplasty as described by Charnley and McKee with unsophisticated cement techniques. Eighty-five percent of survivors are painfree [17] (Fig. 18.14).

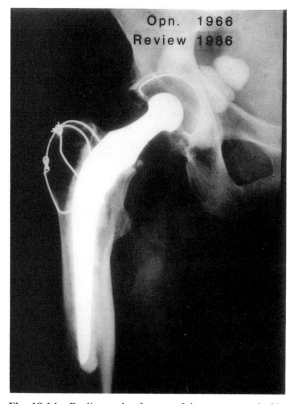

Fig. 18.14 Radiograph of successful asymptomatic 20 year follow up Charnley implant; note the femoral cortical hypertrophy (operation performed by the great man himself!).

Radiological follow-up demonstrates increasing evidence of cement bone lucencies and Charnley observed there were fewer flawless sockets than femoral components. Femoral components that are destined to fracture will do so within 10 years but high acetabular wear rates correlate with loosening due to impingement.

In the second era of cemented hip arthroplasty, post-1975, there remain a relatively low incidence of infection which has been reduced by the advent of systemlc antibiotics, ultra-clean air enclosures and antibiotic incorporation into the cement. The dislocation rates are lower than in the first era probably due to increasing surgeon skill in the technical aspects of component placement. The factors in implant fracture have largely been identified and dealt with by the use of stronger materials. The techniques of bone preparation and cement insertion have developed and are described in previous sections.

The incidence of lucent lines at the cement bone interface with such techniques is greatly reduced and loosening rates are reported to be below 5% [18] in the 5–10 year follow-up.

Simple failure rate or loosening rate curves are not always comparable because they do not include those patients who have absconded from follow-up or those patients that have died. A statistical method of survivorship analysis that has long been used in cancer surgery has now been applied to follow-up of implants [19]. The American literature refers to Kaplan and Meier survivorship tables.

There are critical assumptions in the plotting of any survivorship curve for a group of patients who have had an identical implant. For the results to be meaningful there should be uniformity of implant, technique and age range. Publishing by authors of survivorship curves is to be deplored unless the calculation methods used by the authors are described. Dobbs [19] describes the assumptions that are made in the survivorship curves that he describes:

(1) It is assumed that withdrawals, i.e. patients not traced, are subject to the same probabilities as nonwithdrawals. If there is only a small loss of numbers for follow-up the induced error is small.
(2) It must be assumed that probabilities of implant removal remain reasonably constant, otherwise time life tables are difficult to interpret.

In the described method of calculation it must

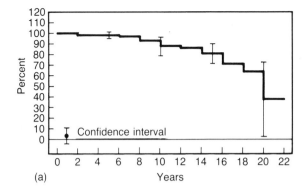

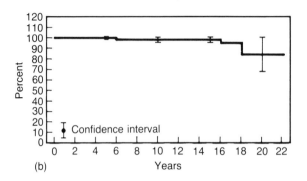

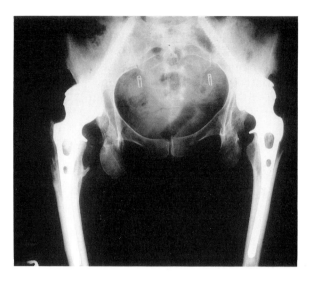

Fig. 18.16 Example of 20 year follow up of successful Ring early design metal on metal non cemented total hip arthoplasty. Note the complete absence of any significant radiolucent lines or osteolysis; note good bony condensation in the upper femur. The feature of note on the acetabular side is some proximal prosthetic migration.

Fig. 18.15 (a) Survivorship analysis of first generation cemented Charnley acetabular components with revision for aseptic loosening or radiographic definite loosening as end point. (b) Survivorship analysis of first generation cemented Charnley femoral components using revision for aseptic loosening or definitive radiographic loosening as end point.

be remembered that in any group of patients there may be some who suffer pain yet retain the prosthesis. Therefore the survivorship curve is a conservative estimate only of any failure rate, and do not include those without symptoms but with significant lucent lines. This method can be used to plot any particular defined aspect of failure. For example, combined results of aseptic revision rates and definite radiological loosening (Fig. 18.15).

Non-cement hip follow-up

Few non-cement arthroplasties have been followed up long enough to compile survivorship curves but the Ring Prosthesis has the longest follow-up (Fig. 18.16). Pain relief is probably inferior to cemented total hip arthroplasty but he observes that low infection rates with ease of revision are desirable features and worth the additional burden of slight discomfort in non-cement arthroplasty. If the results are satisfactory at 10 years with the metal/metal prosthesis later failure is rare.

The early results of the newer non cemented total hip replacement do not match those of cemented (2nd generation) arthroplasty. A 25% incidence of thigh pain at 5 years is recorded and a 30% incidence at 5 years of acetabular osteolysis in some series causes concern for the future.

Biomechanical aspects of implant design

Good cement penetration into trabecular bone can minimize shear and with a non-cement prosthesis suitable interdigitations have the same effect.

Even support for the prosthesis from proximal to distal with any method of fixation tends to reduce the prosthetic stress. Femoral implant failure in cemented hip arthroplasty is more likely if there is good distal support for the prosthesis and proximal loss of support. Such a maldistribution of stress will tend to lead to a concentration at one point and it is at this point, particularly if there are associated implant defects in manufacture, that a fatigue failure will be initiated. With a non-cemented prosthesis a similar situation can arise, for example if there is a porous coat on the whole stem of the prosthesis, and the prosthesis becomes highly incorporated distally and yet proximally minimally incorporated. The stress concentration may lead to implant failure.

Mechanical analysis suggests that:

1. To reduced stem and interface stresses distally there should be a restriction of the length of the stem of the intramedullary prosthesis.
2. The proximal femoral stem should be as thick and as stiff as possible.
3. The distal stem should be relatively flexible as compared to the proximal stem.

Ideally, there should be a large load transferring area. Clearly even stress transfer from proximal to distal is required; therefore the prosthesis should be tapered. A defined step would tend to concentrate stresses. Requirement 3 is also fulfilled by a relatively slender distal femoral stem within a fairly thick cement mantle. An even cement mantle is desirable and a straight stem fulfils this better than a 'banana' stem. Clinical follow-up demonstrates that a straight stem produces fewer failures by loosening than curved stems.

To mechanically limit stresses in the cement the stem should have no sharp edges and to minimize implant stresses the stem should ideally be thicker laterally than medially. This is certainly so in a prosthesis that has a relatively high offset, i.e. physiological neck shaft angle. In a prosthesis with a much more valgoid disposition of the femoral neck, stresses within the implant stem will tend not to be concentrated laterally.

A more recent interesting means of reducing stresses at the interface between the metal shaft and the cement is to pre-coat the stem. Under laboratory conditions methacrylate is bonded onto the femoral stem. The methacrylate cement as used surgically bonds onto the pre-coat and whilst not a true adhesive the methacrylate mantle actually 'sticks' to the metal. Whilst theoretically desirable, such pre-coating may mean that it is virtually impossible to remove the prosthesis should the metal cement composite become loose within the bone.

Another potential complication of this method of enhancing the strength of the metal cement junction is that the metal stem will be less likely to slide within the cement mantle. Whilst no surgeon wishes the prosthesis to subside within a cement mantle, as many studies have shown this to correlate with clinical loosening, there is no doubt that with increasing age the medullary cavity increases in width and Charnley [12] and Ling have found that such settlement or subsidence can occur without there being a fracture within the cement and without there being clinical symptoms or signs of failure. There are two schools of thought on whether the capacity for controlled subsidence should be designed for!

The material composition of the femoral stem should generally be of a high fatigue resistance metal. Few other materials have the fatigue strength. Certainly this is true in a cemented prosthesis where because of the requirements to have an even cement mantle there are very definite limits on the thickness of the metal implant. The only metals that fulfil these requirements are forged, vacuum cast or isostatically pressed chrome cobalt, forged titanium aluminium vanadium alloy and high nitrite stainless steel. A polymer prosthesis for non-cement use is described as isoelastic, i.e. it is stated that its elastic modulus is similar to that of cortical bone. Whilst it is a composite structure in some senses in that it has a metal strengthener, it is not a composite in the sense bone is, with fibre bundles within a matrix. The polymer is isotropic whereas bone is anisotropic. Clinical studies demonstrate sclerosis of the proximal femur, but there are no very long term studies to show the fatigue resisting capabilities of the polymer prosthesis and particulate abrasion debris is likely to cause lucent areas.

Acetabular component

Studies of the acetabular components that have been removed from previously successful total hip replacements show that there is a great variation in the line of wear. A surprising 64% of wear was superolateral, 32% was vertical and only 3.4% was along the accepted line of resultant force R.

A conclusion from this must be that (and these studies were from a study of Charnley acetabular components with a relatively physiological neck shaft angle femoral component) stress analysis does not reveal certain mechanical factors that are induced by total joint replacement or that the abductor muscle force is in some way greatly reduced by the technique of hip operation. Such wear findings support the view of Bombelli that the acetabular component should be positioned relatively horizontal in the line of his 'sourcil'.

The acetabular bone forces are mostly compressive if the axial line of the acetabular component is along the line of the resultant force. To minimize peak stresses it is desireable that there is:'

(1) A large bone implant/cement interface provided this is consistent with a satisfactory placement of the acetabular component in bone of good quality with good cover of the component.

(2) A stiff implant, either thick plastic (Charnley's classic book describes his early photoelastic experiments on this [12]) or metal backing of the acetabular component. Clinical experience with thin cemented acetabular components shows that there is a high rate of failure.

(3) The external shape of the acetabular implant also contributes to the stress concentration. Hemispherical acetabular components have performed well cemented and non cemented. A tighter (more contact pressure) fit at the perimeter in non cemented components produces a more even stress distribution. More complex externally threaded screw designs have failed early with the exception of the original Ring long screwed metal cup. Acetabular components have irregularities on the external surface to key the cement into the plastic. The grooves in the acetabular components on the external surfaces should be no more than a millimetre or two and undercut grooves give the best fixation of the cup within the cement. Deepening or widening the grooves did not increase the bond strength. Slight prominences on the external surfaces of the cemented acetabular component, particularly if these are made of methacrylate, limit bottoming out of the prosthesis on the bone and help maintain an even cement mantle.

Mechanical attributes and tribological aspects of different head sizes can best be considered here.

Charnley [12] advocates a 22 mm head. The mechanical attributes of this are shown in Fig.

(a)

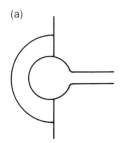   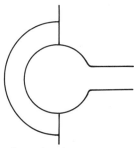

Small head | Large head
Less interface | Larger interface
Less frictional torque | More frictional torque
More load/unit area | Less load/unit area
Less particulate debris | More particulate debris
More penetrative wear | Less penetrative wear

(b)

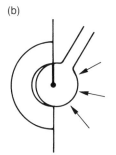   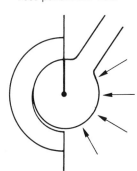

Impingement at less angle of movement Less capsular stretch ∴ less force communication → socket interface **unless** deep penetrative wear

Greater arc of movement before impingement More frictional torque communicated to socket

Fig. 18.17 Tribological characteristics of small and large head sizes.

18.17. (Tribology is the study of friction wear and lubrication.) Clearly with a small head there is a greater load per unit area and this affects penetrative wear – see later. The theory of tribology may be simple but in practice *in vitro* experiments and *in vivo* analyses are much more difficult to interpret.

1. *Friction.* Frictional torque is much less with a smaller head and socket and that between metal and high density polythene is much less than metal on metal. Theoretically, highly polished ceramic on ceramic should have the lowest frictional torque.

2. *Wear.* This can be considered as either wear in depth or volumetric wear. Volumetric wear is much greater with a large head and less with a

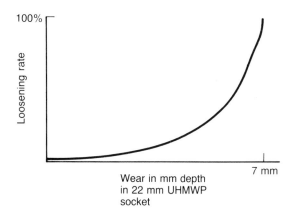

Fig. 18.18 Wear and loosening in patients under 40 years with Charnley THR.

small head, i.e. 22 mm. The wear in terms of depth is much increased with a small head. Wroblewski (Fig. 18.18) describes a high rate of wear in some very young active patients and this correlates in an almost exponential fashion with the loosening rate. Charnley [12] describes an average rate of wear of 0.022 mm per year (penetrative wear). An interesting point is that the wear rate in the second 5-year period of a 10-year follow-up is half that of the wear in the first 5-year period. This may be because of bedding in of the femoral head on the plastic. One factor that Charnley did not look at relates to both friction and wear and is the roughness of the femoral head and the socket of explanted prostheses (abrasive wear). The roughness of the prosthetic surface increases with time and at 5–10 years the surface finish is 0.05 microns, whereas the new implant surface finish is 0.01 microns. Wear is certainly increased if a third body is introduced, i.e. particulate cement 'valve grinding paste'.

3. *Lubrication.* The artificial hip is boundary lubricated, i.e. a layer of liquid adheres to the surfaces. Although lubrication factors can be studied in a laboratory, it is unlikely in the near future they will influence an artificial hip. This will not be considered further.

Implant fixation

The term 'implant loosening' has bedevilled the orthopaedic literature for lack of an agreed definition of the term 'loose'. In some ways it is easier to define what is adequate fixation. A working definition is that 'adequate fixation is present if the clinical result is within defined limits of success and that the result does not deteriorate with time nor is the fixation associated with increasing amplitude of interface movement with resultant pain or osteolysis or bone or implant debris accumulation'. The essential term in such a definition is progression, clinical or radiological.

Radiological progression may differ in cemented or non-cemented implants. The 'lucent line' around the cemented implant at the cement bone junction line is associated with implant failure particularly if 2 mm thick and if that lucent line progressively increases. Such loosening rates may differ on the acetabular and femoral sides of the total joint replacement. In a non-cemented implant progressively wide lucent lines similarly suggest imminent failure; Ring [20] has the longest experience of follow-up of non-cemented implants and describes that a lucent line of up to 2 mm thick in long term follow-up is not an indication of imminent failure of the joint replacement. In non-cement arthroplasty there may be adaptive changes that develop depending on the loading characteristics and the extent of porous coating fixation to bone. Areas of localized load transfer 'spot welding' can be radiologically identified. Adaptive changes can best be seen at junctional areas of porous coating and smooth uncoated stem.

In cemented hip arthroplasty there are radiological features that develop over some years that do not presage failure. An example of this may be increased bony density around the more distal femoral stem, indicating the load transfer to the more distal stem. If the material of the implant stem is strong enough to take the load imposed at the junctional area, fatigue failure is minimized.

Any implant system composed of materials of dissimilar characteristics will have movement, however slight, at the interfaces or junctional area between the components of the system.

Ling [21] details five basic facts of implant fixation.

1. The fixation of an implant system depends on the mechanical interlock created by the surgeon at the time of surgery. There is no doubt that this is true in cemented arthroplasty and the strength of fixation is maximal at the time of surgery but deteriorates with time. With a non-

cement arthroplasty it is likely that there is a less even stress distribution at the metal bone interface initially and a more even load transfer will develop in the course of time. There is no data on whether mechanical security improves with time in a non-cement arthroplasty.

2. Any implantation technique into the human skeleton produces a zone of bone death around the implant. The thickness of the zone of bone death is determined by the techniques of surgery and the materials used [22]. There is no doubt that the thicker the layer of bone death, the more likely that the implant is imperfectly fixed. The devitalized tissue can establish a new blood supply. It is at this critical time following implantation that the type of tissue forms (bone or fibrous tissue) dictated by the mechanical environment of the implant perhaps in the first 3 months post-implantation.

3. The absorption onto the implant surface of a thin film of glycoproteinaceous composition develops within seconds (the interface conversion film). The tissue attachment has to be via such a junctional material. Some materials have a more aggressive affinity for cellular material than others. An example is a recently developed material that appears to have positive tissue affinity is Bioglass. All alloys have an oxide, i.e. ceramic layer on the surface.

4. The bone of the hip deforms with load and the load is imposed by body weight and kinetic energy and by muscle forces.

5. The living tissue bone is constantly being remodelled by osteoblastic and osteoclastic activity. This bone turn over changes with the metabolic status of the patient. The medullary cavity probably increases in width with advancing years.

Ling suggests that there is a fundamental relationship between mechanical effects at a junctional area and its histological or ultrastructural make up.

Mechanical junctional factors

There is a fundamental difference between a cemented (methacrylate) metallic implant and a press-fit metallic implant (non-cemented). In the former there are two junctional areas to be considered: (1) implant cement and (2) cement bone.

The modulus of elasticity of cement is closer to that of cortical bone and therefore junctional stresses are highest between the metal and the cement. Taken overall, however the cement must effectively 'shock absorb' or attenuate stresses from metal to bone.

In the non-cement implant although surface coatings may modify this there are high junctional stresses between a metallic implant and the adjacent bone. The mechanical properties of the membrane in animals around an implant fixed with cement or without cement have the same physical characteristics. The material was Viscolastic and is structurally more capable of resisting compressive rather than shear stresses.

It is likely that it is the different loading characteristics of junctional tissues in a cement fixed acetabular or femoral component that determines the outcome where there are lucent lines, however fine, between the implant and bone. In the acetabular component the junctional tissues are mostly in compression and on the femoral component they are mostly in shear produced by axial or torsional loading. It is probably this that led Charnley in his earlier writing to suggest that there was a different clinical outcome in acetabular and femoral cemented components following the development of radiolucent lines at the bone cement interface.

Histological and ultrastructural features of junctional tissues

Charnley [12] showed in a classic study of retrieved specimens some years after successful cemented arthroplasty that there was a fundamental difference on the femoral and acetabular sides. On the femoral side, there was no thick continuous layer of cellular tissue at the cement bone interface. Live bone was close to the bone cement spheres and there was a thin layer of pale staining material at the interface. There were some cells similar to chondrocytes at the interface. Macrophages were rarely seen and only in association with thicker fibrous tissue and were more common in areas where cement was in contact with bone marrow. No granulomas were seen in successful hips. A characteristic is a scolloping of the junctional area where the bone cement is dissolved away in preparation. This demonstrates conclusively that there was no macro movement, otherwise the delicate bone cement spheres would have been abraded away.

On the acetabular side very different findings were seen. There was no direct bone contact and fibrous tissue of 0.5–1.5 mm thick was seen. This was often modified fibrous cartilage with occasional caseous material islands between bone and cement. There were many histiocytes and occasional granulomas with giant cells. The collagen bundles within the fibrous tissue were parallel to the surface of the acetabular component.

Linder [23], in an electron microscopic study, demonstrated that there could be a non-cellular membrane 0.3–7 microns thick between living bone and cement. This was considered to be uncalcified proteoglycan. Macrophages were seen but they were not associated with resorptive activity. Eng [24] has reported live bone implant contact without intervening fibrous tissue.

Osseointegration and microinterlock

Microinterlock is a description coined by Miller [25] describing an intimate interdigitation of bone cement into trabecular bone. The term can be applied in the interdigitation of bone between irregularities on a non-cemented implant. A working definition in structural terms might be that keyholes that are drilled by the surgeon in acetabular bone before introducing cement that may be from 5 mm to 15 mm could be termed macrointerlock, whereas the forcing of groups of spheres of bone cement between trabecular bone or a similar scale non-cement interface could be termed microinterlock. In the latter, non-cement category mechanical interdigitation of live bone into the roughened surface is rarely technically feasible. Bone marrow and fragmented trabecular bone as a slurry can be forced into the interdigitations. After insertion some osteoblasts will receive their nutrition by diffusion, remaining vital, and it is the surgeon's hope that microinterlock into a porous or roughened surface will take place.

There are few studies on the relationship of the mechanical environment at a non-cement roughened interface to the development of satisfactory bone ingrowth. Albrektsson's [22] classic study used a refined surgical technique with minimal tissue damage and these workers reported loosening of the implants only occurred where

loading was allowed before osseointegration had been achieved.

A definition of osseointegration is that 'normal living bone is in direct contact with the prosthesis'. With a non-cement implant it is the base material or oxide coating; with a cemented component it is the methacrylate that is in contact with the bone. The junctional tissues of both implants are in order: (a) demineralized living bone; (b) proteoglycan; (c) interface conversion film.

The interposition of cellular membranes, fibrous tissue or fibrocartilage by definition describes a state where osseointegration has not occurred.

Failure of implant fixation

If infection is excluded, mechanical or biological failure is the only possible mechanism producing implant failure (Fig. 18.19).

The techniques in cemented or non-cemented arthroplasty that may enhance long-term clinical survival are described in the appropriate sections. Long-term follow-ups of the newer techniques have not yet come to fruition, but it is useful to consider those parameters by which 'loosening' may be judged so that one's own clinical results can be reflected upon. Whilst clinical follow-up in gross terms provides the simplest method of determining patients' satisfaction, interpretation of fine radiological changes may lead to predictive likelihood of clinical failure, certainly in cemented arthroplasty. A study of implant loosening can incorporate: (a) membrane or 'lucent line' thickness; (b) subsidence; (c) migration.

Most observers would agree with Harris that definite loosening is evident by migration. Loosening is probable if there is a lucent line at the whole bone implant interface. The evidence of possible loosening is more arguable, Harris suggests that if more than half the interface has a lucent line possible loosening is likely. Localized osteolysis is more commonly seen with non cemented arthroplasty; infection can be responsible but if excluded the usual cause is a localized build up of particulate implant debris with consequent macrophage activity. Polyethylene debris with its microscopic birefringence even of submicron dimensions can be identified. Micro-

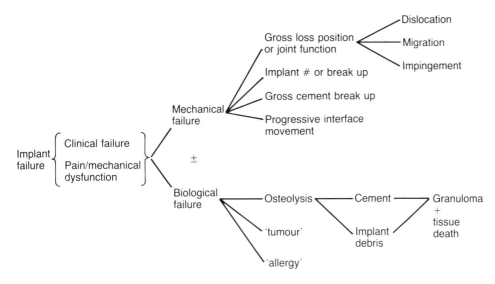

Fig. 18.19   Summary of factors involved in implant failure.

movement at polyethylene metal interfaces *that were not designed to fret or move* have been postulated as a source. Such particles have even been identified alongside the femoral stem of non cemented implants. There is much speculation about the means of transport and theories include joint and interface fluid pressure differences.

Critical objective measurement requires radiographs. The three methods in order of accuracy are:

(1) A standard radiograph of the individual hip with the beam centred at the centre of the hip.

(2) Standard grid radiograph as described by Amstutz. This simplified grid radiograph is simple to use and takes little time to reproduce. The reader is referred to the original article [26].

(3) Stereophotogrammetry as described by Ryd [27] involves a computer analysis of implants where metal ball markers have been incorporated in the bone at the time of surgery. X-rays are taken from a standard position and migration or subsidence of a prosthesis can be measured as accurately as 0.1 mm.

Current status of non-cement total hip arthroplasty including porous ingrowth

In the pre-cement era Thompson and Austin Moore designed implants that are the fore runners of what is used today. Ring in the UK published large series of total hip arthroplasty components fixed without cement. Charnley in his earliest experiments used a press fit.

The general trend towards non-cement arthroplasty is a natural development due to:

(a) The excessive loss of bone stock with failed cemented arthroplasty and the consequent difficulties of revision. There is no doubt that loose non-cement components produce less osteolysis provided particulate prosthetic debris does not develop.

(b) The possible increased susceptibility of cemented prosthesis to haematogenous sepsis.

(c) A possible reduction in the general infection rate in non-cement implant.

For any non-cement total hip replacement system to work there must be:

(a) Primary stability. To achieve this the design of prosthesis must enable there to be as wide as possible area of bone implant contact. The implant must be loaded onto bone of quality strong enough to take the load. To achieve this there must be a wide range of prostheses that fit accurately.

(b) The stress distribution from implant to bone must be of even gradient all around the implant and as low as possible. The design must minimize any tendency to relative movement at the interface. Non-physiological forces should be avoided to minimize bone resorption or loosening, stress transfer being maximal proximally. The force distribution should be such that bone remodelling potential is augmented. Ideally, the design and method of insertion should be such that necessary reparation of the bone close to the implant should be minimized. The technique of insertion should be with minimal bony tissue damage and devascularization, this may not be fulfilled with the extensive reaming necessary to 'fit and fill' suggested as necessary in inserting modern non-cement prostheses. The toxicity of the implant due to ionic insult from interface release or wear products should be minimal.

The factors above are interwoven.

(c) *Porous coating.* Pilliar and Eng [24] have utilized coatings in an attempt to enhance prosthetic fixation. There is no doubt that the condition of primary stability is vital and demands on any supplementary stabilization either cemented or porous coated being therefore minimized. For porous coatings to function and for it to be shown that bone ingrowth is demonstrated histologically in the coating, the following conditions must prevail:

(i)   Primary mechanical stability, as above.

(ii) Pore size. For bone fixation the porous spaces must be more than 100 microns (fibrous tissue fixation takes place if there is less than 50 microns).

(iii) Bone implant apposition. The gap between the bone and implant must not be more than 2 mm.

(iv) Stress transfer. The proof of this function is to demonstrate that a porous coating actually carries load. Eng [24] describes cortical sclerosis at the junctional area between the smooth area distally and the proximal porous coated part of the AML prosthesis at 3 years. Trabecular bone orientation in response to loading induced by a microtextured surface is described. Fibrous tissue fibres also orientate to take the load from such a surface, as opposed to their parallel orientation along a smooth stem.

The author's stem design with proximal macrotexturing has shown no lucent lines in relationship to this surface suggesting bone incorporation. One of the unknown factors in the porous coat implants is the possibility of ionic release. The porous coating enhances the effective surface area of the metal to living tissue interface. Cobalt debris from simulated wear tests injected into experiment animals produced a high tumour incidence; not all authors have been able to repeat this. Sarcomatous lesions adjacent to metal on metal McKee implants have been reported.

The femoral medullary canal width increases with age and how such an expanding skeleton will respond to a non-cement implant is unknown.

Osseoconduction and Induction

It is considered the former is facilitated by the pores in porous coated prostheses filling with blood and bone slurry – the latter [28] is promoted if the surface is coated with a bone inducing agent for example, hydroxyapatite.

The problem of prosthetic retrieval should be considered in the design of an implant. The general view is that if a porous coating should be used at all it should be around the proximal end of the prosthesis and there should be some way of easily exposing the prosthetic bone interface should implant retrieval be necessary.

Eng [24] demonstrated that full length stem coating produced less thigh pain than just proximal coating – users of prostheses fully coated with hydroxyapatite have observed this.

Subsidence is an accurate index of the success or not of a non-cement implant coated as compared to non-coated. This can be assessed by the precise method of stereophotogrammetry.

There is no doubt that the trend is for a porous coating. Hydroxyapatite coatings have reduced subsidence as compared to a control series measured by stereophotogrammetry but the long term outcome is unknown.

There is some concern whether a porous coating applied to a stem reduces the fatigue resistance of the stem. The porous coating therefore should not be applied to a highly stressed area of the stem. Metallurgical studies show that diffusion weld bonding of titanium mesh pads affects substrate forged metal less than sintering chrome cobalt beads to a cast stem base. These findings have implications especially for the more slender prosthetic stems necessary in the narrow medullary cavity of the younger patient. If a stem that was coated throughout its length was to become securely fixed distally and proximal stress shielding was to occur and a distal stem fracture there would be extreme difficulty in removing the distal securely fixed segment of the fractured stem.

The long term benefits of an isoelastic stem are unknown. There is no doubt that proximal bony condensation occurs. Any polymer (with inevitably reduced abrasion resisting characteristics) adjacent to bone may give rise to build up of polymeric debris.

Long term survivorship studies on cemented acetabular components show much poorer performance compared to femoral components in the same study (Fig. 18.15).

Although the first non-cement threaded cups had a high failure rate – hemispherical porous coated metal backed acetabular components appear to perform well – initially they were fixed with screws and same size reamed when ingrowth was seen at the polar contact zone (close to the screw site) but more recent reports both laboratory and clinical suggest under reaming the acetabular by 2 m and impacting the cup giving perimeter contact and better stability and bone ingrowth produces excellent fixation.

There are some reports suggesting particulate debris can derive from a non rigidly held liner or the screws if any holding the cup in. This author's view is that the hemispherical non cemented cups have many advantages in primary and revisional surgery and if the surgeon has confidence in his fit especially in primary THR a factory fitted rigid bond (plastic-metal) acetabular component may be the answer.

On the femoral side the evidence is uncertain in terms of clinical success with pain relief and with less likelihood of microporous bone ingrowth and because of potential removal problems and anticipated stress remodelling changes it is probably desirable to use cemented femoral components in patients over 60 and non-cemented in very young patients.

References

1. Hackenbroch, M. H. *et al.* (1979) Radiological study of 976 arthritic hips, patients under mean age 42. *Arch. Orthop. Trauma Surg.*, **95**, 275–283.
2. Wroblewski, B. M. and Charnley, J. (1982) Classification of osteoarthritis of the hip based on X-ray morphology. *J. Bone Joint Surg.*, **64B**, 568.
3. Bombelli, R. (1983) *Osteoarthritis of the Hip*, 2nd edn. Springer, Berlin.
4. Paul, J. P. (1967) Institute of Mechanical Enginers, 181 (318).
5. English, T. (1978) British Orthopaedic Research Society, Bradford.
6. Rehn, 'Interposition arthroplasty of the hip'. 1930. *Arch. Clin. Chir.*
7. Maquet, P. (1979) Valgus osteotomy results for medial osteoarthritis. *J. Bone Joint Surg.*, **61B**, 424.
8. Morscher, E. W. (1980) Intertrochanteric osteotomy in osteo arthritis of the hip. In *The Hip ... Proceedings of the Eighth Open Scientific Meeting of the Hip Society.* CV Mosby, St. Louis.
9. Osborne, G. (1986) The history of surgical access for hip replacement. *Current Orthopaedics*, **I**, 61–66.
10. Lee, A. J. C., Ling, R. S. M. and Vangala, S. S. (1978) Some clinically relevant variables affecting mechanical properties of cement. *Arch. Orthop. Trauma Surg.*, **92:1**.
11. Hallawa, M., Lee, A. J. C., Ling, R. S. M. and Vangala, S. S. (1978) Shear strength of trabecular bone and factors effecting. *Arch. Orthop. Trauma Surg.*, **92:19**.
12. Charnley, J. (1978) *Low Friction Arthroplasty of the Hip*. Springer, Berlin.
13. Lidwell, O. M., Lowbury, E. J. L. *et al.* (1982) Effects of ultra-clean air in operating rooms on deep surfaces after joint replacement. *Br. Med. J.*, 2, 10.
14. Salzman, E. W. and Harris, W. (1976) Pulmonary embolism fatality rate after total hip replacement surgery. *J. Bone Joint Surg.*, **58A**, 903.
15. Beisaw, N. *et al.* (1987) Dihydrogotamine/heparin prophylaxis of deep vein thrombosis in total hip replacement patients multiple centre trial. *Am. Acad. Orthop. Surg.*, **January**.
16. Amstutz, H. C., Karni, B., Dori, F., Friscia, D. and Yao, J. (1987) The prevention of fatal pulmonary embolism patients under going total hip replacement. *Am. Acad. Orthop. Surg.* **January**.
17. Wroblewski, B. M. (1986) 15–21 year results of Charnley low friction arthroplasty. *Clin. Orthop. Rel. Res.*, **211**, 30.
18. Harris, W. H., McCarthy, J. C. and O'Neill, D. A. (1982) Femoral component loosening using contemporary techniques of femoral cement fixation. *J. Bone Joint Surg.*, **64A**, 1063.
19. Dobbs, H. S. (1980) Survivorship of total hip replacements. *J. Bone Joint Surg.*,**62B**, 168.
20. Ring, P. (1986) Personal communication.
21. Ling, R. S. M. (1989) Mechanical Factors in Implant Fixation. *Current Orthopaedics*, **3**, 168–175.

22. Albrektsson, T., Branemark, P., Hansson, H. and Lindstrom, J. (1981) Osseointegrated titanium implants, requirements for ensuring a long lasting direct bone to implant anchorage in man. *Acta. Orthop. Scand.*, **15**, 155.

23. Linder, L., Hansson, H. A. (1983) Ultra structural aspects of the interface between bone and cement in man. *J. Bone Joint Surg.*, **65B**, 646–649.

24. Eng, C. H., Bobyn, J. D. and Glassman, A. H. (1977) Porous coated hip replacement – the factors growing bone ingrowth – stem shielding and clinical results. *J. Bone Joint Surg.*, **69B**, 95–99.

25. Miller, J., Kraus, W. R., Krug, W. H. and Kelebay, L. C. (1981) Low viscosity cement. *Orthop. Transact.*, **5**, 532.

26. Amstutz, H. *et al.* (1986) The grid X-ray in the follow-up of total hip replacements. *J. Bone Joint Surg.*, **68A**, 105.

27. Ryd, L. (1986) (220) A roentgen stereophotogrammetric analysis of tibial component fixation. *Acta. Orthop. Scand. Suppl.*

28. Furlong, R. J. and Osborn, B. F. (1991) Fixation of hip prostheses by hydroxyapatite coatings. *J. Bone Joint Surg.*, **73B**, 741–745.

29. Gallante (1971) *J. Bone Joint Surg.*, **53A.**, 101.

19

Management of unicompartmental arthritis of the knee

J. H. Newman

Many patients with unicompartmental arthritis of the knee require little in the way of treatment but Hernborg and Nilsson [1] have shown that, in most patients, the natural history of the condition is for a slow deterioration to occur, especially when the medial compartment is predominantly involved. Conservative treatment in the way of non-steroidal anti-inflammatory drugs and physiotherapy may help but many will eventually require invasive treatment. An intra-articular steroid injection can give pain relief, though Dieppe *et al.* [2] believe the improvement is short lived. Arthroscopy is coming to assume an important role, not only because it allows accurate assessment of the joint, but also because a temporary improvement can be obtained in a high proportion of joints treated by arthroscopic lavage alone [3].

When pain persists despite these measures, surgery has to be considered. If the arthritis is predominantly unicompartmental then the options lie between osteotomy, unicompartmental replacement and total joint replacement, with other possibilities such as arthrodesis, debridement [4] or allograft replacement [5] only rarely needing to be considered. Each of these three main procedures has its advocates.

Tibial osteotomy

Tibial osteotomy was first reported as a treatment of osteoarthritis by Jackson in 1958 [6]. Since that time many series have been published with a success rate that has varied from 97% at 2 years [7] to 56% [8]. Most of these series have been retrospective studies with variable criteria for defining success, so evaluation has been hard. It is now generally agreed that the procedure is more satisfactory in the treatment of varus than valgus deformities of the knee, possibly because tibial osteotomy for valgus deformity of the knee usually increases the tibial slope and the tibial spines prevent load transference to the relatively unaffected medial side; in addition, medial collateral ligament instability persists and over correction into varus can easily occur [9].

Theoretically a lower femoral osteotomy should overcome some of these problems with the valgus knee and give a better result. Satisfactory results have been reported [10–12] but the procedure is not widely practised.

In order to obtain a good result from a tibial osteotomy for a varus knee, accurate realignment must be achieved. In the past this has proved difficult and many cases have finished undercorrected; this, combined with other complications [13] has meant that the clinical result has been unpredictable. In addition, Insall [14] has demonstrated that the results of osteotomy deteriorate with time. In his series 97% had good results at 2 years but only 37% were painfree after 9 years. These problems, together with the improvement in the results of knee replacements, mean that there is a much greater need to reassess the indications for tibial osteotomy than was previously the case.

In 1973 Coventry [10] suggested that an upper

tibial osteotomy would do best when performed for early symptomatic unicompartmental arthritis and this has been confirmed by Tjornstrand *et al.* [15] It is now becoming accepted that advanced radiological changes or severe deformity make it hard to achieve a good result after osteotomy. Such cases should be considered for knee replacement.

Unicompartmental replacement

The concept of unicompartmental replacement is attractive because only abnormal surfaces are replaced and minimal bone is resected. Several reports have shown early good results following unicompartmental replacement [14,16–18] but others have been less encouraging [19,20]. Insall and Aglietti [21] presented a particularly worrying report in which initially satisfactory results deteriorated rapidly, and when followed up at 6

years 28% had been revised and only 36% were regarded as good or excellent. However, more than half the cases had undergone patellectomy and it was noted that the curvature of both components was critical so that incorrect positioning could result in binding and subsequent loosening. Both these factors would now be thought of as likely to lead to an unsatisfactory result.

Comparison of tibial osteotomy and unicompartmental replacement [22]

Early experience in Bristol of unicompartmental replacement using the St. Georg Sled prosthesis had been encouraging [23] but a longer term follow-up was clearly needed. Since the obvious alternative procedure was an upper tibial osteotomy, it was decided to carry out a retrospective

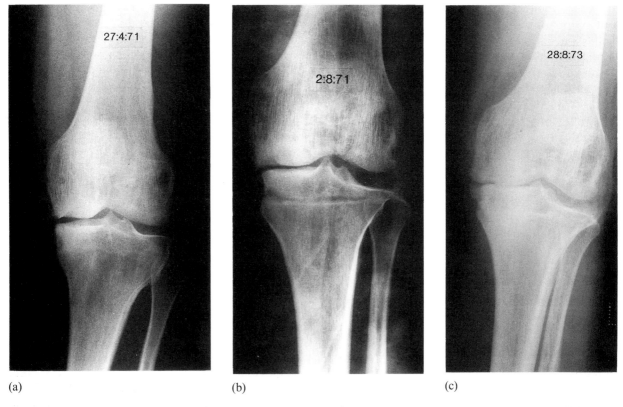

(a)   (b)   (c)

Fig. 19.1   (a, b) Pre- and postoperative radiographs of a 54-year-old female who underwent osteotomy for medial compartment disease. Postoperative alignment was 5° of valgus. (c) Two years later progressive arthritis of both medial and lateral compartments is occurring. Subsequently a knee replacement was performed.

study using the same assessment criteria for both groups. The object was to try to determine whether one procedure was superior to the other, both in terms of quality and longevity of result.

All patients treated in Bristol for osteoarthritis of the knee by unicompartmental replacement or tibial osteotomy between 1974 and 1979 were studied, giving a follow-up period of between 5 and 10 years. Forty-nine osteotomies were available for study and these were compared with 42 unicompartmental replacements. All osteotomies had been performed by resecting a wedge of bone above the tibial tubercle in order to correct the coronal tibio-femoral angle; the fibula was released in a variety of ways (Fig. 19.1). Post-operatively the knee was immobilized in plaster for 6 weeks.

The unicompartment replacements were all St. Georg Sled protheses, cemented in place with a deliberate effort being made minimally to under-correct the deformity.

The selection of the patients for the two procedures was purely determined by the pattern of referral from general practitioners. At that time the unicompartmental replacements were carried out by Mr R. A. J. Baily, the late Mr W. G. J. Hampson and their teams, while the tibial osteotomies were carried out by other Bristol surgeons. There was no evidence of cross referral. The preoperative parameters of the two groups were broadly similar (Table 19.1) and it was

therefore felt that retrospective comparison was justified.

All patients were assessed between 5 and 10 years after operation by history, examination and radiograph where possible. An objective assessment was made using the Baily knee score, which was adapted from that used by the Hospital for Special Surgery and has a maximum score of 50. A score of 35 or more is rated as good, 30–34 fair and less than 30 poor. The radiological features of arthritis were graded according to the system of Kellgren and Lawrence [24] and the coronal femoro-tibial angles were measured on long weight bearing films.

Results

Overall assessment

The unicompartmental replacements show significantly better results than the osteotomies (Table 19.2). Forty-three percent of the osteotomies had a result classified as good, whereas 76% of the unicompartmental replacement group were so classified ($p < 0.01$). Twenty percent of the osteotomies had been revised to a knee replacement whereas only 7% of the unicompartmental replacements had needed further surgery.

Table 19.2   Comparison of overall results in both groups

	Replacement	Osteotomy
Good	32	21
Fair	4	11
Poor	3	7
Revised	3	10

$p < 0.01$

Pain

Although pain represented 30% of the overall assessment, it is often considered the most important factor by the patient. It was therefore assessed separately. Of those patients who had not undergone further surgery, 67% of the unicompartmental replacement group had no pain, while only 26% of the osteotomy group were pain free.

Table 19.1   Comparison of preoperative condition of the unicompartmental replacement and osteotomy groups

	Replacement	Osteotomy
Average age	71 years	63 years
Sex F:M	31:11	38:11
Preoperative deformity:		
Varus	36	33
Valgus	6	16
Average deviation from coronal tibio-femoral angle of 7° valgus	10.2°	9.9°
Average Kellgren–Lawrence score in:		
affected compartment	3.2	3.3
unaffected compartment	1.9	2.0
patello-femoral joint	2.0	2.4

Table 19.3   Incidence of radiological deterioration in compartments

Compartment	Replacement		Osteotomy	
	Deterioration	*No deterioration*	*Deterioration*	*No deterioration*
Affected	–	–	2	15
Unaffected	2	18	12	5
Patello-femoral joint	3	16	8	8

Radiological changes

Not all cases had adequate radiographs to allow full assessment but it can be seen from Table 9.3 that following tibial osteotomy the affected compartment rarely deteriorated but the loaded compartment usually did and the patello-femoral joint deteriorated in 50% of cases. Following unicompartmental replacement with deliberate slight undercorrection, radiological deterioration in the opposite or patello-femoral compartments was unusual (Fig. 19.2).

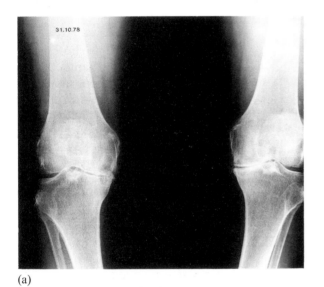

(a)

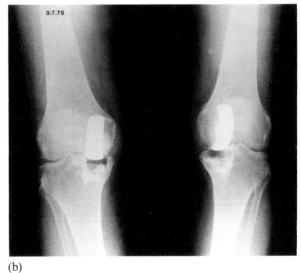

(b)

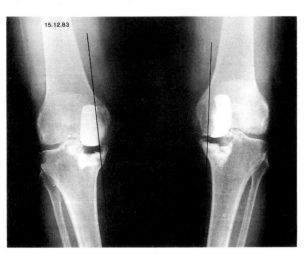

(c)

Fig. 19.2   (a) Preoperative radiograph demonstrating bilateral varus osteoarthritis. (b) Standing radiographs taken 6 months after unicompartmental replacement with St. Georg Sled prostheses. (c) Five years postoperatively there is no evidence of loosening or progressive arthritis. Note the weightbearing line showing undercorrection of the varus deformity.

Thus on the criteria studied, the unicompartmental group appeared to do better when reviewed between 5 and 10 years. The study is open to criticism because it was retrospective and also because the average follow-up of the osteotomies was slightly longer. However, this did not appear to affect the results and in Bristol it seems that patients get a better quality of result and are less likely to need further surgery within 10 years following unicompartmental replacement than upper tibial osteotomy. A more recent review of these patients has demonstrated that the superior results of unicompartmental replacement are maintained at 12 to 17 year follow-up [25].

Although the outcome of the unicompartmental replacements was encouraging, better results can probably be achieved by better patient selection and more accurate component positioning with modern jigs. The choice of prosthesis is also crucial since polyethylene quality and prosthetic design are critical. Possibly longer term survival will be achieved by cementless fixation.

Total knee replacement

Because some of the early reports of unicompartmental replacement were discouraging, some surgeons have not considered the procedure. Such individuals have carried out a total knee replacement when the patient did not appear suitable for an osteotomy. The results of total knee replacement have improved markedly in recent years and good results with a 10-year follow-up have now been reported [26].

With better techniques it is likely that the results will improve still further so that total knee replacement becomes an increasingly attractive option for patients with unicompartmental arthritis. The question that will have to be answered is whether total knee replacement gives better immediate or long term results than unicompartmental replacement.

A comparison of unicompartmental and total knee replacement

When the total knee replacements performed in Bristol during 1974–1979 are compared with the unicompartment St. Georg Sled replacements, it is found that the latter gave 76% good results

between 5 and 10 years compared with 50% good results for the total knee replacement group. However, it should be noted that at the time the predominant total knee replacement being used was a Sheehan arthroplasty and the situation may well be different now that a more modern resurfacing type of arthroplasty is being performed.

Using a standard knee replacement assessment form with a maximum score of 100, the results of resurfacing total knee replacements and unicompartmental replacement have been compared at 2 years. The average score for the total knee replacement group rose from a preoperative figure of 44 to 80, while that for the unicompartmental group rose from 55 to 86. It therefore seems that in Bristol patients undergoing unicompartmental replacement fare slightly better at 2 years than those who have a total knee replacement, but they were a less severely damaged group in the first place.

The only conclusive way to establish the merits of these three procedures is by a prospective trial. The short term results of such a study have shown a slight advantage for unicompartmental replacement in appropriate cases but the long term follow-up is still awaited [27].

Conclusion

Tibial osteotomy is a relatively unpredictable procedure that is not without complications and needs accurate realignment of the knee. It should probably be reserved for younger patients who have early medial compartment arthritis and intact ligaments (Fig. 19.3). For patients with marked unicompartmental arthritis, unicompartment replacement can give good results which do not deteriorate rapidly. However, patient selection is important and the arthritis should be truly unicompartmental [28]. Møller *et al.* [29] have suggested from cadaveric studies that an intact anterior cruciate ligament is necessary for long term survival of an unconstrained implant and recently Goodfellow and O'Connor [30] have presented clinical data to support this theory. In addition, it has been stressed that a flat tibial prosthesis is needed and that over-correction must definitely be avoided in order to prevent deterioration of the opposite compartment. Provided these criteria are met, a predictably good

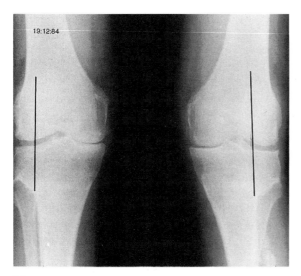

(a)

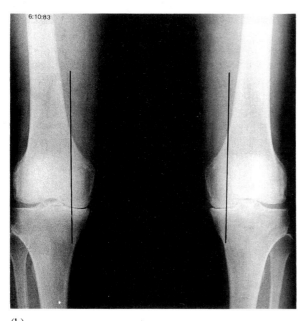

(b)

Fig. 19.3 (a, b) Standing radiographs showing early medial compartment osteoarthritis suitable for an upper tibial osteotomy. The weightbearing line has been transferred from the medial to the lateral compartments (perhaps insufficiently on the left).

result can be expected from the procedure which resects minimal bone, is technically straightforward and which can be easily revised should the need arise [31]. For cases in which the liga-

ments are damaged, or more than one compartment is involved, a resurfacing total knee replacement is probably preferable.

References

1. Hernborg, J. S. and Nilsson, B. E. (1977) The natural course of untreated osteoarthritis of the knee. *Clin. Orthop. Rel. Res.*, **123**, 130–137.
2. Dieppe, P. A., Sathapatayavongs, B., Jones, H. E. *et al.* (1980) Intra-articular steroids in osteo-arthritis. *Rheumatol. Rehab*, **19**, 212–217.
3. Jackson, R. W. and Abe, I. (1972) The role of arthroscopy in the management of disorders of the knee. *J. Bone Joint Surg.*, **54B**, 310–322.
4. Isserlin, B. (1950) Joint debridement for osteo-arthritis of the knee. *J. Bone Joint Surg.*, **32B**, 302–306.
5. Locht, R. C., Gross, A. E. and Langer, F. (1984) Late osteochondral allograft resurfacing for tibial plateau fractures. *J. Bone Joint Surg.*, **66A**, 328–335.
6. Jackson, J. P. (1958) Osteotomy for osteoarthritis of the knee. *J. Bone Joint Surg.*, **40B**, 826.
7. Insall, J. N., Joseph, D. M. and Msika, C. (1984) High tibial osteotomy for varus gonarthrosis. *J. Bone Joint Surg.*, **66A**, 1040–1048.
8. Harding, M. L. (1976) A fresh appraisal of tibial osteotomy for osteoarthritis of the knee. *Clin. Orthop. Rel. Res.*, **114**, 223–234.
9. Shojl, H. and Insall, J. (1973) High tibial osteotomy for osteoarthritis of the knee with valgus deformity. *J. Bone Joint Surg.*, **55A**, 963–973.
10. Coventry, M. B. (1973) Osteotomy about the knee for degenerative and rheumatoid arthritis. *J. Bone Joint Surg.*, **55A**, 23–48.
11. Maquet, P. G. J. (1980) Osteotomy. In *Arthritis of the Knee* (ed. M. A. R. Freeman), Springer, Berlin, Heidelberg, New York, pp. 149–183.
12. Tasker, T. P. B. and Harding, M. L. (1985) Supra-condylar osteotomy for valgus arthritis knees. *J. Bone Joint Surg.*, **67B**, 158.
13. Jackson, J. P. and Waugh, W. (1974) The technique and complications of upper tibial osteotomy. *J. Bone Joint Surg.*, **56B**, 236–245.
14. Inglis, G. S. (1984) Unicompartmental arthroplasty of the knee. *J. Bone Joint Surg.*, **66B**, 682–684.
15. Tjornstrand, B. A. E., Egund, N. and Hagstedt, B. V. (1981) High tibial osteotomy. *Clin. Orthop. Rel. Res.*, **160**, 124–136.
16. Marmor, L. (1979) Marmor modular knee in unicompartmental disease. *J. Bone Joint Surg.*, **61A**, 347–353.

17. Scott, R. D. and Santore, R. F. (1981) Unicondylar unicompartmental replacement for osteoarthritis of the knee. *J. Bone Joint Surg.*, **63A**, 536–544.

18. Thornhill, T. S. (1986) Unicompartmental knee arthroplasty. *Clin. Orthop. Rel. Res.*, **205**, 121–131.

19. Cameron, H. D., Hunter, G. A., Welsh, R. P. and Baily, W. H. (1987) Unicompartmental knee replacement. *Clin. Orthop. Rel. Res.*, **160**, 109–113.

20. Laskin, R. S. (1978) Unicompartmental tibio femoral resurfacing arthroplasty. *J. Bone Joint Surg.*, **60A**, 182–185.

21. Insall, J. N. and Aglietti, P. A. (1980) A five to seven year follow-up of unicondylar arthroplasty. *J. Bone Joint Surg.*, **62A**, 1329–1337.

22. Broughton, N. S., Newman, J. H. and Baily, R. A. J. (1986) Unicompartmental replacement and high tibial osteotomy for osteoarthritis of the knee. *J. Bone Joint Surg.*, **68B**, 447–452.

23. Staniforth, P. and Baily, R. A. J. (1982) St. Georg 'Sledge' resurfacing of the tibio femoral joint. *J. Bone Joint Surg.*, **64B**, 246.

24. Kellgren, J. H. and Lawrence, J. S. (1957) Radiological assessment of osteoarthritis. *Ann. Rheum. Dis.*, **16**, 494–502.

25. Weale, A. E. and Newman, J. H. (1994) Unicompartmental arthroplasty and high tibial osteotomy for osteoarthrosis of the knee. A comparative study with a 12–17 year follow up period. *Clin. Orthop. Rel. Res.*, **302**, 134–137.

26. Insall, J. N. and Kelly, M. (1986) The total condylar prosthesis. *Clin. Orthop. Rel. Res.*, **205**, 43–48.

27. Newman, J. H., Acroyd, C. E. and Ahmed, S. R. (1994) The early results of a prospective randomised trial of unicompartmental or total knee replacement. *J. Bone Joint Surg.*, **76B**, 5.

28. Sarangi, P. P., Jackson, M., Karachalios, T. and Newman, J. H. (1994) Patterns of failure of unicondylar knee replacement. *Revue de Chir. Orthop.*, **80**, 217–222.

29. Møller, J. T., Weeth, R. E., Keller, J. O. and Nielsen, S. (1985) Unicompartmental arthroplasty of the knee. *Acta Orthop. Scand.*, **56**, 120–123.

30. Goodfellow, J. W. and O'Connor, J. (1986) Clinical results of the Oxford knee. *Clin. Orthop. Rel. Res.*, **205**, 21–42.

31. Jackson, M., Sarangi, P. P. and Newman, J. H. (1994) Revision Knee Replacement. Comparison of outcome of primary proximal tibial osteotomy or unicompartmental arthroplasty. *J. Arthroplasty*, **9**, 539–542.

20

Mechanical and degenerative disorders of the lumbar spine

J. S. Denton

Introduction

Back pain is a problem of epidemic proportions. It ranks with headache and tiredness as the commonest symptom of which the general public complain and it causes around half of the population to seek advice from their general practitioners at some time. The cost of back pain in sickness benefit is enormous.

The subject is plagued by the twin difficulties of correctly identifying the source of pain and of finding an effective treatment even for those patients in whom the pain source has been confidently defined. Fortunately, the majority of patients with back pain improve regardless of treatment and only a very few become 'back cripples'.

Classification of back pain

Back pain, like abdominal pain or headache, is but a symptom. It is not a diagnosis. The poor reputation that back pain has among the general public arises largely from the failure to make a diagnosis. Even with the most meticulous enquiry about the history, a detailed examination of the patient and sophisticated investigation, there are occasions when the exact site and source of the pain cannot be identified. Many patients, even though severely incapacitated by their complaint, will be satisfied by an explanation of the nature of their condition and simple advice on how best to come to terms with it in order to minimize the disruption which it causes to their lives.

A rational analysis of the many syndromes of back pain requires a knowledge of anatomy, an understanding of the physiology of pain and some comprehension of the biomechanics of the spine. The chosen classification of back pain is that suggested by Macnab.

Viscerogenic back pain

Backs have fronts. Back pain may thus be derived from any of a number of structures lying in the retroperitoneal space. Common sources of viscerogenic back pain include the kidneys, pancreas, duodenum, malignant infiltration or secondary deposits from remote disease. It is uncommon for back pain to be the only complaint in those patients with visceral pathology. It follows that no assessment of a patient complaining of back pain is complete without an enquiry into the patient's general health, particularly his respiratory, genito-urinary and digestive functions. A careful abdominal and rectal examination is mandatory, as also is an examination of the vascular supply of the lower limbs. Viscerogenic back pain is typically not relieved by rest or aggravated by activity, although occasionally a patient with a posterior duodenal or gastric ulcer penetrating the pancreas may report exacerbation of the pain by stooping or exercise and relief by lying down. On occasion, the complaint of back pain may override the digestive symp-

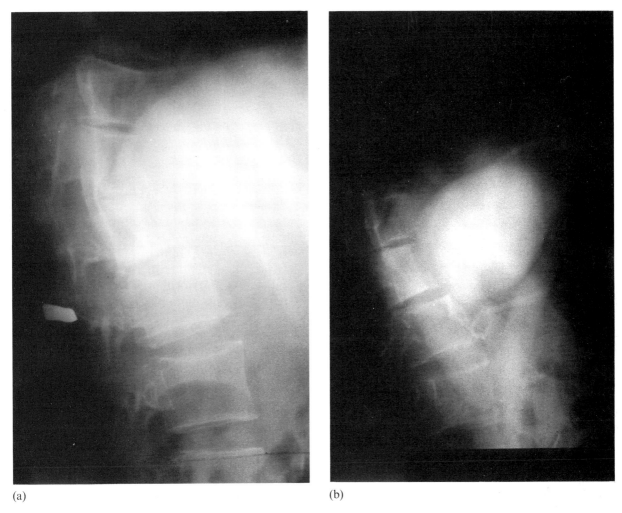

(a)   (b)

Fig. 20.1 Abdominal aneurysm: scalloping of the anterior borders of vertebral bodies and calcification in the wall of the aneurysm.

toms to such a degree that the primary problem may escape the attention of the physician unless the appropriate inquiries are made.

Vascular back pain

An aortic aneurysm may cause severe deep seated boring back pain and abdominal examination may reveal a pulsatile and easily palpable mass. Aneurysmal dilatation of the aorta will not in itself lead to the disappearance of the distal pulses, but such patients may have occlusive vascular disease as well as a propensity for aneurysm formation. The femoral pulses may therefore be reduced in volume or absent. The presence of a thrill or bruit over the femoral artery is a further sign of circulatory disturbance. A scalloped appearance of the anterior borders of the vertebral bodies is often present on the plain lateral radiograph as well as calcification in the wall of the aneurysm (Fig. 20.1).

Neurogenic back pain

The thalamus relays and may record sensory stimuli. Occasionally, a lesion of the thalamus such as a tumour or more commonly an infarct in a hypertensive patient may cause pain in the leg. The pain has a typically bizarre nature which the patient finds difficult to describe. Severe hyperaesthesia may be present, provoked by light touch but not by firm touch such as grasping the limb. Other causes of neurogenic back pain include primary or secondary tumours invading from the vertebrae or arising *de novo* in the meninges, spinal cord or cauda equina. Thus ependymomata, neurilemmomata and neurofibromata are rare but possible causes of neurogenic pain. Occasionally, the syndrome may be clinically indistinguishable from that produced by a prolapsed intervertebral disc with nerve root entrapment. Finally, in childhood, an intraspinal tumour must be suspected.

Psychogenic back pain

True psychogenic back pain is rare but the problem of somatism is not unique to back pain and may dominate the clinical picture. It requires time, patience and a certain expertise to recognize this problem and the management may be outside the province of many surgeons.

Spondylogenic back pain

This category, comprising those causes of back pain arising as a result of pathology in the spinal or paraspinal structures, accounts for the vast majority of patients presenting with a complaint of backache. The pain may arise from bone, joint or soft tissue, the latter being the commonest source. The commoner causes of spondylogenic back pain are discussed in detail in the sections below.

The anatomy of low back pain

The design of the spine arises from a compromise between conflicting requirements. The structure must be capable of withstanding enormous loads yet allow sufficient mobility to perform many activities. Failure of one or more components of the spine will result in one of the recognizable clinical syndromes of backache.

The design of the vertebral column

The cervical, thoracic and lumbar vertebrae articulate with their neighbours by means of synovial facet joints and intervertebral discs. Stability is conferred to the spine by these articulations and their ligaments and associated muscles. A smooth kyphotic configuration in fetal life is transformed by lordotic curves in the cervical and lumbar regions as soon as the upright posture is established.

The intervertebral disc

The disc is a complex structure attached firmly to the hyaline end plates on the adjacent surfaces of the vertebral bodies and within it the nucleus pulposus, a remnant of the notochord, lies towards the posterior half. The tough annulus fibrosus surrounds the nucleus.

In the fetus and during the first years of life, the nucleus pulposus has a blood supply. This diminishes rapidly within a few months of birth and by the age of 8 has virtually disappeared so that the adult nucleus is entirely avascular. Its nutrition is obtained by diffusion of metabolites from the marrow spaces of the neighbouring vertebrae via the end plates and to a lesser extent by a similar process of diffusion through the annulus. The nucleus is composed mainly of ground substances, which consist of a variety of macromolecules held in colloidal suspension. The substances present include glycoproteins and proteoglycans. The latter are strongly hydrophilic and as a result, the water content of the nucleus is high. The diffusion of water into the nucleus gives rise to a hydrostatic pressure within the disc which is resisted by the surrounding annulus fibrosus. As a result, the fibres of the annulus come to lie under tension rather in the manner of the walls of a pressure vessel. The organic content of the nucleus is produced by the cells which lie enmeshed within a loose network of collagen fibrils. Most of the ground substances and collagen are produced by those cells which lie close to the junction of nucleus and annulus. With ageing, the water content and proteoglycan content of the nucleus diminish. This is related to a tendency to fibrosis of the nucleus with simultaneous diminution in cellular activity at the junctional zone.

The annulus fibrosus consists mainly of sheets of collagen fibrils lying in laminae of differing orientations, rather akin to the walls of a tyre. At their ends, they are firmly attached to the cartilaginous endplates of the vertebrae. The orientation of successive sheets of fibrils varies but most lie at an angle of 60° to their neighbours and to the axis of the spine. In this way, they are most favourably disposed to withstand the shear stresses to which they are subjected during load bearing.

The anterior longitudinal ligament is a condensation of the annulus lying along the anterior aspect of the disc and is attached to the endplate. It continues over the anterior aspect of the vertebral body but is easily separated from it. The fibrils of collagen in the ligament are aligned with the long axis of the spine.

The posterior longitudinal ligament by contrast is less robust. It lies in the midline over the posterior aspect of the vertebrae and discs to which it is loosely attached.

The nerve supply of the disc is scanty. Free nerve endings are seen in discs of infants and young children but they degenerate in adolescence, leaving nerve fibres which penetrate only a short distance into the outer layers of the annulus. The main source of nerve endings lies in the fibroelastic tissue attaching the posterior longitudinal ligament to the annulus of the disc. They are likely to be stimulated in a central disc prolapse but not in the more common lateral disc herniation.

Facet joints

The facet joints in the upper part of the lumbar spine lie in the sagittal plane, but lower down the orientation of the facet joints progressively rotates so that at lumbosacral level they lie in the coronal plane.

The role of the facet joint as a cause of back pain has for long been a matter of dispute. Recent imaging techniques have demonstrated pathological changes in these structures so that their importance is more evident.

A concentric articulation is achieved by a convex upper and a concave lower surface though asymmetry is common and may lead to degenerative changes when subject to load bearing. The main movement at the facet joints is gliding to allow flexion and extension. Asymmetric sliding allows lateral flexion. Rotation is limited in the lumbar spine but is brought about by distraction of the facet on the side to which

bending occurs, combined with compression and anterior sliding of the opposite facet; the compressed facet acting as a fulcrum.

Constraints to movement depend not only upon the shape of the facets but also upon the surrounding ligaments and the joint capsules. There are recesses at the upper and lower limits of the joint capsule where multifidus muscle fibres are attached presumably to prevent entrapment of the synovial lining during movement.

Ligaments

The ligamentum flavum is a thick fibroelastic structure which extends from the anterior aspect of the inferior surface of the lamina above to the upper surface of the lamina below. It provides a smooth posterior border of the spinal canal. In flexion it is tight but in extension it tends to buckle so narrowing the anteroposterior diameter of the spinal canal and thus becoming a potential contributing factor to spinal stenosis. It is a bifid structure with a median raphe allowing for easy midline fenestration when the spinous process has been removed. Its attachment to the anterior surface of the upper lamina may interfere with the passage of sublaminar wires.

The interspinous ligament is segmental and is a strong constraint in flexion of the spine.

The innervation of the spine

The innervation of spinal and paraspinal structures follows a complex and variable pattern. The earlier theory that pain was produced by overstimulation of a variety of different receptors has been abandoned since the recognition of specific nociceptive nerve endings. Such receptors have been identified in most tissues of the spine. They are represented by unmyelinated plexiform nerve fibres with free endings ramifying throughout the skin, subcutaneous fat, fasciae, ligaments, bone, periosteum, joint capsules, dura and adventitia of blood vessels.

The neurological anatomy of the lumbar spine has been clarified by the studies of Wyke [1], Paris [2] and Bogduk *et al.* [3]; a pattern has emerged. The ventral and dorsal roots within the central canal are bathed in cerebrospinal fluid and join to form a mixed spinal nerve in the root canal just distal to the dorsal root ganglion but still within the evagination of the dural sheath. As the mixed nerve emerges from the root canal, a branch arises which joins with another from the ramus communicans to form the recurrent sinuvertebral nerve of Luschke. The latter re-enters the spinal canal via the foramen and giving off branches which supply the posterior longitudinal ligament, the fibroelastic tissue attaching the ligament to the disc, the meninges, particularly the anterior surface of the dura, the nerve root sleeves, the ligamentum flavum and the facet joints. The mixed spinal nerve then divides almost immediately into anterior and posterior primary rami. Most of the fibres in the anterior primary ramus are destined to form the lumbar and sacral plexuses. Branches arise which innervate the immediate surrounding tissues of the postero-lateral and lateral aspects of the disc, though with only minimal penetration into the annulus.

The posterior primary ramus innervates the paravertebral muscles and overlying skin as well as the facet joints at adjacent levels. Further branches innervate the interspinous, supra-spinous and intertransverse ligaments. In addition, the posterior primary rami of L4, L5 and S1 send branches to the sacroiliac joints. This simple description belies the wide innervation of spinal structures. Virtually every tissue in the spine is innervated by at least three spinal nerves by virtue of their ascending and descending branches. As a result, referred pain fails to conform to the exact and expected dermatome, which may prove misleading when attempting to identify the level of the source of pain.

Pain pathways in the spine

When nociceptive receptors are stimulated, the nerve impulses are carried in small diameter unmyelinated fibres to the dorsal root ganglion. From here, the fibres enter the cord via the dorsal root travelling in its anterior ramus. The posterior ramus carries large diameter fibres conveying sensations such as proprioception, light touch and vibration sense. As the pain fibres enter the cord, ascending and descending branches are given off which typically span one or two segments. The main fibres and their branches then enter the grey matter of the posterior horn of the cord where they form a synapse with inter-

mediate neurones. From these neurones, most fibres can be traced across the cord where they enter the contralateral anterolateral ascending tract to be conveyed to the brain. Other fibres, via a series of intermediate synaptic connections, project to the motor neurone pools of the muscles of the back and lower limbs. These circuits probably account for the peculiarities of gait and posture which are seen in many patients with back pain.

The gate theory

Within the spinal cord, mechanisms exist for the modulation of pain. Certain of the larger diameter fibres entering the cord through the posterior ramus of the dorsal root relay with neurones within the substantia gelatinosa – a lightly staining area which caps the dorsal horn. These neurones relay with the presynaptic fibres of the nociceptive neurones and inhibit the transmission of pain stimuli across the neighbouring synapses. This is the basis of the 'gate theory'. The application of non-noxious stimuli such as rubbing the skin, gentle heat or even moving the affected source of pain, may be sufficient to reduce the level of perceived pain. The theory may also explain the severity of pain in post-herpetic neuralgia. The destruction of the larger diameter fibres removes their moderating influence on the onward transmission of pain and a more profound painful stimulus thus arrives at the brain.

The gate theory, while still valid, has been modified by better understanding of the modulating influence on pain of descending tracts from the brain. These are conveyed via the reticular formation from the frontal and paracentral regions of the brain. The descending tracts exert their influence via a series of intermediate neurones in the dorsal horns and inhibit the onward transmission of pain impulses in a similar manner to that operating in the classical gate theory.

The anterolateral tract transmits the pain impulses to the brain. Formerly known as the spino-thalamic tract, it is now named according to its position in the cord as recent work has revealed that fewer than one third of its fibres actually terminate in the thalamus. Most of the fibres relay within the reticular formation or other brain stem nuclei; others re-enter the grey matter of the cord to form a synapse with neurones therein. Those with synaptic connections within the thalamus are generally of larger diameter and are myelinated. They project to cortical sensory area 'One' and are chiefly concerned with the location, intellectual perception and recognition of the quality of the painful stimulus.

The frontal area relates to the emotive response and subjective sensation of unpleasantness; the temporal region is concerned with the memory of previous painful stimuli and the hypothalamus regulates the viscerohumoral response to pain, including the changes which occur in the gastrointestinal and cardiovascular systems as well as various hormonal responses.

Communication between these components is achieved by a complex system of association fibres. One component may be modified independently of the rest and there is thus no direct correlation between one and the other. Attempts to quantify pain by measuring visceral responses in a laboratory are unreliable and the best solution is to rely on the well tried method of being a good listener and attending to the patient's complaints and their effect on the quality of life.

Soft tissue injuries of the spine

As with articulated structures elsewhere in the body, the muscles, ligaments and joints associated with the spine are liable to injury. A number of syndromes are described, though it must be admitted at the outset that there is often considerable difficulty attached to the identification of the specific structure which has been damaged.

The acute back strain

The acute back strain is occasioned by activities such as injudicious lifting, falling or other externally applied violence to the soft tissues of the spine. Muscles, ligaments and joints may be torn as the soft tissues tighten to prevent damage to the osseous and neural components of the spine. The patient experiences severe pain in the back, often with ill-defined radiation to the buttocks and thighs. Any attempt to move the injured

structures in the acute stage is confounded by intense muscle spasm, resulting in rigidity of the lumbar spine together with a limp and sometimes profound disturbances in posture. In the absence of symptoms or signs suggestive of a prolapsed intervertebral disc, there is little point in attempting to identify the exact site of the pathology. The treatment is simple. Bed rest is indicated until the worst of the pain has subsided and the patient has begun to mobilize. Adequate analgesia must be provided. Regardless of what treatment if any is applied, the vast majority of patients will make a full recovery from the acute episode in a matter of a few weeks.

Many will benefit from a short course of non-steroidal anti-inflammatory drugs and from a muscle relaxant such as diazepam. If it is possible to locate an area of particularly acute tenderness, infiltration of the region with 0.5% bupivicaine in a dose of around 10 ml may provide instantaneous if short-lived relief. Such manoeuvres probably do not affect the speed of resolution of the pathology, but can bring welcome relief to the patient and encourage him in the belief that his back will eventually recover.

Physiotherapy has little part to play in the earliest phase of the illness. If recovery is prolonged or if the patient is unable or unwilling to go to bed until the symptoms have abated, some form of external splintage must be provided, perhaps in the form of a plaster jacket. It is rarely necessary to continue such treatment for longer than 2 weeks. After this time, efforts should be directed to restoring mobility to the spine and to recovering muscle tone. At this stage when soft tissue healing is under way and the initial hyperaemia and oedema have subsided, a course of physiotherapy may be of benefit, although the great majority of patients will not in fact require it. Local heat, ultrasound, short wave diathermy and megapulse treatment may be applied in conjunction with gentle stretching exercises aimed at breaking down any adhesions which may have formed. The damaged soft tissues will inevitably repair by scar tissue. As long as this scar is prevented from adhering to adjacent structures of different mobility and is protected from further damage by adequate paraspinal musculature, it is reasonable to expect a smooth and rapid convalescence with uneventful return to former activities. Prior to discharge, the patient should be counselled regarding lifting activities at work and taught how to protect his back against further episodes.

The chronic back strain

Some patients do not recover well from an acute back strain. This may be due to inappropriate or inadequate initial treatment, to attempts on the part of the patient to return to strenuous activity too soon or to a lack of resolve on the part of the patient to overcome the illness and rehabilitate himself to what may be seen as an unpalatable if not overtly hostile working environment. Patients who are involved in litigation because of an accident at work which may have precipitated their symptoms can be particularly difficult to manage and it can take a great deal of persuasion that an early return to former activities is what is required in order to rehabilitate their back most effectively.

Much reassurance is needed that the experience of back pain does not equate with progressive structural damage to the spine. The active role of the patient in any treatment programme must be emphasized and it should be made clear that a firm commitment is called for in order to ensure recovery. The patient is not merely a passive onlooker in this scenario. The responsibility for recovery is his as much as the surgeon's.

The long term outlook for patients with a chronic back strain is not good. Very few of those who have been off work for longer than 1 year will return to their former employment and virtually none who have been absent for 2 years or more. The key to prevention of this undesirable situation is the effective treatment of the acute condition.

The prolapsed intervertebral disc

It was not until 1932 that Barr of Boston recognized the existence of prolapse of the intervertebral disc as a cause of back pain. The material which he had removed from his patient's spinal canal had been labelled as chondroma by the pathologist – a common report to obtain from such specimens in that era. In 1934, Barr and Mixter [4] suggested that sciatic pain could be produced from the encroachment of prolapsed intervertebral disc material upon a lumbar nerve root. At first received with scepticism, this concept rapidly gained wide acceptance and it was not long before the intervertebral disc was incriminated as the cause of back pain in the majority of such patients presenting to the orthopaedic surgeon. The balance has now hopefully been restored to a more realistic level and the prolapsed disc has taken its rightful place as a prominent but by no means the sole cause of back pain and sciatica.

Pathology

The changes of ageing in the normal disc do not in themselves cause back pain but render the disc more vulnerable to damage when challenged with loads that a healthy disc in a younger patient would withstand. The stresses required to bring about failure of the disc are debatable but simple compressive loading of the spine will not induce disc failure. The more likely outcome in such a situation is that the vertebral endplate will fail, leading to herniation of disc material into the body of the vertebra and the subsequent appearance on the radiograph of the so-called 'Schmorl's node' (Fig. 20.2). Even when a longitudinal incision is made in the annulus in its posterolateral portion (the most frequent site of annular tears in the patient with the prolapsed

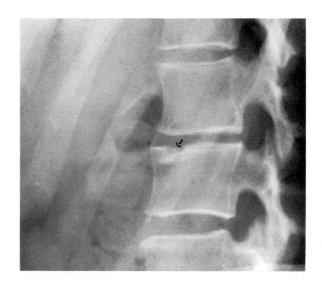

Fig. 20.2 Schmorl's node: herniation of disc material through the vertebral end-plate.

disc), the disc will still herniate into the vertebral body when direct compression is applied rather than fail by a rupture through the annulus [5]. The load required to bring about endplate failure is quoted as between 1800 Newtons and 5300 Newtons by different authors. It is instructive to compare these figures with the normal loads experienced by the disc in everyday activities. Nachemson and co-workers [6] measured the intradiscal pressure in volunteers performing various activities. The L3 disc carries about 60% of the body weight above it – typically 420 Newtons. Sitting or standing in 20° of flexion increases the load in this disc to over 200% of body weight. Forward flexion of 5° alone will increase the load on the disc by 25%.

Compression is certainly of importance in bringing about failure of the annulus but it must be combined with loading in other modalities if other structures are not to fail first. Hickey and Hukins [7] suggest that the combination of compression and rotation is of importance while Adams and Hutton [8] indicate flexion of the compressed disc as being the more likely mode of failure. It is most likely that all three factors are involved. The amount of rotation required to produce failure of the annular fibres of the disc is of the order of 4° [9]. It is unlikely that this can be achieved in the erect normal spine because of the restraint offered by the facet joints. If, however, the spine is flexed, the facet joints will now allow further rotation to occur and the integrity of the annulus will be jeopardized. Reflex protective mechanisms are invoked to prevent such an occurrence. These take the form of involuntary muscle contractions which resist the tendency for the spine to flex and rotate. The application of an unexpected load to the spine in the form of a fall or grabbing at a heavy load to prevent its escaping may, however, overcome these protective mechanisms and expose the disc to loads which can bring about an annular rupture and prolapse of the intradiscal material.

The most common site for the intervertebral disc to fail is just lateral to the posterior longitudinal ligament. It is here that the annulus is thinnest and therefore most vulnerable. A very common clinical finding is the reporting of intermittent backache for some months or even years prior to the sudden onset of severe back pain and sciatica. A possible explanation of this phenomenon is the existence of a small tear in the annulus of the disc prior to the release of the disc material into the canal. The paucity of innervation of the annulus casts some doubt upon this as the true explanation for this phenomenon. The resolution of this difficulty may lie in the invasion of damaged areas of the disc by granulation tissue which carries with it small diameter nerve fibres which could indeed act as nociceptors in the damaged disc. The tears described are generally radially disposed. They arise at the posterolateral corner of the disc, where the annulus experiences its greatest load and occur most commonly in the lower lumbar spine. The concave shape of the posterior border of the vertebral bodies and disc in this region leads to stress concentration at the posterolateral corner of the disc [10]. Furthermore, the lumbar discs, particularly that at the lumbosacral junction, are wedge shaped and carry a greater fraction of the body weight than do discs at higher levels. It is this combination of factors that is thought to predispose the lower lumbar discs to preferential failure given the appropriate mechanical challenge. The radial tear starts centrally and progresses towards the outer margin of the annulus. As progression occurs it may be accompanied by bulging of the disc along the line of the tear but at this stage no communication exists between the nucleus and the spinal canal. This represents a disc protrusion – that is an early prolapse of disc material where the nucleus is still shielded from the spinal canal by layers of intact annulus. Once the tear has reached the periphery of the annulus, the way is clear for the contents of the nucleus to be exuded into the canal – in other words, for the disc to rupture. This may occur slowly or with great rapidity depending upon the mechanical properties of the individual disc and the loading patterns to which it is subjected. Once disc material can be found outside the margins of the annulus, a disc extrusion is said to exist. Initially there is still continuity between the extruded material and the nuclear remnants within the disc. If, however, the extruded fragment becomes separated from the nucleus and lies free within the canal, a sequestration of the disc is said to have occurred. Such free disc fragments may migrate in a cephalad or caudal direction and may give rise to misleading signs when an attempt is made to localize the level of the lesion.

The mechanisms involved in the production of radicular pain are not straightforward. According to Macnab [11], direct pressure on a normal nerve root produces paraesthesiae rather than pain. This observation correlates well with the common clinical finding of lower limb paraesthesiae accompanying back pain in the early stages of a disc herniation, rather than pain. It appears that the nerve root must be inflamed for pain to be produced by direct pressure from the disc. With a longstanding disc prolapse, such inflammation does in fact occur. The herniated disc material irritates the surrounding tissues and an inflammatory reaction is set up with oedema and hyperaemia of the dural sheath of the root. Subsequently, dense adhesions may develop around the root and give rise to clinical features suggestive of nerve root tethering. The cause of the inflammatory reaction is unresolved. It is likely that owing to the avascularity of the disc, the latter occupies an immunologically privileged position and that exposure of the body's immune mechanisms to ruptured disc material may therefore initiate a form of autoimmune reaction. Attractive though this concept is, it awaits rigorous confirmation.

The precise direction in which the herniation occurs is of importance in determining the clinical features of the condition. Occasionally a central disc prolapse is found wherein the disc bursts through the posterior longitudinal ligament. This usually arises very acutely and may be precipitated by trauma. The diagnosis is a matter of great urgency, for there is a severe risk of cauda equina compression developing with subsequent paralysis and loss of sphincter control. The lower limbs are affected bilaterally. Weakness and numbness in the legs are accompanied by loss of perineal sensation and loss of sphincter tone. Unless the situation is remedied by urgent decompression within a few hours, the patient may not recover normal sphincter function and may be left with a residual paraparesis. This type of disc rupture most commonly occurs at the L4–L5 level.

More commonly, the herniation occurs more peripherally, just lateral to the posterior longitudinal ligament. The disc material comes to lie under the root, which is displaced either medially or, in the case of a so-called paramedian disc protrusion, laterally. Characteristically, the root involved is that corresponding to the spinal segment below which the prolapse occurs. Thus, at the lumbosacral level, it is the S1 root which is most commonly affected and at the L4–L5 level, the L5 root is at greatest risk. Atypical patterns of root involvement are well recognized. With a large herniation of the disc two roots may be involved, with disc material impinging upon the root emerging at the level of the prolapse as well as upon that emerging below. Variations in the anatomy of the sacral plexus can give rise to further confusion. It is not uncommon for the fifth lumbar root to accompany the first sacral root and to emerge via the first sacral foramen. Clearly, both roots will be at risk in the event of a lumbosacral disc prolapse.

In the event of the rupture occurring further laterally, the root emerging at the same level may be affected in its extradural course – thus with a lumbosacral disc prolapse, the fifth lumbar root may occasionally be involved rather than the first sacral.

Finally, a sequestered disc fragment may migrate in a cephalad or caudal direction to embarrass nerve roots at other levels or alternatively may become lodged in a root canal, giving rise to a severe local inflammatory response with nerve root tethering. Such fragments may be difficult to detect at surgical exploration unless an assiduous attempt is made to follow the root far out into its canal until it is seen to be completely free.

Clinical presentation

A disc prolapse may occur at any age. Those arising in young patients have special features; an acute prolapse is most common between the ages of 20 and 40 years.

Acute onset

This is often associated with radicular pain and precipitated by lifting a heavy weight. Initially, there may be numbness or paraesthesiae in the distribution of a nerve root with a dull ache in the buttock and thigh. If, for example, the first sacral root is affected, the patient will complain of pain and numbness over the outer aspect of the foot. The pain will be exacerbated by any activity which increases the pressure within the disc such as bending, sneezing or straining at stool. Pain patterns vary and some patients may have minimal backache but severe radicular pain.

Urinary incontinence

Urinary incontinence is serious and indicates that there is pressure on the cauda equina.

Frequently, the acute symptoms subside with rest to a sufficient degree to allow the patient to return to work perhaps with some residual discomfort. Any recurrence of the acute pain may be more severe and take longer to settle down than the first attack; residual symptoms tend to be more pronounced and prolonged.

Motor symptoms are not so frequent and other causes such as multiple sclerosis or an intraspinal tumour have to be considered and excluded.

Physical examination

Posture

In the acute phase there will be paravertebral spasm, loss of the normal lordotic curve and limited spinal movements. The patient may stand with a tilt to one side which disappears on lying down. The explanation for this 'sciatic scoliosis' is not entirely clear. It was formerly thought to be connected in some way with the anatomical relationship of the disc prolapse to the nerve root. Thus, it was said that with a disc prolapse lateral to the root, the patient tended to lean away from the side of the prolapse in order to gain relief from his symptoms; conversely, with a prolapse medial to the root, leaning towards the side of the pain brought relief. This is a highly simplistic and incorrect explanation of a complex phenomenon and in practice, the operative findings often disagree with one's prediction of the exact site of the prolapse. It is likely that the true explanation of this phenomenon involves derangements in the finely tuned postural reflexes which exist at cord level, rather than an obvious mechanical explanation. The matter awaits further clarification. The presence of a sciatic scoliosis is however highly suggestive of the presence of a disc prolapse and in this respect remains an invaluable physical sign.

Straight leg raise

Any increase in tension on an already stretched nerve root will provoke further pain in the distribution of the affected root. The straight leg raise test is most evident in the presence of a disc prolapse affecting the fourth or fifth lumbar or the first sacral nerve roots. Limitation of straight leg raising to 45° or less is positive [12] but there is also variation within the healthy population. A difference between the two sides is more significant, ranging from 15° [12] to 30° [13]. The production of radicular pain in the affected leg when a straight leg raise is performed on the 'healthy' side (the crossed straight leg raise test) is an important sign which gives unequivocal evidence of nerve root tension and is often associated with the presence of a sequestered disc fragment.

The bowstring test

This is another test for nerve root tension. The straight leg raising test is performed to the point where the patient complains of pain. The hip is maintained in this position while the knee is flexed by 5°. This should relieve the patient of pain. Pressure is then applied behind the knee. If this evokes a similar pain to that experienced with straight leg raising, the test is positive.

Likewise, with the straight leg raise being performed just to the point of pain production, forced dorsiflexion of the ankle, internal rotation of the hip or even flexion of the neck may produce a similar positive response.

With a disc prolapse in the upper lumbar region, the sacral nerve roots are unaffected and the straight leg raise and its qualifying tests are normal. However, an equivalent test (the femoral nerve stretch test) is available to test for tension in the upper lumbar roots. The test is performed with the patient lying prone. The hip is passively extended and the knee passively flexed. If pain in a radicular distribution is evoked, the test is positive.

Neurological examination

Neurological symptoms appear at an earlier stage than neurological signs. Consequently, the significance of a normal neurological examination depends to a certain extent upon the duration and severity of the symptoms. The tendon reflexes, muscle tone and skin sensibility

Table 20.1   Typical patterns of neurological abnormality in patients with acute lumbar disc herniation

Level of disc prolapse	Nerve root involvement	Sensory loss	Motor weakness	Disturbance of reflex
L5/S1	S1	Outer border of foot	Calf muscles	Ankle jerk absent or depressed
L4/L5	L5	Outer side of calf and medial border of foot	Extensor hallucis	E.H.L. jerk absent or depressed
L3/L4	L4	Medial side of calf	Quadriceps	Knee jerk absent or depressed
L2/L3	L3	Anterior aspect of knee	Quadriceps	Knee jerk absent or depressed
Central disc prolapse	Cauda equina	Variable pattern in legs; often perineal loss	Variable; may be profound; usually asymmetrical; loss of sphincter control	Variable; corresponds with loss of motor function

Not all patients will display all features for a disc herniation at any given level. Patterns of sensory disturbance, in particular sensory symptoms as opposed to sensory signs may vary somewhat. Patients often find difficulty in localizing sensory symptoms and variations occur in the anatomy of the lumbosacral plexus. In addition, a disc herniation at any given level may affect the exiting root at that level rather than, or in addition to, the traversing root, leading for example to the presence of L5 root signs in a L5/S1 disc herniation.

must be recorded and compared with the normal side. A general neurological examination must be performed in order to exclude either central or widespread disease. A typical abnormal pattern may emerge depending upon which nerve root is affected (Table 20.1).

McCulloch [14] lists five criteria which may be found in the patient with a disc prolapse, of which at least three should be present if a confident clinical diagnosis is to be made. These are:

1. Unilateral leg pain in a sciatic distribution including pain below the level of the knee.
2. Specific neurological symptoms of numbness, paraesthesiae or weakness which can be attributed to the involvement of a single nerve root.
3. Limitation of straight leg raising by at least 50% of normal.
4. At least two neurological signs which may include muscle wasting, weakness, sensory deficit or reduction or absence of a tendon reflex.
5. Myelographic evidence of a disc prolapse. This could nowadays be extended to include computerized tomography or magnetic resonance imaging.

Intervertebral disc lesions in childhood

Most of the clinical features of a prolapsed intervertebral disc in childhood are similar to those seen in the adult. The patient presents with back pain of variable severity which may be of acute or gradual onset. There is sometimes a history of trauma preceding the appearance of symptoms. Leg pain is very common and is not infrequently bilateral. Numbness and paraesthesiae are less prominent than in the adult and motor weakness is an unusual complaint.

The child often presents with a bizarre gait, avoiding the swing through phase of walking by circumduction of the pelvis or by shuffling in those patients with bilateral leg pain in an attempt to reduce nerve root tension by avoiding traction on the sacral plexus. Local cord reflexes may also be involved in the production of this type of gait. The posture may be equally bizarre with marked spasm of the erector spinae muscles and a pronounced list to one side.

Nerve root tension signs are often more striking in the child than in the adult and severe limitation of straight leg raising is the rule. Sensory changes are uncommon but may be present. Usually there are no abnormal motor signs and reflexes are similarly well preserved.

In childhood as in adult life, intraspinal tumours may mimic a prolapse of the intervertebral disc. In the young patient however, such lesions are at least as common as prolapsed discs and every patient with such a presentation must therefore be considered to have an intra-spinal tumour until proved otherwise.

Investigation of the patient with a prolapsed disc

The diagnosis of prolapse of an intervertebral disc can usually be made with some confidence from the history and physical examination alone. The purpose of investigations is to exclude other causes of the patient's symptoms, such as an intraspinal tumour and to identify the level of the prolapse in those patients who require surgery.

In the presence of a disc prolapse, haemato-logical and biochemical investigations will be normal though a full blood count, sedimentation rate and alkaline phosphatase should be obtained in order to assist in the exclusion of more sinister pathology.

Radiography

Plain radiographs of the spine are completely unhelpful in making a positive diagnosis of pro-lapsed intervertebral disc but are essential in-vestigations in order to rule out other pathology. The radiograph will confirm the alterations in the sagittal and coronal contours of the spine found on physical examination. Depending on the length of time which has elapsed since the acute episode, there may be some narrowing of a disc space though this is insufficient to identify the level of the prolapse with any confidence. De-generative changes in the lumbar spine on plain radiography are a common normal finding and may be completely coincidental, appearing at a different level from the prolapse, or may be wide-spread throughout the lumbar spine.

Radiculography

In patients who are to be subjected to surgery, identification of the level of the disc prolapse is important. Water soluble radiculography is still the commonest procedure undertaken for this purpose. It is an accurate method with a true positive rate of over 90%. False positives can occur in cases where there is poor root sleeve filling and false negatives are sometimes pro-duced in cases with a prolapse which is situated

far laterally. Radiculography is not without its complications. Headache, nausea and vomiting are all common complaints following the pro-cedure. Myoclonic spasms, fever, back pain, psychomotor disturbances and chemical arach-noiditis have also been reported. The latter was a much more important consideration in the days of oil based radiography dyes than with modern water soluble agents. The investigation is un-pleasant for the patient not only because of the lumbar puncture involved but also because of the considerable manoeuvring of the subject required to achieve adequate visualization of the nerve roots.

The radiological features seen in the presence of a disc prolapse include extradural indentation of the dural sac, usually with a failure of the affected root sleeve to fill with contrast and in the case of a disc prolapse of substantial size, devi-ation of the nerve root from its normal course (Fig. 20.3). With a disc prolapse situated far

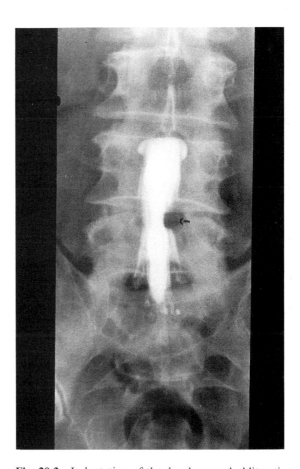

Fig. 20.3 Indentation of the dural sac and obliteration of the nerve root sleeve.

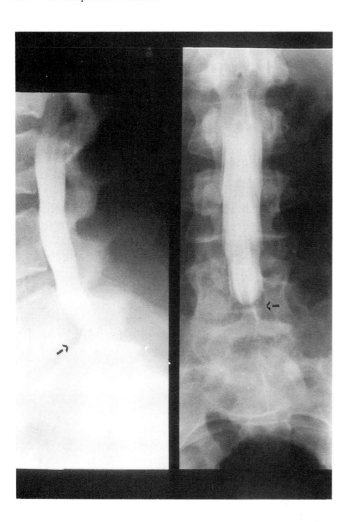

Fig. 20.4 Complete block of contrast medium in a cauda equina syndrome.

laterally, deviation of the affected root or amputation of the root sleeve may be the only changes seen on radiculography. In the event of a massive central disc prolapse resulting in a cauda equina syndrome, a complete block may be seen (Fig. 20.4).

Computerized tomography

The accuracy and increasing availability of computerized tomography has led to its replacing radiculography to some extent. It is non-invasive and lacks complications. The sensitivity of the method is about equal to that of radiculography in detecting prolapse of an intervertebral disc. Certain drawbacks must be recognized. The resolution of the method is less than that of radiculography. The levels at which examination is required must be specified. Migration of seques-

tered fragments of disc material or choice of incorrect level may lead to false negative results. Enhanced computerized tomography with contrast material introduced into the canal as a prior procedure improves the sensitivity of the method. Computerized tomography is more sensitive than radiculography in identification of lateral disc prolapse and in posterior disc prolapse in the presence of a wide epidural space (Fig. 20.5).

Magnetic resonance imaging

Magnetic resonance imaging is a more recent development which is proving to be the most sensitive technique currently available for the detection of degenerative disc disease (Fig. 20.6). Unlike computerized tomography, it is capable of distinguishing nuclear from annular material. It is thus possible to distinguish between disc

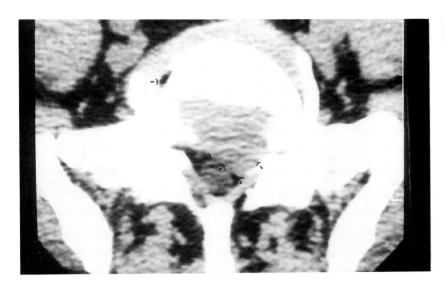

Fig. 20.5 CT scan showing postero-lateral disc herniation.

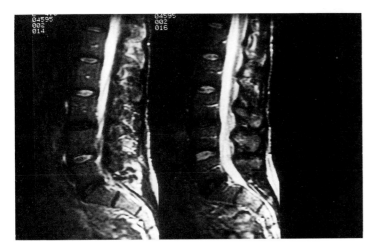

Fig. 20.6 MRI scan showing disc degeneration.

protrusion, disc extrusion and disc sequestration by identifying the relationship of the annulus to the nuclear material under suspicion (Fig. 20.7). This is an important distinction as failure of a patient to respond to chemonucleolysis may result from application of the technique in the presence of sequestrated disc material.

Discography

Discography is seldom performed purely as a diagnostic procedure in cases of suspected prolapsed intervertebral disc. In certain situations where the diagnosis is still in doubt after investigation by radiculography and computerized tomography it may be a useful tool. In addition to the provocation of the patient's symptoms by the procedure, the radiological appearance of the discogram itself may be diagnostic. In a typical case contrast is seen extruding through the annular tear into the epidural space. Discography in conjunction with computerized tomography is particularly useful in visualizing more laterally placed disc prolapses.

The 'investigation of choice' in a patient with a prolapsed disc depends upon the availability of the investigative techniques and upon the degree of confidence with which the level of the prolapse has been identified clinically.

At present, the main limiting factor with magnetic resonance imaging is its lack of availability

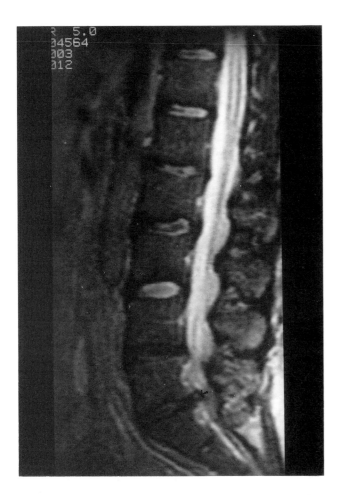

Fig. 20.7   MRI scan showing disc degeneration.

in most hospitals. As it becomes more freely available, it will probably supersede other imaging methods for the study of the prolapsed disc.

If the level of the prolapse can be predicted with any confidence, then computerized tomography is normally the investigation of first choice. If, however, the level of the prolapse is uncertain, radiculography is likely to be more productive, simply because it allows the visualization of several levels in the spine.

Treatment

Most patients with a prolapsed intervertebral disc improve without an operation. In the initial phase, a few days bed-rest, supplemented by analgesia, anti-inflammatory agents and muscle relaxants is beneficial. This treatment should not be prolonged. Patients who have lingered in bed for several weeks following a disc prolapse develop stiff backs, lose muscle tone and most important, they lose motivation. They are extremely difficult to rehabilitate.

Traction gives variable benefit. In order to exert any mechanical effect on the disc, traction of one third of the patient's body weight must be applied. Patients cannot tolerate this and any effect which traction normally exerts is attributable to the enforced bed-rest, relaxation of muscles and to a placebo effect. As with straightforward bed-rest there is no point in continuing this treatment for more than a few days.

As soon as the most acute symptoms have settled, normally within a few days, the patient should be mobilized. A lumbosacral support is often helpful. A course of physiotherapy designed to restore mobility to the spine and to improve muscle tone is the single most useful treatment which can be offered at this stage, a useful adjunct to treatment.

The patient must be given appropriate advice

about sitting posture and avoidance of heavy lifting with reassurance that the symptoms are likely to remain in abeyance as long as the patient continues to treat his back with reasonable respect and avoids activities which are likely to provoke a further prolapse.

Epidural injection

In those patients with persistent but not distressing sciatica and only minor abnormalities on neurological examination, an epidural steroid and local anaesthetic injection is often effective in relieving pain.

The route of administration is either via the L2–3 interspace or via the sacral hiatus. A fine gauge spinal needle is used after preliminary infiltration of the skin with local anaesthetic.

Complications include puncture of the dura, headache, transitory muscle weakness and very occasionally infection.

There is little unequivocal evidence to indicate that patients undergoing epidural injection fare better in the long term than others. Dilke [15] however, in a double blind trial, found that return to work was quicker, reported pain levels were lower and referrals for surgery were fewer in the treated group than in controls and most surgeons would agree that epidural injection is a useful technique in selected patients.

Chemonucleolysis

Chymopapain is a proteolytic enzyme derived from the papaya fruit. It is capable of hydrolysing the protein component of glycosaminoglycans in the disc, as a result of which the disc loses its water-binding capacity and subsequently shrinks. It was isolated in 1941 by Jansen and Balls and was first used in human subjects in 1964. Since that time, it has had a rather chequered history and its use remains sporadic.

The indications for the use of chymopapain are similar to those for discectomy. It is useful in the patient with sciatica secondary to a prolapsed intervertebral disc, which is not settling on adequate conservative treatment. It should not be used in patients with a serious or rapidly progressive neurological deficit, where surgery is to be preferred. It is ineffective in the treatment of

sequestered disc fragments. No patient should ever receive more than one chymopapain injection because of the great danger of a severe allergic response.

The technique of injection is similar to that for discography and indeed a preliminary discogram is a useful step in the procedure, allowing as it does confirmation that the needle placement and disc level are correct. The procedure must be performed under sterile conditions with adequate radiographic control and preferably twin image intensifiers so that simultaneous biplanar visualization of the needle can be achieved.

The injection should be performed under local anaesthesia with the patient sedated but sufficiently aware so that he can communicate with the surgeon. An anaesthetist should be present, however, to control the level of sedation and in case the patient should suffer an anaphylactic reaction to the injection. The latter is the most serious complication of the technique. Other complications include incorrect placement of the injection, infection, thrombophlebitis, radiculopathy, total paralysis, post-injection back pain and headache. Inadvertent intrathecal injection of chymopapain, in addition to being ineffective in relieving the patient's symptoms, has been reported to lead to the development of a Guillain–Barré like syndrome in a number of cases. Puncture of a nerve root during introduction of the needle is a well recognized complication and is probably more common than is generally realized. Although uncomfortable for the conscious patient, this does not seem to give rise to unwanted side effects.

Discectomy

Persistence of sciatic pain after a full trial of conservative treatment is the principle indication for discectomy. Other indications include progressive neurological symptoms, particularly when there is sphincter disturbance, in which case surgical intervention is a matter of great urgency.

The aim of discectomy is to free the patient of sciatic pain and associated radicular symptoms by decompression of the affected nerve root. Before surgery is undertaken, the patient should be warned that the operation will not necessarily cure his back pain. It is often the case that back pain is substantially reduced by discectomy but this is a difficult outcome to predict and surgery should therefore be reserved for those patients in whom the major symptoms are those of sciatic pain, numbness, paraesthesiae or dysaesthesiae in a radicular distribution.

In such circumstances, the results of surgery are good in around 80% of patients as judged by their ability to return to their former employment without disabling symptoms. Sensory blunting in the distribution of the affected root will usually disappear after surgery but motor weakness may not resolve completely and an absent ankle jerk frequently does not return.

Operative technique

The disc is extraordinarily susceptible to infection and for this reason, some surgeons advocate the use of prophylactic antibiotics (typically cefuroxime 1.5 g at induction, followed by two doses of 750 mg 8 and 16 h postoperatively).

For a simple discectomy, the patient is placed prone in the knee elbow jack-knife position. A midline incision is usually employed, though a paramedian muscle splitting approach or transverse incision are equally acceptable. The incision is centred over the offending disc space, a length of about 10 cm giving adequate exposure in the midline approach. The muscles on the affected side are stripped from bone with diathermy in order to expose the spinous process and lamina on the affected side. At this stage, a check radiograph is a useful procedure in order to confirm that the level of exploration is correct. This is normally unnecessary at the lumbosacral level but elsewhere is a very wise precaution. The commonest mistake in surgery for the prolapsed disc is to operate at the wrong level. This is a difficult situation to defend medicolegally, quite apart from the failure to improve the patient by performing the wrong operation.

Occasionally removal of the caudal lip of the lamina of the upper vertebra assists in exposure of the ligamentum flavum. This is, however rarely necessary. A window is created in the ligamentum flavum with a knife and is then enlarged with a fine punch. Deep to the ligamentum flavum, a layer of fat will be encountered with the epidural plexus of veins coursing through it. These veins are often engorged at the site of the prolapse and can cause troublesome bleeding, so

care should be taken to preserve them. Diathermy coagulation should be avoided.

The nerve root lying stretched over the prolapsed disc will then be encountered. The root should be retracted gently to one side in order to allow free access to the disc, taking great care to avoid excessive tension. The bulging disc is then incised. Its consistency is much softer than that of a normal disc and entry to its substance is easily gained by the creation of a small circular window in the most prominent part of the bulge. The disc is evacuated with a combination of punches and curettes, leaving the annulus intact throughout. Great care should be taken not to perforate the disc anteriorly. It is important not to leave any loose fragments of disc in the wound as they are the cause of a vigorous inflammatory response and may migrate into the root canal, causing a recurrence of symptoms. Disagreement exists about how much of the nucleus should be removed. There is no proven advantage in removing the whole of the nucleus and indeed this is normally impossible as remnants will virtually always remain even after meticulous attempts at disc clearance. It is probably sufficient to remove sequestered fragments, bulging disc material and any obviously loose or degenerate fragments of disc which yield themselves easily to the exploring instrument. More assiduous attempts at disc clearance are probably counterproductive.

Following removal of the disc, the root should glide freely throughout its course. A probe should be passed along the side of the root into the intervertebral foramen in order to ensure that there is no stenosis of the root canal. In such circumstances an undercutting facetectomy must be performed, removing enough of the medial lip of the facet joint to ensure complete freedom of the root. The probe should also be passed medially deep to the dura to check for the medial extent of the prolapse and upward and downward to search for sequestered fragments.

If no prolapse is encountered, there should be no hesitation in exploring adjoining levels until definite pathology is found. Puncture of the dura during exploration should be repaired using a fine monofilament suture.

A free fat graft is applied to the window in the ligamentum flavum in order to prevent ingrowth of scar tissue into the spinal canal following muscle stripping. The wound is closed in layers.

Wound drainage is not mandatory but we prefer to use a single superficial vacuum drain led to the site of removal of the fat graft in order to minimise the chance of wound haematoma.

Postoperative care

Immediate relief of radicular pain following surgery is common. The recurrence of radicular pain is frequently due to tethering of the root by scar tissue. The patient should therefore be encouraged to perform straight leg raising exercises from the earliest stages in order to ensure that the mobility of the freed root is maintained. Passive straight leg raising is facilitated by a system of beams and pulleys over the bed.

Postoperative retention of urine is a common complication but is only very rarely due to peroperative neurological damage. If he is unable to void in the supine position, the patient may be stood with assistance. Should this prove unsuccessful, it may be necessary to pass a Foley catheter which should be of fine bore and retained for only 24 h. Voiding is normally successful after removal of the catheter.

It is safe to mobilize the patient following removal of the vacuum drain 48 h postoperatively. Sitting, including the adoption of a sitting posture during activities such as getting in and out of bed, should be discouraged for the first few days. Following this, sitting on a high stool is allowed. Walking is encouraged, though some postural reeducation by the physiotherapist may be required.

The patient is allowed home following wound healing with a programme of exercises and with a lightweight canvas lumbosacral support without paravertebral steels. Normal sitting is allowed at 2 weeks, car travel at 4 weeks and resumption of car driving at around 6 weeks. Patients undertaking clerical or office work may be expected to resume their employment at around 4–6 weeks postoperatively. Those with heavier occupations are likely to remain off work for about 3 months.

Results of surgery

The great majority of patients are relieved of leg pain by surgery and achieve a rapid improvement in their mobility. They must, however, be warned that full recovery of lost neurological function cannot be guaranteed. Some will be disappointed by the persistence of motor symptoms such as foot drop or by the failure of a sensory deficit to resolve. Neither is the relief of back pain assured, though many patients do in fact improve in this respect. Most sedentary workers will return to their former employment but manual workers fare less well. Only around 60% of patients are able to resume their former occupation, and over 20% remain totally and permanently incapacitated. It is important when considering these figures to remember that the most important factor in the outcome is patient selection for surgery. Performing an inappropriate operation on an inappropriately selected patient will inevitably lead to poor results.

In the long term, there is little evidence that patients undergoing discectomy do better as a group than those treated conservatively. The aim of surgery in the patient with a prolapsed intervertebral disc is therefore to achieve a more rapid resolution of radicular pain with a swifter return to work and quicker social rehabilitation than would be the case if conservative treatment alone were pursued. With careful patient selection, confident identification of pathology and meticulous surgical technique, this seemingly modest aim is achievable.

Minimal intervention discectomy

Discectomy can be accomplished by less traumatic surgery than the conventional operation described above. The operation of 'Microdiscectomy' is undertaken via a 2–3 cm incision directly over the affected level. 'Micro' in this context refers to the size of the incision. An operating microscope is used in this operation but its main advantage is to provide illumination into the depths of the wound rather than magnification. Equally good illumination is achievable by the use of specially designed nerve root retractors which carry fibreoptic light into the wound and are also available with a suction tip. The identification of the correct level is obviously more difficult with such a small incision and X-ray control with image intensification is mandatory. Operating table design is obviously an important factor in this context and it is advisable to perform the procedure using a specially designed table attachment. The procedure allows for the removal of sequestered disc fragments and for undercutting of the facet joint should this prove to be necessary. The advantages of the operation are the quicker rehabilitation of the patient and shorter hospital stay. The long term advantages over the conventional operation, if any, have yet to be defined.

An even less invasive procedure involves the introduction of a fine trocar into the disc under radiographic control with removal of the disc by fine rongeurs or by suction. This procedure is normally undertaken under local anaesthetic with the patient sedated. It allows for the removal of only a small quantity of disc material and it is not possible to identify or remove sequestered disc fragments. Rehabilitation, however, is very rapid and short term results in correctly selected patients seem good.

Other recent developments include removal of the disc under endoscopic control by means of a laser. Once again, the technique involves minimal intervention but its long term results await evaluation.

Discectomy and spinal fusion

In simple discectomy undertaken for sciatic pain secondary to a prolapsed intervertebral disc, there is no place for spinal fusion. Attractive though the concept is of fusing the diseased motion segment in order to relieve back pain, the results of such procedures do not justify the added complications and longer recovery rate. Under certain circumstances, spinal fusion may indeed be indicated. These are:

1. Patients in whom there is an element of segmental instability which may have contributed to their symptomatology prior to surgery (for example patients with a spondylolisthesis).
2. Those in whom instability may have been created at the time of operation by the enforced removal of large amounts of bone in order to effectively decompress the root.
3. Those with advanced arthritic change in the facet joints at the level of the discectomy.
4. Those in whom there is a requirement to return to heavy manual work which they were previously unable to perform because of recurrent episodes of incapacitating back pain superimposed upon sciatic symptoms.

Spondylolysis and spondylolisthesis

The term spondylolisthesis indicates a forward slipping of one vertebra upon that below it. The first account has been attributed to Herbineaux in 1782, an obstetrician who described the presence of a bony prominence anterior to the sacrum which could present an obstruction to normal labour. This could have been a spondyloptosis or complete spondylolisthesis. Kilian [16] recognized the abnormal displacement of the fifth lumbar vertebra upon the sacrum and attributed it to a gradual subluxation of the facet joints. He was the first to coin the term spondylolisthesis. The condition is graded according to the degree of slip which has occurred. Based on the lateral radiograph of the lumbosacral spine, a forward slip of up to 25% is grade one, 25–50% grade two, 50–75% grade three and 75–100% grade four. A slip of greater magnitude than this, in which the bodies of the two adjacent vertebrae have lost all contact, is referred to as a spondyloptosis or grade five. It is significant that the area of contact remaining between the two vertebrae in question is not accurately reflected in the system of grading. For example, a slip with 50% forward displacement will leave only 38% of the apposing surfaces of the vertebral bodies in contact. This loss of contact contributes to the continuing tendency for the slip to increase.

Classification

The classification of spondylolisthesis generally adopted is that of Wiltse *et al.* [17]. Five types are described:

1. Congenital or dysplastic, associated with a defect in the lumbosacral articulation and in the neural arch of the sacrum.
2. Isthmic, associated with a defect or attenuation of the pars interarticularis.
3. Degenerative, arising as a result of degenerative changes in the facet joints and intervertebral disc.
4. Traumatic, following severe injury which results in an unstable fracture dislocation of the spine.
5. Pathological, occurring as a result of tumour, infection or other destructive processes compromising the stability of the spine.

Dysplastic spondylolisthesis

This is characterized by a congenital deficiency of the upper sacrum including the articular processes and an extensive spina bifida occulta of the neural arch of the sacrum. The fifth lumbar vertebra is subjected to large shear forces during weight bearing. As a result of the deficient posterior articulations, the lumbosacral junction is unable to resist these forces and the fifth lumbar vertebra slips forward on the sacrum carrying the remainder of the lumbar spine with it. Eventually, the spinous process of the fifth lumbar vertebra comes to lie against the defect in the neural arch of the upper sacrum. Further forward slip does not normally occur but the anteroposterior diameter of the spinal canal may be severely narrowed by this movement, giving rise to compression of the cauda equina. As a secondary feature, a defect or attenuation of the pars interarticularis of L5 may arise allowing a greater degree of slip to occur, similar to that which takes place in the isthmic type 2 spondylolisthesis. The congenital type of spondylolisthesis is commoner in women by a ratio of two to one. Despite the presence of the dysplastic lumbosacral articulation at birth, it is not until the child starts to weight bear that forward displacement of the fifth lumbar vertebra normally occurs. Even then, the slip is usually very gradual and it is uncommon for the diagnosis to be made before the age of 6 years.

Isthmic spondylolisthesis

This type of spondylolisthesis is associated with a fibrous or cartilaginous defect in the pars interarticularis, i.e. a spondylolysis. It is the commonest cause of spondylolisthesis in patients before middle age. The origin of the defect is debatable but most accept that it arises as a result of a stress fracture. Troup [18] has demonstrated that the pars interarticularis is subject to high shear stresses during spinal hyperextension and suggests that a stress fracture may occur as a result of repetitive loading during activities such as gymnastics. Those who indulge in such forms of athletic activity certainly demonstrate a high incidence of spondylolysis. Other authors have proposed a genetically determined cause for the

defect. Certain races such as the Eskimos demonstrate a high incidence of isthmic spondylolisthesis, though whether this is purely genetic in origin or whether it is partly behavioural is open to debate. It is probable that the defect arises as a result of the development of a stress fracture in individuals who for whatever reason have some intrinsic weakness or hypoplasia of the pars interarticularis. The secondary development of an isthmic lesion in the dysplastic type of spondylolisthesis (type 1) suggests that the pars interarticularis may be a vulnerable structure when it is subjected to abnormal loads and lends support to the stress fracture theory of spondylolysis. On the other hand, it is by no means uncommon to find some minor degree of dysplasia of the neural arch of the sacrum or of the lumbosacral articulations during surgery for what appears to be a purely isthmic type of spondylolisthesis. The possibility therefore arises that the two types described are no more than the opposite ends of a continuum. Within this spectrum, varying degrees of dysplasia of any part of the posterior arch of the lumbosacral region may give rise to a spondylolisthesis because of mechanical failure of one of the elements involved in the stabilization of the spine. Failure of one element may lead to failure of another, with further slip occurring. The situation is further confused by the presence of a continuous remodelling process with growth which may alter the morphology and orientation of the facet joints or the pars according to the disposition of the loads on the system. Most commonly, the slip occurs as a result of a lytic defect in the pars interarticularis of the fifth lumbar vertebra (90% of cases) thus causing a forward movement of L5 on the sacrum. In almost all other cases, the slip is between L4 and L5 with a defect in the pars of L4.

Degenerative spondylolisthesis

Degenerative spondylolisthesis is uncommon before middle age. It is frequently asymptomatic and is a common finding on lateral radiographs of the spine taken as a part of the investigation of totally separate pathology. The spondylolisthesis arises as a result of degenerative changes in the facet joints and discs with advancing age. These structures then lose their ability to restrain the

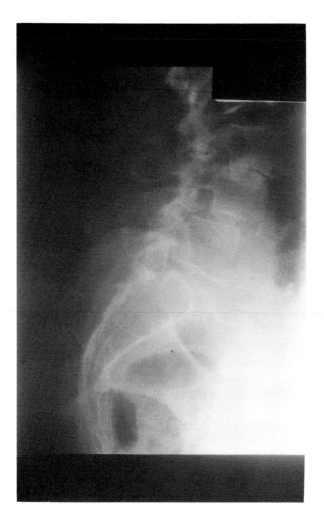

Fig. 20.8   Spinal stenosis due to spondylolisthesis.

spine from undergoing abnormal movements and a gradual slip occurs. Unlike the dysplastic and isthmic types, the level most commonly involved is L4–L5, though it is by no means unusual for several levels to be affected. There is often a discernible degree of osteoporosis present in such patients. This is thought to contribute to the instability of the spine by means of collapse of the subchondral bone in the region of the facet joints, thereby disturbing the normal anatomy of the articulation and allowing subluxation of the joints. Individuals in whom the facet joints are orientated in a more sagittal plane than normal are particularly prone to developing degenerative spondylolisthesis. Other factors which can con-

tribute to the evolution of the condition include obesity and poor paraspinal and abdominal muscle tone. Patients presenting with symptoms attributable to degenerative spondylolisthesis generally do so at around the age of 60. The condition is more common in women by a factor of approximately four to one. The symptoms can take three forms. Firstly, those of segmental instability, with either fatigue pain or momentary subluxation pain predominating; secondly, radicular pain due to nerve root entrapment, usually the L5 root as it rolls over the bulging degenerate L4–L5 disc or the L4 root in the root canal; thirdly, symptoms suggestive of spinal stenosis due to narrowing of the spinal canal at the level of the spondylolisthesis (Fig. 20.8).

Traumatic spondylolisthesis

Traumatic spondylolisthesis may occur as a feature of a major spinal injury, most commonly a fracture-dislocation involving the thoraco-lumbar junction. Its management follows that of all the major spinal injuries and it is doubtful whether such conditions should properly be classified with the other forms of spondylolisthesis. Rarely, a patient may be seen following an acute hyperextension injury to the spine where the radiographic findings are those of a spondylolytic spondylolisthesis. It may be virtually impossible in such circumstances to be certain as to whether or not there was a pre-existing pars defect which has undergone an acute disruption in the injury, or whether the neural arch was previously normal. Occasionally, such acute lesions may be observed to heal following immobilization in a plaster jacket, suggesting that the true origin of the defect was the specific injury in question rather than a pre-existing lysis.

Pathological spondylolisthesis

This may occur in a number of conditions in which the mechanical strength of bone is compromised. Examples are Paget's disease, osteogenesis imperfecta, tumour and infection. An attenuation of any part of the neural arch may develop allowing the slip to occur.

Clinical features

Spondylolisthesis may be totally asymptomatic, even in the presence of an advanced degree of slip. Indeed, such absence of symptoms is the rule rather than the exception in the young child.

The isthmic type of spondylolisthesis characteristically presents in early adolescence with ill-defined low back pain radiating over the buttocks and posterior aspect of the thighs. Frequently, there is a history that a previously athletic child has had to curtail his or her sporting activities because of exacerbation of the symptoms with physical exertion. At this stage, a marked degree of slip may already have taken place. The physical signs are variable. In the presence of an advanced slip, there may be an exaggeration of the lumbar lordosis with shortening of the trunk and an obvious skin crease in the flanks. Palpation of the spinous processes will reveal a step between the fourth and the fifth lumbar vertebrae – the spinous process of L5 is left in its normal position with respect to the sacrum whilst the whole of L4 is carried forward with the body of L5. Some limitation of movement of the lumbosacral spine is present almost universally and there is sometimes localized tenderness at the level of the slip. One characteristic finding is of hamstring tightness with limitation of straight leg raising and a peculiar waddling gait. Typically, the child will walk with a rotatory movement of the pelvis with flexed hips and knees rather than with the normal swing-through gait. Neurological signs are the exception rather than the rule.

Spondylolysis may exist in the absence of a spondylolisthesis. Again, this is frequently totally asymptomatic. Usually, the presentation is of intermittent episodes of mild aching low back pain exacerbated by exercise and relieved by rest. This pattern of symptoms may continue into adult life without ever giving rise to major disability. The age of presentation is therefore highly variable but frequently the patient first presents in early adolescence. As with the isthmic spondylolisthesis, some limitation of movement of the lumbosacral spine is often present, together with an exaggeration of the lumbar lordosis, though to a much lesser degree. Hamstring tightness is much less marked and the gait is usually normal.

The dysplastic or congenital type of spondylolisthesis tends to present with a more acute history than the isthmic type though this is by no means always the case. The age of the patient tends to be somewhat greater, typically middle or late adolescence. The findings on physical examination are generally similar with lumbosacral stiffness and tenderness, hamstring tightness with limitation of straight leg raising and disturbance of gait, exaggerated lumbar lordosis and a step on palpation of the spinous processes. In this case, however, the step will be between L5 and the sacrum, as the whole of the fifth lumbar vertebra is involved in the slip. With the more acute history, spasm of the hamstring and paravertebral muscles may be very marked. The degree of slip tends to be somewhat less than in the isthmic variety so that trunk shortening and skin creases in the flanks are less marked. However, the contents of the spinal canal are more at risk and it is by no means unusual to detect neurological signs of root compression or to elicit a history of sphincter disturbance.

Radiological features

The diagnosis is often revealed on plain radiographs of the spine but oblique views should be taken in order to give a clear demonstration of a lytic defect in the pars. The so-called 'Scottie dog sign' is present in this situation (Fig. 20.9). In the presence of a spondylolysis without a spondylolisthesis, the dog can be seen to be wearing a collar. Once a slip of appreciable degree has occurred, the dog appears to be decapitated.

In the lateral view, the degree of forward slip and hence the grade of the spondylolisthesis is established. The defect in the pars is usually visible though it may not be easy to detect in early cases. In advanced cases, a bony buttress may be visible extending from the anterior border of the sacrum under the anterior longitudinal ligament to the body of L5. In the extreme case, bony ankylosis may occur between the fifth lumbar vertebra and the sacrum and the inferior facets of L4 may abut onto the upper sacrum.

The anteroposterior view usually adds relatively little information. In the presence of a spondyloptosis, the characteristic 'Napoleon's hat sign' is seen (Fig. 20.10).

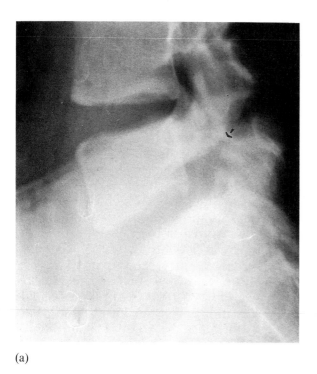

(a)

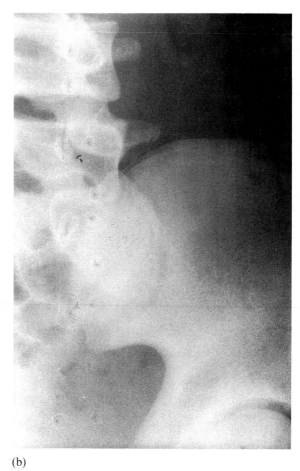

(b)

Fig. 20.9   Defect in the pars interarticularis 'the Scottie dog sign'.

Myelography will give objective evidence of the degree of spinal canal stenosis and nerve root compression. The myelogram may show alarming appearances with marked deformity of the dural sac in spite of minimal clinical symptoms and signs. Often, there is a complete block at the lumbosacral level. Abnormal myelographic appearances are not in themselves an indication for any active intervention in spondylolisthesis, though if surgery is contemplated it should always be preceded by this investigation or, if available, by MRI scanning.

Treatment

Frequently, the symptoms attributable to the spondylolisthesis are so slight that no treatment is indicated. There is a poor correlation between the degree of slip and the severity of symptoms, but as a generalization, slips of lesser degree are associated with less pain. Frequently, mild and intermittent symptoms in childhood and early adolescence can be controlled adequately by the provision of a lumbosacral support and moderation of physical exercise. A course of hamstring stretching exercises is often beneficial. It is essential however, that children presenting with a spondylolysis or spondylolysthesis should be monitored carefully until late adolescence lest the slip should progress.

If the slip continues to increase or if the pain proves intractable in spite of adequate conservative treatment, there should be no hesitation in recommending surgery. The procedure of choice in most cases is a posterolateral fusion *in situ*. If there is evidence of neurological involvement, the procedure must be combined with an adequate decompression of the compromised spinal canal. There is disagreement about the desirability of attempting to reduce the spondylolisthesis at the time of surgery in order to re-establish a normal

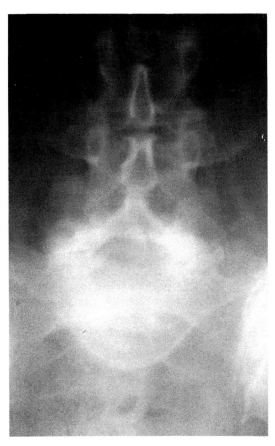

Fig. 20.10 Anteroposterior view of spondylolisthesis 'the Napoleon hat sign'.

anatomical alignment in the spine. In the presence of a severe slip, a combined anterior and posterolateral fusion may be required.

For study of the numerous operative techniques available in this somewhat controversial field further consultation is recommended in the detailed surgical literature.

Spinal stenosis

The term spinal stenosis encompasses a group of conditions in which limitation of space within the vertebral canal contributes to the symptomatology of the disease. Several different clinical syndromes are recognizable within this broad based definition.

The existence of the syndrome classically regarded as representative of spinal stenosis was recognized in 1911 by DeJerine [19], who coined the term 'claudication of the spinal cord'. Verbiest [20] was the first to recognize the association of this clinical syndrome with structural narrowing of the spinal canal. Blau and Logue [21], described six patients with disc protrusions who had exercise related pain and paraesthesiae. They ascribed the mechanism of pain production as compression of the blood vessels to the cauda equina, that is, a form of ischaemic neuritis. Epstein [22] proposed that the pathology lay at nerve root level and described what has become known as the lateral recess syndrome.

Anatomical considerations

There is considerable diversity of shape and size of the normal spinal canal, both between individuals and throughout the length of the canal in any particular spine. The upper lumbar canal is normally circular in cross-section. The sacral canal is triangular. There is a transitional zone within the lumbar spine between these two limits, where the canal may assume a deltoid or trefoil shape. The trefoil shape has well defined apical and lateral recesses, the latter serving to accentuate the length of the root canal. The lateral recess is defined as that part of the central vertebral canal at the pedicular level anterior to the medial aspect of the superior apophyseal joint. It is only the trefoil shaped canal which may be considered to have a lateral recess. The more common dome-shaped canal has a continuous concave posterior surface to the canal and thus the lateral recess does not exist in this configuration.

Various anatomical parameters are measurable in the vertebral canal. The central diameter of the canal in the sagittal plane tends to be widest at the level of the first lumbar vertebra, reducing in size to a minimum at L4 and increasing again at L5. The interpedicular distance is fairly constant from L1 to L3 and then widens progressively over the fourth and fifth lumbar levels. The cross-sectional area of the canal as measured at the level of the pedicles becomes progressively smaller from L1 to L4 but then increases substantially again at the L5 level, to attain a size comparable to that at L1. There is, however, considerable variation between individuals as regards the precise dimensions of the canal at any specified level. This variability is particularly marked at L5. The wide range of cross-sectional areas in the lower lumbar spine is accounted for by variations in the shape of the canal, the trefoil configuration serving to significantly reduce the area as compared to that found in the more usual dome-shaped canal.

The size of the canal in terms of the central sagittal diameter and interpedicular distance is determined by the age of 10 years. This presumably comes about as a requirement for the canal to accommodate its neural contents. The shape of the canal however, may change after this time and thus changes in the cross-sectional area may occur later in life. The trefoil configuration is not seen in young children and if it is to develop, it occurs gradually during adolescence.

The variable size and shape of the vertebral canal is not sufficient in itself to account for the various syndromes of spinal stenosis. Other changes of a degenerative nature are required to produce symptoms. However, such changes, which include bulging of degenerate discs, arthritic lipping of the facet joints, instability secondary to degenerative changes in the disc and facet joints and finally disc prolapse, will all tend to exert their effects on the neural structures within the canal more readily if there is less space available than if the canal is capacious. Other factors can also serve to reduce the area available within the canal. Osteophytes on the cranial lip of the lamina, thickening of the ligamentum flavum with buckling of this structure into the posterior aspect of the canal, particularly during extension of the lumbar spine and iatrogenic scarring following previous exploration are examples of such factors.

Classification

Verbiest [23] described the various subdivisions of spinal stenosis:

> Congenital – due to disturbed foetal development.
> Developmental – due to properties of the neural arch.
> Acquired – due to degenerative changes in the spine.

The classical example of congenital spinal stenosis is achondroplasia. There is impairment of end plate and epiphyseal growth but increased appositional growth. Thus broad, squat vertebrae with short, heavy pedicles and thick, broad laminae are seen. The dorsal surfaces of the vertebral bodies are concave and the discs bulge prominently. The neural contents of the canal are of normal size and as a result of their being accommodated in a canal of small size, may suffer compression over a wide area.

Developmental stenosis implies the presence of a narrow canal with broad, squat pedicles and medially situated posterior joints producing a flattening and stenosis of the exit canals disproportionate to the anteroposterior diameter of the central canal. The articular pillars and laminae may be massive. A typical trefoil shaped canal may ensue. Such patients are initially asymptomatic but problems may develop in later life because of the development of degenerative changes superimposed upon the pre-existing abnormal configuration of the canal.

Clinical features

Any condition which is brought about in whole or in part by the encroachment on the canal of a space occupying lesion will be more likely to produce symptoms if the space within the canal is already limited. Thus, a central disc herniation is more likely to impinge upon the cauda equina if the sagittal diameter of the vertebral canal is reduced. Equally, a posterolateral disc prolapse more readily involves the nerve root in the root canal in the presence of a trefoil configuration. The two classical syndromes in which restriction of space within the canal plays a major part are neurogenic claudication resulting from central canal stenosis and the lateral recess syndrome resulting from nerve root entrapment in the constricted lateral recess.

Neurogenic claudication

The syndrome usually affects men over the age of 50. The presenting complaint is of pain in the buttocks and lower extremities precipitated by walking. The pain is relieved by rest, particularly if the patient sits or leans forward upon a stick. The explanation for this postural effect is the increase in cross-sectional area of the lumbar canal during flexion as compared to extension.

During extension of the spine, buckling of the ligamentum flavum into the canal occurs, whereas when the spine is flexed this structure tightens and does not impinge upon the space within. This postural effect lies at the basis of certain other features of the syndrome. For example, it is often said that the patient can walk uphill for long distances because he tends to bend forwards when climbing a gradient. When coming downhill, however, the spine is extended and the symptoms of neurogenic claudication are more readily precipitated. If present, this symptom serves as a useful feature in distinguishing neurogenic from vascular claudication. Perhaps of more use in this respect is the cycling test. Here, the patient is asked to cycle on an exercise bicycle with the spine in an extended position until the symptoms of neurogenic claudication cause him to stop. After a suitable interval, the test is repeated, the exercise being carried out this time with the spine flexed. A significant increase in the exercise tolerance when the second position is adopted may be expected if the pain is true neurogenic claudication but not if peripheral vascular disease is responsible for the symptoms. In severe cases, the pain may be provoked by simple extension of the spine while standing.

There is often a long history of low back discomfort prior to the onset of leg symptoms. Sometimes there may have been previous surgery to the back, which should raise the possibility of iatrogenic spinal stenosis, particularly if a fusion has been carried out.

Some patients complain not so much of pain as of paraesthesiae or hypoaesthesiae in the legs, again characteristically provoked by exercise. Others complain of a variety of dysaesthetic symptoms in the limbs, on occasion quite bizarre. The sensation may, for example, be described as like having the legs wrapped in cotton wool, like cold water running down the legs or simply as deadness of the legs.

Differentiation of the syndrome from vascular claudication is the most important distinction to be made. The presence of a normal peripheral circulation with good foot pulses excludes the diagnosis of intermittent claudication attributable to peripheral vascular disease. Occasionally, however, the foot pulses may be coincidentally absent and the distinction between the two conditions can then become difficult. Doppler pressure studies may be helpful in this

situation. Occasionally it is necessary to perform angiography in order to establish the state of the peripheral vascular tree beyond doubt.

There are a number of conditions arising from the spine itself which may produce leg pain exacerbated by activity. Referred pain from degenerative disease of the disc and facet joints is occasionally felt to be worse on exercise, presumably due to the motion of the diseased spinal segments during walking. Disc herniation can also produce pain which is increased by exercise but the pain is likely to affect only one leg and other features in the history and examination will normally clarify the matter.

Physical examination of the patient may be remarkably normal. A frequent finding, however, is the adoption of a forward flexed posture by the patient – the so-called simian stance. The patient can normally correct this stance when asked to do so but subsequently readopts it as soon as his attention wanders. Flexion of the lumbar spine is usually unrestricted. There is usually, however, significant limitation of extension and this manoeuvre is likely to be painful. It may cause the appearance of leg pain in severe cases if the posture is maintained for more than a very short period. Straight leg raising is normally unimpaired and it is unusual to find any neurological abnormality.

Lateral recess syndrome

Entrapment of the nerve root in the lateral recess may occur as a result of bone or soft tissue impingement within the root canal. The distribution of pain resembles that of sciatica due to a prolapsed intervertebral disc. Usually, however, it is more severe and is rarely relieved by resting flat on a firm surface. Unlike the pain associated with a herniated disc, it is not made worse if the patient coughs or sneezes. The patient finds it impossible to stand or sit for long periods because of the pain and may have to get up and walk around in order to gain some temporary respite. In others, the pain is made worse by walking.

Many patients have a long history of back complaints. Some will have suffered a previous acute disc prolapse with sciatic pain which subsequently resolved, perhaps leaving a minor degree of backache. Others give a history suggestive of longstanding degenerative disc disease without sciatica and still others have never previously been aware of any problem in their backs. The symptoms which a disc prolapse evokes are dependent in part upon the capacity of the vertebral canal. In patients with capacious canals, even a disc prolapse of substantial size may not cause any embarrassment to the nerve root. With the passage of time, the prolapse is likely to resolve and settling of the disc space may occur. Secondary degenerative changes in the facet joint with osteophytic lipping impinging upon the root canal may then compromise the nerve root and result in the emergence of radicular pain.

The pain of which such patients complain is highly variable in its periodicity and severity. Some victims are tormented by unremitting pain while others carry on for months or years with only minor intermittent discomfort before seeking help.

Clinical examination is equally variable. Straight leg raising is impaired in around one third of patients. In the remainder, it is likely that performing the straight leg raising test relieves the nerve root entrapment by virtue of the passive flexion of the spine which the test produces. Such a manoeuvre serves to open up the intervertebral foramina and lateral recesses and allows more room for the nerve in its course through the root canal. Spinal movements, except for extension, are generally well preserved. Neurological examination is also usually normal.

Pathology

A disturbance of the circulation to the cauda equina or nerve root is thought to be the underlying cause of the various clinical syndromes of spinal stenosis. The mechanism by which such a disturbance operates is purely speculative at present. Either the arterial or the venous side of the microcirculation could be at fault and it may be that either factor can be responsible in a particular situation. Such a circulatory disturbance could be precipitated by a variety of triggers. Restriction of space within the canal arising as a result of degenerative changes within an already stenotic area, the effects of fibrotic scarring from past disease and atherosclerotic changes in the vessels supplying the contents of the canal may combine to bring about these ischaemic changes.

The symptoms of claudication which result probably arise for a number of reasons. The most important of these is the further physical restriction of space within the canal brought about by spinal motion during exercise. In addition, there is an increase in the metabolic demands of the cauda equina during exercise. This may be impossible to meet because of the already compromised blood supply. Finally, the increased venous return from the legs during exercise results in an engorgement of Batson's plexus and further reduces the space available within the canal. Other factors which could play a part in the production of symptoms include intraosseous shunting of blood and disturbances in the circulation of the cerebrospinal fluid. The latter comes about as a result of narrowing of the dural sac and impairment of the free flow of CSF, so preventing the removal of metabolites from the affected area. The adoption of a flexed position allows the flow of cerebrospinal fluid to return to a more normal pattern and thereby brings about relief of the symptoms.

Investigation

Plain radiographs of the spine are of limited use but should nevertheless always be obtained. Measurement of the interpedicular distance in cases of suspected neurogenic claudication is a useless exercise owing to the poor correlation between reduction in this parameter and the presence of symptoms of the condition. Evidence can sometimes be seen on the anteroposterior view of subluxation of the facet joints, particularly in the presence of a lateral recess syndrome. This may help to identify a level in localized disease but is also a normal variation in the ageing spine and more detailed investigation is required before a definitive radiological diagnosis can be made. A common finding on the lateral radiograph is the presence of a degenerative spondylolisthesis. This is seen in up to half of the patients presenting with neurogenic claudication. Again, this finding can be of use in helping to decide which level is involved in localized disease but must not be relied upon without further investigations. Attempts to measure the sagittal diameter of the vertebral canal on plain radiographs are fraught with difficulty. Aside from the difficulties involved in performing the measurement, the technique takes no account of soft tissue structures such as the ligamentum flavum which may be impinging on the canal and is now discredited as a significant aid to investigation.

Some surgeons advocate the use of ultrasound to measure the canal diameter. Porter *et al.* [24] point out that a canal of wide sagittal diameter is incompatible with a diagnosis of neurogenic claudication and that there is a good correlation between the presence of a narrow sagittal diameter as measured by ultrasound and the syndrome of neurogenic claudication. The technique is however difficult to perform accurately and is subject to considerable observer error.

Myelography is invaluable in confirming the clinical diagnosis and in assessing the extent of the disease. It should always be performed if surgery is contemplated. The myelographic findings are variable. Congenital stenosis is often associated with a thin pencil-like column of contrast throughout the affected area. This is also seen in developmental stenoses but is then usually associated with 'waisting' of the column of contrast at several levels over areas corresponding to the discs and facet joints. In degenerative stenosis, the pattern varies according to the direction from which the canal is compromised. Thus, posterior indentation of the column may be seen at several levels corresponding to buckling of the ligamentum flavum. This is always pathological. Anterior defects in the column represent bulging degenerate discs and posterior osteophytes from the margins of the vertebral bodies. Some indentation of the contrast column on its anterior

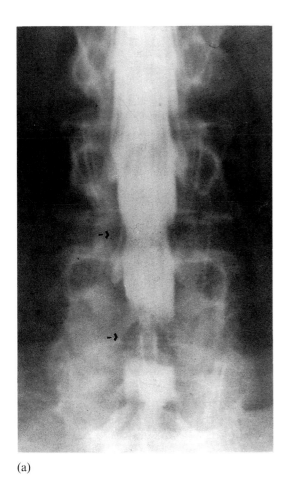

(a)

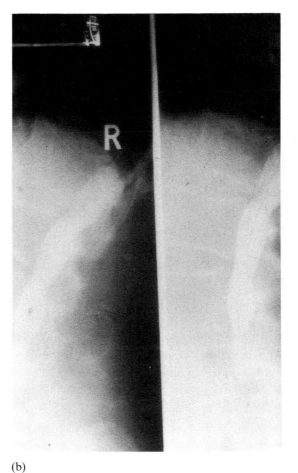

(b)

Fig. 20.11 Considerable deformity of the column of contrast.

aspect is a normal finding in the ageing spine and the appearance may thus not be significant. Posterolateral filling defects correspond to hypertrophy and osteophytic lipping of the inferior facets. The width of the column of contrast is variable but is generally considerably reduced compared to the normal width of at least 15 mm. There may be a complete block of contrast in cases of severe stenosis (Fig. 20.11). It is very important to obtain dynamic studies when performing myelography. Of particular value in this respect are erect films and flexion extension views. The latter may serve to demonstrate the existence of a posturally dependent block in the contrast column. The interpretation of the myelogram in patients who have had previous spinal surgery is particularly difficult. It is important, however, that the investigation be performed in order to exclude conditions such as arachnoiditis which may cause similar symptoms.

CT scanning is a useful technique in that it allows accurate assessment of the canal dimensions and demonstrates the presence of soft tissue intrusion into the canal. The presence of the trefoil configuration, the anatomy of the lateral recesses and their contents and the cranial and caudal extent of the disease are all well demonstrated.

Magnetic resonance imaging appears to hold great promise in the assessment of spinal stenosis. It is as accurate as myelography or CT scanning and is of great value in demonstrating bony and soft tissue encroachment on the canal and lateral recess.

Treatment

Patients with neurogenic claudication may be helped by a programme of physiotherapy including postural advice and by the provision of a lumbosacral support. Such measures generally do not produce a dramatic improvement and the decision must then be made as to whether the patient is to live with his symptoms, with the appropriate modification of activities that this entails or whether he should be offered surgery.

If surgery is undertaken for neurogenic claudication, it is in the form of a spinal decompression. The results are generally very gratifying and there should be no hesitation in recommending surgery to those patients with intractable symptoms. A

dramatic improvement in walking distance often occurs, although some back discomfort may remain. The improvement in the quality of life for such patients is considerable. Some patients will relapse after a period of months or years and start to claudicate again. This is usually due either to arachnoiditis following surgical intervention or to encroachment upon the canal of scar tissue from the posterior surgery. A free fat graft placed over the decompressed dura at the time of surgery reduces the chances of such postoperative scarring developing. If it does occur, a further attempt at decompression may be worthwhile.

If surgical decompression is undertaken, it must be adequate in extent. Hence preoperative investigation must be thorough in order to establish the extent of the disease. By adequate decompression is meant that a free flow of cerebrospinal fluid must be re-established within the affected area. In order to achieve this, the decompression must extend rostrally and caudally until a canal of normal dimensions is encountered. In a typical localised stenosis, this may involve removing the spinous processes and laminae of three vertebrae. Usually it is not necessary to remove the facet articulations to achieve adequate decompression and the risk of postoperative iatrogenic instability is thereby avoided. This is of particular importance in those patients in whom degenerative spondylolisthesis is contributing to the stenosis. Even in such cases, however, the risk of inadequate decompression outweighs the chance of creating further instability and the first priority is to ensure that the decompression is adequate. Occasionally, in order to provide adequate decompression, a large quantity of bone must be removed from the area of the facet joints. The possibility of iatrogenic instability is then very real and serious consideration must be given to performing a fusion of the spine at the same operation in order to prevent this.

In those patients with the lateral recess syndrome, a trial of conservative treatment is worthwhile. As the impingement upon the nerve root is often bony, improvement in the symptoms by expectant treatment may not be as rewarding as in the case of leg pain secondary to a disc herniation. Physiotherapy and a back support help some patients, though the results of such measures are unpredictable. Epidural injections are often very helpful in this condition and non-steroidal anti-inflammatory medications are also worth a trial. Many patients will settle to an extent over the course of time, though a substantial number will continue to complain of some radicular symptoms.

Surgery in this condition is indicated when the pain fails to settle to tolerable levels following adequate conservative therapy. Accurate preoperative identification of the root involved is mandatory. An adequate decompression of the root throughout its course in the lateral recess and root canal should then be undertaken. This often involves considerable undercutting of the lamina and an undercutting facetectomy which should be continued until there is no doubt that the nerve is freely mobile throughout its course. Most patients are relieved of their leg pain by such measures although in a substantial number the relief is incomplete and many continue to complain of low back discomfort.

Fusion of the affected segment is not usually indicated at the time of decompression. Some authors, however, feel that the additional procedure is beneficial in that it eliminates the degenerate facet joints as a potential pain source and thereby reduces subsequent low back pain. Fusion without decompression, however, has no place to play in the treatment of either of the two syndromes of spinal stenosis.

Finally, a small number of patients who present with clinical features of spinal stenosis are shown to have Paget's disease of the lumbar vertebrae. It is thought that a 'vascular steal' phenomenon may operate in this situation which contributes to the patient's symptoms by causing ischaemia of the cauda equina. Such patients may respond to the administration of calcitonin or diphosphonates.

Segmental instability

The term segmental instability implies that there is excessive or unnatural movement between adjacent vertebrae during spinal motion. The spine normally moves in a coordinated manner. In the presence of disturbances in the intervertebral articulations, it is possible that abnormal motion may occur beyond the limits normally set by the restraints of facet joints and soft tissues. Such motion may occur in any of the three axes of rotation of the spine. Anteroposterior instability

produces a spondylolisthesis or retrolisthesis. Lateral instability may be seen in scoliosis. Rotatory instability may occur if there is more pronounced instability on one side than the other.

The question of the definition of instability is a vexed one. The nature and degree of movements seen in the normal spine is very variable between different subjects and between different levels in the same subject and the appearance of what might seem to be abnormal spinal movement does not correlate well with the patient's symptoms. White and Panjabi [25] offer a definition of 'Clinical instability': 'The loss of the ability of the spine under physiological loads to maintain relationships between vertebrae in such a way that there is neither damage nor subsequent irritation to the spinal cord or nerve roots and in addition, there is no development of incapacitating deformity or pain due to structural changes.'

The restraints to motion in the normal spine (facet joints, disc, muscles and ligaments) are strong and considerable disturbance to these structures is required before appreciable instability can develop. Such damage may be produced by trauma to the spine, by degenerative change, or by surgery.

Clinical features

Even gross displacement of vertebrae may produce no symptoms for many years. Complaints of back pain or sciatica are indeed more common in the presence of such vertebral displacement but may be caused by the disease process underlying the displacement rather than by the instability itself.

Two distinct clinical presentations of segmental instability are recognized. The first of these is a reflection of fatigue in those structures which normally limit spinal mobility. The paravertebral muscles and associated ligaments are the principle structures involved. Such patients complain of low back pain, occasionally with radiation to the buttocks and thighs. The pain is characteristically worse after prolonged activity, particularly if this involves stooping forwards for long periods. Thus, such activities as bed making or gardening become impossible. Prolonged standing can also provoke the symptoms whereas lying down produces relief. Obesity or pregnancy exacerbate the problem.

Other patients complain of symptoms primarily while changing position. Rising from a sitting or stooping position is accompanied by a momentary sharp pain in the back. The victim has to use the arms of a chair to assist him in standing up and may be observed to 'climb up his legs' with his hands while standing upright from a forward flexed position. Trick movements may be adopted to achieve an upright posture, such as circumduction of the spine midway through the movement of extension. The presence of such movements on physical examination is a useful clue to the underlying pathology. The pain is caused by momentary subluxation of one vertebra upon its neighbour during the change of posture.

Both types of pain may coexist in the same patient. Other pain patterns may also appear, such as sciatica or symptoms suggestive of spinal stenosis. These, however, are reflections of the underlying disease or of secondary changes brought about in part by the abnormal vertebral motion rather than manifestations of segmental instability *per se.*

Clinical examination is likely to be relatively normal. Hypertrophy of the paraspinal muscles is a frequent finding but may be a normal variant. It is a difficult sign to assess objectively and may in any case be masked as many of these patients are obese. In patients with pain of momentary subluxation, difficulty in regaining the erect posture from a forward flexed position may be noted. Movements of the lumbar spine are often slightly restricted but not grossly so. Straight leg raising is normal and signs of neurological involvement are absent.

Radiological findings

Radiographs of the spine often reveal the presence of a spondylolisthesis or retrolisthesis. In gross instability, there may be lateral displacement of the vertebrae on the A-P film. Traction spurs indicating the unstable segment are a frequent finding. The disc space may be narrowed and accompanying arthritic changes in the facet joints might also be seen, these latter two signs being indicative of the underlying degenerative process. Flexion extension views of the lumbar spine are usually unhelpful. If forward displacement is seen, its degree does not correlate well with the level of pain.

On computerized tomography, gas may be visible in the disc (Knuttson's sign) (Fig. 20.5). This is often associated with instability of the motion segment.

All of the above radiological signs are frequent findings in subjects with no pain. Nevertheless, they may serve as useful reassurance that the diagnosis is correct providing that the history is sufficiently convincing.

Treatment

Many patients can be managed with simple measures such as reassurance that the problem is unlikely to progress relentlessly combined with advice on weight reduction and modification of activities, postural exercises and the provision of a lumbosacral support.

For those patients who fail to improve, consideration must be given to surgical intervention. This will usually take the form of a fusion aimed at restoring stability to the spine. It is particularly important in this situation to be certain that the diagnosis is correct and further investigation may be warranted. Myelography is usually normal in the absence of complicating factors such as secondary spinal stenosis. Magnetic resonance imaging will demonstrate degenerative changes in the disc at the unstable level. In addition, it will hopefully confirm that the disc above is healthy. This is an important consideration as if a fusion is undertaken below an already degenerate segment, a recurrence of the patient's symptoms will almost inevitably occur as a result of the increased loads to which the articulation at this level will be subjected. A normal MRI scan is a useful reassurance that this complication is unlikely to develop. Discography is an alternative useful investigation. A normal discogram will effectively exclude the presence of instability at the level of the investigation. The demonstration of a degenerate disc is useful confirmatory evidence but it is essential to remember that the finding of this abnormality does not guarantee that instability at this level is the cause of the pain. The diagnosis is essentially clinical and the ancillary investigations merely serve to confirm one's clinical suspicions. As with MRI scanning, discography is able to demonstrate the presence of degenerative changes in the disc above the level of the proposed fusion.

The operation offered will usually be in the form of a posterolateral fusion extending out sufficiently far lateral to include the transverse processes. If more than one segment is to be spanned by the fusion, there is undoubtedly a higher incidence of pseudarthrosis. Many surgeons would therefore advocate supplementing the fusion by an implant to stabilize the spine and promote fusion. It is important in such situations to maintain the lumbar lordosis over the fused segment. Failure to achieve this will result in a compensatory increase in the lordosis above or below the level of the fusion and may predispose to the further degenerative changes. Distraction methods, such as Harrington instrumentation, are therefore to be avoided in favour of Knodt compression rods, segmental methods of fixation, such as the Hartshill rectangle which can be contoured to the sagittal curve of the spine or fixation by means of contoured plates attached to the spine by screws passed along the pedicles into the vertebral bodies.

Anterior interbody fusion is also advocated by some authors, although the postoperative complications of ileus, urinary retention and impotence are greater. O'Brien [26] advocates a combined anterior and posterior fusion for gross instability such as in the post-laminectomy syndrome.

The degenerate lumbar spine

Many patients seek help from the surgeon because of symptoms arising from pathological changes directly attributable to the ageing processes of the motion segment. The lateral recess syndrome, central canal stenosis and segmental instability are manifestations of this pathology. Other patients with chronic back pain, however, do not fall into any of these categories.

Typically such patients present with a long history of low back ache which is frequently accompanied by referred pain in the thighs. Their pain is characterized by exacerbations often precipitated by some injudicious activity such as heavy lifting or gardening. Long periods of remission may occur during which the patient may be virtually asymptomatic although mild backache is not uncommon during these intervals. The initial insult to the back often takes the form of an acute disc prolapse with all the typical features thereof. The acute symptoms settle with the course of time and the radicular pain is lost. Thereafter, however, the pattern of chronic grumbling backache interspersed with frequent severe remissions of pain may persist for years.

Physical examination of these patients in between their acute attacks does not reveal very much of value. There is often some restriction of lumbar spinal movement. Straight leg raising is unimpaired and neurological examination is normal. Tenderness over the lower lumbar spine is a frequent finding.

Repeated attacks may leave the patient very apprehensive about his back. Some will restrict their activities for fear of a further attack and as a result may find increasing difficulty in pursuing their occupations and leisure activities.

It is in this group of patients that there is particular difficulty in establishing the pain source. Extensive efforts have been made to categorize the various syndromes of chronic low back pain in the hope of rationalising the management of the individual patient. Thus the concepts of the 'facet syndrome' due to disease of the facet joints, the degenerate disc syndrome etc. have arisen. The more closely one examines these so-called syndromes, however, the more apparent it is that no particular clinical picture is especially characteristic of degenerative disease in one structure of the spine as opposed to another. The attempt to subdivide these patients into such groups is flawed from the outset because so closely are the facet joints, intervertebral disc, ligaments and muscles associated, that dysfunction in one eventually will inevitably lead to equivalent changes in the others. Most patients with low back pain who present to the orthopaedic surgeon will fall into this group. These patients cannot be cured but almost all of them can be helped.

Investigation and treatment

Plain radiographs of the lumbar spine must always be obtained, chiefly for the purposes of excluding other more sinister pathology. Aside from these and routine haematological and biochemical tests such as full blood count, erythrocyte sedimentation rate and alkaline phosphatase, further investigation is usually not indicated unless serious consideration is being given to surgery.

The great majority of patients can be managed with advice regarding general back care, a programme of physiotherapy and occasionally a back support. The active role of the patient in his physiotherapy must be emphasized. It is wrong to reassure the patient that any of these measures will automatically cause the pain to disappear. The patient must be told at the outset that none of the available treatments can reverse the changes that the passage of the years has brought about in his spine. At the same time, he must be reassured that help is available and that while it may not be possible to abolish the pain completely, it should nevertheless be feasible to reduce symptoms to a tolerable level and to go some way towards preventing the severe exacerbations which characterise many of these patients' complaints.

The role of surgery

Occasionally a patient with low back pain uncomplicated by radicular pain, spinal stenosis or instability will be encountered, who despite the best efforts of the surgeon, physiotherapist and orthotist is still severely handicapped by his complaint. The question of surgery must then be given serious consideration. The selection of such patients is a matter of the greatest difficulty. Most of the bad results of back surgery arise as a result of operating on patients without clear indications to do so, in the vague hope that exploration and fusion of the lumbar spine will somehow abolish the patient's complaints. Such a blunderbuss approach has nothing to recommend it. Instead, a painstaking appraisal of the situation must be made, taking into account the psychosocial aspects of the problem as well as the pathological basis of the patient's complaints.

The patient must display a genuine and determined desire to get better. This is by no means always the case. Many patients become locked into patterns of behaviour which provide a form of secondary gain from their symptoms. In such patients, the benefits of the care, attention and sympathy which they reap from their family and friends, the avoidance of unwanted sexual attentions of a partner or the possibility of escape from an unpleasant working environment may outweigh the disadvantages of their backache. Such behaviour may well seem inappropriate to the surgeon, though from the point of view of the patient, it may well offer the least objectionable of the various options with which he is confronted. This neurosis is seldom consciously embraced by the patient but is nevertheless a very real and not uncommon phenomenon and one which will inevitably lead to failure of any surgical measures which may be undertaken. These patients may derive help from the ministrations of a psychiatrist but are unlikely to do well in the hands of an orthopaedic surgeon. Various tools are at the disposal of the surgeon to assist him in his selection of the patient for surgery. Psychological testing of the patient is highly regarded in some circles, the most widely accepted method being the Minnesota Multiphasic Personality Inventory (MMPI). This is a complex and cumbersome questionnaire which is designed to be answered by the patient. There is a high failure rate with the method, many patients having great difficulty in understanding and completing it. Various other attempts have been made to devise simpler systems of psychological assessment, none of which has proved wholly satisfactory and all of which require the expertise of a clinical psychologist in their interpretation. Nevertheless, if it possible to establish with certainty the organic basis of a patient's complaints and if the lesion is potentially remediable by surgery, then psychological testing in one form or other may be a useful addition to the surgeon's armamentarium in arriving at a decision as to whether surgery should be offered.

Surgery in this context means fusion of the painful motion segment. The role of fusion in this situation is the most controversial subject in the whole of spinal surgery and there is very little evidence to indicate that in the long term, patients with this type of low back pain fare any better if they are subjected to surgery than if they are treated conservatively.

If fusion is to be contemplated, there must be no doubt as to the level at which the pathology lies. This is a far from straightforward matter. In certain cases, plain radiological assessment may suggest that a particular motion segment is responsible for the patient's pain; computerized tomography excels at displaying degenerative changes in the facet joints whereas magnetic resonance imaging may show equivalent changes in the intervertebral discs. All such changes, however, may be regarded as part of the normal ageing process of the spine and are therefore insufficient to allow the incrimination of the motion segment under suspicion as the pain source. Provocative tests are, however, available which can greatly enhance the confidence of the surgeon in his clinical diagnosis. Essentially, such tests involve the injection of the facet joints or intervertebral disc under suspicion with hypertonic saline. The injection is undertaken under radiological control. It should accurately reproduce the patient's symptoms, which should subsequently be abolished by injection of local anaesthetic. At the same time as the injection is undertaken, it is useful to obtain contrast studies in the form of a discogram or facet arthrogram, although it must be emphasized that the demonstration of degenerative changes in the disc or facet joint are of less importance than the provocative aspects of the investigation.

If the pain source has been identified with confidence, if the motion segments above this level are demonstrably normal and above all if the patient has been selected with sufficient care, then it is reasonable in certain cases to offer fusion. The operation is most likely to succeed if only one segment is to be fused. Instrumentation may reduce the pseudarthrosis rate and allow more rapid mobilization of the patient. Most commonly, a posterolateral fusion will be undertaken although some surgeons advocate anterior fusion in certain situations or even a combination of anterior and posterior fusion.

Fortunately, very few such patients will come to surgery and the great majority will find that their symptoms can be reduced to a tolerable level by the application of the simple conservative measures outlined above.

Acknowledgement

Figures 20.1 and 20.7 reproduced by kind permission of Professor G. Whitehouse, Department of Radiodiagnosis, University of Liverpool.

References

1. Wyke, B. D. (1969) In *Principles of General Neurology*. Elsevier, Amsterdam, London.
2. Paris, S. V. (1983) Anatomy as related to function and pain. *Orthop. Clin. North Am.*, **14**, 475.
3. Bogduk, N., Tynan, W. and Wilson, A. S. (1981) The nerve supply to the human lumbar intervertebral discs. *J. Anat.*, **132**, 39.
4. Mixter, W. J. and Barr, J. S. (1934) Rupture of intervertebral disc with involvement of spinal canal. *New Eng. J. Med.*, **211**, 210–215.
5. Markolf, K. L. and Morris, J. M. (1974) Structural components of the intervertebral disc. *J. Bone Joint Surg.*, **56A**, 675.
6. Nachemson, A. and Morris, J. M. (1964) *In vivo* measurements of intradiscal pressure. *J. Bone Joint Surg.*, **46A**, 1077.
7. Hickey, D. S. and Hukins, D. W. L. (1980) Relation between the structure of the annulus fibrosus and the function and failure of the disc. *Spine*, **5**, 106.
8. Adams, M. A. and Hutton, W. C. (1981) Prolapsed intervertebral disc – a hyperflexion injury. *Spine*, **7**, 184.
9. Klein, J. A., Hickey, D. S. and Hukins, D. W. L. (1982) Computer graphics illustrations of the operation of the intervertebral disc. *Eng. Med.*, **11**, 11.
10. Farfan, H. F. and Sullivan, J. B. (1967) The relation of facet orientation to intervertebral disc failure. *Can. J. Surg.*, **10**, 179.
11. Macnab, I. (1977) In *Backache*. Williams & Wilkins: Baltimore.
12. Troup, J. D. G. (1981) Straight leg raising and the qualifying tests for increased root tension. *Spine*, **6**, 61.
13. Blower, P. W. (1981) Neurological patterns in unilateral sciatica: a prospective study of one hundred new cases. *Spine*, **6**, 175.
14. McCulloch, J. A. (1977) Chemonucleolysis. *J. Bone Joint Surg.*, **59B**, 45.
15. Dilke, T. W. F., Burry, H. C. and Grahame, R. (1973) Extradural corticosteroid injection in management of lumbar nerve root compression. *Br. Med. J*, **2**, 635.
16. Kilian, H. F. (1854) Schilderungen Neuer Beckenformen und ihres Verhalterns im Lebem. Basserman und Mathy, Mannheim.
17. Wiltse, L. L., Newman, P. H. and Macnab, I. (1976) Classification of spondylolysis and spondylolisthesis. *Clin. Orthop.*, **117**, 23.
18. Troup, J. D. G. (1975) Mechanical factors in spondylolisthesis and spondylolysis. *Clin. Orthop. Rel. Res.*, **117**, 59.

19. De Jerine, T. and Baudouin, A. (1911) La pathologie radiculaire, *Paris Med.*, 386–391.

20. Verbiest, H. (1954) A radicular narrowing from developmental narrowing of the lumbar vertebral canal. *J. Bone Joint Surg.*, **36B**, 230.

21. Blau, J. N. and Logue, V. (1961) Intermittent claudication of the cauda equina. An unusual syndrome resulting from central protrusion of a lumbar disc. *Lancet*, **1**, 1081.

22. Epstein, J. A., Epstein, B. S. and Lavine, L. (1962) Nerve root compression with narrowing of the lumbar spinal canal. *J. Neurol. Neurosurg. Psychiatry*, **25**, 165.

23. Verbiest, H. (1977) Results of surgical treatment of idiopathic developmental stenosis of the lumbar vertebral canal. A review of twenty-seven years' experience. *J. Bone Joint Surg.*, **59B**, 181.

24. Porter, R. W., Wicks, M. and Ottewell, D. (1978) Measurement of the spinal canal diameter by diagnostic ultrasound. *J. Bone Joint Surg.*, **60B**, 481.

25. White, A. A. and Panjabi, M. M. (1978) The problem of instability in the human spine: A systematic approach. In *Clinical Biomechanics of the Spine*. J. B. Lippincott, Philadelphia, Toronto, p. 192.

26. O'Brien, J. P. (1983) The role of fusion for chronic low back pain. *Orthop. Clin. North Am.*, **14**, 475.

21

Surgical management of the cervical spine in rheumatoid arthritis

P. M. Yeoman

The concept that most patients with rheumatoid arthritis involving the cervical spine require surgical treatment is fortunately not correct. There are indications for an active surgical approach but most are confined to those patients who are in need of in-patient care as a result of their disease. Occasionally, young patients may require surgical decompression of the cervical spinal cord but the majority of candidates for surgical treatment have been afflicted by the disease for not less than 5 years; most on average developed the disease between 10 and 15 years before the onset of more serious problems in the cervical spine.

Pathology

Only a few tissues in the body are immune from attack by rheumatoid arthritis but some are more susceptible than others.

Synovial tissue is the first to be affected, and in the cervical spine this is located (1) in the articular facet joints (2) on the posterolateral aspects of the vertebral bodies (3) between the odontoid peg of the axis and the anterior arch of the atlas (4) between the posterior aspect of the odontoid and the transverse ligament of the atlas.

The initial inflammatory process gives rise to swelling of the synovium due to an increased blood flow and oedema. This in turn will cause pain by increasing the tissue pressure or by direct stimulation of nerve endings. Further swelling may encroach on surrounding structures, in particular nerve roots which lie in confined spaces adjacent to articular joints. This elementary introduction forms the basis for a clinical picture and sets the scene for future more serious problems.

Ligaments are also affected more by adjacent inflammation than any direct attack. They become slack and consequently their main function of restraint is diminished thus allowing abnormal movement and possible subluxation of a joint.

Articular cartilage is eroded not only by direct enzyme attack but by deprivation of its nutrition from synovial fluid by a covering of inflammatory pannus, similar to granulation tissue, but extending from the synovium. The pannus may itself cause pressure on nerve tissue or indeed on the spinal cord [1]. It is not uncommon to find plaques of this abnormal tissue embedded between the vertebral laminae. The effect of articular cartilage destruction is simply a mechanical disruption of a joint. It is well established that rheumatoid arthritis initially affects the more mobile and stressed joints, which accounts for the early signs of the disease in the wrist of the dominant limb before affecting other joints. Similarly in the cervical spine the occipito-atlanto-axial complex and later the C5/6 areas are the prime sites for the earliest phase of the disease.

Bone may be eroded by abnormal pressure or destroyed by active resorption. Invariably the bone is softer than normal due to a combination of hyperaemia, active rheumatoid granulation and osteoporosis, which combined with articular destruction and ligamentous laxity will give rise to rapid instability of the vertebral column. Conversely, the opposite affect may obtain if abnormal forces are eliminated so that spontaneous fusion is achieved.

Symptoms

Pain is the predominant concern. It may be localized to the neck; aggravated by movement and related to involvement of the articular joints. Pain may be referred to the occipital area of the scalp from pressure on the posterior primary rami of a cervical nerve and particularly the second or greater occipital nerve. Further spread of pain across the vertex to the frontal area of the scalp mimics the pain of a cervical disc lesion or spondylosis at the level of C5/6, but the pathway is obscure. Peripheral radiation of pain is usually localized to a nerve root distribution and is most common in the upper limbs, but can be confused with the symptoms of a carpal tunnel syndrome which is a frequent manifestation of rheumatoid disease.

Stiffness of the neck is more commonly found on clinical examination than as a complaint, although it can be a distressing problem in juvenile arthritis.

Weakness, loss of balance, paraesthesiae and numbness are all related to spinal cord compression, and when superimposed on the pain, instability, stiffness and deformity on peripheral joints it is very difficult to isolate the true cause of the problem. The onset of these further symptoms is the clue to their more sinister origin because clinical examination may not be helpful. For example, spasticity, clonus or a positive Babinski response are impossible to unravel in patients with stiff and painful joints [2].

Investigations

Radiographic examination of the cervical spine is still the first and most important investigation. The site and possibly extent of the lesion will be revealed and it is still obligatory to obtain lateral views in flexion and extension before embarking on operations requiring general anaesthesia in order to determine any instability of the spine [3].

The occipito-atlanto-axial area and the cervico-thoracic junction are still a problem beyond the compass of conventional radiography.

Nuclear magnetic imaging is undoubtedly the most effective and accurate method of assessment of the structure of the spine, which includes the bone and soft tissues, with a minimal invasive threat to the patient. Soft tissue swelling from rheumatoid pannus may be revealed as a cause of compression of the spinal cord which might have been missed in the past. Multiple levels of disease causing destruction and instability are defined accurately so that surgical intervention can be planned with an increased expectancy of recovery. Almost the entire pathological picture can be displayed, which in turn may confuse and distort the surgical judgement.

Bone scan produces a more refined image of bone structure without all the important soft tissues. It therefore lacks the vital assessment of much of the rheumatoid disease process which can so easily cause spinal cord compression. The introduction of water soluble contrast medium can provide an excellent image of soft tissue infringement, but it involves a more invasive technique for the patient and indeed for the radiologist.

Treatment

Occipito-atlanto-axial level

The joints between the occiput and atlas allow flexion and extension of the head as well as a small range of lateral flexion, but they have been denied any significant study because they are so inaccessible; that is by conventional radiography or surgery. Lateral views of that area are shrouded by the thick mastoid process of the temporal bones. It is not uncommon to find at autopsy a spontaneous fusion of the joints, but it may not occur simultaneously which would account for an oblique range of painful movement of the head. Forward or anterior displacement of the skull may occur depending on the destruction of the joints and this in turn may cause impingement of the posterior arch of the atlas on the overlying occiput; and associated compression may lead to upward migration of the odontoid process of the axis. Atlanto-

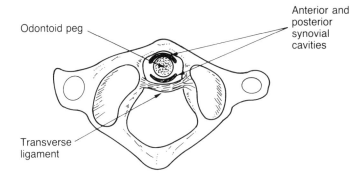

Odontoid peg

Anterior and posterior synovial cavities

Transverse ligament

Fig. 21.1   Horizontal section through odonto-atlantal articulation.

occipital fusion is rarely a practical or indeed necessary surgical procedure.

The axis by contrast is a very real site for problems; mainly related to its odontoid peg and the associated instability between it and the atlas. The odontoid process may become eroded (Fig. 21.1), occasionally it fractures (Fig. 21.2), but in either case it aggravates any instability resulting from laxity of the supporting ligaments (Fig. 21.3). The range of rotation and exaggerated stress from flexion and extension when the

atlanto-occipital joints are fused provides the exact conditions for the deterioration in rheumatoid disease. Hence the reputation that the occipito-atlanto-axial is the prime site for rheumatoid disease of the cervical spine.

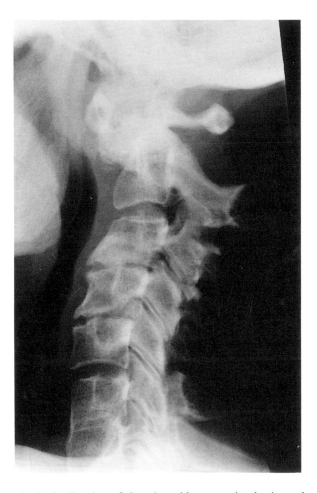

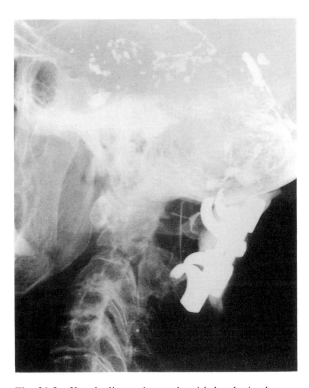

Fig. 21.2   Knodt distraction rods with hooks in the occiput and posterior arch of the axis used for vertical subluxation of the odontoid peg through the foramen magnum.

Fig. 21.3   Erosion of the odontoid peg causing horizontal subluxation of C1 and 2.

Indications for surgical treatment

(1) Presence of spinal cord compression.
(2) Failure to control pain and/or symptoms by wearing a supporting collar.
(3) Failure to achieve stability by wearing a collar [4].

Methods available

(1) Posterior fusion with or without decompression of the spinal cord. The extent of fusion would depend on the area of displacement or instability but generally the occiput is fused to the atlanto-axial complex [5]. Cancellous bone graft is laid on the finely decorticated occiput, posterior arch of the atlas and the laminae of the axis.

Internal fixation is achieved with wires threaded through fine drill holes in the occiput and encircling the posterior arch of the atlas and laminae of the axis [6]. The potentially precarious fixation can be augmented with acrylic cement (Fig. 21.4) [7,8].

(2) Anterior decompression and posterior fusion. This method has the distinct advantage of removing the cause of spinal cord compression which has been identified by an image intensifier; namely the odontoid process. It is a major procedure for a frail old patient and much care is required in the selection.

Cephalic subluxation of the odontoid process

This is undoubtedly associated with destruction of the atlanto-occipital process and deserves special mention in spite of its comparative rarity [9,10]. The odontoid peg can be demonstrated in its elevated position within the foramen magnum (Fig. 21.5). The symptoms are usually those of

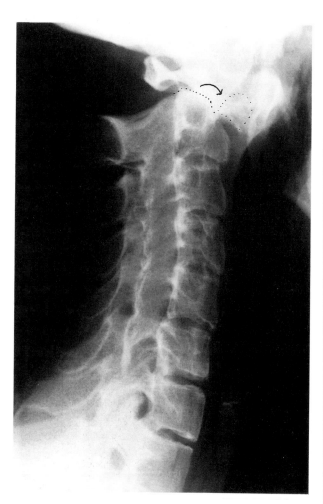

Fig. 21.4 Fracture of the odontoid peg causing horizontal subluxation of C1 and 2.

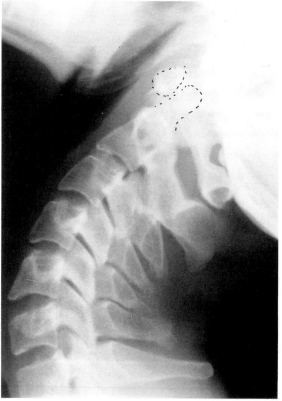

Fig. 21.5 Odontoid peg in extension of the spine.

cord compression with variable signs of an upper motor neurone lesion but with an additional, and often missed, physical sign which is numbness over the side of the face.

Decompression can be achieved by careful resection of the posterior margin of the foramen magnum or by distraction between the occiput and the posterior arch of the axis. The author has used two small Knodt rods as a successful method of distraction; one hook is inserted into a groove made with a burr in the occiput and the other rests on the upper surface of the thick lamina of the axis bone (Fig. 21.2).

Cervical 5/6

Instability may arise at this level either *de novo* or because it has become a junctional area between two fused segments of the cervical spine. The degree of instability will depend on the extent of bone destruction (Fig. 21.6).

Fusion usually involves two vertebrae above

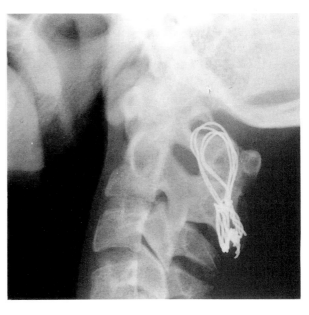

Fig. 21.7 Posterior fusion of C1 and 2 using encircling wires and cancellous bone graft.

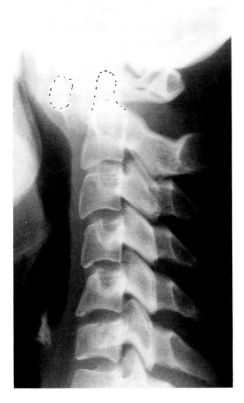

Fig. 21.6 Odontoid peg with subluxation in flexion of the spine.

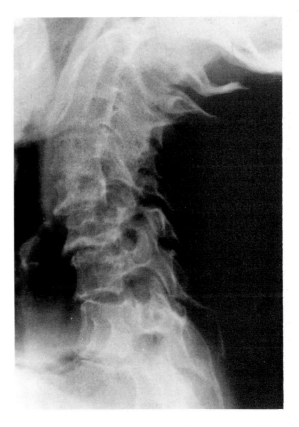

Fig. 21.8 Considerable bone erosion with instability at C5/6 and 'pencil-sharpening' of the spinous process.

and two below the unstable area; and cancellous bone is packed round the decorticated laminae and secured with wire encircling the spinous process (Fig. 21.7).

Decompression of the spinal canal will render the spine more unstable and firm internal fixation is more difficult to achieve; again, the use of distraction rods can provide better fixation than encircling wires but they require transverse holding rods to reduce rotation strain. Acrylic cement may also augment firm fixation (Fig. 21.8) [11].

Multiple levels

Instability and associated compression of the spinal cord may occur at more than one level [12]. In the past this was difficult to identify by myelography unless the contrast medium was introduced both in the cervical and lumbar cisterns (Fig. 21.9). Wide and extensive decompression is required but at the expense of stability, and this is

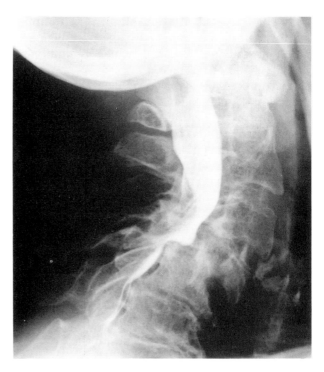

Fig. 21.10   Hartshill rectangle used after wide decompression for multiple level spinal cord compression.

very difficult to achieve by any internal method (Fig. 21.10). Longer holding distraction rods, bone graft and cement are the main components. Anterior fusion is rarely used in these extreme conditions because the vertebral bodies are soft and will not hold any cortical bone graft.

External fixation

It is not sufficient to rely on internal fixation even in a relatively simple two body fusion when a supporting collar is required for at least 3 months.

Block leather or plastic collars with extended vest pieces will provide firmer support and are widely used, but in the frail, aged or grossly unstable necks it is better to rely on the halo-chest fixator [13]. It is tolerated surprisingly well in the most unlikely and unpromising patients. Occasionally it has been used as a most effective single form of management in patients considered to be too ill or frail to withstand a major operation (Fig. 21.11).

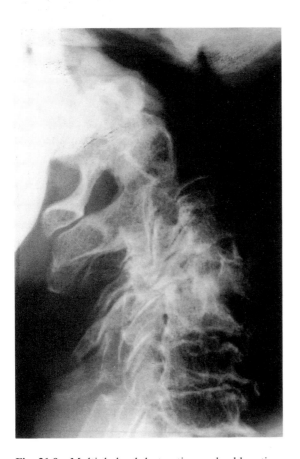

Fig. 21.9   Multiple level destruction and subluxation.

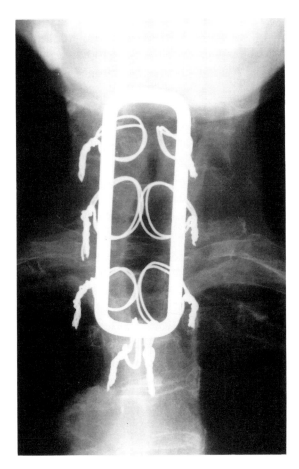

Fig. 21.11 Contrast medium introduced at the basal cistern reveals considerable block at C5/6 but failed to reveal block at lower level.

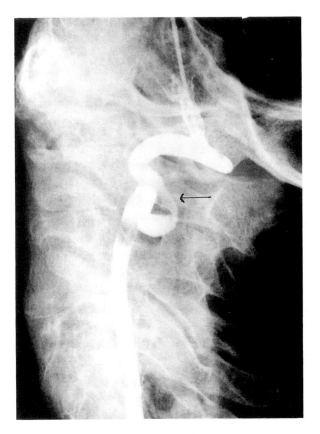

Fig. 21.12 Vertebral artery occluded at base of skull in extension (specimen prepared and artery injected at autopsy).

Conclusion

The hazardous problems of the effects of rheumatoid arthritis of the cervical spine have been outlined. There are reasonably simple solutions for most patients and they are successful. A few have such widespread destruction and osteoporosis that they may be deemed inoperable. It is those patients who are also aged that the halo-chest fixator has been effective; which suggests that perhaps others would be equally helped without operation. Recovery from spinal cord compression is not absolute in spite of apparent successful decompression and there may be a vascular complication in some of the older patients (Fig. 21.12). Spinal artery thrombosis is a difficult enough diagnosis to determine without rheumatoid disease, but it is the most likely reason for some who fail to recover. Finally, the effect of spinal cord compression leads to an unpleasant lingering death and every attempt must be made avoid it.

References

1. Crockhard, H. A., Essigman, W. K., Stevens, J. M. *et al.* (1985) Surgical treatment of cervical cord compression in rheumatoid arthritis. *Ann. Rheum. Dis.*, **44**, 809–816.
2. Christophidis, N. and Huskisson, E. C. (1982) Misleading symptoms and signs of cervical spine subluxation in rheumatoid arthritis. *Br. Med. Jr.*, **285**, 364–366.
3. Ornilla, E., Ansell, B. M. and Swannell, A. J. (1972) Cervical spine involvement in patients with chronic arthritis undergoing orthopaedic surgery. *Ann. Rheum. Dis.*, **31**, 364–366.
4. Althoff, B. and Goldie, I. F. (1980) Cervical

collars in rheumatoid atlanto-axial subluxation: a radiographic comparison. *Ann. Rheum. Dis.*, **39**, 485–489.

5. Heywood, A. W. B., Learmonth, I. D. and Thomas, M. (1988) Internal fixation for occipito-cervical fusion. *J. Bone Joint Surg.*, **70B 5**, 708–711.

6. Brattstrom, H. and Granholm, L. (1976) Atlanto-axial fusion in rheumatoid arthritis: a new method of fixation with wire and bone cement. *Acta Orthop. Scand.*, **47**, 619–628.

7. Bonney, G. and Williams, J. P. R. (1985) Trans-oral approach to the upper cervical spine. *J. Bone Joint Surg.*, **67B 5**, 691–698.

8. Crockard, H. A., Pozo, J. L., Ransford, A. G. *et al.* (1986) Transoral decompression and posterior fusion for rheumatoid atlanto-axial subluxation. *J. Bone Joint Surg.*, **68B 3**, 350–356.

9. Swinson, D. R., Hamilton, E. B. D., Mathews, J. A. *et al.* (1972) Vertical subluxation of the axis in rheumatoid arthritis. *Ann. Rheum. Dis.*, **31**, 359–363.

10. Redlund-Johnell, I. and Pettersson, H. (1984) Vertical dislocation of the C1 and C2 vertebrae in rheumatoid arthritis. *Acta Radiol. Diag.*, **25**, 133–141.

11. Clark, C. R., Keggi, K. J. and Panjabi, M. M. (1988) Methylmethacrylate stabilisation of the cervical spine. *J. Bone Joint Surg.*, **66A 1**, 40–46.

12. Zoma, A., Sturrock, R. D., Fisher, W. D. *et al.* (1987) Surgical stabilisation of the rheumatoid cervical spine. *J. Bone Joint Surg.*, **69B 1**, 8–12.

13. Wang, G. J., Moskal, J. T., Albert, T. *et al.* (1988) The effect of halo-vest length on stability of the cervical spine. *J. Bone Joint Surg.*, **70A 3**, 357–360.

22

Surgical treatment of rheumatoid arthritis of the shoulder

P. J. M. Morrison

Introduction

Symptoms in the shoulder joint are common in rheumatoid disease. Occasionally they are a presenting feature and in hospitalized patients over 50% will admit to symptoms.

Such symptoms are a serious concern to rheumatoid patients. Pain may render life miserable and sleep impossible. Loss of function may make the most mundane tasks of daily living such as dressing, eating and attending to personal hygiene, distressing. Loss of shoulder power may make rehabilitation from other joint surgery more prolonged and difficult. The use of crutches can present a particular problem.

The shoulder complex

Movement of the upper limb involves motion in the joint complex comprising the main glenohumeral joint, the acromioclavicular and sternoclavicular joints and the smooth gliding of the tissues in the subacromial bursa. All these structures may be involved by rheumatoid disease.

Acromioclavicular joint

Local pain, tenderness and occasional swelling of this surface joint suggests involvement, and radiographs (Fig. 22.1) may show erosions and occasionally subluxation of the joint.

Injection with steroid and local anaesthetic may not only determine the proportion of pain arising at this site, but will often settle early symptoms.

Persistent pain is best treated by excision of the outer centimetre of the clavicle but this is seldom

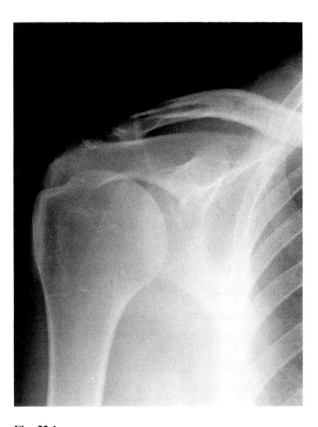

Fig. 22.1

necessary in the author's experience, as an isolated procedure.

The sternoclavicular joint

This joint is relatively infrequently involved. It can usually be settled by instillation of steroid, and only rarely are procedures such as synovectomy or excision of the inner 1 cm of the clavicle (a quite hazardous procedure because of the proximity of the great vessels) needed.

The subacromial bursa

This is commonly affected in rheumatoid disease. Occasionally, it may produce a massive swelling of the shoulder and may occur in isolation or with associated glenohumeral disease.

Affliction of the bursa will usually respond to aspiration and injection of steroid. Occasionally, excision of the bursa is required but this can be an extensive and difficult operation which may damage the deltoid muscle. Associated removal of the acromion must be avoided, but sometimes trimming of the anterior edge of it, if it is specifically impinging on the rotator cuff, may be desirable.

The glenohumeral joint

With involvement of the true shoulder joint, the patient's disability becomes more apparent. The actual onset may be insidious, being masked by an acute flare in the general disease process. Only when this settles does the loss of shoulder function become apparent to the patient and his doctor.

The presenting features are pain and loss of movement. The pain is usually felt all around the shoulder, but often radiates to the root of the neck and onto the outer aspect of the arm; so that the origin of the pain may be mistaken. If there is tenderness, it is usually anteriorly, over the joint.

The loss of function may be slow. The shoulder possesses such a large range of movement in all directions, that the loss of 50% of any modality may produce only minor disabilities, such as difficulty reaching a high cupboard.

However, as motion is progressively lost, there

rapidly comes a point where simple tasks of daily living, such as combing the back of the hair, or washing the neck, become impossible. Almost without warning, the patient is grossly disabled.

Radiographic changes

Early changes may present radiologically as simple osteoporosis. As the disease progresses, erosions can be noted around the neck of the humerus and under the insertion of the supraspinatus tendon (Fig. 22.2). Loss of the joint space and damage to the subchondral plate follow (Fig. 22.3), and ultimately there is destruction of the bony surfaces of the humeral head and glenoid with eventual loss of the normal bone architecture (Fig. 22.4). These changes may progress to secondary osteoarthritis with sclerosis of the bone surfaces.

Usually, the humeral head migrates upwards and this signifies loss of a functional rotator cuff

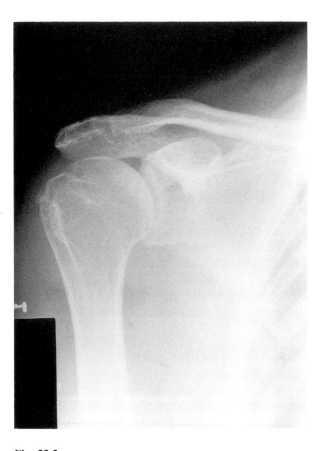

Fig. 22.2

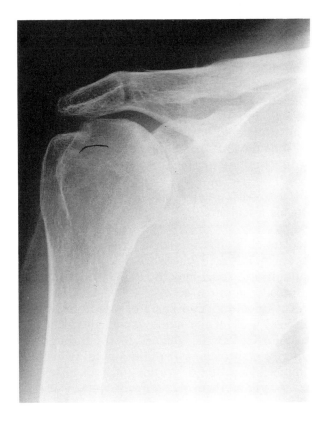

Fig. 22.3

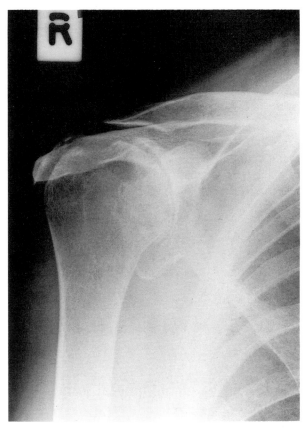

Fig. 22.5

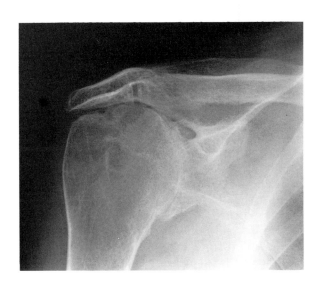

Fig. 22.4

and rupture of the supraspinatus tendon. If the cuff is lost (Fig. 22.5), the dome of the humeral head will articulate with the under surface of the acromion and the root of the coracoid. These surfaces become eburnated.

The glenoid becomes progressively eroded, occasionally allowing the neck of the flattened humerus to articulate with its inferior margin, producing an extraordinary scallop of the humeral neck. The loss of glenoid bone stock may render its eventual replacement difficult because adequate fixation of a scapular component becomes impossible (Fig. 22.6).

The correlation of these radiographic changes and the patient's clinical features and function is quite a close one [1]. The changes were graded I–V in 100 shoulders: it was only when loss of the glenohumeral joint space was apparent (grade IV) that the patient had significant pain and loss of function. Distortion of the humeral head (V) tended to correlate with severe pain and impairment of function.

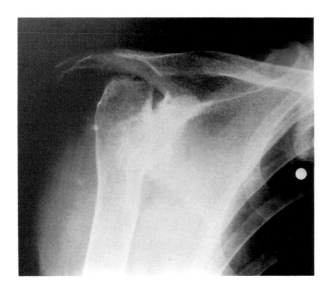

Fig. 22.6

Treatment of glenohumeral joint disease

In the early stages, injection of steroid into the joint cavity (as opposed to the subacromial bursa) may produce dramatic remission of the local inflammation and pain.

However, with persistent pain, and when function is reduced to a level no longer acceptable to the patient, a surgical approach may be advised. The following surgical treatments are available: synovectomy; double osteotomy; glenoidectomy; arthrodesis; interpositional arthroplasty; joint replacement – either half of total.

Synovectomy

This is a neglected operation. It is clear from the writings of Pahle [2] that with good patient selection, a sensible surgical approach, meticulous clearance of the joint and a careful postoperative regime, not only good but long lasting pain relief can be obtained.

In a series of 54 shoulders, only six had required total joint replacement later in a mean follow-up of 5.3 years. The best results are obtained in early cases. A standard anterior approach was used in the later cases, allowing early postoperative mobilization.

As in all series of synovectomies, whatever the joint, a prophylactic procedure in a disease with variable progression is very difficult to evaluate. The earlier the operation is carried out, the more difficult it is to know whether a spontaneous remission could have occurred.

None the less, the pain relief and maintenance of function are impressive.

Double osteotomy

Benjamin [3] has advocated this operation at several joints and published his results on the shoulder as long ago as 1974. They are undoubtedly impressive.

The operation, consisting of osteotomy of the surgical neck of the humerus and the glenoid $\frac{1}{4}$ inch medial to the glenoid fossa, through an anterior approach, is, according to Benjamin, simple. The posterior cortices of both bones are left intact and the osteotomies are not displaced. The arm is supported in a sling and active shoulder exercises are started on the 10th postoperative day.

Twelve patients with rheumatoid arthritis were treated. The abduction range was increased by an average of 50° 'probably due to relief of pain and muscle spasm' Benjamin states. There was no increase in glenohumeral movement observed. Pain relief was very impressive, with 13 of 16 patients (with all forms of arthritis) having no pain, or slight pain only postoperatively. There were no serious complications.

Despite these results, however, the operation is not widely practised, which suggests that the results were not uniformly reproducible.

Glenoidectomy

Wainwright [4] and Gariepy [5] have both written about and advocated this operation.

Wainwright described six patients operated on by a posterior approach removing $\frac{1}{2} - \frac{3}{4}$ inch of the glenoid and maintaining the arm on an abduction splint for 3 or 4 weeks postoperatively.

Pain relief was pleasing: glenohumeral function was poor but because of the pain relief, overall shoulder function was improved. Increased internal rotational movement, however, was very valuable to these disabled patients.

Wainwright reserved this operation for totally disorganized joints with intractable pain.

Gariepy described 12 cases: an anterior approach was used and 7 or 8 mm of the glenoid were removed.

Full removal of the pannus was carried out, the capsule was left open and subscapularis was not overlapped. No postoperative fixation was used and a sling only was worn for 48 hours.

The follow-up was between 1 and 13 years. Relief of pain had been satisfactory in all cases; the range of movement had been improved except where there was severe deformity of the humeral head. Gariepy suggested, therefore, that the operation was best carried out in undeformed joints, where the systemic disease was not too severe and the muscles were good, in other words, early cases.

Although Gariepy says that the operation does not preclude prosthetic surgery in the future, it must surely make such surgery exceedingly difficult and render the fixation of a scapular component of a total shoulder replacement, well nigh impossible.

The author regards this operation, therefore, as a minor salvage procedure for intractable pain and stiffness. As such, it still has a place and he can confirm its usefulness.

Arthrodesis

This operation has been condemned by many authors over the last 30 years. Various reasons have been given but the two main criticisms are, firstly, the fear that the period of immobilization of the upper limb postoperatively will lead to loss of function in all other joints in that limb, and secondly, that the loss of rotation resulting from arthrodesis will greatly restrict simple but important functions of personal hygiene. This is particularly true, it is said, in patients whose other shoulders may be partially restricted.

However, the operation has its advocates and there is no doubt, if well performed, that it can offer great benefit in terms of pain relief and thereby an increase in shoulder girdle function.

The hazards of the operation may have been exaggerated. Arthrodesis is a reliable operation and in a Finnish series the results were remark-

able. Raunio [6] describes a simple three-screw technique and achieved bone union in 90% of patients (37/41). Even in the non-unions, there was sufficient fibrous union to abolish shoulder pain.

All the patients had an increased range of motion – an average total flexion and abduction of 100° before operation and 160° afterwards. But, most remarkably, all patients were able to use the operated limb for eating, combing the hair and were able to take care of their own personal hygiene. Ninety-five percent of the patients were satisfied with their operations.

The technique used involved an anterior approach, removal of all synovial tissue and all remaining cartilage from the head, the undersurface of the acromion and the glenoid. The denuded surfaces are approximated and held with two compression screws passed through the humeral head into the glenoid and one screw passed through the acromion downwards into the humeral head, with osteotomy of the acromion if necessary.

The position of the arm is very important. The aim was to obtain 55° abduction, 25° flexion and 20° internal rotation – an easy hand to mouth position. Postoperatively, a light custom-made thoracobrachial splint was worn for about 10 weeks. The splint allowed exercise of the elbow and hand which is so important to the end result of the operation.

A technique using an extensive compression device has been described. This avoids the need for a splint postoperatively but clearly such a technique is not feasible in many of the osteoporotic damaged shoulders that are encountered in rheumatoid disease.

Thus, there is dispute about the place of arthrodesis of the shoulder.

It should probably be reserved for cases where total joint replacement is contraindicated, or has failed [7]. Nevertheless, the author has been impressed by the confidence and comfort that patients with an arthrodesis seem to exhibit.

Arthroplasty

Interposition with silastic

In 1980 Varion [8] reported a clinical trial of 28 patients with rheumatoid arthritis who had a silastic cup slipped between the humeral head and the glenoid through an anterior approach without removing any bone.

The early results of this seemingly simple procedure were most encouraging with pain relief in all but two patients at a mean 14-month review. A small personal series was also favourable.

However, it seems that in the longer term, the improvement is not maintained. The cups eroded, slipped out of position and fragmented with consequent return of symptoms.

Varion originally stated that the operation was reversible: certainly as at the hip, interposition is an attractive idea if an ideal material could be found to remain in good condition, or if a material could be developed that provoked good quality fibrous cover for the eroded joint surfaces.

Glenohumeral joint replacement

There is no doubt that this surgical procedure should have most to offer the disabled rheumatoid patient. However, even after more than 20 years of evolution its expectations are strictly limited and they are in no way on a par with those achievable at the hip or other major joints. Thus, careful selection and preparation of the patient is vital, if the limited goals and patient satisfaction are to be obtained.

Design considerations

The rheumatoid shoulder presents particular paradoxes to the designer.

1. Absent or poorly functioning rotator cuff musculature makes it difficult for the rheumatoid patient to stabilize an unconstrained implant in elevation and thus achieve good function.

2. Any constrained implant will rely on the fixation of one component in the scapula. The normal human scapula is a thin, light structure. It has been estimated that lifting one's arm carries forces equivalent to the body weight through the articulation. Only at the glenoid and neck of the scapula is there sufficient bone stock to carry such loads and yet in rheumatoid patients, particularly in those patients being referred for shoulder surgery, the bone stock is often grossly eroded and excavated.

3. The space between the humerus and the scapula is extremely limited. Any mechanism inserted must retain the same centre of rotation, otherwise the greater tuberosity will foul the acromion during abduction.

The mean distance between the centre of rotation of the humeral head and the centre of the glenoid dish is only 24 mm.

This awkwardness has led to some radical redesigning of the shoulder mechanism.

4. A normal human shoulder has a remarkable range of movement and this is achieved, to some extent, by a wandering fulcrum of movement. Allowing the fulcrum to move would obviously also reduce the load and torque being carried by the components in a constrained joint. Yet, control of this wandering fulcrum requires muscle balance and strength is often sorely lacking in the patient with rheumatoid arthritis.

5. The shoulder is used mainly in compression but it is sometimes distracted in normal use and a prosthesis must remain stable under all conditions. These considerations have led to the evolution of a number of different designs, none of which has achieved the ideal.

Evolution

As long ago as 1953, Neer [9] produced a hemiarthroplasty replacing the humeral head in a group of patients with fracture dislocations of the shoulder. Hidden within this group, there are patients with secondary avascular necrosis and one patient with primary osteoarthritis.

Neer himself experimented with fixed fulcrum prostheses but in the early 1970s had found them disappointing and returned in 1973 to a redesigned head component and introduced a polythene glenoid surface replacement. This design aimed to provide 'near normal anatomical design'.

Meanwhile, a series of fascinating alternatives were tried, including a group of joints where the anatomy was reversed. This allowed the centre of rotation to be retained by burying the cup (the most difficult component to fix) within the humeral head. The ball was fixed to the scapula. Some of these joints were truly constrained using the principle of the captive ball.

Post [10] of Chicago, introduced two types of prostheses between 1973 and 1977. Forty-three replacements were performed; a few were in rheumatoid arthritis. However, more than half of the first series of prostheses broke or had to be revised. Nearly all his patients had absent rotator cuff function and he regarded his operation by 1980, as a salvage procedure in judiciously selected patients.

Beddow [11] designed a reversed prosthesis where the glenoid ball component was fixed into the lateral border of the scapula, whilst Kessel [12] introduced a simple reversed prosthesis with the ball screwed into the glenoid using a single strong self-tapping screw. The majority of his patients were rheumatoid patients and his early results were most encouraging. In the long term, however, the scapular fixation is bound to be in jeopardy; loosening and breakage of this prosthesis has been seen by the author.

The Stanmore prosthesis, a semi-captive ball and socket implanted in the normal anatomical relationship, provided a stable fulcrum also but in at least eight of 34 patients with rheumatoid arthritis (i.e. almost a quarter), the cup became loose within the period of follow-up.

Lettin in a later article [13] confirmed that patients suffering from rheumatoid arthritis would almost certainly benefit from total shoulder replacement. However, comparisons of different prostheses are few; most reviews being a little coloured by the enthusiasm of the author/designer. Bodey and Yeoman [14] compared 3 prostheses (Stanmore, Kessel and Neer) in 18 patients with rheumatoid arthritis and although the numbers are very small, it is interesting that the Neer hemiarthroplasty performed almost as well as the other two prostheses.

Inevitably, therefore, it is Neer's work that carries the greatest conviction and authority.

A series published in 1982 [15] contained no less than 273 total shoulder replacements, of which 65 were for rheumatoid arthritis. The special difficulties in dealing with this group of patients are detailed, with particular attention to the rotator cuff and its repair. The surgical technique is carefully explained; the follow-up is quite short.

Surgical technique

A deltopectoral approach is used with care being taken to spare the anterior fibres of deltoid. Only

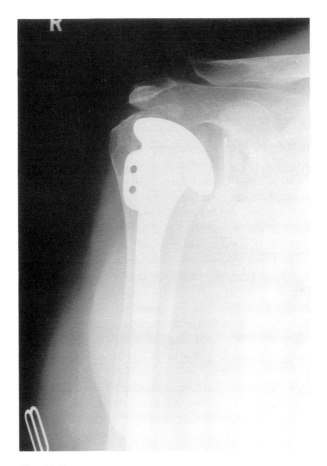

Fig. 22.7

subscapularis is divided. Rotator cuff tears are repaired and great attention is paid to correct tensioning and alignment of the prosthesis.

Difficulties of correctly aligning the glenoid in an eroded bone are discussed and special glenoid components are sometimes used.

Anterior acromioplasty and acromioclavicular arthroplasty are sometimes performed if indicated.

Postoperatively, the arm is placed in a sling and body bandage in normal cases, but an abduction brace should be used if the rotator cuff repair demands it.

Neer has a detailed postoperative rehabilitation programme (Fig. 22.7).

Results

Neer himself reviewed 50 shoulders with rheumatoid arthritis, finding the results to be excellent in

28 and satisfactory in 12, with considerable gains in function and satisfactory relief of pain. Fourteen of these patients had complete rotator cuff tears repaired.

However, Cofield [16] reviewing 77 Neer arthroplasties, of which 29 were for rheumatoid arthritis, reached rather different conclusions. Whilst Neer reported no clinical or definite radiological loosening of the glenoid component, Cofield found eight components definitely loose and 80% of shoulder replacements with a lucent line at the cement bone interface of the scapula. Some of these lucent lines were thought to be significant. Cofield also suggested that the glenoid component needed an improved design. His results were otherwise similar to Neer's.

More recently, Barratt *et al.* [17] have confirmed Cofield's results, finding 10% of radiologically loose glenoid components after $3\frac{1}{2}$ years. They emphasize that osseous support of the glenoid component and functional repair of the rotator cuff are important if glenoid loosening is to be minimized.

Kelly *et al.* [18] deal specifically with rheumatoid arthritis having 42 patients in their series. They note the good relief of pain emphasized in the previous series, 88% of patients had no significant pain. But, for this group, the gains in movement were much more moderate. Elevation was improved by an average of 20°. However, the patients achieved good gains in rotation, leading to an improvement in overall function.

They dispute the significance of the lucent line, that they have also found in 80% of their glenoid components and they were encouraged by the lack of clinical loosening. They expressed doubts about the durability of the glenoid in the long term, however.

The conclusion of all these authors is that non-constrained shoulder arthroplasty merits a place alongside other joint replacements in the surgical management of rheumatoid arthritis. It seems that the 'near anatomical design' of Neer is the one that has proved the most satisfactory in the medium term. There are no cases of humeral component loosening in the series quoted.

Occasionally, cases are mentioned where it has been impossible to implant a glenoid component, but to the author's knowledge, there is no published series of hemiarthroplasties performed for rheumatoid arthritis. Correctly performed, this procedure might have many advantages.

Overall, the objective gains mentioned in series of glenohumeral joint replacements may be small: but all series point out the high patient satisfaction rate.

Recently, the author saw a patient who had undergone shoulder replacement 2 years previously. She was requesting that the other shoulder be similarly treated: a recommendation in itself. The range of movement in the two joints was not dissimilar, however. Certainly the gain from surgery would not have been regarded as statistically significant. The patient, however, had no doubts 'What I can do with the operated arm, I can do comfortably. It makes so much difference', she said.

At present, it is on this limited basis that shoulder replacement surgery should be offered to patients suffering from rheumatoid arthritis.

References

1. Crossan, J. F. and Vallance, R. (1980) Clinical and radiological features of the shoulder joint in rheumatoid disease. *J. Bone Joint Surg.*, **62**, 116.
2. Pahle, J. A. (1981) The shoulder joint in rheumatoid arthritis: synovectomy. *Reconstr. Surg. Traumatol.*, **18**, 33–47.
3. Benjamin, A. (1974) Double osteotomy of the shoulder. *Scand. J. Rheumatol.*, **3**, 65.
4. Wainwright, D. (1974) Glenoidectomy. A method of treating the painful shoulder in rheumatoid arthritis. *Ann. Rheum. Dis.*, **33**, 10.
5. Gariepy, R. (1977) Glenoidectomy in the repair of the rheumatoid shoulder. *J. Bone Joint Surg.*, **59**, 122.
6. Raunio, P. (1981) Arthodesis of the shoulder joint in rheumatoid arthritis. *Reconstr. Surg. Traumatol.*, **18**, 48–54.
7. Neer, C. S. and Kirby, R. M. (1982) Revision of humeral head and shoulder arthroplasties. *Clin. Orthop.*, **170**, 189–195.
8. Varian, J. P. W. (1980) Interposition silastic cup arthroplasty of the shoulder. *J. Bone Joint Surg.*, **62**, 116–117.
9. Neer, C. S. (1955) Articular replacement for the humeral head. *J. Bone Joint Surg.*, **37**, 215.
10. Post, M., Haskell, S. E. and Jablon, M. (1982) Total shoulder replacement with a constrained prosthesis. *J. Bone Joint Surg.*, **62**, 327–335.
11. Beddow, F. H. and Elloy, M. A. (1977) *The Liverpool Total Replacement for the Gleno-Humeral Joint.* Mech. Eng. Publications pp. 21–25.

12. Kessel, L. and Bayley, I. (1979) Prosthetic replacement of the shoulder joint. *J. R. Soc. Med.*, **72**, 748.

13. Lettin, A. (1981) Shoulder replacement in rheumatoid arthritis. *Reconstr. Surg. Traumatol.*, **18**, 55–62.

14. Bodey, W. N. and Yeoman, P. M. (1983) Prosthetic arthroplasty of the shoulder. *Acta Orthop. Scand.*, **54**, 900–903.

15. Neer, C. S. (1982) Recent experience in total shoulder replacement. *J. Bone Joint Surg.*, **64A**, 319–337.

16. Cofield, R. H. (1984) Total shoulder arthroplasty with the Neer prosthesis. *J. Bone Joint Surg.*, **66A**, 899.

17. Barrett, W. P. *et al.* (1987) Total shoulder arthroplasty. *J. Bone Joint Surg.*, **69A**, 865.

18. Kelly, I. G., Foster, R. S. and Fisher, W. D. (1987) Neer total shoulder replacement in rheumatoid arthritis. *J. Bone Joint Surg.*, **69B**, 723.

23

Rheumatoid arthritis of the elbow

P. M. Yeoman

Rheumatoid arthritis is a generalized disease affecting almost all the tissues in the body, and so it should not come as any surprise that the elbow is affected in more than 50% of patients. That does not mean that all require treatment and indeed only a relatively few of the total come to surgery. It is only during the last 15 years that arthroplasty of the elbow has been developed; before the start of this era only a fairly limited number of operations was available and some are still performed with success.

The aim of treatment for patients with rheumatoid arthritis is directed towards the relief of pain; sadly, it is not yet possible to provide a cure by any means. Surgical treatment has to be incorporated into the management of the patient as a whole and is thus regarded as a milestone within the overall medical care. Pain relief by surgical methods is naturally an important aim, but it is not the prime achievement because that can only be guaranteed by robbing the patient of function. In other words, pain could be relieved by an arthrodesis which theoretically would abolish the pain, but in practice it could be a very difficult procedure, fraught with problems and would not contribute to the function of the limb; indeed the patient's existence would be converted from one crippled life to a worse one.

The aims of surgical treatment for the rheumatoid elbow are to provide movement and stability – pain relief will be a bonus.

Movement

The main function of the elbow is to enable the hand to be placed at the optimum position for the patient's use which might be at an angle less than 90° when eating or greater when writing at a desk. Rotation of the forearm has to accompany the range of flexion and extension of the elbow. There are therefore two planes of movement to be considered [1].

Stability

If bone at the elbow is removed either at operation or by disease then the joint will become unstable because the articular surfaces are so designed to provide inherent stability, the surrounding ligaments support the joint but are better served to act as checks against excessive movement. The degree of instability not only depends on the site of bone destruction but its extent. The joint can be transposed into a flail structure, lacking in any direction and resulting in severe loss of function.

Elbow movement and stability related to the entire upper limb

It would be a relatively easy exercise to plan surgical reconstruction of the elbow as an isolated joint, but there are severe restraints on elbow function depending on the shoulder, wrist and hand. For example, a stiff and painful shoulder would mean that rotary movements of the limb would be transferred to the elbow; similarly, a fixed deformity of the forearm or wrist would have the same undesirable effect. In either case the resulting rotary stress imposed on the elbow might hasten the demise of any arthroplasty.It is therefore of importance to restore some part or all of the original function of the elbow without introducing another. Rotary function of the upper limb is just as important as any other but it has to be restored at the wrist, shoulder or both.

Surgical procedures at the elbow

Excision of the olecranon bursa

This is not just a simple little operation because almost invariably the bursa communicates with the joint, and somewhere in the history there may have been some minor infection. The patient may have been gently coerced into agreeing to this minor event as a day case, but the bursa is full of black ingratitude not only for the surgeon but for the patient who may have to endure a long period of repeated dressings because of a sinus; antibiotic cover is essential and the whole affair may result in endless delay for a proposed arthroplasty.

Resection of the head of radius

The indications for this procedure should be confined to those patients with painful restriction of rotation of the forearm, tenderness over the head of radius and only minor erosions on the radiographs. The operation can combine a limited synovectomy from a lateral approach but it must be emphasized that it is unwise to embark on this operation if the disease displays a destructive process in other joints, because it will progress relentlessly in the elbow and rapidly convert it into a useless unstable joint. The early reports of this operation were good, but alas the joints tended to deteriorate after 4 or 5 years [2], and it is only used as a short term palliative procedure.

Arthroplasty

Assessment of the patient's needs are paramount and the important factors are described by Dunkerley in his chapter on the treatment of the wrist and hand; those factors apply to the elbow. The most difficult decision relates to weight-bearing, either at the first consultation with the patient or in the future depending on the activity of the disease. Most of the essential needs of the patient can be restored by an arthroplasty, and these will include feeding, washing, management at the lavatory and gentle housework; all of which are necessary for an independent life.

Moderate weight-bearing may be required to rise out of a chair but a spring loaded seat will ease this burden. Similarly, the patient's needs are better assessed by an expert who is either a physiotherapist or an occupational therapist.

Heavy weight-bearing is the real problem. Walking with the aid of one stick implies that only a small fraction of the body weight is transferred through the upper limb, but the need for two sticks or crutches will throw a great strain on the elbows. It is questionable whether any prosthesis will last the course if the body weight has to be taken regularly through the elbow because the demands upon it and the bone interface would lead to early loosening.

Interposition arthroplasty

This is the prototype of most arthroplasties and has a long history. Many materials have been used to cover the roughened articular surfaces varying from relatively inert gold foil to living triceps muscle. The author reported a series using silastic sheeting; the early results were encouraging but after 3 years the silastic sheet became brittle and tended to fragment. The method was abandoned but not before admiring the better results obtained by using a thicker piece of plastic designed by Helal [4].

Unconstrained prosthesis

The pioneer work by Lowe and later by Roper [5] produced a relatively simple prosthesis with minimal bone resection, but it was soon evident that a stem was necessary for either the ulnar or humeral component because of loosening. The early results were very good but either they were used when the bone stock was poor or the disease progressed and only about 50% success could be secured. This type of prosthesis is still an excellent method for the relief of pain in those patients with good bone stock and no obvious destructive traits in the disease.

Semi-constrained prosthesis

The various designs of semi-constrained prostheses have built-in mobility not only in the lateral but also in the rotary plane [6]. Greater emphasis on the importance of the medial collateral ligament is made by Souter, who considers that rotary forces are checked by this ligament, thus reducing the enormous stress imposed on any prosthesis when heavy objects are being lifted. The ligaments must be restored and this is very necessary if the surgical approach involves detachment of the ligament from the bone. Similarly, if bone is resected then the tension in the ligaments has to be readjusted after insertion of the prosthesis. These principles may appear elementary but have been founded on the causes for loosening.

Ulnar nerve entrapment is an occasional complication of the rheumatoid elbow due to pressure from the tense synovium, but there is a surprisingly high incidence of ulnar nerve lesions resulting from arthroplasty [7]. The author invariably dissects out the nerve as one of the important initial procedures and the nerve should be protected during the entire operation.

The Soutter–Strathclyde prosthesis has been in use for nearly 13 years and the results are impressive. This prosthesis has varying sizes for left and right sides, also various lengths of stem and snap-fit components for use when there has been extensive bone loss and instability.

The tri-axial prosthesis has been used with success by the author for mildly unstable elbows resulting from extensive articular cartilage erosions. The snap-fit connection provides immediate stability and at least 60° of movement can be guaranteed. Rotation of the forearm is not always so successful and it may be necessary to resect the lower end of the ulna in order to restore a useful 90° range of rotation.

Hinge prosthesis

The idea of a straight or even an offset hinge mechanism to replace the elbow is contrary to the accepted movements of the joint. The shearing strains imposed on the prosthesis will undoubtedly cause loosening of one or both components; but this is not the only failure. If the stem and/or cement interface revolve within the bone this will lead to serious loss of bone stock. The stem may penetrate the softened cortical bone or a fracture may develop; these consequences are tragic when they arise in patients who are already severely handicapped by the disease and the results of revision arthroplasty are not particularly inviting [8]. This complication can be avoided by a careful assessment of the patient's disease process, their needs and proper selection of prosthesis. The hinge does not fulfil the requirements.

The stiff shoulder

It is quite apparent that a patient with a stiff painful shoulder has to transfer much of the rotation strains on to the elbow in order to achieve any reasonable function in the upper limb. The best solution is to proceed with an arthroplasty of the shoulder and reassess the function at a later date.

References

1. Torzilli, P. A. (1982) Biomechanics of the elbow. Am. Acad. Orthop. Surg. *Symposium on Total Joint Replacement of the Upper Extremity.* C. V. Mosby, New York, p. 150.
2. Summers, G. D., Webley, W. and Taylor, A. R. (1987) Synovectomy and excision of the radial head in rheumatoid arthritis: a short term palliative procedure. *Clin. Exp. Rheumatol.*, **5**. (Suppl. 2), 115.

3. Yeoman, P. M. (1979) Arthroplasty of the elbow in rheumatoid arthritis using a silastic sheet insert. *J. Bone Joint Surg.*, **61B**, 123.

4. Coates, C. J., Bolton-Maggs, B. G. and Helal, B. H. (1990) Interpositional arthroplasty in the management of rheumatoid arthritis of the elbow. *Rheumatology*, **15(8)**, 1.

5. Roper, B. A., Tuke, M., O'Riordan, S. M. and Bulstrode, C. J. (1986) A new unconstrained elbow. *J. Bone Joint Surg.*, **68B 4**, 566.

6. Inglis, A. E. (1982) Tri-axial elbow replacement: indications, surgical techniques and results. Am. Acad. Orthop. Surg. *Symposium on Total Joint Replacement of the Upper Extremity*. C. V. Mosby, New York, p. 100.

7. Souter, W. A. (1988) In *Surgical Management of Rheumatoid Arthritis*. Wright, London, p. 69.

8. Morrey, B. F. and Bryan, R. S. (1987) Revision total elbow arthroplasty. *J. Bone Joint Surg.*, **69A 4**, 523.

24

Rheumatoid arthritis of the wrist and hand

D. R. Dunkerley

This is a difficult field of hand surgery. Any or all of the many articulations of the hand and wrist, and of the tendons and muscles, may be involved in the disease process. Certain patterns of deformity are seen; the surgeon must be familiar with the patho-mechanics of these deformities. Greater than usual care is required in the selection of patients for surgery, the performance of the operations and the postoperative management.

For each patient the following factors must be assessed:

1. The state of the joints and the function of both upper limbs.

2. The function of both lower limbs. Are the hands required to assist in walking?

3. Timing. While it is not technically wrong to operate while the patient is undergoing a 'flare-up' of his arthritis, it can be unkind, in that the patient may feel unwell either from the arthritis or the treatment. Hand surgery is best deferred if lower limb surgery is contemplated, since crutches or a frame may be required postoperatively.

While hand and wrist operations can be performed under regional nerve block, general anaesthesia is occasionally necessary, for which the anaesthetist must be assured of cervical spine stability. Cervical spine stabilization may therefore need to take precedence, especially if long tract signs are present. The introduction of laryngeal mask airway has, however, greatly reduced the hazards of operating on patients with stiff necks.

4. The patient's ambitions and determination. One needs to know what the patient wants to be able to do, and whether he has the determination to go through with an exacting programme of operations and postoperative therapy.

All this takes time: time to get to know the patient and to give him confidence. Patients with rheumatoid disease are often very trusting of their doctors, and are inclined to accept advice uncritically. This means that the surgeon has an extra responsibility to explain honestly the advantages and disadvantages of surgery.

5. Examination of the hand and wrist. The examination should be more than a catalogue of joint movements or deformities. The mechanism of deformity should be in the examiner's mind and thus govern which features he looks for. It is convenient to examine the following sequence: wrist and inferior radio-ulnar joint, extensor tendons, metacarpophalangeal joints, interphalangeal joints, thumb, flexor tendons. The fingers should be examined for evidence of digital arteritis (Fig. 24.1), a contraindication to hand surgery. The stage of the disease should be noted.

A full assessment must include radiographs, particularly when surgery is contemplated.

6. The patient's manual function. Pain, deformity and functional loss are not always related. It is helpful to have a detailed assessment by an occupational therapist. Great care must be taken to ensure that surgery does not impair function already present.

The hand must be considered as a whole but in the following sections the patho-mechanics of

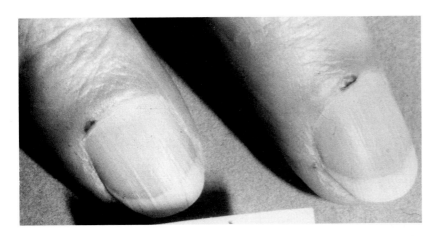

Fig. 24.1 Nail-fold lesions in digital arteritis.

deformity and surgical treatment of each part are, for convenience, considered separately.

The wrist, inferior radio-ulnar joint and extensor tendons

Rheumatoid synovitis may first appear in either the radiocarpal joint or the inferior radio-ulnar joint; sometimes in both at once. Early radiographic changes may be seen as areas of subchondral rarefaction appearing at the inferior radio-ulnar joint and at the insertions of the radiocarpal ligaments on the scaphoid and triquetrum (Fig. 24.2). Later, attenuation of ligaments and loss of bone height, due to articular cartilage loss and bone compression, results in joint laxity. The tendon sheath of extensor carpi ulnaris is often affected, allowing the tendon to displace forwards until it comes to lie anterior to the axis of wrist flexion.

A series of deformities then develops. The carpus translocates in an ulnar direction on the radius. It often also rotates into radial deviation because of the loss of the stabilizing power of the extensor carpi ulnaris (Fig. 24.3). For the same reason the ulnar side of the carpus drops forwards. Thus, the carpus supinates on the radius. This, coupled with dorsal subluxation of the head of the ulna, produces a hollow distal to the ulnar head (Fig. 24.4). Pronation and supination become restricted and painful. Passive anteroposterior movement of the head of the ulna, the so-called piano-key sign, is painful.

In later stages the anterior part of the radial articular surface erodes. The carpus subluxates anteriorly and proximally (Fig. 24.5). Radiographs may also show a collapse of the midcarpal joint: usually the volar intercalated segment instability (VISI) deformity in which the proximal row of the carpus tilts into flexion and the distal row hyperextends (Fig. 24.6). Hodgson *et al.* [1] have described a staging of the disease based on radiographs.

Stage 1: Peri-articular rarefaction with early erosions. The architecture of the wrist remains well preserved but there may be a little rotatory instability of the scaphoid.

Stage 2: While the mid-carpal and radioscaphoid joints are well preserved one or more of the following deformities may be present:

    a. ulnar translocation
    b. palmar flexion of the lunate
    c. flexion deformity of the scaphoid
    d. deterioration of the radio-lunate joint

Stage 3: The mid-carpal joint shows evidence of degeneration. There is degeneration in the radio-scaphoid joint. The carpus subluxes forward on the radius and there may be pseudo cyst formation of the volar lip of the radius.

Stage 4: There is erosion of the volar edge of the distal radius and bone loss in the region of the inferior radio-ulnar joint.

Synovitis of the digital extensor tendons is common in the region of the extensor retinaculum. The synovium may bulge distally and proximally; the distal edge of the bulge can be seen to move as the fingers are flexed and extended.

Rupture of the extensor tendons, including

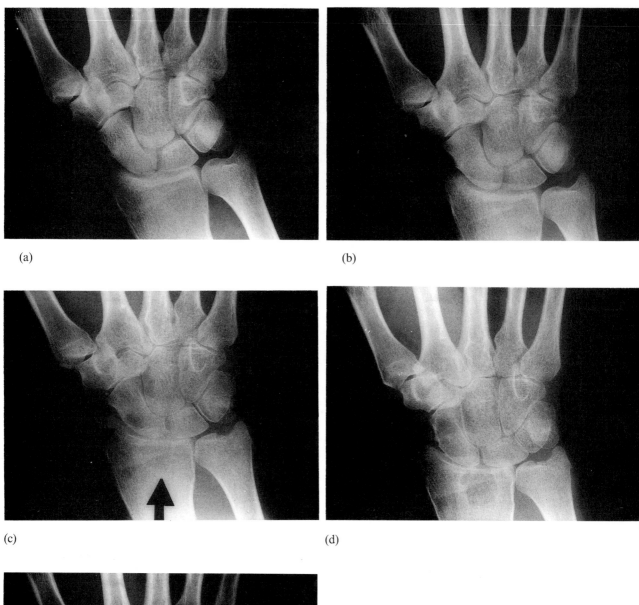

(a)

(b)

(c)

(d)

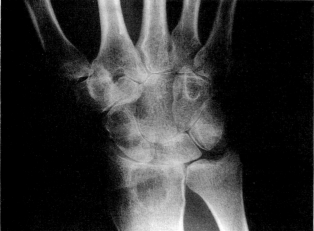

(e)

Fig. 24.2   (a–g) Radiographs taken at 1-year intervals to show progression of rheumatoid disease in the wrist. (a) Normal, (b) early rarefaction of scaphoid-lunate and inferior radio-ulnar joint surfaces, (c) more obvious lesions of scaphoid, radial styloid, radial articular surface and lunate, (d) loss of joint space in radiocarpal joint, erosion of radial surface of scaphoid, early ulnar shift of carpus, (e), (f), (g) rapid progression.

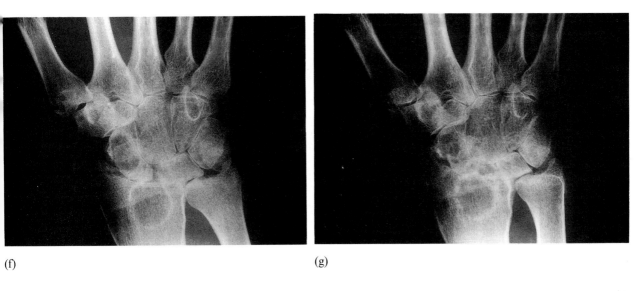

(f)   (g)

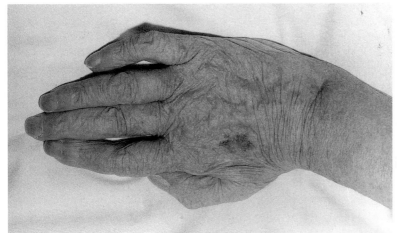

Fig. 24.3   Radial deviation deformity of
the wrist.

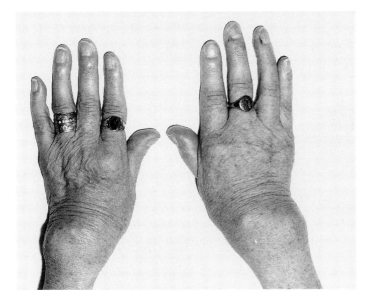

Fig. 24.4   Hollow distal to ulnar head due to
carpal supination on the radius.

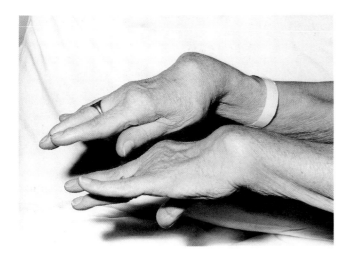

Fig. 24.5 Anterior subluxation of carpus on radius.

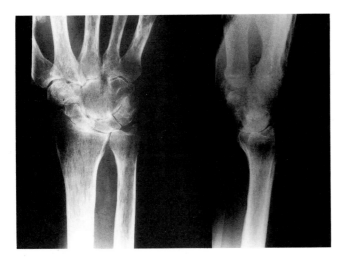

Fig. 24.6 VISI deformity of carpus.

Fig. 24.7 Rupture of extensor tendons to thumb, ring and little fingers.

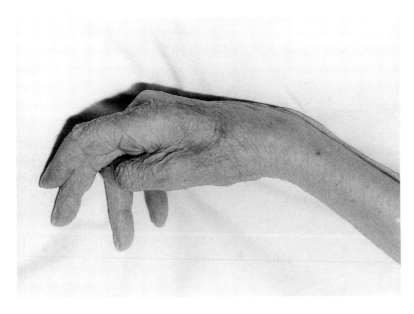

extensor pollicis longus, may occur. Usually, in the fingers, the little finger tendons rupture first, followed at intervals by the others in order. Rupture is often painless (Fig. 24.7).

There are several causes of rupture. It may be due to attrition of the tendons on spikes of bone arising from the eroded ulnar head or radius. The tendons may be invaded by rheumatoid synovium. Ischaemia due to pressure of the mass of synovium under the retinaculum may play a part. Sometimes the two ends of a ruptured tendon are found at operation to be joined by a narrow tube of paratenon.

Surgical treatment

There is a standard surgical approach which gives good access to all these areas. A straight longitudinal incision is made over the midline of the dorsum of the wrist. A straight incision produces less wound healing problems than a sinuous incision. It is deepened down to the extensor retinaculum, preserving the dorsal branches of the radial nerve and ligating as few veins as possible. By gauze dissection the flaps can be reflected at the level between the superficial fascia and retinaculum. The retinaculum is reflected as a flap, usually from ulnar to radial side, and is left attached to the radius between the extensor carpi radialis longus and extensor pollicis brevis tendons. A tongue of the extensor retinaculum can be fashioned on the ulnar side during the reflection. During closure this tongue can be looped round the tendon of the extensor carpi ulnaris to maintain its dorsal position.

Extensor tendons

If the tendons are intact, synovectomy is all that may be required. A very thorough synovectomy may weaken or devascularise the tendons; the synovitis in any case will regress after decompression.

Replacing the retinaculum deep to the tendons decompresses them, protects them from attrition on rough bony edges and diminishes the risk of adhesions.

Ruptured tendons cannot usually be repaired end to end. Tendon transfer or suture of the distal stump to an intact neighbouring tendon is

Table 24.1 Restoration of extensor tendon function

Extensor tendon rupture	Tendon transfer
Little, ring or middle finger alone	Extensor indicis proprius (EIP) transfer
Little and ring fingers	EIP to little finger Attach ring to middle finger tendon
Little, ring and middle fingers	EIP to little Flexor digitorum superficialis (ring) to ring and middle
All four fingers	Flexor digitorum superficialis (ring and middle)
Extensor pollicis longus	EIP or extensor carpi radialis longus

required. A useful plan of treatment is given in Table 24.1.

Tendon transfers from the flexor to the extensor surfaces may be difficult. The flexor digitorum superficialis to the ring finger is most directly routed through a large defect created in the interosseous membrane; some advocate a subcutaneous route via the radial border of the wrist.

Following the operation the MCP joints should be immobilized in extension (with the PIP joints free) for 3 weeks, after which an outrigger splint should be fitted for several weeks.

Inferior radio-ulnar joint

Excision of the lower end of the ulna is one of the most useful and successful procedures in this condition.

Indications for the operation are:

(i) painful subluxation of the head of the ulna,
(ii) severe painful synovitis of the inferior radio-ulnar joint,
(iii) pain or restriction of movement on pronation and supination,
(iv) rupture of one or more extensor tendons.

It is easiest to transect the shaft with a power saw first, about 1.5 cm from the ulnar styloid. The distal stump can be held in a clamp and the soft tissues dissected off the bone.

If this operation alone is performed, post-operative immobilization is unnecessary.

Swanson advocates capping the ulna with a silicone rubber ulnar head prosthesis. Many authors, including the present one, do not find that this procedure confers any benefit and it carries some risk of complications such as dislocation.

Radiocarpal and intercarpal joints

A large number of procedures have been described for the treatment of these joints in rheumatoid disease. Not all have stood the test of time. The following can be recommended:

  (i) Synovectomy
 (ii) Radio-lunate fusion
(iii) Arthrodesis
 (iv) Prosthetic replacement

Synovectomy

Straub and Ranawat [2] described this operation as dorsal wrist stabilisation: essentially a dorsal synovectomy with modifications. The aim of the procedure is a stable, painless, mobile fibrous union.

Extensor tendon and dorsal wrist synovectomy are performed as far as possible. The capsule is carefully repaired and if there is instability crossed k-wires are inserted. The ulnar head is excised. The operation may need to be augmented by transfering the extensor carpi radialis longus tendon to the ulnar side of the hand to restore balance. Plaster support is maintained for 6 weeks; the wires, if used, are removed at 4 weeks. Good results are reported in a long term survey by the originators [3].

The operation is indicated in Stage 1 of the disease. More severely diseased wrists are not suitable for this procedure and arthrodesis or arthroplasty should be considered. Particular contra-indications are fixed deformity, radiocarpal subluxation and a flail joint.

Ishikawa *et al.* [4] have shown that 88% of patients achieve pain relief but there is an increased incidence of ulnar translocation of the carpus.

Radio-lunate fusion

In stage 2 of the disease affecting chiefly the radio-lunate articulation and often accompanied by an ulnar translocation, radio-lunate fusion will confer stability while permitting some movement at the mid-carpal joint. (Chamay *et al.* [5], Stanley and Boot [6] and Ishikawa *et al.* [7]).

Arthrodesis

As in other joints, arthrodesis provides a stable, painless joint without the possibility of future complications. Arthrodesis of the wrist has two further advantages. The wrist functions chiefly in its middle range. Brumfield and Champoux [8] have shown that in normal adults the range of wrist movements required for the activities of daily living is between 35° extension and 10° flexion. Arthrodesis does not, therefore, cause serious loss of function. The other advantage is

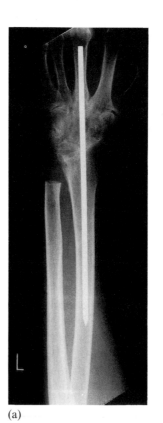 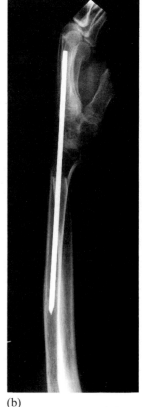

(a)   (b)

Fig. 24.8 Arthrodesis of the wrist using countersunk pin through 3rd metacarpal.

that stabilization of the wrist greatly improves function of the fingers and thumb.

The position in which the wrist should be fused has been the subject of much discussion. The author agrees with Clayton and Ferlic [9] who give good reasons for placing the wrist in a position of 10° of ulnar deviation with neutral flexion-extension.

The technique [10] involves exposing the dorsum of the joints, excising the remains of the articular cartilage, and correcting any collapse of the mid-carpal joint in order to maintain the length. The wrist is then transfixed with a Steinmann's pin driven down the shaft of the third metacarpal and across the wrist into the shaft of the radius (Fig. 24.8). The pin is countersunk into the metacarpal. If any rotational instability remains, a staple or oblique K-wire can be added. To achieve ulnar deviation it may be necessary to put the pin through the radial side of the third metacarpal shaft or between the bases of the second and third metacarpals (Fig. 24.9). Plaster

immobilization for 4–6 weeks is only required if there is still some joint mobility at the end of the operation.

Replacement arthroplasty

This operation is designed to combine pain relief with limited wrist motion. The best results are obtained in the relatively less damaged wrists. The operation is contraindicated in patients who will put heavy stress on the wrists, for example when walking with crutches, in wrists where the bone stock is inadequate to support the prosthesis or where there is severe deformity, especially fixed flexion and subluxation. A particular contraindication to wrist arthroplasty is rupture of the wrist extensor tendons.

Three prostheses have been in use long enough for long-term follow-up reviews to become available. The Volz and Meuli prostheses are true arthroplasties with their respective components cemented into the radius and metacarpus. Swanson [11] developed a one-piece flexible Silastic® implant designed to be a spacer (Fig. 24.10).

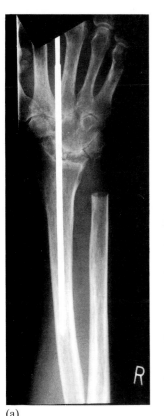 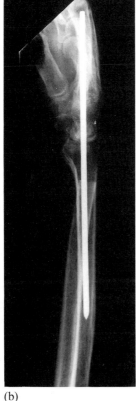

(a)   (b)

Fig. 24.9 Arthrodesis of the wrist using pin between 2nd and 3rd metacarpals.

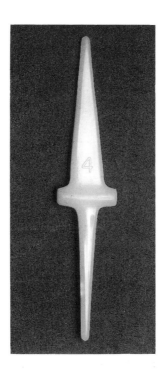

Fig. 24.10 Swanson Silastic® flexible wrist implant.

The Silastic® is soft which protects the bone; on the other hand it is, itself, susceptible to damage from the bone edges and recently Swanson has introduced metal grommets to protect the prosthesis. So far long term studies of this effect are not available.

All these operations are difficult; they require meticulous attention to the positioning of the prosthesis, tendon balance and post-operative care. On the published evidence the Swanson prosthesis, which is the most widely used, leads to fewer complications. The results of all three deteriorate in time.

Advising a patient between arthroplasty and arthrodesis is not always easy. Where arthroplasty and arthrodesis have been compared (sometimes in the same patient) arthroplasty tends to have the advantage in terms of patient acceptability and objective examination.

In planning treatment it can be said that in mild cases of rheumatoid disease with synovitis, the dorsal stabilization is indicated. In more severe cases, where the contraindications to arthroplasty enumerated above do not exist, either arthrodesis or arthroplasty may be chosen, but a successsful arthroplasty is better. Where arthroplasty is clearly contraindicated, arthrodesis is required.

Where both wrists require treatment the best procedure, if possible, is to perform an arthroplasty of the dominant wrist and arthrodesis of the other. The subject is well reviewed by Vicar and Burton [12].

Metacarpophalangeal joints

Synovitis in its early stages can be severe and painful; later the characteristic deformities of ulnar deviation and palmar subluxation occur. A simple staging of the deformities is a follows:

Stage 1: Early ulnar drift alone.
Stage 2: Ulnar drift with palmar subluxation but an intact joint.
Stage 3: Ulnar drift with palmar subluxation and joint damage.

While the primary cause of these problems is attenuation of the ligaments and joint damage, the deformities are produced by unbalanced forces. These may be summarized as follows:

Normal anatomy

The metacarpophalangeal joints have considerable mobility when in extension, allowing sideways and rotary movements. The radial collateral ligaments are longer than the ulnar. In the index and middle finger metacarpals, the slope of the articular surfaces allows more ulnar than radial deviation, and in these fingers the line of the long flexor and extensor tendons means that they tend to pull to the ulnar side.

It has been shown that when the radial and ulnar interossei are stimulated equally the pull of the ulnar inserted muscles is stronger. The arrangement in the little finger means that the powerful abductor digiti minimi muscle is opposed only by the weak third palmar interosseus.

Normal use

In lateral pinch grip the thumb forces the fingers into ulnar deviation. As the radial collateral ligament weakens, the fingers are deviated more. When a tight fist is made, the little and ring fingers become ulnar deviated as the fourth and fifth metacarpals are flexed.

Pathological changes

The radial side of the extensor hood is thinner than the ulnar, and more easily stretched by the synovial proliferation. The extensor tendon is thus allowed to deviate to the ulnar side, and in its extreme position comes to lie in the valley between the metacarpal heads. Adaptive shortening or adhesion of the ulnar intrinsics may occur.

As the joint deviates, the volar plate/transverse metacarpal ligament complex moves ulnarwards, carrying the entrance to the fibrous flexor sheath with it. The flexor tendons then accentuate the ulnar pull. As the extensor apparatus weakens and displaces, the powerful flexors, obtaining a greater moment of force as they are distanced from the metacarpal head, add to the palmar subluxation.

It has been postulated that an external force acting on the metacarpophalangeal joints is the effect produced by radial deviation of the wrist (Fig. 24.11). The metacarpal may be regarded as

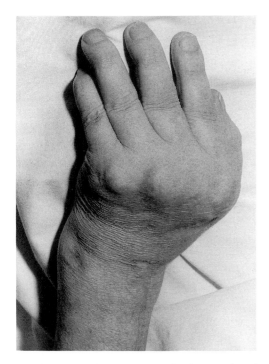

Fig. 24.11 Radial deviation of wrist associated with ulnar deviation of metacarpophalangeal joints.

an intercalated bone in a chain of bones controlled by the long tendons. Once a sideways collapse is permitted at one joint, a zigzag reaction occurs. Thus radial wrist deviation contributes to the opposite, ulnar, deviation force at the metacarpophalangeal joint. However, it is possible that patients hold the wrist in radial deviation to bring the ulnar deviated fingers into line with the forearm.

Surgical treatment

Arthrodesis is never indicated here. The aim is to provide mobile, stable, painless joints. As with many operations for this disease a compromise must be accepted between mobility and stability, and it is rare to achieve 90° of movement with complete stability.

Stage 1. Early ulnar drift alone

Since the joint is intact and there is no palmar subluxation, the aim of surgery is to realign the forces acting on the joint. Synovectomy alone will render the joint more comfortable and increase mobility but it does not correct the ulnar drift or prevent the progression of the disease in the long term.

A mid-line longitudinal dorsal skin incision is deepened through the radial extensor hood. The extensor expansion is reflected off the capsule, which is opened. Synovectomy should be thorough with particular attention paid to removing synovium from between the collateral ligaments and metacarpal head, and from the dorsal lip of the base of the proximal phalanx. It is often difficult to preserve the capsule.

After synovectomy the extensor tendon is centred over the metacarpal head by plicating the radial hood over the dorsum of the tendon. The intrinsic tendons on the ulnar side, including abductor digiti minimi, should be released.

A stronger correction can be provided by crossed intrinsic transfer in which the detached ulnar intrinsic wing is sutured into the radial intrinsic wing of the adjoining finger.

Stage 2. Ulnar drift and palmar subluxation with an intact joint

The procedures for stage 1 can be augmented by the extensor loop operation [13] in which a strip from the centre of the extensor tendon is passed through a drill hole in the dorsal lip of the base of the proximal phalanx and sutured back on itself (Fig. 24.12).

Stage 3. Ulnar drift with palmar subluxation and joint damage

Arthroplasty is required here. The various excision arthroplasties favoured in the 1960s have been replaced by implant arthroplasties. The silicone prostheses of Swanson or Niebauer have emerged as superior to hinged prostheses for this joint. The silicone prostheses are essentially spacers permitting flexion and extension and conferring limited lateral stability. Alone, they do not prevent recurrence of the deformities. Original articles should be consulted for operative details [14,15].

Good functional and cosmetic results can be obtained and late complications are uncommon. However, to achieve good results meticulous

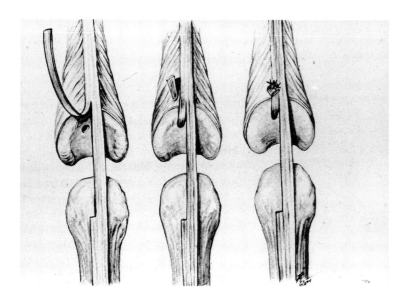

Fig. 24.12   Harrison extensor loop operation. (From Harrison S. H. (1971) *Br. J. Plast. Surg., 24,* 307.)

attention to detail is required, both in the performance of the operation and in the postoperative management.

Interphalangeal joints

Two main deformities are common in rheumatoid disease, swan-neck (Fig. 24.13) and fixed flexion. Both may occur in the same hand.

Swan-neck deformity

The primary causes of the deformity are, with one exception, found in the proximal interphalangeal joint. Hyperextension develops as a result of one or more factors. In normal individuals, hyperextension may occur if congenital joint laxity is present, or after division or excision of the flexor digitorum superficialis tendon. Either of these make swan-neck deformity more likely in a patient with rheumatoid disease. The rheumatoid process can weaken the volar plate and accessory collateral ligaments, and may itself cause dysfunction of flexor digitorum superficialis.

External forces may then accentuate the deformity. Intrinsic tendon tightness is found in a proportion of swan-neck digits, usually secondary to metacarpophalangeal joint disease with ulnar deviation and palmar subluxation. Shapiro [16] points out that loss of length at the wrist, due to a combination of true loss of carpal height and

proximal erosion of the radial articular surface, causes the long flexors and extensors to become less efficient, producing an 'extrinsic-minus' effect.

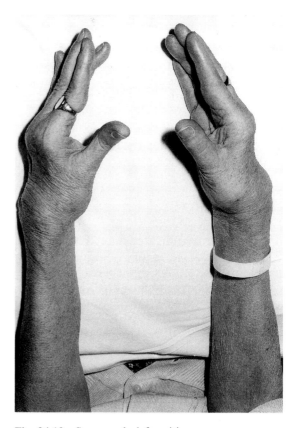

Fig. 24.13   Swan-neck deformities.

Mallet finger is the one exception to the statement that PIP joint disease is the first cause of the deformity. In non-rheumatoid patients with familial joint laxity, mallet finger can produce a secondary swan-neck deformity. This can also happen in rheumatoid disease where the PIP joint is weakened. The loss of tension in the distal extensor tendon allows maximum force to be exerted through the central slip. At the same time, the oblique retinacular ligament is relaxed, and the normal flexion sequence thus broken.

As the deformity progresses the transverse retinacular ligaments stretch, permitting the lateral bands of the extensor apparatus to migrate dorsally until they come to lie dorsal to the axis of rotation of the PIP joint when the joint is extended. They later lose the ability to move in a palmar direction during active finger flexion. In the hyperextended position of the PIP joint the lateral slips are relaxed allowing the DIP joint to droop. With a greater degree of PIP hyperextension the oblique retinacular ligaments come to lie dorsal to the axis of the PIP joint, which finally destroys the flexion sequence of the finger.

When the finger is examined, therefore, the condition of the wrist, MCP joint, long flexor and extensor tendons and intrinsic tendons should be noted. Nalebuff and Millender [17] have described four stages or types of the deformity; their classification is particularly useful because it relates to functional loss (Table 24.2).

Table 24.2   Classification of swan-neck deformity [13]

Type 1: The PIP joint is flexible in all positions of the MCP joint. The MCP joint is usually not seriously affected. Functional loss is slight.

Type 2: PIP flexion is limited when the MCP joint is held in extension or radial deviation, due to a tight ulnar intrinsic. This may follow untreated type 1 deformity or be secondary to MCP joint subluxation.

Type 3: PIP joint flexion is limited in all positions of the MCP joint, but the PIP joint is well preserved on X-ray. Here functional loss is more severe: tip to tip pinch is impossible and the patient develops the 'long pinch' with thumb and fingers extended.

Type 4: PIP joint stiffness with radiological intra-articular damage.

Treatment depends on the stage at which the deformity is seen. Nalebuff and Millender [17] described a series of operations for each type of deformity, but this has been simplified by Souter [18].

The aim of treatment in types 1–3 is to restore active controlled PIP flexion where possible. This can easily be achieved in types 1 and 2 but is more difficult in type 3. The basic operation is a tenodesis on the volar surface of the finger to prevent hyperextension; this can be achieved by either a retinacular ligament reconstruction [19] or a tethering using a slip of flexor digitorum superficialis.

In type 1 the tenodesis alone is sufficient. If the primary cause is a mallet finger, the DIP joint should be fused.

Where the metacarpophalangeal pathology is contributory to the type 2 deformity it should be treated as described above. During this procedure the tight ulnar intrinsic will be released. Tenodesis of the PIP joint will also be required.

Difficulties arise in type 3 because the joint is fixed in hyperextension. This is due to a combination of tight dorsal skin, adherent extensor expansion and tight collateral ligaments. Nalebuff and Millender [17] described a technique for releasing the skin by leaving an oblique incision open on the dorsum of the middle phalanx and allowing it to heal without skin graft. The expansion should be mobilized and the lateral bands allowed to displace volarwards. The central slip may need to be lengthened and the collateral ligaments mobilized. By gentle manipulation flexion can be restored.

Of the two procedures for effecting a tenodesis, the Littler is easier but weaker than the technique utilising a slip of flexor digitorum superficialis. In the Littler technique a strip is mobilized from the lateral edge of one lateral slip. It is left attached distally; the other end is passed volar to Cleland's ligament. Two incisions are made in the flexor sheath at the proximal phalanx level, the strip is passed through them and sutured to itself with the joint held in 45° of flexion. This may seem excessive at the time but stretching of the tenodesis will occur.

The alternative is to mobilize a distally attached strip of flexor digitorum superficialis, taking care that one slip remains intact and the vinculum brevis is not damaged. The strip is passed through a drill hole in the proximal phalanx. After either procedure, the joint is splinted for 4–6 weeks. An extension block splint is used, permitting flexion but restricting extension to 45°.

In type 4, arthrodesis of the PIP joint is the treatment of choice. This may be effected using a Harrison–Nicolle intramedullary peg [20].

Fixed flexion deformity (Boutonnière)

The problem always lies in the PIP joint where synovitis leads to stretching or rupture of the central slip of the extensor tendon. As the PIP joint falls into flexion, hyperextension of the DIP joint occurs. At first this is a secondary effect due to tendon imbalance, but shortening and adhesion of the lateral slips leads to a fixed hyperextension deformity. Initially the patient can oppose to the thumb; later, functional loss occurs because the finger is too flexed to oppose and cannot be extended to grasp.

In the first stage the patient develops an extensor lag at the PIP joint which is often swollen. The lag can be passively corrected. Functional loss, if any, is caused by inability to flex the DIP joint actively. although passive flexion is possible.

In stage 2, the PIP joint deformity worsens and the DIP hyperextension becomes fixed. Finally, the PIP joint becomes fixed in 70–90° of flexion. As the deformity progresses, compensatory hyperextension of the MCP joint develops.

Examination is therefore directed to noting the degree of synovitis of the PIP joint, the degree of active and passive loss of the PIP and DIP joint movements and the actual functional loss. The PIP joint should be radiographed.

In the early stages treatment may be non-surgical. Steroid injection of the PIP joint should be undertaken with the aims of correcting deformity and restoring active movement. The multiplicity of operation described for this deformity in non-rheumatoid patients testifies to the difficulties of achieving a good result. The difficulties are not less in rheumatoid disease.

The steps of the operation are to remove the synovium, tighten or reconstruct the central slip and relocate the lateral bands dorsal to the PIP joint axis. It may be necessary to lengthen or divide the extensor tendon over the middle phalanx to permit active flexion of the DIP joint.

The exact technique will need to be adapted to the findings at operation. Most surgeons use a basic operation, with appropriate variations, and the present author finds Rothwell's [21] operation effective.

When there is joint or irreparable soft tissue damage, arthrodesis of the PIP joint in 30° flexion is an excellent salvage procedure. The extensor tendon should be divided over the middle phalanx to restore active flexion of the distal joint.

The thumb

The problems caused by finger deformities are compounded when the thumb is diseased. A recent survey showed that 60% of thumbs examined were abnormal.

All three joints should be examined, clinically and radiologically, paying attention to the function of the long tendons and intrinsic muscles.

The patterns of thumb deformity in rheumatoid disease have been worked out [22]. These can be simplified by classifying deformities according to the state of the metacarpophalangeal joint.

Flexion deformity at the metacarpophalangeal joint

This is the most commonly seen deformity (Fig. 24.14). At first the deformity is mobile; the joint may be subluxated. Because of the alteration in the pull of the intrinsics the interphalangeal joint

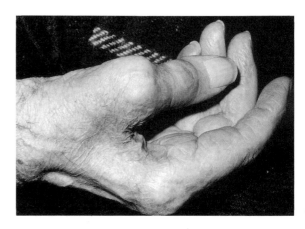

Fig. 24.14   Thumb: type 1: flexion deformity.

becomes hyperextended and after a while the ability to flex this joint is lost.

If, however, the examiner holds the metacarpophalangeal joint in extension, active interphalangeal flexion is at once restored. If it is not, a rupture of the flexor pollicis longus tendon should be considered.

At a later stage both joints become fixed. Before deciding on treatment the function of the carpometacarpal joint must be noted.

Hyperextension deformity of the metacarpophalangeal joint

Here, the deformity of the metacarpophalangeal joint is secondary to a flexed and adducted posture of the first metacarpal caused by disease in

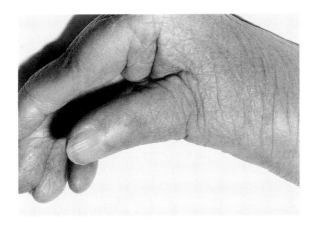

Fig. 24.15 Thumb: type 2: hyperextension deformity.

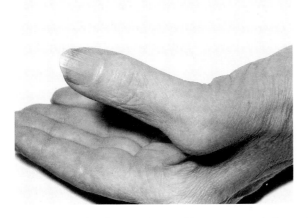

Fig. 24.16 Thumb: type 3: unstable metacarpophalangeal joint.

the carpometacarpal joint. As in swan-neck deformity of the fingers, the terminal interphalangeal joint adopts a flexed position (Fig. 24.15).

Instability of the metacarpophalangeal joint

The whole joint may become loose; laxity of the ulnar collateral ligament is particularly disabling. The interphalangeal joint is also prone to become flail, either alone or as well as the metacarpophalangeal joint (Fig. 24.16).

Surgery

The aim of surgery is to provide a firm post to which the fingers can oppose; of course the fingers may also need surgery to achieve this. One should aim to retain mobility of at least one joint, which ideally should be the carpometacarpal joint. Provided this joint moves, fusion of the other joints is compatible with good function.

Flexion deformity at the metacarpophalangeal joint

Where the deformity is mobile and the joint well preserved the operation described by Nalebuff [23] can be used. The tendon of extensor pollicis longus is passed through the insertion of extensor pollicis brevis and tightened until the deformity is corrected. In more advanced cases with fixed deformity or joint damage, arthrodesis is indicated.

If the interphalangeal joint has become fixed in hyperextension it will need to be fused in 10–20° of flexion.

Hyperextension deformity of the metacarpophalangeal joint

Since disease at the carpometacarpal joint is the primary source of the deformity, this joint should be tackled first. It must not be arthrodesed; arthroplasty with correction of the first web contracture is required. The contracture can usually be released by incising the dorsal aponeurosis over the web, parallel to the first metacarpal. A Z-plasty of the skin of the web may be required.

Fig. 24.17   Swanson Silastic trapezium implant.

The choice of arthroplasty may be difficult. The Swanson Silastic® trapezium implant is designed to articulate with the scaphoid (Fig. 24.17). In rheumatoid disease the scaphoid may be severely damaged, or have been partly resected for a wrist implant. Alternative procedures are to insert a rolled-up tendon, usually palmaris longus, or to use a Swanson convex condylar implant.

Arthrodesis of the other joints of the thumb may be needed to give pulp to pulp opposition.

Instability of the metacarpophalangeal joint

A ruptured ulnar collateral ligament can be reconstructed using a strip of extensor pollicis brevis passed through appropriate drill holes in the bones. However, a degree of rheumatoid invasion sufficient to cause laxity of the ligament usually damages the joint surfaces, and arthrodesis is required.

Flexor tendons

Rheumatoid involvement of the flexor tendons occurs at the site of the synovial coverings. Synovitis may produce restricted movement due to pain, adhesions, triggering and rupture of tendons. In the carpal tunnel the swelling may lead to median nerve compression. Barnes and Currey [24] found that 53% of 45 patients with rheumatoid arthritis had clinical evidence of carpal tunnel syndrome, and a further 16% had impairment of nerve conduction without clinical manifestations.

The carpal tunnel, palm and digits should be examined for swelling and tenderness. The active range of finger flexion may be less than the passive range, which is pathognomonic of flexor synovitis. Digital flexor synovitis may cause the interphalangeal joints to be held in flexion, and the joints can develop fixed deformity due to secondary changes in the periarticular structures. Triggering, if present, is due to nodules catching either at the entrance to the fibrous flexor sheath, limiting flexor digitorum superficialis excursion, or at the superficialis decussation, limiting profundus excursion. Gross digital synovitis stretches the fibrous flexor sheath.

Tendon ruptures may occur, usually in the carpal tunnel or in the palm. They may be clinically disguised by matting of tendons to one another or by the much reduced excursion of all the tendons. The possible causes of rupture have been enumerated by Mannerfelt and Norman [25] as:

(i) granulomatous invasion along the vincula;
(ii) infarction of the vincula;
(iii) attrition due to bony spurs;
(iv) pressure of the flexor retinaculum on weakened tendons;
(v) weakening following steroid injections.

The usual site of bony spurs in the carpal tunnel is the trapezio-scaphoid joint; the most commonly affected tendons are flexor pollicis longus and the flexors to the index finger.

The first line of treatment for flexor synovitis is steroid injection, which can be given into the carpal tunnel or digital sheath. There is probably a small increased liability to tendon rupture after repeated injections.

The diagnosis of carpal tunnel syndrome is an indication for urgent surgical decompression if a steroid injection fails to give relief. The condition is easily relieved if treated early; if neglected the patient has numbness added to the patient's already considerable disabilities.

When should flexor synovectomy be undertaken? The main indications are (i) persistent pain and restriction of movement which has failed to respond to steroid injection, (ii) carpal tunnel syndrome, (iii) triggering and (iv) tendon rupture. Surgery should be undertaken early rather than late [26].

The surgical approach is through a longitudinal incision over the carpal tunnel, with a Z component at the wrist to avoid scar contracture and damage to the palmar branch of the median nerve. In the fingers, zigzag incisions give a wide exposure and excellent scars. The thinner portions of the fibrous flexor sheath may be excised but pulleys should be left at the entrance to the sheath, and over the proximal and middle phalanges. Careful synovectomy is performed; intratendinous lesions can be shelled out but the split in the tendon should be repaired where possible. If there is an obstruction at the decussation of the superficialis tendon one half may be excised back to the palm. The other half should be retained to prevent swan-neck deformity.

Harrison, Ansell and Hall [27] point out that if palmar and proximal subluxation of the base of the proximal phalanx has occurred, the scarring following flexor tendon surgery may make future passive correction of the deformity impossible; this is, therefore, a contraindication to flexor tendon surgery.

Flexor tendon rupture may present problems of management. Direct repair is seldom possible. Tendon grafting is difficult in the rheumatoid hand though some claim good results [28]. The best results are obtained by tendon transfer or appropriate joint fusion. Rupture of flexor pollicis longus or an isolated finger profundus tendon should be treated by arthrodesis of the distal joint. If both flexor tendons to a finger are ruptured the superficialis is excised, leaving one slip. An intact superficialis is then transferred from another finger to the ruptured profundus.

All such surgery will fail unless the greatest attention is paid to postoperative therapy. After synovectomy active movements are started at 5 days. If necessary, extensor assist splints or static splints localizing active movements to certain joints may be used. Therapy needs to be continued for up to 8 weeks.

Provided the postoperative treatment is properly carried out, good results can be obtained in the majority of patients. Unfortunately, recurrence of synovitis may occur. Reports mention figures of 29% [18] and 37% [29] although the recurrence is rarely sufficient to require surgery.

Planning for treatment

While the above account deals with individual parts of the hand the surgeon is faced with a patient whose hands may have many problems. A sequence of operations may be required. Although some advocate combining several major procedures at one sitting [30], it is probably better not to overburden the patient by attempting too much at once. The following are guidelines only and there will be many exceptions. For example, the thumb may be the worst affected digit and need to be treated before the fingers. Decompression of the median nerve for carpal tunnel syndrome takes absolute precedence.

1. Operate on one hand at a time. Occasionally, bilateral wrist surgery may be performed if immediate use of the fingers can be permitted.
2. Operate on proximal joints before distal. Stabilization of the wrist, excision of the distal end of the ulna and extensor tendon surgery, where indicated, should be undertaken first.
3. Flexor synovectomy should usually precede digital joint surgery, and therefore comes next. But, where palmar and proximal subluxation of the metacarpophalangeal joint is present, joint replacement should be carried out first.
4. The metacarpophalangeal joints should be treated before correction of swan-neck deformities. However, an uncorrected severe boutonnière deformity may put a hyperextension stress on a metacarpophalangeal joint arthroplasty and should be dealt with first.
5. Stabilization of the thumb can be combined with any of the other procedures, but if it is left to the last the thumb can be placed in the best position to oppose to the previously operated fingers.

References

1. Hodgson, S. P., Stanley, J. K. and Muirhead, A. (1989) The Wrightington classification of rheumatoid wrist X-rays: a guide to surgical management. *J. Hand Surg.*, **14B**, 451–455.
2. Straub, L. R. and Ranawat, C. S. (1969) The wrist in rheumatoid arthritis: surgical treatment and results. *J. Bone Joint Surg.*, **51A**, 1–20.
3. Kulick, R. G., De Fiore, J. C., Straub, L. R. and Ranawat, C. S. (1981) Long term results of dorsal stabilisation in the rheumatoid wrist. *J. Hand*

Surg., **6**, 272–280.

4. Ishikawa, H., Hanyu, T. and Tajima, T. (1992) Rheumatoid wrists treated with synovectomy of the extensor tendons and the wrist joint combined with a Darrach procedure. *J. Hand Surg.*, **17A**, 1109–1117.

5. Chamay, A., Della Santa, D. and Vilaseca, A. (1983) Radiolunate arthrodesis, factor of stability for the rheumatoid wrist. *Ann. Chir. de la Main*, **2**, 5–17.

6. Stanley, J. K. and Boot, D. A. (1989) Radiolunate arthrodesis. *J. Hand Surg.*, **14B**, 283–287.

7. Ishikawa, H., Hanyu, T., Saito, H. and Takahashi, H. (1992) Limited arthrodesis for the rheumatoid wrist. *J. Hand Surg.*, **17A**, 1103–1109.

8. Brumfield, R. H. and Champoux, J. A. (1984) A biomechanical study of normal functional wrist motion. *Clin. Orthop.*, **187**, 23–25.

9. Clayton, M. L. and Ferlic, D. C. (1984) Arthrodesis of the arthritic wrist. *Clin. Orthop.*, **187**, 89–93.

10. Millender, L. H. and Nalebuff, E. A. (1973) Arthrodesis of the rheumatoid wrist. An evaluation of sixty patients and a description of a different surgical technique. *J. Bone Joint Surg.*, **55A**, 1026–1034.

11. Swanson, A. B. (1973) *Flexible Implant Resection Arthroplasty in the Hand and Extremities*. Mosby, St Louis, pp. 254–264.

12. Vicar, A. J. and Burton, R. I. (1986) Surgical management of the rheumatoid wrist – fusion or arthroplasty. *J. Hand Surg.*, **11A**, 790–797.

13. Harrison, S. H. (1971) Reconstructive arthroplasty of the metacarpophalangeal joints, using the extensor loop operation. *Br. J. Plast. Surg.*, **24**, 307–309.

14. Swanson, A. B. (1972) Flexible implant arthroplasty for arthritic finger joints: rationale, technique and results of treatment. *J. Bone Joint Surg.*, **54A**, 435–455.

15. Goldner, J. L., Gould, J. S., Urbaniak, J. R. and McCollom, D. E. (1977) Metacarpophalangeal joint arthroplasty with silicone-Dacron prostheses (Niebauer type): six and a half years' experience. *J. Hand Surg.*, **2**, 200–211.

16. Shapiro, J. S. (1982) Wrist involvement in rheumatoid swan-neck deformity. *J. Hand Surg.*, **7**, 484–491.

17. Nalebuff, E. A. and Millender, L. H. (1975) The surgical treatment of swan-neck deformity in rheumatoid arthritis. *Orthop. Clin. North Am.*, **6**, 733–752.

18. Souter, W. A. (1984) The rheumatoid hand. In *Operative Surgery* (eds H. Dudley and D. Carter) Butterworth, London, pp. 363–443.

19. Littler, J. W. and Cooley, S. G. E. (1965) Restoration of the retinacular system in hyperextension deformity of the proximal interphalangeal joint. *J. Bone Joint Surg.*, **47A**, 637.

20. Harrison, S. H. (1974) The Harrison–Nicolle intramedullary peg: follow-up study of 100 cases. *Hand*, **6**, 304–307.

21. Rothwell, A. G. (1978) Repair of established post-traumatic boutonnière deformity. *Hand*, **10**, 241–245.

22. Nalebuff, E. A. and Philips, C. A. (1984) The rheumatoid thumb. In *Rehabilitation of the Hand* (eds J. M. Hunter, L. H. Schneider, E. J. Mackin and A. D. Callahan), 2nd Edition, Mosby, St Louis, pp. 681–694.

23. Nalebuff, E. A. (1969) Extensor pollicis rerouting in the rheumatoid thumb – a new operative approach. *J. Bone Joint Surg.*, **51A**, 790.

24. Barnes, C. G. and Currey, H. L. F. (1967) Carpal tunnel syndrome in rheumatoid arthritis. *Ann. Rheum. Dis.*, **26**, 226–233.

25. Mannerfelt, L. and Norman, O. (1969) Attrition ruptures of flexor tendons in rheumatoid arthritis caused by bony spurs in the carpal tunnel. *J. Bone Joint Surg.*, **51B**, 270–277.

26. Nalebuff, E. A. (1969) Surgical treatment of rheumatoid tenosynovitis in the hand. *Surg. Clin. North Am.*, **49**, 799-809.

27. Harrison, S. H. Ansell, B. and Hall, M. A. (1976) Flexor synovectomy in the rheumatoid hand. *Hand*, **8**, 13–16.

28. Moberg, E. (1965) Tendon grafting and tendon suture in rheumatoid arthritis. *Am. J. Surg.*, **109**, 375–376.

29. Dahl, E., Mikkelsen, O. A. and Sorensen, J. U. (1976) Flexor tendon synovectomy of the hand in rheumatoid arthritis. *Scand. J. Rheumatol.*, **5**, 103–107.

30. Stanley, J. K. and Hullin, M. G. (1986) Wrist arthrodesis as part of composite surgery of the hand. *J. Hand Surg.*, **11B**, 243–244.

25

Surgical treatment of rheumatoid arthritis of the knee

P. Bliss

The mechanics of the knee joint with high load and long leverages make the joint vulnerable to progressive changes either from trauma or inflammation.

Rheumatoid disease produces progressive changes in the knee, initially in the surrounding soft tissues but later in the joint surfaces. In the early stages capillary dilatation occurs in the synovium and is more evident than in a comparable stage in osteoarthritis. By contrast, in the capsule the capillaries are only slightly dilated and they run a straight course when viewed by a magnifying arthroscope, but are not adequately seen with an ordinary arthroscope. Subsequent hypertrophy of the synovium with increasing excretion of fluid produces the early clinical picture of a warm swollen joint. Precipitation of fibrin and necrosis of synovial villi arises as a result of cyclical remission and recurrence of the acute inflammation in rheumatoid arthritis. At this stage there is no apparent change in the articular cartilage, but later a progressive and destructive pannus arises which spreads across the articular surface. It may undermine the margins of the articular cartilage before covering the surface, and small erosions may be revealed on the radiographs (Fig.25.1).

The natural history of the disease in juvenile rheumatoid arthritis shows a spontaneous remission in nearly two-thirds of the patients [1], but progression can occur relentlessly or in a series of peaks, often related to physical or emotional stress. The resulting swelling, effusion and pain are together serious problems which may lead to instability, varus or valgus de-

formity, contracture and further destruction of articular cartilage. If this stage is not controlled by medication and suitable rest and splints, then synovectomy should be considered.

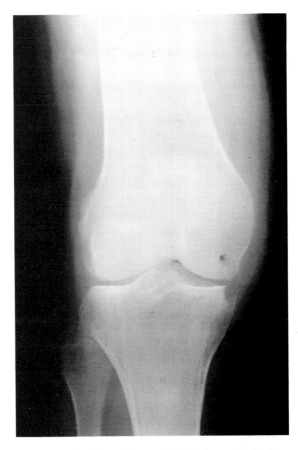

Fig. 25.1 Erosion of the medial tibial condyle in the early stages of rheumatoid arthritis.

Synovectomy

Synovectomy was first performed by Volkmann in 1877 for tuberculosis but in 1900 Mignon reported the operation for rheumatoid arthritis.

Indications

In patients complaining of pain associated with joint swelling due to synovial inflammation, and when free fluid cannot be withdrawn by aspiration due to fibrin deposition. Radiographs should reveal well preserved joint spaces and minimal marginal articular erosion, but there may be some loss of bone density. A steadily rising plasma viscosity is a contraindication to synovectomy but a stable elevated viscosity is not. A more advanced stage of the disease associated with quite definite articular erosions, some fixed deformity and a contracted capsule resulting from 'chemical sympathectomy' are all less favourable indications for synovectomy.

Operation

In essence this is a sub-total excision of knee joint synovium which includes the suprapatellar pouch, medial, lateral and intercondylar recesses with some posterior synovium. A retained area in the proximal part of the suprapatellar region may reduce the tendency for quadriceps adhesions. Degenerate or torn fragments of menisci are also removed. Haemostasis is important, particularly in those fairly active inflammatory joints, and due attention must be paid to the geniculate vessels.

Postoperative care

This is confined to static exercises until the wound has healed; thereafter graduated flexion exercises in the pool or with a continuous passive motion machine are supervised by the physiotherapy team. Manipulation is rarely necessary. Synovectomy carried out arthroscopically either using an electric resectoscope or a mechanical shaver has advantages over open operation but direct articular trauma from repetitive instrumentation is a hazard in inexperienced hands.

Results

A good functional result may be achieved in those patients with monoarthritis in whom the plasma viscosity is stable but elevated, and where there are only minimal radiographic changes. If the resultant good function is maintained for 3 years then there is every chance that it will continue indefinitely. However, although recent surveys [2,3] show promising long term results, the quality diminishes progressively if there are advanced articular erosions at operation.

Juvenile chronic arthritis

This condition introduces other problems including cessation of bone growth or stiffness of joints from a non-cooperative young patient. A review of synovectomy in this young age group

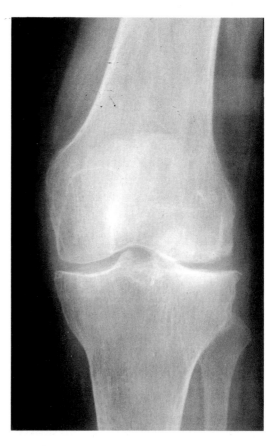

Fig. 25.2 Destruction of articular surfaces in the lateral compartment will not be halted by synovectomy at this stage of the disease.

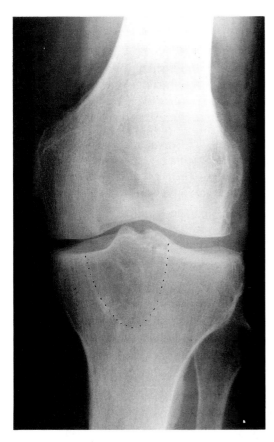

Fig. 25.3   A large bone cyst in the mid-part of the tibia which is a potential hazard.

[4] outlines these extra hazards but in making the decision to perform a synovectomy it is known that cessation of epiphyseal activity and joint stiffness are real complications of the disease. If the child can be relieved of pain, then there is a fair chance that early arthroplasty can be delayed or even avoided. The older the child at the onset of the disease the worse the outlook after synovectomy, and recurrent synovitis is more frequent when the disease is very active particularly in those with polyarthritis.

Finally, synovectomy does not halt the progression of destructive articular damage and indeed these changes may develop in spite of synovectomy but arise in patients with polyarthritis (Fig. 25.2). Progression of the disease not only destroys articular cartilage but causes attenuation of the medial and cruciate ligaments. Bone cysts and destruction of articular surfaces give rise to increasing deformity and disability (Fig. 25.3).

Arthroplasty

The combination of poor bone density and muscle wasting with valgus or varus deformity precludes successful high tibial or low femoral osteotomy to correct alignment and should not be performed for patients with rheumatoid disease although occasional acceptable results are still reported.

Stabilizing the knee joint with collateral ligaments under tension by adequate prosthetic design is the obvious method of management of the more severely damaged knee joint.

In varus deformity the use of a hemi-arthroplasty has been variously reported but it should be noted that in rheumatoid knees the bone density could be questionable and the prosthesis may be unstable and difficult to position. Marmor [5] reports good and excellent results in 106 patients in a series of 137 patients with rheumatoid disease, the better results being in young patients with joint surface destruction. Contra-indications include severe fixed deformities and marked osteoporosis. It is also noted that hemi-arthroplasty used as a bicompartmental implant produced good pain relief but not in patients with angular deformity not correctable by passive stress testing. Unicompartmental replacement tends to be followed by second side degeneration.

A flexion contracture can be corrected by posterior capsular release and excision of osteophytes to stop bony impingement; contractures over 35° require more bone resection.

Correction of valgus deformity is by lateral release from the femur, taking particular care to identify and protect the peroneal nerve; varus deformity is corrected by medial soft tissue release from the tibia to allow realignment of the limb.

Knee prosthetics can be either ligament sparing or ligament resecting and may be constrained, semi-constrained or unconstrained. The patella may or may not be resurfaced.

The meticulous attention to surgical technique in the implantation of knee prosthetics with the correct alignment of the components and adequate fixation reduces the failure rate which in most series is still high. The careful handling of all tissues is essential in order to reduce the incidence of tissue necrosis which is a major cause of wound breakdown. It is recommended that a mid-line or medial curved incision with regard to

Langer's lines is employed. Careful wound closure in layers without tension at the end of the operation, combined with diligent haemostasis and drainage, aim to reduce the incidence of postoperative haemarthrosis and wound haematoma. Recent research has shown that oxygen tensions in the lateral skin flap are significantly reduced in the immediate postoperative period and this relative deficiency is made worse if the knee joint is flexed more than 40° during the first 4 days. The oxygen tension in the skin flaps can be considerably enhanced by supplemental nasal oxygen during this critical time.

The question of perioperative anticoagulant therapy is raised by the incidence of deep vein thrombosis. With serial monitoring of patients using venography and lung scanning, the incidence of vein occlusion is higher than clinically appreciated and appears to be raised with bilateral two stage arthroplasty during the same hospitalisation as opposed to bilateral arthroplasty under the same anaesthetic. Other studies [6] show no difference between bilateral and unilateral arthroplasties, but there appears to be a slightly higher infection rate if second side arthroplasty is performed at a second operation during the same hospitalization or at a later hospitalization.

Assessment of knee function [7] shows that the range of knee movement required for a swing phase of gait is 67° but it requires 83° of knee movement to enable the patient to climb stairs. Slightly more flexion, to 90°, is required to descend stairs and 93° required to rise from a sitting position in a chair provided the femoral axis is parallel with the ground.

Bicompartmental knee joint resurfacing using unlinked femoral and tibial components show, on long term review, that although the success rate was 66%, the failures were due to instability in 13% with component loosening in 7% and infection 3%. Patellar femoral joint pain occurred in 4%.

Deformity of the polyethylene tibial component is a major cause of loosening of tibial elements. This can be resolved in the cementless fixation [1,7] of the tibial component by using a component of adequate thickness to prevent deformation; or by altering the sheer stresses exerted on the tibial component by using a metal plate, possibly with a duocondylar prosthesis with intercondylar stabilization. Thus in the Oxford knee a non-congruent fit allows slippage between component parts which reduces the sheer stress at the prosthetic/bone interface.

Early reports of arthroplasty of the knee using an endoprosthesis suggested major changes in the management of rheumatoid disease in the knee but also contained warnings of the potential complications. Uniaxial hinges with restrictions built into the prosthesis with metal stops to restrict flexion and extension will produce the familiar click [8] and high impact loads transmitted to the prosthetic medullary stems; thus leading to loosening, particularly in the porotic rheumatoid bone. The experience of the Walldius arthroplasty over prolonged usage bears out this complication.

Selecting a prosthesis

The number of prosthetic implants on the market gives rise to concern. A selection is recorded to illustrate the difficulty in making a suitable choice.

The *Stanmore* modification of the simple hinge, by production of a polyethylene bush and introduction of a femoral tibial angle together with long stems improved the clinical results, although retropatellar problems arose and were a major cause for concern. Early good results at 1 year were maintained for ten years. Further review showed that two thirds of patients had pain relief, four fifths of patients had stable flexion to 90°, but one third complained of retropatellar pain.

The *Kinematic* rotating modification of a simple hinge on review [9,10] in use in rheumatoid disease showed approximately 72% excellent or good results but still problems with infection, implant breakage, patella instability and wound healing. Incomplete non-progressive radiolucent lines of less than 1 mm at the tibial bone interface were considered insignificant, clinically, at 2–4 years postoperatively; but there was some progression of the lucent lines in a review of over 1000 Kinematic knees. There were significant complications: infection in 7%, wound healing problems in 5.5%, peroneal palsy in 3.1% and patella instability in 2.2%.

The *Attenborough* stabilized gliding prosthesis showed good functional results in 92% but there were also wound healing problems and serious prosthetic patellar instability.

The *Geupar* arthroplasty [11] carried an infection rate of over 9%.

Thus the hinged prostheses, incorporating modifications to reduce torque forces, still have a high incidence of loosening and infection.

The *Spherocentric* knee allows 15° of internal and external tibial rotation together with 120° range of knee flexion. It is used in grossly unstable knees with severe fixed deformities or metaphyseal bone loss to give improved ambulation in 92% of patients, whilst avoiding many of the problems of a uniaxial hinge replacement arthroplasty. With total condylar knee replacement it was noted that knees with preoperative flexion of more than 100° lost flexion, whilst knees with less than 100° preoperative flexion gained flexion. A preoperative flexion contracture of more than 10° could be corrected at operation but, on retrospective assessment, the longer rehabilitation took to regain flexion the less was the correction of the preoperative flexion contracture.

Bone lysis

Investigations of bone cement interface activity and bone lysis [12] have identified the histological and histochemical characteristics of the tissue layer between the bone and cement. Synovial like cells adjacent to the cement layer, and cell culture of the membrane contain stellate cells which are similar to those found in cell culture of normal and rheumatoid synovial tissue. It suggests that the membrane has the capacity to produce large amounts of prostaglandin E2 and collagenase which may explain the progressive lysis of bone.

As a result of the problems with fixation of the unrestrained components, development towards cementless fixation utilizing bone ingrowth into the implant has continued and the porous coated anatomical total knee [13] and polypropylene finned pegs are now being used. However, these methods of fixation are unsatisfactory when used within insufficient bone stock, or in severely osteoporotic bone or even in dense sclerotic bone where biological ingrowth is inhibited.

Complications

Prosthetic failure [14]

This can be due to obesity of the patient which has to be regarded as a patient failure. By contrast, joint or primary systemic failure may be due to progressive bone weakness, osteopenia or osteonecrosis resulting from steroid therapy.

Patella displacement

The problems which occur with the patellar femoral compartment vary in different reported series from 5% to 30% and do not appear to be specifically related to implant design. Patellar-femoral lateral tracking problems are higher in constrained hinge prostheses. The greater the valgus angle the higher is the tendency to lateral tracking and subluxation [14].

Lateral tracking should be eliminated at operation. If the patella tends to track laterally with the knee flexed to 90° before closure of the extensor expansion, a lateral release should be performed.

Patella dislocation after knee replacement may be due to trauma, incorrect tracking or malrotation of the tibia and should be treated by proximal realignment, lateral release or revision of the components [15].

Malalignment

The mechanical complexities of knee prostheses carry an inevitable failure rate, and varus malalignment, in particular, is perhaps the worst.

Axial rotation malalignment, if left uncorrected, results in a magnitude of increased sheer stresses at the prosthetic/bone interface beneath the tibial component. It will inevitably approach values equivalent to the body weight and result in loosening [16].

Flexion deformity

It is known that a flexion deformity in rheumatoid arthritis is present in over 60% of knees preoperatively, reduced to 17% postoperatively and in only 21% of prostheses requiring revision.

A second procedure results in reduction of flexion deformity to only 8%. Against this is the relief of pain and reduced need for revision found in those patients with the most serious deformities. It is in the light of their multiple problems which are so great that the relief after a successful knee replacement is not outweighed by their limited but hopefully renewed activity.

Aseptic loosening

The management of aseptic loosening of the total knee replacement [11] using intramedullary stems and metal back tibial component has a high success rate for the relief of pain and flexion to 90° with 80% being able to walk for more than 30 min.

Prosthetic infection

The most serious problem for a surgeon is the management of the infected knee prosthesis. Careful tissue handling at operation cannot be over emphasized as well as antibiotic cover and ideal theatre conditions, in order to minimize primary prosthetic infection. It has been shown [17] that micrococci and diphtheroids are frequent causes of operating theatre infections. Late infections due to haematogenous spread should be reduced again by prophylaxis with pre- and postoperative antibiotics for 48 or 72 h. Subsequently all dental procedures [18] likely to cause gingival bleeding should be covered with penicillin or appropriate antibiotics. Similarly, antibiotic cover is essential for all genitourinary and gastrointestinal procedures and particularly drainage of abscesses.

Reviews of knee prostheses [10,19,20,21] have reported that the rate of infections vary between 1.7% and 16%, but stemmed constrained implants have a higher infection rate particularly in rheumatoid arthritic patients. It is reported [20] that superficial infections of the wound with erythema and delayed healing, when aggressively treated, do not present a major problem with regard to prosthetic infection.

All reviews record that revision arthroplasty for aseptic loosening or malposition carry a higher infection rate by a factor of between 2 and 4.

Primary one-stage exchange arthroplasty requires gentamicin impregnated cement and antibiotic therapy initially by intravenous administration followed by oral therapy for at least 3 months. The antibiotic is designed after appropriate operative specimens have been obtained. This method can give a 60% success rate if used in cases of unconstrained knee revision but without impregnated cement and antibiotic cover the success rate falls to only 35%.

Failure to eliminate prosthetic infection [22] leads to the possibility of resection arthroplasty with excision of all necrotic material, particularly the bone cement and bone cement membrane. After excision the patient remains in a long leg non weight bearing cast for 6 months, after which both active assisted and passive assisted exercises are programmed before weight bearing can be contemplated. A knee brace may be necessary to reduce the inevitable feeling of instability.

Arthodesis

The alternative to resection arthroplasty is to attempt an arthrodesis. Three types of arthrodesis techniques have been used most frequently for salvaging a failed total knee implant, namely, external fixation, internal fixation and intramedullary fixation. Care must be exercised to avoid thin skin flaps. Wide exposure with extensive subperiosteal elevation of tissue adherent to the distal femur and proximal tibia is needed to allow adequate mobilization of the femur and tibia. The debridement of necrotic tissue and prostheses removal should avoid fracturing the bone and preserve the maximum bone stock. The previous wide dissection helps the exposure of the prostheses, and pulsatile irrigation is useful in assisting removal of loose acrylic cement from the intramedullary canals and soft tissues. Accurate apposition of bone ends may be aided by the original prosthetic alignment jigs, and it may be necessary to excise the fibula head to allow the femur and tibia to be closely approximated. A short limb is inevitable.

The fusion technique to be employed is selected and the fixation applied. Proper angulation and rotational alignment can be assisted by using small Kirschner wires in the femur and tibia orientated using the original prosthetic jigs.

Flexion must be secure and rigid and any supplemental bone graft, if used, should be applied around the outside of the bone rather than in the medullary cavity where it is liable to form a series of sequestra.

If skin closure is difficult, delayed primary or secondary closure may be carried out.

External fixation

The use of an external fixator may be difficult if the fusion of two hollow tubes or cortical bone is being attempted. But it should be used where rigid fixation can be achieved and when an adequate quantity of cancellous bone is present such as in failed bicompartmental or unconstrained devices.

Internal fixation

The application of internal fixation plates can be more difficult than external fixation. The more extensive exposure required may warrant the application of more than one plate. They can be applied after removal of stemmed hinged or semiconstrained prostheses have resulted in two hollow cortical tubes. The length of time to obtain fusions, up to 12 months, precludes external fixation with its certainty of retrograde pin track sepsis and loss of rigid fixation. The disadvantage of rigid two plate fixation is that remodelling of the bone after fusion may be inhibited and predispose to fracture at the ends of the plate. Thus, after fusion, the plates should be removed.

Intramedullary fixation

The use of a long pre-bent intramedullary nail can be successfully employed on occasions. The technique utilizes the relatively normal bone in the proximal femur and mid tibia to achieve adequate fixation. Careful planning preoperatively is required so that rods of appropriate length and curve are available.

All attempts at fusion must be covered with appropriate antibiotics for at least 3 months.

Failure to control infection either by exchange

of implant, resection arthroplasty or fusion leads to a distressing and disabling discharge from the operation site which, if not controlled, may become life threatening. Reports of failures of knee arthroplasty [19,20] contain a small number of mid thigh amputations. The use of amputation may be in the patient's best interest from the aspect of pain relief, absence of a chronic discharge and a mobile lower limb prosthesis with knee flexion, but the energy requirements and physical muscle power needed to mobilize independently with an artificial limb may well not be possible in a rheumatoid arthritic patient with multiple joint involvement. Consequently, amputation most frequently results in the patient being confined to a wheelchair for the remainder of their life.

References

1. Laaksonen, A-L. (1966) A prognostic study of juvenile arthritis, analysis of 544 cases. *Acta Pediatr. Scand.*, Suppl. 166.
2. Brattstrom, H. (1985) Co-ordinating E.R.A.S.S. long term results after synovectomy for adult rheumatoid arthritis. *Clin. Rheumatol.*, **4**, 19–22.
3. Ishikawa, H., Ohnd, O. and Hirohata, K. (1986) Long term results of synovectomy in rheumatoid arthritis. *J. Bone Joint Surg.*, **68A**, 198–205.
4. Rydholm, U., Elborgh, R., Ranstam, J. *et al.* (1986) Synovectomy of the knee in juvenile chronic arthritis. *J. Bone Joint Surg.*, **68B**, 223–228.
5. Marmor, L. (1982) The Marmor knee replacement. *Orthop. Clin. North Am.*, **13(1)**, 55–64.
6. Morrey, B. E., Adams, R. A., Ilstrup, D. M. and Bryan, R. S. (1987) Complications and mortality association with bilateral or unilateral total knee arthroplasty. *J. Bone Joint Surg.*, **69A**, 484–488.
7. Laubenthal, K. N., Smidt, G. L. and Kettlekamp, D. B. (1972) A quantitative analysis of knee motion during the activities of daily living. *Phys. Ther.*, **52**, 34–42.
8. Matthews, L. S. and Kaufer, H. (1982) The spherocentric knee: a perspective of 7 years clinical experience. *Orthop. Clin. North Am.*, **13(1)**, 173–186.
9. Ewald, F. C., Jawbs, M. A., Miegel, R. E. *et al.* (1984) Kinematic total knee replacement. *J. Bone Joint Surg.*, **66A**, 1032–1048.
10. Rand, J. A., Chad, E. Y. S. and Stauffer, R. N. (1987) Kinematic rotating hinge total knee replacement. *J. Bone Joint Surg.*, **69A**, 489–497.
11. Bertin, K. C., Freeman, M. A. R., Samuelson,

K. M. *et al.* (1985) Stemmed revision arthroplasty for aseptic loosening of total knee replacement. *J. Bone Joint Surg.*, **67B**, 242–248.

12. Goldring, S. R., Schiller, A. L., Roelke, M. *et al.* (1983) Synovial like membrane at bone cement interface in loose total hip replacement and its role in bone lysis. *J. Bone Joint Surg.*, **65A**, 575–584.

13. Hungerford, D. S., Kenna, R. V. and Krackow, K. A. (1982) Porous coated anatomic total knee. *Orthop. Clin. North Am.*, **13, 1**, 103–122.

14. Matthews, L. S. and Goldstein, B. (1986) Biomechanical causes and prevention of failed joint replacement. *Curr. Orthop.*, **1**, 1.

15. Merkow, R. I., Soudry, M. and Insall, J. N. (1985) Patella dislocation after total knee replacement. *J. Bone Joint Surg.*, **67A**, 1321–1327.

16. Kagan, A. II (1977) Mechanical causes of loosening of knee joint replacement. *J. Biomech.*, **10**, 387–391.

17. Bechtol, C. O. (1979) Environmental bacteriology in a unidirectional (vertical) operating room. *Arch, Surg.*, **114**, 784–788.

18. Irvine, R., Johnson, B. L. and Amstutz, H. C. (1974) Relationship with genitourinary procedures and deep sepsis after total hip replacement. *Surg. Gynaecol. Obst.*, **139**, 701–706.

19. Grogan, T. J., Dorey, F., Rollins, I. and Amstutz, H. C. (1981) Deep sepsis following total knee arthroplasty. *J. Bone Joint Surg.*, **68A**, 226–234.

20. Johnson, D. P. and Bannister, G. C. (1986) The outcome of infected arthroplasty of the knee. *J. Bone Joint Surg.*, **68B**, 289–291.

21. Schurman, D. J. (1981) Functional outcome of Guepar hinge knee arthroplasty evaluated with Aramis. *Clin. Orthop.*, **155**, 118–132.

22. Stulberg, S. D. (1982) Arthrodesis in failed total knee replacement. *Orthop. Clin. North Am.*, **13** (1), 213–224.

26

Rheumatoid arthritis of the ankle and foot

J. R. Kirkup

Treatment for the painful rheumatoid foot is a challenge which demands both assessment of current pathology and an appreciation of future changes based on the natural history of a disease process which can involve some 25 closely related joints. Thus the severely disabled foot presents: (i) multiple joint damage, often at different stages of evolution and asymmetrically distributed between the two feet (Fig.26.1), (ii) a commonly progressive yet often erratic pathology which renders the feet elusive targets for considered surgical opinion, and also (iii) problems in management priorities posed by proximal disability especially at the knee.

Clinically it is useful to separate the hindfoot from the forefoot; the former embraces the ankle, subtaloid, mid-tarsal, naviculo-cuneiform, inter-cuneiform and tarso-metatarsal joints, and the latter the metatarso-phalangeal and toe joints. Hindfoot pathology dictates the attitude and stability of the foot, that is whether it is valgus, varus, equinus or calcaneus. Forefoot pathology leads to severe disorganization with dislocation of the toes and callosity problems due to shoe containment and weight-bearing pressures. Whilst both areas may be attacked simultaneously or consecutively, in practice either hindfoot or forefoot disease predominates at any one time.

In a survey of 200 consecutive rheumatoid patients admitted to the Bristol Royal Infirmary and the Royal National Hospital for Rheumatic Diseases in Bath, 104 were noted to have pain or deformity involving the feet, this being second only to the knee as a source of symptoms [1]. Of 204 feet analysed, radiological changes were seen in 176 forefeet (metatarso-phalangeal and toe joints) and 133 hindfeet (124 mid tarsal, 64 sub-taloid and 52 ankle joints); additionally, erosion

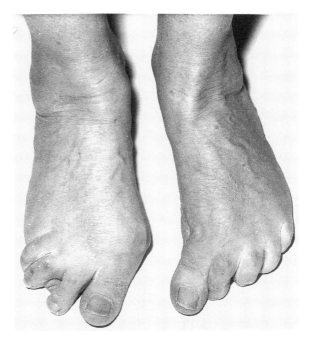

Fig. 26.1 Asymmetrical changes in rheumatoid arthritis. The right foot shows classical hallux valgus with dorsal dislocations of the lesser toes except the fifth which underlies its fellows in a varus position. The left foot shows unusual varus of all the toes and severe flexion of the lesser toes. The right hindfoot is valgus and the left cavo-varus.

of the os calcis was observed in 11 feet, whilst 55 feet assumed a valgus and 2 feet a varus heel profile, It was clear that disease of the metatarsophalangeal and inter-tarsal joints commonly co-existed, whilst the ankle joint often remained intact. Further, unlike the other joints, 55% of radiologically damaged inter-tarsal joints were not a source of complaint at the time of examination. As we will demonstrate shortly, the inter-tarsal joints often ankylose and fuse spontaneously.

Proximal joint disease and the foot

Fixed flexion deformity at the hip and particularly at the knee induces a dorsi-flexed attitude of the foot under load. If fixed flexion persists, a diseased ankle may lose plantar-flexion yet maintain dorsi-flexion. On the other hand, if the knees are straight, fixed equinus at the ankle may result and is a hindrance to walking without a raised heel; such equinus then overloads the forefoot joints.

Valgus of the knee compounds or is compounded by valgus of the foot and may compromise treatment. Generally knee valgus is painful and unstable whereas foot valgus may be pain free and can be stabilized by apparatus. Unless foot valgus is severe and associated with skin breakdown, the knee takes operative precedence. However, severe forefoot disorganization with plantar callosities uncontrolled by suitable shoes, or associated with skin breakdown, takes precedence over both knee and hip disability.

The hindfoot

Natural history

We examined 150 consecutive adult patients attending the Foot Clinic of the Royal National

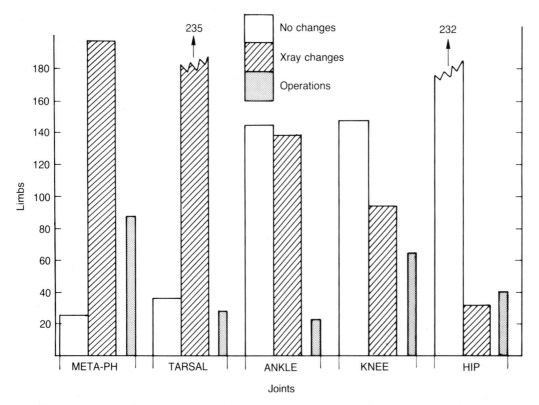

Fig. 26.2 Survey of 150 patients complaining of the hindfoot: radiographic changes and surgical operations due to rheumatoid in 300 lower limbs.

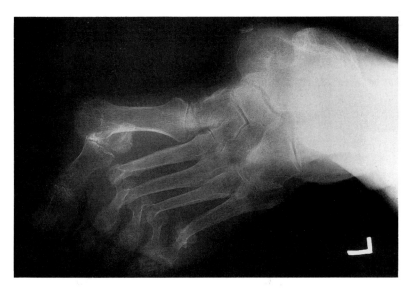

Fig. 26.3 Talo-navicular dislocation with minimal bone destruction: the opacity medial to the weight-bearing talar head was sited in sloughing skin and tendon. The forefoot shows classical destructive changes with dislocation of the hallux.

Hospital for Rheumatic Diseases complaining of the hindfoot, usually bilaterally. All had attended the Clinic for at least 1 year and had proven rheumatoid arthritis present from 2 to 47 years, an average of 15 years. A radiographic survey of the 300 lower limbs (Fig. 26.2) demonstrated joint pathology or previous operation in: (i) 92% of the forefeet, (ii) 88% of the inter-tarsal joints, (iii) 52% of the ankles, (iv) 51% of the knees and (v) 23% of the hips.

As the figure indicates, although the hip was often spared disease, the chance of surgical intervention relative to pathological damage was high. By contrast, surgery for the knee and forefoot was less likely, whilst surgery for the hindfoot was least likely, despite a high incidence of pathology.

Of the 300 feet, almost two-thirds presented a valgus attitude, principally due to inter-tarsal joint subluxation but also due to tilting of the talus in the ankle mortise, or both. Standing radiographs were necessary to measure valgus or varus at the ankle joint. Varus and equinus was uncommon, the latter being associated with ankle joint pathology.

What is understood by radiographic change? Clearly many hindfeet joints manifested narrowing and erosions, leading to joint destruction and often spontaneous ankylosis or arthrodesis. However some inter-tarsal joints without these articular changes were pathologically subluxated and occasionally dislocated (Fig. 26.3). Observation of weight-bearing serial radiographs of individual ankle joints confirmed that changes were often minimal or indeed absent before significant tilting of the talus promoted bone destruction (Fig. 26.4). Fusion was common especially between the joints of the os calcis, talus, navicular, cuboid and cuneiforms. The ankle joint rarely fused and then usually in chair-bound patients; nevertheless, this joint frequently stiffened and developed secondary osteophytosis.

Of 247 surgical procedures performed on these 300 lower limbs, 45 operations (19%) involved the hindfoot and included 28 inter-tarsal and ankle arthrodeses, five osteotomies, two ankle synovectomies combined with tarsal arthrodeses and ten total ankle replacements.

This analysis of 150 patients, supported by more extensive experience, suggested the following:

(i) If the ankle joint is diseased then the tarsal joints are already or will shortly be affected. By contrast, if the tarsal joints are diseased then the ankle joint may escape.

(ii) The tarsal joints commonly ankylose and fuse spontaneously, the ankle joint only rarely.

(iii) Valgus deformity of the foot is common either with or without tarsal ankylosis. Severe valgus and tarsal ankylosis is often associated with subluxation of the ankle joint. Severe valgus and hypermobility sometimes leads to talonavicular subluxation and occasionally frank dislocation.

(iv) Extreme valgus stresses, distorts and fractures the fibula; even the tibia may undergo stress fracture (Fig. 26.5).

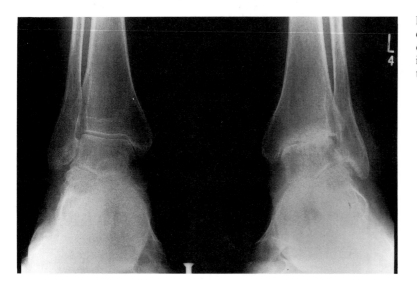

Fig. 26.4 Standing radiographs demonstrating subtalar valgus deformity on the left associated with valgus tilting in the ankle mortise and collapse of the tibia laterally.

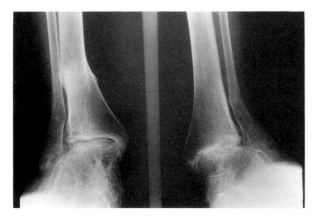

Fig. 26.5 Severe hindfoot disease with bilateral total tarsal ankylosis, in extreme valgus, aggravating ankle disease to cause fibular and tibial stress fractures.

(v) Extreme valgus generates painful weight-bearing callouses opposite the navicular and head of the talus which often progress to skin necrosis.

(vi) Most patients can be treated conservatively.

Hindfoot movements [2]

Accurate measurement of ankle joint movement is only possible by radiological means, for clinical separation from inter-tarsal movement is impossible unless the tarsus is fused. If the tarsus is mobile then significant plantar-flexion of the foot is possible at the mid tarsal joint. It is a practical compromise to measure dorsi-flexion and plantar-flexion actively with the assistance of the clinician passively, when the knees are extended on a couch, using the sole of the foot as an indicator in relation to the shin. Thus if there is fixed equinus of the mid-tarsal joint with mobility in the ankle, the above technique will indicate whether the sole of the foot can achieve a plantigrade position or not, at least when barefoot. Separate movements of the subtaloid, mid-tarsal and other inter-tarsal joints cannot be estimated accurately and the global peritalar movements of foot pronation and supination are a better assessment of foot function, again using the sole of the foot as an indicator.

The theoretical movements of eversion and abduction and of inversion and adduction are considered to equal pronation and supination, respectively. Such movements do not necessarily disappear if the tarsus is fused for they may develop in a painfree mobile ankle. In summary, it is more realistic to determine movement of the foot as a whole in relation to the leg rather than individual joint movements.

The ankle joint

Clinical

This joint is the least likely to be involved in the adult foot. However, in juvenile polyarthritis [3] the ankle is initially the most involved joint, although at a later date the ankle often recovers and the inter-tarsal joints become major targets. Ankle pain is felt diffusely around the joint between the malleoli and should be distinguishable from subtaloid pain, usually felt beneath the lateral malleolus, and talo-navicular pain somewhat distal to the medial malleolus. It is important to ask the patient to indicate with one finger the site of pain when walking.

Admittedly, pain location may be difficult, especially if both ankle and subtaloid joints are active. Even a pain relieving injection may prove uncertain because connections between the ankle and subtaloid joints via tendon sheaths have been demonstrated [4]. Early pain is associated with swelling in the joint itself and frequently the tendon sheaths of the peronei, tibialis posterior and tibialis anterior. Severe pain and swelling are associated with loss of dorsi-flexion and the foot may assume an equinus position. Repeated attacks lead to radiological changes and increasing stiffness. In the later stages tendon swelling often diminishes and both dorsi- and plantar-flexion are lost. A few patients giving a history of an ankle fracture prior to the onset of arthritis find this ankle becomes a target joint and a source of early disability.

Radiology

In the survey of Vidigal *et al.* [1] clinical symptoms and signs were present in 97 ankles yet only 52 developed radiological changes. Persistent disease, however, leads to joint narrowing, followed by subcortical cysts, collapse and joint destruction, stress fractures and secondary osteophytes (Fig. 26. 5) but spontaneous fusion is rare. If the tarsus is ankylosed and in valgus or varus, undue concentration of pressure at the points of contact of the talus in the mortice produces distinct acceleration of destructive disease and disability.

Radiological changes may remain unilateral or if bilateral appear contemporaneously or consecutively.

Conservative treatment

In addition to general treatment, acute flare-ups may require bed-rest and plaster of Paris casts.

Local injections of steroid via an antero-lateral portal [4] often help to keep the patient mobile and can be repeated depending on the general condition, but are best avoided if surgery is being contemplated. When less acute, a cosmetic caliper, an ankle-foot brace or formal below-knee double steels with boots or bootees may assist weight-bearing mobility, especially where there is a correctable valgus or varus posture. However, apparatus is less likely to help when fixed changes develop.

Surgical treatment

If disability persists despite conservative measures and the patient has adequate arterial circulation, surgical relief must be debated. The procedures available are synovectomy, surgical decompression of the lateral compartment of the joint, arthrodesis or replacement arthroplasty.

Synovectomy is mainly directed to adjacent tendon sheaths and can be undertaken as an adjunct to tarsal fusion if synovial swelling does not respond to injection therapy. Good results have been reported in early cases [5].

A valgus foot may cause pain limited to the lateral malleolus by impingement against the calcaneum [6], and resection of the distal fibula to decompress the adjacent talar facet, with local synovectomy, is simple and often provides relief.

In more advanced cases, arthrodesis may be the best option, especially if disability is unilateral, if the peritalar joints remain mobile and if the patient is a large male still employed in moderately heavy work. An antero-lateral approach dividing the fibula at the level of the joint is recommended, which gives ready access and permits correction of deformity if present. When good contact is achieved the position is maintained using staples with the foot in neutral; if the joint is fused in equinus this stresses the forefoot and the knees. However, if there is fixed flexion of the knees, then ankle fusion in slight dorsi-flexion may be required. Unfortunately fusion takes time and requires the patient to be non-weight-bearing for 6 weeks or so and at least 6 further weeks in a walking cast. In our experience, rheumatoid patients do not cope well with compression clamps which often damage the fragile skin of the other leg and can become loose in the os calcis.

Ankle replacement

If severe disability involves both ankles, the question of joint replacement arises because the alternative of bilateral ankle arthrodesis in the presence of previous bilateral tarsal ankylosis and fixed great toes, results in the knees being the most distal mobile joints, a severe handicap when attempting to rise from a chair or lavatory seat [7]. For these patients ankle joint replacement, at least unilaterally, offers significant advantages and moreover a relatively quick return to weight-bearing, unlike arthrodesis.

It is not pretended that ankle replacement has achieved the success of hip replacement and indeed some reports recommend that the ankle prostheses now available are not satisfactory for rheumatoid patients [8]. The I.C.L.H. prosthesis [9] and several other prostheses are constrained and aim to provide dorsi- and plantar-flexion only. We believe that a 'ball and socket' prosthesis is advantageous in the ankle to permit polyaxial movement. The rationale for utilizing a 'ball and socket' or sphero-centric joint is derived from the observation that children with congenital tarsal fusion often have a 'ball and socket' configuration of the ankle with universal motion of the foot, that is the ankle assumes additional subtaloid and mid-tarsal function. If the peritalar joints are fixed, the ankle is subject to pronatory and supinatory strains and thus it is logical to opt for an unconstrained prosthesis with the possibility of polyaxial motion. As with total hip arthroplasty, surgical placement of a polyaxial ankle prosthesis is less critical than that of a uniaxial prosthesis.

No incision is ideal for ankle replacement. Access includes a trans-fibular approach allowing partial subluxation of the joint and a posterior approach [6] detaching the insertion of the Achilles tendon with a block of the os calcis. Bone division, however, retards early weight-bearing, or may result in delayed union and slow rehabilitation. Thus an anterior approach between extensor hallucis longus and extensor digitorum is recommended, taking the vessels medially; this is minimally invasive, provides satisfactory exposure of both malleoli and allows early weight-bearing. Unlike hip and knee replacement procedures, the ankle is not dislocated and therefore, the insertion of the talar component is assisted by os calcis pin traction, to avoid impacting acrylic cement into the posterior compartment of the joint. Careful handling of the skin is also vital as it is often thin and prone to slow cicitrization in patients on steroids.

In 1979, Demottaz *et al.* [10] studied 21 total ankle replacements of which 16 were for rheumatoid arthritis, at an average follow-up of 14.7 months. The follow-up was very comprehensive and included gait analysis and electromyographic studies. Pain relief was considered complete in only four instances, whilst radiolucent lines were present in 19 joints of which two were loose. Seven of the joints were Smith or similar multiple-axis joints whilst the remainder were single-axis articulations principally of the Mayo design. In this small series of short follow-up, no significant difference between the two groups was observed. They concluded that ankle arthrodesis was the operation of choice except for elderly patients with limited mid-tarsal motion. In 1985, Bolton-Maggs *et al.* [8] followed up 41 of 62 uniaxially designed I.C.L.H. ankle prostheses inserted between 1972 and 1981 (mean follow-up 5.5 years), during which the prosthesis was modified several times and both anterior and posterior approaches were used. Of 34 arthroplasties for rheumatoid arthritis, seven were lost to follow-up, five were arthrodesed for loosening and 22 were reviewed. Pain was absent in seven, mild in seven, moderate in five and severe in three. The average range of movement changed from 18° to 23° and walking ability generally was improved. Only six rheumatoid arthroplasties were considered fully satisfactory and it was concluded that total ankle replacement could not be recommended as a long term solution; however, they also observed that arthrodesis in rheumatoid arthritis might be less satisfactory than for osteoarthritis.

Other reports have been more optimistic. In 1982, Herberts *et al.* [11], reporting on 18 I.C.L.H. prostheses at a mean of 36 months and of which 13 were for rheumatoid arthritis, concluded that ankle arthroplasty has a definite place in the treatment of severe arthritis in rheumatoid patients; they considered the osteoarthritic ankle did less well and found a high incidence of loosening and radiolucent zones. In 1984, Lachiewicz *et al.* [12], reporting on 15 uniaxial arthroplasties (14 being of the Mayo type) all for rheumatoid arthritis, at a mean of 39 months, noted gratifying pain relief and rated

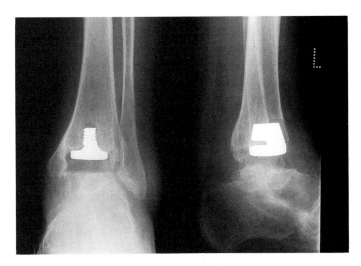

Fig. 26.6 Richard Smith ankle arthroplasty. Note absence of barium in the cement and that the medial malleolus underwent stress fracture following surgery. Joint still functioning at 12 years.

seven ankles excellent and eight good; nevertheless, 11 ankles developed radiolucent lines and six components showed evidence of subsidence.

Our own experience supports the view that arthroplasty benefits the severely disabled rheumatoid with bilateral hindfoot disease. Of 20 polyaxial Smith prostheses (Fig. 26.6) inserted for rheumatoid arthritis in 17 patients between 1975 and 1979, 15 were reviewed at a mean of 7 years; six components were undoubtedly loose mainly in the tibia, yet the patients continued walking, whilst nine had no or little pain although two of these had no movement [13]. This experience suggested that whilst the polyaxial design was safe and not prone to dislocation, the single thickness design restricted choice in accommodating variations of vertical joint space, despite a standard bone resection, due to differing ligamentous tensions between patients. We therefore designed a prosthesis with a polyethylene tibial implant which can be trimmed to size in the antero-posterior plane and is cemented *in situ* under pressure with a special clamp, and steel talar implants of 2, 3, 4, 5, and 6 mm thickness inserted using pin traction (Fig. 26.7). A preliminary report [14] on 25 arthroplasties in 20 patients at a minimum follow-up of 3 years was encouraging; it was noteworthy that having undergone one arthroplasty, several patients asked for surgery on the opposite ankle. A fuller account was presented to the College Internationale de Podologie meeting in 1987, when 24 Smith joints (1975–79) and 66 Bath joints (1980–85) were surveyed. Of the 90 arthro-

plasties, 77 were for rheumatoid arthritis including ten patients with bilateral replacements.

Late infection occurred at 1, 7 and 8 years respectively. No osteoarthritic patients had wound problems. At follow-up, seven patients had died and two limbs were amputated, all for reasons unconnected with their ankle surgery. Ten joints were removed for infection and loosening. Of 71 joints available for follow-up, 47 had no pain or minor pain and only one had severe pain associated with ischaemia. The gain in ankle movement was modest and 12 ankles were stiffer. Of the Smith joints followed for a mean of 10 years 55% were intact; of the Bath joints followed for a mean of 4.2 years 74% remained intact.

If these results cannot compare favourably with current hip and knee total replacement arthroplasties, they resemble the sequelae of hip arthroplasty at its inception and of knee arthroplasty some 15 years ago. Recent innovations including three-part prostheses, two-stage procedures and uncemented components raise expectations that second generation techniques will parallel the evolution of knee replacement.

The intertarsal joints

Clinical

Pain, stiffness and deformity are the principal complaints; more rarely severe varus can produce instability and severe valgus ulceration over the

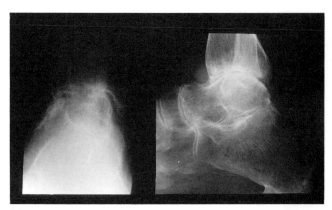

(a)

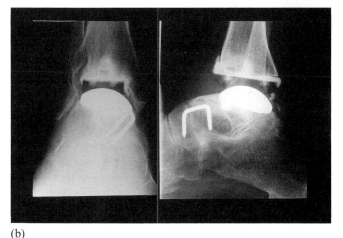

(b)

Fig. 26.7 Bath and Wessex ankle joint. The talar component is 3 mm in height. At operation the talo-navicular joint was found to be slightly mobile and a staple was inserted. Joint still functioning well at 7 years.

medial aspect of the foot (Fig. 26.3); severe valgus may also be associated with rupture of the tendon of tibialis posterior. The intertarsal joints often ankylose spontaneously either in neutral or deformity. If fixed in valgus whilst the ankle joint remains mobile, the fibula distorts or even undergoes stress fracture (Fig. 26.5), causing temporary pain.

The talo-navicular joint can be the first to cause symptoms but generally the patient presents with pain sited beneath the lateral malleolus arising in the subtaloid joint. Frequently this pain is minimal or moderate, or overshadowed by more acute pain in the forefoot, ankle or other joints, and it may subside as the joints quietly ankylose.

Radiology

Despite pain and swelling radiological changes are often minimal. Ultimately joint narrowing,

erosions and cysts appear often commencing in the talo-navicular joint. Spontaneous ankylosis is not infrequent and sometimes the whole tarsus becomes a single osseous entity. Patients with a propensity to subluxation and dislocation develop extreme valgus deformity (see Fig. 26.3).

Conservative treatment

Localized pain in the talo-navicular or subtaloid joints often responds to local injections of steroid and may need to be repeated before eventual ankylosis. More persistent pain is relieved by a below-knee plaster cast but this is not practical when the symptoms are bilateral. Fusion may follow repeated plaster immobilization if the foot can be held in neutral position More chronic pain, especially that associated with mobile valgus deformity, benefits from splintage, either a polyethylene cosmetic splint or steel calipers.

Surgical treatment

The absolute indications for surgery are persistent pain, foot instability and skin necrosis. Stiffness and deformity are not primary indications in themselves and the surgeon is cautioned against believing that complete correction of valgus deformity is a long term possibility, as this often proves illusory (Fig.26.8).

If signs are localized to the subtaloid joint, fusion of this joint alone is recommended. This will prevent pro-supination but preserve dorsi-plantarflexion at the mid-tarsal joint. A lateral approach gives adequate access; to correct minor valgus, bone chips from the malleolus or os calcis can be packed into the joint; more obvious valgus may need iliac crest bone in the sinus tarsi.

When symptoms are localized to the talo-navicular joint, fusion of this joint alone is required, utilizing a short medial incision to excise minimal bone from the articular surfaces and hold with staples or a screw. This blocks all movement in the peritalar joints and causes the undamaged joints to ankylose quietly.

Damage to all the intertarsal joints may result in severe valgus and uncovering of the talar head; for this two incisions are best, one to remove a wedge of bone medially from the talo-navicular joint and the other to excise the calcaneo-cuboid and subtaloid joints. Bone from the talar head and/or the iliac crest can be packed in laterally to aid correction; os calcis osteotomy is sometimes necessary. Full correction of the valgus may

result in supination of the forefoot which must be avoided. Thus a valgus attitude often remains and even after solid fusion in a corrected position, a valgus attitude can recur either in the distal tarsus (Fig. 26.8) or by tilting of the talus in the ankle mortise (see Fig. 26.4).

Nevertheless, tarsal fusions are very successful in resolving pain [15] and would be undertaken more willingly if these did not demand 5–6 weeks non-weight-bearing and up to a total of 12 weeks in plaster.

The forefoot

As indicated above, the forefoot is the most commonly attacked segment of the foot and also rivals the hand in presenting the earliest evidence of rheumatoid disease.

A mobile, painfree forefoot enables the toes to function as a platform for push-off in walking and also contributes to the balance, especially when standing still; if the hallux plays a dominant role, the remaining toes make a significant contribution and therefore it is important to view the forefoot as a single functional unit. Nevertheless, the pathomechanics of rheumatoid damage of the first ray as against the lesser rays is distinct and these differences will be emphasized.

Natural history

In a survey of 100 patients with foot symptoms, we identified deformity of the hallux in 93 patients of which 70 had bilateral changes [16]. This survey demonstrated that at the first meta-tarso-phalangeal joint, the commonest deformity was valgus and involved 60% of the feet, whilst hallux rigidus (dorsi-flexion 20° or less) involved 28% and hallux elevatus (absence of plantar-flexion) involved 10%. These deformities often overlapped and thus some two-thirds of rigid and elevated toes were also in valgus. Rigidus is equated with considerable intra-articular damage often leading to spontaneous fusion, even in a valgus position in some instances, and also hyperextension of the inter-phalangeal joint which, if extreme, forces the toe nail to cut through the upper of the shoe, the so-called 'chisel toe'. Elevatus is associated with inability of the hallux to take weight and also 'chisel toe'

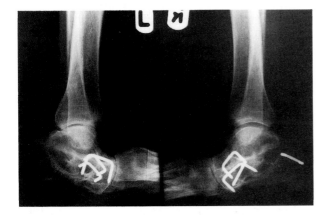

Fig. 26.8   Bilateral tarsal fusions with corrective osteotomy of the right os calcis. Standing lateral radiographs after successful fusions demonstrate valgus recurring distal to the fused segment, at the naviculo-cuneiform joints.

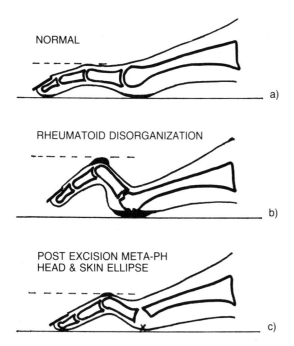

Fig. 26.9 Diagram of lesser toe and metatarsal:
(a) normal, to demonstrate vertical clearance necessary for
toe; (b) rheumatoid dislocation with secondary toe
hammering and increased vertical clearance; (c) following
excision of metatarsal head and plantar skin ellipse.

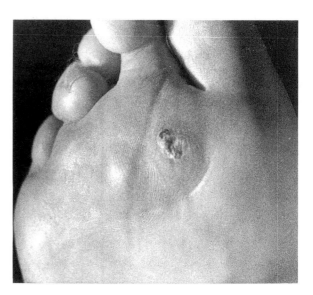

Fig. 26.10 Rheumatoid toe dislocations, metatarsal head
callosities and skin necrosis overlying second metatarsal.

deformity; overall, the latter deformity involved
22% of the feet. Only one foot displayed hallux
varus whilst three first metatarso-phalangeal
joints were truly dislocated.

In another survey [17] we noted that severe
valgus deformity precedes dislocation of the
proximal phalanx laterally between the first and
the second metatarsal heads (Fig. 26.3); dislocation of the phalanx medially and into flexion
is very rare but we observed three great toes
dislocated dorsally. By contrast, at the metatarso-phalangeal joints of the second, third,
fourth and to a variable extent the fifth toe,
dorsal dislocation is the commonest deformity
promoting excess pressure on the metatarsal
heads (Fig. 26.9). At times the lesser toes drift
into valgus without dislocating dorsally.

The metatarso-phalangeal joints

Clinical

Swelling of these joints leads to a complaint of
tight shoes and with progression of the disease,
bunion pressure and plantar pain with callosities,
especially opposite the second and third metatarsal heads; this metatarsalgia is often described
by the patient as 'walking on stones'. Increasing
deformity and unsuitable shoes may result in skin
breakdown and ulceration of the callosities,
sometimes leading to deep infection and bone
destruction. The bunion area does not normally
develop a bony exostosis, and is simply painful as
a result of severe valgus and accompanying metatarsus primus varus; the overlying skin may also
break down (Fig. 26.10). Valgus is only one
component of a three-dimensional deformity and
is associated with tortus, that is medial torsion of
the toe, which may exceed 60° in severe cases [17]
and cause a painful callosity on the medial aspect
of the inter-phalangeal joint. In many patients,
all these problems co-exist.

Radiology

Standing antero-posterior and lateral radiographs should be obtained whenever possible to
assess deformity of the hallux and especially
metatarsus primus varus which can exceed 20°.
Note that the sesamoids remain in constant relationship to the base of the proximal phalanx
even when the latter is severely subluxated or
dislocated (Fig. 26.3). The considerable strength

of the ligaments and tendons connecting the sesamoids to the phalanx prevents dislocation of the hallux more readily.

Standard radiographs display lesser toe dislocation somewhat imperfectly due to overlap, and a tangential view of the metatarsal heads is useful; this highlights the prominence of the heads and demonstrates their destruction to spike-like remnants in severe cases.

Conservative treatment

In the first instance, wider shoes with a lower heel and a simple metatarsal neck support may suffice. If a single joint is persistently swollen, an intra-articular injection of steroid may help. More serious deformity, especially when the toes dislocate, requires the manufacture of special lightweight shoes from plaster casts; such shoes provide increased depth to accommodate the toes and cushioning to relieve metatarsal head pain [18]. Many patients do not require any other measures.

Surgical treatment

Synovectomy of metatarso-phalangeal joints has been advocated but is best undertaken before deformity arises; very few patients are prepared to accept such surgery when local injections and suitable shoes are easier alternatives.

Helal [19] and others recommend tread-levelling osteotomies by oblique section through the distal metatarsal shaft combined with a Wilson osteotomy of the first metatarsal to correct hallux valgus. If the toes are totally dislocated, operative elevation of the metatarsal heads also elevates the toes and hence they remain functionless and special shoes are required to accommodate them. Nevertheless, in early cases with minor toe subluxation, multiple Helal osteotomies can be very successful.

Radical surgery includes excision arthroplasty of all the metatarso-phalangeal joints; experience has shown that removing one or two prominent metatarsal heads is unsatisfactory, for the patient soon returns with callosities beneath the remaining metatarsals. This procedure was first suggested by Hoffmann in 1912, since when it has undergone various modifications. Fowler [20] ad-

vised a dorsal approach to remove the metatarsal heads and bases of the proximal phalanges combined with removal of a plantar ellipse of skin. Kates *et al.* [21] advised a plantar approach to remove the metatarsal heads and their necks leaving the phalanges intact, removing skin from the sole and the insertion of a stabilizing wire into the first ray. If sufficient bone is removed, both these procedures relieve pain and improve the appearance of the foot. In our experience the Fowler procedure leaves the toes rather floppy and weak, whereas the Kates procedure ensures better control of the toes presumably because the attachments to the proximal phalanx are not disturbed. The results of excision arthroplasty of the metatarsal heads are mostly excellent in relieving metatarsal head pain and in improving function generally (Fig. 26.11). Often patients can buy commercial shoes and remain comfortable. However, hallux valgus may recur, for which reason some surgeons fuse the first metatarso-phalangeal joint and claim better long term results. Recurrent metatarsal pain may be the consequence of leaving a metatarsal shaft too long, of a tender scar or to the formation of rheumatoid nodules [22].

Regnauld [23] has advocated removal of the metatarsal heads and implantation on the metatarsal shafts of homograft metatarsal heads and claims these incorporate well. This is a highly skilled and time-consuming procedure and also may be limited by the supply of suitable metatarsal heads. Cracchiolo [24] has advised multiple joint replacements with Swanson silastic implants. This too is time-consuming and also difficult, especially for the smaller toes. Gould [25] recommends silastic replacement of the first metatarso-phalangeal joint and excision arthroplasty of the remaining metatarsals and has achieved good results.

The inter-phalangeal joints

The problems of the lesser toes are generally secondary to their dislocation on the metatarsals, leading to muscle imbalance and flexion or hammering of the inter-phalangeal joints. Severe hallux valgus can induce further deformity by pressure against the lesser toes or by under or over-riding the second and sometimes the third toes.

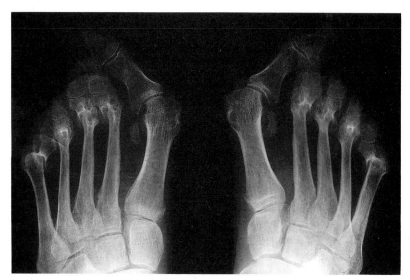

(a)

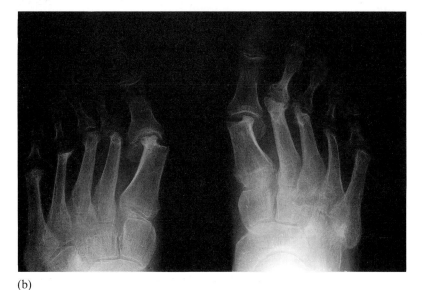

(b)

Fig. 26.11 Severely disorganized forefeet, before and after Kates–Kessel metatarsal head and neck excisions. The right first metatarsal has been over-shortened causing prominence of the second. Note the rounding of the metatarsal stumps; the patient was pleased at 5 years.

Treatment is largely that required for the primary deformity. If inter-phalangeal joint fusions are undertaken alone, full correction of metatarso-phalangeal deformity by tenotomy and capsulotomy is necessary to achieve a planti-grade toe. Partial proximal phalangectomy, sparing the base, is another alternative. Osteotomy of the proximal phalanx can also be applied usefully to re-align toes.

The inter-phalangeal joint of the hallux may present marked valgus or severe hyperextension causing painful callouses whilst the metatarso-phalangeal joint remains normal; arthrodesis of the joint in neutral is best although we have experienced failure when joint destruction has been severe and in retrospect this would have been helped by a cancellous bone graft.

Postoperative care

One penalty of severe forefoot destruction is failure of the toes to take weight, reducing the foot to a static platform whose function ceases at the metatarsal heads. In order to improve toe function, it is essential to alert the patient before surgery that vigorous postoperative toe exercises, especially plantar-flexion, are vital to a good result. These exercises should start during the anaesthetic recovery and be encouraged by all staff. As patients with bilateral plantar incisions cannot take weight until their wounds heal, they have every opportunity to obtain control and power in the toes before walking. Critics of excision arthroplasty rightly observe that it shortens the foot; however, whilst anatomically shorter, the foot proves to be physiologically longer. Indeed the patient who exercises conscientiously can ultimately stand on tip-toe unsupported, despite the absence of all metatarsal heads.

References

1. Vidigal, E., Jacoby, R. K., Dixon, A. St J. *et al.* (1975) The foot in chronic rheumatoid arthritis. *Ann. Rheum. Dis.*, **34**, 292–297.
2. Kirkup, J. R. (1988) *Terminology*. In *The Foot: Disorders and Management* (eds B. Helal, and D. W. Wilson) Churchill Livingstone, London.
3. Arden, G. P. and Ansell, B. M. (1978) *The Surgical Management of Juvenile Chronic Polyarthritis*. Academic Press, London.
4. Dixon, A. St J. and Graber, J. (1981) *Local Injection Therapy*. E.U.L.A.R. Publishers, Basel.
5. Tillmann, K. (1979) *The Rheumatoid Foot*. Thieme, Stuttgart.
6. Benjamin, A. and Helal, B. (1980) *Surgical Repair and Reconstruction in Rheumatoid Disease*, Macmillan, London, p. 204.
7. Kirkup, J. R. (1974) Ankle and tarsal joints in rheumatoid arthritis. *Scand. J. Rheumatol.*, **3**, 50–52.
8. Bolton-Maggs, B. G., Sudlow, R. A. and Freeman, M. A. R. (1985) Total ankle arthroplasty: a long-term review of the London Hospital experience. *J. Bone Joint Surg.*, **67B**, 785–790.
9. Samuelson, K. M., Freeman, M. A. R. and Tuke, M. A. (1982) Development and evolution of the I.C.L.H. ankle replacement. *Foot and Ankle*, **3**, 32–36.
10. Demottaz, J. D., Mazur, J. M., Thomas, W. H. *et al.* (1979) Clinical study of total ankle replacement with gait analysis. *J. Bone Joint Surg.*, **61A**, 976–988.
11. Herberts, P., Goldie, I. F., Korner, L. *et al.* (1982) Endoprosthetic arthroplasty of the ankle joint: a clinical and radiological follow-up. *Acta Orthop. Scand.*, **53**, 687–696.
12. Lachiewicz, P. F., Inglis, A. E. and Ranawat, C. S. (1984) Total ankle replacement in rheumatoid arthritis. *J. Bone Joint Surg.*, **66A**, 340–343.
13. Kirkup, J. R. (1985) Richard Smith ankle arthroplasty. *J. R. Soc. Med.*, **78**, 301–304.
14. Marsh, C. H., Kirkup, J. R. and Regan, M. W. (1987) The Bath and Wessex ankle arthroplasty. Proceedings report. *J. Bone Joint Surg.*, **69B**, 153.
15. Vahvanen, V. A. J. (1967) Rheumatoid arthritis in the pantalar joints. *Acta Orthop. Scand.*, **Suppl.**, **107**, 1–157.
16. Kirkup, J. R. Vidigal, E. and Jacoby, R. K. (1977) The hallux and rheumatoid arthritis. *Acta Orthop. Scand.*, **48**, 527–544.
17. Kirkup, J. R. (1978) Dislocation of the hallux in rheumatoid arthritis. *Chirurg. del Piede*, **2**, 87–93.
18. Dixon, A. St J. (1970) Medical aspects of the rheumatoid foot. *Proc. R. Soc. Med.*, **63**, 677–679.
19. Helal, B. (1975) Metatarsal osteotomy for metatarsalgia, *J. Bone Joint Surg.*, **57B**, 187–192.
20. Fowler, A. W. (1959) A method of forefoot reconstruction. *J. Bone Joint Surg.*, **41B**, 507–513.
21. Kates, A., Kessel, L. and Kay, A. (1967) Arthroplasty of the forefoot. *J. Bone Joint Surg.*, **49B**, 552–557.
22. Morrison, P. (1974) Complications of forefoot operations in rheumatoid arthritis. *Proc. R. Soc. Med.*, **67**, 110–111.
23. Regnauld, B. (1974) *Techniques Chirurgicales du Pied*. Masson, Paris, p. 81.
24. Cracchiolo, A. (1982) Management of the arthritic forefoot. *Foot and Ankle*, **3**, 17–23.
25. Gould, N. (1982) Surgery of the forepart of the foot in rheumatoid arthritis. *Foot and Ankle*, **3**, 173–180.

27

Correction of posture in ankylosing spondylitis

P. M. Yeoman

The flexed posture caused by ankylosing spondylitis is one of the more distressing complaints amongst young adults (Fig. 27.1). It is difficult enough to adapt to a life when the spine is rigid even if that problem develops insidiously, but when the forward vision is restricted to only a few paces ahead the quality of life is seriously impaired. The era is past when rest, firm support, radiotherapy and an assortment of analgesics

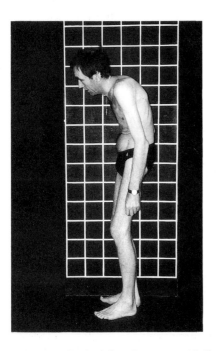

Fig. 27.1 Typical flexed posture with limited forward vision.

were common practice but it left behind a number of patients who have severely flexed and rigid spines. It has been superseded by a regime of exercises and anti-inflammatory drugs backed up by a trained experienced team who can assess and compare the results of their courses of management, which in turn is of benefit to the patient. The diagnosis is made earlier in the course of the disease, and backache in teenage girls may well be the first indication of ankylosing spondylitis. A diagnosis rarely considered 20 years ago for a condition which was thought to be predominantly affecting young men. Ankylosing spondylitis occurs equally between the sexes.

The B27 antigen study has revealed a greater incidence of ankylosing spondylitis among those patients who possess this antigen [1]. There can be peripheral joint changes almost identical with those seen in rheumatoid arthritis and yet it lies within the sero-negative arthropathies [2].

Ulcerative colitis and occasionally Crohn's disease is linked with ankylosing spondylitis [3,4], and either condition can seriously impair the general health of the patient and render them unfit for major surgery. Intestinal low-grade infection from the Klebsiella organism has been incriminated [5] but appropriate treatment has failed to provide more than a brief improvement in the spinal condition.

Pain is foremost in the patient's mind and is the responsibility of the rheumatologist who can employ a variety of anti-inflammatory drugs to good effect. Steroids are rarely used but occasionally ACTH is indicated. Pain developing after a

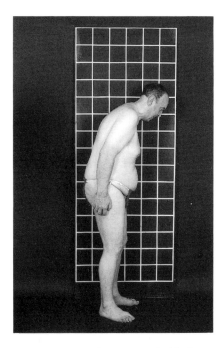

Fig. 27.2 Flexed posture suitable for correction in lumbar spine.

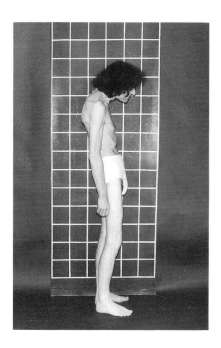

Fig. 27.3 Flexed posture suitable for correction in cervical spine.

reasonably long quiescent period may well be associated with posture and this may not respond to the conservative management.

The flexed posture

The three sites of deformity may be in: the hips, lumbar spine (Fig. 27.2), cervical spine (Fig. 27.3) or a combination of the three. Assessment by the team in hospital includes specially trained physiotherapists who can detect and measure the prime cause of the flexed posture, and thus determine a baseline for the graduated course of exercises. Progress or relapse between these courses can be assessed but most require in-patient supervision on an annual basis, or less depending on the severity of the disease.

Hips

A flexion contracture of both hips in ankylosing spondylitis is not easy to assess with accuracy owing to the rigidity of the lumbar spine. Clinical examination of the patient in the supine position is not possible, which rules out the classical

Thomas' test for demonstrating any flexion contracture in the hips. The patient has to be examined on their side. In the early stages of the disease it should be possible not only to detect but to prevent contractures of the hips [6].

Physiotherapy

Gentle passive movements by the physiotherapist and instruction of the patient to lie face downwards for at least part of the day and night may reduce and even prevent flexion contractures of the hips. The patient's relative should also be instructed on the method of passive stretching of the hips.

Arthroplasty of the hip

This is a well established surgical procedure and both hips can be replaced under the one anaesthetic. The author does not recommend a simultaneous bilateral hip replacement using two surgeons and assistants because of the hazards of blood loss, apart from the obvious technical difficulties. It is better carefully to assess the patient and blood loss after the first operation and only proceed with the second if all is well. In the postoperative period it is essential for the physiotherapist to continue with passive extension exercises of the hips and the patient is encouraged to lie prone for at least two periods during each day for at least 3 months. Heterotopic bone formation and subsequent ankylosis was a particular hazard in the Smith–Petersen era of mould arthroplasty but a recent review in 56 hip replacements [7] has revealed the importance not only of good quality physio- and hydrotherapy but the distance between the acetabulum and the greater trochanter will determine future stiffness and even ankylosis. A small gap between these two points is less likely to succeed.

Indocid has been recommended as a means of reducing heterotopic new bone formation; diphosphonate has not been successful [8].

Osteotomy of the lumbar spine

At first this would appear a formidable task but there are two essential criteria for success: first, not to attempt too great a correction; second, to obtain sound internal fixation (Figs 27.4, 27.5).

The author has always taken an active part in the preliminary scene not only in the anaesthetic room but also in positioning the patient on the operating table. Details can include the correct height of pillows under the chest to allow clearance for abdominal respiration and thus avoid venous congestion in the operating site; suitable padding under the pressure points at the knees and chin; and a check that the table is suitably adapted for breaking in order to accommodate the rigid flexed posture and adjustments for obtaining the proposed correction. A transverse incision in the mid-lumbar area would appear to be the optimum approach because of the clean healing without tension after the correction. In practice, this did not provide the necessary access above and below the osteotomy for applying the internal fixation; a midline longitudinal incision was preferable. The bone was surprisingly soft to resect except on occasions when it was dense and hard around the pedicles, and this called for slow arduous dissection in order to obtain precise clearance for the emerging nerve roots. A chevron shaped osteotomy resection gave the most stable closure, with the axis anterior to the cauda equina [9]. Internal fixation is obligatory, not only to avoid a long period in a corrective

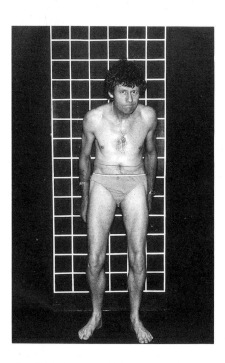

Fig. 27.4 Posture before correction.

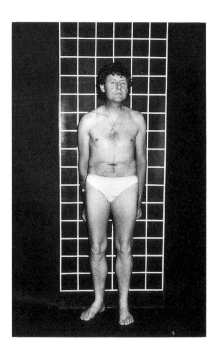

Fig. 27.5 One year after lumbar osteotomy.

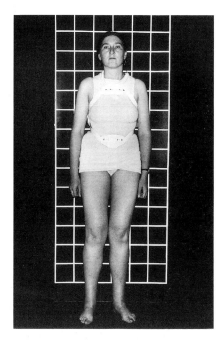

Fig. 27.6 Lightweight spinal brace worn for second period of 6 months.

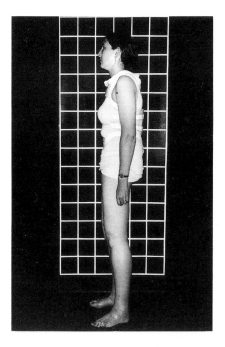

Fig. 27.7 Lightweight spinal brace worn for second period of 6 months.

plaster bed but to achieve stability thus preventing loss of correction or worse, the fatal damage to the cauda equina. Many methods were used [10] and by far the best fixation was obtained by transpedicular screws and interconnecting cables [11]. There is bound to be some loss of correction by any method but in the final group of 17 patients out of a total of 37, there was an average loss of only 6° by the pedicular screws and cable fixation.

In the postoperative period a corrective or supporting corset was worn for 6 months (Figs 27.6, 27.7).

Cervical osteotomy

This can be a formidable task [12]. The bone texture is invariably soft, the cervical canal has less accommodation than in the lumbar area, and there has to be more reliance on external fixation than in the previous account of internal fixation in the lumbar osteotomy. The advice is similar – overcorrection may lead to disaster (Figs 27.8, 27.9).

External fixation is obligatory and halo-vest is the chosen method because it provides safe and reliable external stability and allows the patient to be mobile and return home (Figs 27.10, 27.11).

After the induction of anaesthesia the application of the halo is the first part of the operation. Thereafter it is necessary to position the patient prone on the operating table which has a separate adjustable head piece. A transverse incision may be acceptable and it heals better than a midline longitudinal approach. Sadly the bone texture is relatively soft which makes resection easier but fixation unreliable. The meningeal covering of the spinal cord and emerging nerve roots has to be widely exposed at the site of the osteotomy, which is usually at the level of C5/6 or 7. Closure of the osteotomy is performed as a combined procedure with the surgeon manipulating the patient's towelled head and the anaesthetist on the table controls. Internal fixation is not adequate and consists of encircling wire around the laminae and spinous processes. Occasionally a small metal jaw fixation plate has been used. The halo-vest support may be required for at least 6 months and a collar for a further 6 months. The results reveal a satisfactory angle of correction which has been maintained.

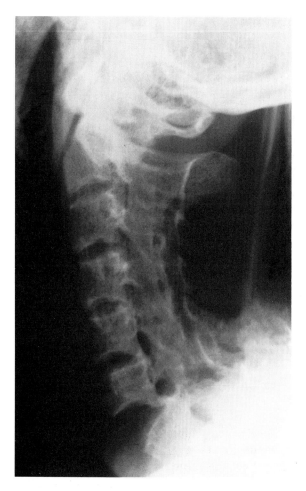

Fig. 27.8   Cervical osteotomy at C6/7 level (maximum correction).

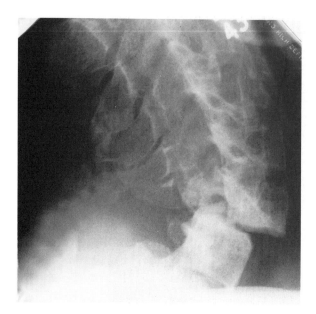

Fig. 27.9   Overcorrection resulting in instability; requiring revision.

Anaesthesia

Perhaps the most important development in anaesthetic technique has been unfairly relegated but there is no doubt that the flexible fibreoptic bronchoscope has made an immense difference; it has transformed a definite hazardous procedure of intubation in patients with ankylosing spondylitis to one of relative safety and reliability. It could be stated that intubation in the past was a hit and miss affair with all the dangers of a failed procedure before embarking on the operation which carried a high morbidity and mortality in itself. Preoperative assessment by the anaesthetist is obligatory not only for appraisal of the rigid neck deformity but to gain the confidence of the patient if it has been decided to perform an 'awake' intubation [13].

Correction without operation

Elderly and others who are unfit candidates for such a major event can be corrected by using an external fixator alone. The halo-vest technique has to incorporate turnbuckle screws with universal joints to allow a slow but steady correction of a few degrees each day. The patients are better in hospital, but not in bed, because problems arise with the apparatus which requires daily adjustment and almost hourly supervision. Some elderly patients develop respiratory problems not only as a result of a rigid rib cage but from the flexed cervical spine; even to the extent of developing a pressure sore between the chin and the chest. Successful correction was obtained without an operation in a select group of five elderly patients. Younger patients who do not have osteoporosis or a recent fracture are not suitable for this method; their spines are unyielding.

Fractures of the spine in ankylosing spondylitis

These patients are as likely to be involved in automobile accidents as any other person but

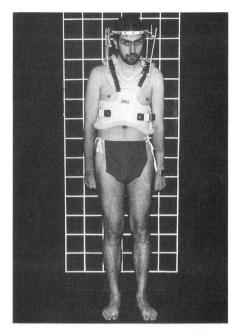

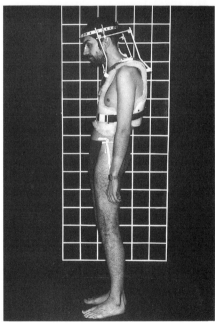

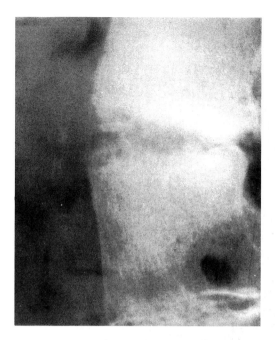

Fig. 27.12 Stress fracture in the lumbar area resembles a chronic infection.

Figs. 27.10 & 27.11 Halo-vest apparatus allows the patient to return home.

they are more at risk if they have a rigid cervical spine [14]. Older patients with quiescent ankylosing spondylitis may suffer a fracture of the cervical spine as a result of trivial trauma, such as a fall from a chair. The opportunity to correct the flexed posture must not be missed. An external

fixator with suitable turnbuckle attachments is indicated. Unfortunately in practice this is not often achieved because time is wasted in making a diagnosis. A fracture is most common at the cervico-thoracic junction, a site which is often obscured on the lateral radiographs by the shoulders, and the fracture is missed. Any patient who develops pain in the neck after a period of remission is deemed to have a fracture until proved otherwise [15].

A stress fracture (Fig. 27.12) may mimic a low-grade chronic infection on the radiographs, and indeed clinically [16]. Brucellosis may be suspected and time is wasted unnecessarily. A bone scan or MRI screening will reveal the site and diagnosis.

Conclusion

The future lies not only in determining the cause of ankylosing spondylitis but in active management to ensure minimal deformity of posture. Already the need for surgical correction of these terrible deformities has diminished and should be confined to special centres.

References

1. James, D. C. O. (1983) HLA-B27 in clinical medicine. *Br. J. Rheumatol.*, **22 (suppl. 2)**, 20–24.
2. Miehle, W., Schattenkirchner, M., Albert, D. and Bunge, M. (1985) HLA-DR4 in ankylosing spondylitis with different patterns of joint involvement. *Ann. Rheum. Dis.*, **44**, 39–44.
3. Moll, J. M. H. (1983) Pathogenetic mechanisms in B27 associated diseases. *Br. J. Rheumatol.*, **22 (suppl. 2)**, 93–103.
4. Hickling, P., Bird-Stewart, J. A., Young, J. D. and Wright, V. (1983) Crohn's spondylitis: a family study. *Ann. Rheumat. Dis.*, **42**, 106–107.
5. Ebringer, A. (1983) The cross-tolerance hypothesis HLA-B27 and ankylosing spondylitis. *Br. J. Rheumatol.*, **22 (suppl. 2)**, 53–66.
6. Bulstrode, S. J., Barefoot, J., Harrison, R. A. and Clarke, A. K. (1987) The role of passive stretching in the treatment of ankylosing spondylitis. *Br. J. Rheumatol.*, **26**, 40–42.
7. May, P. C. and Yeoman, P. M. (1990) Primary total hip arthroplasty in ankylosing spondylitis. *Rheumatology*, **13**, 223–227.
8. Thomas, B. J. and Amstutz, H. C. (1985) Results of the administration of diphosphonate for the prevention of heterotopic ossification after total hip arthroplasty. *J. Bone Joint Surg.*, **67A(3)**, 400–403.
9. McMaster, M. J. and Coventry, M. B. (1973) Spinal osteotomy in ankylosing spondylitis. *Mayo Clin. Proc.*, **48 (7)**, 476–486.
10. Fidler, M. W. (1986) Posterior instrumentation of the spine: an experimental comparison of various possible techniques. *Spine*, **11.4**, 367–372.
11. Weale, A. E., Marsh, C. H. and Yeoman, P. M. (1995) The secure fixation of lumber osteotomy. In press.
12. Simmons, E. H. (1972) The surgical correction of flexion deformity of the cervical spine in ankylosing spondylitis. *Clin. Orthop. Rel. Res.*, **86**, 132–143.
13. Sinclair, J. R. and Mason, R. A. (1984) Ankylosing spondylitis: the case for awake intubation. *Anaesthesia*, **39**, 3–11.
14. Wordsworth, B. P. and Mowat, A. G. (1986) A review of 100 patients with ankylosing spondylitis with particular reference to socio-economic effects. *Br. J. Rheumatol.*, **25**, 175–180.
15. Marsh, C. H. (1985) Internal fixation for stress fracture of the ankylosed spine. *J. R. Soc. Med.*, **78**, 377–379.
16. Yau, A. and Chan, R. (1974) Stress fracture of the fused lumbo-dorsal spine in ankylosing spondylitis. *J. Bone Joint Surg.*, **56B(4)**, 681–687.

28

Musculoskeletal sepsis: current concepts in treatment

R. H. Fitzgerald

Although the incidence of musculoskeletal sepsis has been reduced, septic complications of traumatic and elective surgery of the musculoskeletal system continue to be devastating to the patient. The most efficient treatment of musculoskeletal infections remains prevention of septic complications following the surgical treatment of traumatic injuries and elective reconstructive surgery. Fortunately, there have been numerous improvements, initiated by orthopaedic surgeons, which have the capability of reducing the incidence of postoperative surgical sepsis. Osteomyelitis of haematogenous origin in the child, once a dreaded disease, rapidly responds to specific antimicrobial therapy if diagnosed early. Most adult patients who are afflicted with osteomyelitis sustained a traumatic injury which was complicated by sepsis. Septic complications of total joint arthroplasty have become one of the major complications of total joint arthroplasty. Currently, there are several different approaches to the treatment of the patient with an infected total joint arthroplasty. Unfortunately, none of these approaches has universally resolved the process and preserved the arthroplasty. An infection of the spinal column has been referred to as 'the greatest masquerader', as it can mimic so many other clinical syndromes. Earlier diagnosis necessitates that all physicians become conversant with the initial clinical manifestations.

Prevention of postoperative sepsis

Prevention of septic complications following musculoskeletal surgery includes careful preoperative evaluation of the patient, the selective and appropriate utilization of prophylactic antimicrobial agents, and the use of ultra-clean operating rooms. Many of the elderly patients seeking reconstructive musculoskeletal surgery are malnourished. Jenson and co-workers have found that 10–15% of patients scheduled for total hip arthroplasty are severely malnourished and have evidence of immunodepression. Since protein depletion can adversely influence wound healing and impair humoral and cell-mediated immunity, such patients need to be identified preoperatively to permit nutritional therapy. Identification of such patients can be accomplished by a number of ways.

Anthropometric measurements, biochemical testing, and skin antigen testing provide data which permit assessment of a patient's nutritional status [1]. Anthropometric studies found to be useful in the preoperative assessment for nutritional depletion include measurement of the triceps skinfold and arm circumference in addition to the height and weight of the patient. Biochemical testing should include the serum albumin, serum transfusion and serum transferrin, and serum creatinine concentrations in addition to the total peripheral lymphocyte count and nitrogen balance. When these data are analyzed and suggest nutritional depletion, surgery should be postponed until nutritional therapy can be instituted to correct the problem.

Preoperative evaluation

Preoperatively, each patient should be carefully examined for remote infections which could lead to haematogenous seeding of the postoperative wound with bacteria. The surgeon must inspect such sites as infected hair follicles or sebaceous glands of the skin, necessitating examination of skin of a disrobed patient. Infected toenails are often overlooked during the preoperative evaluation of patients unless the patient examined offer removal of clothes, including shoes and socks. Such infections should be treated before musculoskeletal surgery is performed. Asymptomatic urinary tract infections can usually be identified by the presence of bacteria on a routine preoperative urinalysis. They can then be confirmed with a Gram-stain and urine culture. Surgical intervention should be delayed until the infection has been treated and a sterile urine culture has been obtained with the patient off antibiotic therapy.

Occasionally, patients live symbiotically with chronic urinary infections which are resistant to treatment. The infection can be suppressed during the perioperative period, but the patient has an increased risk of developing postoperative sepsis. This is especially true if the contemplated reconstructive procedure includes the implantation of a foreign body such as an artificial knee or hip prosthesis. Under such circumstances the patient and surgeon must carefully individualize the risk–benefit ratios.

Another area of concern is the prostate in males over the age of 55 years. Such patients should be queried concerning nocturia and urinary frequency. Should the prostate gland feel enlarged to palpation, urological consultation is necessary. When transurethral prostate resection be necessary, it is more desirable to have such surgery performed prior to the surgical placement of orthopaedic implants than to request it postoperatively as urinary catheters are necessary following prostatic resection. Such circumstances certainly place the patient in a com- promised position and increase the risk of haematogenous infection. If a trans-urethral prostatic resection is required, elective musculoskeletal surgery involving the implantation of foreign bodies should be delayed for 12 weeks to allow the resected portion of the prostate gland to re-epithelialize.

Orthopaedic surgeons can overlook the oral cavity during the preoperative evaluation of patients. Although it can be difficult to identify carious teeth, poor oral hygiene is usually apparent. When present, the patient should have appropriate dental examinations and treatment prior to musculoskeletal surgery.

Although such an extensive search for remote infections or potential causes of infection during the preoperative evaluation may seem excessive, it is surprising how often remote infections are responsible for septic complications of total joint arthroplasty. They are simple techniques requiring minimal time and provide both the surgeon and the patient with additional insurance against postoperative infections.

Prophylactic antimicrobial agents

The prophylactic administration of antimicrobial agent has become a well established principle for the reduction of postoperative sepsis. There is, however, some confusion over the application of this principle by surgeons. Should all patients having musculoskeletal surgery receive prophylactic antimicrobial? If not, which patient should and which patients should not? Which antimicrobial agents should be administered and when should they be administered?

All surgeons would agree that those procedures involving the implantation of large foreign bodies necessitate the prophylactic adminstration of antimicrobial agents [2]. The indications for operations involving the application of one or two screws or Steinmann pins are less clear. Certainly, any operation where a dead space which permits the formation of a haematoma should be associated with the administration of prophylactic antimicrobials. Operations requiring 2 or more hours would also justify the prophylactic administration of antimicrobial agents. In general, soft tissue operations, procedures implanting minimal metal devices, and those of short duration are not usually considered for administration of anti-microbial agents prophylactically. However, Henley and co-workers recently reported a statistically significant reduction in the incidence of postoperative sepsis in soft tissue and other musculoskeletal procedures not requiring a prosthetic device lasting 2 or more hours with the prophylactic administration of antimicrobials [3]. Procedures requiring less than 2 hours did not have an associated reduction in the incidence of sepsis. The application of these principles to musculoskeletal procedures must be left to the discretion of the individual surgeon, who is capable of making the wisest decision for each patient.

When the prophylactic administration of antimicrobial agents is thought to be indicated, the surgeon must select an agent that is bactericidal against the microorganisms associated with postoperative musculoskeletal sepsis in his or her hospital. Furthermore, the agent selected should be safe and inexpensive. In North America *Staphylococcus aureus* and *Staphylococcus epidermidis* remain the most common causal organisms isolated from postoperative infections of the musculoskeletal system. Streptococci are the third commonest isolates recovered. Gram-negative bacillary organisms are less common isolates. Thus, a first generation cephalosporin remains an ideal agent for the prophylactic administration to patients having musculoskeletal surgery.

Although some surgeons have advocated the use of a second or even a third generation of cephalosporin as the prophylactic agent of choice, there are few data to justify such recommendations. Occasionally, unique situations in some hospital environments may justify their use on a temporary basis. These agents are no more effective than a first generation cephalosporin against the usual causal organisms and they certainly are far more expensive.

The timing of the administration and the duration of prophylactic antimicrobials remain controversial. Although most surgeons initiate the administration of prophylactic antibiotics during surgery, the duration of administration varies widely. It would appear that most surgeons discontinue antimicrobials 48–72 hours after surgery. There is certainly no need to continue the administration of antibiotics for 5–7 days. In fact, such prolonged administration of antimicrobials appears to permit the development of remote infections. More recently some authorities have suggested that the antimicrobials may be discontinued after one to two doses administered during surgery and in the recovery room. Though such a brief period of administration may prove to be efficacious and cost effective, it has yet to be studied in depth.

Operating room environment

Ultraclean operating rooms, introduced to modern surgery by Sir John Charnley, have remained controversial. All surgeons would agree that if cleansing of the ambient environment can reduce the incidence of postoperative sepsis, it is worthwhile even if expensive [4]. Lidwell and co-workers have presented strong evidence to support the use of ultraclean operating rooms for total hip and total knee arthroplasty [5]. In their multicentre study of nineteen hospitals in which total joint procedures were randomized between a conventionally ventilated operating room and an operating room ventilated by an ultraclean-air system, a statistically significant reduction in the incidence of postoperative sepsis was found with those procedures performed in the ultraclean-air systems (63 of 4133 versus 23 of 3922; $P < 0.001$). Unfortunately, this elaborate and extensive study failed to control the use of prophylactic antimicrobials. The incidence of postoperative sepsis following total hip or knee arthroplasty performed with the prophylactic administration of antimicrobials in a conventional operating room was 24 of 2968 (0.8%). Similarly, the incidence of postoperative sepsis for these procedures performed in a room with an ultraclean-air system was 10 of 2863 (0.3); $Chi^2 = 5.31$, $P < 0.2$. Since the influence of the prophylactic administration of antimicrobial was not randomized, it is difficult to judge its impact on the study. It would appear, however, that total joint arthroplasty performed in a conventional operating room with adherence to strict aseptic techniques, including the administration of prophylactic antimicrobials, can be associated with postoperative infection rates which are statistically indistinguishable from those found in ultraclean operating rooms.

Hill and co-workers made similar observations in a multicentre study of the prophylactic administration of cefazolin. In this randomized, double-blind, placebo-controlled [6] study of ten centres in France, cefazolin statistically reduced ($P < 0.001$), the incidence of deep sepsis following total hip arthroplasty from 35 of 1067 (3.3%) in the control group to 10 of 1070 (0.9%). However, these investigators found 'the rate of hip infection was the same in a conventional theatre with prophylactic antibiotherapy as in a hypersterile theatre with or without antibiotherapy'.

Thus, it would appear that implant surgery must be performed in association with the prophylactic administration of antimicrobial therapy. The role of ultraclean operating rooms awaits clarification from other clinical studies which control the impact of antimicrobial therapy. In the interim, carefully performed implant procedures can be safely conducted in conventional operating rooms where there is strict adherence to aseptic technique and traffic control.

Osteomyelitis

Haematogenous osteomyelitis in the child is not only seen with less frequency than in the past, but is also more responsive to modern therapeutic modalities. Morrissy has demonstrated that minor trauma about the growth plate may be instrumental in the development of acute haematogenous osteomyelitis. The pathophysiological mechanism which is responsible for this 'locus minoris resistentiae' remains to be elucidated. Hobo, however, has suggested that there is limited phagocytic activity by the tissue-based mononuclear cells in and about the physeal plate. Traumatic injuries, although they may be minor in nature, may further compromise the phagocytic defences. The perceived reduction of patients with acute haematogenous osteomyelitis is difficult to explain. Certainly, the overall nutritional status of Western civilization has improved over the past 4 decades. The sophistication of patients and their parents has encouraged early medical evaluation and treatment. Without question, the availability of effective antimicrobials which physicians are willing to administer early have had a decidedly positive influence on the ultimate prognosis of acute haematogenous osteomyelitis. Most children can be cured without surgical intervention. Progres-

sion of this disease process into chronic osteomyelitis is distinctly uncommon in the absence of some major alteration of the immune system by a concomitant disease process.

Osteomyelitis in the adult patient is usually the sequelae of a traumatic injury. In contrast to acute haematogenous osteomyelitis where *S. aureus* and *B-haemolytic streptococcus* are recovered, Gram-negative bacillary organisms are recovered as pure or mixed isolates in almost half of the patients. Methicillin-resistant *S. aureus* is being recovered from clinical material from patients with musculoskeletal sepsis with increased frequency [7]. Essentially all adult patients with post-traumatic osteomyelitis will require a combination of surgical and medical therapy. Recovery of the causal organism(s) from deep tissue specimens and identification of the antimicrobial susceptibility pattern(s) are the first prerequisites of treatment. Surgical excision of foreign bodies, necrotic, and infected tissue must be meticulously performed. In recent years several new surgical modalities have permitted the modern orthopaedist, dramatically to help this group of patients.

The development of external fixator devices has permitted the management of the infected nonunion without introducing additional foreign material into the wound. The use of half-pins as well as transfixing pins permits the surgeon to construct external fixation apparatuses which will biomechanically enhance union. Sixty to 70% of infected non-unions will unite without supplemental bone grafting procedure with eradication of the septic process and the use of external fixation devices.

The availability of local muscle flaps, free microvascular flaps and cancellous bone grafting procedures have permitted the orthopaedist to aggressively treat osteomyelitic foci. Radical local resections, excising infected and poorly vascularized adjacent tissues back to healthy tissue, can now be performed as there are techniques which permit reconstruction of a functional extremity. A local muscle flap can be used in patients with a large defect of soft tissue and bone after debridement of an osteomyelitic lesion if the flap can be elevated and transposed into the defect without compromising its vascular supply [8]. The soleus or gastrocnemius muscle flap are the most frequently utilized flaps to achieve wound closure. The combination of radical

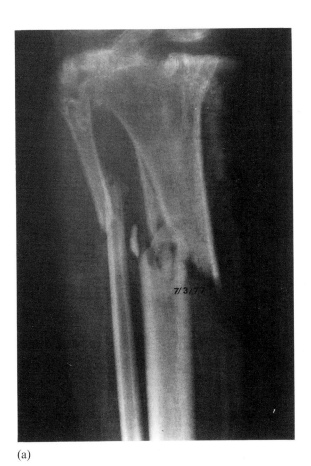

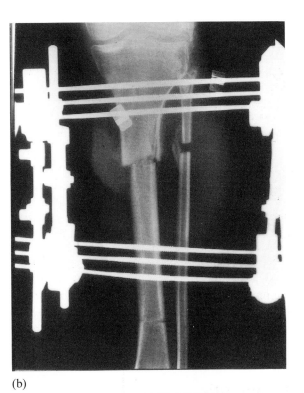

(b)

(a)

Fig. 28.1 Post-traumatic osteomyelitis 7 months following a crush injury to the tibia in a 26-year-old man. There is a 5 × 6 cm open draining wound.
(a) Anteroposterior roentgenogram of tibia 7 months following injury reveals malalignment with obvious non-union. (b) Following debridement the tibia was realigned, an external fixation device applied, and gastrocnemius muscle flap rotated into the soft tissue defect. Subsequently a split thickness skin graft was applied.
(c) Anteroposterior and lateral roentgenograms 18 months following treatment reveal healing with appropriate alignment. No further drainage has occurred 10 years following debridement.

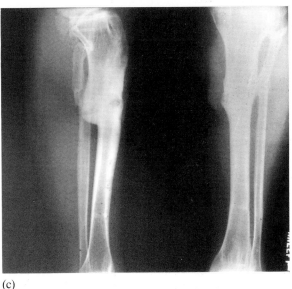

(c)

debridement, wound closure with a local muscle flap, and specific antimicrobial therapy has successfully eradicated osteomyelitis in 93% of the patients treated.

When the infectious process, the radical local debridement, or the anatomic location precludes the use of a local muscle flap, a microvascular free flap composed of soft tissue alone, bone alone or a combination of both is possible. In general, wound closures with a free muscle flap should be the initial goal. If a major segmental, osseous defect exists, it can subsequently be managed with a free fibular flap (or a cancellous bone grafting procedure). Experience with a combined osseous and soft tissue one-staged free tissue transfer has not been as successful.

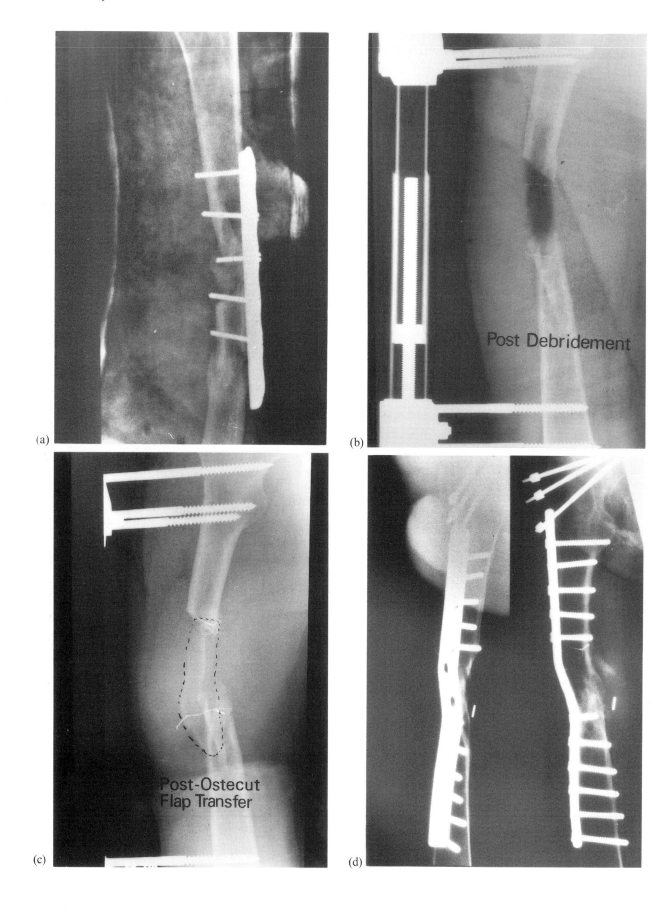

(a)

(b) Post Debridement

(c) Post-Ostecut Flap Transfer

(d)

Although such technically demanding procedures have not been as successful as the local muscle flaps, they have salvaged three-quarters of the patients so treated who in the past would have been relegated to abalative surgery.

Antimicrobial therapy for the adult patient with osteomyelitis should be specific for all of the causal organisms recovered from the deep tissue specimens obtained during debridement. The isolation of mixed aerobic–anaerobic organisms appears to adversely influence the prognosis [9]. The duration of parenteral therapy remains empiric, ranging from 3 to 6 weeks. Experience would dictate that 3 weeks of parenteral therapy followed by 4 weeks of oral therapy in patients with rapid wound healing is adequate. However, when wound healing is difficult to achieve and prolonged, parenteral therapy should be extended. Continuation of parenteral therapy, initiated in the hospital, at home with specialized catheters has proven to be effective [10].

The role of the depot administration of antibiotics utilizing antibiotic-impregnated polymethylmethacrylate beads is currently under clinical investigation. Preliminary studies by Klemm and others suggest that this technique is promising. However, it is disturbing to implant further foreign material into a wound, even temporarily, following a rigorous surgical excision of all necrotic bone, infected tissue, and foreign material. A biodegradable carrier would seem to be more appropriate. Nevertheless, orthopaedic surgeons look forward to the results of a prospective study currently in progress in North America.

Fig. 28.2 Infected non-union of femoral fracture in a 24-year-old medical student. A sinus tract from the lateral thigh incision extends deep to the fracture site.
(a) Anteroposterior roentgenogram reveals an intercalary fracture with non-union of the proximal fracture site.
(b) Anteroposterior roentgenogram following debridement and application of a Wagner apparatus. The intercalary fragment was united to the distal femur but was dead.
(c) Anteroposterior roentgenogram following wound closure with a free-vascularized osteocutaneous iliac crest flap. (d) Anteroposterior roentgenogram 3 months following the free flap. Further bone autogenous grafting and plate stabilization was performed. He is a practising physician without further drainage 7 years later.

Infections following total hip arthroplasty

The dramatic functional improvement following total knee or total hip arthroplasty can be significantly compromised should the procedure be complicated by postoperative wound sepsis. Fortunately, this dreaded complication occurs infrequently. When it does occur, aggressive surgical intervention is indicated in all but a minority of patients as antibiotics alone are ineffective.

Sepsis of a total hip arthroplasty occurs in one of three stages [11]. Stage I infections are those occurring during the immediate postoperative period and usually constitutes a colonized or infected haematoma. Such haematomas are best decompressed with aseptic techniques in the operating room prior to the development of spontaneous drainage. When the latter occurs, secondary bacterial invaders which are usually Gram-negative bacilli have access to the depths of the wound. Surgical decompression of the wound followed 2–3 weeks of specific antimicrobial therapy will eradicate the infectious process in the vast majority of patients.

Stage II infections are those which are associated with minimal symptomatology. Such infections are rarely associated with a febrile response, wound swelling or drainage. Characteristically, the patient will complain of pain, indicating that he or she has experienced pain since the immediate postoperative period. The paucity of symptoms usually delays the diagnosis of sepsis for 12–24 months following surgery. Imaging of the hip with In[111] labelled white blood cells has proven to be an effective diagnostic tool [12]. Patients with Stage II infections will require surgical extirpation of all foreign material to eradicate the infection [13].

Late haematogenous infections of the artificial joint compose Stage III infections. Usually the patient will be free of any symptoms referable to the total joint arthroplasty until the acute onset of pain associated with a febrile response. Infections in this group of patients should be treated with immediate aspiration of the joint. If microorganisms are seen with Gram stain of the aspirate or the aspirate has other features consistent with sepsis, prompt arthrotomy should be performed. Usually the prosthetic devices are found to be securely attached to bone. Treatment in-

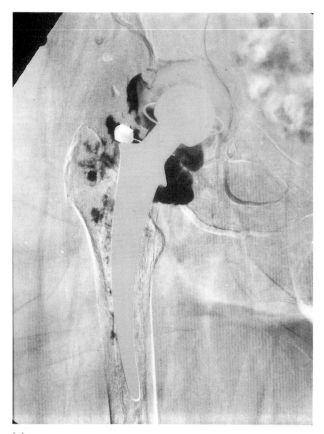

(a)

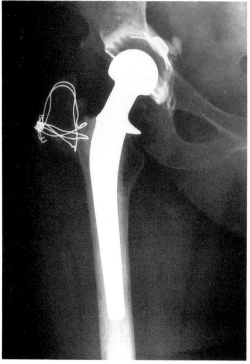

(b)

Fig. 28.3   Infected hip arthroplasty 18 months following a total hip arthroplasty in a 58-year-old school teacher. A two-staged procedure was used to reconstruct her hip. (a) Anteroposterior roentgenogram following resection arthroplasty. *Escherichia coli* was isolated from deep tissue specimens. (b) Anteroposterior roentgenogram following reconstruction of the hip in delayed fashion. The hip was reconstructed 12 months following resection arthroplasty. This roentgenogram was made 18 months following reconstruction. She has a painless hip 5 years following reconstruction.

cludes debridement without removal of the components followed by 4 weeks of parenteral antimicrobial therapy. Unfortunately, many patients with Stage III infection of an implant will experience recurrent infection. At this time, there are no methodologies to predict which patients will respond and which patients will experience recurrent sepsis. The varied clinical response may be related to the development of glycocalyx which is a glycoprotein permitting bacterial adherence to foreign bodies. Glycocalyx also appears to protect microorganisms from exposure to the host defence mechanisms. Unfortunately, there are no techniques which allow the clinician to differentiate those prostheses which have glycocalyx formation from those which do not.

Surgical reconstruction of the septic artificial joint requiring removal of the prosthetic components can be performed in a single stage, two stages or occasionally a three-staged procedure. The treatment of a patient with an infected total hip arthroplasty with surgical extirpation and reconstruction with another prosthesis during a single operation was introduced to the orthopaedic community by Buchholz [14]. This technique was based upon the principle of placing antibodies in polymethyl methacrylate [15]. Careful scrutiny of Buchholz's data suggests that he was more successful with this technique when treating infections which were associated with the isolation of less virulent microorganisms (Table 28.1). He was most successful in the treatment of

infections from which no bacteria could be recovered or those from which he recovered anaesthetic causal organisms. Recurrent sepsis occurred in half of the patients from which Gram-negative bacillary organisms were isolated. In a recent long-term follow-up of some 825 patients treated in Germany, Rüttger reported recurrent sepsis in 30% at 6 years and 50% at 11 years [6]. The preliminary results of a portion of a prospective study in North America suggest that this technique can be highly successful when the patients so treated are carefully selected. Ninety-six percent of 194 patients with an infected total hip or total knee arthroplasty treated at the Mayo Clinic or The Hospital for Special Surgery were free from recurrent sepsis 2 years following surgery.

Delayed reconstruction following surgical extirpation of the infected total joint arthroplasty is certainly a safer technique for the treatment of most deep infections of total joint arthroplasty. The timing of the reconstructive procedure is variable and empiric. Those patients with a less virulent causal organism (Table 28.2) can be reconstructed 3 months following resection arthroplasty, whereas those patients from whom a more virulent causal organism was recovered should have reconstruction of their hip delayed for a year. McDonald and Fitzgerald recently reported an overall success rate of 87% in the management of 84 infected total hip arthroplasties in 83 patients with a staged reconstruc-

Table 28.1 The relationship of treatment and the microbiology of the infection*

Microorganism	Percent with recurrent sepsis
Pseudomonas sp.	47
Proteus sp.	52
Klebsiella sp.	55
Escherichia coli	39
Group D streptococcus	47
Staphylococcus aureus	28
Peptococcus sp.	24
Propionibacterium acnes	16
Sterile	11

* Modified from Buchholz.

Table 28.2 The relationship of the microbiology to the timing of reconstruction

Less virulent causal organisms
Early reconstruction – 3 months

Methicillin-susceptible staphylococci
   (*S. aureus* and *S. epidermidis*)
Anaerobic Gram-positive cocci
   (*Peptococcus* sp. and *Peptostreptococcus* sp.)
Anaerobic Gram-positive bacilli
   (*Propionibacterium acnes*)
Streptococci
   (Excluding enterococci)

More virulent causal organisms
Late reconstruction – 12 months

Methicillin-resistant staphylocci
Gram-negative bacilli
Group D streptococcus (enterococcus)

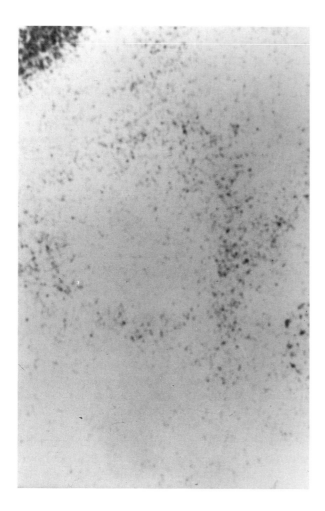

Fig. 28.4   An infected total hip arthroplasty in a 48-year-old woman 1 year following surgery. A one-staged procedure was utilized to reconstruct her hip. Indium image reveals increased uptake in the area of the greater trochanter. She remains pain free 4 years following reconstruction with antibiotic impregnated polymethyl methacrylate.

tive hip arthroplasty. When all of the polymethyl methacrylate was excised during the resection arthroplasty, reconstruction was delayed at least a year, systemic antimicrobials were administered for 28 days, and the causal organism was less virulent. The incidence of recurrent sepsis was significantly reduced ($P < 0.05$).

In the younger patient, a three-staged procedure may be indicated. The younger patient with an infected total hip arthroplasty would appear to be an ideal candidate for reconstruction with a biological ingrowth prosthesis. Frequently, there is insufficient bone stock, especially of the acetabulum following surgical extirpation and treatment of the infection to surgically implant a biological ingrowth prosthetic device. This group of patients can have partial reconstitution of the bony anatomy with the use of autogenous and allogenic bone grafts. Once incorporation of the bone graft has been accomplished, the hip can be reconstructed with ingrowth prosthetic devices. The timing of the bone grafting procedure and subsequent implantation of the prosthetic devices is empiric. Experience suggests the bone grafting procedure can be performed 3 months following surgical extirpation of the infected prosthesis in most patients. The bone graft is usually incorporated to such an extent to support an ingrowth prosthetic device 9 months later. Limited experience with this staged technique has been universally successful to date.

Spinal infections

Infections of the spinal column have historically been difficult diagnostic and therapeutic problems [16]. The diagnosis is frequently delayed, leading to increased morbidity and variable destruction of the osseous structures. Neurological deficits have been reported to occur in a variable percentage of the patients included in retrospective studies. Paralysis has been reported to occur in 5–50% of patients with vertebral osteomyelitis [17]. Hopefully, the introduction of imaging techniques exhibiting greater specificity and sensitivity for septic lesions will permit an earlier diagnosis eliminating or at least reducing the neurological sequelae.

Disc space infections following surgical intervention in the treatment of herniated nucleus pulposus are serious and debilitating complications [18]. Their clinical appearance is heralded by severe back pain with muscle spasms several weeks following discectomy. The surgical incision rarely indicates the sinister nature of the underlying pathology. Needle aspiration of the disc space and blood cultures will permit identification of the causal organism which is usually *S. aureus*. Application of a body cast or hip spica cast to immobilize the lumbar spine will afford the patient pain relief. Specific parenteral antimicrobial therapy should also be administered. Spontaneous fusion of adjacent vertebral bodies usually occurs, resolving the problem.

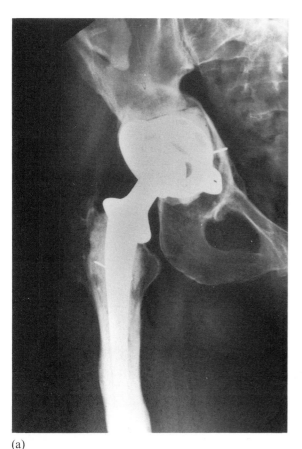

(a)

Fig. 28.5 Infected total hip arthroplasty in a 42-year-old woman who had post-traumatic arthrosis following a fracture dislocation. (a) Anteroposterior roentgenogram after three attempts with debridement to achieve an infected total hip arthroplasty. The acetabular component is obviously loose. *S. aureus* was isolated from a hip aspirate.
(b) Anteroposterior roentgenogram after bone grafts (autogenous iliac and allograft bone) were placed in the acetabulum and proximal femur 3 months following resection arthroplasty. (c) Nine months later an uncemented arthroplasty was performed. This anteroposterior roentgenogram was made 6 months following reconstruction. The hip remains painless 3 years following reconstruction.

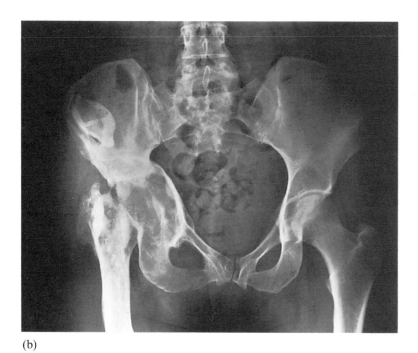

(b)

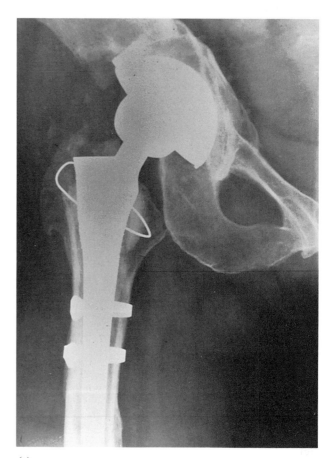

(c)

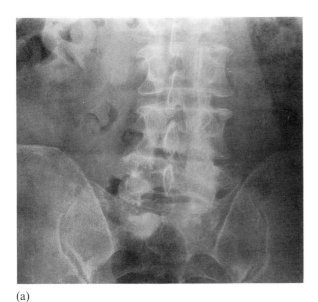

(a)

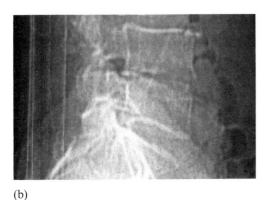

(b)

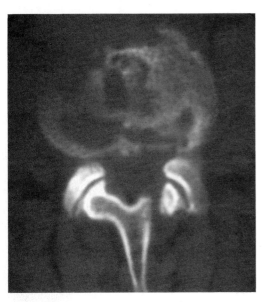

(c)

Fig. 28.6 Disc space infection following laminectomy and discectomy of the fourth lumber disc.
(a) Anteroposterior roentgenogram 8 weeks following surgery reveals asymmetrical collapse of the fourth lumbar disc space. (b) Lateral roentgenogram 9 weeks following discectomy. Narrowing of the fourth lumbar disc space with erosion of the end plates is evident. (c) CT through the fourth lumbar vertebra reveals erosion extending into the vertebral body. Spontaneous fusion of the fourth and fifth lumbar vertebral bodies occurred with cast immobilization.

References

1. Jensen, J. E., Smith, T. K., Jensen, T. G. *et al.* (1981) Nutritional assessment of orthopaedic patients undergoing total hip replacement surgery. In *The Hip*, Proceedings of the Ninth Open Scientific Meeting of The Hip Society (ed. E. A. Salvati), C. V. Mosby, St Louis, pp. 123–135.
2. Hill, C., Mazas, F., Flamont, R. and Eorard, J. (1981) Prophylactic cefazolin versus placebo in total hip replacement. *Lancet*, **April 11**, 795–797.
3. Henley, M. B., Jones, R. E., Wyatt, R. W. B. *et al.* (1986) Prophylaxis with cefamandole nafate in elective orthopedic surgery. *Clin. Orthop.*, **209**, 249–254.
4. Lidwell, O. M. (1983) Sepsis after total hip or knee joint replacement in relation to airborne contamination. *Philos. Trans. R. Soc. Lond. (Biol).*, **302**, 582–592.
5. Lidwell, O. M., Lowbury, E. J. L., Whyte, W. *et al.* (1982) Effect of ultraclean air in operating rooms on deep sepsis in the joint after total hip or knee replacement: a randomised study. *Br. Med. J.*, **285**, 10–14.
6. Nelson, C. L. (1986) Symposium: antibiotic-impregnated acrylic composites. *Contemp. Orthop.*, **12**, 85.
7. Bock, B. V., Pasiecznik, K. and Meyer, R. D. (1982) Clinical and laboratory studies of nosocomial *Staphylococcus aureus* resistant to methicillin and aminoglycosides. *Infect. Control*, **3**, 224–229.
8. Fitzgerald, R. H. Jr, Ruttle, P. E., Arnold, P. G. *et al.* (1985) Local muscle flaps in the treatment of chronic osteomyelitis. *J. Bone Joint Surg.*, **67(A)**, 175–185.
9. Hall, B. B., Fitzgerald, R. H. Jr and Rosenblatt, J. E. (1983) Anaerobic osteomyelitis. *J. Bone Joint Surg.*, **65(A)**, 30–35.
10. Poretz, D. M., Eron, L. J., Goldenberg, R. I. *et al.* (1982) Intravenous antibiotic therapy in an outpatient setting. *JAMA*, **248**, 336–339.
11. Fitzgerald, R. H. Jr (1986) Problems associated with the infected total hip arthroplasty. *Clin. Rheum. Dis.*, **12**, 537–554.
12. Merkel, K. D., Brown, M. L. and Dewanjee, M. K. (1985) Comparison of Indium-labeled-leukocyte imaging with sequential technetium-gallium scanning in the diagnosis of low-grade musculoskeletal sepsis. *J. Bone Joint Surg.*, **67(A)**, 465–476.
13. Fitzgerald, R. H. Jr and Jones, D. R. (1985) Hip implant infection. Treatment with resection arthroplasty and late total hip arthroplasty. *Am. J. Med.*, **78**, 225–228.
14. Buchholz, H. W., Elson, R. A., Engelbrocht, B. *et al.* (1981) Management of deep infection of total hip replacement. *J. Bone Joint Surg.*, **63B**, 353.
15. Wahlig, H. and Dingeldein, E. (1980) Antibiotics and bone cements. *Acta Orthop. Scand.*, **51**, 49–56.
16. Shitut, R. V., Goodpasture, H. C. and Marsh, H. O. (1987) Diagnosing hematogenous vertebral pyogenic osteomyelitis. *Complications in Orthopedics*, **2**, 32.
17. Eismont, F. J., Bohlman, H. H., Soni, P. L. *et al.* (1983) Pyogenic and fungal vertebral osteomyelitis with paralysis. *J. Bone Joint Surg.*, **65(A)**, 19–29.
18. Ford, L. T. (1977) Postoperative infection of lumbar intervertebral disk space. *South. Med. J.*, **69**, 1477.

29

Osteomalacia and osteoporosis

D. J. Baylink and M. R. Mariano-Menez

Metabolic diseases involving the skeleton usually result in either osteoporosis or osteomalacia. Of the two, osteopororis is much more common, yet osteomalacia is more readily cured. Osteoporosis is characterized by a reduced bone density, and osteomalacia is characterized by an increased amount of unmineralized bone matrix. Osteoporosis produces a structurally weakened bone, which increases the susceptibility to fractures and can lead to chronic morbidity and even mortality. The most common osteomalacia that is seen nowadays is that due to vitamin D deficiency. However, the bone pathology in vitamin D deficiency is complex in that mild vitamin D deficiency results in secondary hyperparathyroidism and bone loss, whereas severe vitamin D deficiency results in classical osteomalacia. Thus, the clinical presentation in mild vitamin D deficiency may be similar to that of osteoporosis, whereas the clinical presentation with severe vitamin D deficiency is that of classical osteomalacia, where the clinical presentation is bone pain, usually associated with stress fractures or pseudofractures. It is important to distinguish between osteoporosis and osteomalacia, because the treatment is very different for the two diseases.

Osteomalacia

Osteomalacia is a disorder characterized by defective mineralization of newly produced bone matrix. This leads to an accumulation of poorly mineralized or unmineralized matrix (osteoid). In growing children, impaired mineralization of the cartilaginous growth plates leads to the clinical picture of rickets. However, in adults where the epiphyseal growth plates have closed, only osteomalacia can occur. Recognition of the disease is important, since, in general, it can be successfully treated. The two most common causes of osteomalacia are: (1) vitamin D deficiency and (2) phosphate deficiency. The focus of this chapter will be on vitamin D deficiency, since it is the most common form. Not all vitamin D deficiency results in osteomalacia. Mild vitamin D deficiency results in osteoporosis. It is moderate to severe vitamin D deficiency that results in osteomalacia. In severe vitamin D deficiency, the predominant bone histologic picture is one of the accumulation of excess osteoid. In contrast, in mild vitamin D deficiency, laboratory and bone biopsy findings are indicative of secondary hyperparathyroidism with bone loss and only a modest impairment of mineralization. It is difficult to distinguish between mild vitamin D deficiency and severe vitamin D deficiency in terms of the predominant bone lesion without a bone biopsy. However, this is unnecessary in practical terms, since the management of mild and severe vitamin D deficiency is similar except that with severe deficiency, the treatment period is longer.

Aetiology and pathogenesis

The characteristic feature of osteomalacia is excess osteoid tissue on bone biopsy (Fig. 29.1).

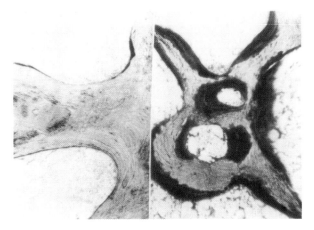

Fig. 29.1 Goldner's stained mineralized sections of bone from a normal subject (left) and from a patient with severe osteomalacia (right) Osteoid appears black and mineralized bone, gray. In the biopsy from the patient with osteomalacia, there is an increased amount of surface covered with osteoid and an increase in osteoid width.

Normally, osteoblasts elaborate new osteoid to replace the bone resorbed by osteoclasts. The osteoid then undergoes maturation before mineralization can proceed. In osteomalacia, the rate of osteoid deposition exceeds the rate of which mineral is deposited, resulting in increased osteoid width. The mineralization lag time (the time between onset of osteoid formation and its' mineralization) is prolonged [1]. The regulation of osteoid maturation and the onset of mineralization is not entirely clear, but both local mechanisms and systemic factors (1,25-dihydroxyvitamin D, [1,25-$(OH)_2$D] serum calcium and phosphate) are probably involved [2]. It is widely viewed that the defective mineralization is due to hypocalcemia and hypophosphatemia, from whatever cause, because a certain solubility product must be exceeded for calcium phosphate salts (hydroxyapatite) to form in the bone. It seems likely that, in addition to the physicochemical effects, serum calcium and phosphorus also have an important local effect on osteoblasts to influence osteoid maturation [3].

Various metabolic perturbations can lead to osteomalacia (Table 29.1), but the most common cause is vitamin D deficiency [4,5]. Mild deficiency results in osteoporosis secondary to increased parathyroid hormone (PTH) secretion, whereas it is the severe deficiency of vitamin D that leads to osteomalacia. A schema of normal

Table 29.1   Causes of osteomalacia

I. Vitamin D deficiency
  1. Parent compound
     a) Dietary deficiency – vitamin D_2
     b) Gut malabsorption – vitamin D_2
        partial gastrectomy
        small bowel disease, resection, or bypass
        bile salt deficiency
        pancreatic insufficiency
     c) Inadequate sunlight exposure – vitamin D_3
  2. Vitamin D metabolite deficiencies
     a) Chronic liver disease – 25-ODH
     b) Anticonvulsant therapy – 25-ODH
     c) Chronic renal failure – 1,25-$(OH)_2$D

II. Phosphate depletion
  1. Phosphate binding antacids – aluminium hydroxide
  2. Renal phosphate leak
     a) Idiopathic
     b) Hereditary
        Vitamin D-resistant rickets
        Idiopathic hypercalciuria
     c) Vascular soft tissue tumour
     d) Metabolic acidosis
        Distal renal tubular acidosis

III. Inhibitors of mineralization
  Etidronate

vitamin D metabolism is shown in Fig. 29.2. The parent compounds are vitamin D_3 (cholecalciferol), which is synthesized in the skin from 7-dehydrocholesterol in response to ultraviolet irradiation, and vitamin D_2 (calciferol), which is found in fortified foods such as milk in the US but not in Europe. Thus, one must have inadequate sun exposure, as well as inadequate intestinal absorption of vitamin D, in order to become vitamin D deficient, as may occur in housebound or institutionalized elderly people [4]. Since vitamin D is stored in the body, and since these stores must be depleted before deficiency occurs, it may take several years before osteomalacia becomes symptomatic in malabsorptive syndromes; e.g. ten years or more after gastric or upper intestinal surgery [6,7]. With adequate exposure to sunlight, it may never become manifest. Other causes of vitamin D deficiency include: (1) chronic liver disease where

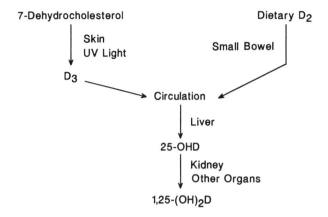

Fig. 29.2 Schema of normal vitamin D metabolism.

there may be impaired conversion of vitamin D_2 and vitamin D_3 to 25-hydroxyvitamin D (25-OHD) metabolite (the D_3 form of which is called calcifediol) [8,9]; (2) long-term anticonvulsant therapy where there may be hastened hepatic degradation of 25-OHD [10]; and (3) chronic renal failure where there may be impaired conversion of 25-OHD to the final, active metabolite $1,25-(OH)_2D_3$ [11].

Physiologic levels of vitamin D (the parent compound) or of 25-HD are inactive and, thus, it is only $1,25(OH)_2D$ that is the active form of this vitamin. Consequently, when we refer to vitamin D deficiency, we are referring to an absolute or relative deficiency of $1,25-(OH)_2D$. Early on during the course of vitamin D deficiency, the level of serum 25-OHD will drop to the point that there is now impaired conversion of 25-HD to $1,25-(OH)_2D$ [4]. This results in a slight decrease in serum calcium which, in turn, increases PTH which, in turn, increases the renal production of $1,25-(OH)_2D$. Thus, with mild vitamin D deficiency, we have a new steady state where the serum $1,25-(OH)_2D$ level is in the normal range but achieves this normal range only by virtue of secondary hyperparathyroidism. The excess PTH mobilizes calcium from the bone and increases renal tubular reabsorption of calcium [12]. At the same time, PTH reduces the renal tubular reabsorption of phosphate, leading to an increased excretion of phosphate by the kidney and a decreased serum phosphate. When the level of vitamin D deficiency becomes moderate to severe, it results in a low serum calcium, serum phosphate and serum calcium phosphate product, all of which impair mineralization [2].

The other major cause of osteomalacia, independent of vitamin D status, is hypophosphataemia [4,13,14] [Table 29.1]. Phosphate is ubiquitous in the diet and is so well absorbed that inadequate absorption is very rare unless phosphate binding antacids are used regularly [15]. Most cases of hypophosphataemia are not dietary but renal in origin. Thus, since serum phosphate is largely regulated by the renal tubular maximum for phosphorus (TmP), hypophosphataemia is usually attributable to a chronically depressed TmP resulting in a renal phosphate leak, either from an acquired or hereditary abnormality (Table 29.1).

As mentioned earlier, long term administration of either the bisphosphonate, etidronate, or fluoride has been found to be associated with inhibition of bone mineralization [16,17]. Awareness of this is important, since these agents are currently being used to treat other metabolic bone disorders; i.e. etidronate for Paget's disease of the bone and for osteoporosis and fluoride for osteoporosis. Etidronate is a synthetic analogue of pyrophosphate, which can inhibit resorption but, at the same time, can inhibit bone mineral deposition, particularly at doses exceeding 10 mg/kg per day [16]. Similarly, long term use of fluoride, particularly at high dosage, can also lead to accumulation of unmineralized matrix (osteoid), which is either partly or solely due to systemic calcium deficiency [18].

Clinical manifestations

The main symptoms in osteomalacia are progressive bone pain, proximal muscle weakness (except in vitamin D resistant rickets, where muscle weakness is not a feature), easy fatigability, and emotional depression [4,5,19]. As the disease progresses, bone pain and tenderness on pressure appear, particularly in the spine, ribs, shoulder girdle, pelvis, and extremities. The pain is aggravated by muscle strain, weight-bearing, and sudden movements. The skeletal pain is usually localized to sites of fractures or pseudofractures. Unless there is a high degree of suspicion, the condition can be mistaken for muscular rheumatism or arthritis. With advanced osteomalacia, skeletal deformities due to softening of the bone and microfractures can occur.

Diagnostic tests

In severe vitamin D deficiency, osteomalacia, serum calcium and phosphate are low, whereas in phosphate deficiency osteomalacia, only serum phosphate is low [20]. In most types of osteomalacia, serum alkaline phosphatase is elevated, although the mechanism for this is not known. In severe vitamin D deficiency osteomalacia, urinary calcium is almost always low because of impaired intestinal absorption of calcium and of the secondary hyperparathyroidism [20]. In contrast, osteomalacia due to idiopathic hypophosphataemia is associated with hypercalciuria [4]. In vitamin D resistant osteomalacia, urine calcium is frequently normal. In osteomalacia additional findings include a low serum 25-hydroxyvitamin D, a low 1,25-dihydroxyvitamin D, and a high serum PTH level.

Radiologically, osteomalacia may present as a nonspecific decrease in radiodensity of the bone due to the decreased mineral content. The trabecular pattern may appear blurred and fuzzy, particularly in severe cases. The distinguishing feature is the occurrence of painful or nonpainful pseudofractures (Looser's zone or Milkman's fractures), which are linear radiolucencies oriented more or less perpendicular to the cortex (Fig. 29.3.) Bone scans show increased activity at these sites. Pseudofractures usually occur symmetrically in the scapulae, ribs, pubic rami, proximal femur, or proximal ulnae [4]. They represent stress fractures in which the healing process is impaired by the mineralization defect but which heal promptly with appropriate therapy (Fig. 29.3).

In fully developed osteomalacia, the diagnosis can be made without difficulty from the clinical history, characteristic serum changes (see Diagnostic Tests), and appearance of pseudofractures on radiography. In subclinical osteomalacia, only a bone biopsy can definitively confirm the diagnosis [4]. However, it is usually not necessary to do an invasive bone biopsy in working up a patient suspected of having osteomalacia. The reason for this is that one can readily detect vitamin D deficiency even when mild by measurements of serum chemistry and, particularly, serum 25-HD. If a low serum 25-HD is found, one can treat this abnormal biochemical marker irrespective of whether or not the patient is known to have osteomalacia (see below) [20].

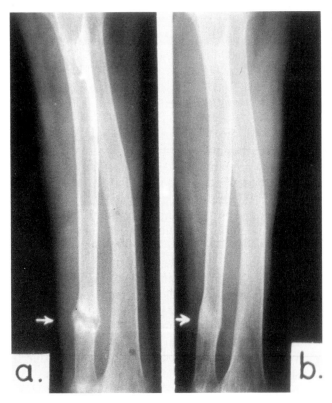

Fig. 29.3 Radiographs of pseudofracture of the ulna in the patient with severe osteomalacia. The pseudofracture before treatment is shown in (a), and the pseudofracture after 3 months of vitamin D therapy is shown in (b).

Thus, nowadays, bone biopsies are usually reserved for complex diagnostic problems [21].

The bone histological features of osteomalacia are increased osteoid width, decreased rate of osteoid maturation; i.e., a prolonged time between the deposition to subsequent mineralization of osteoid [1,22]. Under normal conditions, tetracycline is deposited at the mineralizing front (the interface between osteoid and mineralized bone), as a bright discrete label, whereas in osteomalacia, tetracycline labelling prior to bone biopsy shows widened, smudged tetracycline labels, if the rate of mineralization is significantly reduced, or no label at all if mineralization has ceased completely [21].

Treatment

Identification and treatment of the underlying cause of the vitamin or phosphate deficiency is essential to the management of osteomalacia. For example, maintenance on a gluten-free diet in patients with gluten enteropathy [4], surgical correction of intestinal fistulae or biliary obstruction [8,9], removal of a tumour that has caused osteomalacia (oncogenic osteomalacia) [23], are necessary for optimal patient management. In addition, some form of vitamin D, calcium or phosphate is usually required.

The logical choice for the treatment of the various forms of vitamin D deficiency would be: (1) the parent compound vitamin D (calciferol) for a nutritional deficiency where there is a deficiency of vitamin D_2/D_3; (2) 25-OHD3 (calciferol) for the low serum 25-hydroxyvitamin D seen in chronic liver disease or anticonvulsant therapy [8,9,10]; and (3) 1,25-$(OH)_2$D (calcitriol) for the 1,25-$(OH)_2$D deficiency seen in renal failure [24]. The parent compound, vitamin D, can also be used to treat a deficiency 25-OHD due to liver disease, because, even with liver disease (unless severe), a high dose of vitamin D will result in a normal serum level of 25-OHD [8,9]. In nutritional deficiency, vitamin D 1000 IU/day may be sufficient; but in liver disease, 5000-10 000 IU/day is usually required. The proper dose is determined by monitoring the serum 25-HD. In conclusion, vitamin D is used to treat nutritional vitamin D deficiency and also to treat a deficiency of 25-OHD due to liver disease, whereas 1,25-$(OH)_2$D is used to treat renal disease. Most abnormalities of vitamin D metabolism can be treated with either vitamin D or 1,25-$(OH)_2$D.

It is now appreciated that calcium deficiency per se can lead to osteomalacia and rickets [12,25]. For example, when fluoride stimulates a large increase in bone formation in elderly people who have limited ability to absorb calcium, there is a tendency for calcium deficiency. This calcium deficiency appears to be corrected by the addition of 1,25-$(OH)_2$D therapy [18].

It is important to monitor the patient during vitamin D or 1,25-$(OH)_2$D therapy for two reasons: (1) to make certain that the dose is adequate and (2) to avoid complications from excessive therapy, which, in the case of 1,25-$(OH)_2$D, can be hypercalcaemia. In nutritional vitamin D deficiency, we monitor vitamin D therapy, largely because we need to make certain the patient is adequately treated. Because the dose of vitamin D is usually only 1000 units or, perhaps, slightly more per day, and because this dose, even if continued for a long time, would not be toxic, we are less concerned about toxicity from vitamin D than we are about adequate responses. In patients with nutritional vitamin D deficiency given 1000 units of vitamin D per day, the serum 25-OHD level should return to the normal range within two to three months. This will be attended by a normalization of the low serum calcium and low serum phosphate. However, the elevated alkaline phosphatase may take several months of vitamin D therapy before it declines to the normal level, particularly if the vitamin D deficiency is severe [4,26]. The elevated serum PTH tends to decline as the serum calcium increases to normal. Pseudofractures can show definite evidence of healing within 3 months and are usually completely healed radiographically in less than one year (Fig. 29.3). In nutritional vitamin D deficiency, in addition to vitamin D supplementation, we also recommend at least 1500 mg/day of calcium, since, in order to cure the osteomalacia, the patient must deposit calcium in all of the excess unmineralized osteoid in the skeleton. There is sufficient phosphate in the diet, such that phosphate supplements are unnecessary in nutritional vitamin D deficiency.

Patients who have a low serum 25-OHD as a consequence of liver disease or of anticonvulsant therapy and who are treated with vitamin D are monitored in the same manner as that described above for vitamin D deficiency.

In patients with a deficiency of 1,25-(OH)$_2$D due to renal failure, it is well to start 1,25-(OH)$_2$D therapy early on during the course of renal disease in order to avoid some of the adverse effects on the skeleton of secondary hyperparathyroidism. The oral dose ranges from 0.25 to 1.0 μg per day, depending on the severity of the disease. As mentioned above, we are not only concerned about monitoring serum chemistries to be certain that the patient is having an optimal response, we are also concerned about excessive therapy, inasmuch as the side-effects of this medication can be significant and because it is impossible to predict, from the serum creatinine or from other measures of the degree of renal failure, the optimal dose of 1,25-(OH)$_2$D. The optimal dose is determined individually, based on biochemical monitoring. We routinely monitor serum calcium, PTH and alkaline phosphatase. If the patient has only early renal failure, urine calcium can also be monitored. The urine calcium will be low during the deficiency of 1,25-(OH)$_2$D and will increase into the normal range during 1,25-(OH)$_2$D therapy [20]. With a mild excess of 1,25-(OH)$_2$D therapy, there will be no change in serum calcium but an increase in urine calcium above the normal range of 250 mg/day in females and 300 mg/day in males; with a more severe excess, there will also be an increment in serum calcium. In patients with renal function, it is important not to administer thiazides with 1,25-(OH)$_2$D, because this further increases the risk for hypercalcaemia (thiazides decrease urine calcium excretion by increasing the renal tubular reabsorption of calcium.)

In patients with severe secondary hyperparathyroidism due to renal failure, i.v. injections of 1,25-(OH)$_2$D have been more effective than daily oral administration. Apparently, when 1,25-(OH)$_2$D is given by injection, the blood level of 1,25-(OH)$_2$D reaches a higher peak, as compared with oral administration, without causing hypercalcaemia [24]. The explanation for this is that when 1,25-(OH)$_2$D is given by mouth, it acts locally on the gut to increase calcium absorption, such that there is a preferential effect on calcium absorption over other target tissues such as the parathyroid gland, where it acts to decrease PTH secretion [24,27]. The increment in calcium absorption readily leads to hypercalcaemia, thus

limiting the dose of 1,25-(OH)$_2$D that can be given orally. In contrast, when 1,25-(OH)$_2$D is given i.v., it has equal effects to inhibit parathyroid hormone secretion and to increase calcium absorption, such that a relatively higher dose can be given without hypercalcaemia [24].

In phosphate deficiency states, neutral phosphate salts given at 2 or more grams per day in divided doses will improve bone mineralization. The most common adverse effect with oral phosphate is diarrhoea, especially at doses exceeding 2 g per day. In hypophosphatemic familial rickets (vitamin D resistant rickets), phosphate supplementation should be combined with 1,25-(OH)$_2$D for 3 reasons: (1) phosphate tends to lower serum calcium and increase PTH, which in turn will decrease the TmP for phosphate, thereby lowering the serum phosphate level, which is the main cause of osteomalacia in these patients; (2) these patients have not only an impaired renal tubular reabsorption of phosphate, but they also have impaired renal tubular synthesis of 1,25-(OH)$_2$D; (3) it is important that PTH not be elevated in these patients because PTH decreases serum phosphate and the cause of osteomalacia in these patients is a decreased serum phosphate. (Serum calcium and serum 1,25-(OH)$_2$D are the two major inhibitors of PTH secretion.) Thus, patients with vitamin D resistant rickets should receive large doses of neutral phosphate salts, 1,25-(OH)$_2$D therapy, which may range up to 2 μg per day, and, also, calcium supplements [13].

Hypophosphataemia seems to produce a mineralization defect regardless of the serum 1,25-(OH)$_2$D value. Accordingly, in hypophosphataemic vitamin D rickets and osteomalacia, one frequently sees a low 1,25-(OH)$_2$D serum value, whereas in hypercalciuric hypophosphataemia, there may be a low serum phosphate and a high serum 1,25-(OH)$_2$D. Both of these situations can result in osteomalacia. In practical therapeutic terms, it is important to know the serum level of 1,25-(OH)$_2$D in a given state of hypophosphataemia because, under certain conditions such as vitamin D resistant rickets, 1,25-(OH)$_2$D supplements will be required, whereas in others such as hypophosphataemic hypercalciuria, serum 1,25-(OH)$_2$D may be high and, thus, 1,25-(OH)$_2$D therapy would be contraindicated.

In general, if the patient is receiving 1,25-

(OH)$_2$D therapy and has normal renal function, the risk of hypercalcaemia can be reduced by limiting the total calcium intake to 1000 mg/ daily. If larger amounts of calcium are given, it is essential to monitor the serum calcium at frequent intervals. The advantage of 1,25-(OH)$_2$D therapy is that all patients respond in some manner to 1,25-(OH)$_2$D therapy (with the exception of those rare individuals with mutant 1,25-(OH)$_2$D receptors). The disadvantage of 1,25-(OH)$_2$D is that it is such a potent drug that serious side-effects can occur.

Osteoporosis

In this chapter, we consider osteoporosis in both males and females, but, in our discussion of osteoporosis, we will focus more on female osteoporosis, because this disease is much more common in females than in males. Osteoporosis is defined as a reduction of bone density to a level that increases the risk of fracture with minimal or no trauma.

Osteoporosis is a common and costly disease. For example, it has been estimated that there are almost 20 million people in the US with osteoporosis at a health care cost of about $10 billion annually [28,29]. It is estimated that more than 25% of women over 65 years of age develop osteoporosis, and the prevalence increases further with age [30]. In men, osteoporosis usually becomes manifest in the 7th decade (senile osteoporosis), at which time the prevalence of this disease shows an overall female to male ratio of about 5:1 or greater.

Aetiology and pathogenesis

A variety of conditions can lead to osteoporosis (Table 29.2). Thus, in order to provide appropriate therapy, the underlying disorder must be recognized and corrected. Osteoporosis is classified as either primary, when the cause is not entirely established, or secondary, when the disease can be attributed to hereditary or acquired abnormalities. Primary osteoporosis is much more common than secondary osteoporosis. Of the various types of osteoporosis (Table 29.2), postmenopausal and senile osteoporosis are the most common forms, such that more than 90% of

Table 29.2 Classification of osteoporosis

I. Primary osteoporosis
　1. Idiopathic
　　a) Juvenile
　　b) Young adults

　2. Postmenopausal

　3. Senile (age 65+)

II. Secondary osteoporosis
　1. Associated with hereditable disorders of connective tissue
　　a) Osteogenesis imperfecta
　　b) Marfan's syndrome
　　c) Morquio's syndrome
　　d) Hurler's syndrome

　2. Endocrine disorders
　　a) Cushing's disease
　　b) Hyperthyroidism
　　c) Acromegaly
　　d) Hypogonadism
　　　i) oestrogen deficiency*
　　　ii) testosterone deficiency

　3. Drug induced
　　a) Corticosteroids
　　b) Anticonvulsants
　　c) Heparin

　4. Immobilization

　5. Malignant states – multiple myeloma

　6. Others
　　a) Lactase deficiency
　　b) Malnutrition
　　c) Renal calcium leak
　　d) Cirrhosis
　　e) Alcoholism

*Oestrogen deficiency before physiological menopause, i.e. oophorectomy, some athletes.

females presenting with a low bone density have postmenopausal or senile osteoporosis.

Postmenopausal osteoporosis

Bone loss occurs at the menopause because of the development of an imbalance in bone remodelling; both bone resorption and bone formation increase, but bone resorption increases more than bone formation, and the result is a net reduction of bone density. The skeletal sites at risk for fracture are those composed largely of trabecular bone: the vertebrae, ribs, distal radii and proximal femora, presumably because of the active remodelling in trabecular and endosteal cortical bone at these sites. Eventually, size and number of trabeculae are decreased and the cortices are thin, but the qualities of the bone produced appears morphologically normal (Fig. 29.4).

The dramatic decline in oestrogen production during the menopause is now known to play a predominant role in the postmenopausal acceleration of bone loss, and the mechanism of this oestrogen deficiency bone loss is being disclosed at the molecular level [31,32]. Because most nucleated cells have oestrogen receptors, it seems likely that the molecular mechanism whereby oestrogen affects bone probably includes a direct local action on bones cells, and, also secondary actions on other organs. Thus, oestrogen appears to have a direct action to decrease IL-1, IL-6 and TNFα and increase TGF-β production by osteoblasts, which, in turn, is thought to reduce osteo-

clastic resorption [31,32]. Thus, the increase in bone turnover which is typical of the postmenopausal state is thought to be, in part, a consequence of increased local production of IL-1, IL-6 and TNFα and decreased production of TGF-β. An example of the effect of oestrogen to decrease bone resorption through a secondary mechanism (endocrine) would be the effect of oestrogen to increase serum $1,25(OH)_2D$ and, thereby, improve calcium absorption, an effect which would tend to lower serum PTH and, thus, decrease bone resorption [33]. Despite these recent advances, postmenopausal osteoporosis is still traditionally considered a primary type, because oestrogen deficiency alone may not entirely account for the development of osteoporosis.

A number of factors other than oestrogen contribute to the development of osteoporosis. Genetic and environmental factors, for example, have been found to play a significant role in initiating and modifying the course of osteoporosis. Environmental factors include inadequate calcium intake, smoking, alcoholism and poor physical activity. As much as 70% of low bone density at the peak of skeletal maturity is thought to be genetically determined [34,35,36]. Accordingly, peak bone density is strongly influenced by heredity, race and sex, with males having more skeletal mass than females, and blacks more than whites [37,38].

Senile osteoporosis

While oestrogen deficiency is known to play a dominant role in postmenopausal osteoporosis, the cause of senile osteoporosis (i.e. those presenting with osteoporosis after 65 years of age) is less certain. One of the major advances in understanding this type of osteoporosis is the recognition that the efficiency of calcium absorption declines with age and that this is attended by a progressive increase with age in serum PTH. Thus, it has been proposed that at least one of the causes of senile osteoporosis is secondary hyperparathyroidism [39]. This, however, only represents a subgroup of those patients presenting with osteoporosis who are more than 65 years of age. Some of these patients with secondary hyperparathyroidism will actually have mild vitamin D deficiency as manifested by a decrease in serum

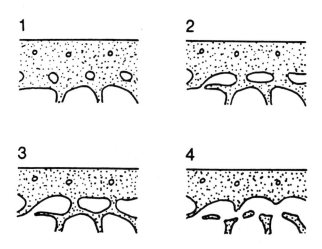

Fig. 29.4 Microscopic structural stages of cortical bone loss. Illustrated are the few successive stages in osteoclast-dependent thinning of cortical bone: (a) shows normal adult cortex; (b) shows enlargement of the subendosteal spaces and communication of these spaces with the marrow cavity; (c) shows further enlargement of these spaces and conversion of the inner third of the cortex to a structure that topographically resembles trabecular bone, with an attending expansion of the marrow cavity; (d) shows perforation and disconnection of the new trabecular structures. Loss of connectivity leads to a deterioration of mechanical performance of the corresponding bony structure. (Adapted with permission from Parfitt, AM, *Calcif Tissue Int* **36 (suppl.)**: S123, 1984).

25(OH)D. Mild vitamin D deficiency has been shown to occur in subjects residing at northerly latitudes [40]. Both of these abnormalities, namely, the decrease of calcium absorption with age and the deficiency of vitamin D, lead to decreased calcium absorption, are readily corrected, and, thus, are important to recognize. Not all patients with senile osteoporosis exhibit vitamin D deficiency or calcium malabsorption. Thus, it is clear that senile osteoporosis is a heterogeneous disease.

The classification of patients with primary osteoporosis into postmenopausal and senile is somewhat misleading [39]. For example, in order for a patient to exhibit fragility fractures in the first ten years after the menopause (i.e. postmenopausal osteoporosis), it seems likely that such a patient, in addition to postmenopausal bone loss, entered the postmenopausal period with a relatively low peak bone density. Thus, the pathogenesis of the osteoporosis in these patients would be more than merely oestrogen deficiency bone loss. Moreover, those patients presenting with fragility fractures after 65 years of age, and thus considered to have senile osteoporosis, could be patients who entered the menopause with a high peak bone density and, as a consequence, did not develop a low enough bone density during the postmenopausal years to develop fragility fractures until after 65 years of age. Thus, patients with primary osteoporosis may develop this skeletal disease as a consequence of the variable expression of several contributing factors which will include: (1) a low peak bone density; (2) a high bone loss rate at the menopause due to oestrogen deficiency; (3) poor calcium absorption; and (4) lifestyle factors (see above). In addition, it seems probable that there are a multitude of other factors that will eventually be disclosed to have a negative impact on bone density in patients over 65 years of age. One such potential factor could be the decline in serum IGF-I that occurs with age [41]. This is known to be an anabolic agent such that a deficiency of serum IGF-1 might lead to a decrease in bone formation.

Clinical manifestations

Osteoporosis is a chronic, progressive, debilitating disease that may remain silent until the patient suffers a fracture, often from minor trauma such as coughing, turning in bed, or bending. Back pain due to osteoporosis is typically aggravated by activity and relieved by rest. The spectrum of symptoms varies greatly, from the absence of pain to severe pain, depending largely on the extent and rapidity with which the fracture occurs and the pain threshold of the patient. For example, some patients have vague back pain without spinal fracture, whereas others have a spinal wedge fracture without a history of back pain.

In patients with osteoporosis, vertebral collapse with back pain is the most common presentation. The patient may complain of two types of pain: (1) there is an acute onset of pain in the area of the crushed vertebrae. This is sharp, severe, radiates laterally and is associated with paravertebral muscle spasm and percussion tenderness over the area. The severe pain may persist for 3–4 weeks and then gradually subside. Lack of improvement in the acute phase within 2–3 months should prompt a search for a possible pathologic cause of the fracture. (2) The other type of pain experienced in osteoporosis is mild, dull, usually described as an aching sensation or feeling of tiredness in the lower thoracic or lumbar area (especially after prolonged standing or activity), and is relieved by rest [42]. This type of pain tends to be chronic.

Progressive anterior wedging in the mid-thoracic spine produces the dowager's hump deformity (i.e. kyphosis), limits chest mobility, and results in loss of height and abdominal protuberance. In contrast, fractures in the lumbar vertebrae are usually collapse of the centrum resulting in a 'codfish' deformity. Hip and Colles' fractures, when they occur in the elderly, are most commonly related to osteoporosis. Hip fracture is by far the most serious complication of osteoporosis and can cause significant debilitation. Mortality from hip fracture exceeds 20% within 1 year [43] and, in those who survive, rehabilitation is often difficult and protracted.

Diagnostic tests

This section will largely deal with diagnostic tests for primary osteoporosis. It should be emphasized however, that the diagnosis of primary osteoporosis is made by excluding secondary causes of osteoporosis. This can usually be done by a history and physical examination and routine laboratory tests, although in some situations, extensive testing may be required in difficult cases to evaluate for secondary osteoporosis. Those diseases that should be considered in working up patients with osteoporosis are shown in Table 29.2 under secondary osteoporosis.

Bone densitometry

The first step in making the diagnosis of osteoporosis is to measure the bone density. This can be accomplished with either dual energy x-ray absorptiometry (DEXA) or by quantitative computerized tomography (QCT) [29,44]. Because osteoporosis is first seen in the spine, these density methods are generally applied to the spine. The other site of special clinical interest is the hip because of the serious clinical problem of hip fracture. The DEXA instrument is the only instrument that can measure hip bone density [45]. For individual patients, we routinely measure both QCT spinal bone density and DEXA hip bone density, because the correlation between spine and hip density is relatively poor. On the other hand, on a population basis, fracture risk can be predicted from a bone density measurement at any skeletal site [46].

The advantage of the QCT for measurement of bone density is that it can be applied to measure only trabecular bone, and, since trabecular bone is metabolically more active than cortical bone, more rapid changes are seen by QCT than by DEXA (measurement of) spinal bone density. The main disadvantages of the QCT approach are: (1) it does not have the high precision of the DEXA measurement; and (2) it is more expensive. The advantage of DEXA bone density measurements is that it is much more convenient than QCT measurements, because QCTs are only available at major medical centres. However, in elderly people (less so in younger subjects), there are frequently age related changes that compromise the validity of the DEXA measurement of the spine. For example there may be a considerable amount of osteophytosis and end-plate sclerosis (from degenerative disk disease) that spuriously increased the bone density value determined by DEXA. Furthermore, extraskeletal calcifications can also spuriously influence the

DEXA bone density. Thus, one can see patients with fragility fractures (spontaneous atraumatic fractures) who have normal bone density by DEXA but have low bone density by QCT. In any case, these potential diagnostic pitfalls with the DEXA instrument should be considered when the DEXA data are interpreted. Interpretation of bone density results is as follows:

1. Bone density that is above the fracture threshold and within 1 standard deviations of peak bone density. This is considered to be a normal bone density.
2. Bone density that is above the fracture threshold but is 1 standard deviations or more below the peak bone density. This is considered osteopenia.
3. Bone density that is below the fracture threshold or below 2.5 SD of young normal mean bone density. This is considered osteoporosis. The spinal fracture threshold for our QCT method is 100 mg/cc, though published fracture threshold values range from 70–110 mg/cc. The spinal fracture threshold for the hologic DEXA is 0.80 g/cm², for the lunar DEXA. 074 g/cm².

Calcium absorption

If the patient has a low bone density (either osteopenia or osteoporosis), the next step is to assess calcium absorption. Unfortunately, there is no commercially available validated test to make this assessment. None the less, we mention this parameter because we feel it is a key aspect of determining the cause of osteoporosis and because, in the future, this parameter will undoubtedly be routinely measured. We assess calcium absorption by determining the 24-hour urine calcium excretion in a patient on a total (diet plus supplements) calcium intake at 1500 mg for at least one week, which is the usual amount prescribed for osteoporotic patients [47]. In patients with either known primary hyperparathyroidism or a past history of kidney stones, this 24-hour urine should be collected while on a low calcium diet of 400 mg/day. The rationale for this test follows: when the patient is on a relatively high calcium intake (1500 mg/day), a 24-hour urine calcium of less than 100 mg/day suggests calcium malabsorption. This level of 100 mg/day is an arbitrary value based on the facts that: (1) urine excretion of

50 mg or less calcium per day while on a regular calcium diet is low, reflecting calcium deficiency or vitamin D deficiency; and (2) a urinary calcium level of 100 mg/day is substantially below the upper normal limit of 250 mg/day and, thus, would not be associated with an increased risk of renal stones. In addition, patients with secondary hyperparathyroidism (i.e. high serum PTH) due to calcium malabsorption seldom have 24-hour urine calcium volume above 100 mg. Therefore, we have defined 100 mg/day as a safe value to achieve with calcium and/or vitamin D or $1,25(OH)_2D$ therapy (see section on Treatment). It should be emphasized that this test to measure calcium absorption is a rational approach but is a test which has not been validated. The major reason for attempting to measure calcium absorption is that one can readily correct a deficiency of calcium absorption either by adding more calcium supplementation or, if this is ineffective, by adding vitamin D or calcitriol therapy.

Of the many serum chemistries that might be ordered during the workup of patients with osteoporosis (as determined by bone density evaluation), our focus is on only two parameters, serum PTH and serum 25(OH)D. We measure serum PTH because we have found high values in almost 20% of our clinic patients, either because of secondary or primary hyperparathyroidism. With respect to serum 25(OH)D measurement, the indication for this test depends upon where the patient resides. If the patient resides in northern Europe and is over 70 years of age, this test should be strongly considered because of a high prevalence of low serum 25(OH)D values in such patients [40]. However, patients living in southern California seldom exhibit low serum 25(OH)D. A low serum 25(OH)D in a patient with normal liver function indicates inadequate exposure to sunlight and, in addition, inadequate dietary intake of vitamin D. Figure 29.2 provides a schema of vitamin D metabolism.

Bone resorption

At the same time calcium absorption is estimated, bone resorption can be measured. This is assessed by 24-hour urine measurements of hydroxyproline/creatinine and is measured in the same urine sample that is used for the 24-hour calcium assessment. Because the diet normally contains hydroxyproline, the patient is placed on a hydroxyproline-free diet the meal prior to and the day of the 24-hour collection. The normal range for urine hydroxyproline/creatinine is quite broad, and there is no general agreement as to what values indicate high resorption. Since, in general, normal premenopausal women lose very little bone [30], we have arbitrarily selected the mean of the normal range for premenopausal women plus two standard deviations as the maximum upper normal limit of bone resorption. This value (in our laboratory) is equal to 25 mg hydroxyproline per gram creatinine. Thus, any postmenopausal patient with a value greater than 25 mg/gram is considered to have increased bone resorption and requires anti-resorptive therapy. If we wish to be more certain about preventing further bone loss, we attempt to achieve hydroxyproline/creatinine values at about 12.5 mg/gram of hydroxyproline/creatinine, which is the mean premenopausal level.

More than 80% of osteoporotic patients in our clinic have hydroxyproline/creatinine values greater than 12.5 mg per gram. Tests other than hydroxyproline can be used to assess bone resorption. These include measurements of urine crosslinks (i.e., pyridinoline/creatinine (PYR/CR) and deoxypyridinoline/creatinine (DPYR/CR) in urine) [48]. These tests are more accurate and are more specific indices of bone resorption than is hydroxyproline. Moreover, these measurements do not require a hydroxyproline-free diet. Normal values for the crosslinks are not as well established as for hydroxyproline. Our preliminary results suggest that the premenopausal mean plus or minus two standard deviations for pyridinoline/creatinine is about 44 ± 34 nM/mM and for DPYR/creatinine 10 ± 9 nm/mm. Because of the relatively large longitudinal variation of serum and urine assays for bone formation and bone resorption, we suggest that therapeutic decisions be made on more than an assay at one point in time.

Other tests that are sometimes used in the evaluation of patients with osteoporosis include radiographic evaluations to evaluate for the presence of fractures and for the possible presence of pathologic fractures. Radiographic features of osteoporosis include diffuse radiolucency, accentuation of vertical trabeculae (because of preferential loss of horizontally oriented trabeculae), cortical thinning, anterior wedging of thoracic vertebral bodies, and biconcavity or 'codfishing' of vertebral bodies [49]. In addition, the radionuclide bone scan is useful in determining whether a compression fracture is old or recent. Increased radionuclide activity at the site of a known fracture indicates ongoing healing (bone formation). The bone scan may also be valuable in detecting the presence of other bone disorders (i.e. metastatic bone lesions and degenerative or inflammatory changes).

Once the patient has had a bone density measurement, a calcium absorption assessment, and a bone resorption measurement, the patient is ready for application of a therapeutic regimen.

Treatment of osteoporosis

In this section, we will discuss the prevention and treatment of primary osteoporosis in females and males, but the focus will be on females because of the higher prevalence of osteoporosis in females. The therapeutic agents available for osteoporosis are shown in Table 29.3. The therapeutic principles that we describe below for the treatment of primary osteoporosis in females also apply, for the most part, to males and females with secondary osteoporosis. The therapeutic goals for osteoporosis are to decrease the pain associated with vertebral fractures and to prevent future fractures. The following are the therapeutic principles which we apply:

1. Patients with calcium malabsorption must be

Table 29.3 Classification of therapeutic agents for osteoporosis

I. Agents that decrease bone resorption
 1. Oestrogen
 2. Calcium
 3. Vitamin D
 4. Calcitonin
 5. Biphosphonates
 6. Testosterone
 7. 1,25(OH)$_2$D or 1αD$_3$

II. Agents that increase bone formation
 1. Fluoride
 2. Testosterone*
 3. Exercise* 4, PTH 1-34

---

* Increases bone formation, but increase in bone density is small.

treated with either vitamin D, larger amounts of calcium, or with either 1,25(OH)$_2$D (Calcitriol) or 1αD$_3$.
2. Patients with high urine calcium or a history of kidney stones should be given calcium supplements with caution.
3. All patients should be placed on an exercise program that should include walking, as well as upper body exercises (i.e., weight lifting) within the limits of the patient's disability.
4. Patients with a high bone resorption rate as determined by urine biochemical markers should be put on an antiresorptive therapy such as oestrogen replacement therapy, biphosphonate or calcitonin. (Only oral and i.v. etidronate and i.v. aredia are available in the US, whereas in some countries other bisphosphonates also are available.)
5. A patient who has a bone density below the fracture threshold should be referred to a treatment centre where the patient can be considered for fluoride therapy.
6. If a patient has severe bone pain from a recent spinal fracture, injectable calcitonin should be considered.

Low bone density is the major determinant of increased fracture risk in osteoporosis. It has

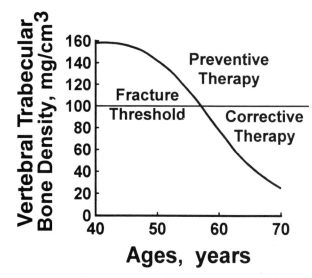

Fig. 29.5 This is a schema of the decline in bone density with age as determined by quantitative computer topography (QCT). The fracture threshold was shown to be 100 mg per cc [44]. In general, patients who have bone densities above the fracture threshold are placed on preventative therapy (see text), and patients who have densities below the fracture threshold are placed on corrective therapy, which includes preventative therapy plus a bone formation stimulator.

been demonstrated that the risk for fracturing in the spine is increased when the vertebral trabecular bone density measured by QCT is 100 mg/cc or less (defined here as the fracture threshold) [44]. A rational approach to therapy would, therefore, be prevention of bone loss when the bone density is above the fracture threshold (preventive therapy) and replacement of bone mass previously lost to a level above the fracture threshold when the bone density is below 100 mg/cc (corrective therapy) (Fig. 29.5). Table 29.3 lists the therapeutic agents (antiresorbers and bone formation stimulators) currently available for the preventive and corrective treatment of osteoporosis. A combination of agents (an inhibitor of bone resorption and a stimulator of bone formation) is usually employed in corrective therapeutic regimens in order to preserve trabecular architecture with antiresorptive therapy to increase bone mass above the fracture threshold and with a bone generation stimulator.

Preventive therapy

If the patient has normal bone density, we recommend preventive therapy using oestrogen, adequate calcium intake, and exercise. Preventive therapy is also recommended for patients with osteopenia and patients with osteoporosis. Patients with osteoporosis, in addition to preventive therapy, also require corrective therapy.

Exercise

It should be emphasized that inactivity can lead to bone loss. A 0.9% per week bone loss has been reported from the lumbar spine in patients on bed rest, and the bone loss was nearly restored with reintroduction of load bearing [50]. This emphasizes the deleterious effect of inactivity and the importance of an exercise program in the treatment of osteoporosis [51]. Based on recent studies, the exercise protocol we recommend includes walking two miles daily and engaging in some type of upper body exercise such as weight lifting (e.g. in an erect standing position – back extended – the patient holds a can of peas in each hand and lifts them over her head. Eventually, as strength improves, the patient should use 5 lb. weights in each hand for this type of exercise.) It

should be emphasized that all exercise should be designed to avoid injury.

Calcium, vitamin D, 1,25(OH)$_2$D and 1αD$_3$ therapy

Intestinal calcium absorption decreases with aging and is further reduced in osteoporotic patients when compared with controls [52]. This can lead to calcium deficiency which increases bone resorption by stimulation of parathyroid hormone secretion, whereas normal or high calcium absorption retards bone resorption. Heaney *et al.* [53] have shown that at least 1500 mg of calcium daily is required in order to overcome the negative calcium balance in postmenopausal women who are not oestrogen treated (Table 29.3). For those patients on oestrogen therapy, 1000 mg of calcium/day is recommended. Dietary calcium may be supplemented with calcium salts (e.g., calcium carbonate, phosphate, lactate, gluconate, or citrate) to meet the increased requirements. Absorption of calcium supplements can be estimated from the rise in urinary calcium (see section on Diagnostic tests).

If the patient has an appropriate urinary calcium excretion after consuming a diet containing a total 1500 mg/day, particularly if the patient also has a normal serum PTH and a normal serum 25(OH)D, this would constitute evidence of normal calcium absorption. The goal of administering calcium is to avoid bone loss and the high bone turnover that occurs with secondary hyperparathyroidism*. If the urine calcium were lower than 100 mg per 24 hours on a 1500 mg diet, the first diagnosis to be considered would be mild vitamin D deficiency which would be reflected by a low serum 25(OH)D. If this deficiency were found, the patient should be treated with at least vitamin D 1000 units daily for 2–3 months (Table 29.3). At this time, the serum 25(OH)D should be normal, and the calcium absorption test should be repeated to document that this has corrected the calcium malabsorption. If the serum 25(OH)D test is normal but the patient has an abnormal calcium absorption test, larger amounts of oral calcium, perhaps up to

* Recent evidence suggests that high bone turnover from any cause has an adverse effect on trabecular architecture (i.e. increases trabecular perforations([54].

2000–3000 mg/day, can be administered in an
attempt to raise the urine calcium up to 100 mg
per 24 hours. In addition, rather than using the
most common forms of calcium supplements (i.e.
calcium carbonates, or calcium phosphate), a
more soluble form of calcium (i.e., calcium citrate) may be prescribed.

If increasing the dose of calcium and/or changing to a different calcium salt fails to increase
urine calcium and decrease serum PTH (if evaluated) after three months of supplementation, cal-
citriol (Rocaltrol) $0.25\,\mu g$/day, or $1\alpha D_3$ $0.5\,\mu g$/
day along with a total (diet plus supplements)
calcium intake of 800–1000 mg/day, is prescribed
(Table 29.3) [20]. (Higher calcium intakes increase the risk of hypercalcaemia). If after one
week of this therapy the 24-hour urine remains
below 100 mg/day, the dose of calcitriol is increased to $0.5\,\mu g$/day and the dose of $1\alpha D_3$ is
increased to $1.0\,\mu g$/day. Larger doses of calcitriol
or $1\alpha D_3$ are not recommended in elderly osteoporotic patients because of the risk of hypercalcaemia. To avoid the hypercalcaemia, patients
on calcitriol or $1\alpha D_3$ therapy are monitored by
measuring serum calcium one week after starting
therapy (or changing the dose). Subsequently,
serum and urine calcium are monitored every
three to six months. Thiazides should not be
prescribed with calcitriol or $1\alpha D_3$, inasmuch as
the vitamin D analogue and thiazides together
further increase the risk of hypercalcaemia (i.e.
thiazides decrease urine calcium excretion and
calcitriol increases calcium absorption, which together tend to promote an increase in serum
calcium).

Antiresorptive therapy

If the patient has a high bone resorption rate, as
determined by measurement of urine hydroxy-
proline/creatinine or urine pyridinoline/creati-
nine, the patient should be placed on
antiresorptive therapy. It is important to detect a
high bone resorption, because there are at least
three different types of drugs to correct this
abnormality; namely, oestrogen, bisphosphonates and calcitonin. On the other hand, if the
patient has a bone resorption rate that is below
the mean for premenopausal patients (see section
on Diagnostic tests), these patients generally

show a poor response to antiresorptive therapy
[55].

Oestrogen replacement therapy after oophorectomy or menopause has been shown to retard
cortical and trabecular bone loss and reduce the
risk of fracturing in the spine, hip, and wrist
(Table 29.3) [56,57,58]. Unopposed oestrogen
therapy increases the risk of endometrial cancer.
To reduce this risk in a woman with an intact
uterus, it is recommended that oestrogen be given
cyclically (i.e., given on days 1–25 followed by 3-
day free period) in combination with a progestational agent (Provera 5–10 mg/day) on the last
10–14 days of the cycle. This cyclic therapy
allows sloughing of hyperplastic endometrium
and, thus, is one means to reduce the risk of
endometrial cancer. There is some evidence that
oestrogen with or without progesterone therapy
may increase the risk for breast cancer. We,
therefore, recommend mammography examinations annually for all patients on oestrogen
therapy.

This cyclic therapy usually causes withdrawal
bleeding, a complication which is unacceptable to
patients more than 65 to 70 years of age. In order
to avoid withdrawal bleeding and, at the same
time, prevent endometrial cancer, a current practice is to give the equivalent of Premarin 0.625 mg
daily every day of the month and, in addition, a
progestational agent such as Provera 2.5 mg daily
every day of the month. After one year of this
treatment, about 75% of patients will exhibit an
atrophic endometrium (and thus have no increased risk of endometrial cancer) without
withdrawal bleeding [59]. The lowest dose of
oestrogen that has been found to be effective in
preventing bone loss in postmenopausal women
is 0.625 mg per day of conjugated oestrogen (Premarin) or its equivalent. Doses higher than
1.25 mg per day are associated with greater incidence of complications without deriving further
benefit to the skeleton. The side effects reported
with high dose oral oestrogens (including intra-
vascular clotting, cholelithiasis, and hyper-
tension) have been ascribed to the so called first
pass effect in the liver. Ingested oestrogen undergoes partial metabolism to less active forms in the
liver before delivery into the general circulation.

The transdermal dosage form of oestrogen,
which delivers oestradiol (E2) through the skin
into the systemic circulation in a constant con-

trolled manner, bypasses the liver and reduces, if not eliminates, the complications attributed to enhanced hepatic effects [60,61].

Because the most rapid bone loss occurs in the early stages of menopause, the earlier oestrogen replacement therapy is initiated, the more effective it will be to prevent the development of osteoporosis. This also holds for other antiresorptive agents. Although oestrogen has its greatest effect to preserve bone density when it is given at the time of the menopause, even patients who are 70 years of age or older will benefit from the antiresorptive effects of oestrogen therapy. However, such patients are seldom inclined to tolerate the menses that occur in many women on oestrogen therapy with an intact uterus. Therefore, we frequently recommend etidronate or injectable calcitonin therapy to elderly osteoporotic patients with an intact uterus.

Although we employ a dose of 0.625 mg/day of conjugated oestrogens or its equivalent at the beginning of therapy, we have found that this dose is not adequate in all patients to reduce the bone resorption rate to the premenopausal value. With oestrogen replacement therapy, the nadir for the decrement in urine hydroxyproline/creatinine is at about 6 months [62]. At this time, if we do not find a normal (premenopausal) bone resorption level, we either increase the dose of oestrogen, or, if this is not tolerated, add another antiresorption agent at a low dose and re-evaluate the patient after another 6 months of therapy. It should be emphasized that, because the time-dependent variation in urine hydroxyproline/creatinine assay is large (i.e., the daily, weekly and monthly variation from unknown causes), the physician may not want to use a single value for therapeutic decision. Thus, the physician may wish to make therapeutic decisions on the basis of two or more similar lab results in sequence.

If a patient has osteoporosis or osteopenia and a normal resorption rate, the patient is still advised to take oestrogen replacement therapy because of the positive actions of oestrogen on the cardiovascular system. Moreover, if the patient has a normal bone density and a normal bone resorption rate, we still recommend oestrogen replacement therapy for the same reasons.

When oestrogen is contradicted or ineffective at the highest tolerated dose (for example, some patients complain of breast tenderness at even moderate doses of oestrogen), we use either etidronate or injectable calcitonin*. The recommended dose of etidronate is 400 mg/day for two weeks out of twelve weeks [63]. It has not yet been established that this dose is effective for all patients. While it is not known when the nadir for hydroxyproline/creatinine is reached on this therapeutic regimen, we suggest sampling at 6 month intervals after commencing therapy. It may be necessary to use higher doses (i.e., more continuous treatment) of etidronate to achieve a premenopausal urine hydroxyproline/creatinine. If so, higher doses should be given with some caution since larger doses of etidronate may cause osteomalacia. If higher doses are used, etidronate should be given intermittently to allow for the healing of the osteomalacia that could be caused by etidronate. It is also recommended that etidronate be given on an empty stomach (i.e., with no ingestion of food for 2 hours before or after, since any calcium in the GI tract will precipitate the etidronate and impair its absorption.) Side-effects to etidronate therapy are minor; we have observed only an occasional complaint of lower gastrointestinal discomfort.

The other agent for antiresorptive therapy is injectable salmon calcitonin (Miacalcin, Calcimar) (Table 29.3). The dose of calcitonin recommended in the PDR is 100 units daily. We are concerned that high daily injections may cause resistance [64]. Thus, we give lower doses (50 units subcutaneously daily), and we give the drug cyclically (3 months on and one month off). Some experts give even lower doses (i.e., 50 units three times weekly instead of daily). However, the theoretical advantage of these lower dose therapeutic regimens have not been experimentally validated. The nadir for the urine hydroxyproline/creatinine following daily calcitonin therapy is approximately three months, at which time the dose can be adjusted as necessary. The major problem with calcitonin therapy is that it must be given by injection. However, the nasal spray form of calcitonin is expected to be marketed sometime in 1995 in the US.

*Etidronate has been approved by the FDA for the treatment of Paget's disease. It has not, however, been approved by the FDA for the treatment of osteoporosis. Thus, the use of etidronate in the US is acknowledged as an off label use.

Corrective therapy

In those patients who have established osteo-porosis (i.e., bone density below fracture threshold with or without fragility fractures), prevention of bone loss by antiresorptive therapy, as described above, is insufficient to eliminate the fracture risk (Fig. 29.5). For example, with 12–18 months of antiresorptive therapy, there is an increase in bone density of about 3–5%, after which bone density stabilizes while the patient continues to receive the drug. If a patient has a spinal bone density as measured by QCT of approximately 50 mg/cc and there is only a 5% increase in bone density with antire-sorptive therapy, the patient on this therapy will continue to be over 48 density points (mg/cc) below the fracture threshold of 100 mg/cc and, thus, at severe risk for an osteoporotic fragility fracture. In order to eliminate this risk for frac-ture or at least minimize the risk, corrective therapy is required (Fig. 29.5). Two forms of therapy have been shown to produce large in-creases in bone density: fluoride and PTH 1-34 (Table 29.3) [65,66,67]. Both agents stimulate bone formation. Thus, bone formation agents can produce large amounts in bone density, whereas antiresorption agents produce small in-creases in bone density. Fluoride is an approved therapy in some countries in Europe and in South America but not in the US. PTH 1-34 is in experimental human trials but is not approved thus far in any country.

One might argue that it would be sufficient to use a bone formation stimulator to replete skel-etal losses without the addition of an anti-resorber. In terms of the increment in bone density produced, antiresorbers contribute only a trivial amount to the combination of anti-resorbers and bone formation stimulators to the increase in bone density. However, antiresorbers tend to decrease bone turnover, and recent studies suggest the higher the bone turnover, the greater the risk for fracture, independent of bone density [68,69]. Thus, antiresorbers not only cause a modest increase in bone density, but they also preserve the trabecular architecture which is important to bone strength. The goal of the combination therapy would be to use bone formation stimulators to increase overall density and to use antiresorptive therapy: (1) to preserve the trabecular architecture; and (2) to decrease remodelling and, thus, decrease surface density of remodelling excavations which serve as stress concentrators on the trabecular surface (stress concentrators would increase the risks of tra-becular microfractures).

Fluoride is a strong bone formation stimu-lator, but its use for osteoporosis remains contro-versial. In the prospective clinical trial published by the Mayo Clinic group in 1990, there was an increase in spinal bone density but no significant decrease in the spinal fracture rate [70]. On the other hand, in a recent study by Pak, there was an increase in spinal bone density and a significant decrease in the spinal fracture rate [71]. In bone biopsies from the Mayo Clinic study, many patients exhibited highly significant morpho-metric evidence of osteomalacia which we pre-sume was, at least in part, due to calcium deficiency [17,18]. It is conceivable that at least part of the poor mechanical performance of the bones in the patients in the Mayo Clinic trial was a consequence of the calcium deficiency osteo-malacia. One difference between the Mayo Clinic study and the Pak study is that, in the Pak study, the amount of fluoride given per unit time was less; thus, the patients would be less likely to develop osteomalacia.

The dose of fluoride used in those studies in which a decrease in spinal fracture rate was seen was about 20 mg of elemental fluoride a day, usually given in two divided doses. One monitors the serum fluoride levels after 2 months fluoride therapy in order to achieve a serum level between 5–10 μM [72]. (The serum sample is obtained in the morning before the dose of fluoride.) A serum level of 5 μM or less is generally ineffective. There is no evidence that serum levels between 10–20 μM have an adverse effect on the skeleton or other tissues; however, serum fluoride levels higher than 10 μM are more likely to be asso-ciated with side-effects from fluoride. The two side-effects seen with fluoride are GI distress and what is referred to as the peripheral pain syn-drome. One only infrequently sees GI side-effects with MFP fluoride or with time released sodium fluoride. In past studies with plain sodium fluoride, up to 50% of patients developed GI side-effects. Thus, currently, the main side-effect of fluoride is the peripheral pain syndrome (i.e., bone pain usually in weight bearing bones, par-ticularly the feet). The cause of the peripheral pain is unknown but probably reflects the stimulation of periosteal bone formation [72,73]. Fluoride therapy may cause calcium deficiency, and this could aggravate the peripheral pain syndrome (see below). Withdrawing the fluoride for 1–3 weeks is usually sufficient to allow the pain to spontaneously resolve. Fluoride is then re-instituted at a lower dose.

All patients on fluoride therapy are monitored for the development of calcium deficiency. Recent evidence suggests that calcium deficiency can occur in fluoride treated patients even on 2000 mg calcium/day and that this can contribute to the osteomalacia seen with fluoride therapy [18]. Indeed, the increased prevalence of stress fractures reported in patients on fluoride therapy may have been due, in part, to the complication of calcium deficiency and osteomalacia. Thus, to avoid calcium deficiency, we monitor our patients for: (1) serum alkaline phosphatase (large increments of more than 100% of basal raise the possibility of calcium deficiency; (2) 24-hour urine calcium, which may drop below 50 mg per 24 hours; and (3) serum PTH, which increases above the basal level. When calcium deficiency occurs, as indicated by the above changes, the patient is treated with larger calcium supplements or with either $1,25(OH)_2D$ or $1\alpha D_3$ to increase calcium absorption [18].

Based on the above discussion, it is apparent that there are three main principles involved in fluoride therapy. First, the dose should be such that the patient has an approximate serum fluoride level of $5–10\,\mu M$. Serum fluoride values at $5\,\mu M$ and below are ineffective. The appropriate serum level can be achieved by adjusting the dose of fluoride. Second, the patient must absorb adequate amounts of calcium either through calcium supplementation or through a combination of calcium supplementation and either $1,25(OH)_2D$ therapy or $1\alpha D_3$ therapy. Third, if the peripheral pain syndrome develops, and one has excluded calcium deficiency, the management of this problem is to discontinue the fluoride for one month and restart the patient at a lower dose, irrespective of the serum level. Even following these general principles there will be patients who do not respond adequately to fluoride with a rapid increase in bone density. We have found that even though there are patients who do not show dramatic increases in bone density early on, almost all patients will show some increase in bone density after several years of therapy.

Treatment of acute vertebral compression fractures

The primary symptom of osteoporosis is back pain, usually associated with a vertebral compression fracture. The acute pain is managed reasonably well with rest and analgesics. The biggest clinical problem that we see regarding acute fractures arises when the patient fails to immobilize herself, in which case, the pain is aggravated and fracture healing is impaired. Ambulatory patients experiencing unusual pain should be at bed rest with bathroom privileges for several days. In addition, particularly if the patient has severe pain, injectable salmon calcitonin at a dose of 100 units per day may substantially reduce the pain [74]. All patients are given a calcitonin skin test before therapy is initiated, and, if it is positive, the patient should not receive this medication. The potential side-effects of injectable calcitonin are flushing and nausea. If these side-effects occur, the dose of salmon calcitonin should be reduced to 50 units per day. If the lower dose is tolerated, then the dose can be gradually increased to 100 units a day, a dose which is necessary in order to control the pain attending acute vertebral fractures.

The above therapeutic management program is for the most part successful, though the physician must remember that osteoporosis is a chronic disease which, thus, requires long-term therapy along with appropriate monitoring of therapy and corresponding drug and dose adjustments.

The therapeutic principles presented above for female osteoporotic patients apply, for the most part, to males. For example, if calcium absorption is low, this is corrected as described above. Similarly, if the bone resorption rate is elevated, the patient is treated with antiresorptive therapy. Unfortunately, we do not have normal hydroxyproline/creatinine values in young male adults (i.e., at time when bone density should be stable), and, thus, we do not have a good estimate of the upper normal limit of bone resorption. Like the treatment of female osteoporotics, if the male osteoporotic has a bone density below the fracture threshold, the patient is treated with fluoride or referred to a centre for the evaluation of fluoride treatment.

In contrast to females, there is a subgroup of male osteoporosis patients who require testosterone therapy; namely, those elderly male patients who have a low serum testosterone (Table 29.3). In these patients, long acting testosterone preparations such as testosterone enanthate or cyprionate can be administered intramuscularly at a dose of about 100–200 mg every 2–3 weeks to correct the low serum testosterone. The optimal dose is one which maintains the serum testosterone in the normal range. We monitor serum testosterone one day after the injection and one day before the next injection.

Testosterone acts to decrease bone resorption and probably also increases bone formation [75,76]. An analogy exists between oestrogen therapy and breast cancer and testosterone therapy and prostate cancer. Accordingly, precaution must be exercised to exclude prostate cancer before testosterone therapy is initiated. Thus, the patient should receive a digital prostate examination as well as a serum PSA before initiating testosterone therapy. Moreover, such surveillance for prostate cancer is continued during the period of testosterone therapy. Testosterone therapy is discontinued if the patient develops evidence of prostate cancer.

To summarize, all patients with osteoporosis should routinely have an adequate calcium intake and an exercise programme. Any secondary causes of osteoporosis should be identified since they are usually treatable. Unless contraindicated, postmenopausal women should be placed on oestrogen to prevent or retard the accelerated bone loss that occurs in the postmenopausal period. Patients with evidence of increased bone resorption should receive antiresorptive therapy. Patients who have a bone density below the fracture threshold should be considered for fluoride therapy. This management programme is successful for the most part, though the physician must remember that osteoporosis is a chronic disease which requires a long period of time to correct the bone density deficit.

Acknowledgements

We thank Ms Jamie Lopez for typing the manuscript, Ms Carol Farrell and Ms Barbara Barr for editorial assistance, and Mr Jerry Bohn and the Medical Media staff for the figures. This work was supported, in part, by a VA Merit Review grant and funds from the National Institutes of Health (AR 31062), the Veterans Administration, and the Department of Medicine, Loma Linda University.

References

1. Baylink, D. J., Stauffer, M., Wergedal, J. *et al.* (1970) Formation, mineralization, and resorption of bone in vitamin D deficient rats. *J. Clin. Invest.*, **49**, 1122–1134.
2. Baylink, D. J., Morey, E. R., Ivey, J. L. *et al.* (1980) Vitamin D and bone. In: *Vitamin D; Molecular Biology and Clinical Nutrition* (ed. A. W. Norman) Marcel Dekker, Inc., New York, pp. 387–453.
3. Howard, G. and Baylink, D. J. (1980) Matrix formation and osteoid maturation in vitamin D deficient rats made normocalcemic by dietary means. *Miner. Electrolyte Metab.*, **3**, 44–50.
4. Baylink, D. J. (1994) Osteomalacia. In: *Principles of Geriatric Medicine and Gerontology, 3rd Edition*, (eds W. R. Hazzard, E. L. Bierman, J. P. Blass, W. H. Ettinger, J. B. Halter), McGraw Hill Inc. New York, chapter 77, pp. 911–922.
5. Frame, B. and Parfitt, A. M. (1978) Osteomalacia: current concepts, *Ann. Int. Med.*, **89**, 966–982.
6. Morgan, D. B., Hunt, G. and Paterson, C. R. (1970) The osteomalacia syndrome after stomach operations. *Q. J. Med.*, **39**, 395.
7. Compston, J. E. *et al.* (1978) Osteomalacia after small-intestinal resection. *Lancet*, **1**, 9.
8. Herlong, H. F. *et al.* (1982) Bone disease in primary biliary cirrhosis: histological features and response to 25-hydroxyvitamin D. *Gastroenterology*, **83**, 103.
9. Compston, J. E. and Thompson, R. P. H. (1977) Intestinal adsorption of 25-hydroxyvitamin D and osteomalacia in primary biliary cirrhosis. *Lancet*, **1**, 721.
10. Davie, M. W. J. *et al.* (1983) Low plasma 25-hydroxyvitamin D and serum calcium levels in institutionalized epileptic subjects: associated risk factors, consequences and response to treatment and vitamin D. *Q. J. Med.*, **205**, 79.
11. Sherrard, D. J. *et al.* (1974) Quantitative histological studies on the pathogenesis of uremic bone disease. *J. Clin. Endocrinol. Metab.*, **39**. 119.
12. Stauffer, M., Baylink, D. J. and Wergedal, J. (1973) Decreased bone formation and mineralization and enhanced resorption in calcium deficient rats. *Am. J. Physiol.*, **225**, 269–276.
13. Drezner, M. K. *et al.* (1980) Evaluation of a role for 1,25 dihydroxy-vitamin D_3 in the pathogeneis and treatment of x-linked hypophophatemic

rickets and osteomalacia. *J. Clin. Invest.*, **60**, 1020.

14. Baylink, D. J., Wergedal, J. and Stauffer, M. (1971) Formation, mineralization, and resorption of bone in hypophosphatemic rats. *J. Clin. Invest.*, **50**, 2519–2530.

15. Carmichael, K. A. *et al.* (1984) Osteomalacia and osteitis fibrosa in a man ingesting aluminium hydroxide anatacid. *Am. J. Med.*, **76**, 1137.

16. Boyce, B. F. *et al.* (1984) Focal osteomalacia due to low-dose diphosphonate therapy in Paget's disease. *Lancet*, **1**, 821–824.

17. Lundy, M. W., Stauffer, M., Wergedal, J. E. *et al.* (1995) Histomorphometric analysis of iliac crest bone biopsies in placebo-treated versus fluoride-treated subjects. *Osteoporosis International*, **5**, 2–17.

18. Dure-Smith, B. A., Farley, S. M., Linkhart, S. G. *et al.* (1993) Fluoride treated patients become calcium deficient despite calcium supplements: correction with 1,25 vitamin D_3. *Fourth International Symposium on Osteoporosis and Consensus Development Conferences*, No. **79**, pp. 146.

19. Baylink, D. J. (1970) Metabolic bone disease. In: *Introduction to the Musculoskeletal System* (eds C. Rosse and D. K. Clawson). Harper and Row, New York, pp. 66–74.

20. Baylink, D. J. and Libanati, C. L. (1994) The actions and therapeutic applications of 1α-hydroxylated derivatives of vitamin D. *Akt. Rheumatol.*, **19** (suppl. 1) 10–18.

21. Gruber, H. E., Stauffer, M. E., Thomson, E. R. *et al.* (1981) Diagnosis of bone disease by core biopsies. *Semin. Hematol.*, **18**, 258–278.

22. Ivey, J. L., Gruber, H. E. and Baylink, D. J. (1980) Measurement and significance of rates of osteoid maturation and mineral accumulation. *Metab. Bone Dis. Rel. Res.*, **2**(S), 207–212.

23. McClure, J. and Smith, P. S., (1987) Oncogenic osteomalacia. *J. Clin. Pathol.*, **40**, 446.

24. Slatopolsky, E. *et al.* (1984) Marked suppression of secondary hyperparathyroidism by intravenous administration of 1,25 dihydroxycholecalciferol in uremic patients. *J. Clin. Invest.*, **74**, 2136.

25. Koo, W. W. K., and Tsang, R. (1984) Bone mineralization in infants. *Progress in Food and Nutrition Science*, **8**, 229–302.

26. Collins, N. *et al.* (1991) A progressive study to evaluate the dose of vitamin D required to correct low 25-hydroxyvitamin D levels, calcium, and alkaline phosphatase in patients at risk of developing antiepileptic drug-induced osteomalacia. *Q. J. Med., New Series*, **78**, 113.

27. Chertow, B. S., Baylink, D. J., Wergedal, J. E. *et al.* (1975) Decrease in serum immunoreactive parathyroid hormone in rats and in PTH secretion in vitro by 1,25 dihydroxycholecalciferol.

J. Clin. Invest., **56(3)**, 668–678.

28. Peck, W. A., Riggs, B. L., Bell, N. H. *et al.* (1988) Research directions in osteoporosis. *Am. J. Med.*, **84**, 275–282.

29. Chesnut, C. H. III (1994) Osteoporosis. In: *Principles of Geriatric Medicine and Gerontology*. Third Edition. (eds Hazzard, W. R., Bierman, E. L., Blass, J. B., Ettinger, W. H., Halter). McGraw-Hill Inc., chapter **76**, pp. 897–909.

30. Mazess, R. B. (1982) On aging bone loss. *Clin. Orthop. Rel. Res.*, **165**, 238–252.

31. Gray, T. K., Lipes, B., Linkhart, T. *et al.* (1989) Transforming growth factor beta mediates the estrogen induced inhibition of UMR106 cell growth. *Connect. Tiss. Res.*, **20(1–4)**, 23–32.

32. Girasole, G., Jilka, R. A., Passeri, G. *et al.* (1992) 17β Estrodial inhibits interleuken 6 production by bone marrow derived stromal cells and osteoblasts in vitro: A potential mechanism for the anti-osteoporotic effects of estrogens. *J. Clin. Invest.*, **89**, 883–891.

33. van Hoof, H. J. C., van der Mooren, M. J., Swinkels, L. M. J. W. *et al.* (1994) Hormone replacement therapy increases serum 1,25-dihydroxyvitamin D: a 2-year prospective study. *Calcif. Tissue Int.*, **55**, 417–419.

34. Smith, D. M. *et al.* (1973) Genetic factors in determining bone mass. *J. Clin. Invest.*, **52**, 2800.

35. Dequeker, J. *et al.* (1987) Genetic determinants of bone mineral content at the spine and radius: A twin study. *Bone*, **8**, 207.

36. Seeman, E. *et al.* (1989) Reduced bone mass in daughters of women with osteoporosis. *N. Engl. J. Med.*, **320**, 554.

37. Melton, L. J., III (1991) Differing patterns of osteoporosis across the world. In: *New dimensions in osteoporosis in the 1990's* (ed. Chesnut, C. H., III). *Hong Kong, Excerpta Medica Asia*, pp. 13–18.

38. Thomsen, K., Gotfredsen, A. and Christiansen, C. (1986) Is postmenopausal bone loss an age-related phenomenon? *Calcified Tissue International*, **39**, 123–127.

39. Riggs, B. L. and Melton, L. J., III (1986) Involutional osteoporosis. *N. Engl. J. Med.*, **314**, 1676–1686.

40. Chapuy, M. C., Arlot, M. E., Duboeuf, F. *et al.* (1992) Vitamin D_3 and calcium to prevent hip fractures in elderly women. *N. Engl. J. Med.*, **327(23)**, 1637–1642.

41. Bennet, A. E., Wahner, H. W., Riggs, B. L. *et al.* (1984) Insulin-like growth factors I and II: Aging and bone density in women. *J. Clin. Endocrinol. Metab.*, **5**, 701–704.

42. Gruber, H. E. and Baylink, D. J. (1981) The diagnosis of osteoporosis. *J. Am. Geriatr. Soc.*, **29**, 490–497.

43. Lewinnek, G. E., Kelsey, J., White, A. A. *et al.* (1980) The significance and a comparative analysis of the epidemiology of hip fractures. *Clin. Orthop. Rel. Res.*, **152**, 35–43.

44. Odvina, C. V., Wergedal, J. R., Libanati, C. R. *et al.* (1988) Relationship between trabecular body density and fractures: A quantitative definition of spinal osteoporosis. *Metabolism*, **37(3)**, 221–228.

45. Dunn, W. L., Wahner, H. W. and Riggs, B. L. (1980) Measurement of bone mineral content in human vertebrae and hip by dual photon absorptiometry. *Radiology*, **136**, 485–487.

46. Melton, L. J. III, Atkinson, E. J., O'Fallon, W. M. *et al* (1993) Long-term fracture prediction by bone mineral assessed at different skeletal sites. *J. Bone Miner. Res.*, **8**, 1227–1233.

47. Heaney, R. P. *et al.* (1982) Calcium nutrition and bone health in the elderly. *Am. J. Clin. Nutrition*, **36**, 986–1013.

48. Bettica, P., Moro, L., Robins, S. P. *et al.* (1992) Bone-resorption markers galactosyl hydroxylysine, pyridinium crosslinks, and hydroxyproline compared. *Clin. Chem.*, **38(11)**, 2313–2318.

49. Pitt, M. (1983) Osteopenic bone disease. *Orthop. Clin. N. Am.*, **14**, 65–80.

50. Krolner, B. and Toft, B. (1983) Vertebral bone loss: An unheeded side-effect of therapeutic bed rest. *Clin. Sci.*, **64**, 537–540.

51. Eisman, J. A. *et al.* (1991) Exercise and its interaction with genetic influences in the determination of bone mineral density. *Am. J. Med.*, **5B (suppl.)**, 55–95.

52. Gallagher, J. C., Riggs, B. L., Eisman, J. *et al.* (1979) Intestinal calcium absorption and serum vitamin D metabolites in normal subjects and osteoporotic patients. *J. Clin. Invest.*, **64**, 729–736.

53. Heaney, R. P., Recker, R. R. and Saville, P. D. (1978) Menopausal changes in calcium balance performance. *J. Lab. Clin. Med.*, **92**, 953–963.

54. Parfitt, A. M. (1987) Trabecular bone architecture in the pathogenesis and prevention of fracture. *Am. J. Med.*, **82**, 68–72.

55. Civitelli, R., Gonnelli, S., Zacchei, F. *et al.* (1988) Bone Turnover in postmenopausal osteoporosis: Effect of calcitonin treatment. *J. Clin. Invest.*, **82**, 1268–1274.

56. Hutchinson, T. A., Polansky, S. M. and Feinstein, A. R. (1979) Postmenopausal oestrogens protect against fracture of hip and distal radius: A case control study. *Lancet*, **2**, 705–709.

57. Weis, N. S., Ure, C. L., Ballard, J. H. *et al.* (1980) Decreased risk of fractures of the hip and lower forearm with postmenopausal use of estrogen. *N. Engl. J. Med.*, **303**, 1195–1198.

58. Riggs, B. L., Seeman, E., Hodgson, S. F. *et al.* (1982) Effect of fluoride/calcium regimen on vertebral fracture occurrence in postmenopausal osteoporosis. *N. Engl. J. Med.*, **306**, 446–450.

59. Marshburn, P. B. and Carr, B. R. (1994) The menopause and hormone replacement therapy. In: *Principles of Geriatric Medicine and Gerontology, 3rd Edition.* (eds W. R. Hazzard, E. L. Biermman, J. B. Blass, W. H. Ettinger, J. B. Halter), McGraw-Hill Inc., chapter 74, pp. 867–878.

60. Chetkowski, R. J., Meldrum, D. R., Steingold, K. A. *et al.* (1986) Biologic effects of transdermal estradiol. *N. Engl. J. Med.*, **314**, 1615–1620.

61. Steingold, K. A., Cefalu, W., Pardridge, W. *et al.* (1986) Enhanced hepatic extraction of estrogens used for replacement therapy. *J. Clin. Endocrinol. Metab.*, **62**, 761–766.

62. Stephan, J. J., Pospichol, J., Schreiber, V. *et al.* (1989) The application of plasma tartrate-resistant acid phosphatase to assess changes in bone resorption in response to artificial menopause and its treatment with estrogen or norethisterone. *Calcified Tissue International*, **45**, 273–280.

63. Watts, N. B. *et al.* (1990) Intermittent cyclical etidronate treatment of postmenopausal osteoporosis. *N. Engl. J. Med.*, **323**, 73–79.

64. Gruber, H. E., Ivey, J. L., Baylink, D. J. *et al.* (1984) Long-term calcitonin therapy in postmenopausal osteoporosis. *Metabolism*, **33(4)**, 295–303.

65. Farley, S. M. G., Libanati, C. R., Mariano-Menez, M. R. *et al.* (1990) Fluoride therapy for osteoporosis promotes a progressive increase in spinal bone density. *J. Bone Min. Res.*, **5(1)**, S37–S42.

66. Farley, S. M., Wergedal, J. E., Farley, J. R. *et al.* (1990) Fluoride decreases spinal fracture rate: A study of over 500 patients. *3rd Intl. Symp. on Osteoporosis, Copenhagen, Denmark*, pp. 1330–1334.

67. Dempster, D. W., Cosman, F., Parisien, M. *et al.* (1993) Anabolic actions of parathyroid hormone on bone. *Endocrine Reviews*, **14(6)**, 690–709.

68. Parfitt, A. M. (1993) Pathophysiology of bone fragility. *Proceedings Fourth International Symposium on Osteoporosis and Consensus Development Conference*, Hong Kong, pp. 164–166.

69. Riggs, B. L., Melton, L. J. III, and O'Fallon, W. M. (1993) Toward optimal therapy of established osteoporosis: evidence that antiresorptive and formation-stimulating regimens decrease vertebral fracture rate by independent mechanisms. Proceedings *4th International Symposium on Osteoporosis and Consensus Development Conference*, Hong Kong, pp. 13–15.

70. Riggs, B. L. *et al.* (1990) Effect of fluoride treatment on the fracture rate in postmenopausal women with osteoporosis. *N. Engl. J. Med.*, **22**, 802–809.

71. Pak, C. Y. C., Sakhaee, K., Piziak, V. *et al.* (1994) Slow-release sodium fluoride in the management of postmenopausal osteoporosis: A randomized controlled trial. *Annals Internal Med.*, **120(8)**, 625–632.

72. Taves, D. R. (1970) New approach to the treatment of bone disease with fluoride. *Fed. Proc.*, **29**, 1185–1187.

73. Schulz, E. E., Engstrom, H., Sauser, D. D. *et al.* (1986) Osteoporosis: Radiographic detection of fluoride-induced extra-axial bone formation. *Radiology*, **159(2)**, 457–462.

74. Gennari, C. (1983) Clinical aspects of calcitonin in pain. *Triangle*, **22(2:3)**, 157–163.

75. Kasperk, C. H., Wergedal, J. E., Farley, J. R. *et al.* (1989) Androgens directly stimulate proliferation of bone cells in vitro. *Endocrinology*, **124(3)**, 1576–1578.

76. Riggs, B. L., Jowsey, J., Goldsmith, R. S. *et al.* (1972) Short and long-term effects of estrogen and synthetic anabolic hormone in post-menopausal osteoporosis. *J. Clin. Invest.*, **51**, 1659–1663.

30

Physics and technology of bone-mineral content measurements

R. R. Price and M. P. Sandler

Introduction

Aside from the conventional radiograph which is used for qualitative evaluation of bone status, there are three primary categories of instruments/ methods which are currently being used for quantitative bone mineral content (BMC) assessment. These are: single photon absorptiometry (SPA), dual photon absorptiometry (DPA) and quantitative computed tomography (QCT) [1,2]. Both SPA and DPA are projection methods, and as such measure the sum of compact and cancellous bone at a specified site in the body. The SPA technique, usually applied to the distal ulna and radius, typically expresses BMC in terms of g/cm. This quantity is a 'linear density' which measures the grams of BMC per centimetre of length along the bone. The DPA technique is used to express BMC in terms of grams per projected cross-sectional area (g/cm^2) while QCT, a tomogaphic methodology, attempts to estimate bone density in terms of g/cm^3.

Each of the above methods is absorptiometric in nature, meaning that by using the known photon absorption properties of bone mineral, one estimates the 'amount of bone mineral' in a given unknown sample. The concepts of how and in what physical units the amount of bone should be expressed is still a matter of some discussion. Fortunately, there has been some degree of agreement in that bone density seems to be an important indicator of bone status. Bone density in this context has come to refer to that portion of the bone which remains when the specimen is

ashed under extreme heat, commonly referred to as bone mineral. The rest of the bone is included under the component which demonstrates absorption properties of soft tissue. Thus, the bone density is expressed as a mass of bone mineral per unit of bone volume (g/cm^3). Since the bone matrix itself is a relatively random network of crystalline structure, estimates of bone density are usually quoted as the mean of many point density measurements over a specified bone site.

In each of the three techniques, bone mineral standards are commonly used for instrument calibration. The phantoms are generally calcium-hydroxyapatite crystals imbedded in a soft tissue equivalent material or dipotassium hydrogen phosphate (K$_2$HPO$_4$) solutions which have been cross-calibrated to actual bone ash weight.

SPA method

The SPA technique, introduced by Cameron and Sorenson in the early 1960s [3,4], has been produced commercially as a compact table-top device for measuring the linear density (g/cm) of bone mineral of the distal ulna and radius (Fig. 30.1). The SPA device typically employs an I-125 source (several hundred millicuries) which is narrowly collimated and rigidly coupled by means of a small C-arm to an opposed scintillation detector. The C-arm is scanned in a rectilinear motion over the region being examined. The transmitted intensity of the beam of mono-

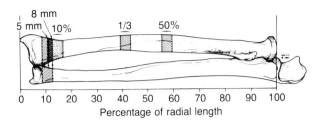

Fig. 30.1 Commonly used SPA sites in the radius and ulna. Distal sites for mixed trabecular/cortical and standard 1/3 from distal end for compact bone site (from [13]).

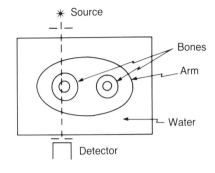

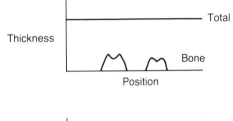

Fig. 30.2 Diagram of the SPA method.

chromatic photons from the source (28 keV) is recorded and used to calculate the average **BMC** of the region.

The SPA technique assumes (also assumed by DPA and QCT) that the body is composed of two components: soft tissue and bone mineral. If the beam of monochromatic photons of initial intensity I_o passes through 't' cm of soft-tissue and 'b' cm of bone mineral, the transmitted intensity, I, is given by:

$$I = I_o e^{-\mu_t t - \mu_b b}$$

where M_t and M_b are the linear attenuation coefficients of soft tissue and bone mineral, respectively, at the energy being used. In the SPA technique, I_o and I are measured at each point of the scan. The attenuation coefficients are constants which have been determined independently through calibration experiments. Calibration experiments usually measure a calibration set of bones which are then ashed to provide the actual BMC.

Since there are two unknowns in the above equation (t and b), the body part must be immersed in water or some other tissue equivalent material (Fig. 30.2) to yield a total thickness (T) which is constant. In this situation:

$$T = t + b,$$

This relationship is substituted into the original attenuation equation which is then solved for the bone content (b).

$$b = \frac{1}{\mu_b - \mu_t}\left(\ln\frac{I_o}{I} - \mu_t T\right)$$

$$b = \frac{1}{\mu_b - \mu_t}\left(\ln\frac{I'}{I}\right)$$

Where

$$I' = I_o e^{-\mu_t T}$$

In this case I' is a constant which is determined by measuring over a site which contains no bone.

Since the SPA method requires the use of an additional material to surround the body part under study, it can conveniently be used only for bones in the extremities.

In assessing bone disease, it is the density of the bone that is of interest instead of the total bone thickness. Total bone thickness is generally not a useful quantity because of its close dependence on the size of the person, i.e. large people have large bones with large thicknesses.

Bone density is determined by using the measuring mass attenuation coefficient (cm^2/g) instead of the linear attenuation coefficient (1/cm) which then in turn yields a mass thickness. Mass thickness has the units of g/cm^2 and is equal to the number of grams of bone mineral per square centimetre of projected areas through the bone. Cameron proposed a further normalization in SPA measurements of the wrist to minimize body size effects by dividing the BMC (g/cm²) by the diameter of the bone to yield a BMC linear density (g/cm). The result of this normalization is to yield a value which is equal to the number of grams of BMC per cm of distance along the axis of the bone.

DPA method

During the mid-1970s several laboratories began developing the DPA technique for assessing the bone mineral content of the lumbar spine [5–7]. During the past decade, this technique has been used to establish well defined values of normal spinal bone mineral mass. The dual photon absorptiometry technique now offers an accurate, inexpensive, and non-invasive test for the early detection of osteoporosis and other demineralizing diseases [8].

As the name implies, DPA utilizes two monoenergetic photon beams. With two beams, there are now two attenuation equations (one for each energy) which can be solved directly for the two unknowns (t and b) without additional material. With the DPA method, it now becomes convenient to examine any part of the body (Fig. 30.3) regardless of the overlying soft-tissue component.

$$I^L = I_o^L \, e^{-\mu_t^L t - \mu_b^L b}$$

$$I^H = I_o^H \, e^{-\mu_t^H t - \mu_b^H b}$$

In the DPA technique; it is possible to solve either for the bone mineral content or the soft tissue content. The solution for the bone mineral content is a follows:

$$b = \frac{\ln\left(\frac{I_o^L}{I^L}\right) - C_2 \ln\left(\frac{I_o^H}{I^H}\right)}{C_1}$$

where,

$$C_1 = \mu_b^L - \left(\frac{\mu_t^L}{\mu_t^H}\right)\mu_b^H$$

$$C_2 = \frac{\mu_t^L}{\mu_t^H}$$

where the superscripts L and H refer to the low and high energy beams, respectively, and C_2 (sometimes called the R-value) characterizes the

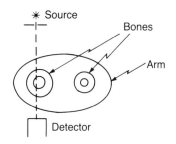

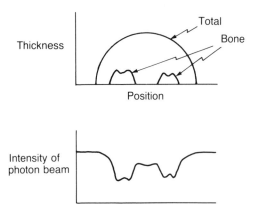

Fig. 30.3   Diagram of the DPA method.

attenuation of the two photon energies in soft tissue. In most DPA systems, the R-value is estimated independently for each patient by making measurements of a body site near to the bone of interest but which in fact contains no bone. (This is equivalent to setting b = 0 in the BMC equation and finding the best value for C_2.) For b = 0,

$$R = \ln(I_o^L/I^L)/\ln(I_o^H/I^H)$$

Errors in estimated BMC can result when R-values measured over soft tissue sites adjacent to bones are not representative of R-values of the bone soft tissue components. Specifically, this condition may arise in elderly osteoporotics where vertebral bone mineral may be replaced by fat rich yellow marrow. Since fat rich soft tissue is somewhat less attenuating than muscle based soft tissue, BMC estimates may be underestimated.

As with the SPA, mass absorption coefficients are used in place of the linear attenuation coefficients so that b is the measured mass per unit area (g/cm²), rather than thickness.

In the DPA method, an image of the BMC

(g/cm²) is created from a rectilinear scan of the region of interest in which the transmitted intensities of both energy beams are measured at each pixel location and then used to calculate the BMC.

DPA source

The most common source use for DPA systems is gadolinium-153. The Gd-153 energy spectrum (Fig. 30.4) is characterized by two primary photon groups. The low energy photon group is actually composed of a complex family of energies. The effective energy of the lower energy group is approximately 44 keV. The upper energy group consists of two energy lines, one at 97 keV and the other at 103 keV with a mean value of about 100 keV.

For *in vivo* applications, thin window NaI crystal is usually the detector of choice. Typical NaI systems will have energy resolutions of about 10% at 100 keV (FWHM) and produce an energy spectrum which does not resolve the internal structure of the two photon groups (Fig. 30.5).

The 44 and 100 keV energies of Gd-153 offer the almost ideal combination of energies in which the bone-soft tissue contrast is optimized with an acceptable beam attenuation.

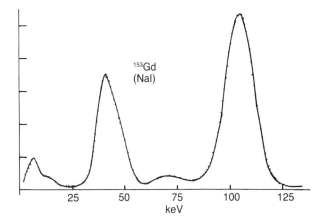

Fig. 30.5   NaI energy spectrum of ¹⁵³Gd.

Scanning apparatus

A computer-controlled rectilinear scanner is used to acquire the dual energy transmission images which are then used to create the intensity modulated BMC images. From the intensity modulated BMC imagers, regions of interest are selected, mean values of mass per unit area are calculated and then compared to the ranges of normal values.

In our laboratory, we have utilized a modified dual-probe nuclear medicine whole-body scanner for our DPA system (Fig. 30.6). This scanner allows great flexibility in the scanner format, making it possible to scan any portion of the body as well as the total body (Fig. 30.7).

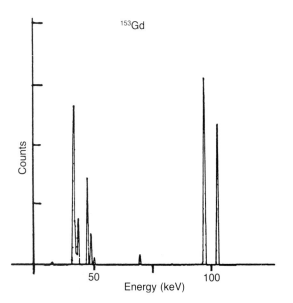

Fig. 30.4   High resolution energy spectrum of ¹⁵³Gd intrinsic germanium detector.

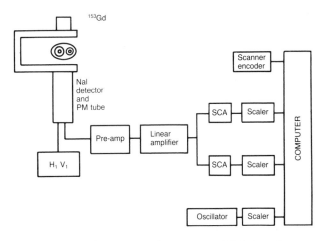

Fig. 30.6   Block diagram of a prototype DPA imaging system.

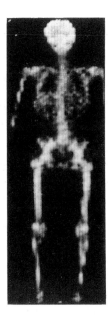

Fig. 30.7 Total body transmission scan at 40 keV (left) and the corresponding derived total body BMC image.

1. Corrections for scatter of 100 keV photons into the 44 keV channel.
2. Dead time corrections for count rate losses.
3. Beam hardening correction due to preferential attenuation of the low energy components of the energy subgroups.
4. Accurate methods for finding the bone edge for accurate calculations of mean values.

An error which has produced a great deal of discussion results from the basic assumption of the method. The basic assumption that the body consists of two absorptive components, bone and soft tissue, becomes a progressively poorer assumption as the fraction of fat increases. This error comes about because the attenuation coefficients which are assumed for soft tissue in the BMC calculation are no longer correct. Interactive corrections for fat contributions are useful in minimizing these uncertainties. Corrections for fat errors are more difficult in the QCT technique.

In our system, signals from the scanner's x and y position encoders, the single analyser pulses from the two photon groups and the pulses from a high frequency oscillator are all monitored and recorded simultaneously by the computer (PDP-11/55). The data are buffered in the computer's memory and then written to a disk at the end of each line. The recorded oscillator pulses make it possible to correct for scanner speed instabilities.

The horizontal sampling rate for our system is variable. Standard scans of the lumbar spine have 256 samples (pixels) per horizontal line (15 cm) and as many lines (3 mm steps) as necessary to accommodate the region of interest. The line stepping distances should be determined by the beam collimator. In our system, the beam is collimated to 6 mm. Commercial systems use beam diameters up to 13 mm. It is the beam diameter which determines the spatial resolution. Spatial resolution will be approximately equal to the beam diameter.

Corrections to the DPA method

In order to achieve a precision of the order of 2%, many corrections must be incorporated into the method. These include:

Imaging site

Early investigators attempted to assess skeletal status by measuring the bone mineral content of the distal ulna and radius and the os calcis. It was discovered that the primarily cortical bone of the ulna and radius was relatively insensitive to skeletal changes (Fig. 30.8). Os calcis measurements, though sensitive to weight-bearing changes, are not closely correlated with spine bone mineral. The lumbar spine or the proximal femur (composed primarily of trabecular bone) have generally been found to be more sensitive indicators of changes in bone metabolism and are currently

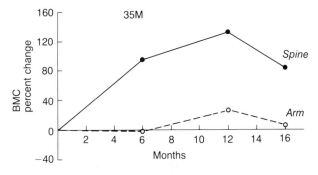

Fig. 30.8 Comparison of the relative change in BMC observed in the spine and wrist over a 16 month period.

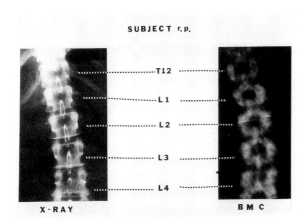

Fig. 30.9 Comparison of DPA image of the lumbar spine and a conventional X-ray in a normal volunteer.

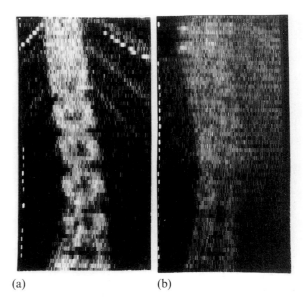

(a)   (b)

Fig. 30.11 (a) DPA spine image of a normal 28-year-old female, (b) DPA spine image of a 72-year-old female with known demineralizing disease.

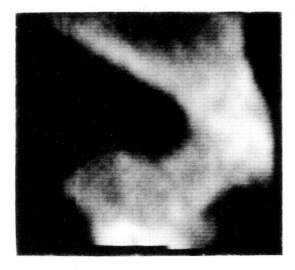

Fig. 30.10 DPA image of the proximal femur.

considered the sites of choice for bone measurements (Figs 30.9, 30.10).

The DPA image

An essential feature of the modern dual photon absorptiometry system is the creation of the bone mineral image. Because of the irregular structure of the vertebral column, it is essential to know what portion of the vertebral bodies are being measured. Figure 30.11 compares DPA images that demonstrate the visual differences between individuals of comparable ages but with quantitatively different BMC values. The image in Fig.

30.11a is a scan of a 28-year-old female who was determined to have normal BMC for her age (Fig. 30.12a). The image in Fig. 30.11b is of a 72-year-old female with significant bone demineralization. The differences in the distinctness of the vertebral bodies and the reduction in overall image intensity are consistent with the measured bone mineral density values. When compared with expected values for normal women of the same general age group, the 72-year-old female was found to have a bone density value over two standard deviations below the mean for her age group (Fig. 30.12b). A value this low immediately identifies her as a member of a high risk group and requires immediate therapy.

Conditions which affect the measured bone mineral contact in DPA scans of the lumbar spine have been identified by Hahner [13].

Conditions which result in falsely high BMC include: significant aortic calcification, hypertrophic degenerative disease, bone grafts, lipoidal in the spinal canal, calcium-containing tablets in the GI tract and barium contrast material in the GI tract. Conditions which could lead to either high or low value of the BMC include: compression fracture, marked scoliosis, spinal deformities, post-traumatic vertebral changes and focal spinal bone lesions. Laminectomy can also lead to a falsely low value of BMC.

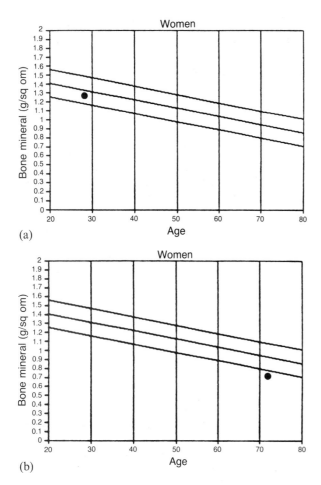

Fig. 30.12 Normal ranges of BMC as a function of age are used to assess those individuals at risk, i.e. those values falling outside the 2-SD limits. (a) BMC of 28-year-old female falls within the normal range of values. (b) BMC of the 72-year-old female falls outside the 2-SD limits and thus identifies this patient as being at risk for fractures.

QCT method

Quantitative computed tomography (QCT) is a method of BMC estimation which was developed as an adjunct to conventional CT scanning. Unlike both SPA and DPA, the QCT technique is inherently tomographic in nature. Because of its tomographic nature, BMC is expressed in terms of true density units (g/cm³) of small user selected regions of selected bones (typically the vertebral body). The tomographic aspect of QCT in principle) allows an estimate of trabecular bone independent of overlying cortical bone. Unfortunately, many factors effect the ability of the

CT method to provide quantitative results and consequently the accuracy with which one corrects for these factors determines the final accuracy of the technique. The primary factor which contributes to the uncertainties in QCT values relates to beam-hardening artifacts. Since CT systems use filtered polyenergetic beams from X-ray tubes rather than monoenergetic beams for isotopic source, the effective energy at a point of the beam will vary depending upon what combination of tissue and bones the beam has passed through in getting to that point. QCT methods typically utilize a beam correction method which employs positioning a calibrated phantom near the bone of interest and forming a QCT scan with the phantom in place. For the lumbar spine, beam projection through other bones is avoided and if the phantom is positioned near the spine, it will be imaged with a beam quality approximately equal to the beam quality seen by the lumbar spine. Other factors affecting QCT measurements are partial volume effects, off-focal spot radiation, reconstruction algorithm variations and subject size and composition. QCT phantoms commonly consist of parallel cylinders filled with different concentrations of K_3HPO_4 which are placed beneath the patient.

A typical QCT scan will report a bone density based upon CT values (Hounsfield Units) from trabecular bone at the midplane of three to four lumbar vertebrae. The CT values are then used to 'look-up' the equivalent bone density using the CT numbers from the phantom cylinders and a calibration data set. The values are then averaged and reported in terms of equivalent g/cm³ of bone.

QCT may utilize either a single CT scan image (usually taken at a relatively low KVp value – 80 KVp) or two CT scan images (one at 80 KVp; the other a heavily filtered scan with KVp > 100 KVp). Dual-energy QCT has been shown to be generally more accurate but at the expense of higher radiation dose to the patient.

A significant uncertainty arises from the QCT method (whether single or dual photon) because of the basic measured quantity (CT number) being related to liner attenuation rather than mass attenuation and consequently being related to true density rather than mineral density. The difference between true density and mineral density being affected primarily by the fat-rich yellow marrow content. It has been shown that QCT measured spinal mineral values are reduced by about 7 mg per 10% of fat by volume at 80 KVp [2]. This effect can result in inaccuracies of 20–30% in elderly osteoporotics. It is estimated that dual-energy QCT may reduce this error to 5% if adequate scan time and radiation exposure are allowed.

Comparison of BMC modalities

The comparison of the three modalities (SPA, DPA and QCT) is usually expressed in terms of two quantities: precision and accuracy. Precision means the ability of the method to reproduce the same measured value. Precision is the factor of concern when the clinical question is whether or not the BMC of a patient is changing with time. Accuracy refers to whether or not the measured value is in fact the true correct value of BMC. Accuracy is important when the clinical question is whether this patient has a normal value of BMC or not.

The precision of SPA is approximately 1% [4]. It should be pointed out again, however, that SPA systems are generally only useful for peripheral sites. The precision of the DPA and single-energy QCT systems are approximately the same and range from 2 to 5%. Dual-energy QCT precision is approximately 4–10% [9–11].

Factors affecting the precision of SPA and DPA relate to the ability of the system or operator to locate the edges of the bones and the ability to carry out adequate corrections for source decay and counting system dead-time. The precision of the QCT method rests largely on the stability of the X-ray tube output and the ability of the operator to accurately reposition the patient and find the same midline region of interest location. The accuracy of repositioning must be within 1 mm in most cases.

The accuracy of each technique relates back to their ability to accurately make a measurement which will yield the value of the bones ash weight. Accuracy determinations are 6% for SPA [4], 5% for DPA [12] and 5–15% for QCT [11].

Radiation exposure

The radiation dose for the SPA method is approximately 10 mrem and approximately 10–20 mrem for the DPA method. QCT values range from 200 to 1000 mrem for single energy measurements to approximately twice these values for dual-energy measurements.

Conclusion

Each of these methods provides relatively accurate methods for measuring BMC status. DPA and QCT are both applicable to the axial skeleton and can be performed on an outpatient basis. Primarily because of its lower radiation burden, DPA may be used for frequent follow-up measurements and may also be a good candidate for a routine screening procedure, especially in those females who are at high risk for developing post-menopausal osteoporosis.

References

1. Price, R. R., Wagner, J., Larsen, K. L. *et al.* (1977) Techniques for measuring regional and total-body bone mineral mass to bone function ratios. IAEA-SM-210/164, *Medical Radionuclide Imaging*, Vol. II, Vienna.
2. Genant, H. K. (1985) Assessing osteoporosis: CT's quantitative advantage. *Diagnostic Imaging*, **August**, 52–57.
3. Cameron, J. R. and Sorensen, J. A. (1963) Measurement of bone mineral *in-vivo*: An improved method. *Science*, **142**, 230.
4. Cameron, J. R., Mazess, R. B. and Sorensen, J. A. (1968) Precision and accuracy of bone mineral determination by direct photon absorptiometry. *Invest. Rad.*, **3**, 141.
5. Price, R. R., Wagner, J., Larsen, K. *et al.* (1976) Regional and whole-body bone mineral content measurement with a rectilinear scanner. *Am. J. Roentgenol.*, **126**, 1277–1278.
6. Wilson, C. R. and Madsen, M. (1977) Dichromatic absorptiometry of vertebral bone mineral content. *Invest. Radiol.*, **12**, 180–184.
7. Madsen, M., Peppler, W. and Mazess, R. (1976) Vertebral and total body bone mineral by dual photon absorptiometry. In *Calcified Tissues* (eds S. Pors Nielsen and E. Hjorting-Hansen), FADL Publishing, Copenhagen.
8. Mazess, R. B., Peppler, W. W. *et al.* (1984) Does bone measurement on the radius indicate skeletal status? *J. Nucl. Med.*, **25(3)**, 281.
9. Dunn, W. L., Wahner, H. W. and Riggs, B. L. (1980) Measurement of bone mineral content in

human vertebrae and hip by dual photon absorptiometry. *Radiology*, **136**, 485–487.

10. LeBlance, A. D., Evans, H. J., March, C. *et al.* (1986) Precision of dual-photon absorptiometry measurements. *J. Nucl. Med.*, **27**, 1362–1363.

11. Genant, H. K., Cann, C. E., Ettinger, B. *et al.* (1985) Quantitative computed tomography for spinal mineral assessment. Current status. *J.* *Comp. Assist. Tomog.*, **9(3)**, 602–604.

12. Wahner, H. W., Dunn, W. L., Mazess, R. B. *et al.* (1985) Dual-photon Gd-153 absorptiometry of bone. *Radiology*, **156**, 203–206.

13. Wahner, H. W. (1986) Bone mineral measurements. In *Nuclear Medicine Annual* 1986 (eds L. M. Freeman and H. S. Weissmann), Raven Press, New York, pp. 195–225.

31

Limb salvage surgery for primary bone tumours

R. S. Sneath and R. J. Grimer

Introduction

Primary bone tumours are rare with an incidence of about 6 or 7 per million per year. In the past, treatment was limited to carrying out an appropriate amputation [1]. In the case of the most common tumour, osteosarcoma, metastases occurred in over 80% of patients within 18 months. Cade, in 1951 [2], appreciating the futility of many of these amputations for osteosarcoma and advocated the more humane approach of treating the primary tumour with radiotherapy followed by a period of careful follow-up. If the patient was free of any evidence of metastases 6 months after radiotherapy the affected bone was removed, usually by amputation. This treatment regime allowed many patients to keep their limbs for the few remaining months of their life, whilst some of the patients who had amputations were long-term survivors, around 20% at 5 years.

From 1970 onwards there was a steady increase in the conservation of limbs by reconstructive techniques for patients with chondrosarcomas, low-grade malignancies, and giant cell tumours [3]. In 1975 and 1976 the treatment of patients with osteosarcoma changed from radiotherapy and delayed amputation to chemotherapy and primary amputation. At this stage it became logical to consider limb salvage techniques for these patients. Late in the 1970s these techniques were also applied to Ewing's sarcoma and the malignant tumours of fibrous origin [4,5].

Over the last 15 years many centres in the world have taken a special interest in the treatment of primary malignant bone tumours. This interest has resulted in the development of teams with special expertise in radiology, pathology, chemotherapy, radiotherapy, bioengineering, physiotherapy and all aspects of orthopaedic surgery. Such a team will usually be led by an orthopaedic surgeon and the team will require at least 100 new cases per year to function efficiently, to gain experience and to have enough experience to develop the specialty through evaluation and research. Therefore, a team needs to serve a population of about 15 million or more to function efficiently, obviously this is not practical in some situations. On the other hand a population of about 100 million is required to be able to collect figures of statistical significance in a reasonable time. The answer lies in cooperation between centres in order that they may draw up protocols of treatment which they can all follow. This cooperation would both provide the necessary numbers for statistics and also stimulate advances in treatment due to the combined enthusiasm of the participants. In situations where the population treated by a team was lower than optimal that team could link into a bigger group in order to absorb the experience and receive the advice of that group.

We believe that it is most important not to encourage too many people to treat bone tumours themselves. We have therefore written this chapter as a source of information and not as a surgical manual, hoping that we may encourage the reader to refer cases to the appropriate centres.

Diagnosis

Diagnosing bone tumours is not straightforward. The presenting symptoms of pain followed by swelling are well known to all, but the rarity of these tumours coupled with the frequency of vague musculoskeletal aches and pains ensures that in many cases the diagnosis is overlooked for a ˙ considerable time. The symptoms which patients experience initially are remarkably consistent no matter what the tumour. The vast majority will start by noticing an ache in the involved part which gradually increases in severity and duration until there is significant pain. The pain may not be affected by activity and is often present at night. Whilst it will initially fluctuate in severity it eventually becomes constant and will only be partially alleviated by mild analgesics. In a few cases there will be no pain and swelling is the initial complaint. In half the cases, swelling and pain are the two presenting symptoms and when these are combined at the end of a long bone then a tumour must be high on the list of differential diagnoses.

A survey of recent cases referred to the Birmingham Bone Tumour Treatment Service has highlighted some of the problems in correctly diagnosing primary bone tumours at an early stage [6].

It surprised us how long patients put up with their symptoms before going to see a doctor, an average of 6 weeks for patients with osteosarcoma, 16 weeks for patients with Ewing's sarcoma and 21 weeks for patients with chondrosarcoma. What was even more concerning was the time after this for a diagnosis to be made and treatment instigated, a further 7 weeks for patients with osteosarcoma, 31 weeks for patients with Ewing's sarcoma and 30 weeks for patients with chondrosarcoma.

The cause of this delay was usually a low level of suspicion. When a tumour was suspected a radiograph was requested and this usually led to the correct diagnosis being made. When the diagnosis was not suspected a variety of treatments were instigated which were invariably of no bene-fit and simply delayed the making of a correct diagnosis.

In all patients the plain radiograph alone invariably led to the correct diagnosis, eventually. In 13 out of 70 cases both the clinician and the radiologist failed to detect the tumour on the initial radiograph although evidence of the tumour was present on retrospective review of the films in all 13 cases.

Factors which led to the tumour being missed included poor quality radiographs and failure to demonstrate the whole of the lesion. Typical of this were the tumours of the distal femur of which 22% were missed on the initial radiograph. The changes which identify the presence of a tumour are well known but easily overlooked. They include ill-defined lysis or sclerosis, periosteal reaction and new bone formation, cortical destruction and localized soft tissue swelling.

The suspicion of any of these on a radiograph should alert the clinician to the possibility of a sarcoma and further investigations should be arranged. If in doubt, a radiograph of the opposite side for comparison is always helpful and readily obtainable. If the abnormality is still questioned a radioisotope bone scan is the investigation of choice. A normal scan will effectively rule out a primary sarcoma, but not necessarily a myeloma, whilst an abnormal scan should lead to further urgent investigation. By this stage a tumour will probably have entered the differential diagnosis but other possibilities such as infection, stress fractures and metastases must be kept in mind.

We found that delays allowed the tumour to increase in size, sometimes making limb salvage impossible. This was most marked with the group who had their initial radiograph reported as normal. This false sense of security resulted in delays of between 2 and 40 weeks before another radiograph was taken, all of which confirmed the correct diagnosis. In this group 58% required an amputation or were found to have inoperable tumours, compared with 15% of the patients who had their initial radiograph correctly interpreted. All the other patients underwent successful limb salvage surgery.

Once the possibility of a tumour is considered then the patient should be properly staged to assess the extent of the tumour both locally and distally [7]. The staging should include either CT or MRI scans of the tumour, CT scans of the chest and a bone scan. This staging process must be carried out before the biopsy.

The biopsy

The biopsy is a most important surgical procedure and should be carried out or supervised by the surgeon in charge of the case. The biopsy needs careful planning to ensure that the correct part of the tumour is sampled and also to ensure that as little normal tissue as possible is violated in order to reduce contamination by tumour cells to the smallest volume of tissue. Careful staging permits a choice of the biopsy route which will take the best sample of the tumour, avoid unnecessary contamination of normal tissues and lie in the operative route for any further surgery required [8].

Mankin *et al.* [9] found that biopsy-related problems occurred between 3–5 times more commonly when the biopsy was carried out in a referring centre. Our study has shown that problems are almost 10 times as common when biopsies are not carried out at a treatment centre. Cannon *et al.* [10] also found that the rate of local recurrence was increased from 7% to 38% in patients who did not have the biopsy track excised at the time of definitive surgery, usually in cases where the biopsy had been done prior to any planning by a surgeon who did not carry out the definitive procedure. At a National Institute of Health conference held in 1985 [11] the conclusion reached about the biopsy was that 'it should only be carried out by a surgeon if he is prepared to carry out definitive surgery also'. We wholeheartedly endorse this conclusion.

Nobody can be absolutely sure of the diagnosis prior to biopsy; therefore if all suspicious cases are referred to an orthopaedic oncology service some will be found to be benign. We accept this situation and consider it to be more preferable than the situation where cases are referred after poor staging and incorrect biopsies.

The surgeon who carries out the biopsy must adhere to the following criteria:

1. The biopsy track must be so placed and described that it can be subsequently readily identified and excised in continuity with the bulk of the tumour.
2. As far as possible no uninvolved compartments should be contaminated when performing the biopsy. Obviously this is not always possible but the route should be as short as possible in normal tissues and avoid intramuscular planes, fatty spaces, neurovascular bundles, bursae and joints.
3. A representative sample of the tumour must be taken. Sampling of reactive tissue at the edge of the tumour and necrotic tumour are two of the reasons for a non-specific histopathological report.
4. There must be complete haemostasis and careful wound closure. A drain should not be used. Direct pressure will usually stop even the most haemorrhagic of tumours from bleeding; bleeding from inside a bone can be stopped by plugging the hole with Sterispon and a muscle plug.
5. Large amounts of normal or tumour bone should not be removed for fear of weakening the bone further. Where tumour tissue is extraosseous this tissue will be sufficient, where it is intraosseous either a core of bone can be removed or the cortex drilled and a medullary sample curetted out. A round hole weakens the bone much less than a square hole of similar dimensions.
6. The biopsy must be correctly labelled and despatched to the pathologist with a representative radiograph.
7. The pathologist must be familiar with bone pathology or be prepared to forward the samples to an expert at an early stage in any doubt about the diagnosis.

The above principles assume that an open biopsy is to be carried out. In specialist centres there may be a role for fine needle aspiration cytology or needle biopsy in selected cases. These techniques rely as much upon the expertise of the pathologist as the technical abilities of the surgeon.

Treatment

Once a diagnosis has been made a plan of treatment needs to be defined. This will involve both surgeon and oncologist in assessing the likely risks and benefits of immediate surgical resection of the tumour against other methods of controlling the tumour. These may consist of chemotherapy, which is particularly valuable for osteosarcoma, Ewing's sarcoma and malignant fibrous histiocytoma, or radiotherapy. Chondrosarcomas do not appear to respond to either chemotherapy or radiotherapy and require surgical resection alone.

The role of surgery is to remove completely the tumour with a surrounding cuff of normal tissue of sufficient dimensions to prevent any recurrence of the tumour. Any compromise of this principle jeopardizes the oncological success of the procedure and except in occasional circumstances cannot be justified.

Enneking [12] has defined four separate margins of resection which can be based on the surgical and pathological findings following a tumour resection. An intracapsular resection implies that dissection has actually occurred through the tumour (such as in curetting a giant cell tumour); a marginal resection has gone through the pseudocapsule around the tumour (as in shelling out a lipoma); a wide resection implies that there is a layer of normal tissue between the resection and the tumour and finally a radical resection is one in which the whole compartment containing the tumour has been removed (as in a disarticulation of the hip for a tumour of the distal femur). If the bulk of the resection conforms with one of the above margins but at one point there has been some tumour spill then this would be a contaminated resection and the risk of local recurrence would be similar to that following an intracapsular resection.

The level of transection of the bone must be planned in advance of the surgical procedure. If the bone is divided and found to contain tumour either macroscopically or on frozen section then it is too late as the surgical field has already been contaminated by tumour spill. Planning the level of transection needs careful assessment of all the staging modalities. Plane radiographs and bone scans are the least reliable two parameters whilst carefully performed CT scans or better still longitudinal MRI scans are the best. Even using these techniques it is still sometimes difficult to assess the end point of a permeative tumour such as Ewing's or central chondrosarcoma and in these situations we would recommend that a clearance biopsy be carried out at the proposed level of transection well before the time of definitive surgery – ideally at the same time as the initial biopsy.

Malignant tumours often form a pseudocapsule around themselves which may appear to be an inviting plane of surgical dissection to the inexperienced surgeon. The pseudocapsule is itself the outer rim of compressed tumour pressing against normal structures and there will always be tumour cells which have bridged across to the adjacent apparently normal tissues so that dissection through this plane will almost inevitably result in recurrence. To obtain a wide resection requires a layer of normal tissue between the plane of dissection and the tumour, and whilst this would ideally consist of a fascial layer many surgeons would consider a few mm of normal muscle tissue to be adequate.

The risk of local recurrence of the tumour is dependent not only on the margin of resection but also on the grade and type of the tumour. The grading of tumours has been standardized by Enneking [12]. The recurrence rate increases as the grade of the tumour increases and as the margin of resection gets less, as would be expected.

The majority of limb salvage resections will obtain either a marginal or wide resection and for high grade tumours there will be a consequent risk of local recurrence. Preoperative chemotherapy will usually result in some shrinkage of the tumour and in these cases the margins of the tumour will often become much better defined (Fig. 31.1) allowing the surgeon to leave more normal tissue intact whilst still achieving an adequate margin [13].

The limb salvage surgeon has to wear two hats – the first and most important is the oncological cap to ensure complete resection of the tumour – and the second is the orthopaedic hat to restore a functioning limb after. The two parts of the procedure are often intimately linked but the former must always take precedence over the surgeon's wishes to retain structures for reconstruction which may jeopardize the oncological resection.

Limb salvage surgery has developed in parallel with improved chemotherapy but the decision whether the limb can justifiably be saved is not only an oncological one. At the end of the day the patient has to be left with a useful functioning limb that is going to be of more use to him than an amputation. Strenuous efforts to preserve the foot following resection of a tumour of the distal tibia should be contrasted with the benefits of an immediate below knee amputation and early fitting of a prosthesis which will undoubtedly give a high level of satisfaction to the patient.

Unfortunately, the majority of tumours occur

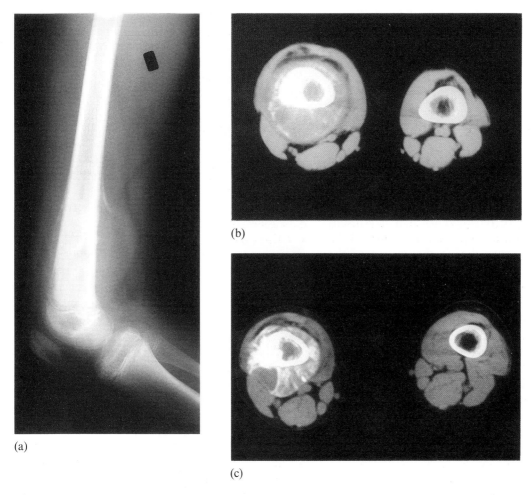

(a)

(b)

(c)

Fig. 31.1   An osteosarcoma of the distal femur (a) showing the CT scan before (b) and after chemotherapy (c) to demonstrate the slight decrease in size of the tumour but the increased mineralization and definition of the tumour.

more proximal than this and in these cases there is usually little doubt that a well executed limb salvage procedure will have considerable benefit over a high amputation. Sugarbarker *et al.* [14] reviewed a group of patients who had limb salvage surgery and compared them with a group who had had amputations. To their surprise there was remarkably little functional and psychological difference between the groups, although the patients who had limb salvage had also had radiotherapy which itself resulted in significant morbidity.

There are few specific contraindications to limb salvage surgery. Inability fully to resect the tumour and gross infection are the two most obvious ones. Occasionally a fulminating tumour can cause such systemic toxicity that an emer-gency amputation is needed to save the patient's life. In most other cases a planned decision can be made. Involvement of the joint by tumour means that an extra-articular resection is required and this may result in such a poor functional outcome that limb salvage is not justified. Involvement of the neurovascular bundle may often suggest that an amputation is required but it may be perfectly feasible to graft the involved vessels if the neural deficit is not likely to lead to too much disability. In the upper limb, particularly where exo-prostheses are of little functional value, every effort should be made to retain a functioning hand if at all possible.

The presence of metastases at diagnosis is a poor prognostic sign but is no contra-indication to limb salvage surgery as the retention of a functioning limb for what is left of the patient's life will enhance the quality of that life compared with an amputation.

Amputations

An amputation will be required if a tumour is found to be too extensive to remove without leaving an adequate margin of normal tissue. Ideally this decision should be made preoperatively but in some cases it can only be made at the time of surgery. All our patients undergoing limb salvage surgery are required to sign a consent form agreeing to an amputation, should it be found to be necessary during the course of the operation.

Limb salvage without reconstruction

There are several sites in the body where bones can be removed without causing serious functional loss. The ribs can be readily resected without much problem although the margins of resection may not be great. Parts of the tarsus and carpus can also be sacrificed. In the upper limb, the distal ulna can be removed with little problem as can the clavicle. The scapula can be removed in total or in part. A partial scapulectomy of the inferior pole leaves no functional disability but a total or even subtotal scapulectomy will result in almost complete loss of abduction of the arm and limit control of rotation of the arm. If the tumour involves the shoulder joint then it may still be possible to salvage the limb by carrying out a Tikhoff–Linberg procedure [15], that is an en bloc resection of both scapula and proximal humerus with the joint intact. This results in a flail shoulder but the hand and elbow still function normally [Fig. 31.2].

In the lower limb a surprisingly large amount of the fibula can be removed without causing disability (Fig. 31.3). Odd case reports also testify to the surprising stability of the knee following resection of a single tibial condyle but this will not usually provide an adequate margin for malignant tumours [16]. Various parts of the pelvis can be resected without recourse to reconstruction. The ischium and pubis can be resected separately or together and the breaking of the

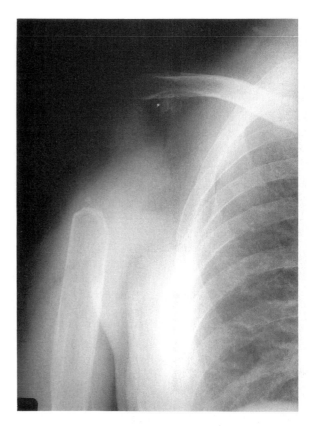

Fig. 31.2   Radiograph of the shoulder following a Tikhoff–Linberg resection for a tumour of the scapula and upper humerus.

pelvic ring in this manner rarely leads to problems (Fig. 31.4). The blade of the ilium can be removed but results in loss of abductor power. If the whole of the ilium is removed then the hip is unsupported and will be free to ride up and down with walking as in pseudarthrosis. A hemipelvectomy may be a better alternative.

Methods of reconstruction

Following resection of the majority of tumours some form of reconstruction will be required. The ingenuity of orthopaedic surgeons has resulted in a huge variety of techniques and has lead to several international symposia on limb salvage, at which attempts to standardize methods of assessment have been made [17]. The benefit of standardized assessment is that very different techniques can be compared to show the oncological success, the functional success and

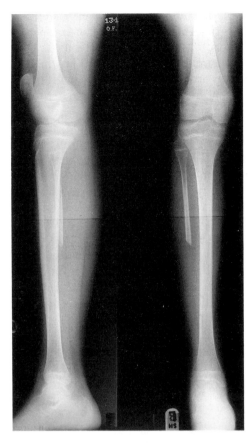

Fig. 31.3 Resection of the distal fibula for osteosarcoma: there was no functional deficit.

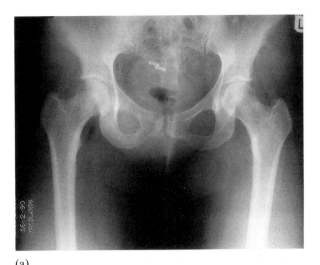

(a)

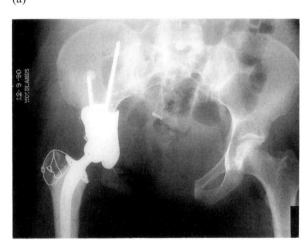

(b)

Fig. 31.4 Ewing's sarcoma of the right pubis and ischium involving the hip joint (a) treated with chemotherapy and resection with endoprosthetic replacement of the hemipelvis and hip joint (b).

the long term success of the procedure. As yet no one technique has been shown to be superior for any one site and thus many methods of reconstruction are practised in different centres.

The principal options available for reconstruction include:

endoprostheses;
allografts;
modified amputation (Van Nes
    rotationplasty);
autografts.

Endoprostheses

Endoprosthetic replacements for the reconstruction of defects left by resection of bone tumours have been carried out for many years [3]. Whilst endoprostheses were initially used for low grade tumours they have increasingly been used to

bridge defects created by resection of malignant tumours.

These endoprostheses can either be custom built for the individual or alternatively a modular system can be used to fit the endoprosthesis to the gap created at the time of surgery [17]. The former method has the advantage that the endoprosthesis will definitely fit the patient and the level of resection of the tumour can be carefully planned in advance, but has the disadvantage of time required to manufacture the endoprosthesis (two to three weeks in most cases) and expense. With preoperative chemotherapy the time factor becomes less important as most chemotherapy regimes go on for between 7 and 12 weeks before there is an interval for surgery. Modular systems have the advantage of availability but the disadvantage that patients come in all shapes and sizes with the result that no system can hope to accommodate them all.

Endoprosthetic replacements for the distal femur, proximal tibia, proximal femur and proximal humerus are all available and have predictable results in terms of function and complications [17].

Endoprosthetic replacements about the knee of necessity require resection of the constraining ligaments of the knee and hence a constrained or semiconstrained type of knee joint will be required. These may then be either cemented in place or alternatively a non-cemented type of fixation can be employed.

The distal femur is one of the most satisfactory sites to replace, providing some part of the quadriceps mechanism can be left intact. Most patients will obtain an excellent range of flexion up to 130° with active extension and a normal gait. Many will be able to partake in limited exercise but should be advised against overactivity because of the risks of mechanical loosening [18].

The proximal tibia is a less gratifying site to replace, as there are often problems with retaining a functioning extensor mechanism and also with providing adequate soft tissue cover anteriorly. These problems have been largely overcome by the use of a gastrocnemius muscle flap for soft tissue cover and reconstruction of the extensor mechanism.

The proximal femoral replacement is really an extended hip replacement but without the muscle attachments of the abductors. These will usually be reattached to the fascia lata at the time of surgery and it is surprising how with time the majority of well motivated patients will lose their Trendelenburg gait and will obtain a very satisfactory functional result [19].

Tumours of the proximal humerus usually involve the deltoid and the insertion of the rotator cuff. In order to obtain an adequate margin of resection some if not all of these must be removed. Despite attempts to reconstruct the rotator cuff most replacements at this site will have limited flexion and little active abduction at the shoulder joint though there will still be ab-

duction at the scapulo-thoracic level. Extension is usually near normal. There will be some control of rotation, which may in fact be more than usual, but the main advantage of these endoprostheses is in providing a stable fulcrum for the elbow and hand to work about. There will undoubtedly be some limitation of the daily activites of living but this limitation pales in comparison with the disability of an amputation [20].

There are a large number of other endoprostheses which can be used to replace defects in the skeleton. These include replacements of the distal humerus, total humerus, proximal ulna and distal radius in the upper limb. In the lower limb it is possible to replace the whole of the femur with an almost imperceptible difference from normal, the mid-part of the femur and the hemipelvis for tumour about the acetabulum. These resections and the endoprostheses to reconstruct them are all infrequently required but in ex-

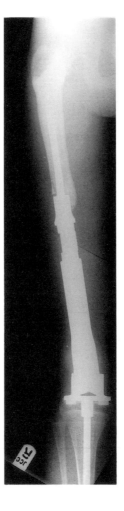

Fig. 31.5 Extendable endoprosthesis of the distal femur.

perienced hands will provide amazingly good functional results.

Endoprostheses can also be used for children for whom continued growth is expected by using passive or active lengthening prostheses. This work is still experimental but in our hands has proved reasonably satisfactory [21] (Fig 31.5).

Endoprostheses provide immediate stable replacements of bony defects with an acceptably low rate of early complications. In the longer term there are predictable complications such as mechanical loosening, infection, wear of the endoprosthesis and occasionally fracture of the endoprosthesis. Mechanical loosening is related to site being least common in the more proximal replacements. In our hands revision for mechanical loosening within 10 years has been necessary for 7% of the proximal femoral replacements, 32% of the distal femoral replacements and 45% of the proximal tibial replacements. Infection is also related to site with an initial 33% infection rate of the proximal tibial endoprostheses reduced to 6% following use of a medial head of gastrocnemius muscle flap to cover the implant.

Revision surgery for a failed implant is becoming increasingly common. Conservation of bone stock is all important and revision before bone stock is lost is becoming more essential, two stage revisions for infection have an 85% success in our hands.

Allografts

Allografts have been less widely used for reconstruction than endoprostheses, largely because of the need to have a large bone bank available for selecting the replacement grafts. The principles and ethical requirements of setting up a bone bank have been described by the American Association of Tissue Banks [22] and considerable experience is available from some centres [23,24]. The allograft types are osteoarticular when one side of the joint is replaced, intercalary when the joint surfaces are left intact and composite when the joint is replaced by a conventional prosthesis.

Intercalary grafts

Intercalary grafts tend to do well because they are relatively easy to fix securely and bone ingrowth will occur from both ends. The stresses on them are less than on osteoarticular grafts and whilst there is an incidence of delayed stress fracture these will usually unite following further fixation and bone grafting. These grafts find use for replacing diaphyseal tumours of the major long bones although tumours at these sites are rare.

Osteoarticular grafts

Osteoarticular grafts present significant problems of storage and preservation of the articular cartilage. They require rigid internal fixation to the remaining bone stock and following resection of a metaphyseal-diaphyseal tumour an extensive graft is usually required. Even though only a small part of these grafts will ever be revascularized there have been some impressive long term functional results [24,25].

Composite allografts

Composite allografts overcome some of the problems of joint stability and mobility that are encountered with osteoarticular grafts but still have the problems of fixation of the graft to the normal bone and also the problem of fixation of the joint prosthesis to the graft.

There have been few publications on the use of allografts for replacing defects created by the excision of high grade tumours. The postoperative chemotherapy that is required in most cases may possibly contribute to the high morbidity of this procedure. Dick *et al.* [26] reported on 27 patients who had chemotherapy and an allograft of some sort. There was a 51% rate of complications including skin necrosis, wound infections, allograft resorption, fractures and nonunions. Despite this, 60% of the survivors were judged to have a good or excellent result. These results are encouraging and certainly suggest the need for further research and experience with this technique.

One of the advantages of an allograft is that on the whole it tends to improve with time and has less likelihood of developing problems in comparison with an endoprosthesis where there tends to be an increased incidence of problems with time. Conversely, allografts require considerable protection for the first 2 years following surgery while union is taking place and in Dick's series they were all provided with a weight relieving caliper until union had occurred. Patients with endoprostheses are able to mobilize fully weight bearing within 6 weeks of the operation.

Modified amputation

The Van Nes rotationplasty was first described by Borggreve in 1930 [27] and subsequently by Van Nes in 1950 [28] for patients with proximal femoral focal deficiency. It can successfully be used to resect large and intraarticular tumours of the distal femur. The distal femur is resected in continuity with the joint and all the tissues of the lower two thirds of the thigh except for the sciatic nerve which is carefully filleted out of the back of the leg. This then leaves a proximal stump of the femur, attached to the lower leg from the top of the tibia down, held together only by the sciatic nerve and its branches. The tibia is rotated 180° and fixed to the proximal femur, and the femoral artery and vein are anastomosed to their respective partners in the lower leg. The length of the new limb is carefully adjusted so that the ankle joint is placed at the same level as the contralateral knee joint. Because the neurovascular bundle has been preserved the ankle will still work even though it is back to front (Fig. 31.6). The advantage of this procedure is that the rotated ankle will now work a prosthesis which can be fitted to the foot and will have both active flexion and extension and is thus more like a below knee prosthesis than an above knee one. After a period of walking re-education most patients will obtain function similar to that of a below knee amputee [29].

The advantages are that there will usually be a very wide margin of resection around the tumour with a low risk of recurrence and that the functional results are good. There can be problems with prosthesis fitting and the ankle/knee joint is subject to increased loading. This procedure can also be used in children where a considerable amount of growth is expected. The amount of growth expected in the resected femoral epiphysis can be calculated from the Anderson and Green [30] growth charts and the resected limb can be made longer by this amount less any growth anticipated in the distal tibial epiphysis (which is preserved). The opposite leg will continue to

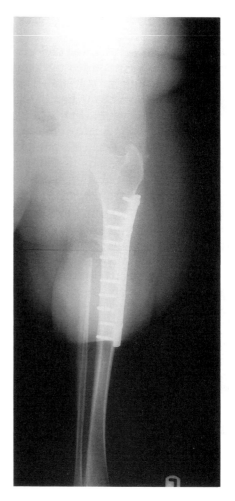

Fig. 31.6   The Van Nes rotationplasty.

grow and eventually the two knees should be at the same level.

Autografts

The role of autografts in limb preservation following tumour resections is really limited to bridging relatively short diaphyseal defects. The only bone which is both readily expendable and of sufficient versatility to be of any use is the fibula. This can be harvested either subperiosteally as a conventional graft or as a vascularized graft with a margin of muscle encasing the peroneal vessels [31].

The fibula has been used to bridge diaphyseal defects of the tibia (Fig. 31.7) and the humerus. It has been used to replace the lower end of the

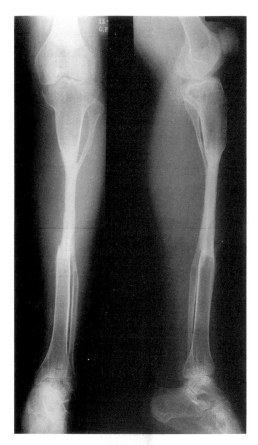

Fig. 31.7 Resection of a diaphyseal tumour of the tibia and replacement with a fibula autograft.

radius and we have used it to bridge defects of the sacroiliac region following resection of tumours there. Others have used it to replace defects in the femur but at this site it often requires supplementation with either internal fixation or another fibula. Once revascularized the fibula will slowly hypertrophy as it adapts to the stresses passing through it, an advantage which does not occur with allografts.

Conclusion

Recent advances in chemotherapy have prolonged survival for all the primary high grade malignant tumours of bone with most series quoting over 50% 5 year survival. This increased survival has meant that more than ever limb salvage procedures are justified in an attempt to maintain as normal a quality of life for this group of patients as possible. Amputations will still be necessary for tumour control and for the complications of limb salvage procedures but in the vast majority of cases a successful limb salvage procedure will provide a considerably better life style for the patient than a high amputation [32].

Limb salvage is a highly specialized field of work, combining complex oncological and reconstructive procedures in the same patient. It is not the sort of work to be embarked upon lightly and quite correctly the majority of this work is now carried out in specialized centres where the multidisciplinary teams are available. Early diagnosis and prompt referral to a specialist centre offers the patient the best chance of prolonged life and successful limb salvage.

References

1. Littlewood, H. (1922) Amputations at the shoulder and at the hip. *Br. Med. J.*, **1**, 381–383.
2. Cade, S. (1951) *Malignant Disease and its Treatment by Radium*, Vol 4. 2nd ed. Bristol, Wright.
3. Burrows, H. J., Wilson, J. N. and Scales, J. T. (1975) Excision of tumours of humerus and femur, with restoration by internal prostheses. *J. Bone Joint Surg.*, **57B**, 148–159.
4. Goorin, A. M., Abelson, H. T. and Frei, E. (1985) Osteosarcoma: fifteen years later. *N. Engl. J. Med.*, **313**, 1637–1645.
5. Sailer, S. L., Harmon, D. C., Mankin, H. J. *et al.* (1988) Ewing's sarcoma: surgical resection as a prognostic factor. *Int. J. Radiat. Oncol. Biol. Phys.*, **15**, 43–52.
6. Grimer, R. J. and Sneath, R. S. (1990) Diagnosing malignant bone tumours. *J. Bone Joint Surg.*, **72B**, 754–756.
7. Enneking, W. F., Spanier, S. S. and Goodman, M. A. (1980) A system for the surgical staging of musculoskeletal sarcoma. *Clin. Orthop.*, **153**, 106–120
8. Simon, M. A. (1982) Current concepts review: biopsy of musculoskeletal tumours. *J. Bone Joint Surg.*, **64A**, 1119–1120.
9. Mankin, H. J., Lange, T. A. and Spanier, S. S. (1982) The hazards of biopsy in patients with primary bone and soft tissue tumours. *J. Bone Joint Surg.*, **64A**, 1121–1127.
10. Cannon, S. R. and Dyson, P. H. P. (1986) Relationship of the site of open biopsy of malignant tumours to local recurrence following resection and prosthetic replacement. *J. Bone Joint Surg.*, **69B**, 492.
11. National Institute of Health (1985) Consensus

Conference on limb sparing treatment of adult soft-tissue sarcomas and osteosarcomas. *JAMA*, **254**, 1791–1794.

12. Enneking, W. F. (1983) *Musculoskeletal Surgery*. Churchill Livingstone, New York.

13. Simon, M. A. and Nachman, J. (1986) The clinical utility of preoperative chemotherapy for sarcomas. *J. Bone Joint Surg.*, **68A**, 1458–1463.

14. Sugarbaker, P. H., Barofsky, I., Rosenberg, S. A. and Gainola, F. J. (1982) Quality of life assessment of patients in extremity sarcoma clinical trials. *Surgery*, **91**, 17–23.

15. Linberg, B. E. (1928) Interscapulo-thoracic resection for malignant tumours of the shoulder joint region. *J. Bone Joint Surg.*, **10**, 344–349.

16. Sharif, D. T. and Braddock, G. T. F. (1988) Knee stability after partial excision of tibial plateau. *J. Bone Joint Surg.*, **71B**, 320.

17. Enneking, W. F. (1987) Modification of the system for functional evaluation of surgical management of musculoskeletal tumours. In *Limb Salvage in Musculoskeletal Oncology* (ed. W. F. Enneking), Churchill Livingstone, New York, pp. 626–639.

18. Roberts, P., Chan, D., Grimer, R. J. *et al.* (1991) Prosthetic replacement of the distal femur for primary bone tumours. *J. Bone Joint Surg.*, **73B**, 762–769.

19. Dobbs, H. S., Scales, J. T., Wislon, J. N. *et al.* (1981) Endoprosthetic replacement of the proximal femur and acetabulum. *J. Bone Joint Surg.*, **63B**, 219–224.

20. Ross, A. C., Sneath, R. S. and Scales, J. T. (1987) Endoprosthetic replacement of the humerus and elbow joint. *J. Bone Joint Surg.*, **69B**, 652–655.

21. Scales, J. T., Sneath, R. S. and Wright, K. W. J. (1987) Design and clinical use of extending prostheses. In *Limb Salvage in Musculoskeletal Oncology* (ed. W. F. Enneking), Churchill Livingstone, New York.

22. Friedlander, G. E. and Mankin, H. J. (1979) Guidelines for the banking of musculoskeletal tissues. *Newsletter, Am. Assn Tissue Banks*, **3**, 2–4.

23. Parrish, F. F. (1973) Allograft replacement of all or part of the end of a long bone following excision of a tumour: report of twenty-one cases. *J. Bone Joint Surg.*, **55A**, 1–22.

24. Mankin, H. J., Doppelt, S. and Tomford, W. (1983) Clinical experience with allograft implantation: the first ten years. *Clin. Orthop.*, **174**, 69–86.

25. Gebhardt, M. C., Roth, Y. F. and Mankin, H. J. (1990) Osteoarticular allografts for reconstruction in the proximal part of the humerus after excision of a musculoskeletal tumour. *J. Bone Joint Surg.*, **72A**, 334–345.

26. Dick, H. M., Malinin, T. I. and Mnaymneh, W. A. (1985) Massive allograft implantation following radical resection of high grade tumors requiring adjuvant chemotherapy treatment. *Clin. Orthop.*, **197**, 88–95.

27. Borggreve (1930) Kniegelenkseratz durch das in der Beinlangsachse um 180 gedrehte Fussgelenk. *Arch. Orthop. Unfall-chir.*, **28**, 175–178.

28. Van Nes, C. P. (1950) Rotation-plasty for congenital defects of the femur. *J. Bone Joint Surg.*, **32B**, 12–16.

29. Kotz, R. and Salzer, M. (1982) Rotation-plasty for childhood osteosarcoma of the distal part of the femur. *J. Bone Joint Surg.*, **64A**, 959–969.

30. Anderson, M. S., Messner, M. B. and Green, W. T. (1964) Distribution of lengths of the normal femur and tibia in children from 1 to 18 years of age. *J. Bone Joint Surg.*, **46A**, 1197–1202.

31. Gilbert, A. (1979) Vascular transfer of the fibula shaft. *Int. J. Microsurg.*, **1**, 100-102.

32. Harris, I. E., Leff, A. R. Gitelis, G. and Simon, M. A. (1990) Function after amputation, arthrodesis or arthroplasty for tumors about the knee. *J. Bone Joint Surg.*, **72A**, 1477–1485.

32

Chemotherapy and radiotherapy in sarcoma of bone and the musculoskeletal system

J. Bullimore

Malignant tumours of bone and the musculo-skeletal system are uncommon and exhibit a wide variety of histological types and clinical behaviour. The site of the tumour and the age of the patient profoundly influence the course of the disease. Treatment of this complex group of tumours requires the combined disciplines of surgery, radiotherapy and chemotherapy.

Radical treatment is preceded by careful clinical and radiological assessment to ascertain the extent of the local disease and to search for metastases. Conventional radiology and computed tomography (CT) scans of the primary site and the lungs, together with an isotope skeletal survey are undertaken. Magnetic resonance imaging, if available, is superior to CT imaging as scans in longitudinal as well as horizontal planes may be produced and the distinctions between tumour, normal tissue and scar tissue more easily delineated. Expert histological assessment of the original biopsy material and of the excised tumour are essential, as treatment is dictated by the histological classification and grading of the tumour and the assessment of the completeness of its excision.

Chemotherapy has become recognized as playing an essential role in the treatment of some malignant bone tumours, notably in patients with osteosarcoma, Ewing's sarcoma and primary lymphoma of bone. Other aggressive neoplasms with a propensity for early haematogenous spread, such as fibrosarcoma, malignant fibrous histiocytoma and haemangiopericytoma are also likely to benefit from its use.

Soft tissue sarcomas are, in general, treated according to their degree of histological differentiation, low grade tumours being treated by surgical excision with or without radiotherapy and high grade tumours having chemotherapy added to the other two modalities, but a uniform approach to their management is not yet agreed.

Management of chemotherapy and its toxicity

Chemotherapy for bone and soft tissue sarcomas utilizes drugs which, if they are to be given most effectively and their considerable toxicity minimized, must be administered only in hospitals where the expertise is available to deal with the complications which may arise. In addition, the timing of chemotherapy in relation to surgery and radiotherapy is critical and a large cancer centre where surgery, radiotherapy and cytotoxic therapy can all be carried out and where close collaboration between the clinicians can be obtained is the safest and best place for this type of treatment.

Prior to starting chemotherapy the haematological, renal and hepatic functions are assessed and rechecked before the start of each drug cycle. If there is failure of normal recovery treatment is delayed and, if necessary, drug dosage modified in subsequent cycles. Extravasation of chemotherapy agents may cause an acute local inflammatory reaction capable of progressing to tissue necrosis requiring skin grafting. For this reason cytotoxic drugs are usually given via a fast flowing intravenous drip either as an infusion or as a bolus injection. 'Long line' catheters inserted into the superior vena cava are increasingly used, especially in the treatment of children, and are kept in place throughout the cytotoxic therapy.

Toxic effects

Both acute and long term toxic effects arise. Of the acute effects, hair loss and gastrointestinal upset with nausea and vomiting are the most common, but more hazardous is the leucopenia which may result in the patient succumbing to overwhelming infection. Measles and chicken pox are life threatening in immunocompromised patients and *Herpes zoster* may become a generalized eruption. Oral moniliasis occurs frequently and may extend into the oesophagus and intestine. Infections with *Pneumocystis carinii* and cytomegalovirus, rarely seen in other branches of clinical practice, are not uncommon in immunosuppressed patients.

Thrombocytopenia may lead to bruising, spontaneous haemorrhage and anaemia. A number of drugs cause cardiac, renal, pulmonary and hepatic damage and cytotoxic therapy must be properly monitored if severe toxicity is to be avoided. Some agents, notably vincristine, are neurotoxic and may give rise to paraesthesia, paralytic ileus and, rarely, palsies of peripheral and cranial nerves.

Late toxicity may include reduced fertility or sterility and permanent impairment of cardiac, pulmonary, renal and hepatic function. There may be impairment of growth and normal development in children and such defects must be monitored in order to correct them as far as possible. The psychological effects of unpleasant treatment require experienced and expert management if both acute and long term disturbance are to be avoided.

Cytotoxic drugs and ionizing radiation are known to be carcinogenic. The study of children with second malignancies has revealed that the risk of developing cancer is 10–20 times greater in patients who have been cured of a neoplasm than that of age-matched individuals from the normal population [1]. Genetic factors have a greater influence in paediatric than in adult malignancy, but there is little doubt that survivors of one tumour are at increased risk of developing a new primary cancer irrespective of age.

The principles of chemotherapy

The rationale of adjuvant chemotherapy is based on the hypothesis that at the time of presentation many patients have micrometastases undetectable by currently available diagnostic means. Cytotoxic treatment given soon after surgery when the residual tumour burden is at a minimum should have the greatest chance of eradicating the disease.

Cell kinetics

Normal and malignant tissues are composed of cells some of which are actively proliferating, some which may be recruited into the proliferating portion and the remainder which are incapable of division. The proliferating portion is termed the growth fraction.

The rate of growth of a tissue depends on the balance between cell production and cell loss. Cell production varies with the size of the growth fraction and the cell cycle time, i.e. the time it takes for a cell to replicate. The cell cycle is a series of events through which a cell passes in order to duplicate, it is divided into phases; G_1, (standing for gap 1), is a short period of preparing to enter the synthetic phase, S. During S phase, purine and pyrimidine nucleotides are built up into DNA using the DNA of the cell as a template. At the end of S, when the DNA and other cell constituents have been doubled, the cell enters G_2 (gap 2), for a short time before dividing in mitosis (M). Following M, the daughter cells may enter a resting phase G_0 or go straight into another cell cycle via G_1.

Cell loss increases as a tumour enlarges and the blood supply becomes inadequate leading to cell death and necrosis. Cells are also lost to the growth potential of the tumour if they become so differentiated that they can no longer divide.

A single dose of a cytotoxic drug kills a fraction of the tumour cells and a similar dose given

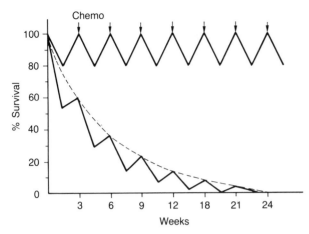

Fig. 32.1 Diagrammatic graph showing the effect of repeated cycles of chemotherapy on normal tissues (e.g. marrow, reflected in the peripheral blood count) upper line, and malignant tissues, lower line.

after an interval will kill the same fraction of the surviving cells, i.e. the diminution is exponential. Similar kinetics apply to normal tissues but normal cells are capable of more rapid repair of cytotoxic damage than malignant. A tumour 1 cm in diameter contains 10^9 cells and the tumour burden, even after surgery, may be many times this number. If a tumour is to be eradicated, chemotherapy must be given repeatedly. The difference in speed of repair of normal and malignant tissues is exploited by using repeated cycles of chemotherapy. Second and subsequent doses of chemotherapy must be given as soon as normal tissue repair has taken place, failure to do so would allow time for recovery of the cancer cells and completely negate the benefit of the

previous cycles. The bone marrow is one of the tissues most sensitive to chemotherapy, and its state is reflected in the peripheral blood. For this reason the return of the blood count to normal levels is taken as an indicator that the other tissues have recovered, and that the next cycle of drugs may be safely given. The optimum interval between chemotherapy cycles is usually 3 weeks (Fig. 32.1).

Chemotherapy drugs

Cytotoxic drugs are most damaging to tissues which contain a large proportion of actively dividing cells. The bone marrow, gut endothelium and hair follicle cells are for this reason particularly vulnerable. Most chemotherapy agents act only on cells in the cell cycle and are termed cycle specific, e.g. cyclophosphamide and doxorubicin. Some drugs act only on cells in a particular phase of the cell cycle and are called phase specific drugs, e.g. methotrexate which affects cells in S phase, and vincristine those in mitosis. There are a small number of agents which damage both resting cells and those in cell cycle. These are termed non-cycle specific drugs, but the damage they inflict is not uniform, being more severe on cells that are in cycle than those that are not; these agents include mustine, the nitrosoureas and ionizing radiation (Fig. 32.2). The cell killing effect of phase specific drugs used over a short time interval increases with dose only until all the cells in the relevant phase have been affected. Thereafter increasing the dose will

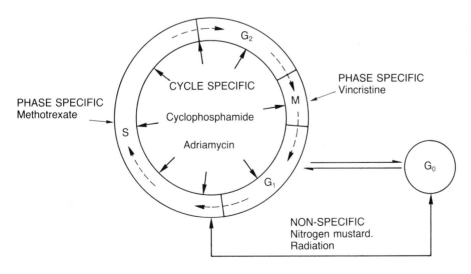

Fig. 32.2 The cell cycle and site of action of some cytotoxic drugs.

not kill more cells. If, however, an S phase specific drug, such as methotrexate, is allowed to act over several days, as cells enter S they are killed. The toxicity of phase specific drugs, therefore, increases with the length of exposure time.

Mechanism of action

Cytotoxic drugs kill cells by inflicting chemical damage and by interfering with their ability to duplicate. Therapeutic cytotoxic drugs fall into the following categories:

Alkylating agents, e.g. nitrogen mustard, cyclophosphamide, melphalan

These form alkyl bonds between the strands of DNA, so that when the two strands are required to split in mitosis they are unable to do so. Abnormal chromosomal breaks occur and the daughter cells produced are non-viable. Nitrosoureas such as BCNU and CCNU have similar properties to alkylating agents.

Antimetabolites, e.g. methotrexate, cytosine arabinoside, 5-fluorouracil

These combine with the building blocks used to construct DNA and interfere with enzyme pathways. Methotrexate is an antimetabolite which interferes with the folic acid cycle; by inhibiting dihydrofolate reductase it stops the production of tetrahydrofolic acid, interrupting DNA and RNA production. The biochemical block may be bypassed by giving calcium leukovorin (folinic acid rescue). Normal tissues more readily utilize the leukovorin than the tumour cells and can be selectively rescued.

Antibiotics, e.g. actinomycin D, doxorubicin

These bind with DNA blocking replication.

Alkaloids, e.g. vincristine, vinblastine, VP16 (etoposide)

Their actions like those of the other groups are not fully understood but it is known that vincristine exerts its action by preventing the formation of the spindle in mitosis.

Others

There are a number of synthetic agents which have been discovered in the course of screening substances with likely formulae for anti-cancer activity, e.g. cis-platinum, DTIC (imidazole carboxamide). These act in complex ways, but frequently include some alkylating activity.

Treatment of malignant bone tumours

Primary malignant tumours of bone account for 1–1.5% of deaths from cancer. Bone cancer occurs at all ages, but is seen most often in young adults and children, comprising 7% of childhood neoplasms. A characteristic of malignant bone tumours is that they metastasize early to lung and later, to other bones and elsewhere. Since the early 1970s there has been an improvement in survival of patients due to the development of treatment which employs the long established disciplines of surgery and radiotherapy together with cytotoxic drugs. Not only have cure rates improved but, encouraged by the local response of the tumours to chemotherapy, surgeons have undertaken limb preserving operations using endoprostheses, thus improving the quality of life both for those patients who survive and those who do not.

Osteosarcoma

The incidence of this aggressive tumour is approximately 3 per million population per year, and although it occurs at any age, it is most common in adolescence. There is a second peak of incidence in the older age group mainly due to the association with Paget's disease of bone. It may affect any bone but is most commonly seen in long bones, 90% occurring in the region of the knee.

Before the advent of adjuvant chemotherapy the cure rate, taken from several historical series, was in the order of 20% [2]. The treatments available were amputation or radiotherapy followed by delayed amputation at 6 months, if no metastases had appeared. The first indication that the cure rate might be improved occurred in the early 1970s, when reports of temporary shrinkage of lung metastases, brought about by chemotherapy appeared. The drugs found to be effective were high dose methotrexate (HDMTX), doxorubicin (adriamycin), and cyclophosphamide. Methotrexate was given at dosages ranging from $1 \, g/M^2$ to $10 \, g/M^2$ or more. An intravenous infusion usually over 6 hours was given, followed by folinic acid rescue. Other drugs used included bleomycin, actinomycin D, and vincristine, but of the early drugs high dose methotrexate and doxorubicin were the most effective.

Following the demonstration of the response of metastases to chemotherapy, it was but a short step to attempt to prevent their appearance by using cytotoxic drugs in prophylaxis. Improved survival of patients treated with adjuvant doxorubicin [3] and high dose methotrexate with vincristine and doxorubicin [4] were reported. There followed a rash of reports on various drugs and drug combinations used as adjuvant therapy claiming projected cure rates in the region of 70%. The reports suffered the criticism of small numbers of patients studied and too short periods of observation. This led to scepticism, as the prophesized major improvements were not realized and five year disease-free survival rates in the order at 30–40% were being achieved. The need for properly conducted controlled studies which would include large numbers of patients was recognized and multicentre trials of adjuvant chemotherapy in non-metastatic osteosarcoma were started.

The Medical Research Council (MRC), in a controlled trial of adjuvant chemotherapy, compared the use of low dose methotrexate ($200 \, mg/M^2$) and vincristine versus low dose methotrexate, vincristine and doxorubicin. Although the appearance of metastases was delayed compared with historical controls, the five year survival was 27% with no significant difference between the two arms [5]. It was not until 1982, when Rosen published the results of his 'T10' regime that hope was rekindled that cure rates in excess of 80% might be obtained [6]. The protocol consisted of preoperative chemotherapy using HDMTX with doxorubicin and bleomycin, cyclophosphamide and actinomycin D (BCD). If on histological examination of the excised tumour 90% was necrotic, the same chemotherapy was used postoperatively. If less than

90% necrosis had been achieved cis-platinum was substituted for methotrexate. Using the histopathological findings to direct postoperative chemotherapy resulted in an actuarially assessed disease-free survival of 92% at 2 years. Other groups have attempted to repeat Rosen's work but although such good results have not been achieved there is little doubt that the T10 regime was more successful than any previous protocol.

A report from the Mayo Clinic that adjuvant chemotherapy had not influenced the survival of patients between 1963 and 1974 [7] gave rise to claims that the improvements in long term survival were brought about by changes in the natural history of the disease rather than by chemotherapy. To test this hypothesis, in 1978 the Paediatric Oncology Group in the United States, started a controlled trial of adjuvant chemotherapy of T10 type given at the time of initial therapy versus chemotherapy delayed until the appearance of metastatic disease. In a short time the delayed chemotherapy group were faring so badly that the trial was terminated [8].

Preoperative (neo adjuvant) chemotherapy is now accepted, based on the results of numerous single arm and randomized controlled trials. Intra-arterial chemotherapy may also prove to have a place. High dose methotrexate intravenously, followed by intra-arterial cisplatin combined with intravenous doxorubicin, was used in the treatment of 164 patients and resulted in a 66% disease free survival at an average follow up time of 54 months [9].

Neutropenia due to chemotherapy limits the dose of drug that may be given safely. The discovery of granulocyte colony stimulating factor (G-CSF) has led to its successful use in preventing or reducing life threatening neutropenia and more speedy recovery of the neutrophil count following cytotoxic chemotherapy. Dose escalation studies are being undertaken to establish if more intensive chemotherapy supported by G-CSF will improve survival. The Medical Research Council (MRC) and the European Organisation for Research on the Treatment of Cancer (EORTC) have undertaken a randomized controlled trial of cisplatin and doxorubicin 3 weekly preoperatively and postoperatively compared with the same doses of the drugs given 2 weekly, with the addition of G-CSF given on days 4 to 13 of each cycle.

Treatment of pulmonary metastases

At the same time as expertise was being gained in adjuvant chemotherapy for patients with no overt metastases, interest was growing in attempts to rescue those patients with lung involvement. The surgical removal of solitary lung

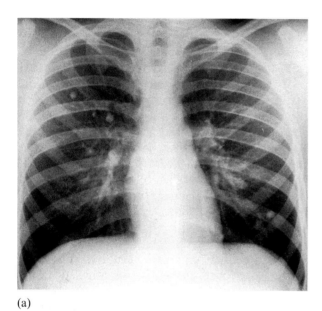

(a)

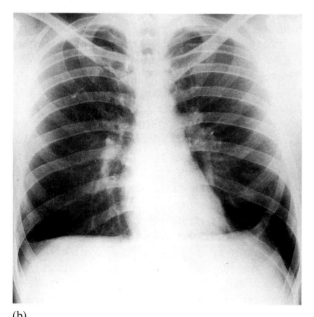

(b)

Fig. 32.3 (a) Radiograph of chest showing multiple bilateral metastases from osteosarcoma. (b) Radiograph of the same patient 12 years from resection of six metastases from each lung.

metastases had had some success, and with the addition of chemotherapy it was hoped that the cure rate would improve. Patients surviving their primary tumour are kept under close surveillance for the appearance of secondary tumours. Regular chest radiographs and CT scans enable metastases to be identified early and many are deemed suitable for resection. Techniques of multiple local resections have been developed so that several lesions may be removed without seriously compromising the respiratory function of the patient. In some reported series, 3 year disease-free survival rates of 40% have been achieved [9]. All patients with pulmonary metastases, and no other evidence of disease should be considered for metastatectomy. One or more cycles of chemotherapy precede resection, using drugs to which the patient has not previously been exposed. Postoperatively chemotherapy is continued for a further 6 months. Patients found to have involvement of the visceral or parietal pleura fare badly and those in whom further lung metastases appear within a year of a previous thoracotomy have a poor outlook [10].

Multiple or bilateral metastases need not be a contraindication to resection. This can be illustrated by two patients of the author. The first, a 15-year-old boy who had six metastases removed from each lung in planned sequential thoracotomies, has remained disease free for 17 years. He leads an active life and has two children (Fig. 32.3). The second, a nurse, who at the age of 17 years had a thoracotomy for removal of the first of a series of 'solitary' lung metastases, is disease free 7 years from her fourth thoracotomy, having survived more than 13 years from the initial appearance of secondary lung tumours. Her nursing training was commenced after the first thoracotomy and in spite of repeated surgery she has returned to normal working duties.

Limb preservation (see chapter 31)

The observation that in some patients extensive necrosis of tumour followed preoperative chemotherapy led to attempts to preserve the limb. Currently pre- and postoperative chemotherapy are used and the tumour resected with the insertion of an endoprosthesis. The majority of limb tumours are suitable for local resection and all patients should be considered for limb preservation. Even when metastases are known to be present the opinion of a surgeon, expert in this operative procedure, should be sought as endoprosthetic insertion is often the best palliative therapy.

Ewing's sarcoma

Ewing's sarcoma was until as recently as the 1960s a tumour with an appalling prognosis. Less than 15% of patients survived 5 years, most of them succumbing to metastatic disease in the lungs and in other bones. Ewing recognized the tumour as an entity in its own right when he first described it in 1921. It is principally a neoplasm of children and young people, 90% occurring under the age of 30 years. Any bone may be involved but the most common sites are the femur and the pelvis. Factors that adversely affect prognosis are the size and site of the tumour and the presence of metastatic disease, the axial skeleton being the most unfavourable primary site [11].

Treatment

Before Ewing recognized the radiosensitivity of the tumour, surgical resection or amputation was the usual therapy. Local recurrence and metastatic disease were almost universal and in subsequent years, radiotherapy became the more common choice of treatment in order to spare the patient mutilating surgery. Radiotherapy techniques improved after 1964, when Phillips and Higinbothom [12] reported higher cure rates and higher local control rates where the entire bone as well as the local tumour and soft tissues extension were included in the treated volume. This change was brought about by the observation that on histological examination of amputated specimens malignant cells often extended throughout the marrow cavity.

In the 1960s more effective cytotoxic drugs were developed and metastatic disease was found to be responsive to them. The agents used included mustine, cyclophosphamide, vincristine and actinomycin D. The encouraging responses led to patients without overt metastatic disease receiving vincristine and cyclophosphamide after completion of radiotherapy and the disease-free survival increased. Other drug combinations were studied, most of which included vincristine, cyclophosphamide and adriamycin in conjunction with a variety of agents such as actinomycin D, methotrexate and BCNU. Survival rates showed further improvement and the US Intergroup Ewing's Sarcoma Study reported, in 1980, a 3-year disease-free survival rate of 56% [13]; Ewing's sarcoma has a tendency for late relapse and the 6-year disease-free survival rate of 49% reported from the Institut Gustave-Roussy using similar chemotherapy is probably a more reliable indication of the cure rate [14]. The combination of ifosfamide and etoposide has been shown to be effective both as initial therapy and in those patients in whom previous chemotherapy has failed.

Chemotherapy is given initially, and provided there is satisfactory tumour reduction, continued for up to four cycles, surgical resection is then undertaken. In the case of limb tumours techniques of limb preservation with endoprosthetic bone replacement may be used. Radiotherapy is only employed if histological examination of the surgical specimen reveals incomplete excision, if the tumour is too bulky for treatment by means of an endoprosthesis or if it is in an unsuitable site for surgical removal. Following irradiation of initially inoperable tumours, when the tumour bulk has been reduced, surgical resection is once more considered. Chemotherapy is continued to complete 1 year. Increasingly, surgical removal and limb preservation in tumours which previously would have been judged irresectable has become possible.

Radiotherapy

Techniques have been designed to reduce the undesirable long term effects of irradiation. Megavoltage external beam irradiation is employed, and when treating a limb tumour care is taken that a length of skin and subcutaneous tissue is left untreated, in order to provide lymphatic drainage, and to prevent the later development of distal oedema. Chemotherapy allows techniques of radiotherapy to be safely modified and when treating children it is now possible to avoid irradiating the epiphysis furthest from the tumour, thus allowing some growth of the limb to continue. Irradiation in the order of 40 Gy in 4 weeks is employed using large fields which include most of the bone. The fields are then reduced to cover the local extent of the tumour and a further 20 Gy in two weeks given (Fig. 32.4). The observation that patients in whom the primary tumour is treated surgically develop less local recurrence but more systemic metastases than those in whom primary tumour is treated by radiotherapy has led to further studies of the use of preoperative radiotherapy.

Tumours of the pelvis present particular problems; both the local recurrence rate and the metastatic rate are high. The tumours are frequently large and the administration of high doses of radiation is rendered difficult due to their proximity to the gut. The radiation fields necessary may compromise the marrow and delay the administration of chemotherapy. When, in spite of preoperative chemotherapy the tumour remains too large to remove, irradiation to a dose of

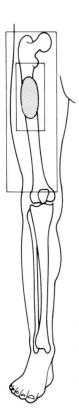

Fig. 32.4 Radiotherapy treatment volumes used in Ewing's sarcoma of the femur, showing the larger volume treated to 40 Gy in 4 weeks and the smaller volume which receives a further 20 Gy. Note the epiphysis which is furthest from the lesion and the strip of tissue medially which are excluded from treatment.

40 Gy in 4 weeks may enable resection to be undertaken. The case of a 20-year-old girl treated by the author illustrates this policy. She was found to have a Ewing's sarcoma of the right iliac bone. There were no detectable metastases, but a large soft tissue component was present. Primary surgery other than hemi-pelvectomy was considered impossible. Following two cycles of chemotherapy consisting of vincristine, cyclophosphamide, doxorubicin and cis-platinum, tumour reduction was insufficient to permit surgery. She received radiotherapy to 40 Gy in 4 weeks using 8 MeV photons, and there followed considerable regression of the lesion (Figs 32.5a, b). Surgery was undertaken 4 weeks from the end of radiotherapy, and chemotherapy was continued postoperatively to complete a year. The patient had no local recurrence (Fig 32.5c) and the cosmetic appearance was good enough to enable her to wear a bikini. She died of metastatic disease 6 years from presentation.

Treatment of metastatic disease

Radiotherapy may result in useful palliation of symptomatic metastatic disease. Localized treatment of metastases or half body irradiation for widespread disease may be effective for several months.

Marrow ablative treatment with chemotherapy or whole body irradiation combined with autologous bone marrow transplantation or the reinfusion of stem cells, previously harvested from the patient's peripheral blood, may result in more prolonged remissions. This type of therapy is now beginning to be used in the treatment of patients who present with poor prognosis disease.

Soft tissue sarcoma

Malignant tumours which arise from the mesenchymal supportive tissues of the body, together make up less than 1% of cancer. They comprise a collection of rare tumours with variable clinical courses and their treatment is far from uniform. As they usually present as a painless lump often on an extremity and noted for some months, their serious nature is frequently overlooked. Malig-

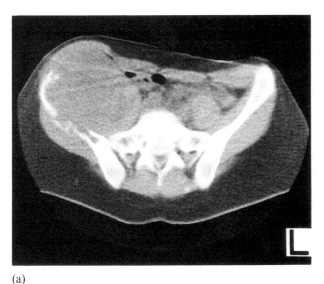

(a)

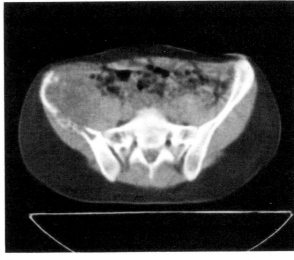

(b)

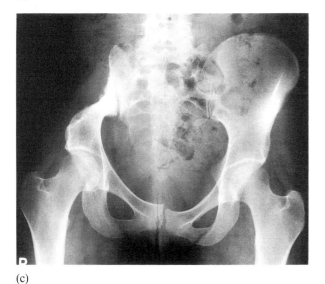

(c)

Fig. 32.5 (a) CT scan of the pelvis showing a Ewing's sarcoma of the right ilium following two cycles of chemotherapy. The oblique line represents the medial edge of the planned irradiated volume. (b) CT scan following 40 Gy in 4 weeks megavoltage irradiation showing tumour reduction. (c) Radiograph of pelvis 2 years from radical resection of the tumour.

nancy may not be suspected and inadequate excision performed.

Malignant fibrous histiocytoma, fibrosarcoma and liposarcoma are equally common and together account for about 50% of soft tissue sarcomas. Synovial sarcoma, leiomyosarcoma, angiosarcoma, and a number of very rare tumours make up the remainder. Soft tissue sarcomas arise most commonly in the buttocks or thighs and may develop in sites of previous injury or old operation scars. They are most common in older age groups, 35% arising in patients over 55 years of age. The commonest paediatric soft tissue sarcoma is rhabdomyosarcoma which accounts for 5% of cancer in children. Rarely, soft tissue sarcoma occurs in patients belonging to families with a predisposition to certain types of cancer. This has been described as the SBLA cancer syndrome and consists of a familial grouping of sarcoma (S), breast, brain and bone (B), leukaemia, lung and laryngeal cancer (L) and adrenal cortical carcinoma (A) [15].

Importance of histological classification and grading

Expert pathology is of great importance in the management of soft tissue sarcomas. A comprehensive study of 1215 sarcomas was carried

Table 32.1   Staging system for soft tissue sarcoma (from Russell *et al.*, 1977)

	Stage	*GTNM parameters*
Key	Stage IA	$G_1 \, T_1 \, N_0 \, M_0$
G: histopathological grade	IB	$G_1 \, T_2 \, N_0 \, M_0$
(1, 2 or 3)	Stage IIA	$G_2 \, T_1 \, N_0 \, M_0$
T: tumour size	IIB	$G_2 \, T_2 \, N_0 \, M_0$
T_1, tumour < 5 cm in diameter	Stage IIIA	$G_3 \, T_1 \, N_0 \, M_0$
T_2, tumour > 5 cm in diameter	IIIB	$G_3 \, T_2 \, N_0 \, M_0$
T_3, invasion of major vessels,	IIIC	$G_{1-3} \, T_{1-2} \, N_1 \, M_0$
nerves or bones		
N_1: biopsy proven metastases to		
regional lymph node(s)	Stage IVA	$G_{1-3} \, T_3 \, N_{0-1} \, M_0$
M_1: clinically evident distant	IVB	$G_{1-3} \, T_{1-3} \, N_{0-1} \, M_1$
metastases		

out by the Task Force for Sarcoma of the Soft Tissues of the American Joint Commission for Cancer Staging and End Result Reporting [16]. An analysis of the natural history of the different sarcomas was made from which a staging system has been derived which can be used as a guide to appropriate management. It combines international TNM staging with histological grading to create a staging system which has relevance to this varied group of tumours (Table 32.1). The tumours are placed in grades 1, 2 or 3 according to the degree of differentiation, grade 3 being the least differentiated. The TNM staging is based on clinical and radiological assessment. The importance of this type of combined staging is that it allows unfavourable histology to outweigh the importance of tumour size when planning therapy.

Radiotherapy

The high rate of local recurrence both of well differentiated and poorly differentiated tumours led to more extensive surgical procedures being undertaken as initial therapy. A marked improvement in local control resulted, being achieved in 70–95% of patients [17]. The cure rate in patients with low grade tumours improved, but not in those with high grade tumours who continued to die from metastatic disease.

Cure resulting from radiotherapy alone in some inoperable low grade tumours led to oper-

able tumours of the extremities being treated by less mutilating surgery combined with radiotherapy. In order to eradicate residual tumour external beam megavoltage irradiation to 60–65 Gy in 6 to $6\frac{1}{2}$ weeks is necessary. There are, however, other types of ionizing radiation which can be used alone or in conjunction with megavoltage photon irradiation. Electron beam and interstitial therapy using radioactive materials such as iridium wire allow locally high doses to be given. It has been argued [18] that if radiotherapy is planned as part of initial therapy there are advantages to it being given preoperatively. The treatment volume may be smaller and the risk of spillage of viable cells at operation lessened. In addition, radiotherapy is not delayed by postoperative complications, and as the tumour frequently diminishes in volume, removal with less extensive surgery is facilitated. Anoxic tissue is known to be radioresistant and a blood supply undisturbed by surgery is an advantage. Histological examination of the excised tumour will confirm the extent of tumour necrosis achieved by the therapy and aid in deciding if a further postoperative boost is needed.

Delayed healing is not a problem if 40 Gy in 4 weeks is not exceeded and surgery carried out within 4–6 weeks of finishing radiotherapy. In this short interval the changes associated with long term radiation damage which may result in impaired healing will not have had time to develop.

Conversely, the use of postoperative radio-

---

therapy has the advantage of immediate surgery, histological information from the whole tumour before it has been altered by therapy, and no anxiety about wound healing. The advantages of preoperative radiation probably outweigh those of postoperative but this is a matter which would be difficult to prove without a controlled clinical trial.

Chemotherapy

Treatment of children with rhabdomyosarcoma now achieves a cure rate in the order of 70% [20]. Preoperative chemotherapy, using vincristine, actinomycin D and cyclophosphamide have been the mainstay of treatment. Doxorubicin and ifosfamide may also be used. If the tumour is then operable, surgical resection is undertaken and if complete excision has not been achieved, postoperative radiotherapy is given. In some sites, such as the orbit or nasopharynx, radiotherapy is the treatment of choice following initial chemotherapy.

The favourable response to chemotherapy seen in rhabdomyosarcoma is not repeated in most other soft tissue sarcomas.

Grade 1 soft tissue tumours virtually never metastasize and do not require chemotherapy. Grade 3 tumours have a high risk of metastatic spread and studies have indicated that this spread is reduced if chemotherapy is given [19]. Drugs such a cis-platinum, doxorubicin and ifosfamide have been shown to be effective in high grade tumours and it is hoped that further evaluation of their role as adjuvant therapy in controlled clinical trials will lead to improved cure rates. To date no clear evidence of benefit has been produced.

Some unsolved problems of therapy

The choice of drugs, the best drug combinations, the duration of cytotoxic therapy and the optimum timing of chemotherapy in relation to surgery and radiotherapy is not yet known. There is now a tendency for protocols to consist of shorter periods of more intensive chemotherapy and it has become usual to give at least part of the chemotherapy preoperatively.

Newer drugs include carboplatin which is

better tolerated than cis-platinum, and epirubicin which is less cardiotoxic than its analog doxorubicin. Confirmation is awaited that they are as effective as their forerunners.

Further assessment of intra-arterial chemotherapy preoperatively or in combination with radiotherapy may prove it to be beneficial in limb preservation and in the treatment of tumours in unfavourable sites. Encouraging reports of the use of doxorubicin and cis-platinum intra-arterially have been published [20].

The way forward to successful therapy for malignant bone tumours probably lies in the direction clinicians are already taking. Integrated therapy using surgery, radiotherapy and chemotherapy is complex and sometimes hazardous, and if the potential benefits are to be reaped, treatment should be carried out in specialized centres where the necessary expertise is available.

References

1. Meadows, A. T. and Hobbie, W. L. (1986) The medical consequences of cure. *Cancer*, **58**, 524–528.
2. Dahlin, D. C. and Coventry, M. B. (1967) Osteogenic sarcoma – a study of six hundred cases. *J. Bone Joint Surg.*, **49A**, 101.
3. Cortes, E. P., Holland, J. F., Wang, J. J. and Glidewell, O. (1977) Amputation and Adriamycin (ADM) in primary osteogenic sarcoma (OS), 5 year report. *Proc. AACR ASCO*, **18**, 297.
4. Jaffe, N., Traggis, D., Frei, E. III *et al.* (1977) Survival in osteogenic sarcoma: impact of multidisciplinary treatment. *Proc. AACR ASCO*, **18**, 279.
5. Report of the Working Party On Bone Sarcoma to the Medical Research Council (1986) A trial of chemotherapy in patients with osteosarcoma. *Br. J. Cancer*, **6**, 513–518.
6. Rosen, G., Capparos, B., Huvos, A. G. *et al.* (1982) Preoperative chemotherapy for osteogenic sarcoma: selection of post-operative adjuvant chemotherapy based on the response to pre-operative chemotherapy. *Cancer*, **40**, 1221.
7. Taylor, W. F., Ivins, J. C., Dahlin, D. C. and Pritchard, D. J. (1978) Osteogenic sarcoma experience at the Mayo Clinic, 1963–1974. In *Immunotherapy of Cancer: Present Status of Trials in Man* (eds W. D. Terry and D. Windhurst), Raven Press, New York, pp. 257–268.
8. Link, M., Gorrin, A., Miser, A. *et al.* (1986) The role of adjuvant chemotherapy in the treatment of osteosarcoma of the extremity. Preliminary

results of the multi-institutional osteosarcoma study. (Proceedings of the American Society of Clinical Oncology, Houston, May 1985). *New Eng. J. of Med.*, **314(25)**, 1600–1606.

9 Bacci, G., Picci, P., Ferrari, S. *et al.* (1993) Primary chemotherapy and delayed surgery for non-metastatic osteosarcoma of the extremities. *Cancer*, **72**, 3227–3238.

10. Putnam, J. B., Roth, J. A., Wesley, M. N. *et al.* (1983) Survival following aggressive resection of pulmonary metastases from osteogenic sarcoma: Analysis of prognostic factors. *Ann. Thorac. Surg.*, **36**, 516–523.

11. Al-Jilaihawi, A. N., Bullimore, J. A., Mott, M. G. and Wisheart, J. D. (1988) Combined chemotherapy and surgery for pulmonary metastases from osteogenic sarcoma: results of 10 years experience. *Eur. J. Cardio-Thorac. Surg.*, **2**, 37–42.

12. Pomeroy, T. C. and Johnson, R. E. (1975) Combined modality therapy of Ewing's sarcoma. *Cancer*, **36**, 47.

13. Phillips, R. F. and Higinbothom, N. L. (1967) The curability of Ewing's endothelioma of bone in children. *J. Pediatr.*, **70**, 391.

14. Razek, A., Peres, C. A., Tefft, M. *et al.* (1980) Intergroup Ewing's Sarcoma Study: local control related to radiation dose, volume and site of primary lesion in Ewing's sarcoma. *Cancer*, **46**, 516.

15. Zucker, J. M., Henry-Amar, M., Sarrazin, D. *et al.* (1983) Intensive systemic chemotherapy in localised Ewing's sarcoma in childhood. *Cancer*, **52**, 415–423.

16. Lynch, H. T., Mulcahy, G. M., Harris, R. E. *et al.* (1978) Genetic and pathological findings in a kindred with hereditary sarcoma, breast cancer, brain tumours, leukemia, lung and adrenal cortical carcinoma. *Cancer*, **41**, 2055.

17. Russell, W. O., Cohen, J., Enzinger, F. *et al.* (1977) A clinical and pathological staging system for soft tissue sarcomas. *Cancer*, **40**, 1562–1570.

18. Cantin, J., McNeer, G. P., Chu, F. C. *et al.* (1968) The problem of local recurrence after treatment of soft tissue sarcoma. *Ann. Surg.*, **68**, 47–53.

19. Suit, H. D., Proppe, K. H. and Bramwell, V. H. C. (1982) Soft tissue. In *Treatment of Cancer* (eds K. E. Halnan, J. L. Boak, D. Crowther *et al.*), Chapman and Hall, London, pp. 607–623.

20. Ragab, A., Gehan, E., Maurer, H. *et al.* (1992) Intergroup Rhabdomyosarcoma Study (IRS) 111: Preliminary report of the major results. (Abstract). *Proc. Am. Soc. Clin. Oncol.*, **11**, 363.

21. Rosenberg, S. A., Tepper, J., Galtstein, E. *et al.* (1963) Prospective randomised evaluation of adjuvant chemotherapy in adults with soft tissue sarcomas of the extremities. *Cancer*, **52**, 424–434.

22. Stephens, F. O., Tattersall, M. H. N., Marsden, V. *et al.* (1987) Regional chemotherapy with the use of cis-platin and doxorubicin as primary treatment for advanced sarcomas in shoulder, pelvis, and thigh. *Cancer*, **10**, 724–735.

Index